THE REDISCOVERY OF INDIA

THE REDISCOVERY OF INDIA

Meghnad Desai

BLOOMSBURY ACADEMIC

First published by Allen Lane, an imprint of Penguin India in 2009

This edition published in 2011 by:

Bloomsbury Academic

An imprint of Bloomsbury Publishing Plc
36 Soho Square, London W1D 3QY, UK
and
175 Fifth Avenue, New York, NY 10010, USA

CIP records for this book are available from the British Library and the
Library of Congress

ISBN 978-1-8496-6350-2 (Cloth)
e-ISBN 978-1-8496-6418-9

This book is produced using paper that is made from wood grown in managed,
sustainable forests. It is natural, renewable and recyclable. The logging and
manufacturing processes conform to the environmental regulations of the
country of origin.

Printed and bound in Great Britain by the MPG Books Group
www.bloomsburyacademic.com

Cover image: Detail of India, from a 1630 Portuguese map of Asia, entitled
Taboas geraes de toda a navegação by Jeronimo de Ataide, João Teixeira. http://
commons.wikimedia.org/wiki/File:Portugues_map_of_India,_1630.jpg [accessed
16/10/2010]

Cover designer: Mark Penfound

To Kishwar
for her constant support and love

CONTENTS

ACKNOWLEDGEMENTS

IN WRITING THIS book I have incurred many debts to the unsung heroes of all my writing endeavours—the librarians. I have been lucky in having access to the House of Lords library where Shorayne Fairweather and her colleagues made available the most obscure documents from within and outside the library. The London School of Economics library also has a rich collection which I have availed of over the years. In Delhi, the India International Centre library is a handy source. I am grateful to all the library staff, front end and behind in the stacks, for their help.

Ranjana Sengupta met me within a month of my starting on this book and she has given me unfailing help and tolerated much authorial misbehaviour along the way. I am grateful to her and Debasri Rakshit for editorial comments and to Mark Penfound for the cover design.

PREFACE

MOST OF THIS book was written between July 2007 and December 2008. Yet, the ideas in it began to germinate in my mind fifty and more years previously. I was seven when India became independent and for the first ten years after that I, along with most others, accepted a well-known view of the nature of India as a nation. I read Nehru's *The Discovery of India* when in my teens. It gave us the basic story, beautifully recounted by a masterful writer.

The story was a simple and seamless one. India had struggled hard against British imperialism but thanks to the leadership of Gandhi, along with his heir and trusted lieutenant Nehru, India had thrown off the foreign yoke. The British had always practised divide and rule and the sad result was the Partition, thanks to Jinnah's fanatic insistence on the 'Two Nation theory', utterly rejected by the Congress party. Post-Partition, and now independent, India was united and hopeful. Its unity was based on a syncretic culture of Hindus and Muslims. The Partition of India had served as a warning to the leaders against any further divisions; the spectre of Balkanization haunted India.

This seamless story was shattered during the 1950s itself. The agitation for linguistic states took a popular anti-Congress form in Bombay where I was growing up, and we could see that despite Nehru's reluctance to grant the demands, linguistic states were popular. What followed in 1959 was much more serious. The publication of Maulana Azad's *India Wins Freedom* shattered the accepted story of India's independence. We learnt that there had been differences and disagreements among Congress leaders as well, and not just between them and Jinnah. Azad's assertion that Nehru might have single-handedly thrown the chance of a united India under the Cabinet Mission plan was shocking and controversial. Newspapers and journals were full of arguments for and against him. India had suddenly become aware that its own history was not a single unit but had rival strands. This is true of most countries; we had just witnessed India growing up.

Bombay state was divided into Gujarat and Maharashtra in 1960, and Bombay city began its new career as the capital of a Marathi-speaking state rather than the commercial capital of cosmopolitan India. I left India for studies abroad, but even as I pursued my career in economics, I kept up my reading and thinking about India and how it became a nation, about the subdivisions within, as much as the big division which caused the Partition.

During the next forty-odd years, I wrote a number of essays, some short and others quite long, on the broad question of the nature of Indian nationhood. These are collected in *Development and Nationhood*, Oxford University Press, New Delhi, 2005. But I did feel that some day I should sit down and write out what I consider the nature of India as a nation and how it came to be what it is. I have been lucky in having colleagues and friends who have been very indulgent of my forays into their special fields. (Their names are in the preface to *Development and Nationhood*.) I have also been fortunate in having access to some of the best libraries at the universities of Bombay, Pennsylvania, California (Berkeley) and the London School of Economics plus, last but not the least, the House of Lords.

Neither friends nor an ample supply of books can be a guarantee against error, and it is with some trepidation that I now put this book forward. It is an ambitious book but it is written by someone who cannot claim to be a professional historian. It is my own, somewhat opinionated, account of how India became a nation and a nation state. I begin with the arrival of Vasco da Gama in 1498 and carry the story down to the present day. I take the creation of the Indian nation to be as much a result of global forces as local ones. I emphasize, more than has been done previously, the 250 years of peaceful relations of trade between Europe and India between 1500 and 1750. The story since 1750 has been much covered, but I do see a continuous—and not totally negative—contribution of the British Parliament and politics to the development of India's constitutional position. It is this, as much as the mass mobilization by the Congress, which has shaped India as it is today. Hence the continuity rather than rupture with the British raj. The Congress also cannot be given the sole credit for the outcome of Independence. The more I read about the period between 1905 and 1947, the more impressed I was about how much a certain hegemonic view of the independence struggle has been put forward since Independence.

India's story, as it fought for Independence, was more than just Gandhi 1921, Gandhi 1930 and Gandhi 1942. There were other parties and leaders, especially the Muslim League and Jinnah, but also the movement of the Dalits and lower castes led by Ambedkar and Naicker, which had their own view of what India should be like after Independence. There were also the Native Princes and the many others who collaborated in the constitutional path charted by the British. There were patriots who rejected the non-violent strategy of the Congress, and dissidents both on the Right and the Left who also fought for the common cause. These aspects have to be given their due weight in the story. The larger perspective, in which the Congress and the British (in India and back home) interacted with non-Congress forces to shape the final outcome, is covered in some detail here. It is important, in my view, to ask whether the Partition was the only possible outcome and, if not, what the alternatives were, and how the one that finally gelled did so.

Along the way, I also pose a number of counterfactual questions: Could India have escaped Western rule as China did? Yes in 1700, but perhaps no by 1750, and definitely not by 1800. What would India have been like had the 1857 rebellion succeeded? Could Gandhiji have delivered swaraj within one year as he promised in 1921? Could India have been a single entity on the lines of the 1935 Government of India Act, or as per the Cabinet Mission plan? The point of asking these questions is to remember that what did actually occur was only one of the many possibilities before it happened. History could have taken a different turn.

The story of India as a nation does not stop at 1947. In fact, it begins then. India has not been so large and so united under a single power any time previously in its history as it has been since 1947, Partition notwithstanding. The sixty-two years since have displayed even greater diversity than the freedom fighters were aware of, and it is the assertion and inclusion of these diversities which is the real success story of post-1947 India. It has not been easy nor peaceable. But it is nothing short of a miracle. India is and continues to reinvent itself as a nation, day after day, democratically and in full view of the world.

I enjoyed writing this book immensely and I can only hope that the readers will also do so. But I must warn them that enjoyment, in my definition, includes getting angry at the author, disagreeing with him, challenging his views and, yet, having the fun which takes you right through to the end.

15 August 2009　　　　　　　　　　　　　　　　MEGHNAD DESAI
London–Delhi–Goa

INTRODUCTION:
INDIA AT SIXTY

IN THE SUMMER of 2007, India celebrated sixty years of Independence. There was a lot to celebrate. Rapid economic growth during the last decade-and-a-half had brought per capita income to the magic figure of $1000. There were still a lot of people below the official poverty line, but if they were one in two when India was thirty years into Independence, now the number was one in five. Indian industrialists were taking over businesses abroad even in the land of their old masters—the British. India was beginning to figure in respectable numbers in the list of billionaires. For leaders of the G8, India along with China was among the new powers—no longer just an 'emerging economy'. India was a nuclear power and a deal struck with the US, controversial in both countries, gave India a privileged status in the nuclear club, much to the chagrin of the rest of the world. No more than it deserved, most Indians thought; perhaps less since it still meant that India had to subject itself to scrutiny by legislators and executive leaders of a foreign superpower.

When India became independent in 1947 its leaders, especially its first prime minister, had high hopes that India would become a moral leader, that it would forge a path of peace and understanding in a world torn apart by enmity between West and East. Nehru, his daughter, Indira Gandhi, and her son, Rajiv Gandhi, were prime ministers of India at the head of the Congress party which enjoyed a large majority in the Parliament for thirty-eight out of its first forty-two years. The high ideals of non-alignment, with a slight tilt towards the Soviet Union, had been the way its foreign relations had been carried out. But by its sixtieth anniversary India had changed—as indeed had the world. The Soviet Union had collapsed, and India as a nuclear power had aspirations to being a global power, not just a moral exemplar. The world was now globalized and capitalism was resurgent. India had become a democracy with fifty political parties, and the Congress was no longer the only dominant player as it had been. Its return to office in 2004, after having failed to come to the top in three out of the five elections since 1989,

1

was itself something of a miracle. The extent of its victory in 2009 surprised many. It was due to one person who revived the fortunes of the Nehru–Gandhi family—Sonia Gandhi.

Sonia Gandhi is an intriguing element in India's colourful polity. Italian by birth, she married into the Nehru–Gandhi dynasty when she met and fell in love with Rajiv Gandhi while she was studying in Cambridge, England to improve her English language skills. Sonia Gandhi inspires as much intense loyalty as loathing. She has adopted India as her home, yet, even after forty years of being domiciled, many are unwilling to call her Indian. She had not wanted to be in politics, nor had her husband, Rajiv Gandhi. But destiny combined with dynasty, plus the burning compulsions of Indian politics, put her husband in the top spot when his mother Indira Gandhi was assassinated by her own Sikh bodyguards in revenge for her determined efforts to root out a secessionist Sikh movement. Sonia was in the prime ministerial home at the time, and cradled her mother-in-law's stricken, bullet-ridden body in the ambulance as they rushed her to the hospital.

Then seven years later Sonia Gandhi's husband, Rajiv Gandhi, was assassinated in revenge for his attempt to help neighbouring Sri Lanka fight a Tamil secessionist movement. He was killed by a woman suicide bomber on the eve of his likely re-election as prime minister at the head of the Congress party after two years out of power. That was 1991. Sonia Gandhi retired to her home and tended her children. But, another seven years brought her back to save the Congress party from a terminal meltdown. Somewhat like Catharine the Great of Russia, she found herself, a person born abroad in another culture, from a family much more humble than the one she had married into, pushed into high politics and low skulduggery by the accident of her husband's death and the expectations that Indians had of her family.

At first, she faltered and had a lot to learn. But in 2004 she led her party to a stunning victory against all expectations, and defeated the incumbent government which had paraded its achievements with the slogan 'India Shining'. She then delivered a blow to her critics by declining to be prime minister, but taking on the management of the fragile coalition she had put together to bring her party to power. Three years later, she once again trumped her opponents by waiting till the end to choose a presidential candidate as unexpected as she was unknown. She split her opposition and secured the election of her chosen candidate with a two-to-one margin. Pratibha Patil, a Congress loyalist, became the first woman President of India, thanks to Sonia Gandhi's capacity as a strategic thinker.

In 2007, the worldwide meltdown was yet some months away. India was celebrating a third continuous year of 9 per cent growth rate of

GNP, 7 per cent per capita. When Sonia Gandhi first arrived in India, the country was a byword for food shortages and famines, of heavy-handed planning which stymied the energy of Indians and kept them in poverty in the name of some ideological shibboleths of socialism. Her husband had made tentative beginnings to break out of that mindset and, after his untimely death, his accidental successor, Narasimha Rao, broke the mould and embarked on a path of liberal economic reform. Now, sixteen years later, India was no longer the basket case it had been when she first arrived. It was being hailed as an economic super power. It had happened not because of her, solely or even largely, but within her time in India. She deserves some credit, however, for having chosen Dr Manmohan Singh, finance minister in the 1991–96 government who had piloted the reforms, to be her prime minister in the United Progressive Alliance (UPA) government that her party headed. Team Manmohan wrought a transformation.

India's arrival as a major economic presence in the global economy, at the outset of the twenty-first century, has taken many by surprise. There are still sceptics at home who are in denial, or even disapproving. They fear the return of colonial dependence, of the East India Company, of the powers of the neo-liberal economic order. Others, mainly from outside India, question whether the growth upsurge in India is sustainable. Whether it is the entry of Walmart into the retail sector or the prospect of foreign investment into India's agriculture, or the exposure of TV viewers to pictures of B-grade movie star Shilpa Shetty being slagged off for being an 'Indian' on the British reality TV show *Big Brother*, Indians have been quick to take offence and react defensively.

On the 150th anniversary of the 1857 War for Indian Independence/ Sepoy Mutiny/Great Rebellion—call it what you will—a small group of British nationals arrived to pay their respects to their ancestors who had fought on the British side in 1857, and had been buried in Lucknow. The local reaction was virulent—they hounded the British visitors everywhere they went, some locals insisting there should be no 'celebration' of the event by the British; the visitors were unwelcome, they said, as they represented the former masters and any celebration would symbolize nothing less than the return of the East India Company. Even sixty years after Independence, some Indians do not feel free, not liberated from their colonial masters, even at home. Hands off India, they cry.

China, in the meanwhile, has been at ease with a flood of foreign investment. Starting from a similar economic base thirty years ago, it has grown at a dizzying double-digit growth rate for nearly three decades, and outstripped India in the GNP growth stakes eight to three. India accelerated gently out of a soporific 'Hindu rate of growth' of 3.5 per cent per annum over 1950–80 to 5.5 per cent in the 1980s, a notch higher in the 1990s after a drastic reform and—at last—in the first decade of the new millennium up to 9 per cent. And yet, many in India, especially in political life, are still hesitant about the new path they have embarked upon. They wish to halt or reverse the globalizing movement, to rein in capitalism and tame it to suit their ideological ends, or merely their parochial interests.

By an uncanny parallel, just as India's economy went into a dynamic upward trajectory breaking with its dirigiste past, its politics came apart in a spectacular way. For forty-two years after Independence in 1947 (bar two years between 1977 and 1979) the Congress party and the Nehru–Gandhi family (again barring two years of Prime Minister Shastri's rule between 1964 and 1966) had been at the helm of affairs in Delhi. Jawaharlal Nehru's prime ministership (1947–64) had been followed after two years by his daughter, Indira Gandhi (1966–77 and 1980–84), and she was succeeded after her assassination by her son Rajiv Gandhi (1984–89). The Congress had enjoyed an overall parliamentary majority in seven of the nine elections between 1947 and 1989, all except for the 1977 and 1989 elections. After the ninth election in 1989, the hegemony of the Congress broke, and since then there has never been a single party majority government in India. The six prime ministers between 1947 and 1989 were matched by seven prime ministers between 1989 and 2009.

The end of Congress hegemony led to challenges to its dominant nationalist ideology—crafted by Nehru and his daughter—of secularism (a balance between the two main religious communities, Hindus and Muslims) and socialism (economic rule by control and protectionism). In December 1992, crowds incited by leaders of the Bharatiya Janata Party (BJP), which champions a non-secular Hindu nationalist agenda, destroyed a sixteenth-century mosque in Ayodhya on the grounds that it was built on the very spot which was the birthplace of the legendary god-king, Rama, the eponymous hero of the epic *Ramayana*. Communal killings followed over the next three months, spreading across India with bomb blasts in Bombay for which the accused, mostly Muslims, were sentenced to fourteen years of jail, later in 2007. The Hindu counterparts of the Muslim terrorists were also named in the Sri Krishna Commission's report, but they are still to be charged. Seventeen years after the Babri Masjid episode, the Liberhan Commission, tasked with inquiring into the circumstances leading up to the events and the persons responsible, reported. The guilty of 1992 are yet to be brought to justice. The law's delays are not impartial. Even secularism has its favourites when it comes to criminal prosecution.

The BJP was rewarded for this temple movement by a victory in 1996, but its majority was too slim to form a government. After a hiatus of two years, while a motley coalition of Left and regional caste parties governed, in 1998 BJP came to power with a coalition, the National Democratic Alliance (NDA), which lasted six years. During this time, a virtual culture war erupted over textbooks of Indian history. Worse was to follow when in March 2002 riots broke out in BJP-ruled state of Gujarat, where hundreds of Muslims were killed in revenge for the fire that engulfed a train carriage carrying fifty-nine volunteers returning from Ayodhya, where they had gone to build a temple in place of the demolished mosque—in defiance of the law of the land. The secular India which Nehru had nourished was about to be taken over by a Hindu India where Muslims would be placed in a precarious condition. Four years earlier, the BJP-led NDA government had exploded a nuclear bomb in defiance of international opinion, signalling India meant to be a strong regional power. Its hostile neighbour, Pakistan responded by exploding its own bomb.

Further challenges faced India in Kashmir where a sixty-year-old dispute with Pakistan continues, with terrorist infiltration from the Pakistani side of the line of control that separates the Indian- and Pakistani-controlled parts of Kashmir, costing India millions of rupees each day to support the large security force it maintains. Terrorists also struck in Bangalore, Bombay, Delhi—even getting close to the Parliament building—and most recently in Mumbai in November 2008. Unrest continued in the North-Eastern edge of India in Assam, where local sub-nationalists denied the right of out-of-state Indian citizens to work in humble jobs such as road building. At the same time, Maoist groups called Naxalites became active in 185 districts spanning across sixteen states. In the period, 2005 to 2007, India lost more security personnel (401) in battles with Naxalites than in Kashmir (370), and twice as many as it lost in the North-East (176). At the same time, fewer Naxalites were killed (549) than the terrorists in Kashmir (1580).[1]

As long as India has been an independent nation, there has been an anxiety about its survival as a single entity. In his brilliant history, *India After Gandhi*, Ramchandra Guha describes how every decade has seen a debate both within and outside India on this topic.[2] Originally, Winston Churchill had insisted that the notion of India had even less meaning than the term 'Equator', and predicted chaos and anarchy after Independence; the riots following the Partition almost vindicated his stand. Ten years later, the anxiety was formulated in terms of 'after Nehru, who?' Later still, after wars with China and Pakistan and two bad harvests in 1965 and 1966, the prediction was made that 1967 was the last election India would ever have. The Emergency of 1975 imposed by Indira Gandhi again raised fears about the survival of India as a democracy. Later still, as Congress hegemony broke and there were battles around mosque and temple, Indians again asked, 'what next?'

Surprisingly, the very lack of a single party hegemony seems to have deepened and strengthened Indian democracy. The scores of new parties which have surfaced in the wake of the erosion of Congress dominance in the 1990s—caste-based and region-based parties—have brought into the fold people of lower castes such as the Other Backward Castes (OBC), Dalits, the people at the bottom of the caste ladder, and tribals. They have used the ballot box to register their group strength and bargain for a better share of the public spoils. Their political agents have learnt the art of coalition-building and leveraging their limited strength in legislative chambers to devastating effect.

This inclusion of the previously deprived people has brought forth strong demands that public sector jobs and places in higher educational institutions be reserved for members of these groups. This is affirmative action, but the deserving are defined by ritual caste criteria rather than economic and social ones. India's Constitution, which was written on liberal democratic lines of the US and UK Constitutions, albeit with a large social democratic component of rights and entitlements, is now threatened with a movement which harnesses the very structures of social inequality to redress their worst effects. The claim to special treatment requires the preservation, not the abolition, of these symbols of inequality. Can India meet the challenge of inclusion and equity, while pursuing rapid growth?

The champions of global India are confident. This class includes company owners as they buy up companies abroad, CEOs who earn multi-million rupees compensation packages, graduates from India's prestigious management and engineering schools—the Indian Institutes of Management (IIM) and Indian Institutes of Technology (IIT)—as they find employers from around the world lining up with exciting job offers at their graduation, and film-makers, actors, fashion designers and beauty queens who roam the London, Paris, New York, Rome circuits. They assert the width of India's democratic culture which allows the reconciliation of conflicting claims in a consensual manner, though it causes delay in the speed of efficient reforms. They are proud of India's nuclear clout, and exult in the new friendliness that the United States is displaying. They point to the more inclusive spirit of India's wealthy who value charity and a notion of trusteeship.

And many more are just happy, for the first time in centuries, to be able to sample the pleasures of sudden and large wealth, like the Delhi elite which holidays in London during the summer months when Delhi's heat is intolerable, just as their erstwhile British rulers fled to Shimla. This class also enjoys an occasional sense of *schadenfreude*. This was most apparent when the premiere Indian business house, Tata Sons, owners of Tata Steel, bought the Anglo-Dutch steel company, Corus.

One component part of Corus used to be British Steel. It is widely remembered in India that just a century previously, a British engineer had doubted whether an Indian could build a steel mill when Jamsetji Tata, the founder of the Tata dynasty, had laid out his plans for Tata Iron and Steel, later Tata Steel. Within just a hundred years, Ratan Tata, the great grandson of the founder, had pulled off this stunning coup. The empire had struck back.

Memories of past humiliations at the hands of erstwhile rulers are the common fare of nationalist ideology. China was never under Western imperial rule as India was, but even there the resentment at having to cede special rights to foreign powers from the first Opium War onwards rankled deep, and became a cementing factor in nationalist and communist ideologies. The sign in Peking's foreign quarters, 'Dogs and Chinese Not Allowed', was to rankle for a long time. China, after all, was Middle-earth and was thrown off to the peripheral extremities in the nineteenth and twentieth centuries. Today, it is regaining its place in the world.

Can India regain its place in the world order?

Regaining is the key syllable here. India, unlike China, was never a unitary or even a single federal state through much of its history. In his fascinating one-volume history of India, John Keay has a diagram showing how much of India's territory was controlled, over the last three millennia, by any ruling dynasty.[3] The contrast with China is striking. For China, once you leave a turbulent period during 300–200 BCE, there is a continuity in state formation. For India, the reverse is true. After the Maurya period of 400–300 BCE, when around 80 per cent of the territory was under central control, you have to fast forward to the Mughal rule which for 150 years, between 1560 and 1710 CE, controlled a similar percentage of territory. By 1850 the British conquest of India had left no major king who could challenge the East India Company, but the 1857 rebellion convinced the rulers not to push their luck too far. Native kings of smaller territories were tolerated and occupied one-third of the land area under the watchful eye of the raj. The Republic of India, proclaimed on 26 January 1950, was the first state which ruled all over India, and controlled a larger area than any other state before, despite the Partition of British India into India and Pakistan.

India as a united polity under a single unified control was born in 1950. It is at once a young polity and a very old culture. The process by which an ancient culture took a millennia to emerge as a political unity is the theme of this book.

INDIA AS A CULTURAL IDEA

India was a cultural idea and a vision of vast wealth which lured foreign conquerors and travellers to its shores. India has been a continuous society for as long as records go back. Hinduism has a history going back to the mists of Indian history. For fundamentalists and even ordinary gullible Hindus, the mists go back scores of millennia. But even hard-headed researchers will date it to 2500–2000 BCE. And yet, there is no written history of India from contemporary sources as there is for China. There are eulogies of minor kings with fantastic genealogies and overblown territorial claims and stories of super-human prowess. There is the superb poetry in the *Rig Veda*, the magnificent epics of the *Ramayana* and the *Mahabharata*, the terse philosophical *Upanishads* and the voluminous *Puranas*, but no historical account. What is now available has been reconstructed from inscriptions, numismatic collections, archaeological finds, and accounts of Greek travellers who visited when Alexander invaded the north-west provinces of India, in what is now Pakistan.

The absence of a written history for much of the period up to 1000 CE is not a puzzle, nor is it a cultural attribute of the Hindus. It has been said that since the Hindus believe in reincarnation, they do not care about history in the ordinary sense; I think this is nonsense. The lack of written history is a symptom of the lack of a single continuous political authority which could have nurtured a school of scribes and recorders. The Chinese have had no problem of having recorded history through their millennia of existence; until the development of secular educational institutions, the writing of history in the West was the monopoly of the Church and the state. The Church was assiduous in maintaining its records and jealous of its domain. Kings wanted to set the records straight, or, at least, bend in their favour. Occasionally, rival claimants commissioned alternative histories. But history writing for many years was a state enterprise. India had no such single state authority and, hence, no history writing.

The only record of ancient India which is about its material reality is a book of statecraft. The *Arthashastra* is from the Maurya period when India had something akin to a single polity. From around 1000 CE, Muslim invaders came to North India through the north-western mountain passes of what is now Pakistan. Written accounts of Indian history and customs begin only with the Muslim chronicles, except for one instance of history written in tenth-century Kashmir—*Rajtarangini*.

Modern historical accounts take their clue from these Muslim chronicles. They were accounts written for the Muslim—at first Afghan and later Mongol/Mughal—kings. They were Delhi-centred as that was the capital of the Afghan kingdoms as they spread and shrank across the centuries—though the capital shifted periodically to Agra or Lahore and once to Daulatabad. Even so, the territories they covered even at best were, by and large, confined to Northern India—what today comprises Pakistan and the Indian states of Punjab, Haryana, Uttar Pradesh, Bihar, Rajasthan and Madhya Pradesh. Bengal to the east and Gujarat to the south-west were in and out of Delhi's control. Mughal rule never reached eastwards beyond Bengal to Assam and the hilly regions of what were once called the North-East Frontier Area—Manipur, Tripura, Arunachal Pradesh and Nagaland. The last effective Mughal emperor, Aurangzeb, spent the final twenty-five years of his life trying to extend Delhi control further south from where his illustrious ancestors had left the empire's boundaries. Briefly he succeeded, and Mughal hold on India reached its highest extent in the late seventeenth century. Yet, the Deccan (from *dakshin* (Sanskrit), or *dakkhan* (Prakrit/Hindi)) was to be his graveyard. Farther south, Kerala and parts of Tamil Nadu remained beyond Mughal reach. Even this control was lost when Mughal rule weakened after Aurangzeb's death.

British historical writing built on that tradition, and since the British saw themselves as successors to the Mughals, Delhi remained the focus of their attention even though the capital was in Calcutta till 1911.One could even argue that by the time the capital moved to Delhi, the end of British rule was nigh. The British claim was that they established order over all of India and gave a reality to an entity which did not exist before they conquered the various parts of India. The rising nationalist movement, from the second half of the nineteenth century onwards, fought this claim hard. It asserted, as do many nationalist movements everywhere, that the nation was one and timeless. The fact that for much of its history what was now India did not have a single ruler, was explained away by various devices, including foreign (Muslim) invasions, centrifugal tendencies that were a result of personal ambitions, treachery and artificial divisions fomented by foreign (British) rulers, and so on.

Of course, a more effective counter to the British assertion that India lacked a single ruler for much of its history, would have been the history of Europe, which in size is comparable to India. Indian nationalists could have pointed to the breakdown in European polity after the fall of the Roman Empire. Charlemagne tried to regain control over Western Europe at least in the eighth century CE, and established what came to be known as the Holy Roman Empire across continental Western Europe. Europe was divided into two different political and social formations on either side of the Elbe from the end of the first millennium CE and, indeed, each region west and east of it, fragmented into separate kingdoms.

The puzzle is not that India was not a single polity, but why anyone should have thought it should be one. Yet, the idea that India was—and should be—a single political entity through its entire history, and if it was not special causes had to be evoked to explain such episodes, became a central tenet of Indian nationalism. The dominance of British intellectual discourse prevented Indians from defining the ground on which they chose to fight. The ground of the nationalist ideological struggle was determined by the way the British constructed India's history. By denying that India could be a single entity, or even a single idea, the British asserted—simultaneously—that Britain was such a single entity and that India was not. Nationalists had to counter this by asserting that India was a single nation like Britain and unlike Europe. Balkanization became the one fear haunting the nationalist ideology, and political unity was raised to the highest status for the nation to define its identity.

Yet except for China, no human population of India's size has been united under a single ruler for as long as these two have been urban civilizations. The United States is a larger country in terms of size. But it started small at its independence in 1783. It became large by absorbing sparsely settled territories by purchase (Louisiana) or conquest. Czarist Russia became a continental empire, during the second millennium CE from fifteenth century onwards, when the Muscovite kingdom spread its wings wider. Yet Russia, even by the eighteenth century, was large in size, not in terms of population. India was not an exception as the British asserted, but the rule. China was the puzzle to be explained. Europe took till 1957 to unite six nations in a single treaty as a community, and it has taken another fifty years for the European Union to cover most of Europe, and the process is still not complete. Even so, the European Union is far from being a single political entity that India is today.

Political unity is, then, not easy to establish and maintain. England is another example: there was no single English nation till after the Norman invasion of 1066 and then, perhaps, a single united kingdom only after the Wars of the Roses in the fifteenth century. Wales was conquered early on in the thirteenth century, and Ireland in the sixteenth, but the Union with Scotland took till the seventeenth century when James I united the two crowns and a formal union took place in 1707. Ireland was formally added to the British Empire in the late eighteenth century. Along the way, there was a murderous civil war engulfing all the three kingdoms—England, Scotland and Ireland. So Great Britain had become a single country only with the advent of the nineteenth century. Then, of course, it split in the early twentieth century when Eire became independent. Within the next fifty years, demands for regional autonomy grew in Scotland and Wales, while Northern Ireland remained a theatre of dissident violence till the end of the twentieth century.

France was a large single kingdom, but Germany did not become a single national entity till 1870. Indians were too dazzled by their British masters to throw British history at them. Instead, Indians went about inventing the mythical single Indian nation for all times; they did not even see how different India was, even in Asia, when compared to China.

China is a huge land mass whose political boundaries were extended by military conquests. But it is an unusually homogenous society with the Han people comprising more than nine-tenths of the population. Chinese and foreign (Manchu) rulers took advantage of that homogeneity and maintained central control by fashioning an effective bureaucracy.

India is a large land mass with a bewildering array of languages and religions, of ethnic groups and races. Even within the dominant religious community—the Hindus—the constant emphasis is on differentiation by ritual status in addition to the differences due to regional distances. Thus, during the summer of 2007, a controversy broke out as to the existence of a bridge built between India and Sri Lanka by Rama, the same mythic god–king whose birthplace in Ayodhya had led to the riots of 1992. It was asserted by some that the proposal to dredge a channel in the Palk straits, which separate India and Sri Lanka, should be abandoned since it was the site of the *Rama Setu*, the bridge built by the monkey army which helped Rama to secure a victory over Ravana, king of Lanka and the man who had abducted Rama's wife, Sita. The Archaeological Survey of India submitted a report to the Supreme Court that there was no evidence of a human construction which could be proved and added, rather gratuitously, that it did not think Rama had actually existed.

All hell broke loose as the BJP and its Hindu religionist allies protested that the government, led by Sonia Gandhi, an Italian Catholic, was denying the deepest beliefs of the Hindu majority of India. While the government quickly retracted, the law minister (of a secular, socialist, democratic republic) loudly asserted his government's abiding belief in Rama, his existence, as well as his divine status. But the Dravida Munnettra Kazhagam (DMK), the party which rules Tamil Nadu and partners in the ruling coalition led by Sonia Gandhi's Congress party at the Centre, countered by saying that as far as they were concerned, the *Ramayana* was a North Indian epic which recorded the humiliation of the Dravidians of the South by the Aryans of the North, and that Rama was a myth and, if not, no god of the Dravidians of the South.

The interesting thing about this somewhat arcane piece of politics is that it revealed that the story of Hindu India itself is not a uniting story. The serious divide in India is not just between Muslims and Hindus, which the secular vision is trying to overcome, but between the Hindus of the various regions. No single hegemonic account of India's ancient culture is tenable any longer. The ancient epics, which are claimed to be the building blocks of eternal India, are themselves divisive, since they tell the story of India from a North Indian viewpoint. One needs to rethink India not from a North Indian hegemonic perspective, but in its regional differences out of which a single India is only now being forged. Understanding how India can become one from its manifold diversity, and how it can attain plurality in this diversity rather than some false unity, is the theme of this book. We need to begin with India's diversity before we can assert its unity.

Indeed, India before 1947, before Independence and Partition, was even larger, a whole subcontinent. It was the size of Europe without the European part of Russia. Europe itself has a chequered history with many quarrelling and divided kingdoms. And yet, British rulers and historians professed to be bewildered by the multiplicity of Indian kingdoms and rulers with their quarrels and intrigues, wars and unions as these (to them at least) strangely named dynasties fought for their attention. Indian history was not very different from continental European experience. Reading, for example, Italian history any time from Dante to Mazzini, reveals similar tales of petty quarrels and mindless intrigue against a superb cultural and artistic backdrop. German history is no different. A reader of Thackeray's *Vanity Fair* will appreciate that the many small principalities of Germany that Becky Sharpe passes through, were not unlike the many native kingdoms of India. There is also in Eurocentric accounts of modern history a bias towards Western Europe and a neglect of Eastern Europe (a bias shared by Adam Smith, Hegel and Karl Marx as they constructed their stadial accounts of universal history) paralleling the North/South division in Indian history.

Indian nationalists, then, should not have been dazzled by British accounts of India's lack of unity, its multiple centres of power or with the British equation of order and indeed 'civilization' with unitary political control. Perhaps, the British had a similar view of European history being a mess, but the Indian nationalists responded not by saying that India was just like Europe, but exactly the opposite. They asserted that India had always been a unit, but that its unity was disrupted by foreign invaders, local traitors and collaborators. Once Western education became entrenched in the three seaports of Calcutta, Bombay and Madras (now known as Kolkata, Mumbai and Chennai respectively), and an elite cognizant of British history formed itself by the last third of the nineteenth century, its response was to assert that India was one, and that the assertion by the colonial rulers that India was never an entity, but just a jumble of races and languages and faiths, was false.

There were some problems with this nationalist boast. There was no single theory of why India should be considered a nation. Indeed, there *is* no single theory of Indian nationalism. This lack of a single story of why India should be considered a single nation was at the heart of the Partition of India, where the two principal visions collided. Mohammad Ali Jinnah, the leader of the Muslim League and the founder of Pakistan, said that there were two nations—one Hindu and one Muslim—within India. The Congress party denied this, at least for a while, until it saw power being denied to them if they—the party of Indian nationalists— did not agree on Partition.

Yet, even then, there were rival stories to the one the Congress told as to why India should be thought of as one. The Hindu religious parties wanted India to be seen as a Hindu nation in which minorities professing other faiths lived at the sufferance of the majority. Other minorities, the Sikhs for instance, wanted a nation defined just for the Sikhs in Punjab. In South India, the Dravidians, even though Hindu, were virulently anti-Brahmin and had a different notion of what Hindu society should be like, which their Northern brethren did not share. The leader of the Dravid upliftment movement, E.V. Ramaswamy Naicker (who was known as Periyar) agreed with the leader of the Dalits in the North, Dr B.R. Ambedkar that independent India under Congress dominance could well, potentially, be not as friendly to their communities as the foreign rulers were.

The pre-Independence nationalist had to argue that the nation was timeless with its origins in the hoary past; that the present rule by alien powers was degrading the nation whose glory could only be restored by getting rid of foreign rule. India's long history and large land mass were obstacles to any such simple idea. For one thing, the nation that went back into the mists of antiquity was Hindu, though Hinduism itself had evolved around the first millennium BCE. The incoming Indo-Europeans (they were called Aryans till Hitler made the term an ugly one) won over and absorbed the people living in the urban culture of the Indus valley and several other tribes scattered all over India. The ur-nation was thus Hindu.

Muslims had come to India in two separate waves. As traders they came to South India, as the Arabs had come from the Gulf and the Red Sea since pre-Islamic days. In the North, they came as armies of conquerors. The conquerors' idea of India was confined to the North, which is where Partition took place. Yet, Muslims lived all over India, and as many live in India today as in Pakistan—around 140 to 145 million. Jinnah's argument was that there were two nations, but what he got were two nation states, both with a large Muslim presence, one where Muslims were in overwhelming majority, and the other where they remained the largest minority. Later in 1971, Pakistan split between

Pakistan and Bangladesh since even the Muslims of old Pakistan were not a unity, but divided along linguistic and cultural lines.

The Congress party asserted that India was a syncretic union of the two faiths with a rich culture which drew on both Hindu and Muslim traditions; that India could and should be a single nation state once the British rulers left. Yet, though this theory failed to win the argument before Independence, it continued to define the nationhood of India—at least of the large portion which remained after the Partition of India. Even this idea of a syncretic culture was Northern, excluding the South as well as the North-East Frontier Area. In the South, Muslims were integrated in a different way, and Hindus divided by caste between Brahmin and non-Brahmin who were hostile to each other. Sikhs had been unhappy at the Partition in which they were clubbed together with the Hindus, and nursed the dreams of a separate nation, Khalistan—a dream which was to turn into a nightmare in the 1970s and 1980s. The Dalits, the ritually untouchable fifth of the population, had their own reasons for not buying into the Congress story.

These are, alas, not historical issues. They still haunt India today. In the 1960s, the unhappiness of the South about the adoption of Hindi as the national language led to violent agitations which shook the integrity of India. The South seemed to be heading for secession. But a compromise was reached by Prime Minister Shastri, Nehru's successor, and the deadline for adopting Hindi as the sole national language—1965—was postponed forever with a guaranteed maintenance of the status of English (the alien tongue) on par with Hindi. In the 1950s, Ambedkar had already led Dalits out of Hinduism into Buddhism in a mass conversion, and Dalits became much more radical, critiquing the upper-caste reading of India's ancient glorious past, as it was a past in which they had always been marginalized and exploited. They rejected Gandhi who wished to fold Dalits into Hinduism; instead of Gandhi the Dalits celebrated their own leader, Ambedkar.

In the North-East, the Nagas, who live on the border with Burma, maintained that they were never colonized by the British, but had been tolerated as an autonomous nation. They have fought inclusion into the Indian Union ever since the inception of independent India. Jammu and Kashmir fell athwart of the two-nation theory, since it had a Hindu king and a Muslim majority population, and this has led to three wars between India and Pakistan. The demand for Khalistan exploded in the 1970s, and its violent suppression by the Indian Army cost Prime Minister Indira Gandhi her life. Assamese students are agitating for nationhood, though less violently than the Sikhs did for Khalistan.

Yet, India has prospered as an economy and survived as a nation state. The unravelling of Congress hegemony, both in parliamentary and in ideological terms, proved a stabilizing factor rather than a divisive one. Inclusion has become the single agenda item for politicians of democratic India. The inclusion of the poor people and of regions which have not prospered as others, and also of the deprived communities—Scheduled Castes and Scheduled Tribes (SC/ST) and Other Backward Castes (OBCs) as well as Muslims and poor Christians, Sikhs, among others—has been carried out through a political and legislative effort, not perfect nor even consensual but still accepted by the country at large. The two categories overlap; the poor are often SC/ST and OBCs, but there are poor in the upper castes and also among the non-Hindu minorities who are outside the purview of caste-based reservations. The political process is currently absorbing their demands. Indeed, the voting strength of these groups means that politicians are rushing—regardless of arguments of economic efficiency or benefits and costs of the reservation policies—to grant whatever is asked. Muslims, being non-Hindu, cannot claim to be within any of those categories. Their welfare, thus far neglected, has become a politically contested issue. Christians need to claim that they, too, have castes among their numbers to qualify for the benefits of inclusion.

India, thus, has to look in two opposite directions. One is a cosmopolitan, competitive global economic direction, a world where trade is getting freer with low or no tariffs and markets opening out for India's products and services as much as India's capital. The world is dying to do business with this India, to lend investible funds, hire its graduates and receive its money in return. This is a world in which India has been scoring great gains in recent years. This is the world in which India Inc. has arrived with a bang.

The political system is looking in another direction—championing social protection, and focusing its mind on how to put impediments to competition based on merit in the access to jobs and places in higher educational institutions. The vision here is neither cosmopolitan, nor even secular (though this is hotly denied). The policy privileges Hindu society's caste divisions, and thus validates the argument of the pre-Independence days by Hindu parties that India is a Hindu nation. Policies towards non-Hindu minorities are hastily thought out, inadequate, late add-ons. The social protection being promised is a throwback to the bad old days of the licence-permit raj, which in 1991 India began leaving behind. Its vestiges remain, since hiring and firing is still difficult for large firms, and bankruptcy a long drawn out and painful process. The private sector is no longer restricted in much of its economic activities of investment and exports, but now suddenly faces further restrictions on who it can hire. At the same time, if up to 49 per cent of places in higher educational institutions are reserved on grounds of caste rather than non-religious criteria of deprivation and need, how will India Inc. guarantee a supply of good personnel which can let it compete around the world?

The reason why this is worrying is that India is a democracy and, in a democracy, the voters' will should and will prevail. A meritocratic system would be much more efficient though also more selective, even elitist. The parties arguing for social protection are unmindful of the costs of what they propose. Indeed, one could argue that the new growth impetus has made their economically costly policies affordable. But there is another dimension to this policy. One may wish to be relaxed about the social protection if the costs to India Inc. are containable. But this is not guaranteed. Parties of the Left, and, indeed, of the Hindu fundamentalist Right argue against the economic liberalization as such. They would rather revert to the hoary old days of the Hindu rate of growth on the grounds that liberal economic reform leads to increasing inequalities (the Left), or that India should be free of foreign capital (the Left and the fundamentalist Right).

If these were just debating points, again, one would not worry. But inequalities of growth—real and perceived—across classes and regions are at the root of some of the violent conflicts in India today: the Naxalite wars and the Assamese student rebellion; even much of the strife between Hindus and Muslims are due to the distortions of growth. The answer is not lower growth or an even less liberal economic policy, but a more rapid growth and a better functioning polity. Yet, India's central problem today is a well-functioning economy and badly dysfunctional politics. If India is to sustain rapid and equitable growth, it has to do something about its politics—of course, within its democratic framework.

But even more than the economics of growth, it is the misreading of Indian history and the failure to accommodate genuine diversity in the national story, which accounts for tensions across the land—between the North-East and the rest, the North and South, between Hindus and Muslims, among the Hindus as also among the Muslims. Ideologies imposing a false unity, be they the Nehruvian secular–syncretic vision or the Hindutva vision, are false trails which need to be abandoned.

India needs a politics of poverty that delivers freedom from poverty. To do that it has to tackle the poverty of its politics. It also needs a story of why it is a nation and that story has yet to be told in a way that cements, and does not divide, the nation.

THE ARGUMENT

My argument in this book is that many of India's problems lie in a flawed understanding of its own history. Both nationalist and British historians have contributed to this process. Like a patient with a psychological problem, India needs to revisit its birth traumas as a nation. The remedy may be quite radical if one is to rearrange the patient's psyche so s/he can be well again.

The key is in history. Not the history going back into its hoary past, back to the mists of time, to Aryan arrival in north-west India, but to the outset of India's induction into global history, at the time of Vasco da Gama's arrival in Calicut in south India in 1498. India's nationhood, like that of the majority of nations around the world, was conceived and shaped in response to the impact of this globalizing shock.

This way of beginning our argument is deliberately provocative. I argue that India would not have been thought of as a single national entity, let alone an administrative/political unity, in the absence of a 300-year-long process of competition between European maritime powers on its soil as part of the global conflict for imperial domination, which began in the last decade of the fifteenth century and ended on the battlefields of Waterloo. The triumph of the British, I shall argue, saved India from the fate that Europe experienced after the fall of the Roman Empire—Balkanization into myriad separate nations. The British fought with European armies in Europe as well as in India, and with many Indian rulers over a hundred years between 1750 and 1850. By 1858, when the Crown took over from the East India Company, British India had been formed. This then led to some definition of the boundaries of India, once the Afghan wars had ended and Kabul was out of reach. An administrative unity called India was created by 1870. The nationalist discourse in India was born around this time.

It was, then, the reverse cycle of the erosion of British power starting sometime during the Boer War at the end of that century, which precipitated the final movements of India's move to freedom. Britain's war effort in the First, and even more the Second, World War accelerated this process. Much, of course, was done in India for that freedom, but it could not have succeeded, nor can it be understood, if we do not see India in its global context. It is because India's quest for freedom is seen entirely in its local context and with a false notion—or perhaps many false notions—of what makes India a nation, that accounts for much of the grief of the past sixty-odd years.

PART I

CHAPTER 1

THE VASCO DA GAMA
MOMENT

INDIA WAS A cluster of several open regional economies, many of which were trading by land and sea with the world; in the process the country acquired a reputation as a site of fabulous wealth. Where had this wealth come from?

Though a settled country for millennia, in 1500 India's population was about 100 million—less than a tenth of the populations of India's constituent parts today—the constituents being India, Pakistan and Bangladesh. The country had large regions which were basins of fertile land with good diversity of crops, forests and, of course, mountains and deserts. But with only 100 million to sustain, there was no need to reclaim land or clear forests. We don't know how the ordinary peasantry fared since many of the accounts of fabulous wealth are by travellers describing royal processions and life in royal courts. But we do know there were handicrafts and manufactures which catered to the luxury markets created by the kings and their retainers. It was this wealth which attracted invaders to the North and traders to the South.

South India has been a maritime trading region for millennia. All along the coastal areas bordering the Arabian Sea, the Indian Ocean and the Bay of Bengal, merchants have sailed in and out of local ports, carrying an amazing variety of goods. The Roman Empire as well as the Persian one traded with the South extensively since BCE. Southern India was well integrated into the nexus of world trade, eastwards with the Archipelago and China, and westwards with the Gulf and the Red Sea. North India was a part of Central Asia and traded along the routes which connected the land masses of Europe with Central Asia all the way to China, the Silk Route being the most famous example. While armies had poured into North India via the Khyber and Bolund passes for both loot and conquest, the South had been free from such incursions.

South Indian kings had spread their rule to the countries now known as Malaysia, Indonesia, Cambodia and Thailand. There is no record of a reverse 'invasion' of India in the South.

TRADE WITHOUT DOMINION, 1498–1750

The arrival of the Portuguese in South India in 1498 began a phase of Indian history in which it became part of a global power system. Unlike North India, which was part of the Central Asian power system, South India's maritime links with the Gulf countries to the west and the Indonesian archipelago to the east were long established. It was this maritime link that now connected South India with the new power system. The Iberian countries were first off the block among the European powers when it came to overseas exploration and empire building. Ships were becoming light and fast and they could carry cannon, which made them effective weapons of warfare on the high seas. They could also undertake long journeys.[1] With newly acquired geographical knowledge about the shape of the world and new navigation instruments, Europe was ready to explore the rest of the world. Having driven the Muslim armies out of the Iberian Peninsula, the Christian West was ready to expand its sphere of influence. The Pope in his infallible wisdom had divided up the world between Spain and Portugal, with the dividing line running somewhere near where Brazil is today. All land to the west of this line belonged to the Spaniards and the east to the Portuguese. It was not the first time the Pope had dealt in property which did not belong to him.

What the explorers were looking for was India, and wherever they made a landfall they described the natives as Indians. On the western shores of the Atlantic the Spanish found America, rich in land and natural resources and relatively sparsely populated—before the disease the Europeans brought decimated the locals. They destroyed urban settlements that they found—of the Inca and the Aztec cultures—and proceeded to extract as much gold and silver as they could by dragooning the native population to work in mines and, when necessary, supplementing this with slaves shipped from their African outposts. This land became, over the next half-a-millennium, Latin America; only the fact that the islands to the north had been named the 'West Indies' and the term used for the native peoples was 'Indians', are signs that remind us that the original quest had been for India.

Asia, unlike Africa and America, already had a dense population in many of its regions and many long established urbanized cultures. The capacity for technological knowledge in Japan, China and Korea and what is now Indonesia and India, was in advance of most European countries. In fact, China was famous for its wealth and the wisdom of its mandarins; so much so that the great French Enlightenment philosopher, Voltaire was to contrast the stupidity of the French Bourbon kings with the wisdom of the Chinese emperors.

Europe and Asia were never separated by the ocean, forming a contiguous land mass over which caravans could travel from Venice to the heart of China—as Marco Polo's travels bear witness to. There was trade through the roads and by sea right up to the Egyptian ports on the Red Sea and the Gulf. What the Europeans did not know—and had not explored—was the Pacific route to Asia. That was yet to come. So, in the meantime, the race was on to find the passage to India. The Portuguese won that race.

WHERE WAS INDIA?

So eastwards went the Portuguese in search of spices which they were sure they would find in India, though as John Keay says, '. . . the words "India" and "Indies" had no precise geographical connotation. They were used indiscriminately to describe anywhere east of the Cape and west of the Azores. Thus the Spice Islands might be regarded as part of "India" and Goa as somewhere in the "Indies".'[2]

What the Portuguese circumnavigation of the Cape of Good Hope achieved was to remove the capacity constraints on East–West trade which meant a sea journey to the Red Sea; then the goods had to be lugged across the land to the Mediterranean and finally put on a ship to Venice. Now, at reduced cost and with fewer middlemen, goods—spices and textiles for instance—could be taken by sea from Asia to Europe. India was joined up to Europe via the Arabian Sea and the Indian Ocean.

Of course, India had never been entirely closed off from the continental politics of Central and West Asia. During much of its history the frontiers of North India—Indostan or Hindustan (land of the Indus) as it was called—extended up to Kabul where the Kushan Empire flourished in the second century CE. Niccolao Manucci, travelling in India in the seventeenth century, remarks of the river Narmada: 'Its waters divide the lands of the Deccan from those of Industan, which word means "*Gentile*dom".' It was this land, Industan to which incursions from West Asia, of Arab, Afghan and Persian armies, using the mountain passes of the North-West, became routine after the advent of Islam in the seventh century CE. This is not only the route the Indo-Europeans (Aryans) were supposed to have taken when they came to India, but Alexander the Great, too, came this way in the fourth century BCE. The Mongols used these passes when they came from Central Asia. Timur arrived first, but stayed only temporarily; Babur, the first of the great Mughals, more permanently. North India was then very much a part of Central Asia—South-Central Asia rather than South Asia as it is thought of now. Its trade was linked by roads to the Silk Route and hence to Chinese and West Asian markets. The traffic was quite heavy on the land routes and traversed as much by traders as soldiers. Reading the memoirs of Ibn Battuta who came to India in the fourteenth century, it becomes clear how closely knit the Islamic world was from Morocco to India and China.[3]

South India was relatively immune from these Central Asian connections. Southward penetration by North Indian kings remained patchy until Akbar in the sixteenth century; then Aurangzeb extended the Mughal Empire's borders even further south in the seventeenth century. But even that territorial control was short lived. South India was culturally connected to the North as much of the philosophical thinking in Hinduism came from the South, for instance, the teachings of the great savant Sankara in the eight century CE. But politically it was autonomous. Again, John Keay in continuation of the previous quote says:

> As seen from the crow's nest of a European merchantman, the south Asian subcontinent, like the Far East, comprised several distinct trading areas—the Coromandel coast, the Malabar coast, Bengal, Gujarat etc. Each belonged to a different and independent state with its distinctive language and its particular productions; each was historically and commercially linked to various trading areas in east and west Asia; and each was separated from the others by weeks, even months, of sailing. For the Jacobean navigator, as for his employers in England, India as a political entity simply did not exist.[4]

A contrary view is put forward by Burton Stein:

> By the seventh century, 'India' was conceived both by the people of the subcontinent and by Chinese and other visitors as extending from the Himalayas to the southern tip of the Indian land mass. No longer was a distinction drawn between the northern, or continental, portion and the long peninsula that spread southward from the Gangetic heartland of the ancient Aryans. The integration was acknowledged in the dharma texts of post-Gupta times, which accepted that there were customs—the touchstone of the sacred law—that were different, but no less valid, in the south . . . But Chinese Buddhist pilgrims sojourned in southern lands considering them part of the India where they may find Buddhist texts and savants. By the seventh century, in fact, a single complex system of political, ideological, economic and cultural relations and institutions obtained over the whole of the subcontinent; southern peoples participated fully in the evolving history of India and it was in the south that many of the religious practices of the medieval age were first manifested.[5]

WHAT WAS INDIA?

There is no contradiction between these two statements by two distinguished foreign historians of India, though the India they describe was a thousand years apart. Stein is speaking of India as a Hindu society in which the religious practices permeating the cultural, political and economic spheres had matured. Along with the religious belief system had evolved a social structure with a caste system which had religious sanction that gave a certain uniformity to Indian society across all regions. The religion was unlike the monotheistic religions of the Abrahamic family.

The people of the Indus Valley civilization, which flourished around 2000 BCE, had built an urban civilization of some sophistication and archaeological evidence indicates they worshipped animistic gods. The incoming Indo-Europeans, on the other hand, were a nomadic, pastoral people, and had at the outset a pantheistic religion—expressed in the hymns of the *Rig Veda*—Vedic Brahmanism. This was much like Greek and Roman religions with many gods behaving in larger-than-life, yet human fashion—somewhat like Hollywood and Bollywood celebrities today with a similar pecking order among the gods. Indra, the god of rain and thunder, was the head of the Vedic pantheon; Agni was the god of fire and the subject of many hymns in the *Rig Veda*, and the pantheon included the gods of the wind and the sun—and many others.

Most experts agree that what emerged by the end of the first millennium BCE was a synthesis of the two belief systems with the 'dark' gods—Shiva, Vishnu and Kali—emerging as dominant and the Vedic gods increasingly marginalized.[6] This synthesis was helped by the emergence of a rival belief system which challenged Vedic Brahmanism. The message that Gautama, the Buddha, preached in the sixth century BCE was spread by organized bands of monks trained in large universities and monasteries. Buddhism's simpler approach to salvation and its critique of Vedic Brahmanism's animal sacrifices and elaborate rituals appealed to many people, especially among the castes one or two notches below the Brahmins.

There are conflicting views as to whether Buddhism was an independent religion which successfully rebelled against the then prevalent Vedic Brahmanism with its emphasis on sacrifice—yajna—or whether it was merely one of the many variants of Hinduism; Jainism was one such variant which also broke away from Hinduism, but stayed a minority practice and did not, unlike Buddhism, spread outside India. In one sense, these rival belief systems were proposing a simpler monotheistic structure in place of the myriad gods of Vedic Brahmanism. An influential view has been that Buddhism represented the changing class structure of ancient India, which saw the merchants emerging as a powerful group, posing a challenge to the warrior Kshatriyas and the Brahmins who were ritually dominant. It represented, moreover, the transition from a pastoral to an agricultural mode of production. Damodar Kosambi, perhaps India's most original Marxist historian, championed this approach, though others argue—more conventionally—that Buddhism is merely a branch of Hinduism and did not acquire the full paraphernalia of a religion until after its migration out of India.

As the historian N.N. Bhattacharya says:

> Buddhism [was] one of the numerous offshoots of the Vedic religious tradition. It wanted to project the 'enlightened one' [Buddha] far above the natural gods of the Vedas ... The process of such supercession began in the post-Rigvedic age when the early Vedic nature-gods were first subordinated to Yajna, elevated to the position of the world principle in the Brahmanic literature, and then to *brahman*, the all-pervading cosmic self of the Upanisads. Two common features are conspicuous in the whole process. The first is the marked decline in the position of the Vedic nature-gods which was probably caused by man's increasing mastery over nature ... Although in a religious sense the concept of *brahman* later culminated in the growth of monotheism based on the equation of the sectarian Supreme Beings with the Upanishadic Absolute, the basic concept was based on the equation of the cosmic self with the human individual self ... Buddha humanly incarnated by the historical Buddha apotheosised to the status of the Supreme Being in course of time.[7]

Either way, Buddhism was organized as a proselytizing movement with the *sangha* as the active agency of monks. It received royal patronage most notably from Emperor Ashoka, who in the third century BCE spread its message across India with a series of strategically placed inscriptions. The struggle between Vedic Brahmanism and Buddhism lasted over nearly a thousand years from the sixth century BCE till the eighth century CE. But even by the end of the last millennium of BCE, Hinduism had emerged as a simpler, more appealing religion. Its many gods were replaced by the three major 'dark' gods. Interestingly, Brahma, a 'white' god, though called the 'creator' and one of a trinity with Vishnu and Shiva, was quietly sidelined and temples dedicated to him are rare. Rituals became simpler and *bhakti*—devotion to one or more of the major three gods—replaced Vedic practices. Sacrifices largely ceased to have animal killings and became 'vegetarian'. The somewhat esoteric and intellectually forbidding corpus of late Vedic philosophy embodied in the *Upanishads* was simplified in the *Bhagavad Gita*, the central text of post-Vedic Hinduism. All the previous paraphernalia of the *Vedas* and the *Upanishads* continued, however, as the better educated and learned Brahmins were in charge of the rituals. For ordinary people, it was the worship of the gods that mattered, so they did whatever the Brahmins told them.

In the eight century CE Sankara debated with Buddhists and the various schools of Hindu philosophy and established the hegemony of the high philosophical doctrine of *Advaita*—the non-dualistic principle of a universal presence or *Brahman* (not to be confused with the caste label, which I shall spell in the Western style as 'Brahmin'). It was a monist rather than a monotheistic resolution of the multiple contradictions of Vedic Brahmanism. The many gods of Hinduism were retained for the ordinary worshipper but at the high intellectual level, Hinduism was furnished with a lean analytical doctrine. Whatever the merits of this philosophical battle, it exiled Buddhism from India and established Hinduism as the universal belief system.

As a belief system, Hinduism is unusual in not having a name for itself. The term is derived from the Persian word 'Hindu', itself derived from the river Indus or Sindhu and the 'ism' is a Western addition. It is also called *sanatan dharma* (perennial philosophy). Yet, it is unlike other religions in that it has no single god, no single Book and no Church hierarchy to enforce religious practice. There is no confession and no priesthood with a divine sanction. It is a complex mesh of many belief systems which share a common ancestry. Hinduism has remained popular because it is a multi-tiered belief system ranging from worship of simple local gods—the serpent god or the small-pox goddess, for instance—to the two main gods, Shiva and Vishnu and the mother goddess, Kali, and higher still, the philosophy of *Advaita/Upanishads*. As there are no methods of practice laid down, there is ample choice for the worshipper to be as simple or as elaborate as s/he wishes. One could believe in many gods, in one god or merely in the monistic principle of the Brahman, or all at once.

What gave the Hindu society a semblance of unity is not so much the belief system but the caste system. Across India, wherever Hindus lived, they could identify the Brahmins as the highest caste which was entitled to ritual honour and often material concessions from the ruling authority. The system was defined at a macro-social level by the *varna* system or the four-fold caste division—Brahmins, Kshatriyas, Vaishyas and Shudras. At the bottom, beyond the pale were the Dalits—the pariahs who were outside the system and yet exploited by it. Within the macro-social structure there rose a complex morphology of *jati*, of which there were hundreds in the interstices between the four (plus one) division. While the details of the jati names and status varied by region, the top position of Brahmins was uniform across the country as was the pariah status of the Dalits. In between these limits there was a lot of flexibility possible since there was no overarching authority to assign each jati a precise rank relative to the others.

In the absence of a Church and a Book, the system was sustained by the ubiquitous presence and acknowledged authority of the Brahmins, as mentioned before, along with the ability of orthodoxy and superstition to sustain a hierarchical structure rooted in the accident of birth. It was a decentralized but ideologically resilient system of oppression where women and lower jatis were at the receiving end of the many sanctions which could be administered by the local elders of the dominant caste groups. Many of these sanctions were codified in a treatise attributed to the sage Manu—*Manusmriti*, literally the 'Laws of Manu'. Since the upper castes had a monopoly over knowledge and often a predominant share of the assets, especially land, which was tilled by the lower orders, the power structure had ideology as well as material force at its disposal. There was also the belief in reincarnation, which meant that rewards for good behaviour were not available in this life for the poor and the punishment for bad behaviour was postponed for the powerful. It was not until the advent of Western rule that the hierarchies of the caste system were mapped and the British even undertook the impossible task of assigning precise status to the myriad jatis. The emancipation of the lower castes, and especially the Dalits, did not begin till after the arrival of the Europeans.

The three top castes, Brahmins, Kshatriyas and Vaishyas, were upper castes entitled to an access to education, though only the Brahmins could learn Sanskrit, and read and recite sacred texts. The Shudras and the Dalits below them were denied education or profitable occupations. Since caste is defined by birth, there was no individual mobility up the ladder, though later in the modern period some amount of jati mobility up the ritual and economic ladders, did take place. It was only after the opening up of education to all Indians, once the British established a modern education system, that the calcified structures of Hindu society began to crack.

Thus India at the end of the first millennium CE presented the world with a single society and a rich and complex belief system. The belief system ranged from animistic worship to the heights of monistic philosophy. Yet, the society was deeply unequal and hierarchical. As a belief system, Hinduism does not believe in equality even in theory and not at all in practice. The inegalitarianism of Hinduism has been celebrated by the French anthropologist and political philosopher, Louis Dumont in his classic study of the Hindu caste system.[8]

The philosophical glories of Vedic Brahmanism were not for the lower orders; monotheism or monism, bhakti or rituals, they could neither acquire the knowledge to grasp these subtleties nor the social power to challenge it till the advent of modernity in the nineteenth century. Unlike in other societies, Hinduism denied the consolation of religion to its most oppressed. They could not enter temples nor could they access the priestly castes to perform their marriage, birth or death rituals. And yet they were tied to the system that degraded them by the compulsions of hunger and the inability to escape.

The consolidation of Hinduism achieved by Sankara in the eighth century CE had received a severe jolt when Muslim armies came from the North-West. This was the expansionist phase of Islam as it had emerged in the seventh century CE out of Arabia. Its westward expansion had taken it as far as Spain and eastwards it came to India by the end of the first millennium CE. As a single-Book, single-God religion with a fierce iconoclasm as its central tenet, Islam was everything Hinduism was not—a hard as against a soft religion, an intolerant religion sure of itself as against a multi-tiered complex belief system, an egalitarian faith as against an inegalitarian one.

As they came down the Khyber pass, Muslim armies were able to conquer territory quite quickly. Although their initial forays were merely to loot and destroy idols in temples, soon Afghan kings established a permanent presence in North India. Muslims also proselytized, often at the point of a sword, but also the message that Allah would give them equal status with other believers appealed to the downtrodden lower orders in Hindu society. The fragmented political structure of North India with many rival Hindu kingdoms did not stand much chance against the incoming armies. There began for North India a long period of Muslim domination.

Unlike its earlier rivals such as Buddhism or Jainism, Islam did not engage in a religious debate with Hinduism. There are no accounts of great debates between Hindu scholars and Muslim ones as there are of debates between Muslim, Jewish and Christian philosophers in Moorish Spain. Individual travellers such as Alberuni and Ibn Battuta did show some curiosity about Hinduism, but by and large no interaction took place in the sense of a dialogue. Hinduism withdrew within its own protective walls which were immune to mere ideological attack. In North India there was, for many centuries, a stand off between the Muslim kings who levied a tax on the infidels, and Hindu kings who periodically fought them or aligned with them.

There was eventually a slow growth of a syncretic culture in North India, largely a product of the royal courts, which drew from the music, the language and the culture of each community. The many lower caste converts to Islam did not abandon their beliefs in their local gods, and some sophisticated Muslims took an intellectual interest in the upper reaches of Vedantic monism. Sufism, a deviant sect of Islam, is suffused with elements of Hindu mysticism and espouses universal love. Across North India Sufism, as well as a practical syncretism of the lower caste converts, gave a semblance of peaceful coexistence between the two belief systems. Soon, Indian Islam also began to give rise to cults of local saints whose graves became places of pilgrimage for Muslims as well as many Hindus, who just added another god to their large pantheon. Thus the *dargah* (grave) of Moinuddin Chisti of Ajmer in Rajasthan became a place of worship for all communities, so much so that some of the groups who were marching to Ayodhya, to destroy the Babri Mosque in December 1992, sought the blessings of the holy saint before committing their act of anti-Islamic vandalism.

Some Muslim kings were tolerant of the idol worshippers among their subjects and often rescinded the infidel tax—*jaziya*. Akbar, who was the third Mughal emperor, and the one who consolidated the Mughal Empire, was curious about all religions and conducted dialogues with Hindu, Christian and Muslim scholars—at his death some Jesuit priests even hoped for his late conversion to Catholicism. He even established his own variant of a syncretic religion, *Din-e-Ilahi*. But the religion died with him.

Akbar's reign stood out like a solitary beacon of tolerance and generosity among the many Muslim kings. He intermarried with Hindu royal families and, for a couple of generations after him, the tolerant phase of Mughal rule continued. The fierce intolerance of the last great Mughal emperor, Aurangzeb, reverted to form. After his death, the unravelling of Muslim rule in India and the advent of the British changed the balance between the two principal religions of India. The history of their coexistence presents episodes of cooperation and of conflict, with scholars emphasizing one or the other, depending on whether they wish to highlight the tolerant, syncretic phase or the conflictual, intolerant one. The result is that by the end of the eighteenth century CE, India was not the vision that Burton Stein presented in his quotation, nor was it a Muslim society.

The South, where Muslims had first gone as merchants and not as conquerors, had a very different historical trajectory. Muslim kingdoms were established as extensions of Northern kingdoms, but they had to contend for control with large and thriving Hindu kingdoms, for instance, the Vijayanagar and the Maratha kingdoms, right up to the eighteenth century. The interaction of Islam and Hinduism was qualitatively different and much less fraught in the South than it was in the North, though, it must be said, that the topic has not been given the same kind of attention as its North Indian variant. The fact remains that India was different, North and South. Similar is the much neglected story of the North-East of India—Assam and the hill tribes on the modern borders of India with China and Burma—whose cultures retain a distinct shape and has not been studied to the same extent as North, or even South, Indian culture.

In this respect India was much like Europe of the time of, say, Charlemagne at the end of the eighth century. The Roman Empire, which had united Europe, was in decline. Such unity as there was in Europe was shaped by Christianity, yet political authority was fragmented in various large and small kingdoms. There was, and continued to be for centuries, a division between Western and Eastern Europe, the dividing line running through the River Elbe where the Roman Catholic Church gave way to the Greek Orthodox Church. By the seventeenth century, Western Europe was having convulsions due to the religious schism caused by Martin Luther. India was also, by then, no longer just a Hindu society but a mixture of Islam and Hinduism. The relation between the two religions was—and continues to be—a combination of conflict and cooperation.

India was thus a cultural plurality, dialectically shaped by unifying moments as well as episodic ruptures, and a fragmented polity, rarely united under a single king. This was as true of the seventh century as of the seventeenth. The Jacobean sailor thought in terms of political entities since he had to do deals with whoever was in authority at the port where his ship landed. While Chinese scholars looked at the cultural unity since they had no dealings with political authorities.

THE SHAPE OF INDIA

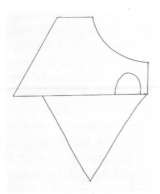

It is best to think of India as a sum of two shapes. At the top is a pentagon with a base going across from the Makran coast in the west to the Naga Hills in the east. The left side of the pentagon rises from where the border of today's Pakistan with Iran is, up to the Pamir mountains. Then a short flat line goes across the Karakoram range. On the east the line rises from the border with Myanmar in the Naga hills to the top where the Brahmaputra enters India. The fifth side is not a line but an arc which traces the Himalayan range. This is North India. The South is an inverted triangle with its apex at Cape Comorin and two straight lines, east and west, joining up the flat base of the pentagon near the Rann of Kutch on one side and the Sunderbans on the other. This is not an exact but a suggestive description since it is a linear approximation of a very non-linear shape.

The point of this thought experiment is that it helps to think of these two parts as only loosely articulated for much of India's history. The difficulties of transport across land with bad roads and lurking robbers made rapid, or even regular, movement North to South difficult. Intrepid walkers and itinerant holy men and Brahmin preachers did traverse the length and breadth of the land, but for the majority, life was local and depended on whether you lived south or north of the Vindhya mountains.

Moreover, the ecology of the two shapes is also different. Each contains regional economies which, in the past, flourished appropriate to the soil, climate and ecosystems. North India is dominated by the Doab, the large land mass watered by the Ganga and the Yamuna and the various river systems which join them. This is a fertile alluvial plain whose possession determined the fate of the Delhi kingdom. The Doab traverses the states of Uttar Pradesh and Bihar of present day India and ends in Bengal where the confluence of the two rivers breaks up again into various branches. Up north and west of the Doab is the land of the five rivers—the Punjab, which is now divided between India and Pakistan. Outside the Doab leading up to Bengal and the Punjab, the northern part is dry and hilly; Sind and Rajputana along with the Thar Desert are hilly or arid regions. The South is accessible by sea and even the Ghats, which shelter the interior from the sea coast, are not an insurmountable obstacle. Regional economies are along the coast— Gujarat, Konkan and Karwar, Malabar, Coromandel and Golconda coasts as well as the large Deccan Plateau.

It is difficult to think of India as separated in this fashion. We think of it as one single nation state, but to imagine this was not possible till the advent of the railways and trunk roads in the late nineteenth century. India was an idea, a social order; it was not a geographical unity with precise boundaries until after the last Anglo-Afghan War (1893) when the Durand Line was drawn separating India from Afghanistan—before that Kabul was often part of the Mughal Empire. Other borders in North India have not been so solid—for instance, the Younghusband expedition in early twentieth century fixed a border with Tibet. But this was contested by the Chinese, during the India–China border dispute of the 1950s, in the north in Aksai Chin, as well as in the north-eastern areas in what is called Arunachal Pradesh today, leading to the 1962 war between India and China. The Indian state of Nagaland, on the southern edge of the North-East at the border with Burma (Myanmar), has seen constant tensions between New Delhi and the leaders of the Nagaland movement for the last sixty years. Even so, from late nineteenth century onwards, there was a shape to India which had not existed in the centuries before. So, in looking at India in the 1500 to 1750 period, it helps not to project our more recent visions of the nation back on to the past.

NORTH INDIA

North India was largely a land-bound continental economy deriving its revenue from land, inland trade and some overland trade. The handicrafts industry, along with other flourishing industries, catered mainly to the luxury demands of the royal courts and the aristocracy. We have very limited knowledge of ordinary people's living standards, but travellers' accounts relate the impressive luxury of the royal households and the very humble consumption levels of the rest of the population. The fabled riches of India seem to have been highly concentrated in the hands of the noble elite.

Ibn Battuta, being a learned man of some repute, upon arrival in Delhi in the fourteenth century CE, was awarded a salary of 5000 dinars by Mohammed Tughlaq, to be paid from the revenue of two-and-a-half villages. Soon after, he was made a *qadi* (judge) in Delhi, and his stipend went up to 12,000 dinars with an equal amount as cash advance plus a horse and saddle and robes of honour. This was at a time when a soldier was paid a monthly salary of about twenty dinars and the average family lived on about five dinars a month.[9] Even then, he got into debt because he had to emulate other noblemen who gave outrageously expensive gifts and competed with each other in spending money they did not have. Ziya al-Din Barani, a courtier-cum-historian at the Tughlaq court, writes, 'If one of the nobles bestowed fifty horses in his wine party and gave robes to two hundred persons, another noble hearing this would feel jealous, and try to give away a hundred horses and to bestow robes on five hundred persons.'[10]

Ibn Battuta soon owed 55,000 dinars. Around this time, in 1335, six months after his arrival, a famine broke out in North India which lasted seven years and as Barani reported, 'thousands upon thousands of people perished of want.'

Things moved slowly on land in those days before the advent of railroads and much of the transport of goods was by bullocks which clans of *banjaras* plied up and down the perilous roads carrying low-value bulky goods. They were provided armed guards by the local ruler or by the private merchants who employed them. People walked, and the better-off moved about in palanquins, and the higher up they were, the larger the retinue they carried with them. Francois Bernier relates that when Aurangzeb went to Kashmir for a health cure, 36,000 soldiers, tent carriers, cooks, tailors and dress makers, among many more, went along to feed, clothe and serve the higher generals and the *zenana*—the harem which accompanied him. When the emperor left it, Delhi was emptied, as all accompanied him. There must have been close to 100,000 people in Aurangzeb's retinue. Scores of elephants and horses and camels were harnessed as the entourage made its way slowly from Delhi to Lahore and then northwards into Kashmir. Elephants and men died along the way due to the hazards of weather and treacherous land slips. The life of the ordinary person was cheap.

A retainer called a *mansabdar* was obliged to maintain a certain number of armed men and horses, the number varying according to rank. There were sixty-six ranks of mansabdars who maintained armies which ranged from as little as ten retainers all the way to 5000 and beyond. In the Mughal era, an officer of 5000-rank kept 340 horses, 100 elephants, 140 camels, 100 mules and 160 carts. He was paid Rs 30,000 per month and granted a *jagir*, like Battuta was, to collect the revenue of a number of villages. Of course, what he actually exacted could be much higher than the official rate. This is when a servant was paid three or four rupees a month at most, and an unskilled labourer got half that much. Shireen Moosvi has calculated that there were 1671 officers of various categories in 1595 and their salaries absorbed about 83 per cent of the total revenue.[11]

Yet, the basic necessities of life were very cheap indeed. Abul Fazl, a courtier-historian at Akbar's court, recorded many such facts about daily life in his *Ain-I-Akbari*. An unskilled worker's daily wage would purchase him 18 lbs of millet or 14 lbs of gram and 4.5 lbs of milk. Ghee, a real luxury, would take two days' wages for a pound. Pelsaert, travelling in Akbar's times, mentions that the poor in Agra consumed it regularly. In his study of standards of living in Akbar's time, Ashok Desai claims that in the late sixteenth century the consumption level of the ordinary people was as high as it was in 1961, though other critics have remarked that he probably had wages of the royal servants as his base; away from the imperial palace, things were a little less grand. But even if he was right, there seems to have been a deterioration in the next couple of centuries even before the advent of colonial rule. Thus Moosvi concludes that per capita income measured in terms of wheat purchasable was 13 per cent higher in 1595 than it was in 1910–11, though she admits that if one took cloth as the comparator, with cheap industrial production, the relative positions might reverse. These are, of course, all calculations based on life in the royal capital for which the information is provided by the court historian. In the rural areas, where the vast majority lived, things were grimmer.[12]

Of course, North India was not a single economy. With high transport costs and bad roads it could not be. Also, kings made much revenue from tolls and cesses on the movement of goods, from which the favoured few got exemptions. Trading companies put much effort into obtaining such exemptions from internal taxes. Thus, the English East India Company pulled out all stops in 1715 with *forty tons* of presents to petition Emperor Farukhshiyar for a *firman* which would exempt the Company's trading from all internal tolls. As Keay relates it:

> Carrying the presents and the mission's trade goods, 160 bullock carts, each loaded with half a ton, creaked along in single file. Twenty-two more oxen hauled the cannon, also destined for the Emperor, while 1200 porters bent beneath an assortment of loads which included the mission's chintz-lined tents and a selection of richly furnished palanquins. Amidst this concourse, ten hackeries, some fifteen camels and an assortment of horses and ponies jostled for road space. The troops, to a total of 600, patrolled the flanks and guarded front and rear. In all the caravan must have been fully a mile long; when in early May (a month after it left Patna) it reached the Ganges at Benares, the mission's diary records four days of 'ferrying over our goods'.[13]

Still it was worth it, and after having hung around the imperial court for seventeen months, the Company was granted its wish—and just in time since within a year Farukhshiyar was murdered. The Company was to use this firman in its battle forty years later with the Nawab of Bengal, Siraj-ud-Daula, and leverage its possession of all of Bengal thereafter.

The more important regions of the North included, firstly, the stretch from the North-West Frontier up to Delhi. The westward frontier here could be all the way to Kabul. Enterprising young men seeking a career in the Mughal army and more humble people from West Asia and Persia plied down this road. This region had the five rivers of the Punjab and the Indus in particular was a vital lifeline. It did not then have the canals which were to transform Punjab into a granary in the late nineteenth century. Another region was the Doab, with the confluence of the Yamuna and Ganga and the many other rivers which ran into them; it was the heartland of the Northern economy. Beyond that was Bengal which was a separate regional economy connected to the seafaring regions of South India. The region beyond Bengal—Assam (Kamrup) and the rest of the North-East—was in a limbo of uncertain allegiance. Borders were fluid here and many tribes occupied the vast territory which today straddles India and Burma. Back on the western front, Sind and Rajputana were arid areas. Rajputana's kingdoms were often at war with the Delhi sultans and only Akbar was able to include it in his empire through intermarriage, though not without resistance from some families—the Rajput clan of the Sisodias being one example. Central India had mineral resources as well as good agricultural land for cotton cultivation. These economies were, however, loosely articulated and, though we think of India as a single economy today, it would be an anachronism to extend that idea back to the fifteenth century.

SOUTH INDIA

The South was a different world. There was immense inequality, of course, with kings as well as temples amassing fabulous wealth. The various regional economies which comprised the South—Gujarat, Konkan and Karwar, Malabar, Coromandel and Golconda—were open trading economies using their access to the sea to their advantage. Bengal was more akin to these regional economies than to the continental North, thanks to its access to the sea, and in fact there was a lot of inter-regional trade between Gujarat and Bengal using the sea lanes. The Europeans soon discovered that such trade was even more profitable than East–West trade.

The Deccan was an inland plateau and here the land was drier and life harder. We know less about wages and prices in this part of India since we lack an account such as Abul Fazl's. Wages in western Deccan were said to be a rupee per month for artisans such as blacksmiths in the seventeenth century, and their helpers got just a third of that. The eastern Deccan had higher wages than the western Deccan. One account states that labourers' wages were as high as Rs 5 per month in the late seventeenth century.[14] The daily sustenance of many village artisans was provided for by the village householders on a sort of rota basis in lieu of services performed by them when required. This system, known as *jajmani*, prevailed much more widely in the South than in the North, though recently some anthropologists have questioned the basis for this belief.[15] If such a system was as widespread as it is claimed to have been, then the village afforded some security to these artisans. I would guess that the merchant class was rather larger and more independent in the various regions of the South than was the case in the North, since they were less dependent on the royal courts for their living. For one thing they did not need royal concession to trade; moreover, by and large, the kingdoms did not provide any maritime protection to the merchants, so the merchants did not have to pay out large sums for this security.

Five famines occurred in the Deccan—at least those we know of—during 1630–31 and 1702–04 which were severe, and minor ones in 1655, 1682 and 1684. Famines were frequently followed by plagues. In famine years revenue would be remitted by the kings and local landlords; if severe, there would be free kitchens and grain would be brought in from surplus areas. Wars and plunder added to the miseries and invading Muslim armies are said to have reduced the population in the Deccan by a quarter in the late 1640s. We have only the occasional snapshot for the odd year on such matters as no statistics were recorded at the time.[16]

THE IMPACT OF EUROPEAN ARRIVAL

It is the relative autonomy that the South enjoyed which was breached in 1498. Although the European traders did not conquer it, and their trade affected, indeed even stimulated the economy, they changed the power equations in maritime trade in the Indian Ocean. The Portuguese bought spices to begin with—pepper especially, but also cloves, cinnamon, ginger and indigo. They began by asserting a monopoly over shipping routes in the Arabian Sea and tried to bar Indian merchants from them. They soon realized that the more profitable alternative was to tax the traders—that is, extract protection money from traders who had for centuries traded in the Red Sea and with Gulf countries. The Portuguese won a monopoly for the procurement of pepper from the Raja of Cochin, which meant that the local pepper producer got a lower price than he would have from other traders. When the Dutch replaced the Portuguese in the seventeenth century they, too, got a similar concession. There seems to have been no concerted effort by any South Indian Empire, Vijayanagar for instance, to counter these monopolies. Until the 1570s, when Emperor Akbar was fully in command in the North, there was no real challenge to the Portuguese; in any case, Mughal defences were land-based and their naval power was weak. As Om Prakash says in his masterly book on pre-colonial India, 'The Portuguese were able to enforce such an arbitrary and high-handed requirement essentially because of the near absence of effective naval capability on the part of Indian and most other Asian states.'[17]

Of course, what broke the Portuguese monopoly of the seas were developments in Europe. Spain and Portugal (which had merged for a few decades) lost out to the Dutch and then to the English in Europe during the sixteenth century. From the end of the sixteenth century onwards, Portugal concentrated on its empire on the two sides of the Atlantic—Brazil and Angola–Mozambique—while Spain had much of the rest of South America and an extensive empire in the Pacific.[18] It was the two 'emerging' European powers—the Netherlands and England—who began extensive trading in India by the seventeenth century and, by the second half of that century, the French joined them. Each of these new traders was a private enterprise—East India Companies—with some state sanction from home and not a state enterprise as the Portuguese were. Their demands were different. The Dutch spice trade had shifted to the Indonesian archipelago and textiles were the main export out of India. Tapan Raychaudhuri has described how the Dutch settlement in Coromandel stimulated the local economy as a result of their demand for textiles for export.[19] But Bengal and Gujarat also benefited. In the textile trade there was none of the monopoly procurement which there was in Malabar pepper.

ECONOMIC BENEFITS OF EUROPEAN TRADE

The Portuguese and their successor European trading powers engaged in intra-Asian trade which was more profitable, as well as trade with their home bases. Mercantilist sentiments were satisfied if the trading companies financed their European trade from their Asian trade profits. The Iberians had the advantage of being flush with the treasure from South America which sparked off, what John Maynard Keynes has called, 'the century of inflation' between 1550 and 1650. This treasure, as it was spent by them, gave much stimulus to the trade with Asia. The transmission mechanism of the treasure, largely silver, was such that most of it came to Europe via the spending of the Iberian kingdoms. Spain went through what today we would call the Dutch Disease. Its economy was pretty much ruined due to the influx of silver.[20] But the rest of Europe benefited from Spanish and Portuguese demand for imports. This, in turn, stimulated demands for Asian spices and textiles, which the Dutch and the English were able to pay for with bullion since they could sell none of their goods to the Asians. Some of the silver was used by the Portuguese directly to finance their pepper trade.

Angus Maddison estimates that between 1500 and 1700, Spain and Portugal shipped 308 metric tons of gold and 33,668 tons of silver. In the next century, which does not impact on India, 1400 tons of gold and 39,157 tons of silver. The British and Dutch East India Companies between them shipped 10,045 tonnes of gold and silver in silver equivalent terms between 1600 and 1780.[21] Maddison does not say how much Portuguese silver came to India during its trading heyday from 1500 to 1650. This would be a rough measure of the export surplus the South Indian regional economies enjoyed.

The effects of trade on an economy are better understood in terms of Adam Smith's theory of trade rather than the later Ricardian doctrine of comparative advantage. Smith posits that trade awakens dormant resources into action since he does not assume full employment of resources at all times as Ricardo does. Thus, the impact of the extra demand for spices and textiles would have harnessed many households, which previously did not cultivate these spices or spin and weave, to engage in producing the extra spices and textiles.

Om Prakash confirms this prediction:

> The increase in the output of export goods in the subcontinent in response to the secularly rising demand for these goods by the Europeans would seem to have been achieved through a reallocation of resources, a fuller utilization of existing productive capacity and an increase over time in the capacity itself . . . In the case of textile manufacturing, for example, artisans engaged in the activity on a part-time basis seem to have increasingly found it worth their while to become full-time producers and to relocate themselves in the so-called *aurungs*—localized centres of manufacturing production, where the Europeans were increasingly concentrating their procurement through the intermediary merchants.[22]

The upsurge in textile imports from India led to the predictable protectionist demands in England by 1700, seeking a ban on printed textiles from India which was easily evaded by exporting white textiles to be printed elsewhere in Europe. Even a ban on the use or wear of printed calicoes did not dent the trade. In light of recent protests by European manufacturers about Chinese textile exports under the WTO regime, one can only say the world has come back to where it was in the 1700s! To quote Om Prakash again, 'Such perceived threats of a "deindustrializing" Europe in response to the invasion by Indian textiles, however, makes one wonder as to which, between north-western Europe and south Asia in the early modern period, was the "core" and which the "periphery".'[23]

The available data do not permit any quantitative assessment of this impact. At the level of the Indian economy as a whole, the impact of trade on the local economies of Coromandel or Malabar or Konkan and Karwar does not register. However, only if we think of the Indian economy as a sum of many separate local economies, can we gauge the impact of trade. Angus Maddison estimates that for the period between 1500 and 1800 the economy had nil growth in per capita income—$550 (Maddison dollars) between 1600 and 1700, and a mild decline ($540) in the next fifty years, though population is estimated to have risen from 135 million in 1600 to 165 million in 1700 and 185 million in 1750.[24] It must be said, however, that if the accounts of pre-colonial trade are anything to go by, the Indian economy could not have been as stagnant as Maddison's estimates claim. The only other possibility could be that the North of India was declining as South grew, but we have insufficient information to conclude that.

Om Prakash's findings leave little doubt that Gujarat, Coromandel and Bengal were growing in this period, though the growth in Malabar was, perhaps, less rapid.

> An increase in trade being beneficial for a country is an axiom: in India's case the 'bullion for goods' character of the European trade considerably enhanced its positive implications and indeed turned it into an important instrument of growth in the Indian economy ... The growing level of monetization in the economy, in turn, facilitated reform measures such as the growing conversion of the land revenue demand from kind to cash, which led to a further increase in market exchange and trade. The growing availability of precious metals in the system also helped the rise of banking firms, and generally became an important factor in facilitating the expansion of the Mughal Empire.[25]

A direct connection between the outflow of silver from South America to Spain and imports of silver into India has been traced with a gap of five to ten years. Indian money supply—which was silver-based (178 grains troy), for the standard denomination *rupiyah*—trebled between 1591 and 1639. There was a slowdown for the next forty years and again the growth resumed in 1684. All silver which came in was minted into coin, while the gold which came in went into hoard, kept by goldsmiths. By the seventeenth century the exchange ratio between gold and silver was similar in India to that in Europe. In consequence of this influx there was a price revolution in India just as there was in Europe. Irfan Habib estimates that the rate of inflation was around 2 per cent per annum over the 150 years, 1600–1750. Real wages did not keep up with the inflation, though the evidence varies by region and type of worker, with a redistribution towards merchants and artisans as well as those whose incomes were paid in real terms, such as the revenue farmers.[26]

THE CHANGING CONTEXT IN
EIGHTEENTH CENTURY

It is from the late seventeenth century onwards that the English and the French began their hundred-year war, extending from 1695 to 1815. By the end of this period the Dutch had been marginalized in European warfare and had left India for Indonesia. The first effects of the Anglo-French rivalry were felt in 1744 during the War of the Spanish Succession in Europe. While the trading companies in India were not inclined to fight, naval squadrons arrived from France and England for a skirmish off the Coromandel coast. Both Companies were paying allegiance to the Nawab of Carnatic. The English appealed to him for protection against French attacks. The Nawab obliged but tardily; the English had surrendered to the French by then and conceded Madras. To punish the French, the Nawab turned his army on them, but Dupleix defeated him with a much smaller but more disciplined army. This was a new departure in many ways. As Parry says:

For the first time, Europeans had made war among themselves on Indian territory; they had defied the authority of their overlord, a major Indian ruler; they had defeated, with surprising ease a formidable army which the ruler sent against them, so demonstrating that cavalry, elephants and large numbers were no match for small forces possessing heavy fire power and [relatively] good discipline.[27]

Robert Clive was to exploit this knowledge more effectively than Dupleix, using the tactic of training Indian soldiers with British officers for the battle at Plassey a decade later. Indian rulers also emulated this tactic, hiring European officers to train their armies. In the next phase of the Anglo-French saga in the Seven Years War (1756–63), fought mainly in North America and the West Indies, England defeated France and this proved to be a decisive turning point, not only in Europe but more so in India. The French tried various alliances with local rulers— Hyder Ali for instance in the 1780s, but eventually lost out to the British in India. But this initial advantage of the British was short-lived. Whatever the glow of triumph which envelops the Battle of Plassey, it was neither the pivotal encounter as British imperial historians have claimed, not did it ensure irreversible British domination, as many Indian nationalists have argued. India was not that easy to conquer. As we shall see later, it took ninety more years till the British East India Company could claim to rule over the whole of India.

From 1500 till 1750 the interaction of the West with India was peaceful and trade driven. It was also during these 250 years that in North India, as in South India, wars between various kingdoms and dynasties, whose fortunes waxed and waned, left India without a serious power or state which ruled over a substantial part of its landmass.

The Vijayanagar Empire, which was flourishing when the Portuguese arrived, had declined by 1600, as had its rival, the Bahmani kingdom. On the other hand, there was no substantial power ruling over all of the North in 1500; but by 1600 Akbar had established a commanding position over much of North India up to Kabul and had even made inroads across the Vindhyas. The Mughals held out the possibility of a long running all-India dynastic rule, but again within 120 years that prospect vanished. The dissolution of the Mughal Empire was mainly at the hands of the Marathas and the Sikhs. The Maratha Empire enjoyed a good run for about a century from 1660 to 1760, and then collapsed over the next fifty years after its defeat in the 1761 war with the Afghan king, Ahmad Shah Abdali.

It is worth asking what other directions Indian history could have taken, by adopting a comparative perspective. This will be done at several points in this book. This is not a procedure which ever satisfies everyone and there are methodological debates about its validity. But it is well to remember that a counterfactual account is not a forecast. What happened in real life was only one of several possibilities. It is worth speculating what *could* have happened if that one possibility had not been realized and another had. Of course, there are always myriad possibilities. One has to pick and choose the more likely ones.

COUNTERFACTUAL BOX

India in 1700

In 1700 the Mughal dynasty had almost total control over the entire territory of India. There were irritants to Mughal rule, for instance the Marathas and the Sikhs, and the reach of the Mughal army did not quite cover Assam or Malabar. There were many European trading factories—Portuguese, Dutch, English, French, Danish—but they all hugged the coastline along the South.

At this stage the Western nations had not established a commanding lead in technology except for the ship mounted with light cannon. This was soon grasped in India but while the technology of iron-making was still primitive and small scale, the military advantage was marginal. We have to remember that the Western advantage over Asia does not really take a leap till the Industrial Revolution, which was still decades away. Commercial capitalism had come to Asia just as much as to Europe, though with different characteristics.

Had Mughal rule not gone into a long decline of 150 years after Aurangzeb's death in 1707 but continued vigorously, India would have been in a similar situation to China at that time. For China the Opium Wars and the concessions forced on it by the trading nations were still in the future. But even when they came—and though the Chinese nationalists resented them bitterly—China stayed a single nation state. The analogy is not exact, of course, but India could have stayed a single kingdom ruled by a 'foreign' dynasty, just as China was ruled by the Manchus. In 1911 China became a republic and though its next forty years were plagued by weak central control, warlords, civil war and Japanese occupation, China emerged from these experiences in 1949 strong and united.

That could have been India's trajectory. Whether it would have been able to adopt Western technology and science as they developed (assuming for the time being that there was no prospect of an autonomous spurt of industrial innovation in India) and resist European expansion which came later in the century, is a moot question. The nearest analogy in that respect is the Ottoman Empire. It was also immensely powerful in 1700, but failed to adopt the new technology early and sufficiently well to be able to resist continuous nibbling at its frontiers by the Habsburgs and the Romanovs. When the empire collapsed in 1920 after its defeat in the First World War, it split into many independent territories which became disunited and disaffected—and are so to this day.

Thus India could have had continuous Mughal rule which in 1700 looked pretty solid. Yet, its future trajectory could have gone either China's way with predatory European traders winning concessions at its edges, and yet remaining united up to the early twentieth century. Alternatively, it could have gone the way of the most powerful Muslim kingdom as of 1700 and ended up defeated and disunited. It could have been many different nations as West Asia is today.

What changed, of course, was that by 1750 there was no single powerful authority though the Mughal emperor in Delhi claimed suzerainty over a large territory. But the empire was Balkanized and many independent *satrap*s had emerged in Awadh, Hyderabad and Bengal. The Maratha kingdom spanned much of central India and the Deccan and organized raids deep into the South and into Bengal. The Mughal emperor was bankrupt as the flow of revenue to Delhi had ceased. Long distance overland trade routes became more dangerous—travelling in the mid-seventeenth century, Tavernier, Bernier and Manucci noted the constant possibility of being robbed on the highways, even within the Mughal Empire. Decentralization of power—though militarily weakening—was not necessarily bad for the economy. Burton Stein took the view that the collapse of the Mughal central authority was a good thing for the economy.

> It is claimed that new, smaller states with efficient tax-gathering procedures replaced the Mughal military imperial order, that market networks proliferated and became to a degree interlinked, that a more prosperous agriculture came into being with increased commodity production as a result of rural investments by the revenue farmers of the time, that all of this was buoyed up by an ever-increasing level of international trade in which Indian artisans, merchants and especially bankers played key and lucrative roles, and that this phase of political economy obtained until the first quarter of the 19th century.[28]

Tapan Raychaudhuri took a similar view in his contribution to the debate sparked off by Morris David Morris's revisionist article on Indian economic history.[29] Such views go against the conventional wisdom of nationalist historiography. It was firmly established in Indian nationalist thought that it was when the Centre became weak that India was open to foreign takeover. In preparations for prospective independence, the Congress party drew up a planning blueprint in which a strong central authority was essential not only for political independence, but economic development as well. It would cost the country thirty years of low growth, though perhaps the problem was not so much central control as the policy chosen which may have cost quite as much.

But yet again, what changed in 1750 was not so much internal to India but involved events in Europe. India was not of major concern to either the French or the British government since the East India Companies were private trading enterprises. But war meant booty and the local agents could not be relied upon to be sufficiently restrained by their company directors who discouraged expensive military adventures. The defeat of the French by the English in the Seven Years War had not yet altered the balance of power in Europe—that was to take another fifty years.

By 1750 the Dutch had given up any territorial ambitions they might have had in India. In the late seventeenth century they had fought wars with England. At that time the Dutch were the leading financial power in Europe having gained independence from Spain. But within the next fifty years the English surpassed them, both as a financial and as a military power. The last Anglo-Dutch war was fought in Europe in the 1780s, but by that time the Dutch had fallen far behind the English in fighting strength. They were soon conquered by the French after the Revolution and became dependent on England for their eventual independence. The Portuguese, meanwhile, had lost interest in India, and were content to simply hold on to what they already had. So the battle was left to the French and English East India Companies to fight it out as proxies for their governments back home.

The outcome—an English victory—was not a foreseeable certainty ahead of the time. Though they won the Seven Years War, the British were isolated during the first half of the French Napoleonic wars between 1793 and 1815. Victory, when it came, took a lot of diplomacy and some hefty subsidies to European continental kingdoms to provide mercenaries. In history, *ex ante*, there are always alternative possibilities. It is *ex post* and especially in hindsight, that outcomes look inevitable. Imperial history then gilds the lily a bit more to prove to the colonized that their masters were and are invincible. Later, I shall examine the reasons for the English victory over the French and for the steady surrender of different Indian kingdoms over the next hundred years, so that by 1850 the British conquest of India was complete.

COUNTERFACTUAL BOX

India in 1750

In 1750 India was divided into a number of small and a few large kingdoms. In a way it was back to its usual pattern to which only the Maurya period and the Mughal one were exceptions. The continuation of the Mughal emperor in Delhi was a symbolic rather than an effective presence. The major difference with the past 3000 years was the presence of four or five European powers who were vigorous trading and military nations and whose military technology was superior to that possessed by the Indian kings. Indeed, gunnery in many kingdoms was the preserve of hired Turkish or European officers. Innovations in arms were taking place in Europe, not in India.

If no single European nation had emerged victorious, what shape would India have taken? India's size is such that it can easily sustain many independent 'nations'. This is not as bizarre an idea as it may sound, in the twenty-first century after sixty years of Independence, for two reasons. Firstly, relative to what it was in 1750, India is today split into three nation states—India, Pakistan and Bangladesh. Secondly, for a continent as large as Europe, the surprising outcome is not that it would be Balkanized, but that it would be united into a single entity when, through the greater part of its history, it was not a single state.

Had India been divided into many nations as Europe is today, what would it have been like? There are two comparative examples which offer a clue. One is, of course, India's present federal structure. Individual states such as Uttar Pradesh or Tamil Nadu or Maharashtra are large enough to be countries in their own right and larger than most nation states of the world today. They are part of the Union of India, but that is one outcome the reasons for which we seek to explore in this book.

It is quite likely that not only would India have been a collection of many separate nation states, but they may even have been foreign colonies until well into the mid-twentieth century when Asia and Africa won their anti-colonial struggles. Thus, Tamil Nadu could have been French-speaking and Bengal either Dutch- or English-speaking. Maharashtra may have been Portuguese-speaking, Gujarat, English-speaking and so on. There would have been many nation states (or perhaps kingdoms) in the Doab and the Punjab which could have been run by local chieftains as they were till a hundred years after 1750. Indeed, some Princely States such as Hyderabad had dreams of an independent existence even in 1947.

How plausible is this? Again, two examples are available. One is South-East Asia where Malaysia, Indonesia, Vietnam, Cambodia, Laos, Thailand, Burma (Myanmar), all in close proximity to each other (and with a total population less than that of India) ended up being ruled by Dutch, British, French and local rulers. The entire region could easily have been Dutch or English or French despite the many different languages spoken. We think of them today as separate nation states, but that is an accident of history.

The other example is Sub-Saharan Africa. Again it is a continent or, at least, a substantial part of one. It too had some early foreign incursions by the Portuguese and the Dutch. But in 1884 at the Congress of Berlin, European nations, normally rivals, collaborated in a 'carve-up' of Africa among themselves. If the English and the French had not settled their battle the way they did in Europe, every European power could have stayed around in India and nibbled away at the edges. At some stage, when the bankruptcy of the Mughal power was obvious, and none else had taken its place from within the cast of Indian rulers, there could have been a similar carve-up of India.

The possibility that existed in 1700 for India to be single and independent like China (see previous box 'India in 1700') was lost by 1750, unless—by some miracle—the Maratha Empire had found within itself the will to establish and maintain all-India rule. By 1750 Balkanization, the usual pattern of Indian history, was much more likely with, rather than without, foreign presence. The outcome which did happen was, again, only one of the ex ante possibilities in 1750.

CONCLUSION

The 250-year period 1500–1750 is interesting from our contemporary viewpoint. This is because the colonial experience which followed made the nationalist movement suspicious of foreign trade and foreign capital as devices which enslave. The earlier period is an example when India, despite not being a single political entity, was a major trading power with the West and trade was unhindered by military domination. India had a competitive edge not only in textiles and some spices, but also in many other exports such as food grains which it regularly supplied to the islands in the Archipelago and to Gulf countries. In nationalist historiography, this long episode is downplayed, if not ignored altogether. British historians are also keen to write a seamless account of East India Company's domination more or less from the time it established its first factories in Surat in the early seventeenth century. In fact, the rivals in the pre-colonial period—the French, the Dutch and the English—were *equals* and the final victory was, echoing the words of the Duke of Wellington after Waterloo, 'a damn'd close run thing'. Yet, India's benevolent experience of trading as equals with European powers is worth recalling since India has re-emerged as a strong competitor in the global economy. Yet, there continues to be a suspicion of foreign trade and foreign capital in some nationalist and Left quarters. The reason for this lies in the historiography of Western imperialism.

Latin America's experience with Spanish and Portuguese imperialism, almost contemporaneous with these 250 years, was much worse. The Iberian countries were interested in extractive industries—gold and silver mining—and exploited the local 'Indian' population mercilessly. They also supplemented the labour force by importing slaves from Africa. Of the 9.4 million slaves who survived transatlantic shipment, 5.2 million went to Brazil and Spanish America, 3.8 million to the Caribbean and 0.4 million to the USA.[30] We have already seen the data for exports of gold and silver from South America to Spain and Portugal. Many contemporary debates about colonialism are influenced by this shameful episode in the European expansion overseas in the centuries following 1492. Marxist writers such as Andre Gunder-Frank and Paul Baran reflect in their works the searing experience of Latin America both under Iberian imperialism and then de facto American domination of the Western hemisphere.[31] India as a colony was, of course, the largest in the British Empire but unlike Latin America it had had a trading relationship with Europe for 250 years before foreign domination was established. It is this experience which needs greater attention than it has had thus far as India emerges as a powerful global economic player.

CHAPTER 2

THE ENGLISH TURN

IT IS COMMONLY said that colonialism integrated the Indian economy into global markets and altered India's export pattern from manufactures to agricultural products, as much through coercion as by reason of market forces. In fact, as we have seen in the previous chapter, India, or at least regions of South India and Bengal, was integrated into the global economy in the seventeenth century when three or four European trading nations were competing for India's exports. India's trade with the Archipelago and the Gulf region consisted of coarse textiles and food grains. The finer textiles went to Europe along with pepper, though Indonesia replaced India as the major source not only of pepper but of all spices.

What British rule did was to cut Indian trade off from the rest of the European economy and harness it to the British economy, and later to the British Empire in South-East Asia and Africa. The Dutch followed a similar process in Indonesia (then called the Netherlands East Indies) and the French followed suit in Indo-China. British rule, therefore, narrowed India's trade exposure. It was a rerun—on a much vaster scale—of the 120 years when the Portuguese tied Malabar's pepper producers to their exclusive buying and cut the region off from other traders (though there were leakages and evasions). India's economy thus became narrowly directed to the British economy, and as the latter's fortunes waxed in the nineteenth century and waned towards the turn of the twentieth, India's economy had to adjust accordingly.

The colonial experience also tied India to the British political system—to the Parliament, the bureaucracy and the monarchy. Britain was never the monolith which nationalist historians have made it out to be. The differences of party and class within Britain, and the changes these two categories underwent during the two hundred years of colonial rule over India, also require serious analysis. In the mid-eighteenth century, British parliamentary politics was dominated by factions who depended on aristocratic patronage; party labels were an uncertain guide to ideological differences. The king interfered in cabinet formation and dismissed ministries he did not like. This began with George III who was the first in the three generations of Hanover kings to understand enough English to interfere. The situation, therefore, revolved around what were essentially a King's Party and the Opposition. The electorate was narrow and consisted of scores of rotten boroughs with voters who were securely under the thumb of their aristocratic patrons.

India became the football of party politics at Westminster almost from the moment of the East India Company's victory at the Battle of Plassey in 1757. An infamous scandal of the time concerned the vast personal fortunes that Robert Clive and other East India Company traders—the nabobs, as they were called—had accumulated. Clive was aware that the Company was in no fit position to take on the task of governing what they were about to acquire. Even before the award of Diwani of Bengal in 1765, Clive had written to the Prime Minister William Pitt the Elder, that in his view it was not desirable for the East India Company to rule India and that the British government should take over this role. He was ignored. Pitt was busy with the war with France, and in any case felt taking on the governance of India was fraught with dangers. His fears had to do with the powers of patronage that India would bring to British politics.

If India came under British government control, it would greatly expand the king's opportunities for patronage. If Parliament—or rather the House of Commons—controlled the Company, then a patron to rival the king could be set in place and the faction in power could buy the votes required to perpetuate its dominance. But if the patronage was left in the hands of the East India Company, its directors could buy and sell parliamentary influence at will. Therefore, a desire to control the affairs of the Company existed in the ministry of the day, but fell short of actually initiating moves for a takeover. The new rulers of India, the East India Company, were not sovereign—they had someone looking over their shoulders. Previous rulers of India, Hindu or Muslim, were not subjected to Reports of Select Committees and Debates in Parliament or held to account for failing to fulfil not just British standards of behaviour, but what an influential set of persons—for instance the eminent eighteenth century parliamentarian, Edmund Burke—imagined Indian standards to be.

From the early intimations of power to the period between the late 1750s and 1785 when even more territory came into the Company's purview, India was the subject of many turbulent debates and much jockeying by rival factions for control. The year 1784 marked the passage of Pitt's India Bill which established a Board of Control to oversee Indian affairs. Pitt's bill was, in fact, the second India Bill. Charles James Fox, the Whig leader whom the king regarded with disfavour, had tried to pass his own India Bill. The Commons passed it but the king had it blocked in the House of Lords and Fox resigned as prime minister. But even after the passage of Pitt's Bill, there was a long backlog of resentment to work through as Burke (who was in Fox's group) tried to impeach Warren Hastings in a trial which lasted over seven years at the bar of the House of Lords.

Indians in the medieval period were not unused to rapacious rulers, and often the king of one region would think nothing about looting another. This is how military campaigns were financed by the Afghans, the Mughals, the Marathas and Hyder Ali. There was no bar on Hindu kings looting Hindus, Muslims looting Muslims and, of course, cross-looting as well. People had become accustomed to the heavy burdens of revenue demands, and often extra labour services as well, from their kings and emperors. Yet, these were local rulers, *Indian* rulers. They operated within a moral framework which they shared with their subjects. In those days religion and deeply entrenched notions of religious duty permeated all spheres of daily life; kings feared the afterlife—if not any payback in this one—for misdemeanours and injustices. My point is, conventions may have limited their cruelties.

The new rulers were different. J.H. Parry has captured the novelty of maritime empires. In essence, his argument is that the maritime empires stood in contrast to land-based empires in one respect. Within land-based empires, such as the Habsburg or Romanov or Ottoman, there was a seamless extension of power over neighbouring territory. An overseas empire is spatially discontinuous, and its foreignness stands out like a sore thumb. This is not a matter of race—the Australian resentment of the English reveals this clearly. Siberia and Australia were both penal colonies, but while one seemed just an extension of St Petersburg, the other was thousands of miles away separated by water. Yet, few will agree with J.H. Parry when he says rather provocatively, 'Even the British in India were not much more alien, and probably never more unwelcome or oppressive, than the Chinese in Tibet; though the Chinese have merely re-asserted, brutally and effectively, a loose suzerainty which had existed for centuries and was recognised by the British themselves.'[1]

The British were, indeed, alien; whether or not they were unwelcome is a question we need to examine. They were also oppressive even when they thought they were reforming or 'civilizing' India. Some of the oppression may seem—in retrospect—beneficial, for example, the reform of sati. But the sense of oppression stemmed from a lack of public legitimacy for the acts the British carried out. The Indians did not share the same moral universe; nor could they influence any action the British chose to pursue.

As far as the Chinese case is concerned, paradoxically, if we think of Tibet as a 'nation' today and not as a Chinese province, it is also because two hundred years of European imperial expansion spread ideas such as nationalism which date from no earlier than mid-eighteenth century at the earliest. Before that there were kingdoms and subjects, sometimes slaves; but no nations or citizens or nationals. The vast literature of nationalism agrees on that, if on nothing else.[2]

Parry's definition of empires, given at the very beginning of his book, is apt here.

> Wherever an organized group of people, or their rulers, have reduced other, alien groups, or *their* rulers, to the status of subjects, tributaries or subordinate allies; or have sent some of their number to settle in distant places and subsequently retained control of the settlements: there were the makings of an empire ... Since the later eighteenth century ... in normal English usage the word has described a particular kind of political organization, a super-state, comprising a metropolis and dependencies.[3]

WHY DID THE ENGLISH WIN AGAINST THE FRENCH?

The English East India Company's victory over its European rivals is *the* crucial event of the late-eighteenth century. It was not predictable ex ante. France had a larger population than Britain and hence a larger land army. Britain had a larger navy but despite Nelson's legendary triumph at Trafalgar in 1807, the French navy was not substantially inferior. Following the removal of James II, the last Stuart king, in 1688, Britain had a financial revolution through the eighteenth century with the establishment of the Bank of England, the National Debt and the Sinking Fund. With these institutions the British government could borrow at much cheaper rates than the French king could. French finances were crippled by its century-long war; indeed, this was one of the causes for the French Revolution.

The key to the financial revolution was, paradoxically, that unlike the French king, the British king did not have unlimited powers of taxation— the long struggle for liberty in English history had taken the form of a fight to limit the powers of the Crown to tax. From the time of the Magna Carta in the thirteenth century, the aristocracy and the Commons wanted to bind the hands of the Crown. The Commons grabbed the privilege of sanctioning taxes which the Crown always needed to wage wars. The aristocracy wished to subject the Crown to a rule of law. It was this restraint on the king which assured the financial markets that the tax revenue would be predictable and that the Crown would not get into unsustainable debt. Robert Walpole, as the First Lord of Treasury (the first proper prime minister), institutionalized National Debt and from then on public finances were transparent, if not prudent. As the Crown came under parliamentary regulation, so did the East India Company. Indian kings were not subject to parliamentary or aristocratic control; the only restraints were periodic coups and beheading of legitimate and even illegitimate successors—as the events of the final decades of the Mughal Empire demonstrated. The power of the Mughal emperor was absolute but precarious, if not maintained by personal prowess in arms. They were often in hock to merchants, but eventually their power to behead demanding lenders meant that lending to kings was also precarious business. The French king was a greater master of his aristocracy as compared to his British counterpart, and could summon his parliament. But when recalled, parliament did not always grant the French king what he wanted. The very restraint the English king faced, and the French king did not, made the English king a good risk as a borrower for the merchants and bankers who had money to lend. The French king's absolutism inspired suspicion that one's lendings may never be paid back.

WINNING BENGAL: THE BATTLE OF PLASSEY (*PALASHI*)

None of the reasons given above is sufficient to explain the English East India Company's success in edging the French out of India. Chance and individual leadership no doubt played a part, as did Anglo-French peace treaties concluded after their wars in Europe. The French had taken Madras during the 1740s, but it was restored to the English at the Treaty of Aix-La Chapelle which ended the War of Spanish Succession in 1748; similarly, the English took Pondicherry in the Seven Years War, but it was restored to France at the Peace of Paris in 1763. Clive sailed to Calcutta from Madras and took Chandernagore in 1757. It was then that the Battle of Plassey took place—and Clive's victory was by no means inevitable. But win he did, and from then on the Company's coffers were full—as were Clive's pockets.

The Battle of Plassey was not much of a battle in military terms as a business deal. The French and the English had, by their battles in the Carnatic campaigns, impressed upon Indian rulers that here was serious military talent, and it was available to the highest bidder. This is how the British East India Company was inducted into the transaction. The transaction was that Mir Jaffar, the Chief of Army Staff of the Nawab of Bengal, had signed a blank cheque for Clive to come and remove Nawab Siraj-ud-Daula and place him (Mir Jaffar) on the throne. In return, Mir Jaffar promised he would keep the troops under his command out of the fray. Behind Mir Jaffar was the new emerging commercial class—the traders and the bankers who had prospered during the last 150 years off exports matched by imports of silver and gold. Jagat Seth, for instance, had an international banking network which made him a powerful man—but, alas, not in the eyes of his feudal lord. The old nawab—Ali Vardi Khan—had been respectful; the new nawab—Siraj-ud-Daula, who had just succeeded to the throne in 1756—was haughty and arrogant. Jagat Seth's man, Ami Chand, was one of the nawab's bankers. He was brought into the conspiracy, but he wanted 5 per cent of the treasure which Mir Jaffar would get when he became nawab. Clive had different and better ideas.

The fighting stopped after four hours on 23 June 1757 because heavy rain intervened. Until then Mir Jaffar had not changed sides. Clive went back to his tent to change into dry clothes. Siraj-ud-Daula ordered the withdrawal of his artillery. Major Kilpatrick saw his chance—and in defiance of Clive's orders—charged with a small detachment of his troops. 'Clive rode on the scene breathing fire at Kilpatrick but was soon shouting for reinforcements.'[4] Mir Jaffar's troops stood by watching as the rest of Siraj's troops withdrew.

Siraj's 50,000-strong army was effectively reduced to 12,000 due to treachery compounded by confusion. With only a four-to-one advantage, he had no chance. He lost 500 men and Clive lost four Europeans and fourteen sepoys. Thus ended what later became famous as a decisive battle for the foundation of the British Empire. It has caused much agony and intense soul searching on the nationalist side on how it could have come to pass. Dr Biplab Dasgupta, an economist and a leading member of the Communist Party of India (Marxist) (CPI(M)), sums it up: it was 'the improbable takeover of a country as big as India, by a mere trading company that originally came to India to do business and make profits, from a land that was several thousand miles away'.[5]

This is a mirror image of British historiography which makes the Battle of Plassey such a pivotal event. One explanation which nationalist historians advance is treachery by Mir Jaffar and the nawab's banker whose silence was bought by a promise of 5 per cent of the nawab's treasure. He was promised this, but was double-crossed by Clive as 'we blush to write it', Macaulay commented disapprovingly. Macaulay minded the commercial cheating more than the disloyalty of Mir Jaffar. Yet, one needs the idea of a nation to be loyal to, to be a traitor. No such idea was around. As Dasgupta concludes, 'The ordinary masses, bereft of any idea of a nation, and used for a long time to invasions and palace coups, did not care whether it was a *Habsi* (a word for Abyssinian, i.e. Black African, in Indian languages) or a traitor or an Englishman on the throne. The elite was too concerned about its own safety and position in the new order to have any sense of shame.'[6]

Dasgupta's explanation for the debacle is almost epic, but well within the Indian Marxist tradition.

> Palashi was a contest between two modes of production, not between two armies or two people. It was not, in a historic sense, a contest between Bengalis (Indians) and Englishmen (or Europeans). While Siraj represented decaying and degenerate feudalism, the East India Company symbolized the world-wide rising power of nascent capitalism, with both contradictory features—on the one hand its dynamism, scientific outlook, secularism, rationality and global perspective, on the other its ugly, selfish, utterly dishonest, mercantilist face.[7]

The Battle of Plassey was, in fact, nothing of the sort. It was a single, contingent event and English rule over all of India did not, in any sense, become inevitable as a result of that one battle. English rule remained a fragile possibility for the next fifty years at least, if not the next ninety. Bengal had escaped being captured by the Marathas only due to the sheer tenacity and luck of Ali Vardi Khan who had managed to fend off many attacks. It could easily have gone the other way, even after Plassey. It is necessary, therefore, to place Plassey in context. The victory did give Clive the licence to replace Siraj by Mir Jaffar. This was hardly a new or a shocking event. The annals of the years since the death of the Mughal emperor Aurangzeb in 1707 record that Delhi had witnessed multiple and repeated betrayals and double-crossings. The difference was in the single-minded way in which Clive and every one of the Company's traders saw this as an opportunity to extract as much loot as possible from Mir Jaffar.

If at all there was a struggle between two 'modes of production', it was between the feudal-aristocratic mode of the nawabs and the Mughal emperor which extracted rent from land and thrived on warfare, on the one hand, and the emerging commercial capitalism of Jagat Seth which was still fragile and dependent on the aristocracy for its security, on the other. The latter exemplified the people who wanted guarantee of their private property and a stable, business-like government. Jean-Baptise Tavernier, the Frenchman who travelled across India in the seventeenth century, gives an account of his experience of selling a valuable jewel to a previous nawab of Bengal; he got cheated on his payment and had to curry favour with the nawab's underlings to get the proper amount. The newly rich of Bengal wanted something better and safer. They were the future and they sided with their commercial capitalist cousins from England.

The end of the Seven Years War with the Peace of Paris in 1763 confirmed the dominant position of the English East India Company over its European rivals in Bengal. This meant misery for Bengal. As Parry says of the Company's employees, 'Few of them felt any responsibility towards the people of India; officially, indeed, they had no responsibility, for the Nawab still reigned and ruled and the emperor was still, at least nominally suzerain . . . They fleeced the local populations, through their assumed privileges of duty-free internal trade in Bengal, which threatened to put local traders out of business.'[8]

The duty-free internal trade was what the Mughal emperor, Farukhshiyar, had granted way back in 1717. Now, with a tame nawab at their command, the Company traders could fully exploit that concession which before had meant bribing local rulers at each stage. The forty tons of presents would prove an investment worth making.

THE DISASTROUS DIWANI

A more decisive battle was fought at Buxar in 1764, 'perhaps the most important battle the British ever fought in South Asia',[9] where Company troops led by Hector Munro (Clive was stuck in Brazil on his way back to Calcutta from London) took on Mir Kasim (the latest puppet the English had made nawab of Bengal), Shuja-ud-Daula, the nawab of Awadh (Oudh) and Emperor Shah Alam II—and won.

Clive arrived in Calcutta and the Treaty of Allahabad was signed between Shah Alam II and the Company after the battle. The emperor granted the Bengal *diwani* to the Company, along with possession of Allahabad and the revenues of the surrounding country in return for twenty-six lakh rupees. The Company also agreed to protect the emperor who at this time was a fugitive from his capital, without money, without troops and wholly dependent on the English for his daily bread. With that defeat the Company could dream of lording over all of North India. The humiliation of the losers was pitiable. As Keay says, 'The Emperor . . . having first been perilously seated on a throne constructed from a suitably draped armchair perched on top of Clive's dining table, had ceremoniously conferred on the Company the *Diwani* of Bengal . . .'[10]

The diwani meant only the job of collecting revenue for the emperor. Nawabs used to appoint their own *diwan*s. But the Company took its task to be not just *collecting* but *maximizing* the revenue. The haphazard exploitation by the Mughal officers were replaced by eager corporate greed. As Clive wrote to the directors of the Company, 'The whole Moghul Empire is in our hands . . . we must indeed become the Nabobs ourselves in fact, if not in name . . . we must go forward, to retract is impossible . . . if riches and stability are the objects of the Company this is the method, the only method, we now have for attaining and securing them.'[11] He, of course, asked for money to recruit more men to fight; the directors, on the other hand, wanted to retrench. The diwani, however, was the answer the directors had been waiting for. Clive promised it would bring in £2 million.

James Mill, who thirty years later wrote a multi-volume history of British India as a job application to the East India Company (and got the job), writes scathingly about this matter:

> The most pernicious perhaps of all the errors into which Clive exerted himself to mislead the Company, was, the belief which he created, that India overflowed with riches, the expectations he raised, and on which the credulous Company so fondly relied, that a torrent of treasure was about to flow into their laps. And such expectations were adverse to the best use and improvement of resources, they only hastened that disappointment and distress which their inconsistency with the matters of fact rendered a necessary consequence.[12]

Mill, as an economist, had hit the nail on the head. India appeared fabulously rich to travellers and conquerors. But, as we saw from the data on wages of ordinary people, it was a country of millions of poor people exploited ceaselessly to provide large fortunes for a very small elite. If you descended from the Khyber pass to loot Delhi's palaces, you would not go far wrong, as Nadir Shah and many other invaders realized. But to husband the land for a lot of money over a long period required policies to raise productivity and improve the condition of the ordinary masses. Neither the old rulers nor the new ones were to reward the Indian masses with much in that respect. Again, as Mill was to say, 'Though nobody should believe it, India, like other countries, in which the industrious arts are in their infancy, and in which the law is imperfect to render property secure, has always been poor.'[13] The size of India and its large population also misled many observers. In modern terms the total GDP may have been large but per capita income was low and, of course, very unequally distributed. Yet, the idea that India was prosperous in the eighteenth century and that only the foreign rulers impoverished it, was to persist. Two centuries later, the newly independent country was to rely on the same mantra—that the mere removal of foreign rule would guarantee the end of the drain of resources and India would suddenly regain its age-old prosperity. Hard lessons had to be learnt then, as in the late eighteenth century. But this is to anticipate our story.

The demand for diwani, rather than a stake in the territorial sovereignty of Bengal, was partly because the Company even then was not sure of its strength. To be formally subservient to the Mughal emperor served its purpose in two ways. Firstly, it meant that the burden of administration was still borne by the existing Mughal officers or their counterparts employed by the Bengal nawab. Secondly, it meant that the government back home would leave the Company alone, since were it to acquire sovereign powers and yet be under the suzerainty of the emperor,

George III would technically become a vassal of the Mughal emperor, and Whitehall would not countenance that.

It is also worth noting, despite what Dasgupta says, that the one thing the Company avoided is the ambition that the Marathas—the other rising power in India during the late eighteenth century—entertained. This was to capture power in Delhi and rule over all of India. The Marathas wrecked themselves in 1761 in a straight fight against Ahmad Shah Abdali from Afghanistan, who also had his eye on Delhi. The Company avoided a formal capture of the Delhi throne till 1857. It proceeded to capture territory far away from Delhi. Its orientation was sea-bound and South India was its preferred hunting ground. It was well into the next century, after defeating the Marathas in a succession of battles lasting thirty years, that the Company turned its attention to the North. The common aim of the many invaders from the North-West had been to make a beeline for Delhi; this was not how the Company thought of India. At least, in that it reflected commercial capitalism rather than feudalism.

This large sum which the diwani netted made a fundamental alteration to the economics of trade in Bengal. Now, the Company did not need to bring in bullion to finance its purchases. Bengal's export surplus was bought with Bengal's revenue, and when it got to London the pounds sterling collected went into the Company's coffers. No wonder there followed a boom in the Company's stock and like all bubbles, it burst a few years later leaving a lot of sad faces. It also brought the British government to actively regulate the Company.

THE NEW GOVERNANCE OF THE COMPANY IN INDIA

From the outset of the Company coming into its diwani rights, two things happened. The Company's economic affairs were transformed with all the new revenue promised. The king and Parliament began to notice the rise of a new corporate power; unlike India the affairs in Britain were conducted in a framework of laws and rights, especially property rights. This, however, happened only after some initial bouts of misrule.

The British Government became concerned when the early phase of diwani brought ruin to the Bengal peasantry. Clive had promised the directors of the East India Company a profit of £2 million, but it was an overestimate. Not knowing the extent of the overestimation, the revenue demand was pitched very high by the Company. Back in London the dividend was sought to be raised by the Company, though it needed permission of the ministry to do that. The Company was operating under a charter and was not free to do what it liked.

The actual income disappointed the Company's directors and soon there was the need for bullion to be sent to Calcutta to finance the trade. This was because the expenses of the army and the Company officers increased as the Company began to behave like just another local nawab, entering into intrigues and secret treaties with now this, and then another local chief, to aggrandize itself. 'The English Company ... was [to] become a regal, as well as a commercial body; the money which was paid for remittance into their treasury in India was absorbed in the expense of the government.'[14] A revenue surplus of £5.5 million was earned between 1761 and 1772, but the excess of exports to London over imports from England was £3.85 million. The Company also used to divert its revenue from India to buy goods in China for export to England, as this saved draining gold from England—an investment valued at £2.4 million. In the end, there was a deficit of about three quarter of a million pounds which had to be met from the Company's own funds in London. The Company's employees were also trading on their private accounts and claiming exemption from local duties. They remitted their private profits via a bill drawn on the Company's account in London. However, the Company did not receive money from Calcutta to honour these claims. As of March 1773, in London, the Company had £7.8million (round figures) in credit and debts of £9.2 million, a shortfall of £1.4 million. Its trading surplus on India and China was £4.3 million. The net capital value was thus £2.9 million for a company which had issued capital of £4.2 million. Thus, a capital loss of £1.3 million had been incurred despite all the 'exertions' of Clive et al.

The directors were alarmed but so was the Parliament whose members soon began to notice the adverse effects of Company rule. There was not only a shortfall in the promised revenue, but within five years a severe famine decimated Bengal.

The reason for the shortfall in revenue was not hard to seek. There would have been some fall in demand for luxury products from the now displaced aristocrats. Also, the ceaseless exploitation of their monopoly powers by Company traders must have meant a squeeze on the incomes of the non-agricultural producers. In such circumstances, with fragile income entitlements, a harvest failure was the last straw. In the famine of 1769–70, up to a third of Bengal's population died. Not having any experience of ruling, the Company also did not relent nor did it provide the relief measures that any Indian king would have done. Instead, as Adam Smith observed:

> In rice countries, where the crop not only requires a very moist soil, but where in a certain period of its growing it must be laid under water, the effects of drought are much more dismal. Even in such countries, however, the drought is, perhaps, scarce[ly] ever so universal as necessarily to cause

a famine, if the government would allow free trade. The drought in Bengal, a few years ago, might probably have occasioned a very great dearth. Some important regulations, some injudicious restraints imposed by the servants of the East India Company upon the rice trade, contributed perhaps, to turn that dearth into famine.[15]

A combination of parliamentary and Company directors were put in to advise and control the governor of Bengal, who was superior to the other two governors—of Bombay and Madras provinces—and hence also called governor general. This was because by virtue of the charter under which it operated, the Company was a subject of the king. The legal position was that, 'In respect to such places as have lately been acquired or shall hereafter be acquired by conquest, the property as well as the dominion vests in your Majesty, by virtue of your known prerogative, and consequently the Company can only derive a right to them by your Majesty's grant . . .'[16]

Thus began a two-tier government. The Company made appointments but Parliament ensured that its affairs were under the scrutiny of the Crown and Parliament. The Company appointed governor generals and governors and the Crown exercised control via Parliament. Parliament passed Acts in 1773 and 1784 regulating Company government in India. The 1773 Act put the governor general at the mercy of a council where he was often overruled. Warren Hastings was the guinea pig for this experiment. He ended up being so frustrated with his council that he had a duel with Philip Francis, a member of his council. Though he did not kill him, he earned himself the lifelong enmity of Francis who returned to England and became an MP and then sought revenge.

In the context of British history at this juncture, India was not the principal item of business. There was a rebellion in the thirteen colonies of North America, and Parliament and George III were preoccupied with that issue. Here were the 'cousins' of the British revolting for the right to tax themselves with their own representatives rather than pay the homeland. Lord North was much blamed as prime minister for losing America. The radical journalist and politician, John Wilkes, had been agitating about the corrupt Parliament elected on a limited franchise in 1780. By the time Pitt became prime minister in December 1783, five governments had served within two years. Pitt was only twenty-four years old at this time and there was still a war on with the French. As a wag put it:

A sight to make surrounding nations stare,
A Kingdom trusted to a school boy's care.

Yet, Pitt was to surprise his mockers and rule as prime minister for the second-longest period in British history—nearly twenty years—second only to Robert Walpole. India was to be one of his first priorities since Fox's India Bill had been the bone of contention between the House of Commons which had passed it, and the House of Lords which rejected it.

Pitt's 1784 Act repaired the problem which had plagued Hastings, and made the governor general much more his own master. There was also the thorny issue of how to bring the Company under some sort of government control. Fox's India Bill transferred the powers of the Company to commissioners elected by Parliament. But the king suspected Fox of taking all the powers of patronage in his own hands. Burke had hoped to be one of the commissioners. Pitt's Act gave the power to the king working through the Parliament. That act set the pattern by which India was ruled for the next seventy years. A Board of Control appointed by the government with the Crown's approval supervised the governance in India from London, as well as the reformed Governor's Council on the spot in Calcutta.

The Company's charter came up for renewal every twenty years and, at last in 1813, the Crown recognized the Company's control over its Indian territories 'without prejudice to the undoubted sovereignty of the Crown of the United Kingdom etc. in and over the same'. It was only in 1858 that the two-tier government was replaced by the Crown taking over the government of India.

THE IMPEACHMENT OF WARREN HASTINGS

Early on in this two-tier relationship came the impeachment of Warren Hastings. Hastings has had a better press recently, but for many decades Edmund Burke's denunciation of Warren Hastings fed nationalist rhetoric in India. In Burke's critique of Hastings, the nationalists found an indictment of Company rule by a British parliamentarian renowned for his superb oratory. Yet, Burke is a strange hero for the Indian nationalist movement to have chosen. K.M. Panikkar names Burke, along with William Jones and Macaulay, as the three Englishmen (Burke was Irish, but let that be) who will be remembered in Indian history: '. . . the moral indignation which one of the greatest minds of the time felt and expressed in undying words against the oppression, tyranny and corruption by his countrymen in India can well be claimed . . . to have put an end to the period when moral considerations did not enter into the government of India'.[17] If one were to accept this judgement it would confine the 'amoral' period of British rule to around twenty years, at most between 1765 and 1785. One does not need to accept such a drastic shortening of the period of amorality of British rule. Yet, Burke's fascination for Indians remains a puzzle.

Generations of Indian nationalists were moved by Macaulay's florid account of the impeachment of Hastings. But, I would argue that Burke's rhetoric has blinded the Indian readers about his partisan pleadings and his opportunistic career. He never did complain about the condition of the Irish of his day, perhaps willing to forgive the discrimination his countrymen suffered for being Catholic, a religion not favoured by the Glorious British Constitution of which he was such a staunch defender. In Britain he is now regarded as a pillar of Conservatism, with his celebration of the Old Order in his passionate attack on the French Revolution—*Reflections on the Revolution in France*—which elicited scathing rejoinders from Tom Paine and Mary Wollstonecraft. Burke was very much a politician of his times and was, all his life, a hired pen and did even better as a hired larynx. His eloquent testimony against Hastings and even before that, his attack on the East India Company at various sessions of the House of Commons, is what mostly lives of his work in India.

Burke's denunciation of Hastings is so much a part of Indian nationalist memory that it is necessary to examine the whole episode again. This is because Burke's criticism was not free of partisan prejudices and, in many crucial ways, played upon the Parliament's ignorance of Indian affairs. To re-examine the case against Hastings which Burke presented, it is proper that we go into some details about what Warren Hastings was doing and why. Then we can look at the trial itself.

Warren Hastings was the first British ruler of India to try and understand the culture of the people he was meant to rule. Along with Sir William Jones the great Orientalist (a word I use with admiration despite much recent abuse of the term 'Orientalism'), he initiated the translation of Sanskrit and Persian classics. Jones translated the legal codes of the Hindus and Muslims to the best of his knowledge, consulting local scholars. The idea was that Indians should be ruled according to the laws they were used to being ruled by. As Hastings wrote to the directors, the reforms he proposed in Company governance did not include 'one which the original constitution of the Mogul Empire had not before established . . . and rendered familiar to the people'. His ambition was to 'found the authority of the British government in Bengal on its [Bengal's] ancient laws'.[18] This was, perhaps, a romantic idealization of what the actual reality was in the India of those days, but the English took the tales they were told by the pundits and the maulvis seriously. They tried to rule by the book or by the Sacred Books. As in sex and cooking, so in governance—books can only take you so far. It is doubtful if Bengal or India had a system of laws analogous to the English Common Law which Hastings and Jones were seeking in their Sanskrit and Persian texts. What there was, was arbitrary, royal rule-bound by religious scruples and perhaps fear of what may happen in the afterlife, even personal magnanimity on occasions—but hardly a *system* which could be called reliable. If there was justice meted out by the community, at least in Hindu communities it was biased in favour of the upper castes and perennially against the Dalits and women of all castes. (Women did not fare much better under Muslim sharia law either.)

The problem lay with Hastings acting as if he was one of India's many local rulers. He had spent his entire career in India, starting in a humble position as a writer (a clerk) at £5 per annum in 1750, and rising via working in the warehouses of the Company, to the very top. He was the last governor general to be appointed without any interference by the Cabinet or the king. He was also the longest serving governor general of the British possessions in India—thirteen years from 1772 to 1785. He had seen Clive use his guile to exploit the divisions within the Indian elite as well as the decay of the Mughal Empire. He had observed the new emerging powers of Mahadji Scindia, the Maratha general who prospered after the defeat of the Maratha forces in 1761. He was wary of the rising power of Hyder Ali in Mysore on the edge of the domain of the nawab of Carnatic who was under de facto protection of the Company. Within seven years of the grant of the diwani, the political situation in India had become even more fluid. So Hastings decided to become a player rather than a bystander in the unravelling of the Mughal Empire. This was to cost him dear with the parliamentarians back in Westminster.

He also antagonized the Company traders by abolishing all inland duties, so they were no better off than anyone else in Bengal. By now, with the emperor reduced to a non-entity, Hastings could grant freedom from local duties to everyone just as Farukhshiyar had done for the Company. He simplified the revenue collection system. Annual collection by the nawab's officers had to be supervised by Company's men to ensure no leakage. Hastings changed the system by farming out land on five-year leases. It reduced the opportunities for corruption and made revenue more predictable.

When the Maratha general, Mahadji Scindia, offered protection to the Mughal emperor, Shah Alam II, the emperor gladly accepted. When he had first passed under the Company's protection, he had persuaded his vassal, the nawab of Awadh to give Clive two districts in Awadh and in return the Company had paid him twenty-six lakh rupees. The emperor now wanted the two districts to go to Scindia but they were not his to give away. Hastings saw this as an opportunity to cut expenses and stopped paying the money and accepted the fact that the emperor had found a new protector. The Company garrisoned the two districts and recouped its twenty-six lakhs. He passed over the two districts to the nawab of Awadh. When the nawab wanted to attack the Rohillas, Hastings offered the Company's troops as mercenaries.

Hastings may have thought that he was behaving like a native raja, but back home Burke saw red. He waited till Hastings came home and then moved the House of Commons to impeach him. For Burke, Hastings had simultaneously violated the sanctity of treaties as one should not in a European context, and failed to follow the proper ritualistic respect for the Great Mughal, as he should have in the Eastern context. Burke had been studying Indian affairs assiduously years before he took on Hastings. The Regulating Act of 1773 was passed by the Rockingham ministry of which he was a member. When again the North–Fox coalition was briefly in power in 1783, he spoke on Fox's India Bill. He was a scourge of the Company in Parliament. Yet, in his dual insistence on Western legality and Eastern decorum, he frequently got things wrong. Soon after Pitt's return to power in May 1784 with a majority which surprised and infuriated Fox and his faction, in July 1784 Burke made a passionate speech on the case of Almas Ali Khan, a minor official of the nawab. This was the beginning of his sustained attack on Warren Hastings which was to climax two years later into a resolution for impeachment. A recent author who is quite appreciative of Burke's writings on India, has called it 'one of the most oddly dramatic of Burke's India performances'.[19] Burke alleged that Hastings had ordered the assassination of Almas because he was resisting extortionate revenue demands. Burke had found evidence in form of a letter of Hastings. What he did not know was that Almas intercepted that letter himself, settled his revenue conflict and 'managed to live in complex and not unprofitable relation with the British for another twenty-five years'.[20]

When this was pointed out, Burke's reaction was to see it as a conspiracy of British interests to undermine his proof of their atrocities. 'Every new rebuff to him becomes conflated with new evidence of abandoning Indian peoples. Parliament's complicity with tyranny in the guise of ordinary political procedures of debates, elections, and rules becomes a version of the sham legalism of Hastings's Indian rule.'[21]

Legalisms of parliamentary procedures were indeed to frustrate Burke and his friends when they tried to impeach Hastings. It started auspiciously for Burke though, despite his faction being a minority in the House of Commons. As James Mill says:

> We have now arrived at the period of another parliamentary proceeding, which excited attention by its pomp, and by the influence upon the public mind of those whose interests it affected, much more than by any material change which it either produced, or was calculated to produce upon the state of affairs in India . . . It appeared to those whose interest it still was

to arraign the government in India, that the most convenient form of the attack could assume was that of an accusation of Mr. Hastings.[22]

The trial in the Commons began on 18 February 1786. The long time it took to come to conclusion can only be understood if we look at the procedures which had to be adopted by Burke. The House of Commons had to first agree to impeach Hastings. Then the House of Lords had to sit in judgement. Each House had (and still has) its own peculiar habits which it does not give up. Urgency is not valued as much as sticking to proper procedures.

The procedure in the Houses of Parliament is to 'move for papers' when you want some issue to be discussed. Burke moved on 18 February 1786 a motion for a variety of papers. A long debate followed with Henry Dundas replying for the government. Each accusation had to be debated separately and papers had to be asked to be moved. By 4 April Burke had put twenty-one accusations on the table. (One more was added later in May.) There being other business, it was not until 23 January 1787 that Burke got the House to agree to send to its Committee the motion to impeach Hastings. On 25 April the Committee reported back to the whole House. There was another debate with John Wilkes opposing the motion to impeach. As Wilkes said, there was a demand to impeach but why was there no demand to compensate the victims of Hastings's policies? The answer was that MPs wanted the theatre of revenge on Hastings for all that had angered them since Clive's mischief at enriching himself and his fellow nawabs in Bengal, but did not want to spend any money helping the victims (who in Burke's view had suffered from Hastings policies in Bengal). But he was in a minority and the impeachment was now to go to the House of Lords.

The scene then moved to the House of Lords, which had to sit as the highest court of the land in Westminster Hall, the oldest extant building in Westminster to this day, which was then used as a court of law. This impeachment, however, was special since it had been brought by the House of Commons before the House of Lords, so all the peers had to sit and judge. Over the seven years that the trial took, as the Lords heard the arguments as and when they could spare time from their legislative deliberations, a third of the original peers—around eighty of them— died, to be replaced by their heirs.

It was high theatre for Londoners. On 13 February 1788, the impeachment trial opened in Westminster Hall. As magnificent structures go, it is hardly possible to do better than this large and high-ceilinged hall with a hammer-beam roof which has stood on its site by the Thames since before the Norman conquest in 1066. Before the peers arrived in their procession in the Hall, the galleries were filled. The Queen was there herself with her three daughters in the Duke of Newcastle's gallery, 'dressed in fawn-coloured satin, her head-dress plain, with a very slender sprinkling of diamonds'. The Duchess of Gloucester was there with the young Prince and the ladies were all in morning dresses, a few with feathers and variegated flowers in their headdress, 'but nothing so remarkable as to attract public attention.' The mistress of the Prince of Wales, Mrs FitzHerbert, was there. The prosecutors from the Commons, Burke, Fox and their friends—'managers' as they were called during the trial—were in full dress, but some of the 200 MPs were not—some even arrived in boots!

The excitement was not to last for ever. The impeachment resolution against Hastings passed by the Commons on 4 April 1786 contained twenty-two charges, the first nine of which dealt with his conduct towards the Mughal emperor, the Nawab of Awadh, and the Raja of Benares as well as others about his behaviour with respect to Company officers. It took the clerk of the House of Lords two days to read out all the charges. Many of the charges pertained not to what Hastings had done but what the Nawab of Awadh had done, for example, to his mother and grandmother—the Begums of Awadh—because, as the charge said:

> That contrary to justice and equity, and the security of property, as well as to public faith, and the sanction of the Company's guarantee, Warren Hastings authorized the Nabob of Oude, a dependant or vassal of the East India Company and over whom he possessed an entire and absolute command, to seize upon and confiscate to his own profit, the landed estates of his mother and grandmother, his kindred and principal nobility, as also the personal property of the two princesses; and that in the enforcing of these measures against the latter, they with other females of the royal family, their servants and dependants, were treated with atrocious indignity and barbarity, in obedience to his injunctions and commands.[23]

I have given this charge in its entirety because the general impression is that Hastings was cruel to the begums. The charge is that he did not stop his vassal 'over whom he possessed an entire and absolute command'. How Burke thought Hastings could command Shuja-ud-Daula to do as ordered is hard to understand. He clearly misread the nature of the treaty between the two. Shuja was a vassal of Shah Alam, if of anyone, whom he treated with scant respect, and not of Hastings. Hastings was also accused of stopping the payment to Shah Alam—which of course he had done because he thought he had been freed of the obligation to protect him since Mahadji Scindia was doing it.

In any case, Burke was to have his day or rather many days before the bar of the House of Lords. His opening oration lasted four days—15, 16, 18 and 19 February. Much of the oration concerned Devi Singh who was supposed to have been given the contract to collect revenue, for five years of a district, 'improperly and for corrupt ends'. When complaints arrived against him at Calcutta, he retaliated by raising his demands. Burke's account of the miseries visited upon the poor peasants and their families was so moving that as the shorthand reporter wrote, 'In this part of his speech, Mr. Burke's descriptions were more vivid—more harrowing and more horrific—than human utterance on either fact or fancy, perhaps, ever formed before. The agitation of most people was very apparent—and Mrs. Sheridan was so overpowered she fainted'.[24]

Or in the more decorative prose of Macaulay:

> The energy and pathos of the great orator extorted expressions of unwonted admiration from the stern and hostile Chancellor, and, for a moment, seemed to pierce even the resolute heart of the defendant. The ladies in the galleries, unaccustomed to such displays of eloquence, excited by the solemnity of the occasion, and perhaps not unwilling to display their taste and sensibility, were in a state of uncontrollable emotion. Handkerchiefs were pulled out; smelling bottles were handed round; hysterical sobs and screams were heard: and Mrs. Sheridan was carried out in a fit.[25]

Burke's tale was horrifying with people beaten up with bamboo canes till blood gushed, flogged, tied together and women, with their nipples torn off, dragged to prisons. Yet, as James Mill remarks, 'our readers must see that Mr. Hastings cannot be responsible for [the above mentioned cruelties], unless it shall be proved that he was privy to, and countenanced the barbarities'.[26] Burke was quoting a report by Paterson, a commissioner who had been appointed by Hastings to investigate the complaint. Hyman Horace Wilson, who edited Mill's *History* in the 1850s and who wrote a running commentary on the text, remarks in continuation of Mill's comment, 'Burke's oratory on this occasion was liable to still more serious censure. It was a tissue of falsehood. In any case, the cruelties of Deby Sing, in collecting his rent, could not be charged upon Hastings; for, as soon as he heard or knew of them, he displaced him and that in so hasty a manner so as to expose himself to the charge of having acted with so much severity towards Deby Sing.'[27] Paterson was also quoted by Hastings's lawyer, Mr Law as saying, 'he has publicly disavowed ... the encomiums of Burke'.

Burke concluded his four-day oration in a dramatic finale. Again as Macaulay has said:

> At length the orator concluded. Raising his voice till the old arches of Irish oak resounded, 'Therefore,' said he, 'hath it with all confidence been ordered, by the Commons of Great Britain, that I impeach Warren Hastings of high crimes and misdemeanours. I impeach him in the name of the Commons' House of Parliament, whose trust he has betrayed. I

impeach him in the name of the English nation, whose ancient honour he has sullied. I impeach him in the name of the people of India, whose rights he has trodden under foot, and whose country he has turned into a desert. Lastly, in the name of human nature itself, in the name of both sexes, in the name of every age, in the name of every rank, I impeach the common enemy and oppressor of all!'[28]

Fox then asked the House of Lords to pronounce upon each accusation. Much argument followed between the two sides and at the end the peers withdrew to make up their minds. Coming back on the 22nd they said all the charges had to be heard first before judgement could be given on any of them. This was a decision which favoured Hastings and it was carried out with a three to one majority. So it went on for days on end. At each stage the prosecution's demands were rejected by the peers.

The trial dragged on. Very often, Burke pressed on with issues which were not listed in the charges or which were horrifying instances of tragedies, but not in any way Hastings's fault. In a sense the accumulated anger against everything which had happened in Bengal since 1757, all the lootings and oppressions which Clive inaugurated and got away with without reproach, were now being laid at Warren Hastings's door. Burke did not wish to bring up those days since he knew that Clive was a hero to many and many of his 'nabob' friends were still in the Commons. So he said:

There is a secret veil to be drawn over the beginnings of all governments. They had their origin, as the beginnings of all such things have had, in some matters that had as good be covered by obscurity ... Prudence and discretion make it necessary to throw something of that veil over a business in which otherwise the fortune, the genius, the talents and military virtue of this Nation never shone more conspicuously.[29]

So Burke could draw a veil over all Clive had done and even the famine of 1769–70, since that was the 'genius' and 'talent', and so on of the realm. Hastings, if anything, had tried to reform the administration and was much more considerate to the people of Bengal than any of his predecessors. The king and the peers were sympathetic to him. On the 146th day of the trial, on 13 January 1795, seven years after it had started, the time had come for the House of Lords to begin its judgement.

An elaborate procedure had to be now followed. A committee of the House was formed to decide 'the mode of giving judgment on trials of high crimes and misdemeanours'. This is because impeachments were few and far between. Francis Bacon had been impeached and there were impeachments during the English Civil War. But that was more than a century ago. The report of the committee was then referred to the whole

House on 2 March 1795. Then the House decided upon the advice of the Lord Chancellor, its presiding officer, that the peers would decide on each charge three times—first as a committee of the whole House, then as the House itself and, finally, as judges in the Westminster Hall. There was a lengthy debate on each of the twenty-two charges. At each stage the peers rejected all the charges against Hastings. Of course, each peer had to be asked individually from the Woolsack by the Lord Chancellor whether he found Hastings guilty of a particular charge or not.

On 23 April 1795 all the peers, sitting in Westminster Hall as judges, had declared Hastings not guilty of all the twenty-two charges. It had been a long, gruelling task. By the time the trial ended, a revolution had broken out in France and its king had been guillotined. Burke had fallen out with his friend, Fox on the issue of the revolution and gone over to Pitt's side. He had worn himself out on this one question. As a sympathetic author has recently written:

> Burke undertook and sustained the Hastings impeachment from a position of ever-increasing isolation, even within his own party. After surprising initial success in the Commons, given the factional political bitterness of the time, the impeachment campaign of seven years also terminated with defeat in the Lords in 1795, an outcome that had been predicted as virtually inevitable from the start. The end of the trial had the virtue of finally releasing Burke from what many, by 1795, had come to regard as a fifteen-year monomania.[30]

Nevertheless, his rhetoric inspired generations of Indians and let them embarrass their colonial masters about what one of their own had said about another of their earlier incarnations. Stripped of the partisan context of the times and read on its own, Burke convinces us that he is indeed describing the ruin wrought by Hastings during his rule. Yet, what he speaks of in, say, his indictment of Devi Singh's cruelties could have been—and was—happening all the time under every rule across India, and went on happening in many Princely States and everywhere else where big landlords wielded power over poor peasants. His many charges concerning the Mughal emperor or the Nawab of Awadh are not charges against Hastings' conduct per se but Burke's imputation of what a lord–vassal relation involves, as if it was a legal contract signed in Westminster while preserving the delicacies—as Burke envisaged—which ruled social relations in feudal India. By ignoring what had happened under the predecessors of Hastings and putting all blame on him, Burke was also fashioning a baroque defence of the British rule. The harassed Warren Hastings, a victim of parliamentary rivalries, lived on but a broken man. He was compensated by the Company with an annuity of £4000 and £50,000 was lent to him interest free towards his costs.

CONCLUSION

Hastings was the last governor general to come from the ranks. After him all the appointments were made from the peerage and with the king's approval. There was also a warning that British rulers of India should shy away from 'going native'. The notion of Hastings and William Jones, that there was wisdom in the traditions of India which could improve governance if only the British knew more about them, was quietly dropped. Lord Cornwallis, who had surrendered to the American guerrilla armies at Yorktown, was now restored to his honours and made the governor general in succession to Warren Hastings. Within twenty years of the award of diwani, the Parliament had rectified the oversight of the government and began to wield direct control over the Company's possessions in India.

CHAPTER 3

REVENUE, REFORM AND RENAISSANCE

THE BRITISH ARISTOCRACY TAKES CHARGE OF INDIA

Charles Cornwallis was, in many ways, a typical member of the ruling elite of the British Empire in the last quarter of the eighteenth century. Born in 1738, he was the son of an earl. He contested the local family seat for the House of Commons but soon succeeded his father in the House of Lords. Cornwallis began the tradition whereby governor generals of India would not be like Clive—soldier adventurers—or even like Warren Hastings who began as an ordinary employee of the Company and managed to rise to the top. They would be from the landed aristocracy, sometimes the heir to title and fortune, as was Richard Wellesley, Lord Mornington or, as in the case of Lord William Bentinck, the second son of the Earl of Portland. Even John Shore, a long-time Company employee who had risen to be a member of Hastings's council, was made a baronet before being appointed governor general. The aristocrats usually had an army background, typically after public school and, sometimes, a university education as well. They sat in Parliament and would have travelled across Europe regularly. They had a stake in the country and the empire. Investment in agricultural improvement was fashionable and sometimes profitable as well, and they were keen to show themselves as improvement-minded when it came to their land. Some were conservative in their outlook while others were fired by an evangelical zeal for propagating the Christian faith when they went abroad. But they all wanted the empire to thrive. To that extent, they could be called imperialists.

But having said that, there were differences among them as well. In the previous century the British Isles had been through a series of religious battles, often narrowly labelled the English Civil War, which ended in England with regicide, then a Protectorate and, after the restoration of the Stuarts in 1660, a bloodless Revolution in 1688 which removed the last English king who would profess Catholic sympathies. Since then Scotland at first, and then by the end of the eighteenth century, Ireland, had been formally added to the Union. The isles became the United Kingdom. In the century when the Mughal Empire was breaking up, the British Isles were coming together.

The dominant group was the English Anglican aristocracy to whom the other groups and classes—the Anglican English middle and working classes, Welsh and English Nonconformists and Catholics, as well as Scottish Presbyterians and Irish Protestants and Irish Catholics—ceded primacy. Thus, the distinction of class added to that of religion in defining British public life. The British viewed their society as hierarchical and cellular with religion, region and class being the vectors which constructed the cells.

Even within the ruling classes, there were differences. Though party lines were not rigidly drawn, there was a Whig/Tory distinction in their views of how to rule at home or abroad. Whigs were radical and swore by the 1688 settlement which restricted the king's powers and wanted Parliament to be supreme. They disliked George III since he tried to control Parliament. Tories were more sedate and generally supported the king and the established order. But Pitt, who was their most successful prime minister, steered the party in a more reformist direction. He supported Wilberforce's anti-slavery campaign and didn't push electoral reform only because he knew the king was strongly against it. He wished for tolerance for Irish Catholics—and Cornwallis was one with him on that—but again George III would not hear of it. The rigidities of the Old Order were eroding, as George III approached the end of his life. Within four years of his death, there was voting reform which began the long democratizing process in British politics that extended the franchise widely.

The fifty years between 1776 when the American Declaration of Independence was proclaimed and 1826, by which time Mexico and South America had been liberated from Iberian imperialism, were revolutionary for the western hemisphere but also for western Europe. From here on, except for Canada, the Falkland and the Caribbean Islands, the American continent was free of European imperialism. Spain and Portugal lost their American possessions *because* they had lost power in the European context. Their royals were displaced by Napoleon, and subsequently only restored at home, not in America. After that upheaval Asia and Africa became the destinations of European imperialism. But even then, it was the fluctuating fortunes of these countries *within* Europe which determined who got what in the two continents. The fact that Britain emerged victorious in this struggle shaped the history of India as much as that of imperialism itself.

Britain also went through a transformation of its self image in the thirty years following the loss of the North American colonies. The advent of the French Revolution with its regicide shook Europe and entangled Britain in a twenty-two-year war (1793–1815) with France, often without allies, while European powers fell to the French assault like ninepins. The Whigs split on the issue of the revolution. Fox and Burke quarrelled and Burke emerged as the great defender of conservatism. There was radical protest in Britain which had to be put down sternly and rebellion in Ireland (with French support) which had to be met with force. Ireland was integrated into the United Kingdom with Irish MPs sitting in the House of Commons for the first time. Wartime inflation added to the unrest on political grounds and the French threat of invasion across the Channel was ever present. But after Waterloo the British felt vindicated in their own gradual system of change and adaptation, and their stand against any revolutionary enthusiasms. The British Way had been victorious and after 1815, British confidence in their way of life was to be undimmed till, perhaps, after the Second World War.

Yet, even then the Whigs—they became Liberals later in the century—stuck to their love of reform and even, to some extent, revolution—though only abroad. Some Pitt-ite Conservatives—William Bentinck for instance—and Whig aristocrats took to Christian evangelism, inspired by William Wilberforce's success in abolishing the slave trade through the passage of the Slave Trade Act of 1807. Still, by and large, Conservatives spoke for the status quo and aristocratic guardianship of the Constitution. Liberals were for the dismantling of barriers to free trade internally and internationally. Conservatives put their faith in paternalism and in the preservation of pre-market societies. The imperialists were thus not a homogenous lot. As the personnel changed and, indeed, as British society evolved, so did their policies at home and in India.

Cornwallis had fought a brave campaign in North America but it was his surrender at Yorktown in 1781 which was the effective end of the British efforts to retain their empire in America. He was not blamed for the loss and was Pitt's choice for the governor general's post in India, the first to be appointed under Pitt's India Act which gave the governor general power over his council, something which Warren Hastings had wished for but never did have. After his return from India, Cornwallis served as Lord Lieutenant of Ireland, and in his last year returned to India as governor general but did not live long. He thus served the empire in its three large possessions—North America, India and Ireland—in high positions while also being active in domestic politics.

Starting with Cornwallis, for the next sixty years the British Empire in India expanded and consolidated itself. Lord Mornington (Richard Wellesley), along with his brother, Arthur Wellesley (later the Duke of Wellington), who was serving in the army, was especially aggressive in his designs. All the time the directors of the East India Company, who were expecting to earn a profit from trade rather than pay for the battles and intrigues in India, were bitterly against such adventures. Yet, each expansion brought more land and, hence, more land revenue within the Company's control. The successive governor generals knew that it was politics in Parliament and the Cabinet which decided their fortunes, and not the Company directors. So they went ahead with their plans. The remnants of Indian rulers in post-Mughal India—Tipu and the Marathas, and later the heirs of Ranjit Singh—were mopped up; by the 1850s much of the old Hindustan and the Deccan were under British control, either directly as British India or under paramountcy as Native States. Meanwhile, the more militaristic of the governor generals proceeded to wage war against Burma and Afghanistan with success in the east, but failure in the north-west.

By the second decade of the nineteenth century, British rule had replaced the Mughal Empire. One could say that the period between the death of Aurangzeb in 1707 and the Fourth Anglo-Maratha War in 1818, was an interregnum in India. After the Maratha defeat, it was clear that the British did not face any serious military challenge from any Indian ruler or even from the French. Simon Bolivar had led his troops through many nations of Latin America (as we call it today) and secured the end of Spanish and Portuguese Empires, but there was no such leadership then which was a focus of anti-British forces in India. Also, while Spain and Portugal had weakened over the past century, Britain had become stronger. A new empire heralding a new dispensation had begun in India. Along the way it became midwife to the Indian Renaissance.

SOWING THE SEEDS OF THE INDIAN RENAISSANCE

It did this by challenging the local elite about their society and culture. The awe with which William Jones and Warren Hastings regarded the old culture was replaced by a Christian certainty of the benighted nature of heathen India. Yet, Jones and his collaborators in the Asiatic Society had already created the conditions for the locals to be able to rise to the challenge. They had been shown glimpses of their ancient civilization after centuries of Brahmins monopolizing and hoarding such knowledge. The Asiatics—the amateur British officers and soldiers—continued to pursue their interests in a splendidly amateur fashion, discovering India's history and religion. Indeed, their efforts created what we know today as 'the Idea of India'.

It has become fashionable lately, among post-colonial writers, to regard as sinister British attempts to learn about India's history and geography and their efforts to measure and map Indian society. Following Edward Said's critique of orientalism and Michel Foucault's ideas of power as a control instrument, the British are denigrated for their systematic attempts to understand their empire—Nicholas Dirks[1] is a good example of this school, while Bernard Cohn[2] is more balanced. Cohn anticipates much of the post-colonial critique but with a more sympathetic understanding of British rule than is found in subsequent writings on the subject. For the post-colonial, the British did not just learn the Indian languages, but as John Marriott puts it, 'a programme was launched to appropriate Indian languages to the exigencies of colonial rule'.[3] Bernard Cohn also speaks of the British 'invading the epistemological space' of the Indians.

Such expressions are based on false analogies. Languages cannot be 'appropriated'. Language is, and ought to be, a public good which none can appropriate as a private commodity (though literacy can, and has often been, denied to the majority. I discuss this below.) If I use your language, you are not thereby deprived of your ability to use it. Indeed, as more people use your language, the wider is the circle over which you can communicate without the difficulty of translation. As the British learnt Indian languages, Indians began to learn English. Should we say the Indians appropriated English? (Incidentally, are Indian businesses and students and politicians better off today than, say, the Chinese because they did appropriate English?) By speaking of appropriation, a false image is created of something being stolen. Epistemological space, also, is unlike private space; it is not exclusive to anyone. One no more 'invades' it than appropriates the air one shares with others.

Literacy, especially in Sanskrit, was indeed treated like the possession of the Brahmins from which other lower-caste Hindus and non-Hindu Indians were excluded. They were not allowed to read it, even if they wished to, and could not speak it. This was done by social control backed by religious superstition just as the Christian Church had restricted the knowledge of Latin and resisted translations of the Bible for centuries. Caste distinctions and domination of the lower castes by the Brahmins were not British inventions. Reading the scriptures was punishable by death for a non-Brahmin as the story of Sambuka in the *Ramayana* illustrates. It was not simply the learning of languages; many forms of knowledge were limited to a prescribed circle and anyone flouting these rules was severely punished. In the *Mahabharata*, for instance, Eklavya, a man from a low caste is penalized for learning archery (a preserve of royal princes) by having to cut off his own thumb. Dalits and lower caste people were not allowed to aspire to literacy or any skill other than their traditionally ascribed one.

Far from appropriating the languages, the British liberated them from this narrow caste monopoly and disseminated them to any and all Indians who wanted to learn them. A Shyamji Krishnavarma, who became a scholar of Sanskrit despite being a Vaishya, or a Bhimrao Ambedkar, a Mahar, who possessed doctorates from the universities of London and Columbia, was unimaginable, had the colonial rulers not 'appropriated' Indian languages which allowed all Indians to read them in printed books and magazines.

Raja Rammohun Roy was a harbinger of these emerging forces in Bengal when he argued for modern knowledge rather than just Sanskrit and Persian. He had 'sanguine hopes', he wrote on 11 December 1823 to Lord Amherst, the governor general, that the new rulers would spend money on 'Mathematics, Natural Philosophy, Chemistry, Anatomy and other useful Sciences' rather than Sanskrit, which he said would 'load the minds of youth with grammatical niceties and metaphysical distinctions of little or no practicable use to the possessors or to society. The pupils there will acquire what was known two thousand years ago, with the addition of vain and empty subtleties since produced by speculative men, such as is already commonly taught in all parts of India.' Sanskrit, he said, 'is well known to have been for ages a lamentable check on the diffusion of knowledge'. He contrasted the stagnation of knowledge in India with the progress of science in the West. 'In order to enable your Lordship to appreciate the utility of encouraging such imaginary learning as above characterised, I beg your Lordship will be pleased to compare the state of science and literature in Europe before the times of Lord Bacon with the progress of knowledge made since he wrote.'[4] The point was made that European knowledge was not prized because it was European, but because, since Bacon's introduction of the scientific method in the early seventeenth century, stagnant European knowledge— much like Indian knowledge until then—had been revolutionized. It was Enlightenment rather than imperialism that Roy was applauding.

Roy knew that as a public good, knowledge was a double-edged sword. As the imperialists charted India, their subjects also used those very charts to organize their resistance. Before the advent of the British, the only thing which could be said to have provided a uniting framework to India was either the Mughal administrative framework or the cultural framework of Brahmin domination in every part of the country. These were both partial frameworks. The Mughal administrative structure essentially covered North India—the Doab and Bengal. The Brahmin framework united caste Hindus and oppressed the lower castes and Dalits. Neither represented India as the new generations from early nineteenth century came to know it.

Muslims had written a history of North India—at least since the advent of Muslim rule in the second millennium CE. There had been no attempt by the Brahmin elite or, indeed, any other Hindu leaders to write a pre-Muslim history or to preserve the country's cultural heritage as, for instance, monuments, perhaps because many of the monuments were Buddhist. The old tradition of inquiry into astronomy and mathematics died sometime towards the end of the first millennium CE in India, and Muslim scholarship also began to atrophy across the arc of Islam, stretching from India to Spain by the fourteenth century at the latest. While the Mughal royal courts helped create a syncretic culture of music, costume, dance and cuisine, no synthesis of the analytical or scientific inquiry occurred between the Hindu and Muslim streams of knowledge, unlike in Spain where Islamic influences gave impetus to philosophical dialogues between Jewish, Christian and Muslim scholars. Akbar's curiosity about the many faiths is the one, and often cited, exception to this general apathy about knowledge. Rote learning and orthodoxy had become the inferior substitutes for knowledge and inquiry in India centuries before the Europeans arrived.

What the British brought to this dormant society was curiosity, a faculty which the traditional elites—Muslim and Hindu—sadly lacked. The Enlightenment had been spreading across Europe with its insistence on empirical rather than supernatural explanations of natural phenomena since the mid-seventeenth century, with each of the major nations— France, the Netherlands, England and Scotland—playing its part. By the late-eighteenth century its roots in England and Scotland were strong enough to have penetrated all ranks of the elite and knowledge became prized as valuable in itself. The new generations wanted to know about the history and the laws and social practices of their own society, as much as the causes underlying their progress. Adam Smith, the father of political economy, and Adam Ferguson, the Scottish philosopher and historian, began a discourse on the rise and decline of civilizations. The project of universal historiography, which the eighteenth century Enlightenment inaugurated via Montesquieu, Smith and Ferguson, was furthered by Hegel and Marx. Its central concern was always Eurocentric and sought to explain how their particular corner of western Europe had emerged triumphant when, but two centuries previously, China and India were powerful. The rise and fall of civilizations were studied, starting from Greece and Rome whose decline was the theme of Gibbon's multi-volume masterwork, *The Decline and Fall of the Roman Empire* (1771–88). China and India seemed to have suffered the fate of Rome, but why they did so was the subject of much speculation. Governance in the form of despotism was one clue for the decline of Rome and perhaps this was true in the case of China and India as well. Hence, a study of Indian history and culture was pursued, both to understand India and to improve it—at a profit, of course.

In this process the British undertook the improvement of India more systematically than reform at home. There soon developed a symbiotic relationship between the improvement in India and that in England. As a recent biographer of John Stuart Mill, one of the most distinguished employees of the East India Company, says in the context of Mill's submission to Parliament resisting the abolition of the Company in 1858, 'For all its terrible faults, the East India Company was also born of the Enlightenment, and was interested in the pursuit of knowledge and reason.'[5]

Paul Johnson, in his magisterial *The Birth of the Modern 1815–1830*, echoes this:

> The East India Company set up various menageries, specializing in birds, mammals and reptiles, and all these institutions carried out regular and elaborate expeditions to collect specimens and acquire information, gradually spreading their activities to the great mountain ranges of the north, and to the jungles of northern Assam, Ceylon and South East Asia. The purpose was not merely scientific—one object was the establishment of the great Assam tea-growing industry—but the research effort established for the world the basic knowledge of the natural history of south Asia.[6]

This is not just pro-imperialist propaganda. Bernard Cohn, an acknowledged precursor of post-colonial studies, puts it as follows: 'The process of state building in Great Britain, seen as a cultural project, was closely linked with its emergence as an imperial power, and India was its largest and most important colony.' Moreover, he argues, it is not merely the fact that the British officials and soldiers were ruling in India, it was that 'the projects of state building in both countries—documentation, legitimation, classification, and bounding, and the institutions therewith—often reflected theories, experiences, and practices worked out originally in India and then applied in Great Britain, as well as vice versa.'[7]

Britain and India began the journey to modernization in tandem, except that in Britain there was parliamentary government with a small but increasing role for some of the ruled—the middle classes by the 1830s, and the working classes in stages from 1867 onwards—while in India that aspect of self-rule was to be delayed by a century-and-a-half. But in Britain the reformers were still far from the power they would gain only decades after the Reform Act of 1832. In India their young students—the East India men—had a free hand to experiment and implement radical schemes. The ideas of Jeremy Bentham and David Ricardo were tried out twenty to thirty years before they were applied in Britain. Thus, the fact that India is a modern democracy with a civil service and a framework of laws is not an accident. Its roots go back to the early years of the nineteenth century.

The British began the process of understanding and mapping India even before they became rulers, but accelerated the process after 1765 when they came into the Bengal diwani. They taught themselves Sanskrit and Persian with the help of the local elite and began a systematic analysis of the classical and local languages. They wrote and printed grammars of those languages. They translated (rather badly to begin with) law books for use in courts. They began exploring ancient monuments, especially those dating before the twelfth century, and retrieved their history for the Indians. Buddhism, as we know it today, was literally dug up from the soil and recovered from Pali texts by the amateur Asiatics of the British Army and the revenue officers of the Company. They sketched wherever they went, collected coins and artefacts and dug where they felt they could discover more.[8]

Portuguese Imperialism as a Contrast

Post-colonial critique has concentrated on the British case especially in the first few decades after 1765. This is perhaps because the records of these efforts are in English and secondly, because these efforts took place in Bengal, which was for many decades the most politically conscious province of British India. But it is useful to contrast the British case with an older imperialist state.

An earlier example of European imperialism which had colonized India— Portuguese—shows a very different approach to the exigencies of colonial rule. Adhering to ideas that pre-dated the Enlightenment, and moreover as a Catholic power, strongly counter-Reformationist, the Portuguese relied on conversion as a surer way of winning over their subjects than the appropriation of local languages or the recording of local culture and practices. Although it was a Portuguese scholar, Duarte Barbosa, who had first studied caste, the Portuguese showed no inclination to map the caste system. Their subjects could stay Brahmin as far as they were concerned, as long as they became Christians. It was their souls which mattered.

There was a strong Jesuit presence whose efforts were aimed at winning the souls of the natives, learning their languages—not so much to rule them better, but to convey to them the truths of Christianity. The first printing press in India was started in Goa in 1556, two centuries before the Baptist Serampore Press opened in Bengal. The Jesuits embarked upon the translation of the catechisms, confessionaries and other such material to Tamil, the language of Tamil Nadu—a place far away from Goa, as they felt that the impoverished Parava fishermen on the east coast were more likely converts. The Paravas were trying to escape conversion to Islam and sought the help of the Jesuits. Thus began the printing of texts in Tamil and, later, the first Tamil grammar book and dictionary by Henriques and even some original Tamil writing by Beschi—both Jesuits. The Lutherans later competed for the souls of the Tamil poor resulting in more printed books. All this took place decades before British efforts in Bengal.[9]

Even so, Portuguese imperialism did not liberate and disseminate knowledge in the same way the British did. The local language of Goa, Konkani, languished despite a grammar text produced by Thomas Stephens in 1640. This is because the rulers insisted on Portuguese being taught in local schools under Portuguese rule from the outset. By 1684 Portuguese support for local language had stopped altogether and only Latin and Portuguese were used officially. Had this continued, Goa would have relied on imported Portuguese to work the system. The local elite, as it was before the advent of the Portuguese, would have been totally marginalized. Eventually, a compromise was worked out with the local social hierarchy retaining its caste and its lands while giving up its religion. Catholic Brahmins became Lisbon's leading collaborators as conversion allowed them to hold on to their lands. The Portuguese Empire lasted twice as long as the British in India, but the modernizing effects of the latter were sadly missing in the former. This is because the Enlightenment did not affect the Catholic kingdoms of Iberia the way it did Britain and France. Even among imperialisms there are differences which need to be studied.

Ruling India was seen as a serious matter for the British. After the chaos and misrule of the ten years following 1765, the reform of the administration became a constant theme in the British Parliament. Warren Hastings's reforms were frustrated by his lack of power and the freedom of the Company agents to trade, as they exploited the firman granting freedom from tolls to drive out the native traders in Bengal. This was soon to be remedied by Pitt's India Act, followed by Cornwallis's more successful reforms. Company agents became paid public servants. A college was established, first in Calcutta and then, more effectively, in England which trained future Company servants to work in India. India thus had a better trained public service than the mother country itself. Indeed, one could say that India brought civil service reform to Britain, fifty years later, when the Northcott–Trevelyan reforms were adopted by Whitehall.

Fort William College, established by Wellesley in Calcutta, also spawned imitators. Hindu College in Calcutta began to train the local elites in Western knowledge. Soon, a Hindu College was set up in Poona (Pune as it now is), and then colleges were founded in Bombay and Madras. These institutions had one novel feature which had been absent earlier: admission was not based on caste status. Thus, non-Brahmins could access available knowledge on the same terms as Brahmins. Of course, to begin with, Brahmins and other upper caste elites predominated in the student body, but the mould had been cracked. Eventually, even the Dalits could study in the same schools and colleges as the upper castes. The democratization of access to education had come from the imperialists. This was just one of the many paradoxes unleashed by the British rule in India.

British culture began to be absorbed and emulated by small groups of Indians first in Bengal, and then spread to the areas around Madras and Bombay. India's national consciousness, dormant as of 1800—years of division into local kingdoms having prevented the formation of a 'national' consciousness—developed in reaction to the imperial challenge. The many forms it took will occupy us in subsequent chapters. The British conquest of Indian territories was the catalyst of this process. Let me start with the conquests first.

THE MILITARY CONQUEST OF INDIA

How did a small island, smaller than Bengal, rule over a large subcontinent like India? This has been one of the great debates among Indian nationalists. Plassey sets the tone of this debate—a betrayal by enemies within, by traitors who sold the motherland for a pittance. But, as we saw earlier, Plassey was a small episode, and it did not secure India for the British except by hindsight. It was the Battle of Buxar (1764) which was the more serious military success. After that the British had to fight their wars—with Haidar (1766–82), then Tipu (1782–99), and then the Marathas (1775–82,1803–05,1817–18)—against armies which had modern guns as well as soldiers trained by French or Dutch officers. Indian rulers were quick to obtain the hardware along with the personnel required to teach them how to use it. Yet, the final outcome was never in doubt, as I argue below. Stories of the exceptional bravery of individual generals such as Haidar or Tipu or Mahadji Scindia are told even today; and yet they lost. After 1818 there was no prospect of an independent India. Why this was so has to be examined.

The difference lay not in the hardware, not in *modernization*, but in the software, in *modernity*. This is best seen by recalling the Battle of Asaye (1803) which Max Boot, a historian of warfare, considers among the most crucial of all modern battles. This was fought in the region of Maharashtra between the British led by Arthur Wellesley, later the Duke of Wellington, and the Maratha forces led by Daulat Rao Scindia and Raghoji Bhonsle.[10] The Marathas had 11,000 Infantry; the British had 3300, of whom 2000 were Indian sepoys. At the end the Marathas lost 1200 men with 4800 wounded; the British lost 428 with 1156 wounded.[11] What explains the disparity in numbers of those who fought and those who died? Why did the smaller army win and the larger army lose?

Boot attributes the British victory to the process through which warfare had been developed systematically in the West over the previous two centuries:

In the 1590s, the Mogul Emperor, a contemporary of Queen Elizabeth I and King Philip II, commanded more than four million warriors—a force bigger than any army in Europe until the twentieth century ... Until the mid-1700s, the notion of Europeans conquering these ancient civilisations was generally regarded as too fantastic to contemplate ... It would have been hard to predict in 1614 or even 1714 that by 1914, 84 per cent of the world's land surface would be dominated by Europeans ... By 1800, Europe had already conquered 35 per cent of the world, and industrialisation had made almost no impact on warfare by that point. The British Empire reached its heights under Queen Victoria because it was able to exploit the manpower and financial resources of India—an entire subcontinent whose conquest was well under way by 1800 but had barely begun by 1700.[12]

The main change had been in the way soldiers were regarded. Armies became permanent careers and this meant undergoing regular training in the barracks. Hospitals were established to treat the wounded. Engineers studied ballistics and designed lighter, more effective artillery. The French four-pounder—a gun that could shoot a four-pound ball of gunpowder—Boot tells us, became lighter at 600 pounds rather than 1300.[13] Above all, European armies were trained as a group through drill and discipline; they fought as a team, while Indian soldiers fought one-to-one in individual combat. For Indians battles were matters of individual glory; for the European armies it was the victory of the side which was important.

When the Marathas fought the Mughals or even the forces of Ahmadshah Abdali, both armies shared a similar code of warfare. Each was a collection of individual soldiers put together by various vassals and junior officers, and the soldiers received no formal training from their masters. There was no drill, no uniform, no common identity which bound soldiers together as members of a company, a regiment or even an army.

> Equipping and managing an army requires an administrative apparatus whose members are chosen at least partly on merit, who receive a secular technical education, and who perform their duties relatively honestly and efficiently and without excessive favouritism to family and friends ... Above all what was needed was an openness to new ideas and a willingness to evolve beyond old ways of doing things ... In sum *to fight like Europeans you had to become "European"*. You had to adopt at least some of the dynamism, intellectual curiosity, rationalism, and efficiency that has defined the West since the advent of the Gunpowder Age.[14]

It is this modernity which enabled the British to win their wars even if they lost the odd battle. Indeed, Max Boot attributes the dominance of Europe over Asia and Africa to the creation of modern warfare. Mornington (later the Marquis of Wellesley), with the help of his brother, Arthur Wellesley (later the Duke of Wellington), quadrupled the size of the British empire in India—'an achievement worthy of Napoleon'.

Arthur Wellesley received a knighthood and Mornington a marquessate when they went back to England. After their departure India was more or less secure, though there were still battles ahead, notably in Punjab. One outcome of all this was that the British created a modern European-style Indian army which exists to this day not just in India, but also in Pakistan.

BUILDING A NEW ORDER:
RELIGION, REFORM AND REVENUE

As they conquered more provinces, the new rulers also systematically 'settled' them. This meant measuring and recording the lands cultivated, with details of the crops grown as well as field notes on the local people, their habits and institutions. Land revenue systems were tried out, partly adapting what was already there and partly reflecting the new doctrines of 'political economy' that were being bandied about in Europe. There was also a new 'state' being built with a new system of law and justice. Here again, intellectual trends in Britain were influential.

Warren Hastings's attempts at translating Hindu and Muslim law and implementing them in the courts had been sincere and could have provided a good model for future governance, but the hostility with which Parliament treated him, discouraged his successors from 'going native'. At the same time Britain itself was undergoing profound political and social turmoil from which it emerged with remarkable confidence with its own model of government. The challenge posed by the French Revolution and the two decades of Anglo-French wars led to much dissidence and near revolutionary conditions in Britian, which were effectively and harshly suppressed. Their triumphant emergence from that experience convinced the British that they had seen off the excesses of reform and that this demonstrated the superiority of their own Constitution.

Yet, against this complacence was set the radicalism, not only of Wilberforce, who had battled to end slave trade and for parliamentary reform, but also of the political philosopher, William Godwin, whose plea for justice inspired the generation of Wordsworth and Coleridge, and led to an examination of the extent to which life could be better for ordinary citizens. Malthus, and later Ricardo, was pessimistic about the perfectibility of the human condition, while Edmund Burke's venomous attack on the French Revolution and his stout conservative defence of the Constitution angered many radicals. Tom Paine and Mary Wollstonecraft penned their replies vindicating the revolution and castigating British reactionaries, while Jeremy Bentham promoted his rational and utilitarian approach to reform. The Clapham movement of ardent Christians propagated the reform of morals, at home and abroad, in Parliament and elsewhere, in public life. India was high on their list for reform. James Mill's multi-volume history of British India and its disdain for all things native in India reflect these new trends. Mill was a utilitarian and an economist who had befriended Ricardo. The bulk of his eight volumes is a detailed account of what the East India Company did. His assessment of old India is harsh and dismissive, but the main object of his concern is an examination of how his fellow countrymen behaved and misbehaved in India. He went on to work for the Company as a writer, rising to the post of Chief Examiner of Correspondence, as did his more famous son, the economist, John Stuart Mill.

India was thus not just an empire; it became a project. The Company had kept the evangelical hordes, who wanted to bring the light of Christianity to the benighted heathens, at bay. As Cornwallis wrote to the Bishop of Salisbury on 27 December 1788, 'The success of the Portuguese Missionaries in the Malabar Coast does not hold out any very encouraging prospect to us as their converts are the poorest and most contemptible wretches in India.' This was based on anti-Catholic prejudice as well as new British confidence. Portugal, after all, had now become a client state of the British. But apart from the failure of the Portuguese, there was another strong argument against proselytizing activities in India. Cornwallis continues in the same letter, 'It is likewise a matter for serious consideration, how far the impudence or intemperate zeal of one teacher might endanger a Government which owes its principal support to a native army composed of men of high caste, whose fidelity and affection we have hitherto secured, by an unremitted attention not to offend their religious scruples and superstitions.'[15]

Even so, the Christian missionary was sure of his cause. Each renewal of the charter brought complaints on this score till Parliament relented. The wisdom of Cornwallis's words was to be proven within twenty years when there was a mutiny by the army at Vellore Fort. Here, 1800 Indian sepoys and 400 British soldiers were guarding the family of Tipu Sultan in July 1806. The decision to make soldiers wear caps with leather straps spread fears that the *firangis* were aiming to convert the sepoys. In the mutiny, which lasted just a day, 350 sepoys and 114 British soldiers died, including some officers. William Bentinck was then the governor of Madras. As he recalled later, all the British 'went to bed in the uncertainty of rising alive'. It revived the spectre of the Terror in the French Revolution. Charles Grant, then high up in the East India Company but not yet the leading figure he became later, said to Bentinck how the mutiny showed 'symptoms . . . most alarming and in a great degree new in our Indian history'. As an evangelist Grant did not want to blame the missionaries. Bentinck, however, knew 'that the primary cause was the turban and the interference with caste marks which had roused the soldiers' fear for their religion'.[16] The insistence that sepoys wear head gear with a leather insignia had led to trouble. The fault was the army's but, meanwhile, the parliamentary situation in London had changed and Bentinck lost his chance of staying on, or being considered for the bigger job in India for twenty years, as a result. A further fifty years on, excessive zeal for conversion of Hindu and Muslim soldiers cost the Company the power to rule over India. As we shall see later, the reforming zeal came to a crashing stop after 1857 and the missionaries were taught to stay in their place.

Cornwallis set himself two tasks—to root out corruption in Company servants and settle the question of land revenue in Bengal. He blamed the corruption among the Company servants on their dealings with the Indians. He thought the latter were irremediably corrupt, a prejudice which he held almost a priori and did nothing to revise. The answer lay in separating the two nationalities as they conducted business of government. This was a contrast to Warren Hastings's approach, and began the racial divide between the rulers and the ruled which lasted for the next 150 years. He also dispensed with Hastings's insistence on using the laws of the Hindus and Muslims in courts of law. Law courts were, from now on, to reflect British practices. Thus were laid the foundations of what became one of the enduring legacies of the British to India—the legal system.

But the issue of land revenue was urgent. Pitt's India Act directed the Company 'to inquire into the alleged grievances of the landholders, and if founded in truth, to afford them redress, and to establish permanent rules for the settlement and collection of the revenue . . .'[17]

The result was the Permanent Settlement. It settled the revenue assessment for Bengal zamindars in perpetuity. After Hastings's efforts at farming out lands for five years to curb harsh revenue demands, this was the logical extension. The assessment was carefully done: recent records of revenues paid were examined and an average was found. Bengal province (which then included the states of Bihar and Orissa), was assessed at £3,109,000 and Benares at £400,000. The Permanent Settlement has, since, sparked much debate on whether it was a good thing or not and whether it signified a fundamental revolution in agrarian relations. Those who want to castigate British imperialism as having damaged India take the view that this was a radical and alien restructuring of the system. Cornwallis is criticized for attempting to create the prototype of an English landlord class—the zamindars—in the hope that they would improve cultivation. Little did he know, critics aver, that Indian landlords were not the entrepreneurial kind and would not invest in improvement.[18]

A more balanced view, not only of the reforms in Bengal, but in other presidencies as well, is that the British just tidied up what they had already seen on the ground. Far from a radical restructuring of the system of agrarian relations, they merely consolidated it. What they did introduce as an innovation—which came as a shock to the first generation of zamindars—was their insistence that the annual assessment had to be paid on time. Indian aristocrats were not used to being asked to play by any set of rules. The insistence on prompt payment of revenue and, even worse, confiscation of the land for non-payment, were issues which caused much trouble in Bengal at the outset of the Permanent Settlement. The idea that the land which they owned could be taken away for non-payment and sold to the next successful bidder was a shock to the elite of the old system. Status had begun to give way to contract. A rule for property was as binding on the property owners as the rules for the rest of the society. This was a shock to the feudal notions of *zamindari*.

The prompt payment of revenue required a modicum of efficiency in administering the lands and engaging enough peasants to cultivate it. Not all zamindars displayed such efficiency. Thus, in the first two decades, there was a major turnover of owners. In Orissa half the zamindars—about 1500—changed between 1804 and 1818. In Bengal and Bihar a more fragile estimate is 40 per cent between 1793 and 1806. After this initial upheaval, the system settled down to a double permanence of settlement and of owners.

What caused the initial upheaval was that the revenue rate had been jacked up in the years between 1765 and 1790. The famine of 1769–70 had depopulated Bengal by death and migration. A lot of previously cultivated land needed peasants to resettle it. As time went on, Bengal re-populated and the lands began to bear the yield which justified the settlement. The value of land rose and Bengal zamindars became fabulously rich. They spawned a host of intermediaries who all lived off the rising surplus they could extract from the land, leaving just a subsistence for the cultivator. It is clear that after paying the permanent settlement to the government, there was a lot left to spend for the layers of intermediaries and the zamindar himself. Indeed, through the nineteenth century Bengal remained prosperous, becoming the leading province for intellectual, literary and cultural matters. A lot of these activities were carried on by the *bhadralok*, the gentlefolk, who were, more often than not, the class living off the surplus rent that the peasants generated. Bengal began to suffer from the limitations of zamindari only in the twentieth century, and one interesting point is that there was no famine in Bengal till 1943.

In other parts of the British conquered territories, the same strategy of adapting existing institutions for revenue collection was followed. The difference was that existing practices were codified. Measurements were made of lands and their revenue potential. A bewildering variety of rights in land existed, for example in South India where at first zamindari was adopted along with a settlement with individual farmers— a system which came to be known as *raiyatwari* (or 'ryotwari' as the British called it). Bentinck was influential during this process in his capacity as governor of Madras. As the purpose was to collect as much revenue as was feasible, the Permanent Settlement became less popular, and the Ricardian idea that the rent on land rose as population and income increased with time persuaded the Company's officers to skim off the rising rent on land The raiyatwari arrangement allowed this as the revenue assessment could be periodically revised. Much of South India as well as the Maratha lands in Bombay presidency were converted to raiyatwari by mid-nineteenth century and the variety of rights in land was reduced and regulated. In North India the settlement was with whole villages via the leading families. This was called the *mahalwari* system. It was also not a British invention, but what they thought was local practice.

The different models for revenue settlements confirmed and deepened the differences among the local economies. The British ruling classes were not like the French who would have taken a single rational approach to a problem such as revenue settlement and to other issues such as weights and measures and decimalization of currency. The British may have become the new masters of Europe, but they were imbued with conservatism, not just when Cornwallis was governor general but for decades after. They believed in maintaining local institutions, relying on local gentry to collaborate with them and make only such improvements as would enhance and regularize the revenue.

The land was settled by these cautious and careful arrangements— measuring lands, clarifying the nature of rights and confirming local arrangements. But while the revenue settlements were conservative, the law reform, the challenge of Christianity and the spread of education were revolutionary. The resulting impact was a tremendous cultural upheaval in the parts where the British ruled directly. It was not something India had ever experienced before; India had not even thought of itself as India. That was the major shock in the century to follow after Cornwallis's departure.

WILLIAM BENTINCK:
THE FIRST OF THE BRITISH MUGHALS

When William Bentinck (1774–1839) returned to India in 1828 as governor general, twenty years after his initial stint in Madras as governor, he was conscious that a new order had been consolidated. The

Marathas had been dealt with and, in a long Burma campaign, Assam—
a region that even the Mughals had not conquered—was added to
British India by the time Bentinck departed for the second time, and Sind
and Punjab would follow by 1850, along with Kashmir. The British were
creating a *nation* in their new empire, which covered more territory than
the Mughal Empire ever had. As George Norton, the judge advocate of
Madras, wrote in a letter to Bentick in 1835, his predecessors had been
mostly 'occupied in acquiring, in consolidating, and in adjusting the
English dominion in India. But it rested with your Lordship first to
introduce *nationality* (if the word suffices) in the system of policy
advocated as most fitting for its future prosperity, and for the times.'[19]
Bentinck himself wrote to a friend that 'all India now virtually composes
one empire'. British rule was 'more firmly fixed than that of any
sovereign from the time of the first Mahommedan invasion'.

Yet, the British were 'strangers in the land' and were 'the objects of
dislike to the bulk of those classes' who had influence, courage and
vigour—those who constituted its army and the local loyal gentry. The
fears of Vellore had not been forgotten. Others shared this view.
Macaulay, who was to join Bentinck in 1834 as a member of his council,
thought 'we were strangers' and 'a serious check in any part of India
would raise half the country against us'. An Anglo-Indian from Calcutta
said, '*All* British subjects live here by sufferance. A legitimate claim to
the sovereignty of a single foot of soil cannot be established except on
ground of good government.'[20]

The answer, then, was to make 'the happiness and improvement of the
people, the first and last objects' of the government. As Charles Trevelyan,
who also held the post of Madras governor and worked with Bentinck
in India, said, Bentinck had been the first governor general to place 'our
dominion in India on its proper foundation, in the recognition of the
great principle that India is to be governed for the benefit of the Indians'
though, as he added, 'the laws of God are so happily adjusted that, in
benefiting the natives, we also benefit ourselves'. Bentham's doctrine of
utility asked the ruler to pursue the welfare of the people but did not rely
on a notion of God to justify it—only utility. Added to this was a deep
belief in Christianity; it was not only the proper way to rule but was also
profitable.

By now, the British had turned 180 degrees away from the admiration
of William Jones and Warren Hastings for things Indian. India, in the
new view, had been rendered irremediably corrupt due to the 'despotism'
it had endured for centuries. To our modern ears, this may sound like
the kettle calling the pot black. The contrast was not, however, between
despotism and democracy, but between good and bad despotism. Even
among the radical utilitarians, democracy based on wide franchise had
not won the day. Bad despotism was government which disregarded the

well-being—material and spiritual—of its subjects. As John Stuart Mill was to write in his classic essay *On Liberty*, 'Liberty, as a principle, has no application to any state of things anterior to the time when mankind have become capable of being improved by free and equal discussion. Until then, there is nothing for them but implicit obedience to an Akbar or a Charlemagne, if they are so fortunate as to find one.'[21] A lifetime of working in the East India Company had convinced Mill of the benefits of benign colonialism, a 'government of leading-strings the one required to carry such a people the most rapidly through the next necessary step in social progress ... I need scarcely remark that leading-strings are only permissible as a means of gradually training the people to walk alone', a sort of 'self-abolishing imperialism'[22] as Alan Ryan, a British philosopher has called it. To do Mill justice, he thought the same of the Greeks as the British working classes—in his view the latter were yet to deserve a franchise.

Thomas Babington Macaulay, who was no favourite of the Mills—father or son—faced massive criticism when he expressed similar views in his attempt to reform the ways in which the British in India could be brought to trial:

> The political phraseology of the English in India is the same with the political phraseology of our countrymen at home; but it is never to be forgotten that the same words stand for very different things at London and at Calcutta. We hear so much about public opinion, the love of liberty, the influence of the Press. But we must remember that public opinion means the opinion of five hundred persons who have no interest, feeling or taste in common with the fifty millions among whom they live; that the love of liberty means strong objection to every measure which can prevent them from acting as they choose towards the fifty millions, that the Press is altogether supported by the five hundred, and has no motive to plead the cause of the fifty millions.
>
> We know that India cannot have a free Government. But she may have the next best thing—a firm and impartial despotism.[23]

Bentinck came from the Benthamite stable and had been something of a radical in his European appointments. He had tried to foment a republican revolt in Sicily, much to the embarrassment of the British foreign office, during the Anglo-French wars. By the time he arrived in India as governor general, his view had been formed. 'Nationality meant that India should be united, great, imperial, rich, enlightened and perhaps, one day, self-determining.' He set about instituting a number of reforms, some of which worked and many did not, 'because of the fetters and contradictions of British rule within which Bentinck was working'.[24]

Of the things that did not work, some were visionary. Bentinck wanted to move the capital of British India to the north. Over the years he mooted to an unconvinced Company Meerut, Allahabad, Delhi and Agra as possible seats of government. 'The Governor-General', he wrote, 'would never willingly agree to give up, with Agra, "the brightest jewel of its crown", its position "amid all the scenes of past and future glory; where the Empire is to be saved or lost", [which] gave it "a charm which will soon burst through the cloud of old commercial associations and prejudices in favour of Calcutta".'[25]

Bentinck also wanted free settlement of British in India, a policy which was supported by the new elite, including such eminent Indians as Dwarkanath Tagore, who looked forward to 'further advantages from the unrestricted application of British skill, capital and industry to the very many articles which this country is capable of producing.' Rammohun Roy thought 'the greater our intercourse with European gentlemen, the greater will be our improvement in literary, social and political affairs'. Bentinck wanted long leases for indigo cultivators, since sugar and coffee planters already enjoyed sixty-year leases. He also wanted an influx of 'capitalists' who would build large steam mills or grow strains of tobacco to compete with the United States.

Neither the world nor, indeed, the East India Company directors were ready for what we might term today as 'liberal economic reform'. Settlement was out of the question in a nation which still smarted from the revolt in North America of British settled abroad. Once free passage was allowed to all and sundry, who knew what kind of people would end up in India? The British ruling classes had as little trust in its own poor and working classes as, perhaps, in the 'dark heathens'. Mountstuart Elphinstone, an old India hand, feared that the migrants would breed Eurasians and foster 'contempt and dislike for blacks', much as had happened in the Portuguese enclaves in India.

The abolition of *sati*, the Hindu upper-caste practice of widow immolation, remains controversial to this day. It exemplifies the divide between a cosmopolitan view of human rights and a culture-centric one. Being the Christian evangelist that he was, Bentinck had no doubt about the rightness of what he was doing. Orientalism would have defended and protected sati; utilitarianism, with its universality and the added certainty of evangelical Christianity, had no such qualms. But for the modern Indian elite—from Radhakant Deb, who opposed Bentinck's reform of sati in the nineteenth century, to contemporary social scientists such as Ashis Nandy today—the sati question remains an error on Bentinck's part. Sati may have been a part of the organic culture of upper-caste Hindus, but the pathetic position it accords to a widow as a non-person cannot be in tune with any modern notion of the value of individual life. Later political leaders, such as Gandhi and Nehru, had no doubt that Bentinck was right, and the Indian Parliament incorporated the ban in legislation after Independence. Yet, the sati question touches one of the deepest divides in Indian society. Why this is so will be seen as we come to the diverse ways in which the Indian Renaissance expressed itself.[26]

The most successful among these reforms was, of course, the introduction of English instruction. Macaulay has received the most credit for it, and he was certainly its most articulate advocate. But it was Bentinck who willed it and so arranged the debate that he would win the argument. Money had been set aside—Rs 1 lakh for education of natives following the 1813 Charter Act. This had crept up to Rs 4 lakhs by the time Bentinck came to decide on how best to spend it. A debate had been raging for some years in the General Committee for Public Instruction (GCPI). The orientalists, who included James Prinsep, William McNaghten and H.H. Wilson, were all for Persian and Sanskrit—after all, the Company had been putting money in that direction. The new younger hands who had recently come from England, such as Macaulay and Trevelyan, wanted English. We have already seen that elite opinion in Calcutta, as exemplified by Rammohun Roy, was in favour of English and modern European knowledge. Bentinck was firmly on the side of teaching English. India, he thought, like England, needed a 'national' language. While Wilson thought all vernacular languages could be Sanskritized to create a single national language, Bentinck and Macaulay plumped for the option that Rammohun Roy had already championed. According to a modern post-colonial historian, Macaulay 'provided spurious legitimacy for Bentinck to dismantle the Orientalist educational programme and install one promoting European literature and science'.[27]

I take the view that of all the many positive and negative acts of British rule in India, Macaulay's Minute had the most far-reaching effect on the creation of modern India, up to and including its current emergence as a dynamic economic presence on the global scene. It is, therefore, important in my view that this Minute be looked at carefully and the implications of its revolutionary impact understood.

MACAULAY'S MINUTE ON EDUCATION

Macaulay's Minute on education was central to the decision to introduce English as a medium of instruction in India. It is a document which has become notorious due to one or two memorable phrases. Two may be cited here before looking at the Minute in detail.

On the Uselessness of Oriental Literature

I have read translations of the most celebrated Arabic and Sanskrit works. I have conversed both here and at home with men distinguished by their proficiency in the Eastern tongues. I am quite ready to take the Oriental learning at the valuation of the Orientalists themselves. I have never found one among them who could deny that a single shelf of a good European library was worth the whole native literature of India and Arabia. The intrinsic superiority of Western literature is, indeed, fully admitted by those members of the Committee who support the Oriental plan of education.

On Teaching English to the Natives

In one point I fully agree with the gentlemen to whose general views I am opposed. I feel, with them, that it is impossible for us, with our limited means, to attempt to educate the body of the people. We must at present do our best to form a class who may be interpreters between us and the millions whom we govern; a class of persons, Indian in blood and colour, but English in taste, in opinions in morals, and in intellect. To that class we may leave it to refine the vernacular dialects of the country, to enrich those dialects with terms of science borrowed from the Western nomenclature, and to render them by degrees fit vehicles for conveying knowledge to the great mass of the population.[28]

Even in these two quotations one can see that once put in the context of the whole paragraph, the notorious phrases, 'a single shelf of a good European library' etc. and 'Indian in blood and colour but English in taste' etc., appear much milder than they sound on their own. In the first assertion of the superiority of Western knowledge, Macaulay takes care to cite the views of those who disagree with him on the GCPI. Unlike James Mill, Macaulay seems to have read some of the literature, albeit in translation, that he is criticizing. But, as he says later in the Minute, like Rammohun Roy he doubts the usefulness of oriental learning once one passes from 'works of imagination to works in which facts are recorded and general principles investigated'. There was, by the early nineteenth century, no new writing in Sanskrit on astronomy or mathematics or any others sciences for well nigh a thousand years. Even in Arabic and Persian new knowledge had ceased being generated by the mid-fifteenth century. Macaulay was no expert in these matters, but his instinct was not wrong.

Macaulay has an arrogant, florid style. It was part of his persona to offend people, especially public figures whose reputations were widely esteemed. He was a severe critic of James Mill's *Essay on Government*—a treatise on utilitarian model of government—and wrote a devastating critique of it in the *Edinburgh Review*. John Stuart Mill said Macaulay was 'an intellectual dwarf, rounded off and stunted, full grown broad and short, without a germ or principle of further growth in his entire being'.[29] Stuart Mill, from Leadenhall Street at East India Company's offices, disagreed with Macaulay on the question of oriental learning, as we shall see later. Macaulay's dismissal of the totality of oriental learning is certainly arrogant, but he is able, in the same Minute, to point out how backward England was once on the same terms. He draws the analogy of Greek and Latin as useful sources of knowledge for Europeans, in the late fifteenth and early sixteenth centuries, when the European Renaissance occurred.

> At that time almost everything worth reading was contained in the writings of the ancient Greeks and Romans. Had our ancestors acted as the Committee of Public Instruction has hitherto acted; had they neglected the language of Cicero and Tacitus; had they confined their attention to the old dialects of our own island; had they printed nothing and taught nothing at universities but Chronicles in Anglo-Saxon and Romances in Norman-French, would England have been what she now is? What Greek and Latin were to the contemporaries of More and Ascham, our tongue is to the people of India.[30]

This shows that Macaulay's dismissal of oriental literature was not 'racist' as one would say in modern terms. It was universalist since he makes the same argument, by analogy, against the Anglo-Saxon and Norman-French. England in the fifteenth century was shrouded in ignorance of any serious knowledge of the sciences or philosophy. This knowledge was preserved and transmitted by the Arabs to Europeans, but Macaulay did not think that made a case for favours to Arabic.[31] He was to say later, in his capacity as president of GCPI, in the context of ordering books, 'That the Saracens a thousand years ago cultivated mathematical sciences is hardly, I think, a reason for our spending any money in translating English treatises on mathematics into Arabic.'[32] Money was scarce and had to be spent on what mattered. So, Macaulay's point was not who brought the knowledge to Europe but how the knowledge available then could best be conveyed to Indian students. English, though a foreign language for Indians, was the key. Europe could have missed the boat if it had rejected Latin and Greek as alien tongues which they had almost become in the Dark Ages—indeed his Minute later cites how during the previous century-and-a-half, Russia had acquired a large educated class 'nowise inferior to the most accomplished men who adorn the best circles of Paris and London'.

This was done, Macaulay says:

> Not by flattering national prejudices; not by feeding the mind of the young Muscovite with the old woman's stories which his rude fathers had believed: not by filling his head with lying legends about St. Nicholas; not by encouraging him to study the great question, whether the world was or was not created on the 13th of September; not by calling him a 'a learned native' when he has mastered all these points of knowledge; but by teaching him those foreign languages in which the greatest mass of information had been laid up, and thus putting all that information within his reach.[33]

The conclusion at the end of this double example is inevitable. 'The language of Western Europe civilized Russia. I cannot doubt that they will do for the Hindoo what they have done for the Tartar.'

We noted above Max Boot's assertion that British-led armies won battles against superior forces in India because of modernity and not modernization—that is, because of attitudes rather than material tools. The example of Russia that Macaulay cites has to do with the reform Peter the Great instituted in Russia, whereby he forced Westernization on the old society. In European as much as in non-European societies, under self-rule as in Japan and later Turkey, or alien rule as in India, the imperative of modernity has been inescapable. Japan started after 1868 and Turkey under Kemal Ataturk after 1920. In India the beginnings were made in the first half of the nineteenth century. It was an alien power that instigated it, but it is not obvious that the internal forces that existed within India could have instituted such changes endogenously.

The driving force of the next quotation—and indeed the entire debate—was scarce resources. Money that was available was not enough to educate the 'body of the people' in either oriental languages or English. Then the issue becomes, how can these scarce resources be best used? Elsewhere in the Minute, Macaulay criticizes the practice of giving bounties to students for learning Sanskrit or Persian as he thinks that 'it never can in any part of the world be necessary to pay men for doing what they think pleasant and profitable. India is no exception to this rule. The people of India do not require to be paid for eating rice when they are hungry or for wearing woollen cloth in the cold season ... Why then is it necessary to pay people to learn Sanskrit or Arabic?'[34]

Macaulay argued that the Charter Act of 1813 was being wrongly interpreted by the champions of traditional learning. 'We have a fund to be employed as Government shall direct for the intellectual improvement of the people of this country. The simple question is, what is the most useful way of employing it?'[35] After dismissing the claims of oriental languages as we see above, Macaulay moves swiftly to his message, 'We have to educate a people who cannot at present be educated by means of their mother tongue. We must teach them some foreign language. The claims of our own language it is hardly necessary to recapitulate. It stands pre-eminent even among the languages of the West.'[36] Macaulay then goes on to describe how a knowledge of English will give 'ready access to all the vast intellectual wealth which all the wisest nations of the earth have created and hoarded in the course of ninety generations.'

His prescience about the role of English in the world at large is uncanny:

> In India, English is the language spoken by the ruling class. It is spoken by the higher class of natives at the seats of Government. It is likely to become

the language of commerce throughout the seas of the East. It is the language of two great European communities which are rising, the one in South Africa, the other in Australasia; communities which are every year becoming more important and more closely connected with our Indian Empire. Whether we look at the intrinsic value of our literature, or at the particular situation of this country, we shall see the strongest reason to think that, of all foreign tongues, the English language is that which would be the most useful to our native subjects.[37]

Those who had been paid to learn Sanskrit or Arabic or Persian could not find jobs and hence needed further subsidy. 'They represent their education as an injury which gives them a claim on the Government for redress, as an injury, for which the stipends paid to them during the infliction were a very inadequate compensation.'[38] They are not wrong, Macaulay admitted, since their education 'procures for them neither bread nor respect'. The conclusion follows that, 'it is the bounty money paid to raise champions of error. It goes to form a nest, not merely of helpless place-hunters, but of bigots prompted alike by passion and by interest to raise a cry against every useful scheme of education.'[39] Anyone who has witnessed similar agitation against the withdrawal of any subsidy in India today will readily recognize how astute Macaulay is about such psychology.

He had his critics. John Stuart Mill was one whose low opinion of Macaulay I have already quoted above. While Macaulay was in India, Mill was working in Leadenhall Street for the East India Company and was closely involved in examining the correspondence on this question. He disagreed with Macaulay. Mill's view was that the Indian elite had to be kept on the British side and they would, in turn, 'act extensively upon the native character and ... produce elementary books and translations.'[40] As it happens, this was also Macaulay's strategy except that he wanted to do it through English rather than oriental languages. Mill was overruled. Macaulay had, after all, threatened in his Minute to resign if he did not get his way. As his recent biographer records, Mill felt 'the annoyance of one having for years (contrary to the instincts of his nature which are all for *rapid* change) assisted in nurturing & raising up a system of cautious & deliberate measures for a great public end ... finds them upset in a week by a coxcombical dilettante litterateur who never did a thing for practical object in his life.'[41]

Great thinker though he was, John Stuart Mill was wrong in his low valuation of Macaulay's work in India. Mill worked all his adult life in the East India Company and retired only when the Company lost its charter after 1857. Yet, his impact on India is hard to discern when compared with Macaulay's. And Macaulay had four years compared to Mill's thirty-four. It is important to understand how Macaulay made so much difference during his short stay in India.

MACAULAY IN INDIA (1834–38)

Thomas Babbington Macaulay went to Trinity College, Cambridge, and then was called to the Bar. His father, Zachary Macaulay, was active in the abolition of slave trade and served as governor of Sierra Leone, but he lost his fortune in a crash and Thomas Babbington had to make a living by his wits. He acquired a reputation as a reviewer and a literary critic which enabled him to earn a living. His reading was vast, especially in the classics as well as in many modern European languages. He was elected to Parliament in 1830 for a pocket borough (a constituency which was in the pocket of the local lord) and then, after the Reform Act of 1832, became the member for Leeds. But it was not until he was appointed member of governor general's council in India at £5000 per annum, that he felt himself free of money worries. On the voyage to India he records, 'The catching of a shark; the shooting of an albatross; a sailor tumbling down the hatchway and breaking his head; a cadet getting drunk and swearing at the captain'.[42] Landing at Madras in June 1834, he was delighted at all he saw: 'To be on land after three months at sea is of itself a great change. But to be in such a land! The dark faces, with white turbans, and flowing robes: the trees not our trees: the very smell of the atmosphere that of a hothouse, and the architecture as strange as the vegetation.'[43] He was summoned to Ootacamund where Bentinck was spending the hot summer months. Climbing the Nilgiris, he thought he was seeing 'the vegetation of Windsor Forest, or Blenheim, spread over the mountains of Cumberland'. Ooty had 'very much the look of a rising English watering place' and the governor general was '. . . all that I have heard; that is to say, rectitude, openness and good-nature personified'.[44] They hit it off immediately and Macaulay accomplished much in the one year he overlapped with Bentinck; afterwards he went on to become a key member of the governor general's council.

He got down to work immediately. The Minute on education was written within nine months of his landing in Madras. But he was on to a bigger project. 'I have already entered on my public functions, and I hope to do some good. The very wigs of the Judges in the Court of King's Bench would stand on end if they knew how short a chapter my Law on Evidence will form.'[45] This was the prelude to his other achievement which has lived on as long as his advocacy of English—his contribution to the commission which was entrusted with the codification of penal law which eventually became the Indian Penal Code. It still stands on the statute book and has been much less revised than acts of similar kind.

A clause in the 1833 Charter Act had allowed 'the appointment of a Commission to inquire into the Jurisprudence and Jurisdiction of our

Eastern Empire'. Macaulay was the president of the commission, and he directed the commission members to draft a Code of Criminal Procedure. He is credited as the principal author of this piece of law, and was most assiduous in his search for the best possible code. It took another twenty-five years before the Indian Penal Code was officially law, but few doubt his contribution. His code has lived a long time, and as one of his successors, Fitzjames Stephen, said, 'It reproduces in a concise and even beautiful form the spirit of the law of England, in a compass which by comparison with the original may be regarded as absurdly small. The Indian penal code is to the English criminal law what a manufactured article is to the material out of which it is made.'[46]

The genius of Macaulay was that, while arguing for education in English he was a universalist, who cared not for the local circumstances but derived his policy from general principles. Thus, what worked in Europe during the Renaissance and in Russia under Peter the Great was, in his view, just as applicable to India. But his genius was also in knowing local psychology. How else could he have formulated a criminal law code which is perfectly adapted to Indian habits and circumstances?

BENTINCK'S ACHIEVEMENTS IN PERSPECTIVE

Macaulay's contemporary, Bentinck, is rightly regarded as the first reforming governor general. Though it is the sati question which looms large in the way historians view his tenure, the issue of English education should also stand to his credit; moreover, it was during his regime that judicial reform was taken up. His desire to further primary education in vernacular languages languished after he left, if only because military campaigns had resumed and there was, as always, the perennial excuse of lack of resources.

But in education as in law, the primary impetus came from Parliament— the setting aside of Rs 1 lakh for education in the Charter Act of 1813, for instance, and the proposal to establish a commission in the Charter Act of 1833. The appointment of Macaulay also was due to his parliamentary career. Whatever any individual governor general did, military campaigns apart, was overseen by the British Parliament. India, as we have seen above, had become a project, a laboratory, where experiments in the improvement of governance could be tested. In this respect, the initiatives with which Bentinck and Macaulay are associated— law and language—have stood the test of time. They were crucial to the building of modern India.

It may be—and has been argued by both nationalist and post-colonial historians—that the British could experiment with India because they wielded absolute arbitrary power which they had usurped militarily. That is true, but so had every other previous ruler of India—after all, none of them had been popularly chosen. And it is not that past rulers had not experimented with India. Akbar had tried his hand at religion with dismal results. Jahangir's much vaunted system of justice died with him—even granting that it was as good as legend makes it out to be. No monies are recorded to have been set aside by any Mughal emperor for the 'revival and promotion of literature and the encouragement of the learned natives of India, and for the introduction and promotion of the sciences among the inhabitants . . .'[47] as the British Parliament did in 1813. No universities survive from three hundred years of Mughal rule; nothing, for instance, comparable to Al-Azhar in Cairo.

The issue is not that the rulers were alien—as this only gets us into a sterile argument about whether the Mughals were alien or Indian. Nor does it matter that they were despotic—after all, few regimes up to the nineteenth century were anything else. The rapaciousness of the English occupation of Bengal in the first thirty years after Plassey is recorded by the British Parliament itself, and is to be deplored. But we have no comparable, detailed record of the rapaciousness of Afghan and Mughal kings and the frequent invaders and marauders who preyed upon India. For the ordinary peasant household working away in a village, it mattered little whether the loot was spent in London, Samarkand or Agra. But the long-term benefits of education through the English language, and the establishment of a system of justice independent of personal imperial whim, are what have lasted to benefit India.

THE INDIAN RESPONSE TO THE REFORMS

Whatever Bentinck may have thought of his possessions, India was not a single unity in 1835. The three presidencies of British India were going their separate ways. The pace of social and political change was different in these provinces and even within each province, as between the urban capital and the 'mofussil'—a quintessentially Raj word.

The response of the local population was also diverse since there were class and caste differences among them, as well as religious differences as between Hindus and Muslims. Much of the response that we know of came from elite upper-caste Hindus. The response of the lower castes and the Dalits, as well as of Muslims, would surface later in the nineteenth century. Within the elite upper castes a divide opened up between the modernizers, including Raja Rammohun Roy and Dwarkanath Tagore, and their more traditional fellow subjects, Radhakant Deb for instance. The responses were centred on religion and social reform. The attack of the Christian reformers on Hindu religion and those who practised it led to acquiescence by some who sought to establish new religious movements—the Calcutta-based Brahmo Samaj being among the best known, with its efforts to 'Christianize' Hinduism. The opposing groups were those who tried to revive and protect a more orthodox version of Hinduism.

The Renaissance story is inevitably centred on Hindu populations of the presidencies. Indeed, in every presidency of British India, religion was the first line of defence by the local elite whenever they felt themselves under attack. It was also the terrain over which reformers and traditionalists within each community clashed. In the Bombay presidency, for instance, the Prarthana Samaj was the reformist movement while the Arya Samaj was revivalist, and the latter spread, most prominently, to North India later in the nineteenth century. When a distinctive Indian nationalism took shape in the second half of the nineteenth century, religion was an important ingredient of it. The pioneers in these movements were often employees of the new order. In Gujarat, which by and large welcomed British rule as a respite from Maratha depredations, the employment of educated Indians was opened up by the 1820s. The founder of the Prarthana Samaj, Bholanath Sarabhai was employed as *munsif* in the judiciary. Mountstuart Elphinstone, the governor of Bombay Presidency, had followed the lead given in the Madras presidency by Thomas Munro by taking on Indian employees in clerical and judicial posts.

It is said by post-colonial critics that imperial rulers thrust their culture upon a helpless slave nation and that Indian culture was forever after distorted from its true nature. There was violence not only of a physical kind but also psychological, as one culture conquered another. But that is to take too simplistic a view of the various regional cultures which the British encountered. The dominant Brahminical culture was so insular that they could only interpret the arrival of the white-faced rulers as the advent of the *kaliyuga*, the era which would herald the imminent arrival of Kalki (the being who would destroy the world). They regarded the foreigners as *mlechcha*—impure and unclean. But, more significantly, the regional elites in each of the three presidencies dealt with the onslaught of Christian as well as modernist discourse by the rulers in a nuanced way. Rammohun Roy was already a monist as a result of his Persian and Arabic training before he encountered Christianity. The Brahmo Samaj was his response, but he distanced it from contemporary Christianity which he found superstitious. Radhakant Deb, while opposed to the abolition of sati, was all for women's education. The British were catalysts to forces which were already dormant in the old society, but also pushed things along by imparting education in Western science and philosophy.

The enlightened Indian did not give up his religion. The Brahmo Samaj remained an esoteric Bengal phenomenon. But even there, sectarian differences between Roy and other leading Bengali figures, notably Kesab Chandra Sen and others, drove the new converts back to Hinduism—albeit a refined version, stripped of its most obviously oppressive features. The reformed Bengali was Westernized in his living room but orthodox Hindu in his bedroom and kitchen. In Brahmo Samaj meetings and lectures, there would be a passionate critique of Hinduism and the caste system, but back inside the house the women seldom agreed with the views expressed, and marriages continued to be arranged along caste lines. Even the Tagores married child brides, as in respectable families no woman could remain unmarried beyond the age of puberty. This, indeed, was the response of all of Macaulay's children across India. A new, refashioned Hinduism was constructed reviving the *Upanishads* and the more monotheistic aspects of Vedant philosophy. This co-existed with all the orthodox worship and rituals. Again, it was the women who stuck to the old-time religion, leaving it to the men to pontificate.

In western India the reform movements took place in the big cities—Bombay principally, but also Pune and Ahmedabad. In Bombay, unlike in Calcutta, three communities interacted—Marathis, Gujaratis and Parsis—who also spoke their own version of Gujarati. The Parsis had been first off the block to adapt to Western ways. They moved to Bombay from Surat early in the eighteenth century and were largely engaged in shipping and finance. Parsis also took the lead in starting a newspaper, the *Bombay Samachar*, as early as 1822. Newspapers were to form a major weapon in the hands of the new elite, both for the reform of Indian society and for the struggle against foreign rulers.

The Gujaratis were primarily in finance and traders in cotton, but there were also many teachers and essayists among the Gujarati Brahmins and they took to Western education enthusiastically. Among the Marathis, the modernizers were teachers and writers. Yet, Christian criticism of Hinduism had less impact on western India—the Prarthana Samaj, for instance, never did acquire the following the Brahmo Samaj had. There was, however, a vigorous reform movement in which the Gujarati essayist and poet, Narmadashankar Dave took an active part. His newspaper, *Dandio*, published in Surat, was loudly reformist. Along with Karsandas Mulji (his fellow graduate from the Elphinstone Institute in Bombay), the reform movement reached a peak in the maharaj libel case. In this they exposed the corrupt morals of a Vaishnavite maharaj (priest) and won the libel case brought against them. The nationalist and reformer, Dadabhai Naoroji, also a young graduate of Elphinstone Institute (later College), joined them and started the Gnan Prasarak

Mandali (the Society for the Diffusion of Knowledge) which operated in Gujarati, Marathi and English. They opened a school for girls, and by 1855 there were nearly 750 girls on the rolls. Bombay also saw a lot of civic activities in which Gujaratis, Marathis and Parsis came together. Bombay municipality became a major civic body for the training of the local elite in democratic politics.

In Madras presidency the situation was different yet again. There was a strong local culture deeply rooted in Tamil and with a caste system which was much more Brahmin-dominated than the other two presidencies. There was a strong Christian influence in education, but it failed to erode the dominance of the Brahmins.

There was also a secular ingredient. This came about as a result of the education in English-medium colleges such as Hindu College established in Calcutta and Pune, and later in the 1850s, the new universities established in the presidency headquarters. The Jesuit order soon added to the colleges which were imparting a Western education. But by all accounts, Bengal, or rather Calcutta, was the first to experience what has come to be called the Bengal Renaissance. This movement began in the 1820s as a result of the founding of Hindu College and was led by a teacher, Henry Louis Vivian Derozio, who though dying young, left a powerful impression upon his young Bengali students. The access to Western literature had the impact that Macaulay and others had hoped for. Curiosity was now implanted among the youth and they began to experiment with literary forms in Bengali, as well as writing in English. Their study of the history of Britain inspired them to retrieve their own history.

This secular, Westernized stream of Indians in the different provinces was influential in shaping the ideals of a modern Indian government whenever it came. Their aspirations were moulded by the British example, of course, and they took to heart the eloquence of Burke and Pitt and Fox. This secular, Westernized Indian stream was also, by and large, reformist in areas such as widow remarriage and child marriage but not, as yet, advocating reform of the caste system or the abolition of untouchability. These were the forces across the three presidencies which were to constitute the first recruits for the long struggle for Indian Independence. The secular and the religious individuals often overlapped or changed positions as the reforming ideas came closer to their own lives. Much of the complexity of contemporary debate on religion and secularism has its roots in the early-nineteenth century beginnings of the Indian Renaissance.

CHAPTER 4

THE GREAT DIVIDE:
FROM COMPANY TO CROWN

IF YOU GO to Horse Guards Avenue off Whitehall in London, across from where tourists flock to see the Guards in their fancy costumes, you come across the statue of a Gurkha soldier. Beneath the inscription at the base it lists the battles the Gurkhas fought over the years for the British government. The Anglo-Gurkha War of 1814–16 introduced the British to the fighting prowess of the Gurkhas and they were recruited like other 'peoples' the British had defeated in battle—the Jats, Marathas, Sikhs—as the century progressed. What we see is that the Gurkha regiments, and indeed many other regiments of the Indian army, were constantly engaged in battles within and outside India for much of the period between the establishment of the army in the mid-eighteenth century and Indian Independence in 1947. During the Napoleonic wars in the nineteenth century they were helping the Netherlands defend their possessions in the Indian Ocean against the French and then handing it back to them; they also fought in many British wars in Africa or in what we now call the Middle East. They fought all over India in campaigns and in Burma, which meant a loss of caste for the Brahmins among them as they had crossed the waters (Bay of Bengal). Even in the Afghan campaign they had crossed the Indus, and this was foreign territory as far as the Indian regiments were concerned.

The Indian army was made up of Indian soldiers led by British officers who trained them. As we saw in the accounts of Plassey and Buxar and Asaye above, the same raw material that was available to any Indian king was honed into a superb fighting force by the British. As new territories were conquered, the local soldiers were recruited into the Indian army. The ratio of Indians to the British was 9:1 and the army was an indispensable and, indeed, an economical tool for the global British Empire. The large population of India provided the best resource for the army.

Military campaigns went in cycles. Through the nineteenth century ambitious governor generals embarked on expensive campaigns and the Company's directors, sitting in London, complained. Then came retrenchment and a few years of relative peace which meant low-intensity wars. Bentinck's rule coincided with such a period. But overall military activity was unrelenting. Lords Amherst and Auckland ventured into Burma and Afghanistan; Dalhousie mopped up Punjab after the death of Ranjit Singh and Sind was ruthlessly annexed by the soldier-general, Sir Charles Napier, on grounds that were highly dubious. Dalhousie also changed the rules whereby Indian kings were allowed to adopt an heir if they had no successor. The new rule, called the Doctrine of Lapse, stipulated that kingdoms without direct heirs were to pass into British control. Finally, in what is universally thought to be the most blatant and unnecessary British takeover of them all, the Nawab of Awadh was deprived of his possessions solely because his lifestyle was considered decadent by the Company. Awadh had been loyal to the Company and though the latter had provided for his security, they had also extracted a handsome sum from the nawab for this service. The nawab had few, if any, tasks of governance, but was an active patron of poetry, dance and music. The annexation of Awadh proved to be the proverbial final straw for the people.

As he departed from India after eight years as governor general, the Marquis of Dalhousie was a satisfied, not to say, a smug man. As a later account of the 1857 uprising said, 'Counting up his treasures, the Governor General was certainly enabled to announce a most extraordinary accession of territory during the years 1848 to 1855. The Punjab, Pegu, Nagpoor, Oude, Satara, Jhansi, Berar, Ungool, Darjeeling, Khyrpore, the Carnatic, and Tanjore all became British for the first time.'[1] In his parting message to the Company, Dalhousie also added: 'Seven years ago, the heir-apparent to the King of Delhi died. He was the last of the race that had been born in the purple. The Court of Directors was accordingly advised to decline to recognise any other heir-apparent and to permit the kingly title to fall into abeyance upon the death of the present king, who even then was a very aged man. The Honourable Court accordingly conveyed to the government of India *authority to terminate the dynasty of Timur* whenever the reigning king should die.'[2] The Court of Directors was, however, reluctant to proceed with such a move; despite the fact Dalhousie proudly reported, 'The grandson of the king was recognised as heir-apparent; but only on condition that he should quit the palace in Delhi in order to reside in the palace at Kootub; and that he should as a king, *receive the governor-general of India at all times on terms of perfect equality.*'[3]

This, then, was the apotheosis of the farce which took place in 1764 after the Battle of Buxar when Robert Clive sat the Mughal emperor, the blind Shah Alam, upon a chair and had him grant the diwani to the East India Company. The Great Mughal had been reduced to a king of Delhi and it was incumbent on his successors to treat the governor general as an equal. The early years, when the King of England refused to allow the Company to sign treaties in his name lest he become a vassal of the Mughal emperor by implication, had now turned into a situation when the appointee of the Court of Directors of the Company, albeit under a parliamentary charter, now flaunted himself as an equal to the Shah-in-Shah.

It had been clear, since Bentinck's time at least, that the ambition of the governor generals was growing. Bentinck modelled himself on the Mughal emperor and wanted to move the capital to Agra or Delhi as we saw above. Dalhousie's action in asking the King of Delhi to vacate the Red Fort and move to the Qutab area appears part of the same growing self-confidence. For a Company which was always watching its pennies, and indeed loved Dalhousie for the extra £4 million from Awadh that he had added to the revenue of £30 million in 1855, it was a surprisingly overweening gesture. And it proved to be so.

The annexation of Awadh was Dalhousie's last act before leaving India; he reported to the directors that a complete civil administration and resident military force had been organized even before the annexation had taken place and that the soldiers of the nawab were now 'contentedly taking service in British pay'. As to Indian soldiers in all other regiments, he was sanguine 'the position of the *native* soldier in India has long been such as to leave hardly any circumstance of his condition in need of improvement'. This was to prove a fatal misconception.

Dalhousie's feelings of triumph were not without some solid foundations. Railroads had been introduced as had the telegraph. A Grand Trunk Road from Calcutta to Delhi had been extended to the Sutlej, now that Punjab was part of the empire, and plans were drawn up to extend it to Lahore and Peshawar, a magnificent stretch of 1500 miles 'available for commercial and military operations'. The civil service had been reformed with open recruitment, though for the British only. An Indian doctor, Chakravarty, educated in England, had won for himself a commission as an assistant surgeon in the Company's service. The branding of convicts—'a semi-savage practice'—had been stopped. A commission had been established to open universities in Calcutta, Bombay and Madras. A department of education had opened in Calcutta with directors-general of public instruction in all the presidencies, and the Company had by a dispatch 'sanctioned a most extensive education scheme for the whole of India', including 'all possible encouragement to the establishments of female schools along the lines of the Hindoo ladies' school in Calcutta.' A civil engineering college, too, had been started at Roorkee followed by colleges in Calcutta, Madras, Bombay, Lahore and Poona.

Though he was proud of his military and civilian achievements, Dalhousie was careful to add a caveat which proved prophetic after the most serious uprising the Company faced in its decades of rule. In his final report, he said 'No prudent man, who has any knowledge of Eastern affairs, would ever venture to predict the maintenance of continued peace within our Eastern possessions. Experience, frequent hard and recent experience, has taught us that war from without, or rebellion from within, may at any time be raised against us, in quarters where they were the least to be expected, and by the most feeble and unlikely instruments. No man, therefore, can ever prudently hold forth assurance of peace in India.'[4] Here was Bentinck's fear being repeated, the constant feeling that 'the moral mass of India is, to almost all of us, an absolute blank'.[5]

MUTINY OR REBELLION OR WAR OF INDEPENDENCE: 1857

The uprising which took place in 1857 had a short curtain raiser in the personal revolt of Mangal Pandey, a soldier in the 34th Bengal Infantry stationed in Barrackpore, in March 1857. He was summarily tried and shot. It was the much more serious revolt in Meerut in May that sparked off a rebellion which in one way or another lasted for a year and more. Men of the 3rd Native Cavalry and the 20th Native Infantry summoned the 11th Native Infantry to join in a revolt on 10 May. The rebellious troops freed their comrades who had been punished the previous week and overcame their European officers. They then marched to Delhi. It surprised and shocked the British who, despite the fears they had expressed to each other (as we have seen above in Bentinck's letters), never really expected such a sustained and militarily effective battle. Since these were soldiers they had trained themselves, they had little doubt about the fighting capabilities of the troops they were facing.

Much of the action on both sides was confined to the Doab region— the old Awadh kingdom and some surrounding kingdoms recently annexed by the British. In modern terms it was Uttar Pradesh, Uttarakhand, Madhya Pradesh and Bihar which provided the theatre for action. The rebel soldiers lacked leadership. They chose Bahadur Shah, the last Mughal king, as their symbolic leader, but he had neither the will nor the capacity for military leadership. Like the last Nawab of Awadh, Wajid Ali Shah, Bahadur Shah was a poet with the pen name of Zafar and was, like most Mughal princes, a sensualist. Sporadic leadership was provided by Nana Saheb, the scion of the last peshwa of the Maratha kingdom defeated in 1818, and more resolutely, by Rani Lakshmi Bai of Jhansi, who had been deprived of her kingdom upon widowhood and had cause to hate the British.

As we saw in the battle of Asaye, the many instances of individual bravery were not sufficient for victory, nor was it enough that the soldiers had genuine grievances. The injustice, and even the illegality, of annexations added to the fuel which lit the conflagration, but it was not enough to bring down British rule. What counted in the end was the leadership of officers and the discipline of troops. It was, after all, a military affair, despite some participation by the civilian population. The troops in Bombay and Punjab fought loyally on the British side against their fellow soldiers from Meerut. But they were also backed up by a large contingent from Britain itself. The empire had just fought a battle in Crimea and trouble had broken out in Iran just before 1857; and after the Indian crisis it would be engaged in battle in China—all during the second half of the 1850s. But it proved strong enough to withstand what was the largest revolt Britain ever faced in its most valuable possession.

What was the nature of the Indian army? As a contemporary account published soon after the events explained:

> Under an ordinary state of affairs, and without reference to the mutiny of 1857, the Indian army is in theory a strange conglomerate. The Queen *lends* some of her English troops, for which the Company pay[s]; the Company enlist[s] other English troops on their own account; they maintain three complete armies among the natives of India who are their subjects; they raise irregular corps or regiments in the states not so fully belonging to them; they claim the services of the troops belonging to certain tributary princes, whenever the exigency arises; and the whole of these troops are placed under the generalship of a commander-in-chief who is appointed—not by the Company, who have to pay for all—but by the Queen or the British government.[6]

In the Bengal presidency army, there were two regiments of light Cavalry, fifteen of Infantry and one battalion of 60th Rifles—all Queen's troops. Then there were six battalions of European foot artillery, a corps of Royal Engineers and two regiments of European fusiliers supplemented by three brigades of mixed native and European horse-artillery, three battalions of native foot-artillery, ten regiments of native light Cavalry, seventy-four regiments of native Infantry and one regiment of sappers and mines—all paid by the Company. There were, further, twenty-three regiments of irregular native Cavalry and twelve regiments of irregular native Infantry, a corps of guides and one regiment of camel corps plus sixteen regiments of local militia and contingents from Gwalior, Jodhpur, Malwa, Bhopal and Kotah. In all there were 1,50,000 men in this one presidency army alone. There were, in addition, armies of the Bombay and Madras presidencies.

In the Bengal Infantry four-fifths were Hindu and the rest Muslim, while in the Cavalry three-fourths were Muslim and the rest Hindu. As before, the grievances were about the possible loss of religion and about secret plans to convert soldiers to Christianity. Missionaries were not lacking who proudly proclaimed such intentions; the possibility that the cartridges issued to soldiers in the native army were greased with beef or pork fat incensed Hindu and Muslim soldiers alike. Given the later reputation of the British to 'divide and rule', it is astonishing that the cartridges managed to offend both Hindus and Muslims of the Bengal presidency army. The cartridge question had been brewing since the early 1850s. These grievances were, no doubt, further inflamed by the annexation of Awadh from where many of the soldiers came and whose nawab was, after all, the last powerful Muslim king in all of North India.

Eventually, after much horrendous cruelty as well as genuine humanity and loyalty on both sides, the rebellion was defeated and contained. It was a complex multi-layered event and has led to many debates about its causes and consequences. Even the term we use for it has varied over the years as fashions have changed among Indian and British writers. From Sepoy Mutiny to Revolt and Rebellion to Peasant War, War of Indian Independence—authors have brought their own interpretations to the events.

This is not surprising. Major historical events in any nation's life are always subject to debates which revise and reinterpret the way in which each generation thinks about them. The American Civil War, as well as the English Civil War or the French Revolution, have been live topics for charged debates in which opposite positions have been taken about the significance of the action. The events of 1857 are no different. For my purpose, it is the way in which the events have been debated which is of more import than the events themselves which are well covered.

In the decades following 1857, much of the writing supports the British side. The sense of shock and indeed of betrayal by loyal troops plus the sensationalist depiction of rape and pillage of British women and children led to many 'best-sellers' in fiction and in books covering the history of 1857. For the British public and, indeed, for the British Empire, this was a deep and rude blow. After 1857 there was a sea change in attitude as far as official policy was concerned. The enthusiasm for reforming Indian society evaporated and any plans for further annexations of native kingdoms were put on hold. Kings, or 'Native Princes' as they were called, were to be flattered and kept loyal by titles and gun salutes and favours. They were the dependable allies. Recruitment for the Indian army was to conjure up the notion of martial races, races that conveniently lived in regions far from the locations of the rebellion. The newly conquered territories of the north-west and Punjab became the reservoirs of manpower; the Gurkhas, too, were major recruits.

Queen Victoria, taking over the control of India from the East India Company, in her proclamation of 1858 promised to respect the religious beliefs of all her subjects. Indeed, she promised to treat her Indian subjects as she treated her other subjects everywhere else across the empire. So powerful was this message that a later leader of the fledgling Indian National Congress, Surendranath Bannerji, called the proclamation India's Magna Carta. He was not alone. Mohandas Gandhi used the proclamation to argue that Indian indentured labourers in South Africa had been conferred the rights to be treated as the loyal subjects of the empire thanks to the proclamation (it did not get him very far).

On the Indian side, there was a strange silence on the events of 1857, at least in terms of printed material. The new elite of educated Indians were firmly on the side of the Company. Narmadashankar Dave, a graduate of Elphinstone Institute, a social reformer and a formidable writer of essays, celebrated the victory of the Queen's forces:

Now we sincerely pray
That rid of all obstacles,
May the Queen have a glorious reign.

His fellow Gujarati, founder of the Prarthana Samaj and the first judicial officer appointed under Elphinstone's policy, Bholanath Sarabhai, agreed: 'Compared to other rule, the British rule is far better and may God continue it for ever'. Gujaratis had not forgotten the Maratha raids on Surat and elsewhere. Luckily for India the Almighty did not grant Bholanath his wish.[7]

The main losers of 1857 were perceived to be Muslims. It was the Mughal king who had been the leader of the rebellion, and it was his authority which the rebels sought to re-establish. Although Hindu and Muslim soldiers had combined in the act of rebellion as well as in their choice of Bahadur Shah as the leader, the onus in the following years fell on the Muslims. This is why one of the first Indian writings on the 1857 events was by Sir Syed Ahmad. His concern was to urge Muslims to reassert their loyalty and adapt to British rule by taking up Western education. He wanted to apologize unreservedly for the actions of his co-religionists and declared that his task would be to reorient them towards loyalty.

The first significant text on 1857 is by Vinayak Damodar Savarkar. Fifty years after the events, it was he who researched and wrote the book which characterized the events as India's War of Independence.

Savarkar was from Poona, a Maharashtrian Brahmin and someone in whose memory the triumph and tragedy of the Maratha Empire, which came ever so close to founding a Hindu Empire in India, were vivid. Savarkar's subsequent career as a leader of the Hindu nationalist movement and his alleged role in the assassination of Mahatma Gandhi (he was acquitted), have made any evaluation of his work a partisan affair. But he was the first Indian historian to write on 1857, and it was he who labelled it the War of Indian Independence.

By the time he wrote the book, the Indian National Congress, established in 1886, had been around for over twenty years. Its stance was loyalist, moderate and parliamentarian. It was an elitist movement but, at least, the idea that there was a nation called India which had demands that could be articulated by an annual congress—not a political party as yet—had taken hold. The maharajas and nawabs and nizams stayed away from this gathering. This was a meeting of commoners, albeit elite commoners. These elites, mainly Hindus and Parsis from across India, were now gathering for the first time on a secular platform to discuss political demands. I shall revert to the Congress below. For the present I wish to emphasize that the notion of an *Indian nation* was born only in the last quarter of the nineteenth century. This is what enabled Savarkar to call the events of 1857 a War of Indian Independence. Had someone of his calibre and opinion written in the immediate aftermath of 1857, they would have lamented the failure to restore the Mughal Empire or the Maratha dream of a Hindu Pat Padshahi.

Jawaharlal Nehru, the most articulate writer of Indian modernity, was unhappy with that label. He saw the events of 1857 as premature and pre-modern, a feudal reaction which was bound to be defeated as it was not in consonance with the flow of history. Nehru, along with many Indians of his generation, adopted a version of the Marxist theory of history in which progress happened in a linear and predetermined fashion—where primitive Communism was followed by slavery and then by feudalism, which was followed by capitalism and then socialism. This scheme had been designed mainly for European, or more specifically, western European history, to which, for Marx, even Russia could be an exception. Marx had left all of Asia in a strange bag labelled 'Asiatic Mode of Production'. But Indian nationalists, especially of Left-wing sympathies, ignored all that. By the time they came to use Marx in their analysis, the Bolshevik Revolution had converted Marx's writings into a dogma which had to be imbibed as universal truth. To them 1857 was a feudal reaction and was doomed to defeat as it defied the logic of progress.[8]

The ambivalence of most nationalists—those who did not take a Hindu religious view of Indian nationality—about 1857 was reinforced on the centenary of the event in 1957. By then India was an independent and sovereign democratic republic. The government appointed a committee of historians to celebrate the event. The volume was tersely titled, *1857*; the members could not agree on whether it was a war of independence, a feudal reaction or a peasant war.

This ambivalence is well reflected in K.M. Panikkar's *A Survey of Indian History*, a Nehruvian text from the 1950s—if any can be so named. In two paragraphs separated by half a page, Panikkar writes: 'It is true that all the leaders of the rebellion came from among the great dispossessed: but all were united in the object they had in view; the expulsion of the British and the recovery of national independence. In that sense the "mutiny" was no mutiny at all, but a great national uprising.'[9] 'Seen in true perspective, the mutiny is important only from two points of view. In the first place, it was the last effort of the old order to regain national independence and honour, and though stained by cruelty, it was a heroic effort of a dispossessed people to reassert their national dignity. In the second place, it is the Great Divide in modern Indian history, as the policy, practice and ideals of the government that followed differed fundamentally from the government of the Company which it displaced.'[10]

The 150th anniversary in 2007 did not yield any better results. There was a restaging of the march from Meerut to Delhi but it was a damp squib. Many books were published on all sides of the argument. Bollywood contributed a film based on the life of Mangal Pandey, but even this ran into controversy because he was depicted as less than perfectly virtuous. Progressive Left opinion had moved away from the old dogma and was more willing to recognize the liberation aspects of 1857. There was also a more assertive anti-imperialism than in 1957, but by 2007 India had emerged as the second largest investor in UK and the lingering anti-imperialism was more nostalgic than real.

It is possible, in our perspective, to give a more definite answer to the question of whether the uprising of 1857 represented a War of Indian Independence or was the last throw of an Old Order. But first the concept of the 'nation', for which the soldiers were rebelling, has to be defined. None of them had the idea of the 'nation' which would, fifty years later, inspire Savarkar and which Rabindranath Tagore wrote about in his famous anthem, *Jana gana mana*, a few years after that. It was not Bharat, comprising of 'Punjab, Sind, Gujarat, Maratha, Dravid Utkal, Banga', but Industan as Manucci called it. It was a revolt of the Doab along with its surrounding areas. It was what the Mughal Empire had shrunk to by the days of Shah Alam. It was Awadh writ large, along with the environs of Delhi. It was the Hindustan which had lost the battle of Buxar in 1765, backed up by the losers of the Maratha wars or their heirs.

This is not to belittle the achievements of the rebellion. If there had been an independent nation free of the British, comprising what is now Uttar Pradesh, Uttarakhand, western Bihar, north-eastern Rajasthan, Madhya Pradesh and Delhi, it would have been a large, populous nation. (I assume that Jhansi and Awadh would have joined this victorious kingdom). In post-Independence India, these areas return a third of the membership of the Lok Sabha and comprise around three hundred million people. It was, by and large, an Urdu/Awadhi-speaking nation (a language that would later be called Hindustani). It was the Old Order because it was the last to be formally included in the Company territory. Unlike the Bombay, Calcutta and Madras presidencies, where education was already set to flourish and new factories and railroads established, Hindustan was still hoping for the re-establishment of the Mughal Sultanate.

The apposite comparison is with Latin America and its liberation in the 1820s. By then Portugal and Spain had been weakened by the French wars, and in Simon Bolivar the many separate countries of South America had a superb leader. The war of liberation from Spanish rule lasted a decade and more, but eventually Bolivar won. The liberation was carried out in stages with Venezuela and Colombia becoming independent first, followed by Ecuador and Peru. Brazil took on a junior scion of the Portuguese royal family and declared independence, but with a monarch. Bolivar did not succeed in uniting all of South America into a single entity but his dream is still a powerful ideal. The Indian soldiers did not have such leadership. In Tantia Tope and Lakshmi Bai they had individual heroes but not military generals who could harness large troops in strategic battles. Of course, Spain and Portugal were weak in the 1820s which Britain in the 1850s was not, but as mentioned above, it was engaged militarily in Crimea and then in Persia just before, and in China after its Indian battles. To have engaged the British Empire in a battle for over a year was no mean achievement.

The rebellion of 1857 is perhaps most remarkable precisely for the one characteristic which has not been highlighted. It was indeed a sepoy rebellion—a leaderless army of soldiers, most of them from peasant communities of North India who had habitually been commanded and seldom, if ever, took any initiative. This army, starting from Meerut on 10 May 1857, marched to Delhi and sought leadership from Bahadur Shah, which he failed to give. In subsequent months the army seems to have marched under its own orders, with inadequate or no leadership; yet, despite this, it sustained action over more than one year. In this fact at least, the rebellion was like many other peasant movements.

The rest of India—can we call it the New Order—was unaffected by the events in Hindustan. Given the commercial origins of the Company, it was in the three port cities that the New Order had taken shape. It was here that Western education had begun and local elite had found employment in the revenue and judiciary departments. These were still pre-railroad days and distances were still vast. What was happening in the North did not touch the people in the port cities and their hinterlands. The troops of Bombay and Madras presidencies fought loyally for their British masters. The Sikhs, the most recently conquered, were even more loyal and were to become a bulwark of the Indian army for the next century and more. The Western-educated elites of Bengal and Bombay and Madras, who were all crafting their own separate 'Renaissances', were unmoved by the events. They would be the modern writers and historians of India and they wanted no part of it. Assiduous research has turned up an odd revolt here or there in these regions, but at the time these scattered uprisings did not bother the British.[11]

CREATING INDIA

It is during the fifty years that followed 1857 that an India was conceived that was to later become the object of liberation by the Indian elite. It was to be consciously forged from the separate regional and religious elements, from a society divided by caste and class. What did the trick was the fashioning of an ideology of nationalism. A story had to be told to explain why this enormous land mass was not just a society or a civilization, but a nation and a single nation at that. This ideology had to address the scepticism of alien rulers who questioned the very notion of an Indian nation. To counter such opinion, the rulers felt that the time had now come to undermine any such idea since, had there been a nation, the British would have perished in 1857. Scepticism about the nature of the country they were ruling would now be de rigueur in the academic halls of Oxford and Cambridge which trained the new generations of Indian hands.

But it was too late. The tools for fashioning the ideology of a nation were provided by the education which the foreign rulers had themselves established. The glorious past of India was recovered in accessible form and the history of the nations of Europe was available in books. The French Revolution and the Greek war of independence, the regicide of the English and the constant struggle of the British people to enlarge the freedoms available to them from their government—all this knowledge was absorbed and used. The rhetoric of Burke was turned back on the rulers.

The rulers also played an important, if inadvertent, role in this process. While denying that India was a unity, they created an administrative entity which, for the first time since the death of

Aurangzeb—if not for the first time ever—gave a *shape* to 'India'. As K.M. Panikkar says:

> The most notable achievement of British rule was the unification of India. British rule may be said to have given substance to the idea of a national State which India had inherited from the Moghuls ... A conscious process of unification was set afoot, the object of which was not merely to secure the effective exercise of British authority in Indian States, but weld the whole of India into one country. Railways, posts and telegraphs, currency, salt administration—these were the external forms through which this unity was achieved.[12]

The administrative structure and the railroad, posts and so on were, however, only the hardware of nationhood. What was necessary and, in fact, very difficult, was to provide the story—the narrative as to *why* India should be seen as a unity. Indeed, not one but many competing stories were available and have not lost their appeal even to this day. It is not just that 'unity in diversity' is a slogan and not a story, but the very fact that many nations can coexist within a unified framework of administration came as a shock in 1947. But that is to run ahead of our account.

One lesson was learned after 1857. The British Empire was not removable by military means. Sporadic individual acts of violence were carried out again and again, in Bengal or in Punjab or in Maharashtra. The martyrs of these actions, even today, form a corpus whose role in the final achievement of independence is disputed. The British were ousted not by native military tactics but by the methods of debate and protest the Indians had learned from the British. The examples of the chartists and the trade unions were absorbed and used creatively by many Indians in pushing for political reforms, rather than the desperate tactics of Jacobite rebellion which got Bonnie Prince Charlie sentimental sympathy but no independence for Scotland. In learning these methods and turning them on their rulers, Indians proved to be smarter students than Macaulay had expected. It is this story which we need to follow.

The first task was to forge a story—a narrative—as to why India was a nation. But at the same time, there was the urgent task of addressing the criticisms that Christian missionaries levelled at the practices and beliefs of the Hindu religion and society. The shock of 1857 had muted the voices of the missionaries, and they were never again to push their luck as they had in the four decades preceding the event. But now within the Hindu community, some were conscious of the need for reform, and in each region there was a reform movement, by its nature uneven, but still impressive. This task would no longer be undertaken by the government: no more Benthamite or Claphamite reform; the Mutiny had put paid to that. So 'civil society'—to use a modern phrase—had to undertake the agitation for reform on its own. Many local associations were formed to reform Hindu society—whether for widow remarriage or to raise the age of marriage beyond childhood, or for the right of women of certain castes to wear blouses rather than an unstitched piece of cloth.

Of course, Hindu society was not a single unit. As we have seen before, the only uniting element was the Brahmin caste which dominated culture across the country. But now, after decades of Western education, there was a split even at the top. The elite reform movements were all upper-caste oriented. The consciousness of the oppressed lower castes, especially the Dalits, was also transformed by the advent of Western education. But here, again, the struggle for social equality on part of the lower castes was different in different regions. It was in Maharashtra and in the Madras presidency that the anti-Brahmin struggle took its most acute form. Indeed, when it came to their demands, the Hindu elite fought for parity with the colonial masters, while the oppressed demanded equality with the elite. Even while the narrative of a single nation was being constructed by the elite, there were fissures in its texture.

Nonetheless, while there was vigorous activity among the Hindu elite and the oppressed on the subject of reform and self-improvement by absorbing the newly available knowledge, Muslims as a people suffered a setback. Unlike the Hindus, they had been the ruling community in North India up to the absorption of Awadh and in the South, in Hyderabad. Arabic and Persian were official languages in British India, but steadily, as English judicial practice and English law were introduced by Cornwallis, Macaulay and others, Muslims felt marginalized. Their failure to take to the new education was perhaps understandable since North India, where the majority of Muslims lived, lagged behind the port cities in these matters. The 1857 Mutiny was blamed on them, perhaps only because Bahadur Shah was the symbol of resistance. In the Crimean War, which the British fought against the Russians, the Ottoman emperor (who was also the caliph) was a British ally. The British had expected Muslims in India to feel grateful for their championing of the caliphate, but despite the caliph's injunction to support the British, *fatwa*s were issued to Muslims by Indian maulvis to fight the British. This deepened suspicions of Muslim disloyalty.

The pace at which Muslims took to Western education and social reform was qualitatively different from the Hindu response. It was to take a sustained effort on the part of the leaders of the community to overcome the initial lag. Moreover, similar to the situation among the Hindus, the forces of religious revival were as powerful as those of reform, if not more so. Sir Saiyad Ahmad was the leader of the movement to present the British in a more favourable light to the wider

Muslim community. Assiduously loyal, he tried to convince his fellow religionists that the path forward was through Western education. In the region where the Muslims were most numerous, Western education had not yet penetrated the extent to which it had done in the port cities. That is why he fought for, and won, the establishment of the Muslim Anglo-Oriental College in Aligarh. But he had a battle with the orthodox sections of the community in trying to convince them that social reform was necessary. A most significant development, in this context, was the Deobandi movement which adopted a revivalist line while, at the same time, not absolutely rejecting the usefulness of Western education. The battle was over reform of the society.

There were, thus, at least three major social groups—even if we ignore regional variations: the Hindu upper-caste Western-educated elite, the lower castes and Dalits and the Muslims. The uneven pace at which Hindus and Muslims adapted to the New Order influenced the fashioning of the nationalist narrative. Even among the Muslims there were regional differences. In the port cities Muslims joined with Hindus and Christians to access education. But the possibilities of a separate path for Muslim modernization were charted as early as the 1870s. It was a subterranean force hidden under the larger force uniting to fight the foreign ruler for independence, but it was there nonetheless.

THE COMING OF MODERN POLITICS

A crucial step in the process which eventually led to Independence was the hesitant introduction of a small element of consultation in the governance of India. In 1861 the Legislative Council was expanded at the presidency level to include Indian representation. These were nominated rather than elected members. By this time Britain had experienced nearly thirty years of middle-class franchise, but the big extension of franchise was yet ahead. Even the champion of liberty, John Stuart Mill, supported neither secret ballot nor votes for the working class. Yet, for India this began the modern process of collaboration in which the local elite apprenticed itself to a simulacrum of the parliamentary process; they could at least talk if not wield any influence, to say nothing of power. It was one avenue along which the demands of the elite could be advanced. Local government along modern lines was introduced in the 1880s and, by the end of the century, the Imperial Legislative Council also included representative members. These were indirectly elected from the presidency councils.

In the history of the Independence movement, these developments and the personnel who took up these positions have been downgraded, if not ignored, altogether. The story of Indian Independence is told very much as a story of the Indian National Congress, and how it changed from a docile and loyal organization to a moderately radical one in the early twentieth century, with the Partition of Bengal followed by a radical mass movement under Gandhi's leadership in the aftermath of the First World War. It is through rejecting the constitutional path and taking up street level agitation that success is said to have come. Within thirty years of Gandhi taking over the Congress and making it into a political party, Independence had arrived.

Yet, if independent India became a democracy and remains so, the antecedents to the agitational mode should not be forgotten. There was a lot of training in the modus operandi of parliamentary democracy, even though power did not reside in the legislature. Indeed, the Congress conducted itself along democratic lines throughout its pre-Independence existence, and procedural points of election and passing resolutions by a vote were important to its legitimacy. Even as Gandhi's agitations took to the streets, there were Congressmen who fought the elections to the newly reformed councils in the 1920s and only gave up towards the end of the decade. Legislative activity was resumed in 1937. The Congress formed ministries in many provinces and only resigned at the outbreak of the war. When Independence did come, it was more in the spirit of continuity with what had gone before, rather than a radical rupture. It was the replacement of one elite by another. The new elite was home grown and hence legitimate; and it instituted democracy at the outset. But even the agitational mode which was adopted from 1919 onwards was, despite its rejection of the participatory parliamentary alternative, in the end a collaborative strategy which preserved power in the hands of the elite at Independence. They had gone to jail and made sacrifices for the Independence movement, not cynically but genuinely. There was never any doubt about who would take over power when the British left. I will establish why this was so in the sections that follow; it is sufficient to say at this point that it was the opening of the legislative consultative door which introduced the new elite to politics.

Politics served a most important function for the nationalist movement. While reform movements were divisive battles within each community, politics was unifying as it was directed at a common source. Even if British rule was not yet seen as 'the enemy' in the 1870s or 1880s, all demands were directed to the alien ruler. Every member of every elite faction had something to gain from the demands made to this single source. Very soon a narrative could be constructed as to why this alien rule was an obstacle. In a society lacking cohesion and fragmented along religious and caste lines, the foreign presence became a unifying element.

Nationalism is an ideology, and all ideologies have a common thematic structure. There is a golden past, a miserable present for which the subject of the ideology is not responsible, but some external agent is. Removal of the external agent leads to the promised golden future which recaptures the glorious past. Communism has primitive communism which is a golden age; Capitalism in the present is miserable because of exploitation by the capitalist. A proletarian revolution will restore the golden age of mature communism. This will take the society back to a stage where everyone will be happy, very much like the age of primitive communism. Nationalism asserts that the nation has been ageless and when it was free in the past, it was a golden age. An alien ruler has visited misery upon the nation, impoverished it and bound its hands and feet. But once the alien ruler is expelled by the shedding of blood of the nation's martyrs, then rivers of milk and honey will flow again. The nation will be free once more.

The nation has to be a united entity admitting no divisions of class or caste or religion. It has to construct its history before the arrival of the alien power in a way which highlights harmony and peace and prosperity which was uniformly experienced by all members of the nation. The alien ruler harms all equally and must be shown to be the cause of current miseries. The removal of the alien ruler is thus urgent and is the only effective way of restoring peace and prosperity.

As I have already shown, in India sections of different communities blamed their fellow Indians for their misery. Oppressed caste leaders, such as Jotirao Phule, were convinced that the enemy was the Brahmin, who was himself an alien who arrived as an Aryan invader and usurped power from a land where all were Kshatriyas, and who was responsible for creating the caste hierarchy by abrogating spiritual authority. Brahmins across India—North and South—were not averse to the flattery of European Indologists who projected them as being part of an Indo-European Aryan elite who had arrived in India three to four millennia previously. For them, this bolstered their claim to be treated on parity with the British who were also fellow Aryans. But if this was the case, what was the Indian nation?

There were also, historically, divisions between regions and peoples. Thus, Maratha depredations were resentfully recalled in Bengal and Gujarat. The great epic *Ramayana* was denigrated in the South as a story of the Northern conquest of Southern peoples. The river Indus was perceived as the boundary beyond which a Hindu suffered pollution and loss of caste. Macaulay's hope that the new graduates in English knowledge would help develop their vernacular languages was more than fulfilled. But because languages were useful as modes of identity construction, purification movements broke out. Hindi had to be distinguished from Hindustani and Urdu by sanskritizing its words which, the purists claimed, had been polluted by Urdu influences. In a subtle way, the message of the language purists was that Hindi was for Hindus and Urdu was for Muslims—who were alien. Tamil speakers became aware that Sanskrit words had crept into their language which had a continuous history of use comparable to any other language, and unlike Sanskrit. Languages in South India wanted to emphasize their non-Sanskrit origins.

A further problem arose with the very notion of alien rulers. If Aryans were seen to be practically natives and not alien, Muslims were handy scapegoats as alien rulers who had ruined the nation by their conquests, oppression and so on, but had then been supplanted by another layer of alien rule. Integrating Muslims into the national narrative, therefore, became a major challenge to the ideologues of nationalism.

Thus constructing a nationalist narrative in a multi-lingual, multi-religion country was a challenge to which the elite had to respond. They were the new Brahmins who, despite their small numbers, would provide a unifying framework to the nation. They had to because they were at the head of the queue wanting to grab representation in the legislative councils and other official positions. They wanted to be able to compete for the Indian Civil Service and have respectable positions in the army and the judiciary and the executive.

While the representation which was granted remained small and select, with no whiff of election, the elite strategy of mobilizing like-minded people together from across India was an effective response. The Indian National Congress, founded at Bombay in December 1885, was a creation of concerned Englishmen such as Alan Octavian Hume and William Wedderburn who brought together what can only be called Macaulay's children. The seventy-two delegates came from all parts of India, and this is where the truly revolutionary nature of the Congress lay. No previous such gathering, secular rather than religious, peaceful rather than military, had existed in India. The very words 'Indian' and 'national' were challenges thrown at the rulers who were busy denying that such a thing as an Indian nation existed.

Those who came were prosperous, well-educated and conversant with English. They commandeered special railway carriages to arrive at their destinations at each annual gathering. They had studied their British history and memorized the great parliamentary debates in the House of Commons. They favoured the Liberal over the Conservative as a more likely friend of India—perhaps more in hope than expectation. They came mainly from the cities of the presidency—Calcutta, Bombay and Madras—to begin with—but then also from Pune and Ahmedabad. They included such luminaries as Pherozeshah Mehta, Dadabhai Naoroji, Badruddin Tyabjee, W.C. Bonnerji, M.G. Ranade, K.T. Telang, G. Subramanian Iyer and Viraraghavachari. They had cut their teeth in local associations, for instance, the Madras Mahajan Sabha, the Pune Sarvajanik Sabha, the Bombay Presidency Association—all bodies which were innovations for Indian civil society, despite the presence of such Indian terms as 'Sabha' or 'Sarvajanik' in their names.

The Congress was unique in being All India. Indeed, it is remarkable that the expression 'All India' denotes geographical coverage that merely 'India' seems to lack. In comparison, 'All American' is not about geographical coverage but cultural type. But All India is indicative of how much the universality of geographical coverage was valued. Indian nationalism had one dimension which was acceptable to all: this was its territorial definition. It may have had several languages and religions, tribes and castes and so on, but the territory was a single unit. India was defined by its extent. This is probably the primary reason why Partition was such a shock to the nationalist sentiment when Independence came in 1947, and why Balkanization has been a continuing nightmare for the political leadership. But, again, this is to race ahead of our story.

The official reaction to the Congress, as and when it came, was not singular. The governance of India had altered a little in 1858 and now the Secretary of State for India had a cabinet post with a council comprising of old, retired India hands to advise him. The governor general was also a viceroy in his dealing with the Native Princes and with neighbouring foreign powers. And the debates on policy making had four parties at least. There was the governor general and the bureaucracy in Calcutta; the Secretary of State and India Office in Whitehall; there was also the Parliament; and in India, there was the white population.

Differences of political party mattered as much as they do in such circumstances. The evolution of famine policy is an example of the interaction between the many sides of Indian governance and political party differences. The Liberals did believe in free trade in food grains, internally and in international trade. The Conservatives were suspicious of traders and championed the landed interest. The Liberals believed in balanced budgets and political economy, the Conservatives treated such matters with distrust. Lord Cranborne (later the Marquess of Salisbury), when he was the Secretary of State for India in 1866, faced the news of the Orissa famine with alarm. But political economy, Cranborne found, was worshipped as 'a sort of fetish'. It reigned supreme in Calcutta and no help was given, when it was needed, to the starving people. As his biographer writes:

> With two Councils, two finance ministers and two local Governors, Cranborne's efforts against the famine, though strenuous, were largely unavailing. During the parliamentary debate that followed, 'Quoting from Blue Books, Cranborne showed how, especially as there had been a famine the year before, officials such as Beadon [the Lieutenant Governor of

Bengal] had been 'walking in a dream ... in superb unconsciousness, believing that what had been must be, and that as long as they did nothing absolutely wrong, and they did not displease their immediate superiors, they had fulfilled all the duties of their station.' Around three quarters of a million people died because, as Cranborne put it, Beadon chose 'to run the risk of losing lives rather than to run the risk of losing the money'.[13]

Thus, when he became Secretary of State for India next time around in 1874 and there was a famine again in Orissa, he asked for and got a loan of between £6 and £10 million (more than what was spent on the Irish potato famine). Lord Salisbury (as Cranborne had become on succeeding to his title) wanted to ban food exports from India, but Northbrook as a Liberal opposed this. He more astutely introduced famine relief works and paid workers out of the funds Salisbury had made available. 'Even if it should turn out that you have made too large a provision,' Salisbury wrote to Bengal famine commissioner, Sir Richard Temple, 'it will be much better than to have lost life by the slightest deficiency in supply'.[14] From here on famine policy combined free movement of food grains and relief works to provide purchasing power for the needy.

On the other hand, when Lancashire manufacturers feared Indian competition, it was the House of Commons which lobbied the government to impose duties on Indian manufacturers, much to the chagrin of Calcutta. Agitation by Indian leaders succeeded in imposing a countervailing duty on imports but only after some delay. Thus Calcutta also had its occasional success in face of the Parliament back home.

Since early on, the Congress leaders knew that they too would have to operate on many fronts: petition the governor general, agitate to have representation in the Legislative Council but also lobby the MPs in London and, if necessary, the government in Whitehall. Dadabhai Naoroji became the Liberal Party's MP and Mancherji Bhownagari was the Conservative MP, both during the 1890s. Indian leaders cultivated MPs such as Charles Bradlaugh and Keir Hardie to argue India's case. They had grasped that they needed to use the factions and divisions in the system, despite the formidable obstacle the imperial power presented to their demands in India. Dadabhai Naoroji started the East India Association in Britain to plead India's case. This practice of lobbying London was continued right up to 1947 with the India League led by Krishna Menon, and friends of India were consistently sought in the House of Commons.

Meanwhile, things had been changing in Britain as well. The year after the Congress was inaugurated, the Liberal Party split on the question of Irish Home Rule. Liberal Unionists led by Joseph Chamberlain joined the Conservative Party. The Liberals had a return to power in

1905 but after 1922 went out of office, and from then onwards they disappeared from the front rank of British politics. The Labour Party partially replaced the Liberals, but the dominance of the Conservative and Unionist Party gave it power for twenty of the thirty years between 1916 and 1946.

During this period franchise had been extended first in 1867 and then again in 1886 and 1916, so that all male adults had voting rights. Women won partial suffrage in 1916 and then parity with men in 1928. The period after 1886 also coincided with doubts in Britain about its capacity to sustain the top position in world economy as competition from Germany and USA threatened its hegemony. Then, towards the end of the century, the Boer War shook the nation as the British suffered their first defeat abroad in a century. As the Victorian era ended and the twentieth century began, Britain faced the world with considerably less confidence than it had at the start of the previous century.

It was in this context that Indian leadership began to articulate its demands about tariffs, the rupee–sterling exchange rates, agricultural relief, as well as the right to take the Indian Civil Services (ICS) examinations. These were all-India matters. From the beginning the Indian leadership showed a serious knowledge of the economic issues and, in fact, Dadabhai Naoroji's *Poverty and UnBritish Rule in India*, forged a powerful critique of the impact of imperial rule on India. It is remarkable that the sophistication of the Indian leadership in these matters matched—if not bettered—that of any anti-colonial movement anywhere else. Indeed, it set the model for anti-imperialist movements around the world.

This stemmed from the fact that even though their highest demands were strictly in the context of the British Empire continuing for the foreseeable future, they saw themselves as potential rulers. They may have been Non-Commissioned Officers (NCOs) then, but they aspired to lead from the front as and when allowed to do so. Thus, their principal concern was to show that they were deserving of such trust. And yet, the logic of facing a despotic foreign rule, itself subject at home to a democratic Parliament under a constitutional monarchy, meant that the logic of numbers was sooner or later going to tell. The Congress would be faced with the question: who was it speaking for?

The crisis came with the proposal to partition Bengal presidency into two administrative units. Bengal had always had a dual structure. The governor general resided in Calcutta, and, since he was also overall head of the administration, there was also a lieutenant governor. Orissa and Bihar were with Bengal in a single presidency. It contained 30 per cent of India's population in 1901. It did not seem absurd to suggest that Bengal should be administered in two units rather than one. Population pressure had been rising in Bengal as the Permanent Settlement had provided a century of stable ownership and unlimited opportunity for the subdivision of land among competing tenants. There had been ecological changes, thanks to frequent shifting of the river complex as it came down into Bengal after the confluence of many more rivers to the original duo of Ganga and Yamuna. Jute had become a viable commercial crop in addition to rice, and it was cultivated in the eastern parts of India. There was also a communal separation along east–west lines. Muslims, who were peasant tenants, were settled in the east; their landlords were, for the most part, Hindu zamindars settled in Calcutta on the western edge of Bengal.

Curzon was not unaware that the division of Bengal would provoke the Congress, but he was also anticipating a weakening of Bengal, which had been the driving force in the national renaissance since the 1820s. Bengal's agrarian economy was, however, past its peak. Land values, as multiples to their revenues, had been shrinking since their peak of over ten in the 1860s.[15] Bengali youth had become radicalized by reading the patriotic novels of Bankim Chandra Chatterji, who gave Bengal and India its first anthem in *Vande mataram*. This was a slogan and a recurrent theme of his novel, *Ananda Math*. The novel and the slogan-salute to the mother evoked the worship of Kali, and thereby also the motherland. This was a Hindu revival in a modern idiom. Bengali youth, sensitized to their situation by their education as well as the slim prospect of gainful employment in the few jobs available in the local bureaucracy, were flammable tinder. The Partition of Bengal provided the spark.

From its elite nature, the Congress was roused into mobilizing and recruiting larger numbers. Numbers were mobilized not just in Bengal, but in Bombay presidency and Punjab and, indeed, across the urban centres in India. While the moderates in the Congress leadership—Gokhale and Naoroji—protested politely, radical leaders—Bal Gangadhar Tilak, Bipin Chandra Pal and Lala Lajpat Rai, representing Marathi, Bengali and Punjabi-speaking regions, respectively—launched the *swadeshi* (own nation) movement. This called for the boycott of British products, buying only Indian ones instead. This was effectively about cloth in which India was now acquiring a capacity for machine manufacture, rather than just yarn, which it had been manufacturing since the mid 1850s.

The anti-Partition movement had multiple impacts on the notion of an Indian nation. Firstly, a regional question was seen as a national issue. Curzon's scheme of dividing Bengal united Indians across the land. Yet, in mobilizing the recruits, leaders used Hindu symbolism. Tilak pioneered the use of Hindu festival—such as the celebration of Ganesha Chaturthi and Dussehra, the festival which marked the defeat of the villain Ravana by Ramachandra, prince of Ayodhya and God on earth—to unite Hindus of all castes. Punjab, which Lala Lajpat Rai represented, was heavily influenced by the Arya Samaj, a revivalist as well as purifying movement in Hinduism. Hindus constituted around 65 per cent of the total population and Muslims around 30 per cent, with the other minorities standing at around 5 per cent. So it is no wonder that any mass mobilizing strategy would be Hindu oriented. Yet, this was divisive since Muslims, who stood to benefit from a government closer to where they toiled in East Bengal, were not included in the struggle against the Partition of Bengal. The slogans were Sanskrit—*Vande mataram* and swadeshi, the mobilizing festivals Hindu—centring on the Hindu gods, Ganesha and Rama—and the nation being thus appealed to was the majority of the people, but not all. Thus, the first time the Congress broke out of its elite status and connected with the more numerous, though still well-educated, upper strata in the urban centres of new India, it lurched into a religious national narrative.

Bengal had already been inflamed by the cries of *Vande mataram* and its youth was prepared to kill for the motherland. Three years after Partition, Khudiram Bose and Prafulla Chaki made an unsuccessful attempt on the life of Douglass Kenford, a district judge, and while Chaki committed suicide, Bose was hanged. The protests following this incident broke the Congress into rival factions. Tilak, who defended the revolutionaries, was deported to the Andaman Islands by the British where solitary confinement was his punishment. His sacrifice, the first prominent leader to go to jail, set the pattern for the future. The moderates, though still numerous in the Congress, were now on the decline. The future belonged to a strategy which would mobilize the broader strata of middle-class urban youth and take to the streets. The British Raj was to be defied rather than just appealed to.

It was a successful strategy. Curzon was eased out, though more because of his quarrel with Herbert Horatio (later Field Marshall) Kitchener, who was then commander-in-chief of the Indian army, than because of Bengal. Within six years, in 1911, Bengal was reunited. But 1911 was also the occasion of a *durbar* (a grand gathering held in Delhi) for the new King Emperor George V; it was announced at that durbar that the capital would shift to Delhi from Calcutta. It had taken eighty years for Bentinck's dream to be realized. What had been implicit in Dalhousie's desire to be treated as an equal of the Mughal Emperor had been exceeded in that the new king emperor was now the new great Mughal installed in Delhi, leaving behind as his nizam the viceroy of India, Lord Hardinge.

George V was the first king emperor who held a durbar in India, but also the last who died as emperor of India. At the silver jubilee of his reign in 1936, few could have thought that his successor (after the abdication of Edward VIII, his eldest son and heir), George VI, would preside over the cessation of India from the empire. By 1935 the British Parliament had already debated and passed the longest piece of legislation it had ever considered. It was the result of a process which had begun in 1928 and climaxed in the Government of India Act 1935. It was, for all practical purposes, the blueprint of the future Constitution of independent India. The fact that independent India had a different shape than that envisaged in the 1935 Act is what we must pursue in the following chapters.

CHAPTER 5

THE SETTLEMENT

CURZON DEPARTED IN a huff. His quarrel with Kitchener as to the relative powers of the viceroy and the army chief annoyed Whitehall. He was for civilian control over the military and Kitchener wanted to be the only power in military matters. Curzon lost in the immediate context, but his insistence on civilian control was to become a central plank of the British government's policy in India and a valuable legacy to its successors.

Curzon delayed leaving India till the Prince and Princess of Wales arrived on a visit, and expressed his own romantic view of the empire while welcoming the royal couple to Bombay on 9 November 1905:

> For where else in the world has a race gone forth and subdued, not a country or a kingdom, but a continent, and that continent peopled, not by savage tribes, but by races with traditions and a civilization older than our own, with a history not inferior to ours in dignity or romance; subduing them not to the law of the sword, but to the rule of justice, bringing peace and order and good government to nearly one-fifth of the entire human race, and holding them with so mild a restraint that the rulers are the merest handful amongst the ruled, a tiny speck of white foam up in a dark and thunderous ocean?[1]

Curzon understates the use of sword in winning India, but he makes clear that, to the British imperialist, India was special. It was neither like the White settlements of Canada, Australia and New Zealand, nor like the newer territories of Africa. Only about 5000 British officials were attached to Indian governments at the Centre and in the provinces. They were all on limited time tenure and would go back home to retire. There were to be no colonial settlers in India, unlike Africa or any of the White Commonwealth countries. India was ruled in collaboration with the local elite, whose modern leaders had been clamouring for even greater collaboration. Curzon uses the word 'race' in a much looser sense than we would today, but he was aware that the British people ('race' as he called it) had won over the territory of the Indian peoples ('races'). It was the task of the nationalist movement to deny the plural and assert that a single people inhabited India. Many of the forty-odd years that followed Curzon's speech were to be spent in negotiating a settlement between the tiny speck of white foam and the dark and thunderous ocean of the Indian peoples.

During the four decades between 1905 and 1947, these negotiations were initiated by the British Parliament, the effective power ruling India, in a series of pronouncements and laws and carried out in assemblies and councils, in conferences in India and in Britain—as well as on the streets where the protesting Indians were met with lathi charges and tear gas. There were industrial strikes and peasant riots. There was also a lively—though minority—tradition of the incendiary bomb or attempted assassination, where young men and women carrying out these acts willingly risked death. There were religious nationalists and atheistic communists, as well as non-violent Congressmen and women who brought about the final surrender of the British.

This story is told nowadays in monochrome, wherein it appears that Gandhi and the Congress fought for, and obtained, the freedom of India. The British are portrayed as monolithic imperialists, who only divided and ruled till they were defeated by Gandhi's cleverness. The narrative focuses on events after the First World War and encompasses Gandhi's struggles in 1920 and 1930 and 1942. There is collective amnesia both about the many constitutional understandings which advanced the cause of independence as well as the militant, often revolutionary, violent movements or, indeed, any and all non-Congress efforts in the independence battles.

Yet, to understand why India today is a thriving democracy and a successful economy which can deal with the world on its own terms, we need to explore the richer history of the struggle for Independence. When Independence came, it came as a transition, not a disjuncture (Partition notwithstanding); the new elite were at pains to achieve a smooth passage from the old to the new—so much so that the first prime minister, Jawaharlal Nehru, was often called the last viceroy. But he was also a great democrat, and therein lies the delicious paradox of India's freedom struggle.

Jawaharlal Nehru relates in his autobiography that he outshone his fellow students at Harrow by being the only one to know the members of the Liberal Cabinet which had taken office in 1906 with a landslide victory under Henry Campbell-Bannerman. He would have also known, doubtless, that in 1908 Herbert Asquith succeeded Campbell-Bannerman and led one of the most radical governments in modern times. It established the beginnings of a welfare state and cut the power of the

House of Lords to size so that the elected chamber would henceforth dominate. War broke out in August 1914, and by the summer of 1915 there was a wartime coalition of the Liberals with the Conservatives and Labour. Lloyd George split the Liberal Party, replaced Asquith as prime minister in 1916, and with Conservative support, won the 1918 election and stayed in office till 1922. The Liberals were never to regain power for the rest of the twentieth century. In the next twenty-five years—till India gained Independence—the Conservatives were in power for twenty years and Labour for five but in three fragments: 1923–24, 1929–31, 1945–51. Constitutional progress was initiated either by Liberals or by Labour, never by Conservatives.

The Liberal government under Asquith and the coalition under Lloyd George inaugurated two of a series of constitutional settlements, the so-called Morley–Minto and Montagu–Chelmsford plans, which suggested reforms that were designed to go beyond the appointed, or indirectly elected, representation of Indian legislators devoid of an electorate. There had been abortive attempts—mainly in the House of Lords—to introduce representative Indians in the viceroy's executive council or in the central and provincial legislative councils in the 1890s. MP Charles Bradlaugh had even introduced a Home Rule Bill in 1889, but it fell due to his death soon after. Curzon had been more successful, while Undersecretary of State for India in 1892, in getting a bill through which allowed bodies such as the British Indian Association, chambers of commerce, etc., to nominate sixteen additional members to the Imperial Council, one of whom later would be Gopal Krishna Gokhale. This was far short of the kind of representation that the Congress had asked for. The British Parliament, however, knew of the elite nature of the Congress. As Curzon said, 'You can as little judge of the feelings of and inspiration of the people of India from the plans and proposals of the Congress party as you can judge of the physical configuration of a country which is wrapped in the mists of early morning, but a few of whose topmost peaks have been touched by the rising sun.'[2]

With the new Liberal Cabinet the time for change had obviously come. Britain had just been through a bruising battle with the Boers in South Africa and the Irish issue was always alive, not the least because the eighty-three Irish MPs in the House of Commons supported the Liberal Party. The Liberal Party had been committed to Irish Home Rule for a quarter of a century, if not longer, and Gladstone's impatience to grant it had split the party in 1886. The Liberals were thus well aware of aspirations around the empire for greater autonomy. The Bengal disturbances were seen as a sign that all was not well in India.

Even the Prince of Wales, later the King Emperor George V, during his visit in 1905–06, had come to see the writing on the wall. He wrote to one of his courtiers:

> Personally I think we have now come to the parting of ways, we cannot let things rest as they are. We must either trust the Natives more and give them greater share in the Government or anyhow allow them to express their views; or else we must double our Civil Service, the latter have now got out of touch with the villages on account of the great increase in their work, it is now all office work, where formerly they went amongst the Natives every day, who learned to know them and trust them.[3]

In November 1908, on the fiftieth anniversary of Victoria's Proclamation, the King Emperor Edward VII published a message to the Indian people announcing the extension of representative institutions. Congress moderates like Gokhale and Dadabhai Naoroji, fighting for their corner against Bal Gangadhar Tilak and the extremists, were relieved. In December 1908 John Morley, as Secretary of State for India, introduced a bill in the House of Lords on behalf of the government, and soon after, he and Minto, as governor general, announced a moderate introduction of franchise and elections in the imperial and provincial legislatures. The 1892 reforms had failed to widen the basis of representation. Of the newly 'elected' members 45 per cent were professional middle class and 27 per cent landholders; there was not a single Indian businessman. Now, twenty-eight members were to be added who would be non-official, chosen by a combination of direct and indirect elections. Thus, half of the members were to be non-official (Indian) and some of them were to be elected by an electorate on a narrow-based franchise. The members had no actual power, and were only to debate issues rather than decide upon them. Predictably, even the moderate wing of the Congress found this inadequate. But, as in each subsequent such concession, the Congress complained about the size of the loaf, then, sooner or later, proceeded to swallow it.

The presence of a Liberal government in 1906–10 was not an insignificant element in this development. Tilak had been sentenced to six years of transportation to the Andamans for his support of violent methods. By now a section of Indian youth had taken to attacks on British personnel in India and in Britain, having learnt to make bombs. Anushilan was a Bengali youth movement which sought to hasten independence by attacks on foreign rulers. Similar movements sprang up in Maharashtra—indeed Savarkar encouraged young Indians studying in London to follow their example. These movements were, however, judged by Whitehall for what they were—nuisances rather than serious threats, and the Liberal government did not hold back its small constitutional concession. It had been equally indulgent to Irish terror attempts. A Conservative government was unlikely to have taken a similar position.

Once the principle of popular (albeit based on a narrow franchise) representation had been introduced, the question of whom these legislators were to represent arose. The Congress, of course, took the view that since they comprised the educated, well-to-do and the secular, they should have the right to represent Indians. The British did not view India the way the Congress did: they saw India as a cellular society made up of many fragments defined by region, religion, caste. They did not just divide India into two communities, but many, and held on to this view throughout the negotiations for constitutional concessions. What is more, the British saw their own society as made up of numerous, carefully-graded hierarchical groups, such as the aristocracy, gentry, middle classes and working classes, and the indigent. The Catholics had been discriminated against till 1830 and Jews and Nonconformist Christian sects had to overcome their disadvantages in public appointments across the nineteenth century. In Britain itself the franchise had been guardedly extended from the top to the bottom over the previous seventy-five years but even then, not all workers and no women were enfranchised by 1909.

The British thought of other societies in the same way as they did their own. In South Africa, for instance, where the British had just concluded a war against the Dutch Boers, the native Black Africans had been caught in the crossfire. There they had also seen Zulu rebellions and Gandhi's attempts to win rights for the Indian immigrants and Boer resistance to it. Thus, they viewed South Africa as a divided society. Similarly, Ireland was also split north and south by religion since Protestant migrants from Scotland in the sixteenth and seventeenth centuries had settled in and around Belfast. The Catholics in Ireland had been persecuted, and their co-religionists in mainland Britain had been discriminated against for centuries. Ireland had a situation where most landlords were Protestant and their tenants Catholic, much as Bengal had Hindu landlords and a largely Muslim tenantry. In Australia, another British possession, there was tension between the English and the Irish migrants, to say nothing about the conflict between them and the indigenous peoples of the island continent. In New Zealand the Maoris had come to a truce with the English migrants, after a long and bitter history. The British thus knew of divided societies across their empire. This is why twenty-eight seats were allocated as twelve indirectly elected from the provincial legislatures, seven by landholders from various provinces, five by Muslims, two by chambers of commerce representatives and, finally, two by representatives of Indian business. Three seats were reserved for minorities or special interest groups.

The nationalist movement has consistently accused the British of following a divide and rule policy and—especially after 1909—deliberately introducing separate representation for Muslims. Maulana Mohammad

Ali, who joined with Gandhi in the Khilafat movement in the 1920s, put it perhaps more truthfully: 'We divide and you rule.' (Some say he was quoting Gandhi.) The Congress was not trusted by Muslim leaders such as Sir Syed Ahmad Khan, who wanted Muslims to regain the trust of their rulers, not by making demands and protesting, as the Congress did, but by being extra loyal. He had started the United Patriotic Association in 1887, just two years after the Congress. In response to Congress demands that half the members of the legislative councils be elected, Sir Syed said that due to their numbers and a lower level of education, Muslims could lose out in such a scheme, even if special provisions were made for them; the Muslims had to take a slower path than what the Congress wanted. This was a strategy for making up lost ground since 1857, if not earlier. The Muslims had also been excluded from the Bengal agitation and were alarmed that the Congress did not appreciate the advantages to them (the Muslim community) of a Muslim-majority East Bengal. One Muslim grandee, Nawab Salimulla of Dhaka, had joined his fellow Muslim zamindars from UP to form a delegation led by the Aga Khan to lobby John Morley in London as representatives of the All India Muslim League. This is regarded as a watershed event in the history of India and Pakistan.

Of course, a few Muslims belonged to the Congress as well as the League. Mohammad Ali Jinnah, a brilliant barrister who had pleaded Tilak's case, was a promising young Muslim leader in both the assemblies. Certainly, one should not read history backwards and think, as many have done, that the die was cast for the eventual Partition of India in 1907 when the League was formed. Nor is it necessary to see the British as arch manipulators of an innocent and guileless Indian leadership led into separate electorates against its wishes. The British did not view India as made up of a homogenous mass of Indians, free of divisions of religion or region, language or caste. Of course, they had an incentive to highlight the differences, but did not manufacture them.

The truth is simple though painful. By 1909 the Congress had failed to construct a narrative of Indian nationhood which was inclusive, either of the diverse religions or even of all sections of Hindu society, especially the lower castes. Its concerns were elite concerns—jobs, seats in legislative councils, tariff protection and the rupee–sterling exchange rate. Lower caste leaders such as Jotirao Phule from Maharashtra and Iyothee Thass, a Dalit from Tamil Nadu who converted to Buddhism, did not credit Congress with any concern for their interests. The first foray of the Congress into an even moderate extension of its appeal in 1905 was based on Hindu religious mobilization. But even so, this was upper caste. With 'Vande mataram', a Sanskrit poem, as its anthem, the Bengal agitation largely ignored its majority Muslim population and its concerns.

The many 'nations'—social communities defined by religion and caste status as well as region and language—in India had not yet been brought together by the Congress leadership, nor for that matter was the League yet inclined to mobilize the Muslim masses. As the franchise expanded, numbers became even more crucial and as each side tried to mobilize its demographic strength, it played on the separate rather than the common identities.

The Congress was willing to take up the offer of the Morley–Minto reforms despite its unhappiness about the separate seats for Muslims. It also wanted much more than half the non-official places in the Legislative Council. Yet, the new reforms were a further step to inclusion in the imperial power structure. There was to be Indian representation in the executive councils. In March 1909 Satyendra Nath Sinha, who eventually became a member of the Imperial War Cabinet during the First World War and the only non-White hereditary peer, became the first Indian to join the governor general's executive council.

The proportion of reserved seats, around 30 per cent, was in line with the population proportions (with similar proportions in the provincial legislatures), and had the Congress taken a broader view, it could have regarded the reserved seats as protection for a large—indeed the largest—minority. Sumit Sarkar is typical of nationalist historians who take umbrage at such minority reservations. He says, 'Electoral rules were also made markedly invidious: the income qualifications for Muslim voters being considerably lower, for instance, than for Hindus. It must be added that though officials and Muslim leaders always talked in terms of entire communities, in practice only particular elite groups among Muslims were being preferred throughout by government policy.'[4] Muslims were poorer than the rest of the population and, indeed, even after a century remain poorer, sixty years of Independence notwithstanding. Muslim incomes were lower than those of Hindus or Parsis, and so it was not a bad thing that a lower limit was fixed for their community to ensure similar sized electorates. Nor were Muslims unique in having elite representation; the Congress was also an elite body, and the non-Muslim seats were filled by members of the elite as well. Of course, given the lower income limit for Muslims, their elite were poorer than the Hindu elite. But even a progressive historian like Sarkar, who is aware of the inequalities, is convinced that everything done for the Muslims was a British plot.

In 1911 the new King Emperor George V came back to India five years after his previous visit as the Prince of Wales, but this time for a coronation durbar. Here was the apotheosis of the Mughal pretensions of the British raj. The new viceroy, Hardinge, had 40,000 tents constructed in Delhi, which was to be the new capital fit for a new Mughal Empire.

He boasted that he had 90,000 rats killed in a single month. The royal tents were silk-lined and carpeted to reassure the Queen Empress, who was not happy with the idea of 'roughing it'. The King Emperor failed to enter Delhi on an elephant for reasons of economy, and rode a horse instead. It made his entry rather obscure, and unlike what any Indian prince would have tolerated. But the purpose of the durbar was served. As the *Times* reported:

> Enthroned on high beneath a golden dome, looking outwards to the far north whence they came, their Majesties the King-Emperor and Queen-Empress were acclaimed by over 100,000 of their subjects. The ceremony at its culminating point exactly typified the Oriental conception of the ultimate repositories of Imperial power. The Monarchs sat alone, remote but beneficent, raised far above the multitude, but visible to all, clad in rich vestments, flanked by radiant emblems of authority, guarded by a glittering array of troops, the cynosure of the proudest princes of India, the central figures in what was surely the most majestic assemblage ever seen in the East.[5]

If it was the most majestic assemblage ever in the East (which is open to doubt), it was never to be repeated. George V was the only King Emperor to hold a durbar in India and the last King Emperor to die as such. His heir, George VI, would preside over the dissolution of the British Empire in India within a decade of his rule. New Delhi was built by Edward Lutyens for the British rulers, but was to be enjoyed by the rulers of independent India. As a portent to the new order in prospect, the Gaekwar of Baroda, Sayaji Rao III, appeared before the King Emperor stripped of his jewellery, in ordinary clothes and turned his back as he walked to his seat 'after a perfunctory obeisance'.[6]

THE GREAT WAR AND ITS AFTERMATH

The next stage of the extension of the franchise and of representation in the legislatures was to come within ten years, but Britain, India and indeed the world had been transformed by then. The First World War, or the Great War as it was called, was fought on a mass mobilization basis across Europe, and the subjects of each European Empire were harnessed as soldiers to fight on the side of their masters. Indian soldiers had fought for the empire in the Middle East and in Africa, but never in Europe. They had never seen their masters defeated or desperate. For four years, a massacre took place across the fighting fields of Europe. Even before its end, the Czar of Russia fell, bringing an end to centuries of Romanov rule and two more imperial houses—the Austrian Hapsburgs and the German Hohennzollerns—were brought down. A democratic republic—the USA—was crucial to the victory of the western European empires—British, French and Dutch.

Britain had suffered two years of reverses and deaths by thousands. It had been a shock to the ruling classes to meet such resistance on the battlefield. The officers were soon blamed for the reverses; the soldiers were, it was said, 'lions led by donkeys'. The Suffragette movement had proved to be one of the most radical and, indeed, violent movements since the Chartists and by 1918, women had won the right to vote, though only for those over thirty. Men had also won an extension of franchise. Trade unions had emerged as powerful institutions, thanks to full employment and their contribution to the war effort. When Lloyd George took over from Asquith in 1916, Britain's fortunes turned. Britain emerged by 1918 as a victorious power, but the victory required the entry of America on the side of the Allies. At Versailles for the post-war negotiations, India along with Australia, Canada and South Africa was a full member of the five-nation delegation led by the British prime minister, Lloyd George. This was in recognition of India's war effort.

The contribution of the Indian army cannot be overestimated. Its numerical strength was just the simplest part of its contribution. Two million Indian soldiers—the largest single contribution to Allied war effort—fought during the conflict and were noted for their bravery in Flanders and Gallipoli and Mesopotamia. Many native states had contributed. The Maharaja of Jodhpur, even at seventy years of age, insisted on escorting his heir and nephew to the front. Besides Jodhpur, the Bikaner, Kishengarh, Patiala and Sachin kings volunteered for service along with their armies. Many in the Congress and the Muslim League encouraged India's war effort. Mohandas Gandhi, returning from South Africa via London, made recruitment a vital part of his campaign in India. He was awarded the Kaiser-i-Hind medal for his contribution. Indian soldiers impressed the Europeans. 'It was the performance of India which took the world by surprise and thrilled every British heart.'[7]

India also bore all the expenditure of her army fighting overseas, which was a departure from normal practice. This meant between £20 and £30 million per year, when the total revenue was only £100 million. It further gifted £100 million to the imperial coffers at the end of the war, adding 30 per cent to its national debt. Loans of £75 million were raised, and to finance the purchase of food stuffs provided by India for the war effort, the US treasury was approached for sale of enough silver to coin the millions of rupees needed.

Britain had problems nearer home. There was dissent in Ireland and, in 1916, there was a rebellion in Dublin when the Irish Republican Army (IRA) took over the general post office. Within four years Ireland had won Home Rule. Not until 1917 would the Allies see the tide of the war turn in their favour. But it was in that year, impressed by the contribution the Indian army had made, that the next crucial step was taken. The coalition government had been preparing for some advance on the Morley–Minto reforms. Curzon, now back in Cabinet, had drafted some proposals. Austin Chamberlain, as Secretary of State for India, had developed them, but it fell to Edwin Montagu, as the new Secretary of State, and hitherto a long standing critic of the government in India from Liberal back benches, to announce on 20 August 1917 that, 'The policy of HMG with which the Government of India are in complete accord, is that of increasing participation of Indians in every branch of the administration, and the *gradual development of self-governing institutions, with a view to the progressive realisation of responsible government in India as an integral part of the British Empire.*'[8]

Montagu announced he was to go to India 'to consider with the Viceroy the views of local governments, and to receive the suggestions of representative Indians and others.'[9] The bar to Indians receiving commissions in the army was to be removed and nine Indian army officers were to be gazetted for such promotion.

Just a month previously, on 12 July, Montagu as a backbencher had denounced the government in India as 'too wooden, too iron, too inelastic, too antediluvian to be of any use for the modern purposes we have in view'.[10] He was teased during the question hour about this, but demurred. Later, in the report he wrote jointly with the viceroy, they called it 'the most momentous utterance ever made in India's chequered history'. Superlatives were obviously in fashion when it came to India.

Yet, no independent India was on the cards, but then in 1917 even the Congress had not asked for Independence but only Home Rule. As with the White colonies, there was a steady series of progressions euphemistically labelled as 'responsible government' and 'self-government' which conceded a measure of local representation but within an overarching imperial executive control. Then came 'Dominion Status' which was only mooted during the war, and defined later in the Statute of Westminster in 1931. But by 1918, the White colonies were practically at the Dominion Status stage. The Irish were demanding Home Rule and, indeed, that was the demand which Gladstone was trying to meet when his party split in 1886. He tried again in 1892 only to be thwarted yet another time by the House of Lords.

When the Cabinet discussed the draft of the statement Montagu was to make, even Curzon admitted that 'the free talk about liberty, democracy, nationality and self-government which had become the common shibboleths of the Allies' required some gesture towards India.[11] Yet, he was chary of using 'self-government' in the statement, as was Balfour. Hence it became the more moderate phrase 'gradual development of self-governing institutions' in Montagu's statement. There were to be self-governing institutions which would lead to responsible government—a code word proposed by Curzon himself for the Indian majority on the Executive Council. There was no firm promise about democracy, but the text implied the steady growth of a small franchise. Montagu went off to India soon after and, along with Chelmsford, toured various parts of the country consulting the provincial legislatures and other opinion on this issue.

There followed a Montagu–Chelmsford Report in 1918 setting out the details. This was prepared after reports had been laid before Parliament examining the feasibility of the proposals. Lord Southborough's committee had concluded that the expanded franchise would be fifty-seven times larger than that under the 1909 Act. It amounted to as many as 6.375 million voters by 1926 (yet, still only 2.8 per cent of the population). Another committee had looked at the splitting of portfolios. The Montagu–Chelmsford Report itself disagreed with the principle of separate electorates, but the evidence they had received while consulting representative opinion in India led them to conclude that the 1909 decision was irreversible.

The proposals were put in an Act passed in 1919 which split the executive at provincial levels, with portfolios in 'soft' areas such as health and education assigned to non-official, i.e., Indian, members and hard subjects like finance and defence going to the British. Diarchy, as it was called, was to be a first trial in the ability of the new elite to govern. Parliament was to review the progress under the Act at the end of ten years.

More noticeably, there was an expansion of separate electorates and reserved seats. The case of Muslims has attracted much attention; Sikhs also got separate representation. But what has been less noted is the special status given to lower castes. Thus, in the legislative council of Madras, twenty-eight out of sixty-five seats were reserved for non-Brahmins. Yet, the Justice Party which had been formed as an anti-Brahmin party, protested about the small numbers. This was a move which Congress could not benefit from as it was seen as a Brahmin party in Madras. Even a small amount of guarded democracy was enough to bring to light the fissures in the Indian nation as the different sections of the population—'nations'—started hustling for the head of the queue. Indians had learned from all they had read about the West that once you have elections, numbers count. The presumption of the Congress that it was the sole representative of Indians was challenged at the first hurdle.

ENTER GANDHI

What transpired, however, was to launch the Congress on a twin-track strategy whereby it would transform itself from an elite gathering to a fighting political party, as well as a player in constitutional negotiations. It had already been radicalized by the First World War, and taken up the demand for Home Rule along the lines of a similar movement in Ireland. There was also a deliberate move to overcome the divisions between Hindus and Muslims in electoral matters. At the Lucknow meeting of the Congress in 1916, Mohammad Ali Jinnah successfully moved a Hindu–Muslim accord to unite against the British. Muslims conceded separate electorates in seven states where they were a minority, half the elected seats in Punjab and a third of the central legislature. Thus the Morley–Minto effect of separate electorates was being dealt with amicably by the Congress and the Muslim League. But this was to prove an irrelevance as Mohandas Gandhi entered the scene, and changed the nature of Indian politics.

Mohandas Karamchand Gandhi was, and continues to be, a complex multi-layered personality, hard to grasp and difficult to subject to a proper critique. *Time* magazine named him as one of the three most significant personalities of the twentieth century besides Albert Einstein and Franklin Delano Roosevelt. The Father of the Nation, and indeed the pilot of its march to Independence, Gandhi looms large in any history of India in the post-First World War period. His name has been appropriated by the Congress, not only to sanctify its often dubious politics, but also to hegemonize any proper history of the Independence movement. After Gandhi's entrance into politics, his role eclipses everyone else's. We are invited to believe that single-handedly and non-violently Gandhi delivered India's freedom. Congress was at his side, his tool for the struggle. What was good in the march to freedom was due to Gandhi and the Congress, and what went wrong—Partition for instance—was due to the divisive forces of communal parties, both Hindu and Muslim.

I distance myself from such simplistic accounts. Gandhi's role was the largest and the most pivotal. But, by the same token, his errors and miscalculations were also crucial to the direction the freedom struggle took. His genius is undeniable, and his example has inspired struggles elsewhere, most notably in the USA, in the Civil Rights movement in the 1960s led by Martin Luther King. But in India, Gandhi's detractors have grown rather than diminished, especially as it concerns the Dalit parties. In what follows I shall chart my course, making clear where it is my own view rather than the accepted history of India's freedom struggle. The present state of India cannot be understood without critically understanding Gandhi's triumph and his shortcomings.

The most remarkable thing about Gandhi is his willingness to expose his life and thoughts to the public throughout his political career. So we know a lot about him, but on his own terms. There has been a lot of further research on his life, and this forms a corrective to some extent. It is his enemies or, at least, those who were not completely captivated by his charm, who often have better insights into Gandhi than his devotees.

Gandhi learned his way around politics while a student in London. Unlike almost all other Indians who studied in London, he sampled a lot of British political life, especially the radical, dissident, quirky side of British politics. His vegetarianism brought him into contact with anarchists and socialists, esoteric Christian sects and food faddists and health quacks. In the Vegetarian Society he learned the rudiments of organizing and persuading others of an unpopular minority cause. But he also saw the ferment in British politics as trade unions and radical Liberals attempted to democratize it—where Charles Bradlaugh challenged the necessity of swearing an oath upon taking his seat in Parliament and Keir Hardie brought the working man's views into Parliament. Through his fellow vegetarian socialists such as Edward Carpenter, Gandhi would have known of the Chartists, a mass movement in the 1840s which was almost totally non-violent and which posed many radical demands to change British politics. Even as they lost, their influence continued via trade unions, and within twenty years of the great Chartist march in London, their demand for extension of franchise was implemented. The trade union movement also continued the tradition of peaceful mass action to establish workers' rights. What it required was organization, patience and solidarity. The lessons were not lost on Mohandas Gandhi.[12]

He then plunged into politics in South Africa. Here he represented a rainbow coalition of Indians of all religions and all classes—Muslim merchants, Gujarati bania traders and Tamil labourers. He had to organize this minority to fight for respect and rights against overwhelming odds. Unlike the leaders of the Congress in India, he would not expect polite dismissal or arrogant contempt; he faced prison and bullets and beatings. He petitioned local governments and went up to London to the imperial government. He organized his motley crew of semi-literate men and, more remarkably, women in their struggle for decent treatment. He spent thirty years of his life in South Africa, and though he did not win as much as he demanded, people around the world and in India began to see the unique qualities that he brought to any political struggle.

He was one of the elite—an English barrister, as he insisted on calling himself during his stay in South Africa. But, he had been thrown into the midst of a struggle where there were no other fellow members of the elite. He was the sole leader who had to use his talents at petitioning and pleading. He demanded and inspired total loyalty from his followers, and did not promise any easy successes. He changed those who followed him by removing fear of those in power. He truly *empowered* them.

Gandhi bided his time when he entered Indian politics. He first established his totally different style—of dress, of travel, of speech from the rest of the Congress leadership. He took part in a couple of non-political movements—indigo farmers in Champaran and textile workers in Ahmedabad, where he had his ashram—just as he did in South Africa. For Gandhi the personal was political and, indeed, all politics was personal.

The Congress had been a loyal organization advancing its cause for gradual improvement in representation without challenging the established order. It had tasted blood in the Bengal Partition affair, but had gone back to its polite ways. This was not Gandhi's way. He also could not just join the Congress. He had to lead it. Soon, however, a tragedy occurred which broke the old mould and radicalized Indian politics. Gandhi's time had come.

Gandhi in South Africa, as in India, professed to be a loyal subject of the Crown. Even in his days of leading agitations against the British Empire, he professed friendship, often of a personal nature, with viceroys and their families. Few have appreciated that this was the style not just of parliamentary opposition, but even extra-parliamentary agitation in Britain which was (suffragettes apart), by and large, loyal. Demanding change, but doing it peacefully, had been the British way, unlike the French who took to the streets. There is, of course, a history of violent outbreaks, but it is their infrequency in British history which is striking. The Peterloo massacre, as it is called, where the police fired on a peaceful crowd in Manchester in 1817, had only five victims, and that is the most vividly remembered event in the history of British radicalism. Gandhi had imbibed this history and he adapted this logic to Indian circumstances.

A FRIGHTFUL EVENT

For Indian history, the most important consequence of the Great War was that the consciousness of the soldiers had been transformed. Their horizons had expanded, and when they returned, they had seen and could retell the many instances when their masters were in retreat. The returning soldier added a whiff of the cordite to the atmosphere in post-1918 India. By then the Bolshevik Revolution had taken over Russia, and everyone could see that the peasant soldiers had been crucial to Lenin's victory.

The British had been grateful for the soldiers to fight in the killing fields of Europe, but in India they were wary of the returned soldier who had come back with new ideas in his head. Ireland was exploding in the aftermath of the war. In India, after nearly fifty years of stable prices and slow but steady growth—about half to 1 per cent—in per capita income per annum between 1860 and 1914, the war had disrupted supplies and raised prices. There had been forced recruitment of soldiers in Punjab, and resentment ran deep. War had also induced the British to permit greater industrial growth than previously, and the industrial working class, though small, was growing fast. India also had, by this time, a formidable local press which, in English and local languages, informed readers of political developments. The *Pioneer*, *Amrit Bazaar Patrika*, *Kesari* and many other newspapers were awakening the dormant Indian middle classes to their plight.

Rushbrook Williams succinctly describes the effect of the war:

> For India, the war possessed—nay, still possesses—a twofold significance. It was in the first place, a transient if exhausting crisis in the history of the British Commonwealth: a crisis in which India bore herself bravely: contributed substantially to the cause of victory, and vindicated once and for all her attachment to the person of the king. But it was also something far more significant. It was a wind from the West, fanning to a blaze the embers of old Nationalist ambitions, bearing with it the spark of new fires which readily seized upon combustible elements already heaped together.
>
> Strange enthusiasms were kindled: unfamiliar ideals furnished fuel to the flames. A furnace glowed, and into its fires the polity of India passed.[13]

A panicky government in India passed the Rowlatt Act as a weapon to incarcerate and control likely dissidents. The unofficial members of the central legislature had opposed it, but they had no power to influence the decision. Gandhi decided the time had come for agitation. He launched the very Indian notion of *hartal*—shops shut and tools down. In his own conciliatory way he fixed Sunday as the day, instructing shop workers to make up for the lost day another time. He did this independently of the Congress by founding the Satyagraha Sabha under his leadership. Gandhi travelled around the major cities spreading his call for a hartal on 6 April 1919.

The unilateral launch of an unusual agitation without consulting anyone else was to be typical of Gandhi's forays into mass action. As in South Africa, he expected total obedience to his orders from his followers, as well as an understanding of his unconventional methods. What happened was like a spark to a dry haystack. People decided that the time had come to rebel, and they were hardly likely to show restraint, having been so badly off for so many years of the war. Gandhi declared, within a fortnight of the day of the hartal, that he had committed a 'Himalayan blunder', and on 18 April called off the satyagraha. This was to be a recurrent pattern, where he found his followers inadequate vehicles of his moral leadership.

But he may also have been reacting to a tragedy which struck just five days previously. In what was easily the vilest attack on innocent civilians ever in the history of British rule, on 13 April 1919, a week after the first hartal, General Dyer fired at peaceful protesters in Jallianwala Bagh in Amritsar. It was an unprovoked and vindictive act, meant to strike terror not only in Amritsar but throughout the Punjab. Eighty years later Queen Elizabeth II conveyed an apology for this act, the only imperial act for which such an apology has been given.

The House of Commons debated the issue of Dyer's sacking and the Jallianwala Bagh episode on 8 July 1920. Edwin Montagu put up a staunch defence of the Cabinet's decision to retire Dyer. He was faced by hostile Conservatives, many of whom disliked Montagu because he was a Jew and welcomed any excuse to contrast his style with that of an 'Englishman'. Thus his opening speech in the debate, denouncing Dyer's act as terrorism, inflamed pro-Dyer Tories: 'Once you are entitled to have regard neither to the intentions nor to the conduct of a particular gathering, and to shoot and to go on shooting with all the horrors that were here involved, in order to teach somebody else a lesson, you are embarking on terrorism, to which there is no end.'[14]

As he was being barracked by pro-Dyer Tories, Montagu added, 'Are you going to keep hold of India by terrorism, racial humiliation and subordination, and frightfulness, or are you going to rest it upon the goodwill and the growing goodwill of the people of your Indian Empire?'[15] The chief whip, reporting to Lloyd George on the debate, disapproved of Montagu's style. He wrote, 'Under interruption, Montagu got excited when making his speech and became more racial and more Yiddish in screaming tone and gesture, and a strong anti-Jewish sentiment was shown by shouts and excitement among the normally placid Tories of the back bench category.'[16] It was then that Balfour, who was in charge that evening, decided to deploy Winston Churchill. As the minister for war and responsible for ending Dyer's employment, Churchill was the person to defend the decision and, as a good parliamentary speaker, win back the debate after many more people attacked Montagu.

Churchill rescued Montagu by making a powerful speech against Dyer. He criticized Dyer for resorting to a doctrine of 'frightfulness'. 'What I mean by frightfulness is the inflicting of great slaughter or massacre upon a particular crowd of people with the intention of terrorising not merely the rest of the crowd, but the whole district or country . . . Frightfulness is not a remedy known to British pharmacopoeia. This is not a British way of doing business.'[17] He urged for 'that spirit of comradeship, that sense of unity and of progress in cooperation which must ever ally and bind together the British and Indian peoples'.[18] He told the House that he had informed the army council, which had unanimously supported Dyer's dismissal. He added that even if they did not do so, he would recommend to the Cabinet that Dyer be retired from the army. He went on to say:

> However we may dwell upon the difficulties of General Dyer during the Amritsar riots, upon the anxious and critical situation in the Punjab, upon the danger to Europeans throughout that province, upon the long delays which have taken place in reaching a decision about his office, upon the procedure that was at this point or that point adopted, however we may dwell upon all this, one tremendous fact stands out—I mean the slaughter of nearly 400 persons and the wounding of probably three or four times as many at the Jallian Wallah Bagh on 13 April.
>
> That is an episode which appears to me to be without precedent or parallel in the modern history of the British Empire. It is an event of an entirely different order from any of those tragical occurrences which take place when troops are brought into collision with the civil population. It is an extraordinary event, a monstrous event, an event which stands in singular and sinister isolation.[19]

Churchill's vision of the empire was, at this juncture, not dissimilar to what Curzon said on his departure:

> Our reign in India or anywhere else has never stood on the basis of physical force alone, and it would be fatal to the British Empire if we were to try to base ourselves only upon it. The British way of doing things ... has always implied close and effectual cooperation with the people of the country. In every part of the British Empire that has been our aim, and in no part have we arrived at such success as in India, whose princes spent their treasure in our cause, whose brave soldiers fought side by side with our own men, whose intelligent and gifted people are co-operating at the present moment with us in every sphere of government and of industry.[20]

Churchill was a romantic imperialist. For him the imperial relation between Britain and India was special. His father, Lord Randolph Churchill, whom he idolized, had been Secretary of State for India for a few years. He had himself been posted in India in the Hussars, and spent his time in Bangalore bored by inaction, but improved himself through extensive reading. He had sought thrills in the Malakand and anywhere else on the North-West Frontier he could engage in battle. He held the view that the empire was a force for good and that, in ruling India, 'frightfulness' was unnecessary and excessive. In 1921 his name was mentioned as a possible viceroy to India when Chelmsford came home (in the event, the job went to Rufus Isaacs, the Marquess of Reading). He was to be disillusioned of his romanticism, and retreated into a perpetual denial that Indians may want to get rid of the British.

This made him bitter, in the end, towards the empire, but in 1919 he had no doubt where he stood, nor did Montagu and the Cabinet.

But as far as Whitehall was concerned, the pursuit of reform was not to be derailed. Thus, only three months after the Jallianwala Bagh massacre, on 5 June 1919, Montagu rose in Parliament, during a five-hour debate on India, to make his announcement that he would be bringing a bill to implement the Montagu–Chelmsford Report of 1918. By that time India had been represented at Versailles by Lord Sinha, the Maharaja of Bikaner, and Montagu himself. Thus, India was being treated on par with the White Commonwealth countries of Canada and Australia, which were also delegates. As Montagu said during the debate, 'I can only repeat that these things [that is, India being at Versailles and at the inaugural conference for the International Labour Organization (ILO)] together with the place occupied by my friend and colleague Lord Sinha in the House of Lords commit this House and Parliament to the view that this position is only justified if you can raise India to the position of a sister nation in the British Empire, and it is wholly inconsistent with subordination'.[21]

Montagu went on to tell the House that a majority of provincial governments in India 'do not like that portion of the Montagu–Chelmsford form of government which is known as "diarchy" and they have said so forcibly'.[22] So, the House must produce alternative proposals. When the bill came to Parliament, it was referred to a joint committee of both Houses to take evidence on the alternatives and make recommendations. The British Parliament had begun its involvement with governance of India in the 1760s, and it would not give up that activity till 1947. In the 1919 Act, one important clause laid it down that within ten years the workings of the reforms would be examined by a parliamentary committee composed of members of both Houses.

Montagu's peroration, when he introduced the bill at second reading on 6 June 1919, was a call to the Indian people:

> The future and the date upon which you realise the future goal of self-government are with you. You are being given a great responsibility today, and opportunities of consultation and influence on other matters in which for the present we keep responsibility. You will find in Parliament every desire to help and to complete the task which this Bill attempts, if you devote yourselves to use it with wisdom, with self-restraint, with respect for minorities, the great opportunities with which Parliament is entrusting you.[23]

But it was now too late. In a fundamental sense, after Jallianwala Bagh the trust was lost. The Indian leadership could never again believe that such events would not recur, nor could they ever again accept the measured pace to freedom on offer from London passively. India would engage actively in the process of *attaining its freedom rather than just receiving it*. Jallianwala Bagh finished, for ever, any chance of India retaining the imperial link in any fashion. Dyer had trumped Parliament.

SWARAJ WITHIN ONE YEAR

Under Gandhi's leadership, the Congress moved from a mild and loyalist umbrella organization to a mass political party ready to fight. Members were recruited at the small subscription of four annas, quarter of a rupee (4d in the then British currency), so as to make it widespread. Provincial and district level offices were opened up for the Congress party across India. There was a working committee elected by delegates to an annual conference. Gandhi quickly established his sole leadership of the Congress. Tilak died in 1920, and established leaders such as Chittaranjan Das were willing to acquiesce to Gandhi's leadership in the aftermath of the Jallianwala Bagh massacre. Others such as Tej Bahadur Sapru, a liberal, and Jinnah were horrified by his style and the religious idiom used in his political agitation. Jinnah withdrew from the Congress. But the tide was with Gandhi.

Once again the catalytic event was provided by Europe. The victorious Allies had planned to dismember the Ottoman Empire, even before the end of the war. A secret treaty—the Sykes–Picot Agreement—hatched by the foreign office and Quai d'Orsay, outlined how the Allies would take over different regions of the empire. In this, Iraq and Palestine were to go to Britain, Syria and Lebanon to the French, and so on. But the most serious blow after the war was that the sultan would lose his power over all the regions, except what is now Turkey, and his caliphate would be taken away from him and given to the sheriff of Mecca. In addition to all his woes, the sultan would be challenged by an army officers' revolt headed by the charismatic modernizer, Mustafa Kemal. Kemal defended Turkey when the Greeks invaded Anatolia in 1919, and defeated them in a three-year war, winning the title 'pasha'.

India, at this time, had the largest Muslim population in the world, despite the fact that Muslims were in a minority. (South Asia remains the largest Muslim subcontinent even today, except that it is broken into three jurisdictions—India, Pakistan and Bangladesh.) Muslim leaders— not the landed gentry, but merchants and religious teachers—had already seen the dangers looming ahead and had started an agitation in defence of the sultan. They wanted him to retain the caliphate and be left with sufficient territory to be able to defend Islam, and insisted that the holy places of Islam should stay under Muslim sovereignty. The Sykes–Picot Agreement had been made public by the Bolsheviks upon coming to power, and Allied treachery was exposed. Palestine being under British rule would mean that one of Islam's holiest places was to be taken away from Muslim control. Muslim masses in urban areas of India were moved to action under a central Khilafat committee. The movement was radicalized by Maulana Mohammad Ali and Shaukat Ali.

Gandhi saw this as a superb opportunity to harness Muslims to the cause of Indian Independence. He came out in support of the Khilafat movement on a platform of Hindu–Muslim solidarity. The injustice of Jallianwala Bagh and the humiliating Treaty of Sevres imposed upon the sultan could now be fused in a single struggle against the iniquities of the British Empire. Yet, the implication was that Muslims could only be enthused to fight for a pan-Islamic cause while the rest would join for Jallianwala Bagh, an Indian issue. The coming together of a Muslim political struggle which had religious overtones suited Gandhi's strategy of using religious symbolism and religious rhetoric as devices for political mobilization. His own version of Hinduism was more akin to a Christianized Brahmo Samaj plus a simplified monotheism based around the character of Rama, the hero of the epic, *Ramayana*, with all ceremonial aspects of Hindu practice stripped away for a Bhakti-based ecumenism, reminiscent of the sixteenth-century poet, Kabir.

Gandhi was not the first leader to harness religion for Indian nationalism. The Indian response to Western rule had always contained a religious core, with revival and reform as the two paths. The Arya Samaj was revivalist, while the Brahmo Samaj and Prarthana Samaj were reformist. The Muslims also had Sir Syed Ahmad Khan advocating reform and Westernization, though of the society and not of the religion, and the theological school at Deobandi wanted to meet the challenge of modernity through education as well as revivalism. There were even other revivalist movements such as that of the Barelvi school. For Hindus, with their religion confined by and large to India, religion could become a vehicle for nationalism. For Muslims, Islam was always a universal religion with its roots and headquarters outside India. For Hindus lacking a single book, a single church and a single founder, the possibilities for rewriting and reinterpreting religious texts were infinite. For Muslims the Book was unalterable and the Prophet undeniable.

At the turn of the century, a powerful force for melding Hinduism as a vehicle for Indian/Hindu nationalism was provided by the charismatic figure of Swami Vivekananda. He acquired the glamour of a Western reputation by his presence at the World Council of Religions in Chicago in 1892. Through his lectures and his mission, he constructed a muscular theory of Hinduism which was tolerant, yet militant. His teachings influenced Bengali youth who translated the message into a violent movement much in evidence during the agitation against the Partition of

Bengal. Aurobindo Ghose, later a philosopher–saint, was inspired by Vivekananda to formulate a theory of an Indian nation based on Hindu philosophy and religion.

Aurobindo Ghose's nationalism was woven around the concept of the mother goddess, Kali in whose honour the poem 'Vande mataram' had been composed by the novelist Bankim Chandra in his novel *Anand Math*. This poem had become the anthem of the nationalists in the Bengal agitation. Aurobindo wove together the notions of mother goddess and motherland:

> It is not until the motherland reveals herself to the eye of the mind as something more than a stretch of earth or a mass of individuals, it is not till she takes shape as a great divine and Maternal Power in a form of beauty that can dominate the mind and seize the heart, that these petty fears and hopes vanish in the all-absorbing passion for the mother and her service, and patriotism that works miracles and saves doomed nations is born ... Once that vision has come to a people, there can be no rest, no peace, no further slumber till the temple has been made ready, the image installed and the sacrifice offered. A great nation which has had that vision can never again be placed under the feet of the conqueror.[24]

In Western India Bal Gangadhar Tilak had also forged a militant Hinduism taking as his text the *Bhagavad Gita*, which forms part of the epic *Mahabharata* and is in the form of a dialogue between the god, Krishna and the great warrior, Arjuna. If there has to be a single text for Hinduism it is this or, at least, Indian nationalism has made it so. Tilak's militant Hinduism derived much from the history of the eighteenth-century Maratha Empire, which projects Shivaji, the first Maratha king, as an iconic figure. It was directed against foreigners, but this category included Muslims as former rulers and the British, both being classed as *mlechcha*—the impure, polluted ones.

Gandhi's national appeal was based on a distinctive and much more ecumenical version of Hinduism. While in London he had come in contact with Christian sects and became a proselytizer for esoteric Christianity, a sect which was very individualistic and based its approach on personal perfectibility imitating the sacrifices and life of Jesus Christ. He never converted to Christianity, but absorbed much of the message of esoteric Christianity into his version of Hinduism. This was helped by Annie Besant's book *Esoteric Christianity*, in which she interprets the Christian message in light of the *Bhagavad Gita*. His doctrine of *ahimsa* derived much from Jainism and Gujarati Vaishnavism, both of which were pacific, non-violent belief systems. Gandhi's reading of the *Gita* was militant yet non-violent, the struggle being against all forms of untruth—British rule, the practice of untouchability, modern machinery and all vices of eating, drinking and pleasurable sex. It was his own lifestyle, with its simplicity and the garb of the poor peasant, that made him a universal symbol of Indian-ness.

If the Congress needed a narrative of why India was a nation, it now had *a person who was the story*. Gandhi became, for all practical purposes, for India and the world, the image of India, especially during the twenty-five years he dominated politics after his entry in the post-war period. This is not to say he convinced everyone. Bengal and Maharashtra were to retain their own brands of nationalism. There was also only a tenuous link with social movements in South India, which were anti-Brahmin. Gandhi and his movement dominated the heartland of India—the Doab, central India—the territory of the 1857 rebellion, as well as his own home state of Gujarat. He had his followers elsewhere, but in Punjab, Madras, Bengal and Maharashtra (except in Bombay), his writ was often challenged. But in 1920, the tide was with him.

Gandhi urged the boycott of elections to be held under the new reforms. The older generation of leaders joined reluctantly, while the younger generation was enthusiastic. The Nehru father and son pair—Motilal and Jawaharlal—illustrated this divide perfectly: Motilal would have contested elections but Jawaharlal was against it. Gandhi launched the Non-cooperation movement in December 1920, taking complete command of the Congress in his hands. Reflecting the elite background of the Congress, one demand of the movement was the renouncing of titles conferred by the British, resignation from the civil service, police and army. A more serious platform was non-payment of taxes. There was to be boycott of foreign goods, withdrawal from government educational institutions and the opening of national ones in their place. The aim was the attainment of Swaraj by all legitimate and peaceful means. Indeed, Gandhi promised swaraj within one year.

Gandhi had gained much experience in South Africa of conducting similar campaigns, and he had been able to control them effectively. But, in India, he was launching something on a much bigger scale, both geographically and in terms of numbers. Hardly any time had been really spent in acquainting the masses with his methods, and the appellation of Mahatma gave rise in the credulous to the belief that here was a god-like magician capable of miracles. A countrywide agitation broke out in a way never seen before, even in 1857. There had been peasant riots in India through the nineteenth century and into the twentieth. There had been army revolts and industrial strikes. But this was a nationwide conflagration. It was also, like the 1857 rebellion, a Hindu–Muslim joint effort along with Sikhs, Parsis and other religious minorities. This was perhaps the first movement in which the many fragmented 'nations' of India came together on a single platform.

It was also, alas, the last time that this happened. Gandhi's movement had come at a time when there was a great deal of unrest and some of it, inevitably, took a violent turn. Police and army repression, present from before the end of the war, had intensified. With Gandhi's call, many disparate struggles found a new legitimacy for their actions. They had not been told about Gandhi's reservations about such tactics. But thousands gave up their places in schools and colleges, resigned from government jobs, went to prisons and demonstrated in every way they could in public places. For a people who had been cowed down by a century of foreign rule and who had become timorous, this was liberation. It was their first taste of the power of mass action, and they were willing to go all the way with their leader.

The government had seen nothing like this, and the viceroy, Lord Reading, urged the Secretary of State to take some step, for instance a Round Table Conference, to discuss the demands. The Prince of Wales was due to visit India and a semblance of peace would be desirable, if it could be managed. But suddenly, after a year of high-intensity struggle, Gandhi ordered suspension of the movement on 11 February 1922. Violence had taken place at Chauri Chaura, a village in Gorakhpur district of the then United Provinces (now Uttar Pradesh) on 5 February 1922. A mob, enraged by days of police violence, had burned twenty-two policemen alive. Gandhi gave up the struggle. Most remarkably he decided this unilaterally, consulting no one else, neither Congress leadership nor his Muslim partners, Maulana Mohammad and Shaukat Ali who had brought out their followers for the struggle. Muslims were, on the whole, poorer and less likely to have good government jobs, less well educated and with fewer teaching jobs. Yet, they had responded, and theirs was a more costly sacrifice in material terms as compared to all other communities.

There have been many debates as to why Gandhi did this. In the tradition of nationalist historiography, especially the Congress's hegemonic kind, this was totally unexpected but was, at the same time, a tactical piece of genius. Ultimately, Gandhi, and Gandhi alone, had to be in charge. He did not consult the Congress either in launching his *satyagraha* in the light of the Rowlatt Acts, nor did he do so this time around. The Congress was faced with a force majeure to which it had to concede. The viceroy received a polite letter from Gandhi. He admitted in this letter that, 'I confess that I did not—I did not attempt to—succeed in weaning them [the party of violence, that is, Muslims under the Ali brothers' leadership] from violence on moral grounds, but purely on utilitarian grounds.'[25] To his followers he said, 'The drastic reversal of the whole of the aggressive programme may be politically unsound and unwise, but there was no doubt that it was religiously sound . . .'[26] If there was a Himalayan blunder that Gandhi made, it was this.

The Khilafat agitation was in many ways a peculiarly Gandhian tactic. It sought to define the Indian nation by appealing to the primordial forces of religion, albeit the religion of the largest minority. Yet, the pan-Islamist agitation for a caliphate was misjudged. Mustafa Kemal Pasha moved in 1921 to establish an independent government in Ankara and abolished the caliphate in 1922. He proceeded to modernize Turkey by making it secular, imposing Western dress, banning the *fez* for men, removing the veil for women and adopting Western script for the Turkish language. Thus, the Khilafat movement fought the British imperialists against something which the Turkish people themselves welcomed—the abolition of caliphate as a signal of the advent of modernity. Gandhi had thus sided with a pre-modern, if not an anti-modern, movement among the Muslims for a nationalist platform. A parallel Hindu struggle would have been to re-establish sati, or the beheading of Shudras for learning Sanskrit as Rama had done.

But the worst aspect of Gandhi's conduct in the entire agitation was his launching of a nationwide non-violent movement with little preparation and no teamwork from his fellow leaders. He was right when he understood after Chauri Chaura that his followers were not committed to non-violence as a moral principle as he was; they saw it as an instrument to use, since he had promised swaraj within one year. It remained so until Independence. Gandhi plied his own lonely moral furrow with satyagraha, and Congress saw this as a convenient political tactic. Gandhians became a devoted, even fanatical, little band around the Mahatma, while the Congress became a mass organization concerned with the grubbier aspects of anticipating and, when it came, enjoying political power. They suffered his unilateral leadership since they could not devise an alternative. But they never took non-violence or any of the rest of his constructive programme—rural uplift, khadi spinning, cleanliness, etc.—seriously. Once Independence came, Gandhism died almost as soon as Gandhi did.

The long term effects of Chauri Chaura were much more serious. Gandhi had, indeed, created for the first time a truly national platform, bringing together the two principal disparate 'nations' around a single issue. The issue may have been pre-modern, but it was anti-imperialist. The British were disturbed, and Reading as viceroy was ready to offer some negotiations which moderate Congress leaders such as Chittaranjan Das would have been happy to accept. By suspending the movement, Gandhi took the pressure off the British.

He also lost the support of the Muslims. Again the nationalist, Congress-sponsored historiography denies this, but after Chauri Chaura, Muslims never again trusted Gandhi or the Congress. They had suffered relatively more than the others as they had given up their recently won government jobs and places at colleges and universities. What was offered as substitutes—national universities such as Jamia Milia or Gujarat Vidyapith—never became the high quality institutions which the older established universities were. The bulk of the agitators returned to their British-established institutions and resumed their jobs. The Muslims realized that they had made a blunder in following the pied piper of satyagraha. After Chauri Chaura, only a few Muslims stayed with the Congress. These Congress Muslims gave an ecumenical look to the Congress, but they were untypical of Muslim leadership.

COUNTERFACTUAL BOX

Could India Have Been Independent in 1922?

Hindsight imposes an inevitability on what happened, and soon there are ways of rationalizing the past. But it is worth asking if India could have succeeded in obtaining Home Rule, if not independence, in 1922 had Gandhi not suspended the struggle. The reasons for doing so are partly to subject the Congress hegemony to a critical analysis, and to put Indian history in a broader context.

In 1921 the British government had just given up an attempt to impose a settlement on the Irish nationalists which would have led to Home Rule, but with two separate Parliaments, in Belfast in the north and Dublin in the south, one Protestant-dominated and the other Catholic. In 1920 legislation had been passed to grant Home Rule to Ireland, but a vicious civil war had broken out because of the resistance in Ulster backed by Edward Carson, a Tory MP and a die-hard Unionist. The Irish, north and south, had driven Whitehall to a stalemate and a surrender. While a United Ireland remained unaccomplished, for the first time in two centuries a part of the British at home seceded. Dublin got its self-government on par with other White Commonwealth countries. One reason for British concession to the fighting IRA was the unpopularity which the violence by the British Irregular Black and Tans caused in America. By now, America had emerged as the world's most powerful nation, and Britain was becoming aware of its altered status. Ireland had been integrated into the Union at the end of the eighteenth century and departed 120 years later. Eire became independent in 1937 and a republic in 1949 after the war, during which it maintained neutrality.

The end of the Austro-Hungarian Empire had given birth to new nations in Europe—Hungary, Austria, Czechoslovakia and Poland. The Ottoman Empire was to break up into many nations, some under League of Nations trusteeship of France and Britain. The Russian Revolution had thrown down a challenge to the imperial powers and, despite the Allied blockade, the Red Army had defeated the White Russian counter-revolution by 1922. The American government had preached self-determination at Versailles, and the idea of independence had been legitimated by the League of Nations.

Thus in 1922, the British were capable of being defeated. There was also a lot of trouble in Europe with Germany and Greece, which was occupying Lloyd George. The coalition was divided and was soon to fall apart. The Non-cooperation movement was the largest rebellion against the British, even larger than 1857, although without professional soldiers. Britain had just gone through two years of inflation and was in a severe deflationary crisis. It was to remain in torpor for the next ten years as far as the economy was concerned. The weakness in Whitehall was exploitable.

Also by 1919, the principle of an eventual Home Rule-type of destination for India had been conceded by the Montagu–Chelmsford Report. The movement could have accelerated the journey to that destination. The Marquess of Reading was already exploring a Round Table-type offer. That could have been the catalyst. There is no reason why India could not have had Home Rule by the mid-1920s had Gandhi not unilaterally let the British off the hook.

CHAPTER 6

WESTMINSTER TAKES CHARGE

THE RESUMPTION OF THE CONSTITUTIONAL ROAD

The end of the first Gandhi-led struggle led to two paths. The first was the constitutional one, in which Parliament chugged on regardless of what was happening on the ground in India. The elections based on the 1919 reforms were held and Congress sprang a faction—the Swarajist Party—which took the constitutional road and contested elections. Some of the pre-Gandhi leadership, including Chittaranjan Das, Vithalbhai Patel and Motilal Nehru, entered the legislative councils. Jawaharlal Nehru took to municipal work in Allahabad, as did many others of his generation across India. This activity kept the Congress alive as a party, while Gandhi went into a quiet retreat. Only he could excite the Congress to take the radical path. But he was not ready.

After he was released from jail, Gandhi took to propagating his constructive programme of rural uplift, khadi spinning and cleanliness, from his ashram. He wrote his autobiography, *The Story of My Experiments with Truth*, continued his hectic journalistic activity and despite this masterly inactivity, kept a watchful eye on what was happening elsewhere in the political arena. A quiet quinquennium followed the *sturm und drang* of the Khilafat agitation.

The Congress had now come to an anomalous position. It was no longer a supplicant, loyalist organization. It was a political party. But since it had vested its sole leadership in Gandhi, it had to wait till he gave the orders for a new struggle. For Gandhi his constructive work was just as important for freedom as his agitation. For his followers the priority was freedom, and not constructive work. Gandhi had taken a fierce objection to all Westernization and all modernization since his debate with Savarkar in London in 1909. Savarkar was advocating a militarist, independent India based on the models of Garibaldi and Mazzini of Italy, but defined as a Hindu republic. Gandhi was appalled by this vision and argued that Europe, far from being the ideal, was the Devil itself, which India had to reject. Gandhi's answer was *Hind Swaraj*, which he penned on board the ship taking him back to South Africa. Written in Gujarati as a dialogue between an editor and a reader—almost on the model of the *Bhagavad Gita*—it argues the case against Western medicine, machinery and all forms of modernity.

The Congress's members did not swallow this message completely, though a few Gandhians did. Younger Congress members, such as Jawaharlal Nehru and Subhash Chandra Bose, were more influenced by socialism which had become the fashion after the war, especially since the Bolshevik Revolution in Russia and the emergence of the British Labour Party with its Fabian socialist roots. For them modernity was part and parcel of the package which would make India a great and powerful country when Independence came. Western industry and mechanization were the tools of modernization, which India had to adopt with enthusiasm. In this they agreed with Savarkar, with whom they disagreed on much else.

The central disagreement between them was, of course, on the nature of Indian nationhood. Savarkar took the view that Hindutva— 'Hinduness'—was the defining characteristic of Indian nationhood. Savarkar was an atheist unlike Gandhi and like Jinnah. Yet, his name is associated, like Jinnah's, with a religious brand of nationalism. He wanted all Indians, regardless of religion, to acknowledge that they were Hindus by origin in the land where they lived, though, at some stage in the past, they may have converted to other religions. This was aimed mostly at Muslims, who were cast as original Hindus forcibly converted by the conquering Afghan or Mughal kings. Christians were also put in the same bag. Of course, the Parsis were not by any description converted, but they were too small to matter. Jains and Sikhs were honorary Hindus in any case. For Savarkar, acknowledging Hinduness, whatever your religion, was the price of membership of an Indian nation.

The Congress would oppose this philosophy from the beginning. After Chauri Chaura, the Muslims may have deserted the Congress, but the Congress party never, in principle, excluded the Muslims or any minority. Its leadership remained predominantly caste Hindu, even Brahmin, except for the bania who led them and his Gujarati helper, Sardar Patel. But the Congress defined Indian nationhood as their leader had taught them—ecumenically and inclusively. They took the view that distinguishing between Indians by religion was inappropriate. All Indians were the same. This is the liberal doctrine; but in a party dominated by caste Hindus it was also conveniently majoritarian. The Muslims wanted some protection against being swamped by the majority Hindus. It was to take the Congress much struggle and ultimate failure to understand this position. To give special protection to ethnic fractions within the population is today labelled as a 'consociational' approach. The Congress was not ready for consociationalism.[1]

Chauri Chaura signalled an end of communal harmony and riots between Hindus and Muslims became frequent across North India—precipitating many of Gandhi's fasts. In the United Provinces alone, ninety-one riots were recorded between 1923 and 1927. Parallel with the Muslim League, the Hindu Mahasabha came into being to argue the orthodox Hindu nationalist cause, both against the ecumenical Hinduism of Gandhi and Muslims. Much as Tilak had done, the Hindu Mahasabha believed that the Independence struggle was against foreign rule, both present and past. Hindus had to repossess their nation, which they had lost to Muslims at the end of the first millennium CE and then again to the British in the eighteenth century.

The Congress remained an umbrella party in as much as many Hindu Mahasabha leaders belonged to it as well, though, by now, very few Muslim League members did. Indeed, at this time the League fell into a low state as it had always been a constitutional and loyalist organization, and not an agitational one. It was never a mass-based political party, but followed the old elitist path of influencing the British for a larger wedge of legislative membership and jobs in official capacities. The leadership was now mainly with Uttar Pradesh zamindars and religious leaders; Jinnah, a rare modernist, was in a minority.

THE SIMON COMMISSION AND THE NEHRU REPORT

The next catalyst to action in India was again provided from outside. Article 84A(1) of the Government of India Act 1919 had stated:

> Within [amended from 'At the expiry of'] ten years after the passing of the Government of India Act 1919, the Secretary of State with the concurrence of both Houses of Parliament shall submit for the approval of His Majesty the names of persons to act as a commission for the purposes of this section.[2]

By 1927 a Conservative government had been in power for three years, and Secretary of State Lord Birkenhead decided that rather than wait the full ten years for the expiry of the stated term for appointing a commission, he would keep the initiative in Tory hands and jump the gun. By the due date—1929—elections would have taken place, and there was no guarantee that Tories would be re-elected. Hence, the amended 'within' rather than 'at the expiry of' ten years. Parliament had to nominate the members and, as per normal practice, parties were consulted in both Houses. The commission so appointed was 'to invite the Central Legislature to appoint a Joint Select Committee chosen from its elected and nominated unofficial members which would draw up its proposals in writing and lay them before the Commission',[3] though this advice was not meant 'to limit the discretion of the Commission in hearing other witnesses'.

Thus, this was to be a long process starting first with the commission consulting in India, and then reporting to Parliament. Then a joint committee of both Houses would deliberate on the proposals, but after consulting Indian legislatures and 'other bodies' while doing so. The next step was to throw the ball back to the government in power to formulate the further stage for responsible government. Since technically India was still ruled by Parliament which appointed the viceroy/governor general, this was the august body taking its task of imperial governance seriously. In the event, the entire process was to take eight years and the final outcome was the Government of India Act 1935, the longest piece of legislation debated and passed by Parliament until then and not exceeded till the Government of London Act 2000.

Yet, it was not a straight, smooth path as laid down by Birkenhead. The seven members nominated were to be led by John Simon, a Liberal Party bigwig, who was later, as Viscount Simon, to be Lord Chancellor. The other members were Lord Burnham and Lord Strathcona, both Conservatives, Edward Cadogan, Colonel Lane Fox, Victor Hartshorn and Clement Attlee, all from the House of Commons, two Conservatives and two Labour. As a Tory, Birkenhead did not wish to see much advance on Montagu–Chelmsford. The choice of Simon was a safe one. Given the disarray in the Liberal Party and the Tory majority, the only radical members were Hartshorn, a miner and an MP from a mining constituency in South Wales, and Attlee, who was a very junior MP. Burnham owned the *Daily Telegraph*, Lane Fox was a fox hunting Tory and brother-in-law of the new viceroy, Lord Irwin, later Lord Halifax.

Attlee was very reluctant to be a member. He had two small children and a third was on the way, and his wife Violet would not appreciate his going away to India. He also did not think it would help his career. Elections were due soon, and he did not want to lose out his chance of becoming a minister in case Labour came back to power after its short regime in 1923. Ramsay MacDonald knew the Simon Commission Report would be unpopular with his party, and did not want any senior Labour MP associated with it. Personally, he was quite radical about India, but he could sense that the Labour Party was now in the league of the top two and success could elude him at the next election if something precipitate was to happen on India which he could not control—such as an offer of Home Rule. Thus it was that a 'gas and water socialist' became member of the Simon Commission. No one, least of all himself, could have foreseen that Attlee was to be the man of the moment when twenty years later India became independent.

Whatever the plans and intrigues of Birkenhead and MacDonald, the appointment of the Simon Commission with no Indian members caused an outrage in India across all parties (the Justice Party in Madras and Unionist Party in Punjab were exceptions). Of course, if the membership was to be confined to members of the two Houses of Parliament (the Act was not clear on this, but it would be the normal presumption that only members of the two Houses could serve on the commission), the only MP of Indian origin who could have been appointed was Shapoorji Saklatwala, but he was a communist and not liked by MacDonald.

The Simon Commission was boycotted wherever it went in India during its two visits, from 3 February to 31 March 1928 and 11 October 1928 to 13 April 1929. As Attlee's biographer says, 'They arrived in Bombay two weeks later [after leaving London on 19 January 1928]. Their reception was mixed. Large crowds met them carrying banners bearing the words "Simon Go Back", though there were also smaller parties carrying leaves and flowers. The former regarded the Statutory Commission as the latest expression of Britain's determination to maintain its Raj. For the latter, the arrival of the commission heralded the next advance towards self-government.'[4] When they got to Delhi, 'They had been led to expect that they would be able to rub shoulders and hobnob with Indian politicians and prominent citizens. In fact they were either greeted with reserve, or cut dead.'[5]

But Simon and his commissioners were not daunted. They had a task to perform, and they went about it assiduously. Their Indian counterparts in the central and provincial Legislative Councils had set up a parallel Indian central committee, which also submitted its report under the chairmanship of Sir Sankaran Nair in December 1929. The Simon Commission even sought permission to tackle the subject of Princely States, which were, until then, not in the framework of any reform proposals. But if self-government was to come with any element of representative government, this was a thorny question which would have to be faced.

The Simon Commission Report runs to 700 pages in two volumes, and its evidence from the joint committees with the central as well as the provincial legislatures plus two volumes of unofficial witnesses adds a further sixteen volumes. The first volume not only surveys the workings of the Montagu–Chelmsford reforms, but is a primer in social, economic and political conditions of India in the 1920s. The second volume is its recommendations, which were quite moderate, but they were overtaken by events in India.

Birkenhead did not clarify whether he had to appoint a parliamentary commission from members of the two Houses. He was provocative in saying Indians could not be trusted to come to a unified view in any case. This stung the leadership in India into action. Gandhi was still in his retreat, but the constitutional tendency—Sapru, Jinnah and Motilal Nehru—got together to produce a Dominion Status Constitution themselves. This exercise, which became known as the Nehru Report, came from an All Party Conference chaired by Motilal Nehru.

Jinnah had made the first move as early as March 1927 for Hindu–Muslim unity, just as he had done at the Lucknow Congress–Muslim League meet in 1916. He persuaded the Muslim League to give up separate electorates for joint electorates with reserved seats. He did not carry everyone with him in the party but persisted. The number of seats was to be proportional to the population, one-third overall in the central legislature and in each province as per the proportion. Punjab and Bengal were Muslim-majority provinces, and three more Muslim-majority provinces were to be created—Sind, Balochistan and North-West Frontier. Sind was then part of Bombay province, but its separation was on the cards.

The Congress accepted this offer at its December 1927 Madras session. But its Hindu Mahasabha associates were furious, especially about the Muslim-majority provinces. There were negotiations and compromises. But finally, at the All Party Conference in (ironically) Lucknow in August 1928, the Nehru Report was finalized. No concessions were made for the provinces. Only at the central legislature were reserved seats conceded. Sind was to be separated only after Dominion Status. The Congress thus succumbed to the Hindu Mahasabha's blackmail. This was partly because at the most recent elections in 1926, the Mahasabha had trounced the Swarajists; but also because, although Gandhi and the Nehrus kept the Congress on an ecumenical secular path, beneath the façade its heart beat to a Hindu tune.

Another dimension along which the battle was fought was whether India would be a federation or a unitary state. The Mahasabha was all for a unitary state, since that would be a majoritarian powerhouse. The Congress would only say that while the Centre and the provinces would have the powers as of then as embodied in the Montagu–Chelmsford Act, residual powers would go to the Centre. Jinnah wanted much more devolution, especially if separate electorates had to be conceded. For then, at least in the Muslim-majority provinces, there could be significant ways in which Muslim lives could be bettered. Jinnah tried again for unity at the December 1928 All Party Conference in Calcutta. He suggested that the reserved seats be treated as a transition measure till adult franchise was established, but did want Sind to be a province immediately. He appealed to the delegates, 'We are all sons of this land. We have to live together ... Believe me there is no progress for India until the Musalmans and Hindus are united.'[6]

Jinnah's plea was rejected, and he rejoined the hardline group in the Muslim League with whom he had broken to work on the compromise. He described his rejection at the Calcutta Conference as 'parting of the ways'. His first attempt in 1916 was rendered irrelevant by Gandhi's rejection of the Montagu–Chelmsford scheme. His new attempt was rejected because the Mahasabha leader, M.R. Jayakar, commanded more Congress support than he could. Jinnah left India for London, and resumed his practice at the Bar there. The Nehru Report is subtitled 'An Anti-Separatist Manifesto', but it proved to be just the opposite.

Despite this failure which presaged later trouble, the Nehru Report is a full-scale Constitution-making exercise. It has eighty-seven articles and two schedules laying down the central and provincial subjects. Its main theme is communal representation with which the main text ends. Among its signatories are, besides Motilal Nehru, Subhash Chadra Bose and Maulana Azad from the Congress, as well as Madan Mohan Malaviya, M.S. Aney and M.R. Jayakar from the Mahasabha, Tej Bahadur Sapru and Annie Besant from an earlier generation. Jawaharlal Nehru acted as secretary to his father, Motilal, but did not sign the report. The most radical proposal in the Nehru Report was for full adult franchise for men and women. This was, in terms of those days, unprecedented in most democracies. Despite this radicalism, the Nehru Report failed to provide a blueprint for an independent India, which could command a consensus. Birkenhead was not that far wrong.

The two paths which had opened up after Chauri Chaura were the constitutional one and Gandhi's agitational one. They were both modes of negotiation with a powerful foreign ruler. The Nehru Report saga showed that the constitutional elite could not present a united front to the British Parliament. Thus, whatever the Simon Commission might report, the ball was now in the British court. The Congress would have to fall back upon Gandhi to make any progress.

Gandhi could see that Dominion Status was perhaps the most that could be expected, and it was not yet on offer. But it was the end point of the Montagu–Chelmsford process; self-government meant government by the elected representatives, but under the tutelage of a governor general appointed by the Crown. This had been the offer to the White Commonwealth.[7] In trying to draft a Constitution for Dominion status, the Nehru Report had already jumped the gun. But Jawaharlal Nehru was impatient with such pusillanimity. At the Madras Congress in 1927, where Gandhi was absent, he had pushed through a resolution in favour of Independence. This was too fast for Gandhi. So, at the next Congress meet in 1928, he got the resolution modified. The 1928 Calcutta resolution asked for Dominion Status by the end of 1929, failing which Congress was to resume civil disobedience. Gandhi knew the British way of negotiating. He would go one step at a time, but keep the pressure up by putting deadlines, which he knew would not be possibly met. Gandhi had got the train back on the right track; if the signals would just go green, he would advance. His purpose was not merely a further stage in India's Independence, but also the retention of the Congress's claim to be in sole charge, as and when the occasion came. For this goal, the Congress had to put a distance between itself and the other political parties who were wedded to a more constitutional path.

THE WESTMINSTER COUP

Once again, the next step in India's Independence struggle was shaped by what happened in the British Parliament. Elections were called as the Simon Commission set sail for Southampton from Bombay in April 1929. By the time the commission had submitted its report, Labour had come into office, though without a majority.

Labour had polled as many votes as the Conservatives and got 288 seats to the Conservatives' 260 with Liberals on fifty-nine. Ramsay MacDonald was prime minister and it would be his task to present the Simon Commission's Report to Parliament, and ask it to appoint a joint committee of both Houses to deliberate upon it as had been laid down in the 1919 Act.

But events took a different turn. Edward Wood, a minister in the Baldwin government, had been appointed viceroy in 1926 in succession to Reading. Lord Haig, who had led the army in the war, was suggested, but the king thought a civilian would be better and plumped for Edward Wood. He was given the title Lord Irwin, though he would eventually succeed to his family title of Halifax. Irwin went to London after the election had secured a Labour victory. He conferred with MacDonald and Baldwin. Irwin had seen the rising impatience in the younger Congress leaders, and also the agitation, which began as anti-Simon but went on to other struggles. The British economy's stagnation since it had returned to gold standard in 1924 had impacted the Indian economy adversely. So, he decided to accelerate the response. With Labour rather than his own party in office, he seized his chance. He urged MacDonald to call a Round Table Conference, a demand which had been on and off the table since Reading toyed with it during the Non-cooperation movement.

MacDonald was no stranger to India or Indian questions. He had travelled to India with his wife in 1909 just as an ordinary tourist while he was an MP. In his book, *The Awakening of India*, he had noted, 'India is the home of the poverty-stricken.' For days he and his wife saw 'nothing but thin bodies toiling, toiling, trudging, trudging, trudging; or pinched bodies worshipping, worshipping, worshipping with a sadness that one sees in no other temples'.[8] He had been a member of the Islington Commission, which was charged with investigating the 'Indianization' of public services in 1913, and had spent four months in India then. MacDonald had already said in May 1928, 'I hope that within a period of months rather than years there will be a new Dominion added to the Commonwealth of our nation, a Dominion which will find self-respect as an equal within the Commonwealth. I refer to India.'

MacDonald knew that Simon was too cautious to recommend Dominion Status, as indeed was confirmed when the report came out in June 1930. The Simon Commission recommended 'responsible government' in provinces, and negotiations between the British government, the Indian government and the Princely States about an arrangement at the Centre. The dimension of Princely States, hitherto absent in any reform, had suddenly struck Simon while in India. The Congress had also begun to question the authoritarian nature of native states, and founded the All India States Peoples' Conference in December 1927. Congress wanted the transfer of paramountcy—subordination of Princely States to the Crown via the viceroy—to an independent Indian government. The Nehru Report, in Article 85, had plainly asserted the right of independent India to such power. From the simple first steps about share of seats in the Imperial Legislative Council, which Congress asked for in 1885, things had moved much farther. A self-governing India was clearly on the cards. The uncertainty was about its nature and its Constitution. Irwin had now moved the train on.

On 31 October 1929, Irwin declared that 'the natural issue of India's constitutional progress is the attainment of Dominion status.' There had been some collusion between MacDonald as the new prime minister and Irwin. The Simon Commission, being a statutory commission, had a claim to have its report laid before Parliament before the next step in the constitutional journey. But everyone had seen through Birkenhead's ploy and Tories had lost majority. MacDonald did not consult any member of the commission, least of all Attlee. He had however talked to Baldwin, via an emissary, because Baldwin was on his summer holidays in Aix-les-Bains. Thus, a bipartisan truce was arranged on the question of India between the two leaders—MacDonald and Baldwin. Baldwin was unlike previous Tory leaders. He was from the trading classes, and not the aristocracy. He did not have the sentimental imperialism of Curzon and Churchill, but the pragmatic approach of Lloyd George and some of the radical Liberals now out of power.

Baldwin's fellow Tories had other ideas. To Winston Churchill, this 'stitch-up' was an abominable insult of parliamentary procedure. He liked Irwin, and thought of him as a friend. He also disliked Baldwin and, after the defeat in 1929, very much fancied his own chances as Leader, if he could only challenge Baldwin. But Churchill had drifted in and out of the Conservative party through his career, and had only come back on the eve of the 1924 election. He was a 'big beast' with his own following of about fifteen to twenty MPs. Churchill fancied that Baldwin's collusion on India would outrage the Tories, and this could be his chance.

There was an adjournment debate on the Irwin announcement in the House of Commons on 7 November 1929. This had a history of its own. The *Daily Mail* had a leak the previous week alleging that Baldwin had sold Simon down the river. This was on the day before the Irwin statement came out. David Lloyd George then put down a private notice question which, as per convention, a minister had to answer. Baldwin on that occasion denounced the newspaper. William Wedgewood Benn, as Secretary of State, was evasive and on 4 November he refused to answer a question put down by MP Kingsley Wood about a statement George Lansbury had made anticipating the official response. The issue then came to a head with an adjournment motion, which is a House of Commons device to debate a particular question a backbencher has raised.

Baldwin felt his honour impugned, so he opened the debate and explained that he had been approached by the prime minister's private secretary to agree to the announcement, but only on the understanding that Simon had been squared. He then found out that Simon had not agreed to Irwin's statement; MacDonald had just out-manoeuvred everyone. Baldwin defended Irwin against any charge of wrongdoing. He said, 'I will only add that if ever the day comes when the party which I lead ceases to attract to itself men of the calibre of Edward Wood then I have finished with my party.'[9] Baldwin added that he wanted to be sure that whatever Irwin had promised was in line with the 1917 statement by Montagu, and asked, 'whether this statement implies any change in the policy hitherto declared or in the time that this status may be attained'.[10]

Baldwin could sense that behind him his backbenchers were not with him. The Tory imperialists thought he had sold out. So he tried his hand at the superlative as others had done when speaking on India in the Chamber:

Far away in time, in the dawn of history, the greatest race of the many races then emerging from prehistoric mists was the great Aryan race. When that race left the country it occupied in the western part of Central Asia, one great branch moved west, and in the course of their wanderings they founded the cities of Athens and Sparta; they founded Rome; they made Europe, and in the veins of the principal nations of Europe flows the blood of their Aryan forefathers ... At the same time, one branch went south, and they crossed the Himalayas. They went into the Punjab and they spread through India, and, as an historic fact, ages ago, there stood side by side in their ancestral land the ancestors of the English people and the ancestors of the Rajputs and of the Brahmins. And now, after eons have passed, the children of the remotest generations from the ancestry have been brought together by the inscrutable decree of Providence to set themselves to solve the most difficult, the most complicated political problem that has ever been set to any people of the world.[11]

Whatever one may think of the historical accuracy of the passage, it was clear that Baldwin was telling his backbenchers to suspend their racial prejudices and acknowledge Indians as their cousins. The House was being asked to consider an extension of the 1917 declaration which 'our people have to consider at the very time that we are making a great political experiment of our own—when we are entering for the first time into complete democracy with manhood suffrage. It does not make our task any easier. No man can say yet whether we, with all that political strength behind us, are going to make a success of our democracy.'[12] Universal adult suffrage had come to Britain only in 1928 and Baldwin was right to be apprehensive, because the newly enfranchised women had sentenced his party to its defeat.

Churchill had 'sat forward glowering and unhappy' during Baldwin's speech. It was to him and others of his 'diehard' friends that Baldwin addressed a part of his peroration: 'What I would put to the House and to my hon. Friends behind me is this—when self-Government or responsible Government is attained in India what is the position of India in the Empire? ... Nobody knows what Dominion status will be when India has responsible Government, whether that date be near or distant, but surely no one dreams of a self-governing India with an inferior status. No Indian would dream of an India with an inferior status, because that would mean that we had failed in our work in India.'[13]

Lloyd George, who followed Baldwin, was out of the loop. He had not been consulted by MacDonald. For him the issue was: could Simon be set aside without his explicit permission, and had such permission been granted by Simon? Lloyd George could boast: 'I was the head of the Government that introduced these reforms. I presided over the Imperial War Cabinet that sanctioned the terms of these Declarations in reference to the future self-government of India ... These Declarations were considered carefully, not by a British Cabinet; they were considered during the War at imperial Cabinets where there were representatives of every Dominion in the British Empire. India was also represented. They were made in the name of the King Emperor.'[14]

The issue then was: did the new announcement amount to a change of policy, a more ambitious goal than self-government? 'Whether by the Declaration which has been issued recently the impression has been created in India that there is a change of policy, that we have departed from that pledge, that we have gone far beyond it, and that there is an absolutely new departure which was not contemplated in any of these pledges.'[15]

In replying to the debate from the government benches, Wedgewood Benn, the Secretary of State, was brazen. He admitted that Baldwin's consent was contingent upon the agreement of Simon. The Marquess of Reading, the most recently retired viceroy and the leading Liberal, was against Irwin's declaration. Simon was also of the same opinion. Benn had to be frank about his disregard of all the contrary advice. 'What did the Government do? They governed ... The Declaration was a restatement, and an interpretation of the Montagu policy ... The Montagu policy stands as a cardinal article of faith in British policy towards India.'[16]

Benn assured the House that Irwin's announcement had been well received in India where 'in recent years there had grown up a feeling, and that it had been constantly said, that British policy was altering, that the tone was altering, that sympathy was gone, that the days of Mr. Montagu were past.'[17] He cited the Reuters telegram from Delhi: 'The effect of the statement may be summed up as having at a stroke removed the tension from Indian politics and reintroduced a spirit of confidence and trust between Government and governed and delivered a blow to the Independence movement which has hitherto been gaining daily adherence among Congress men.'[18] Irwin had obviously been following the Nehru–Gandhi tussle about Independence closely.

So, Benn was able to announce the details of the Round Table Conference which was going to be held in any case after the discussion of the Simon Report by Parliament: 'Representative Indians will now have the opportunity of coming forward and expounding their views and pressing their solutions, supported by all the arguments and all the conviction which they can bring to bear. They will have direct access, and their views will be heard and considered, not at some remote stage when the opinion of the Cabinet is already declared, but at a stage when everything they say will be heard in time, with an open mind.'[19]

Later, after the end of the first Round Table Conference, Wedgewood Benn explained in a speech at Chatham House on 17 February 1931:

> When the Simon Commission was appointed a great deal of resentment was expressed in some quarters in India because it was composed exclusively

of Englishmen. Under the Act of 1919 it might have been a mixed commission, but it was decided by the wisdom of those who set it up (i.e. our Tory rivals who were then in power) that it should be purely British. A large section of Indians therefore refused to co-operate by giving evidence or in any other way although large numbers of others did co-operate ... This Round Table Conference was intended to make good this deficiency felt by so many Indians in that they have been asked to co-operate actively in the framing of the new Constitution.[20]

Baldwin's speech, and the subsequent debate which I have covered at some length, show that the question of India's constitutional progress was now causing concern in the British Parliament. Indeed, British democracy was itself evolving as it faced India's demand. That evening the government got away with it, and the adjournment motion was not put to a vote. Had the House divided, the divisions within the Conservative party would have come to a head more quickly than they did over the next two years as Churchill threw a massive tantrum on the question of India. He eventually resigned from the Opposition front bench, and went to the back benches to express his diehard rejection of the MacDonald–Baldwin truce on Irwin's plans. The Round Table Conference went ahead as planned.

PURNA SWARAJ—NOT DOMINION STATUS

As laid down in the 1919 Act and, indeed, given the way the British regarded the nature of Indian polity, the list of invitees was quite ecumenical. In modern parlance, the British saw many stakeholders in India—elected members of the central and provincial legislatures, representatives of political parties, representatives of religious groups including Muslims, Hindus and Sikhs, and women as well as untouchables. This was the cellular view of Indian society. The Congress had other ideas.

Soon after the Irwin announcement Gandhi, along with some leading Congress signatories of the Nehru Report, had let it be known that they would attend the Round Table Conference subject to the Congress having majority representation and it discussing Dominion Status. This was faster than MacDonald–Benn could move and, moreover, they never regarded the Congress as the Congress saw itself—as the most important, if not the sole, representative body for India. The British were committed to the due process through which these constitutional changes could happen.

During the adjournment debate, even Lloyd George had championed gradualism. He had given the example of Canada:

Canada did not attain Dominion Status immediately. It began with self-government of the provinces. It took nearly a generation before you had confederation. [An Hon. Member: 'And rebellion'] No; rebellion had nothing whatever to do with it. It was a voluntary act, and, after very long reflection and discussion and careful adjustment between the provinces, it took nearly a generation before you converted self-government for the provinces into confederation for the whole of Canada, and even after confederation it took nearly another generation before Canada attained what is now known as Dominion Status.[21]

As in Canada, so in Australia, gradualism had been the order of the day or so, at least, it looked in retrospect. MacDonald and Benn could not and would not change the well-tried methods of gradualism and inclusive consultation. Their commitment was to the process laid down, and that involved some consultation with Indian groups, followed by proposals from the government, and then a joint committee of both Houses and so on. Things had been different in the cases of South Africa and Ireland. In India the British did not face an armed revolt, just a cunning negotiator. But for the Congress to have insisted on a precondition of majority representation, when it was not even a majority of the elected members on the central assembly, may have been a mistake. The Congress was not to know that work would be done at the Round Table Conference which would determine the basic shape of the Indian Constitution. It chose to miss the pivotal event. It took this gamble since its aim was as much to retain hegemony as to win Independence. To be in sole control was Gandhi's constant concern. He wanted Independence on his own conditions.

As he said to the *Manchester Guardian* on the eve of his next act of defiance in March 1930:

I don't believe that the slightest good for India can come of the Round Table Conference in London. I would like to spare the world the melancholy spectacle of Indians fighting against Indians in a foreign country, but this is what the Conference would lead to, as it is composed at present. I shall waste no time. I expect my movement to be successful. I hope that my movement will not lead to deeds of violence, but even in this case there can be no going back for me. Yes I supported the Nehru Report once; but many things have changed since then.

I admit that this may be my last chance, and if I do not seize it, it may never come again. The revolutionary and, of course, violent movement has gained ground heavily. The need for speediest action is absolutely clear. The question of religious antagonisms and the problem of the native States are subordinate questions and cannot be solved until we have power in our own hands. I do not believe that there is any solution to the Indian problem except the one I have now proposed.[22]

It is clear from this interview, which was republished in the above summary form in the *Hindu* on 11 June 1930, that Gandhi was getting impatient. On the one hand, he had abandoned the Nehru Report and downgraded the problem of religious antagonism in the order of priorities. Kathryn Tidrick cites Gandhi as saying to C. Vijayaraghavachariar, a signatory of the Nehru Report, 'My solution to the [Hindu–Muslim] problem is so different from what is generally expected. I am more than ever convinced that the communal problem should be solved outside of legislation and if, in order to reach that state, there has to be civil war, so be it. Who will listen to a proposal so mad as this?'[23]

This was not just an idiosyncratic outburst. Gandhi broke off relations with Maulana Shaukat Ali with whom he had collaborated during the Khilafat agitation. The story as to why this happened is confused, but the essence was that Shaukat Ali was unhappy with the Nehru Report's conclusion on Muslim seats and blamed Gandhi as having been behind it. For Gandhi the priority was Independence and the communal issue was to be solved later. The Muslims saw the priority the other way around.

The second major consideration for Gandhi was that he feared losing control of the Independence movement to younger, more hot-headed Indians who were developing their own ideas about Independence. To counter them, Gandhi had to force the issue. The trump card the Congress could play, which none of the other parties represented at the Round Table Conference could, was that Gandhi could bring thousands of volunteers on to the streets of Indian cities and unleash hundreds of farmers who would go on a rent and revenue strike.

After having held Nehru back in 1928, Gandhi overruled the wishes of all the provincial Congress committees who wanted him as president and chose, unilaterally once again, Jawaharlal Nehru as the president for the Lahore Congress of December 1929. Gandhi had seen that the anti-Simon agitation had released radical forces. Youth movements were springing up and Nehru and Subhash Bose were its heroes. Communists were making an impact across the world with more than a decade of the Russian Revolution behind them. The young looked to communist and socialist ideas for the future formation of India. While neither Nehru nor Bose were systematic socialist thinkers, they endorsed the ferment which was in the air. Nehru had been to an anti-colonial conference in Brussels, and was much influenced by the communists and fellow travellers that he met from across the colonial world.

So Gandhi was happy to recruit Nehru to his side. He had been quiet since Chauri Chaura and, while everyone appealed to him to return to active leadership, he sensed that if he led a movement prematurely, the hotheads among the youth could once again embarrass him. To be in sole charge of the agitation, he had to choose the time and nature of the next struggle. He could see the power of the younger generation in Nehru. Jawaharlal is, he said, 'undoubtedly extremist, thinking far ahead of his surroundings. But he is humble and practical enough not to force the pace to the breaking point. Steam becomes a mighty power only when it allows itself to be imprisoned.'[24] The supreme strategist that he was, Gandhi knew he needed troops, but only if he could discipline them. Jawaharlal would be his chief instrument in controlling the young. Jawaharlal was forty years old at this juncture; the Mahatma was sixty.

Thus, it was that just when Irwin hurried Westminster into debating Dominion Status for India, Jawaharlal Nehru asked the Lahore Congress to take a pledge for purna swaraj. Nehru proclaimed himself a socialist and a republican. He and Bose were eager to launch the struggle for Independence, but Gandhi had other ideas. For the time being, the only action was to take a pledge for Independence on 26 January 1930, while all waited for Gandhi to devise the next step. He moved in a conciliatory manner and gave Irwin an eccentric eleven-point list of demands mentioning along with prohibition, cuts in government spending, reform of the Central Investigative Department (CID) and abolition of the salt tax. Many younger Congress members thought this was poor substitute for non-payment of land revenue or other taxes. Irwin and Benn were not impressed.

The British government had a severe economic crisis on its hands. The collapse on Wall Street and the bank failures in Vienna and elsewhere were creating a deep recession, which would turn into the Great Depression before long. The MacDonald government would eventually fall on the issue of spending cuts and reduction of unemployment allowances. But that was yet a year off. In the meantime, the government in India was in no mood to consider economic conditions for Congress acceptance of the Irwin offer.

Gandhi launched his second great struggle, in March 1930, by marching from his ashram in Sabarmati to the coast at Dandi, where he would challenge the salt monopoly enjoyed by the government by making some salt himself. Salt may have seemed trivial, and Nehru said it did not keep him awake at night, but it was an idiosyncratic choice for other reasons. The British had acquired the salt monopoly as part of the diwani rights in 1765, since salt was taxed by the Mughals. By 1929 the government did not have a monopoly on salt making. But making salt required a licence for which a fee had to be paid. In 1925, 35 per cent of the total amount of salt consumed was from government sources, 30 per cent was imported from abroad and 35 per cent was made by private manufacturers under licence. In 1929–30, salt contributed

Rs 6.35 crore (just under £5 million at the exchange rate then prevailing) to the total revenue of Rs 91.39 crore (about £70 million) of the British government in India. To protect its salt monopoly in the previous century, the government had built a large fence across north India separating British India from the native states of Rajputana. The fence had proved ineffective. Salt had been taxed at Rs 2.50 per maund (82 lb or 37 kg) in the nineteenth century. The tax had moved up and down subsequently but, since 1924, it had been Rs 1.25 per maund. It was a small thing, but since the beneficiary was the government rather than Indian landlords or businessmen whom Gandhi did not wish to antagonize, salt could mobilize millions. It was something each person could defy the mighty government about.

This time he did not launch an agitation across the country, and did not include the Congress officially in his plans. Indeed, from here on until 1942, Gandhi would not involve the Congress as such, but relied on chosen volunteers. Congress members did, of course, respond to his call, but they were not his responsibility any longer. This was to be a *Gandhian* struggle along with chosen followers from the ashram, seventy-eight people in all. He anticipated being arrested, and after that anything could happen, as he had told the *Manchester Guardian*. He set off on 12 March 1930. This was his last gamble; he was an old man running out of time. Or so he thought. He got to his destination on 6 April and broke the law by making salt. He had made his point.

Of course, what no one had foreseen, as Gandhi alone had, was the symbolic power of a sixty-year-old man marching 22 miles a day with a small band of devoted followers defying a mighty empire. Gandhi had discerned the power of the new media of cinema and radio. Film newsreels were shown in every cinema house across the world by agencies such as Pathe and Movietone. Gandhi was first-rate documentary material, and millions across the world saw, in dark cavernous cinema halls for the first time, the legendary brown man known as Mahatma taking on the cause of the poor by fighting over an essential ingredient of daily living. The propaganda gains were immeasurably large.

This time although Gandhi had said that the movement had to be non-violent, he did not insist as he had earlier in 1922—calling off the movement at the first sign of trouble. Indeed, in 1942, when he launched his third and last struggle, he let the others do as they pleased as long as his own example illustrated the power of non-violence. He was not arrested either before, during or at the end of his march. In the meantime, people began to agitate in any way they could. Jawaharlal was arrested on 14 April but Gandhi was not till 5 May. A group of fifty young revolutionaries broke into the Chittagong armoury, shooting the sentries and torching the building. Two platoons of the Garhwal Rifles refused riot duty in Peshawar. But soon, Congress committees took charge and, despite their leaders being in jail, carried on a largely non-violent campaign.

Even so, the salt struggle was not as widespread as the 1921 Non-cooperation movement. There was no longer Hindu–Muslim unity. The Congress was now mainly a Hindu organization, except for some Muslim National Congress members such as Abdul Hameed Ansari and Maulana Azad. Yet, thousands went to jail, women as well as men, and a new generation of young people was recruited to the cause. There was also a significant shift in support from Indian industry and business, which donated money to the Congress. The shrewd businessmen could sense that Congress could eventually be the custodian in any transition to Independence, and they had to hedge their bets. In any case, the Depression had dried up British markets, and imports were costly, while the Indian rural economy had suffered a collapse in agricultural prices. The Indian economy was latched to the British one. Earlier, the British economy had grown and dominated the world—as in the decades before the Great War; now it was slipping in the world league, and was no longer an engine of dynamism. Britain tried to harness the empire via imperial preference, a sort of protectionism within the British Empire, but, in the main, when economic recovery did come to Britain, it was the home market which was important and not the empire.

THE ROUND TABLE CONFERENCE

On 30 November 1930, the King Emperor opened the first Round Table Conference in the Royal Gallery of the House of Lords. This is a long and richly decorated room, next to a small anteroom—the Princes' Chamber—beyond which is the Chamber of the House of Lords. The Royal Gallery is noticeable for its two huge paintings of the battles of Trafalgar and Waterloo on opposite walls, many portraits of royalty, stained glass windows with coats of arms of various lords and a gilded ceiling marked with VR—Victoria Regina. It is so large that during the Second World War, while House of Commons met in the Chamber where the Lords normally sit, the Lords met in the Royal Gallery. It was a fitting place for Indians and their rulers to sit across a single table on a formal basis of equality for the first time in two centuries.

The Round Table Conference met from November 1930 to January 1931 without the Congress attending. Around ninety attended, among whom were Indian states' delegation, including many maharajas; members of every political party except the Congress, including signatories of the Nehru Report such as Jayakar and Sapru, but also Jinnah, Fazlul Haq and B.S. Moonjee of the Hindu Mahasabha and Dr B.R. Ambedkar; the gifted orator Srinivas Sastri; businessmen such as Sir Cowasjee Jehangir, H.P. Mody and Sir Chimanlal Setalvad; Sir B.N. Mitra, the journalist; B. Shiva Rao and the Sind grandee, Sir Shah Nawaz Khan Bhutto, father and grandfather of two future prime ministers of Pakistan (a distinction he shares with Motilal Nehru). The Aga Khan was there, as were the Khilafat leaders, Maulana Mohammad Ali and Zafrullah Khan. Women were represented by Begum Shah Nawaz and Mrs Subarayan. The British Cabinet was there—MacDonald, Wedgewood Benn, Lord Chancellor Lord Sankey and four others. MPs and peers from other political parties were present, including the former viceroy Lord Reading and the future Secretary of State for India, Sir Samuel Hoare.

This was a unique event. Inaugurating the conference the King Emperor said, 'Never before have British and Indian Statesmen and Rulers of Indian States met, as you now meet, in one place and round one table, to discuss the future system of government for India and seek agreement for the guidance of My Parliament as to the foundations upon which it must stand.'[25] He was aware of the pressure of events. The East was no longer unchanging or even moving at a leisurely pace. He noted 'a quickening and growth in ideals and aspirations of Nationhood which defy the customary measurement of time'.

MacDonald, who spoke next, was equally fulsome:

> We are now at the very birth of a new history ... We have met to try and register by agreement a recognition of the fact that India has reached a distinctive point in her constitutional evolution. Whatever that agreement may be, there will be some who will say that it is not good enough or that it goes too far. Let them say so. We must boldly come out and appeal to an intelligent and informed public opinion. The men who co-operate are the pioneers of progress. Civil disorder is the way of reaction.[26]

The gist of the problem was soon stated:

> And when I come to the representatives of British India, I am mindful, it is true, of India's different communities and languages and interests, but I am reminded still more of the quickening and unifying influences which have grown up irresistibly from her contact with Great Britain and also and still deeper, of the aspirations for a united India which were in the minds of her philosophers and her rulers before the first English trader set foot on her shores.[27]

Pleasantries over, the conference reassembled the following Monday at St. James's Palace. The moderate and constitutionalist loyalist Sir Tej Bahadur Sapru was forthright in his opening speech:

> We have come here across the seas in the midst of the gibes and ridicule of our own countrymen ... I have realised from the beginning the grave

dangers of the Civil Disobedience movement to my country ... Never before in the history of India, never before even in the Mogul period of history, has India been governed by agents and sub-agents.

What is the system that you have established? It is the system of Parliamentary Sovereignty, sovereignty exercised by some 600 odd members of Parliament ... and you are attempting to exercise that sovereignty over 320 million people living 6000 miles away from the centre of your political power ... Ultimately it comes down not to Parliamentary Sovereignty but to the Sovereignty of half a dozen men in England and half a dozen men in India.[28]

The crucial speech was the one that followed. The Maharaja of Bikaner, who had served as one of the delegates to the Versailles Conference, put forward the idea that in any eventual Dominion Status, the Princely States would join with British India to form an All India federation. At that time, without the benefit of hindsight we have today, this was a radical move. If the British had given back the sovereignty to the princes or even retained their treaty relations, the Balkanization of what we now know as India would have been complete. British India would have been independent and princely India would have retained its treaty status with the British. The Maharaja of Bikaner's radical move said India was a single entity because it was a geographical unit, within which the two political arrangements co-existed. They could then be brought together in a single constitutional unit. Thus, India was defined by the way the British had drawn its boundaries with the paramountcy relation with princes and direct rule over British India.

The case for the 'depressed classes' was put forth eloquently by Dr Ambedkar. He said the 43 million depressed people were a fifth of the total population, suspended somewhere between serfdom and slavery with servility as their birthmark.[29] 'What is worse is that this enforced servility and bar to human intercourse due to untouchability involves not merely the possibility of discrimination in public life, but actually works out as a positive denial of all equality and opportunity and the denial of those most elementary of civic rights on which human existence depends.'[30]

He acknowledged that, for the depressed classes, the British had been 'deliverers from age-long tyranny and oppression by the orthodox Hindus'. The depressed classes had repaid that debt by fighting in the army. But now he wanted to be rid of the bureaucratic form of government and replace it with a government 'of the people, by the people and for the people'. But he was wary of the democracy about to be bestowed. 'The depressed classes feel that they will get no shred of the political power unless the political machinery for the new Constitution is of a special make.' The leadership was made up of 'intelligentsia, a very necessary and a very important part of Indian society ... drawn from its upper strata' which had 'not shed its narrow particularism of the class from which it is drawn'. This is why, Ambedkar thought, 'the problem of the depressed classes will never be solved unless they get political power in their own hands'.[31]

The Congress demand for swaraj was not problem-free, since 'the idea of Swaraj recalls to the minds of many of us the tyrannies, oppressions and injustices practised upon us in the past and the fear of their recurrence under Swaraj. We are prepared to take the inevitable risk of the situation in the hope that we shall be installed, in adequate proportion as the political sovereign of the country, along with our fellow countrymen.'[32]

Here was a significant departure from the Congress view of India as a seamless whole led by the Mahatma. Ambedkar pointed to the underclass which existed and, indeed, continues to exist as a nation within India, despised and denied human dignity by fellow Indians. The Nehru Report had not even addressed their problems, subsuming them under Hindus. Just as Muslims were asking for separate status for fear of being swamped by the Hindu majority in a democracy, Ambedkar was asking for protection from Hindu upper caste majority.

Of course, the tricky problem was always going to be the Hindu–Muslim question. The Nehru Report had led to 'a parting of ways', as Jinnah had said. The Congress and the Hindu Mahasabha were not willing to concede the demands of the Muslims for separate electorates, or even proportional representation in Muslim majority provinces. Jinnah in his speech started by stating how he was at one with all the other groups. Addressing his hosts, he said, 'We have a greater and far more vital interest than you have because you have the financial or commercial interest and the political interest, but for us it is all in all.'[33] But after that he had to come to his basic contention: 'I almost said there are four parties, not forgetting the other smaller minorities, such as the Sikhs and the Christians and not forgetting for a single moment the depressed classes. But there are four main parties, sitting around the table now. There are the British Party, the Indian Princes, the Hindus and the Muslims.'[34]

But there were further divisions to contemplate. There was Mr B.V. Jadhav, for instance, who argued that the Marathas wanted their special position to be acknowledged in any constitutional arrangement. Thus, you could believe India was a single unity, or that it was two nations—Hindus and Muslims, or that Hindus were divided into caste Hindus and depressed castes or even Brahmins, non-Brahmins and depressed classes, but you still had Sikhs and, to a lesser extent, Christians to deal with. The various interest groups on display in

London were not the mere creation of the imperialists. They had always been there, but faced with the prospect of Independence and some form of electoral democracy, each group had begun to set up its stall for the foreign rulers to look at before they scuttled. Of course, at that date, there was no immediate idea of scuttling or even Dominion Status.

Ramsay MacDonald was aware of how difficult the problem of minorities was going to be. He had chaired the Minorities Subcommittee of the conference. On 14 December 1930, he wrote in his diary, 'Yesterday a Moslem-Hindu gathering at Chequers [the PM's weekend residence] showed the worst side of Indian politics ... India was not considered. It was communalism & proportions of reserved seats.'[35] But Sikhs also proved intransigent, insisting on 20 per cent of seats in Punjab and against 50 per cent going to Muslims. There was no settlement of this prickly issue at the end.

Still, the Round Table Conference did some foundational work. The most important was the commitment of the princes that in any future scheme of Dominion Status, they wished to be part of the arrangement, of the All India Union. This was significant since, until then, all constitutional agitation had been confined to the Constitution of British India. The princes were ruled not by British Parliament, but by the Crown via the viceroy—hence the significance of the King Emperor opening the Round Table Conference. The Maharaja of Bikaner's initiative in proposing the federal solution including the princes was a decisive move, more so than even the Nehru Report, which had wanted paramountcy powers, but not with any idea of including the native states in the Union.

Wedgewood Benn listed 'federation' as one of the three major achievements of the Round Table Conference. The other two were, according to him, 'responsibility' and, as he called it, 'a jargon phrase, Safeguards'. 'The Princes are not prepared to enter into a federation unless it is a federation which is responsible, in which instead of being face to face with an autocratic Power as at present, they are face to face with a Federal Executive in which they themselves play a substantial part.'[36]

So responsibility meant that 'the Central Legislature of the federation must have the Executive responsible to it'. Wedgewood Benn was addressing the sceptics who did not wish to relinquish power, or, even if they did, had second thoughts about being accused of irresponsibility, if all went wrong once India was self-governing.

Safeguards were, of course, going to restrict the extent of responsibility. But Wedgewood Benn was at pains to argue that this was how all the Dominion Status countries had approached their present status, and so would India. The two areas in which safeguards were to be put were defence—'the assistance of British forces for some long time'—and the difficult realm of finance to guarantee the stability of Indian credit to allow India 'to borrow in the money markets of London and elsewhere at a reasonable rate'.[37] Even mild nationalists, such as Sapru and Setalvad, knew that these safeguards, especially currency and credit, were for Britiain's benefit much more than India's. After all, the sterling was wobbling on the edge of massive devaluation and exit from the gold standard, even as the delegates met. It was the balance of trade surplus of India and its sterling deposits in London which shored up the pound. The army also fought more for the empire outside India than at home. Safeguards were unacceptable to Indian nationalists. The only difference was between those who were willing to accept them as transitional and those who were more impatient.

The most crucial decision the conference made was to commit India to a federal structure, though with much greater powers to the constituent units than to the Centre. Of course, a federation was always the obvious solution, since that was how the governance of British India had evolved. After the first Round Table Conference, it was clear that decisions were being made for the eventual shape of an independent India, though no one was willing to utter the 'I' word as yet. On offer was a limited Dominion Status with defence, external affairs and finance in British hands.

There were detractors, of course, and Churchill was the principal one. Speaking to the West Essex Conservative Association at Epping (near his constituency), Churchill articulated the doubts of the imperialists about the Round Table Conference:

> I was however surprised and alarmed at the sudden landslide of opinion which took place upon that Conference and at the impression which was created throughout this country and in India that all the three parties were in agreement in principle to set up a federal constitution under Indian ministers responsible to an all-India Assembly. Still more was I alarmed when this enormous departure was itself presented as only a temporary and transitory arrangement soon to give place to what is called 'full Dominion Status' for India, carrying with it the control not only of law and order and of finance but of the Army, and the right to secede from the British Empire.[38]

A clearer picture of what actually came to pass could not have been better presented, if only to show the usefulness of paranoia as a predictive device.

CHAPTER 7

GANDHI, IRWIN AND CHURCHILL

WITH THE PRESENCE of British troops and no control over the currency and credit as the best on offer, many in India thought this was not what they had been promised by Irwin. But then, as far as the British were concerned, this was not a final settlement. This was one stage in the daisy chain of deliberations, outside and inside Parliament, which was to lead to a Constitution. The dialectic of the process now moved away from London and back to Delhi. Irwin again took initiative. Gandhi was released a week after the Round Table Conference ended on 19 January 1931. Gandhi wrote back asking for an interview. He was perplexed, since in spite of the large number of people arrested, and the attention the struggle received, the results of the Round Table Conference were less than what he had hoped for. As he said to Irwin, a devout Christian, 'somehow or other, in the present case, I have missed the guidance of the inner voice'.

Winston Churchill immediately saw red. On 26 January 1931, the day Gandhi was released by Irwin with Baldwin in support of the decision, he wrote, 'I reached my breaking point in my relations with Baldwin.' There was a debate in the House of Commons the next day, and MacDonald robustly defended the decision saying that the only alternative concession to Gandhi's release was 'Repression and nothing but repression . . . the repression of the masses of the people.' Churchill denounced the government's policy as wanton, reckless and incontinent. But Baldwin repudiated Churchill from the front bench. He talked glowingly of a United States of India and pledged his support. MacDonald noted in his diary, 'Winston was distracted . . . Baldwin's throw-over of Winston was complete.'[1] Two days later Churchill resigned from the Opposition Business Committee, as the Shadow Cabinet was known in those days.

For Churchill, 'This supreme question of India which is no ordinary question of politics but involves the life of the British Empire', was now the litmus test of Tory principles, and he was willing to fight for his position. At the Free Trade Hall in Manchester on 30 January 1931 he called Gandhi 'a fanatic and an ascetic of the fakir type well known in the East' and warned that 'the loss of India, however arising, would be final and fatal to us. It could not fail to be part of a process which could reduce us to the scale of a minor power.'[2] Yet again, Churchill was prescient, though wrong in his opposition to India's aspirations. But from here on he exiled himself to the back benches and spent the next eight years in wilderness, where no one took him seriously, be it on India or on the dangers of the rise of Hitler.

Robert Rhodes James, a biographer of Churchill has said of his tantrum on India, 'By the violence of his speeches and the exaggeration of his images he had grievously debased the coinage of alarmism. Many of Churchill's phrases used in the India controversy were to be subsequently repeated in another context, with inevitably lesser impact. The description of the Indian nationalist leaders ... was striking, but was not likely to make comparable descriptions of genuinely evil men more credible.'[3]

The Gandhi–Irwin meeting was unprecedented in the history of the British Empire. Gandhi had no formal status, either as elected leader of a political party or as prince of a native state, to expect equality with the viceroy. Yet a private person, a subject of the King Emperor was able to meet the viceroy on equal terms and negotiate a 'pact'. This was a treaty between an imperial power and a subject. Churchill was outraged. 'When Mr. Gandhi went to the seashore a year ago to make salt he was not looking for salt. He was looking for trouble. He was looking for a means of flouting the Government and compelling them to arrest him. Now he has compelled the Government to recognise the propriety of his action. He has elevated his deliberately-selected breach of the law into a trophy of victory, the significance of which, believe me, will be appreciated from the Himalayas to Ceylon.'[4]

It was the fault of his old friend Edward Wood, now Lord Irwin.

I notice that Mr. Gandhi speaks of Lord Irwin in terms of strong approbation. It is no more than just. In the course of this year, the Viceroy has fostered the growth of Mr. Gandhi's power to an extent almost inconceivable, first by neglecting to arrest him until his breach of the Law had gradually attracted and riveted the attention of all India; secondly, by arresting him when they did for his breach of the Law; thirdly, by not trying him upon any known charge or proceeding against him by any recognised process of the Law but confining him under some old Statute as a prisoner of the State; fourthly, by attempting to negotiate with him when he was still in prison; fifthly, by releasing him unconditionally; sixthly, by negotiating with him as an equal and as if he were the victor in some warlike encounter; seventhly, by conceding to him as a permanent emblem of triumph the legalisation of the very practice which he had selected for the purpose of affronting the Government.[5]

Gandhi's meeting with Irwin has been described as a meeting of 'two uncrucified Christs'. Delhi had just recently been occupied as the new capital of British India, and the Viceroy's House (later the President of India's house—Rashtrapati Bhavan), where they met, was a massive monument to the grand style which Lutyens had adopted for Delhi. You walk through a massive open front garden, after which there are many steps to climb as you get to the top where you are received. Churchill, in his most quoted lines on Gandhi, brought to life the spectacle for everyone in case they did not feel as much outrage as he did. 'Mr. Gandhi, a seditious Middle Temple lawyer now posing as a *fakir* of a type well-known in the East, striding half-naked up the steps of the Viceregal palace, while he is still organising and conducting a defiant campaign of civil disobedience, to parley on equal terms with the representative of the King-Emperor.'[6] (In fact, he went through a side door helped by an English bodyguard, and did not climb up the stairs.) This was a sentence Churchill had worked on for a few days. The 'fanatic and an ascetic of the *fakir* type well-known in the East' in his speech of 30 January 1931 had now been honed to perfection as Churchill talked around the country against Gandhi and Irwin. He had met Gandhi during the South African years when Gandhi was insistent on styling himself as an 'English barrister'. Churchill could now see the transformation and its effectiveness in getting his way in negotiations.

Irwin was pious in his Christianity, but still a shrewd negotiator. While the spectacle did much for Gandhi's and the Congress's prestige, the final outcome of the discussions was a triumph for Irwin. Gandhi negotiated solo, and while he kept the Congress Working Committee informed, he did not take its advice. Irwin did not concede Gandhi's demands about removal of the salt laws, or about inquiry into police conduct. On his part Gandhi promised to halt the civil disobedience and the boycott of foreign cloth, while Irwin promised to release the prisoners who were in jail for non-violent civil disobedience. The Congress accepted the invitation to the second session of the Round Table Conference, but had to accept the agenda, which had already been agreed on at the first Round Table Conference—federation, responsibility and safeguards.

Churchill kept up his attack from the back benches and at every Conservative party gathering he was invited to address. Having heard of the details of the pact, his conclusion was chilling:

To abandon India to the rule of the Brahmins would be an act of cruel and wicked negligence. It would shame forever those who bore its guilt. These

Brahmins who mouth and patter the principles of Western Liberalism, and pose as philosophic and democratic politicians, are the same Brahmins who deny the primary rights of existence to nearly sixty million of their fellow countrymen whom they call 'untouchable', and whom they have by thousands of years of oppression actually taught to accept this sad position. They will not eat with these sixty million, nor drink with them, nor treat them as human beings. They consider themselves contaminated by their approach. And then in a moment they turn around and begin chopping logic with John Stuart Mill, or pleading the rights of man with Jean Jacques Rousseau.[7]

He was equally forthright about the proposal that India could use its tariff autonomy against British cloth rather than have Congress boycotts. He averred that Muslims wore more clothes than Hindus, and so would suffer more from the tariff. 'What are we to think of a proposal which places 70,000,000 Muslims where they will be bled and exploited and made to pay through the nose by this group of Hindu Capitalists who are the Chief subscribers of Mr. Gandhi's party fund?'[8] No wonder Baldwin said of Churchill that he spoke 'as George III might have done had he been endowed with the tongue of Edmund Burke'. But after 1930 Baldwin had made up his mind irrevocably that India was to be his great mission. His fondness for Irwin meant that he would do everything, including risking the wrath of Churchill and many in the Conservative party, to support MacDonald and Irwin on India.

Gandhi had won prestige but little else—despite all the trouble since the rejection of the first invitation to the Round Table Conference, the salt struggle and the boycott of cloth, and so on. Jawaharlal reportedly wept when he saw that the safeguards had been accepted by Gandhi. Nehru had been asking for full Independence and a swift end to British rule. Irwin thought Jawaharlal's intransigence 'impossible', and added, 'he appeared to have no spirit of peace and all his utterances left a clear impression on my mind that he certainly regarded the present arrangements as an uneasy truce . . .'[9]

The Congress Working Committee was very disappointed. Irwin, the 'Holy Fox' as he was to be called later, had outfoxed Gandhi. Irwin correctly diagnosed Gandhi's weakness to flattery by an Englishman, and took full advantage of it. We have Gandhi saying to Irwin, 'When you . . . use your best arguments, it does not always have much effect on me, but when you tell me that Government is in a difficulty and cannot do what I want, then I am inclined to capitulate to you.' The better alternative would have been to be unaffected by the plea of helplessness on part of the government, but capitulate to their best arguments. Irwin had appealed to Gandhi to have faith in British sincerity and to forget about civil disobedience. Gandhi concluded that the viceroy was 'strong, straight, capable, firm and a democrat'.[10] Jawaharlal, quite rightly, was of the opinion that Irwin was just an average Englishman, no more, no less.

In his interviews to the press after the pact, Gandhi tried to reopen the issue of safeguards. He clearly hoped that he would be the sole negotiator at the Round Table Conference, in a one-to-one combat with the British. The reality was, however, more mundane. The Congress chose to send Gandhi as their sole delegate (though Sarojini Naidu was also present on her own as women's representative). This confirmed his unique status. As he said, he did not need advisers: 'My adviser is God ... If I had any idea to take advisers I would have taken them as delegates.'[11]

Before his departure he tried to seize the initiative again on the Hindu–Muslim question, as it had been left undecided at the first Round Table Conference. He began to make, quite unilaterally, some eccentric 'offers' to his Muslim detractors. At the Jamiat-ul-Ulema Conference in Karachi on 1 April 1931, we have Gandhi saying, 'I do not wish to act like a Bania. I wish to leave everything to the honour of the Muslims. I would like you to put down whatever you want on a blank sheet of paper and I shall agree to it.'[12] He indicated that Jawaharlal concurred. There was a problem with the image of the Congress. 'It is not right to say that the Congress is a Hindu organisation. What is the Congress to do if Muslims would not care to go into it?'[13] Yet, the Congress was 'the swaraj Government in embryo. Its prestige is ever so much superior to that of the British Government and the Congress President is greater than the Viceroy.'[14] All this was said notwithstanding the fact that just the previous week Irwin had turned down his request of a reprieve for Bhagat Singh and hanged him, much to the disgust of Congress members.

He persisted six days later at a press conference: 'My own personal view is ... that of full surrender to any unanimously expressed wish of the Mussulmans and Sikhs. I would like the Hindus to see the beauty of the solution.'[15] Of course, he knew that Hindus would not agree, nor would his own band of nationalist Muslims. So, the required unanimity was unlikely. This was also a ploy he had used on the issue of untouchability. He had wanted all Hindus to unanimously agree about its abolition. In both cases he well knew that his conditions would not be met. Jinnah's demands, which were first accepted by the Congress and then rejected due to the Mahasabha's objections, had majority Muslim support. But not among Congress Muslims. Gandhi knew there would be no unity either among Muslims or among Hindus.

Irwin was gone by the summer of 1931 to be replaced by Willingdon, who was much less Christian in spirit. The Gandhi–Irwin pact was in tatters and repression had resumed. The Congress did not get the special status it had asked for and began thinking of withdrawing participation in the Round Table Conference. But Willingdon managed to get Gandhi to Simla and gave him the minimal reassurances required. Willingdon said to Wedgewood Benn, 'He may be a saint; he may be a holy man; he is I believe quite sincere in his principles; but of this I am perfectly certain, that he is one of the most astute politically-minded and bargaining little gentlemen I ever came across.'[16]

As he left India for the Round Table Conference on 29 August, Gandhi was despondent. He 'must bear the cross, alone and to the fullest extent',[17] he wrote to Rajagopalachari. Zaverchand Meghani, a Gujarati poet of the day, wrote a memorable poem exhorting 'Bapu to swallow this last draught of poison'. So off went Gandhi 'with God as my only Guide. He is a jealous Lord. He will allow no one to share His authority. The horizon is as black as it possibly could be. There is every chance of my returning empty handed.'[18]

He was not wrong in this fear. The Conference was conducted as a resumption of the one that had risen in January 1931, though much had changed in the meanwhile. The British political scene had suffered one of the worst traumas it has ever known. The MacDonald Labour Cabinet was almost evenly divided on the necessity of making economies in the midst of mass unemployment. The sterling had to be defended, and that required international loans. As part of that, the pittance that the unemployed received as dole had to be cut. After dividing eleven to nine in favour of the cuts, MacDonald went to the Palace and gave his resignation. But the king asked him to form a national government, with the Conservatives and the Asquith Liberals. MacDonald agreed, and the Labour Party split the day after Gandhi set sail for London. A new election was called as the new coalition Cabinet sought a fresh mandate. In the ensuing election the Labour Party was wiped out. On 29 October 1931 when the results were announced, Conservatives got 471 seats, MacDonald's National Labour thirteen and the old Labour Party forty-six. The three Liberal factions—Lloyd George, Herbert Samuel and John Simon—divided up around seventy seats among themselves. The national government had a majority of 556. MacDonald remained prime minister, but Wedgewood Benn was replaced by Samuel Hoare as Secretary of State for India.

The resumed Conference convened on 7 September in the midst of an election campaign, and rose again on 1 December 1931. The British delegation had changed since the government had changed. MacDonald and Hoare were supported by Baldwin, who was now Lord President (that is, Leader in the House of Commons). There were also changes on the Indian side. The most notable was, of course, Gandhi's attendance, but also present were Sarojini Naidu, Shaukat Ali, G.D. Birla, the trade union leader V.V. Giri, Pandit Madan Mohan Malaviya and Sir Purushottamdas Thakurdas. Mahadev Desai attended as a member of Gandhi's staff. Gandhi's disciple and admirer, Madeline Slade (Meerabehn), daughter of a British naval officer, also accompanied them in her private capacity.

By now the positive atmosphere of the first Round Table Conference had dissipated. Baldwin was cooperating fully with MacDonald, but now with him having the majority, he had to listen to his backbenchers who were less enthusiastic about the outcome. The two great fears that were typically bothering the Conservatives were, 'that we were handing over India to a set of agitators who were not real leaders of the people, and secondly that we were not taking proper steps to safeguard our trade, . . . a vital question to the large contingent of Lancashire members who were in politics for that'.[19] (The Hindu–Muslim issue continued to be as troublesome for MacDonald as it had been the previous year.) Gandhi tried again his offer of April 1931. In an interview with the *Sunday Times* he is quoted as 'prepared to go "the whole hog" [hardly an apt image while negotiating with Muslims] without the slightest reservations. He would sign a blank paper and leave the Muslims to write in it what they considered the truth and he would then fight for it.'[20] Muslims were not to fall for such tactics. They wanted separate electorates, and they wanted them from the British before any grant of Dominion Status, much less full Independence, which was the demand of the Congress. Muslims did not think their status in a post-British India was for Gandhi to guarantee, blank paper or no blank paper.

There was a contradiction at the heart of Gandhi's negotiating stance with the Muslims. He claimed that the Congress was not a communal party, that it was universal. Yet, in making offers to Muslims of a blank cheque, he was casting himself as a leader of the Hindus, indeed the sole leader. The Congress, after all, had to be, if not solely at least largely, a Hindu party, if it was bargaining on behalf of the Hindus. Of course, it was not solely a party for the Hindus, as the Mahasabha was. Nor was the Congress the sole, or even the largest, party for Muslims since its adherents did not represent the majority of Muslims, as Shaukat Ali had reminded him. The entire negotiation was a non-starter.

The Congress did not get the special status it had craved for and, perhaps, thought it deserved. It could bring India to a standstill by its agitation, but in London it was one among many and not even *primus inter pares*. Hoare was no Wedgewood Benn, and did not have the latter's natural sympathy for India's interests. By 8 November 1931 the Congress Working Committee was asking Gandhi to come back. He ignored them as he had done often before.

MacDonald's biographer tells us what happened at the British end while the Round Table Conference was going on:

On November 11th, MacDonald and Sankey (the Lord Chancellor) dined with the Indian Liberal leaders M.R. Jayakar and Sir Tej Bahadur Sapru. They agreed to what MacDonald described rather optimistically in his diary as 'a good plan for settling India' by which the work of drafting a federal constitution would be started around May 1932, while legislation granting autonomy to the provinces would be passed around July—thus meeting the Indian fear that if provincial autonomy preceded self-government at the centre, self-government at the centre might be indefinitely postponed. Next day, Hoare agreed to the plan, and the Cabinet Committee on the conference decided to recommend it to the Cabinet. On November 13th, however, the Cabinet watered it down almost beyond recognition— sticking to the notion of a two-stage advance to self-government, with provincial autonomy coming first and self-government at the centre later, but insisting that the commitment to federal self-government should be phrased in a way that would make it possible to withdraw it if the Indians failed to settle the communal problem themselves.[21]

Soon, it got worse. The Conservative majority wanted no assurance to be given at the Conference until Parliament had debated the issue. MacDonald 'stood alone'. After much to-ing and fro-ing, MacDonald was able to tell the final session on 1 December of his commitment to the federal solution. He had been working on his speech at Chequers over the weekend 'Harassed & head giving pain & working slowly and badly'. But when he finally did give his address closing the Conference, he was frequently interrupted by cheering Indian delegates, and Gandhi congratulated him on driving the Conference 'with pitilessness worthy of a Scotsman'.

Gandhi himself had spoken the previous night, indeed early on the morning of 1 December. The preceding twenty-four hours had been one of his 'silent' days. His personal routine was not to be upset by a small matter such as constitutional advance for India. So he would not react to speeches made at the plenary session. But at 12.15 a.m. he made his speech for which he had been sent to the Round Table Conference.

He started by reminding the Conference that he had already submitted a report to the Federal Structure Committee that 'the Congress claimed to represent over 85 per cent of the population of India, that is to say the dumb, toiling, semi-starved millions'. Why he left out 15 per cent is not clear, since he claimed to represent the princes as well. He continued, 'All the other parties at this meeting represent sectional interests. Congress alone claims to represent the whole of India, all interests. It is no communal organisation; it is a determined enemy of communalism in any shape or form. Congress knows no distinction of race, colour or creed; its platform is universal.'[22] He wanted to tell the British public that 'Congress is capable of delivering the goods'. The many other parties at the Conference 'claim—I hold unjustifiably—to represent 46 per cent of the population of India. The Congress, I say, claims to represent all these minorities.'

He blamed the Hindu–Muslim quarrel on the British. 'It [the Hindu–Muslim quarrel] is coeval with the British advent, and immediately their relationship, the unfortunate, artificial, unnatural relationship between Great Britain and India is transformed into a natural relationship when it becomes that you will find Hindus, Mussulmans, Sikhs, Europeans, Anglo-Indians, Christians, Untouchables will all live together as one man.'[23]

The implications of this speech were clear. The British must negotiate only with the Congress. Once Independence was granted, the communal problem would sort itself out. There was no need for any special electoral arrangements. Few at the Conference were ready to go along with this simple hegemonic argument. Congress had lost Muslim support with the Chauri Chaura decision. Then again, it had lost a chance with the Nehru Report, in amending it at a late stage to freeze Jinnah out. Now at the Round Table Conference there was no progress, because there was a large gulf between Congress and Muslim delegates. Had the Congress included Muslims in its delegation, it could have held some of its ground. But now the ball was back in the British Parliament's court.

Outside the Conference Gandhi was a popular hero. This was his first visit to London in fifteen years. The last time he was there in 1916, he was on his way home to India from South Africa via London. He was not an unknown quantity then, but now he was a world figure. He enjoyed the love and adulation he received. Narayan Desai, the son of Mahadev Desai, in his outstanding four-volume biography in Gujarati, titles the chapter on the Conference itself 'The Cup of Poison' in reference to Meghani's poem I mentioned earlier, but the chapter about the events outside the Conference he titles, 'A Mouthful of Nectar'. Gandhi's decision to stay in the East End, his visit to the textile workers in Lancashire, his simplicity, which contrasted with the pomp of the King Emperor, his ready wit and his availability to journalists meant a huge boost to his personal standing and, by implication, to the standing of the Congress. Now, abroad as at home, Gandhi was Congress, and Congress was Gandhi. In the middle of a miserable Depression winter, he brought cheer to the working classes of Britain. But he returned home empty-handed as he had feared.

THE MACDONALD AWARD AND ITS CONSEQUENCES

From the British viewpoint, the Round Table Conference was always a stage, within the procedure laid down by Parliament, on how to take the Montagu–Chelmsford reform forward. (A third session of the Round

Table Conference was held in late 1932 but lasted only five weeks and, again, the Congress did not join it.) The only difference was that Irwin and MacDonald had jumped over the Simon Report and speeded things up a bit. But the Round Table Conference could never have granted anything unilaterally, since Parliament had to approve. Now, with the new parliamentary situation MacDonald was only effective as long as the Tories tolerated him. The decision to leave the gold standard soon after the national government took office, had made economic recovery possible. The first half of the 1930s saw a revival in UK economic activity based on the domestic market. But once recovery was assured MacDonald could be cast aside, though the Tories chose not to do so till 1935.

So the ball, as far as India's constitutional position was concerned, was in Britain's court. Parliament proceeded to receive the report on the Round Table Conference from the government, and appointed a joint committee of both Houses of Parliament on Indian constitutional reform to develop various themes—finance, federal structure, franchise, etc. These committees sat in Britain, and travelled to India to take evidence. They also co-opted Indian members. The process was to climax in a report by the joint committee to Parliament, on whose basis the government would draft a Government of India Bill for Parliament to debate and pass. The end of the Round Table Conference was a signal for Parliament to begin its processes.

In India, the first half of the 1930s was, by contrast, a period of low intensity protest, much frustrated by the relentlessly repressive attitude of Willingdon. The government having changed colour in Whitehall, the viceroy was sure he would face little criticism for being harsh, and much displeasure from Churchill and his 'diehards', if he was to give any concessions to Gandhi and the Congress. Gandhi, upon his return, tried to relaunch the agitation, but Willingdon would give him no room for manoeuvre. Throughout 1932 Gandhi was in and out of jail, but rendered ineffective. He took to his untouchability campaign as a diversion. But even here he had to face up to a basic contradiction. For all his sympathy with the untouchables, and his renaming them as *harijans* (the children of Hari or God), he was reluctant to take on the caste Hindus in their opposition to any improvement in their condition. Untouchables (despite the recent usage of the term Dalit to refer to this community, I use the old word 'untouchable' because this was the word in use at that time; use of Dalit in the 1930s' context would be an anachronism) could not enter temples, nor could they draw water from wells and reservoirs from where caste Hindus drew their water. They had to confine themselves to the unclean jobs of scavenging, dealing with dead animals and garbage disposal and live on the outskirts of villages, facing frequent unprovoked violence. Upper caste men raped their women, 'untouchable' though they were. Gandhi wanted Hindus to agree *unanimously* to reforms such as temple entry, but this merely gave veto power to the most extreme of orthodox Hindus. His sincerity was not in doubt, but his tactics, as in the Hindu–Muslim case, left something to be desired for effectiveness.

Once again, it was an external shock which revealed the fragility of his position. Ambedkar had been a real success at the Round Table Conference. His eloquent address had been impressive, and he patiently negotiated his own case, while the focus was on bigger issues, for instance Hindu–Muslim unity or Dominion Status for India. His success came with MacDonald's announcement of an award on 4 August 1932. This gave untouchables, or 'depressed classes' as the then expression was, separate electorates on the same basis as Muslims.

There was here a golden opportunity to see such separate electorates as a form of affirmative action for communities who had fallen relatively behind in economic and social progress. Thus, by clubbing Muslims with untouchables, the Congress could have argued that the separate electorates were not based on religion but on relative deprivation. Alas, the Congress refused to see them that way; they took the view that here was another 'divide and rule' ploy by the imperialists.

Gandhi went on a fast to reverse the separate electorates award to the untouchables. For six months before MacDonald had announced the award in August 1932, Lord Lothian was travelling around India with a parliamentary committee, inquiring into the franchise as part of the next stage in the constitutional process. But Gandhi did not wish to speak to him; he chose to speak only to the British prime minister or the viceroy. Then, in August, while in Yerawada Jail, he announced his fast. This fast was the final sacrifice, and it was being undertaken for the untouchables. 'It was a fast for the sake of the most downtrodden; to die for the lowliest would be the purest self-abnegation.'

Gandhi's fast unto death put Ambedkar on the spot. He had won vital concessions from the British for his people. He did not trust Congress to deliver any benefit to the depressed classes, as he had said at the Round Table Conference. Before the British left India, he wanted security for the depressed classes from caste Hindu majority rule. Ambedkar was one of the most talented people India has ever had in its politics, and this is independent of the fact that he was a Mahar, one of the untouchable *jati*s. Indeed, Mahadev Desai reports a conversation with Gandhi, when Gandhi expressed surprise that Ambedkar was an untouchable. He always took him to be a Brahmin (how else could he be so clever?).[24] That handicap he overcame, but he never forgot his people, and more than anyone else, Gandhi not excluding, he fought for the untouchables.

Gandhi wanted the separate electorates for the untouchables to be removed. He wanted them to be part and parcel of the Hindu electorates. This despite the fact that the Congress hitherto had paid no attention to their cause. The Nehru Report had been silent, and the Congress had not, on record, ever passed a resolution until then which championed their cause. Gandhi wrote to the government: 'My intimate acquaintance with every shade of untouchability convinces me that their lives, such as they are, are so intimately mixed with those of the Caste Hindus in whose midst and for whom they live that it is impossible to separate them. They are part of an indivisible family ... There is a subtle something quite indefinable in Hinduism which keeps them in it *even in spite of themselves*.'[25] Thus untouchables not only live 'in the midst' of Hindus but they live 'for' them. Slavery can be defended on similar terms, since the slave owners look after the slaves, feed and clothe them. Orthodox caste Hindus did not even have to do that. Untouchables were denied access to temples, such being the 'subtle something' of Hinduism.

Ambedkar fell under tremendous pressure once the fast began. Yet, he proved to be quite a tough negotiator. He was one of the very few who did not succumb to the charms or the charisma of the Mahatma. Jinnah and Savarkar were two others. He called the fast 'a foul and filthy act'. Ambedkar understood clearly that he could not rely on the caste Hindus reforming themselves even with Gandhi's help. He wanted the guarantee of political power for his people. The fast concentrated Congress minds. Here were Gandhi and the Congress now negotiating as the agents of caste Hindus. Ambedkar's intransigence paid off. The 'epic fast', as it has been called by Pyarelal, one of Gandhi's biographers and close disciples, lasted seven days. Finally, the separate electorates, which would have secured seventy-one seats, were given up by Ambedkar and he got, instead, 148 electorates in which the Dalits were to have reserved seats. Ambedkar had won himself more seats, though it was on the basis of untouchables 'belonging' to the Hindu electorate. As Mahadev Desai noted in his diary for 14 September, 'Is Ambedkar an extreme Mussalman or what? He has no Hindutva in him. But he reacts to pressures when it comes from all around him. He is even arguing that untouchables are a separate community from the Hindus.'[26]

The reserved seats mechanism was a special one. In each reserved seat constituency, four candidates would be selected from among proposed candidates, who were untouchables, registered in the constituency. From within them the winning candidate would be elected at a proper ballot by all voters, untouchables and others. Thus, there would be no separate electorates in which untouchables voted exclusively for untouchables. This was only granted for the central legislature.

Gandhi plunged himself in anti-untouchability activity, though even today, the caste Hindus are less than completely reformed in their behaviour towards the untouchables. But nearly eighty years after that fast, it is clear that it is electoral power which the Dalits (as the untouchables have renamed themselves) have to thank for such progress as there has been. It is Ambedkar's reputation that has risen in the Dalit's estimation. Just before his death he quit Hinduism with its 'subtle something', and led a mass conversion to Buddhism.

The Congress was now clearly the principal agent for the majority caste Hindu population. It also had other minorities—Parsis for instance—with it. Some Muslims were with it, as were Sikhs. But when electoral politics loomed for real, each minority had to look after itself. The Congress developed a 'hub and spoke' system by recruiting leaders of each minority as its agents to corral together votes for the party. This meant that the larger of the minorities—Sikhs and Muslims and Dalits, for instance—had their Congress and non-Congress factions.

The agreement between Ambedkar and Gandhi was called the Poona Pact, but Gandhi himself did not sign it. It was signed by leaders of the Congress. It is a breakthrough in Indian politics, for many reasons. It was the first constitutional provision negotiated entirely among Indians who had no official standing, and yet accepted by the British government. This could have been the model for a Hindu–Muslim pact, but that never happened. It was also an innovation in terms of British electoral practice, which did not, itself, have reserved seats. But for the Congress it was still a victory because now it could run Dalit candidates on a Congress ticket and rely on caste Hindu voters to get them elected. Congress Dalit candidates thus had to win caste Hindu support, and had, therefore, to be conservative in their social attitudes. Ambedkar won a better number of seats for his people, but they did not get the benefit as per his original agenda which was much more radical.

The next five years were quiet ones for Gandhi and the Congress. Dissatisfaction with Gandhi was beginning to show. One view held that although he had created the fighting machine that the Congress party was, he had so far not delivered a success. The salt satyagraha, though spectacular as theatre, did not advance the case of the Congress at all. The first Round Table Conference was missed and, at the second Round Table Conference, Gandhi was a failure. His legendary negotiating strength was in one-to-one encounters or in small conclaves, where his primacy, or at least his parity, was granted as a starting point. With all his efforts he had had no success to report in alleviating the position of Indians in South Africa by the time he left, despite twenty years of struggle. In India sixteen years had passed since his return, and while many had been emboldened to defy the government and go to jail, and trained in democratic practice within the Congress party, there was not much to show as result. Vithalbhai Patel, who was the elder brother of Sardar Vallabhbhai Patel, Gandhi's principal assistant and the Speaker (president) of the central Legislative Council, a leading constitutionalist Congressman, wrote to a friend and fellow Gujarati, Dadubhai Desai after the second Round Table Conference: 'All has been ruined [the actual Gujarati phrase is *badhu bafai gayu*—the cooked dish is overboiled]. I blame Gandhi for this. He does not accept anyone's advice. All he knows about is Satyagraha and little else.'[27]

The younger generation was getting impatient. Its vision was not clouded by religiosity. They were inspired by the new wave of socialism and wanted to wage a militant struggle, not only against foreign rule, but also against the landlords and capitalists at home. They were modernists, while Gandhi was against all forms of modernity. They were Westernized in their ideas, while he was anti-Western in his outlook, despite his education in London. They saw their struggle against imperialism as a political one. He saw it as a moral one. There was bound to be a certain distancing between Gandhi and the Congress. He shrewdly saw this, and resigned from the Congress in 1934, though that did not mean he did not run the party. They indulged him, while hoping to do without him. That however proved impossible, and again the catalyst came from abroad.

ATTLEE'S VISION FOR INDIA

Soon after the Round Table Conference, the government issued an award (August 1932) and a White Paper (March 1933), and then Parliament proceeded with its committee work. The White Paper promised provincial autonomy—end of diarchy and an All India federation of British India and the native states. Its one permanent contribution to the Indian Constitution was the concept of *scheduled castes and tribes*. Appendix VIII of the White Paper lists Scheduled Castes, but includes within it Scheduled Tribes as well. What it showed, however, was that in his own quiet way, Ambedkar had been very effective in getting his point across, that the depressed classes deserved special treatment. Seventy-five years later the category of Scheduled Castes and Tribes has, if anything, acquired greater importance.

The White Paper had to be debated in Parliament and, then, a resolution moved to appoint various committees to look into aspects of the White Paper, such as franchise, federation, finance, minorities. It was an intensive process, but it ended in a report of the Joint Committee on Indian constitutional reform. The report backtracked from the bold declaration of Irwin about Dominion Status. The caution on part of the national government was because politicians with a long memory could recall that the Liberals had split on Irish Home Rule, which had strengthened the Conservative party. Could it be that now the Tories would split on India?

The joint committee was dominated by Conservatives, since they had the large majority in the Commons as well as the Lords. From among the forty-six Labour MPs, it fell to Clement Attlee to be one of the four Labour members of the joint committee. The committee was chaired by Linlithgow, who had chaired the Royal Commission on Indian Agriculture and who would soon be viceroy. Labour members wanted a much more radical report, but, as expected, they got nowhere.

Attlee was cautious, even as he pushed the committee beyond provincial autonomy which was its horizon. His concerns were wider. He wrote a draft for his Labour parliamentary colleagues, in which he expressed his fears and hopes. For what he was to become eventually, as much as a reflection of his contemporary thinking, the draft deserves some attention. He was not 'persuaded that it is either possible or desirable to follow the Westminster model', but 'his overriding anxiety was to ensure that Britain would not establish a new Dominion in India which would abandon the poor and politically weak to the oppression of traditional and the new Indian elites'. He, of course, included Congress among the 'new Indian elites'. As a socialist, though a moderate one, Attlee 'hoped that class-based politics would replace communalism in drawing political allegiance'. He distrusted the Congress's claim to speak for all Indians, and 'feared that the new constitution would perpetuate rather than reduce social inequalities and injustice'. He thought 'separate electorates were detestable, as they would exacerbate communal differences, but inevitable in the short term given the strength of the differences'.[28] Since the Congress was made up of disparate forces, he expected it to break up once self-government had been attained.

The report erred on the side of caution, as was expected. At the Centre the executive was to retain its powers in defence and foreign affairs, with the other subjects being dealt with by ministers chosen by the governor general from members of the central assembly. Reserve powers were with the governor general since the devolution, such as it was, was reluctant. Rules of federal finance, which were to linger for decades, were laid down here. At the provincial level, diarchy was to be done away with and autonomy given. There was to be full popular government at the provincial level.

But with provincial autonomy, the central legislature had to be a federal assembly. But then, in addition to this British India federation, there was the issue of the Princely States joining a federation. Thus, the central assembly was to have elected members from British India (250) and nominated members from the Princely States (125). There was to be an Upper Chamber where princes would send their nominees (104) and British India its elected members (156).

The report had one minority dissent, and that was from Attlee. He formed his dissent in the form of an alternative draft report. Attlee was sensitive to Indian nationalism: 'We desire to give the fullest possible expression to the national consciousness and to make provision by means of a reformed constitution for the living forces of Indian Nationalism to be harnessed to the tasks which confront any government in India.'[29] But nationalism by itself was not enough.

> We are not unmindful that unless political changes result in giving a better life to ordinary citizen, they are of little value. We are not blind to the fact that in India, as in most parts of the world, the masses of the people are the prey of economic exploitation. A change in the constitution which would put India's rural population and urban wage-earners at the mercy of a politically dominant section in possession of economic power might very well intensify the very evils which we desire to be eradicated. While recognizing the public spirit and zeal for reform of leading Indian statesmen, we cannot but recognise the fact that the majority of the active and politically minded Indians belong to the privileged well-to-do classes, that the Hindoo social system is based on inequality and in India as elsewhere, the power of wealth in politics is inevitably strong.[30]

On minority rights Attlee took a forthright view: 'The state of Europe today provides an abundance of instances of oppression of minorities by majorities. It is unnecessary for us to emphasise the very grave divisions in India caused not merely by the rivalry of the great Hindu and Muslim Communities, but by the existence of many minor communities, and by the existence of the very numerous Depressed Classes.'[31] Therefore, he did not approve of separate electorates, but took the view that, *faute de mieux*, there was little else the committee could do. 'The division of the electorate into watertight compartments and the allocation of seats according to the numbers of various religious communities seems to us to cut very deeply at the roots of a real system of democratic government; but we can only hope that in course of time, a realisation of their common citizenship may lead the contending communities to sink their mutual suspicions and animosities.'[32]

Attlee also saw the dangers inherent in provincial autonomy preceding central self-government:

> India has been united for a short period of time relative to her long history. While the sentiment of nationalism is strong, there are powerful tendencies towards Provincialism. There is a grave danger that if responsibility were conceded in the Provinces and not at the Centre there might be a growth of separatist feeling ... We consider it is essential the Centre should be, as it were, the focus of Indian Nationalism. At the present time the Congress

appears to very many Indians as the most vital expression of their
nationalist aspirations, and it has been a regrettable fact during the years
which have elapsed since the Montagu-Chelmsford Reforms that Congress
has been to a large extent a body functioning outside the Constitution. It
is our desire that Indian Nationalism should find its full expression within
the Constitution, and we think this is only possible if real responsibility is
given at the Centre as well as in the Provinces.[33]

Attlee's dissenting report is not very well known. But here, in a
remarkable way, is the blueprint of what was to happen after 1945. The
1935 Act federation was never established, precisely because not enough
Princely States signed up. There is some evidence that they were egged
on by Conservatives in Britain to delay and dither. They paid the price
eventually by being abolished when Independence did come, and it came
under a Labour government presided over by the lone dissenter. But all
that was unknown in October 1934 when the report was published.

What still remained was to frame the bill with all the detailed
provisions for division of powers between the Centre and the states and
the concurrent list, etc. The bill was introduced in the House of
Commons in February 1935. There were 473 (325 excluding Burma)
clauses and sixteen (ten excluding Burma) schedules. Churchill called it
'a gigantic quilt of jumbled croquet work, a monstrous monument of
shame built by pygmies'. In the House of Commons, where normally
bills are 'sent upstairs' for the committee stage, constitutional bills have
to be taken by a committee of the Whole House (which is the normal
practice for all bills in the House of Lords). An unprecedented thirty-
seven days were allocated for the Government of India 1935 Bill. The
total number of days including all stages was forty-three, and a total of
1951 speeches were made, taking 15.5 million words occupying 4000
pages of Hansard. This was, as I have mentioned earlier, the longest bill
discussed by British Parliament until the end of the twentieth century.
The official policy was to speed the bill through. The small numbers on
the Labour benches wanted to push things faster, while Churchill and
the 'diehards' wanted to slow things down.

The second reading debate, which normally takes a day or two at
most, took four days. Hoare opened for the government on 6 February
1935. He knew that the main criticism he had to fend off came from
behind him from the Conservative back benches. So he put it thus, 'Let
us face realities. The real danger in India is not Congress, or Communism,
or misgovernment; it is irresponsibility. As long as Indian Assemblies
have no responsibility to govern, so we must expect negative criticism,
and even mischievous obstruction.'[34]

Attlee moved the Opposition motion saying, 'no legislation for the
better government of India will be satisfactory which does not secure the

goodwill and co-operation of the Indian people by recognising explicitly India's right to Dominion Status . . . And which does not . . . secure to the workers and peasants of India, the possibility of achieving by constitutional means their social and economic emancipation.'[35] He pointed out that the bill had no support in India, whatever Hoare may say. 'There was as a matter of fact rejection by all the live movements in India, not only by Congress and the Liberals, but by Labour and by many people classed as Moderates.' This was because, of course, 'The keynote of the Bill is mistrust. There is no trust at all. India is not to have control of its foreign affairs and her finances. Indians in the Provinces are not fit to deal with terrorism.'[36]

The nub of the matter was conservatism. 'The legislature is to be overloaded with Conservative interests, landlords, commerce and the like. Second chambers are to be set up. The conclusion to which one comes on looking at the Bill is that the definite decision has been that India is to be ruled by the wealthy and the privileged. The curious thing is that even these people are not trusted.'[37]

'The assumption on which [Conservative] Members act is that things are fairly satisfactory in India, and that we are to take the very greatest care that they do not go wrong. I say that things are most unsatisfactory in India, and that we want very big changes.'[38] Attlee talked about slums and low wages and the usurious interest rates charged by rural moneylenders. He did not just want Dominion Status for India; he also wanted real economic and social change.

Churchill spoke on the last day, 11 February, just before the final speeches. His was the longest speech in the debate. He began by reminding everyone how Irwin had jumped the gun, and the Simon Report had been shelved. Dominion Status was nonsense. He was worried about the welfare of the masses of India in this great bill and in all these reports and commissions.

> We complained that the welfare of the Indian masses is virtually ignored in all theses reports—their agriculture, their education, their hospitals, their water, their forests, their labour standards, their social services. The Imperial Power divests itself of interest in and control over all these matters, grasps solely what is essential to its own self-interest, and, with a shrug of its shoulders, leaves this enormous peasant proletariat to take their chance in the inexperienced hands of whatever may be the dominant party in the different provinces or in the Central Legislature.[39]

He was in no mood to leave, or even admit that the British were an alien power in India:

> None of it is true. We are no more aliens in India than the Mohammedans or the Hindus themselves. We have as good a right to be in India as anyone

there except, perhaps, the Depressed Classes who are the original stock. Ordinary Indians preferred British officers over one of their own. Any Hindu would prefer to have his case dealt with by a British officer than by a Mohammedan, and vice versa. Talking about going to people of your own race and language and so forth, when Mr. Gandhi had his appendix removed he was very careful to insist upon a British surgeon.[40]

Churchill mixed arrogant paternalism with a disbelief that the Indian ability to wield power could be better than the British. His romantic imperialism could not admit that there could be better rule for India than what the British Empire had delivered. But his time was gone. George Lansbury, leader of the Labour Party said: 'We draw from India ... enormous wealth in the form of salaries, pensions, travelling allowances, holidays and so on, in addition to very considerable sums in dividends and repayments for loans of public works. If we remained in India and spent the money there the wealth which has to be sent to this country, I do not believe that the people of India would be living under the conditions they are living under today.'[41] What was more, the empire was paid for by Indians.

> While the British connection may have built railways and while the British connection may have protected them, the Indian people have found all the money required for these purposes, and the maintenance of the British Army is a terrific strain on the resources of the country. It is not that India is a poor country, but that her population is very poor. Something like 63½ per cent of the money raised at the Centre has to be spent on the Army, the cost of which has tremendously increased because it is a British Army and not an Indian Army.[42]

The big gap in the debate was that no one spoke for India, except, perhaps, the Labour Party. Lansbury reminded the House, 'The voice of India ought to be heard in this country either through broadcasting or in some other way ... We declared at our conference at Blackpool for self-government and self-determination for the Indian people ... India is to be from our point of view a partner of her free will in the British Commonwealth of Nations. This Bill does not fulfil that principle at all.'[43]

Lansbury was telling some home truths to the large masses on the Tory benches, for which he was not liked. 'We may have the British flag flying over the seven seas; we may even have the greatest finance houses in the world; but here right in the heart of the Empire, we have a mass of people decaying both mentally and physically because we cannot find them the means of livelihood. What benefit is it that we rule in India if masses starve or are semi-starved here? What benefit is it to those in my constituency and in other constituencies whatever you may do in India?'[44]

When Baldwin got up to reply, he asserted the view of British having united India. 'It is due to us that there is any unity in India from which she has been estranged for centuries. That is due solely to us. We have established the rule of law and order, we have created the credit of India, we have run railways all over India, and we have built up a great system for the relief of famine and the prevention of disease. We have organised agricultural and veterinary services. We have developed institutions for education and for research. All these will go on.'[45]

The electorate was going to be 35 million, five times the electorate for the 1919 reforms. 'The representation of the Depressed Classes is being increased out of all knowledge.' He finished by saying, 'Let us welcome into our Commonwealth of Nations the Indian people, the majority of whom, I am confident, have no greater ambition than to see their country play a worthy part in the Commonwealth. We have, as I said one day in this House, no secular feud with the Indian peoples as, alas, our people had in Ireland. Let us in offering what we believe to be a precious gift, do it in no huckstering spirit.'[46] The motion was passed 404 to 133. The bill went on through its various stages till in June 1935 it passed its third reading by 386 to 122 votes and then passage through the House of Lords on 24 July. It became an act when it received royal assent on 2 August 1935. Thus, in eight months, a mammoth bill was passed, and this itself represented a eight-year process, began when Birkenhead appointed the Simon Commission in 1927.[47]

Among other things the Act established the Reserve Bank of India and a National Railway Authority. Powers were shared out between the Centre and the provinces along with a concurrent list. The Scheduled Castes and Tribes list was made. A federal court was established. Orissa and Sind were set up as new provinces and Burma was hived off separately. The skeleton of independent India's Constitution is very much here. As Butler recalls, 'When, in 1954, I stayed with Nehru in Delhi, he affirmed without hesitation that our Government of India Bill, founded as it was on Dicey and Anson, the two great constitutional lawyers, was the basis of the Independence Bill itself.'[48]

That is not, however, the way Nehru and many others felt about the bill in 1935. In a letter to Lord Lothian, Nehru quoted Tej Bahadur Sapru, though without explicitly naming him, as saying of the 1935 bill, 'the quintessence of the most venomous opposition to all our national aspirations'. Lothian was trying to argue the British Liberal line that this was the way gradual advance was best made. But by now Nehru had lost patience. 'Between Indian nationalism, Indian freedom and British imperialism there can be no common ground.' The act was 'the new charter of slavery'. Congress was wedded to the idea of sabotaging the federation. Nehru was ready: 'We shall fight to our utmost strength, and the primary object of our creating deadlocks in the provinces and making the new Act difficult of functioning, is to kill the federation. With the federation dead, the provincial end of the Act will also go and leave the slate clean for the people of India to write upon.'

Nehru was to be proved right, but not in the way he had envisaged. The federation died, but not because Congress killed it. It was stillborn because not enough Princely States joined. The provincial part of the act became unworkable after a while, but more because of the breakout of the Second World War and Congress ministries resigning than anything else. The people of India did write a new Constitution, but not on a clean slate. The slate was soaked in blood, and the India which emerged from the process, twelve years later, was a truncated version of what the 1935 Act was meant to help govern. After the 1935 Act, there was never another constitutional bill passed by Parliament which dealt with that larger India. The next time around there would be India and Pakistan formed out of the India of the 1935 Act.

CHAPTER 8

THE RUPTURE

ONE INDIA OR MANY?

The 1935 Act did one more thing which no previous piece of legislation had done. It defined the boundaries of India. Once Burma was hived off, the rest of British India along with the Princely States was India; indeed, the expression 'All India' increasingly came into use at this time. What was ruptured in 1947 was this 'All India', which was not formally defined until the proposal was made by the Maharaja of Bikaner that the Princely States would merge into an All India federation at the first meeting of the Round Table Conference. This simple, and somewhat shocking, fact has never been admitted. Had the British not suspended their policy of annexation which Dalhousie did so much to promote, and which was held to be one of the major triggers for 1857, they could have easily absorbed all the Princely States. All India then would have been British India. Their reluctance to conquer and their reliance on the loyal princes to provide ballast may have been helpful to them, but it was a headache for the nationalists. Luckily for everyone, except in the north with Kashmir, everywhere else the boundaries of India were in British India. (Since the boundaries of 'All India' were never to be the boundaries of independent India, I intend to use the expression All India for pre-Partition India where I need to distinguish between pre- and post-Partition India. Of course, after 1947 the expression All India continued to be used for the smaller India.)

The territorial boundaries of India (not as a society but as a state) had fluctuated through the Mughal era. Kabul, for instance, was once a part of the empire, though Assam never was. The four Afghan Wars that the British fought finally put paid to the idea of Kabul being an outpost of British India. The Durand Line was the border between Afghanistan and India. Dinshaw Wacha, a moderate Congress leader in the pre-1914 period, complained about the money spent on 'the disastrous invasion of

Afghanistan in 1878–80, and now sought to be perpetuated by the establishment of permanent military posts far beyond the physical boundaries of India on the West, for the maintenance of which costly railways . . . have been constructed.'[1] Of course, it was never clear before where the western boundaries of India were. The Hindu soldiers, who took part in the 1857 rebellion, thought crossing the Indus meant loss of caste since the Indus was *kaala pani* (literally, the 'dark waters/ocean'). The North-West Frontier, too, was a scene of constant battles to establish control. These were the badlands where the young and bored Winston Churchill had transferred himself from Bangalore to seek some adventure. To this day it is a troublesome area.

During Curzon's rule, in 1903–04, Col Francis Younghusband had led an expedition to Tibet to determine the borders of India and Tibet. He had to withdraw without conquering Tibet, since no one in London wanted the purpose of the expedition to be conquest. So a compromise was put together. This was a sign of how weak the Chinese had become, who thought of themselves the suzerain of the territory. The expedition was regarded as a humiliation by the Chinese nationalists. The conquest of Assam and Burma brought the tribal areas of Nagaland and the adjoining hills into British India. This region, termed as the North-Eastern Frontier Area (NEFA), has since been an ambiguously defined border. The Nagas in the south on the border with Burma never formally accepted British sovereignty, and the maps left these areas blank or only hazily delineated. In the north of the same region, the border ran with Bhutan and Sikkim as well as with Tibet, where China's suzerainty was only grudgingly acknowledged by imperial Britain. Jammu and Kashmir were parts of All India because of the 1935 Act. The Andaman and Nicobar Islands fell within Indian territory—they had once been a part of the Chola Empire in the eleventh century, then for the next seven centuries they were independent until the British recaptured them in the eighteenth century. Geographically, their location is closer to Burma or indeed, Malaysia, than to India. The nationalist movement never questioned that the boundaries of All India were the ones set by the empire. Whatever deplorable and even fiscally irresponsible adventures may have secured them, once they were there, they were All India's boundaries.

In the narratives of Indian nationhood, which the Congress or the Mahasabha or even the Muslim League put forward, India was primarily a North Indian entity—a Doab plus Punjab plus Bengal affair. Sir Syed Ahmad, in a very conciliatory speech in Patna in 1883, had described how Muslims had come to India along the same route as the Hindus had. 'Gentlemen, just as many reputed people professing Hindu faith came to this country, so we also came here. The Hindu forgot the country from which they had come, they could not remember their migration from one land to another and came to consider India as their homeland *believing that their country lies between the Himalayas and Vindhyachal.*'[2]

The ideology of Aryans coming to India and civilizing it is very much a North Indian upper-caste Hindu narrative. Muslims are foreign invaders, it avers, and they must acknowledge that they live in a Hindu nation; if not, they have to be exiled. Sir Syed's account is therefore interesting on two counts; it says Hindus and Muslims in the North are both from outside and that the South is beyond their national boundary. The Mahasabha, obviously, would not agree: the whole emphasis of its narrative is on the Muslims being émigrés, not the Aryans. The same logic is extended to Christians, whether Anglo-Indians, Indian Christians or Westerners.

The Congress absorbed this narrative, but went further. It glorified Buddhism along with Ashoka as a corrective to Vedic Brahmanism. A distinctive character of the Congress version was to absorb Muslim history in a creative rather than a hostile fashion, which was the Mahasabha's line. The Mughals, more than the Afghans of the Delhi Sultanate, were the heroes here. The Mughal Empire was seen as a template of the Indian nation state.[3] The Congress narrative relied on the extent of India being roughly what the Mughal Empire had aspired to cover, with the story of a syncretic culture emerging from Hindu–Muslim interaction in the northern royal courts. It was this India which was enslaved by the British according to the Congress nationalist narrative.

There was a distinctive formal attempt to fuse together Islam and Hinduism. Akbar was always a hero in the Congress narrative for his tolerance of all religions as well as for his attempt to found a national Indian religion, Din-e-Ilahi. It died with him. There were other examples of the fusion of Islam and Hinduism—but this was the elite Hinduism of the *Upanishads*. Dara Shikoh, the son of Emperor Shah Jahan, had translated the *Upanishads* into Persian and though, or perhaps because, he lost to the intolerant Aurangzeb his chance of succeeding to the throne, he was much lionized in the syncretic narrative. Maulana Azad, who was the highest ranking Muslim leader in the Congress from 1936 till his death in 1959, also made an attempt to see the meaning of the *Upanishads* as reflected in Islam, though for him Islam was the larger absorbing truth. Much of this, however, had no relevance to the bulk of the Hindu or the Muslim population. It was an elite (British as well as Indian) story for elite consumption. What mattered, when push came to shove, was how ordinary people viewed their own and the other religion. The Congress was to be surprised when it found out.

But India was more than just a collection of religious communities—Hindus and Muslims and Sikhs. This was one way of viewing India. But this was not enough, nor did it speak for the entire country. The Dravidian people's position in Indian culture has always been an afterthought in the nationalist narrative, though integrated more in the mid-twentieth century than before. Gandhi's vision of India was much more inclusive since he had worked with Tamil and Gujarati Muslim immigrants in South Africa. He could even read Tamil, unlike most Northern leaders. His son, Devdas was married to Lakshmi, the daughter of Rajagopalachari, a Tamil Brahmin and the Congress's face in Madras province. But this was his personal story. The Congress narrative stayed narrowly North Indian, where even Bengal was marginalized after the departure of C.R. Das.

Even more glaring was the narrative's obliviousness to the entire North-Eastern region—the Assamese, the Naga, the Khasi, the Garo. It is only in Appendix VIII of the White Paper of 1931, with its Schedule of Castes with some castes marked with asterisk as 'Primitive Tribe', that the aboriginal people get a formal admission as people of India. But even here, the list does not cover the parts which were not among the eleven provinces. The Assamese are in along with the scheduled castes, but the territory between Assam and Burma is not explicitly mentioned. There had been censuses since mid-nineteenth century, and the Anthropological Survey had got to work. These 'original' inhabitants, untouched by 'the civilizing mission' of Vedic Brahmanism and, later, of Hinduism, were among the people of India, but uncomfortably, if at all, a part of the narrative of Indian nationhood.

The Muslim League narrative emphasized the minority position of the Muslims, but as a separate 'community' (becoming designated as a 'nation' late in the 1930s) from the Hindus. There was pride that Muslims had overrun North India as conquerors and ruled it for eight centuries. But this was not the issue since it was the Muslims who, as the last rulers, were dispossessed by the British. The two communities—Hindu and Muslim—had co-existed (though with no intermarriage and little social mixing except among the aristocracy) under an alien government in an undemocratic set up, where the numerical strength of each community signified little. As late as 1883, Sir Syed was saying, 'India is home to both of us. We both breathe the air of India and take the water of the Holy Ganges and the Yamuna . . . We are living and dying together. By living so long in India, the blood of both have changed . . . Thus, if we ignore that aspect of ours which we owe to God, both of us, on the basis of being common inhabitants of India, actually constitute one nation.'[4]

This way of looking at the nation was to change soon as issues of representation, jobs and 'Indianization' of public services began to emerge. With an elective democracy in prospect the superior numbers of the Hindus, constituting a possible permanent majority, were seen as a threat to the rights of the minority. Sir Syed was a loyal British subject, and willing to take whatever the British chose to give. The Congress began, in 1885, a more positive approach of demanding, ever so politely, much more much faster. Religion, which had been something one could forget, now became a solid identifier for political favours. This became the narrative even with Sir Syed Ahmad, and the Muslim League was the institutional expression of it.

The dispossessed minority had to be loyal and seek favours from the alien rulers, hoping they would resist a democratic urge and treat the two unequal communities equally well. For Sir Syed this was not a religious matter, and the answer was not some multi-faith dialogue or fusion. His stance on Islam was a modernizing one, on the lines of Mohammed Abduh who had adopted a pro-British position in Egypt and pushed a modernist agenda. This was also the prevalent current in Turkey, where the Tanzimat movement had struck out in a pro-Western direction in the second half of the nineteenth century. The modernizers in Islam at this juncture did not mind being pro-Western, because they were fighting the forces of religious obscurantism. Sir Syed's was a secular struggle for the rights of the large minority.[5] He was as secular as it was possible for a nineteenth-century Muslim leader to be. He has been compared to Raja Rammohun Roy, though, obviously, it was not possible for him to found a new sect like the Brahmo Samaj within Islam.

Once Morley–Minto had opened up the Pandora's box of representation, the League played the minority card rather than the dispossessed former ruler card. Jinnah's Lucknow Pact followed by his attempts in 1928 with the Nehru Report were possible half-way houses, which reposed trust in the majority to guarantee the rights of the minority by some electoral seat-sharing agreement. He was not successful, as the Congress chose instead to snuggle up to the Mahasabha. The 1935 Act gave another chance to revisit the thorny issue of Hindu–Muslim accord on seat sharing and minority rights.

The Muslim narrative was fragmented along the lines of revivalist or reformist. The appeal of revival was great and integrated the Indian Muslims into a pan-Islamic movement centred in Istanbul, the capital city of the Ottoman Empire. There was, however, a conflict among the revivalists themselves between viewing Indian Muslims as part of the pan-Islamic community which owed primary allegiance to the caliphate (re-established by Sultan Hamid in 1876 when he banned the Tanzimat), and regarding themselves as Indian nationals, fighting for independence against the British. Jinnah regarded the revived caliphate as 'an exploded bogey'. The Ali brothers and, at that time, even Maulana Azad were among the fundamentalists who believed Muslims had to look to Istanbul and the caliph for unity across the *ummah*. A third position was to seek British protection against a possible post-British Hindu tyranny.

When Gandhi fought the British on the Khilafat platform, he recruited the obscurantist wing of Indian Islam. He did not know of, or perhaps was hostile to, the pro-Western movements in Turkey, which had been suppressed by the sultan. His anti-European diatribe in *Hind Swaraj* saw little difference between anti-imperialism and anti-modernism. Jinnah left the Congress in disgust because he could not abide the obscurantists. Worse was to come when Kemal Pasha abolished the caliphate. As Aijaz Ahmad has written:

> It is generally recognized that key leaders of the Khilafat Movement, such as the Ali Brothers and Azad, were utterly dumbfounded at the fact that the Turks would themselves abolish the Osmanli caliphate and dynastic rule, and the movement entirely unprepared for the denouement, petered out in confusion ... Why in other words had they staked the passions of Indian Muslims on the fate of a moribund institution, namely the Osmanli caliphate, which had been exceedingly unpopular with the great majority of its Turkish and Arab subjects since its revival by Hamidian despotism in the 1870s?[6]

Jinnah's narrative, when he returned to India four years after his disappointment with the Nehru Report, was not based on a historical account. It was narrowly focussed on rights. It was Jinnah's genius to grasp that the way to overcome the disparity in numbers was to designate the communities as 'nations'. India was thus not a single nation as the Congress would have it, but a collection of nations, among whom two were prominent. When Nehru said there were two sides to the dispute—British imperialism and the Congress, Jinnah is reported to have said, 'No there is a third side; the Indian Muslims.' The Indian nationalist narrative always regarded this as a divisive and somehow British-inspired tactic—similar to its reaction to the scheduled caste issue raised by Ambedkar. There was however a case for Jinnah, if one looked at the prevailing larger picture.

There was a new mode of discourse in Europe since the break-up of the Austro-Hungarian Empire. This process saw a proliferation of nations come into being, many of which had large minorities, often of Austrian–Germans, the previous rulers. During the second reading of the 1935 Bill, Attlee had mentioned how minorities were being badly treated by majorities across Europe. Ireland had split on the eve of Home Rule into a largely Catholic South and a Protestant North, with a minority population of the other sect within the borders. Within four years of

Attlee's speech, it would be the German incursion into Czechoslovakia to protect the German-speaking minority in Sudetenland, which would warn the British that a war was looming. The persecution of the Jews was to follow in the late 1930s, and their annihilation soon after. Germany was an old nation, but going through a revanchist phase. In Hungary, Czechoslovakia, Poland, there was an upsurge of primordial nationalism, which bore down on the minorities which had previously been their masters. Nations which had just become independent after 1918 took a majoritarian view, since the nation was ethnically defined on a linguistic basis or worse yet, on a racist one.

Today we know better, or so at least we believe. In Northern Ireland, a century-old conflict between the Protestant majority and the Catholic minority persisted, with power and patronage firmly in the hands of the Protestant majority and the deprived minority driven to using terrorism to register its protest. Its southern neighbour, the Irish Republic had a Catholic majority and similarly ignored non-Catholic rights. Dreams of a United Ireland kept the conflict alive. It was in 1998, after two decades of efforts by UK and the Irish Republic, that a solution was found. It recognized that the two communities of unequal size had parity in terms of democratic power when it came to constitutional change, and each had to independently approve of any constitutional change. The South renounced its dream of uniting the two parts. This was a consociational arrangement rather than a majoritarian one.[7]

If more lessons were needed, Europe learned, yet again, from the break-up of Yugoslavia that majorities can indulge in ethnic cleansing, that is, genocide of their minorities. Even Sri Lanka witnessed the persecution of a Tamil minority by the Sinhalese majority, and the result was a civil war lasting twenty-eight years. Majorities can be oppressive, even democratic ones, as Sri Lanka's case shows. But at the time of the debate in the 1930s, such lessons had not been learnt. Nationalism in its first flush in India did not wish to share power in a consociational fashion. The next twelve years were to unfold the drama as these narratives, substantially North Indian, became a battleground. Until the prospect of a self-governing democratic India became realistic, nationhood could be defined hazily, its territorial boundaries fluid in time and space. But if there were to be an India which ruled itself even under the Dominion Status arrangement, there had to be a story: What was this 'India' which was to be self-governing? Which 'self' or 'selves' were to rule India? It was in the interstices of the self-governing provinces, but with the elusive prize of an All India federation beckoning, that the clashing narratives played out their dramas.

PROVINCIAL 'NATIONS'

The battle of the national narratives came across a new barrier, which had been building up quietly, and which did not possess a single narrative. This was the result of the separate development of the various regions of British India, which made the entire territory a heterogeneous collection of pieces of uneven size. This is not to say that there was homogeneity before the British arrived. The small degree of centralization during the period since 1857 as well as the growth of the railroad, newspapers and postal services reduced the heterogeneity somewhat, but also awoke new forces of regional identity such as the growth of modern literature in local languages and an awareness of local histories. The diversity of the provinces was, of course, not just in terms of size. Their development had taken varied paths, mainly because the land tenure systems had been different—zamindari in Bengal and Bihar, ryotwari in Madras and Bombay and canal settlements in Punjab. (There has been an endless debate as to whether these land tenure systems were innovations imposed by the British or whether the British took over what was already there and simply systematized the operation. I take the latter view. Punjab's canal systems were, of course, an innovation.)

The industrial and commercial developments, which had taken place since the mid-nineteenth century, had been concentrated in the towns and hinterlands of Bombay and Calcutta and, to a lesser extent, Ahmedabad. Madras had less industrial development. Military recruitment in Sind, Punjab and NWFP meant that local elites had strong loyalist links with the army and British civil service. To use a catch phrase, 'bourgeois' development had taken place in Bombay and Bengal and, to a lesser degree, in Madras, while NWFP, Punjab and Sind were 'feudal'. UP and Bihar had seen some, but not much, urbanization—very few new towns, for instance, and only a small amount of industrial development. They were in-between the 'bourgeois' and the 'feudal' stages. (I use these expressions as mere labels and not as fully developed Marxist categories.)

There was also a class divide which followed the religious divide, but differently in different regions. In UP and Bihar Muslim landholders were dominant and, though there were some Hindu landowners as well, the bulk of the peasantry was Hindu. There was a nascent Muslim middle class in these provinces, as also in Bombay. In Bengal, however, the landlords were Hindu and the peasantry Muslim. In Madras the divide was not religious, but within the Hindu social system, for instance between the Brahmins and the rest. This was also a live issue in the Maharashtra parts of Bombay province, while in Gujarat the commercial castes dominated the Brahmins. A peasant caste, the Patidars, had emerged through the late nineteenth and early twentieth centuries as a formidable upwardly mobile group of commercial farmers. It was the genius of Sardar Patel to mobilize this group for many agrarian struggles that Gandhi launched against the British.

The many provinces were defined each as a local 'nation', or several local 'nations', or, at least a 'people', who, with some ingenuity, could be placed in the Hindu/Muslim/Others grid; but there were substantial differences within and among these categories. The Sikhs were a big group in Punjab as were the Christians in the South. The intra-Hindu conflict between Brahmins and the rest has already been mentioned. Even among Muslims, there was a social and cultural distance between the poor Muslim peasantry of Bengal and Assam or Sind and Punjab, and the aristocratic pretenders of UP and Bihar or the large landowners of Sind and Punjab. There was an urban Muslim population, largely self-employed and poor with a thin layer of the educated, some of whom held government jobs. In South India, Muslims had first come as traders and not as conquerors. Their social and economic position was also different in Kerala as against Hyderabad. But the differences between the interaction of Hindu and Muslim cultures, north and south of the Vindhyas, have not been much appreciated.

Language was another marker of heterogeneity, since each province had one, or sometimes, even two languages, with their own script and literature. Bombay had Marathi and Gujarati and Madras had Tamil, Telugu, Malayalam and Kannada within its borders. All South Indians were called 'Madrasis' by the North Indians late into the 1950s, much to their annoyance, as they pointed out that they were as diverse from one another as the Marathi- or Gujarati- or Bengali-speaking were from each other.

The notion that a nation must have a single language loomed large in the nationalist consciousness of the Congress. An earlier generation of Congress leaders had been happy with English. As Surendranath Bannerji said to the Student Association of Calcutta in 1878, 'We are not separated by language; English supplies us with a common medium of communication, and removes one of the greatest difficulties to national union.'[8] With Gandhi's entry and the creation of a mass party, the Congress saw this as inadequate, hence the attempts to make Hindi/Hindustani—the principal language of the Doab and Delhi—the national language of India. Northern India was the battleground among Hindus and Muslims, and often literally so. This meant that there was one vociferous group who wanted to expunge Urdu/Muslim traces from Hindi and sanskritize it, insisting on using the Devanagari script. This was part of the Arya Samaj movement's demand in the last quarter of the nineteenth century, something which made Sir Syed uneasy as he could see the de-skilling of Urdu-reading Muslims when it came to jobs. The syncretic champions of Hindustani wanted the script to be both

Urdu and Devanagari. Gandhi ecumenically used both scripts in his weekly *Harijan*, and often received hostile post on that account. The battle was as much within the Congress parties of UP and Bihar as with the Hindu Mahasabha. None would admit the political lingua franca of Indian nationalism was English. The leadership in the Congress spoke English with their colleagues from other provinces and their local language among themselves. Hindi was difficult for the South Indians to master, and even a Gujarati like Sardar Patel had problems with it.

The 'provincial' nationalism was not assertive, but power resided in the provinces. It was thus crucial to the development of Indian nationhood that in the period of clashing narratives, there was this silent but powerful force arguing for provincial autonomy and identity. The single nation narratives preferred a strong Centre, which would define a single India, a single language and a single national identity—Indian; at the same time many in the provinces fought for devolved authority and separate regional identities. Unfortunately, this battle was also to be scarred by the Hindu–Muslim divide in North India and shape events in a way no one had foreseen.

PROVINCIAL AUTONOMY IN ACTION

The 1935 Act had given substantial self-government to eleven provinces of British India. This self-government was to be exercised by directly elected members of the Legislative Assembly, who were to form a government under the chairmanship of the governor of the province. These provinces were unequal in size, and in their religious and caste mix. The total number of seats was broken down into general and separate electorate seats. The reserved seats for scheduled castes were part of the general seats as a result of the Poona Pact. There were separate electorates for Muslims, Sikhs, Anglo-Indians, Europeans, Indian Christians, Commerce and industry, landholders, university, labour and women. The main issue was the number of general and Muslim seats. This division varied according to proportions in the population. The Muslim majority states were Punjab, Bengal, Sind and NWFP. But the majority of the Muslim population of India lived in Muslim minority provinces, such as UP and Bihar. It was the first time ever in Indian history that parts of India were to be governed by people elected from her own population. The overall control of the British remained, with all those 'safeguards' and the dominant position of the governor general and the provincial governors.

The distribution of seats is revealing, both as to the size of a province and to its population mix. There were 1585 seats in all, of which 808 were general (Hindu) and 482 Muslim. Scheduled caste seats (151) were a part of the general category as a result of the Poona Pact between Gandhi and Ambedkar. There were forty-one seats for women overall, twenty-four for tribal and backward area representatives (seven in Bihar, nine in Assam and five in Orissa), fifty-six for commerce, thirty-eight for labour and thirty-seven for landholders. In the following table, the number of seats for the general, scheduled caste and Muslim categories are shown separately with the remaining categories as Others. Apart for the Sikhs who had an allocation in Punjab and NWFP, the resulting pattern shows where the Muslim majority provinces were. But together, these four provinces—Bengal, Punjab, NWFP and Sind—had 270 seats, while the minority Muslim provinces had 212 seats. These numbers formed the background to later discussions about power sharing and, eventually, for Partition.

Distribution of Seats by Religion and Caste

Province	Total	General (Scheduled Caste)	Muslims	Sikhs	Others
Bengal	250	78 (30)	117	–	55
Madras	215	146 (30)	28	–	41
Bombay	175	114 (15)	29	–	32
UP	228	140 (20)	64	–	24
Punjab	175	42 (8)	84	31	18
Bihar	152	86 (15)	39	–	27
CP/Berar	112	84 (20)	14	–	14
Assam	108	47 (7)	34	–	27
NWFP	50	9 (0)	36	3	2
Orissa	60	44 (6)	4	–	12
Sind	60	18 (0)	33	–	9
Total	1585	808 (151)	482	34	261

The Congress went through one of its regular turnarounds. Since 1921 it had alternated between two phases—Gandhi on the (non-violent) war path with the Congress on the streets; the other phase had Gandhi in his ashram with the Congress in the assemblies. In 1923 the Constitutionalists had started the Swaraj Party and entered the assemblies under the 1919 Act after Chauri Chaura. After the salt agitation and subsequent failed agitations, Congress again contested elections for assemblies and won fifty-three out of the seventy-five seats open to Indian members in the Central Legislative Assembly still operating under the 1919 Act.

Now faced with a lull on the part of the Mahatma, the Congress decided to participate in the elections based on the 1935 Act. It was a decisive move in many ways. Gandhi and the Congress were cool to each other, though without a formal break despite the former's resignation from ordinary membership. But the Congress was also split. It was between Sardar Patel, who was the organizing genius, and Nehru, who was the political orator and mass mobilizer. Gandhi had declared his hand and designated Nehru as his successor. Patel had his legitimate claims; he accepted the decision but the tension remained between the fiery Left-wing ideologue Nehru and the pragmatic Rightist Patel. They were to be the crucial team for the next fifteen years till 1950 when Patel died. (It has been suggested by some cynics that Gandhi chose Nehru over Patel because he was a Brahmin, while Patel was from a 'backward' caste. I doubt this. Nehru was younger and obviously the person who could keep the younger, more radical generation with the Congress. It proved to be a brilliant choice, perhaps the best of the many that the Mahatma had to make in his lifetime.)

The young radical socialists would have chosen not to participate in the elections, as their leader Nehru preferred a mass movement based on a class strategy of mobilizing peasants and workers. But the more moderate Congressmen, including Sardar Patel, Rajendra Prasad and Rajagopalachari, who saw Congress as a universal rather than a class organization, were for entry. The moderates won, thanks to Gandhi's influence on Nehru. In the event, Congress proved to be a formidable election winning machine. The active agitators, who had come to the succour of rent strikers in the villages and courted arrest in the cities, were now harnessed to election winning. The Congress was now ready for its eventual avatar as a political electoral machine.

The elections proved the strength of the Congress as the leading national party, but it also showed that it did not command support among the Muslims. But the Muslim League also did not command Muslim loyalty. Congress won a majority in five out of eleven provinces—Madras, Bihar, Orissa, the central provinces and Uttar Pradesh, and also a near majority in Bombay—eighty-six out of 175. It had contested only fifty-eight Muslim seats, and won twenty-six of them.

Thus, Congress established its claim as the largest single political force, winning 711 out of 1585 seats. Excluding the Muslim seats it won 683 out of 1103 seats, a 62 per cent success rate, though not the 85 per cent Gandhi had claimed at the second Round Table Conference. The Congress could be said to be the lead party in the heartlands—the five states where it had majority as well as Bombay—but not in the periphery. All the provinces where Congress won became part of post-Partition India. The only province it could claim in the periphery was NWFP, where Khan Abdul Ghaffar Khan's Red Shirts supported the Congress. This accident gave Congress the semblance of an All India party which it was not.

But, while Congress did not make a major breakthrough in the periphery, the Muslim League failed to make any impact at all. Out of 482 seats for Muslims, it won only a hundred. The Muslim vote went to provincial rather than national parties in Punjab, Sind and Bengal. In Punjab it contested only seven seats out of eighty-four and won two. In Bengal it won thirty-eight out of 117 seats and, in NWFP, none.

Having fought the elections and won, there was still the issue of taking office. Many in the Congress were ready to take office. But there was a split between the Right and the Left. After all, Nehru had said they would wreck the federation by entering the assemblies. So he was against taking office under British imperialism, a situation which had not arisen under the 1919 reforms. Nehru had been explicit about what that meant, 'Imperialism sometimes talks of co-operation but ... the ministers who accept office will have to do so at the price of surrender of much they might have stood for in public ... That is a humiliating position ... disillusion with us will spread across the land ...'[9]

To reconcile these two positions, the Congress tried to lay down preconditions for taking office which would restrict the powers of the governor. Since no other party had asked for it, Lord Zetland, the Secretary of State for India, was not inclined to bend solely for the Congress. It is important here to avoid the perils of hindsight: in 1937 it was not clear, even after the Congress had won a majority of non-Muslim seats, that it would rule India in the near future. Its claim to being the potential ruling party could yet be resisted on pragmatic grounds by the viceroy. The British position had not moved an inch. They were not about to entertain the Congress's exalted view of itself as the sole party in India. Thus Zetland restated his objection in a House of Lords debate on 8 April 1937, two months after the elections, that to give in to Congress would be 'a grave breach of faith with the minorities and others in India who have been promised the protection against the arbitrary rule of a majority ... reserve powers are an integral part of the Constitution ... they cannot be abrogated except by Parliament itself and ... the Governors cannot treat the Congress as a privileged body which is exempt from the provisions ... by which all Parties are bound.'

A near farcical situation developed with the Congress seeking a fig leaf which would cover its acquiescence in the 1935 arrangements. Gandhi tried to suggest a compromise formula which would square the circle—that the Congress wanted power but did not wish to appear to be collaborating with British imperialism. But Linlithgow and Zetland were not Irwin and Wedgewood Benn. There was no give. In the meantime, minority parties had formed governments in provinces where the Congress had won majority and were helping themselves to the fruits of power. Eventually, as has happened so often, the Congress compromised with a small concession from Linlithgow. But there was still Nehru to please. After struggling with his conscience and having been persuaded by Gandhi of his importance to the national cause, Nehru acquiesced. Faced with the prospect of limited power, the Congress, as always, took the half-loaf, though grumbling all the while.[10]

Elections confirmed the fears of Muslim leaders that if push came to shove, the Hindu majority would dominate the Muslim minority. In UP the Congress had won a majority. There was an expectation, indeed a pre-poll understanding that it would form a coalition government with the League, but it refused to do so. The Congress was into coalitions in some provinces, but not with the League as partners. This episode is often said to be the beginning of the final rupture which led to Partition, but that is with hindsight. The problem was a clash of visions about the nature of Indian-ness in a democratic set up. Even where they did not have a majority, there was no coalition of the Congress with the League. In Bengal the Congress had hoped Fazlul Haq of the Krishak Praja Party would invite it into a coalition, but in the event, the antagonism of Bengali Hindu landlords to agrarian reform (which would benefit their Muslim tenants) meant there was no agreement. Fazlul Haq went with the League whose anti-reform landlords were in UP and Bihar, not Bengal. In Bombay the chief minister designate, B.G. Kher (whom Patel imposed over the legitimate claims of K.F. Nariman, a Parsi who was the Congress leader) wrote to Jinnah about plans to form a coalition. Jinnah insisted that Gandhi rather than Kher write to him proposing the scheme. Gandhi did not feel like obliging, and gave one of his 'inner voice' replies: 'I wish I could do something but I am utterly helpless. My faith in [Hindu–Muslim] unity is as bright as ever. Only I see no daylight out of the impenetrable darkness and in such distress I cry out to God'.[11] God obviously said no. Jinnah cleverly got another stick to beat the Congress with.

For Nehru and his socialist colleagues in Congress, it was class rather than religion which was the major demarcation category among citizens. Nehru especially, being an atheist, regarded religious belief as a sign of economic backwardness which would erode with progress. His was a liberal democratic vision mixed with the recently fashionable Marxism of the Popular Front, which Stalin had launched in 1935. His more conservative Congress colleagues were religiously inclined, and Hindu, with the rare exception of Maulana Azad. For Patel and Prasad and Rajagopalachari, the Congress's claim to represent India was based as much on Gandhi's ecumenical persona and charisma as on a Hindu majoritarian calculus. Nehru did not see India as consisting of Hindus and Muslims, but of rich and poor, with Congress on the side of the poor. His colleagues knew better. Nehru did not wish for a coalition with the League in UP because of its reactionary policies; his colleagues were just happy not to have to share power with the League.

Jinnah had been persuaded to return from England when the prospect of elections under the 1935 Act came up. But he was not as yet a popular mass leader. He could see that in the new atmosphere, the League would have to transform itself into an electoral organization. It also had to prove its claim that it was the sole representative of the Muslims. For this he had to face a double obstacle. In the two large Muslim majority provinces—Punjab and Bengal—there were powerful local parties which had no time for the League. The Union Party led by Sir Sikandar Hayat had a stranglehold on the Punjab assembly and did not wish to make itself a Muslim party. In Bengal the Congress had been weakened since Chittaranjan Das died and Subhash Bose had taken over. More conservative Congressmen, such as B.C. Roy, disputed Bose's claim and Gandhi managed to force Bose out of the Congress presidentship when he tried to seek a second term in 1938. The Muslim majority of Bengal had chosen to cast their lot with an agrarian reformist party—the Krishak Praja Party. Its leaders, Fazlul Haq and H.S. Suhrawardy, had strong local roots and championed the cause of Muslim peasantry and Calcutta's urban Muslims respectively, while Congress membership reflected Hindu landlords and urban middle-class bhadralok. Jinnah had to recruit Haq to the Muslim cause and also win over Punjab somehow. He also had to establish a League presence in Sind and attempt to do so in the NWFP.[12]

Jinnah's problem was that the Muslim League's mass base, such as it was, was in UP and Bihar, with some support from the Muslim merchants of Bombay city. It was here that it had its active members, where the majority of Muslims lived, even though, paradoxically, they were not Muslim majority provinces. So UP was the chosen battleground for challenging the Congress on the streets. Nehru had noticed that the Congress had failed to win many Muslim seats, so he launched a Muslim membership recruitment campaign for the Congress ('mass contact' was the new mantra of the Popular Front politics across Europe). Jinnah could see that the Muslim vote, as of 1937, was neither with the League nor with the Congress. There was everything yet to fight for before the All India federation became a reality. He set about making the League into a mass party.

The breakdown in the coalition arrangements in UP, which the League believed the Congress had promised, was leveraged by Jinnah into a mass agitation about Hindu majoritarian rule being anti-Muslim, and alleging Congress atrocities against Muslims. On its side, the Congress encouraged the singing of *Vande mataram* which, since the Bengal Partition of 1905, had been a Congress anthem. Yet, it was based on the identification of Kali, the mother goddess, with India, the motherland, and leaders such as Aurobindo Ghose had instilled it with mystic religious significance. Was the singing of such a quasi-religious Sanskrit poem, in schools and colleges and at public gatherings, a nationalist act or a Hindu celebration? The Congress flag was flown over public buildings, and saluted. Thus, in singing a Sanskrit poem as the national anthem and saluting the Congress flag, the Congress seemed to say that India was synonymous with the Congress. But was this the case or was the Congress only one of the parties, albeit the largest one in India? The presumption that the Congress was the sole body capable of representing India was to be the principal weapon the party wielded in the next ten years. It was to cause a lot of problems.

It was this presumption and the reigniting of communal riots, which Congress governments were alleged of having dealt with by an asymmetric treatment of Muslim as against Hindu rioters, which formed the gist of Jinnah's mass protest about 'Congress atrocities'. Even though Nehru soon persuaded the Congress Working Committee to forbid the singing of *Vande mataram* (and thus sparked a low intensity quarrel which persists to this day as to the status of the song in a secular India), Jinnah had now got the bit between his teeth. He had rattled the UP Congress government. Congress failed to recruit many Muslim members; indeed Nehru confessed to Rajendra Prasad, 'there is no doubt that we have been unable to check the growth of communalism and anti-Congress feeling among the Muslim masses'.[13]

Provincial autonomy proved to be a useful apprenticeship in democratic self-government, even under strained circumstances. There were politicians across India who became ministers and assembly members, and got to grips with practical issues. As an agitational movement, the Congress was embarrassed when it had to wield police powers and allow the use of *lathi*s, which they had previously felt on their own backs. Of the top leadership of the Congress, only Rajagopalachari became chief minister of Madras, his home state. This was necessary because the Congress was fighting with the Justice Party, and had to widen its appeal. The Congress also tried its best to pursue a reformist programme, both in the agrarian sphere and elsewhere, implementing Gandhi's programme of prohibition. In non-Congress provinces like Punjab and Bengal, the parties in power were also successful in creating a basis for the devolution of political power, as and when an All India federation came about. The arrival of the federation was slowed down by the reluctance of the princes to sign up, no doubt encouraged by the conservatives who wished to see no increase of power to the nationalist movement. Had the federation been implemented despite its many concessions to the reactionary princes, time and patience may have worked out a gradual solution to the contradiction of Congress being a party in power, while at the same time opposing British imperialism. This was not to happen. Once again, the focus of action determining India's future shifted back to Britain.

WAR IN EUROPE

The decade of the 1930s had been turbulent in Europe. On the one hand, the horrendous effects of mass unemployment had taken their toll on Britain, where hunger marches were seen for the first time ever; but the 1936 elections still returned the National government, now openly Conservative, to power. Baldwin became prime minister again, and MacDonald was out of office. The Labour Party improved its strength from forty-six in 1931 to 154, but the National Party, mainly Conservatives, had 432, down from 556 in 1931, but still a large majority. Attlee surprised everyone by being elected leader, replacing Lansbury. The Marquis of Zetland became Secretary of State for India and Linlithgow, who had chaired the joint committee of both Houses on constitutional reform as well as the Royal Commission on Indian agriculture, became the viceroy/governor general. Churchill, still on the back benches, was now warning against the dangers of German rearmament, but he was ignored, as he was on India. The public mood was pacifist. The Labour Party was for disarmament, and for making the League of Nations an effective organization.

But Mussolini in Italy and Hitler in Germany had thrown down a challenge to liberal democracy and *laissez faire*. The fascists had their origins in socialism. Though they had now become violent and racist movements, they were able to generate full employment in their economies using the weapons of state credit and military expenditure. They were the first to introduce planning in a mixed economy. In the USSR also there was planning and full employment, though the horrors of collectivization had imposed a great cost on the rural population. But clever propaganda by Comintern had disguised such tragedies as the class war against the peasantry, and the USSR was still seen as a challenge to capitalism. In France there was a growing fascist movement and, even though socialists won the elections in 1936 under Leon Blum, they were beleaguered by myriad economic problems. America had seen a revival under the New Deal, and Roosevelt was trying to experiment with proto-Keynesian policies which promised to save liberal capitalism.[14]

The year 1935 may have been the last one when Europe was still in some sort of peace. In Asia the Japanese assault on Manchuria, which was later extended further into China, had already begun. Hitler's rearmament started in earnest soon after as he reoccupied the Ruhr, while the old Allies stood by, helpless. Mussolini invaded Ethiopia, and the League of Nations was paralysed into inaction. Franco displaced the democratically elected republican government in Spain, and a civil war of murderous proportions started, which became a rehearsal for the coming war. In 1938 Hitler demanded territorial concessions from the Allied powers, especially the Sudetenland region of Czechoslovakia. Neville Chamberlain, who had succeeded Baldwin as the British PM, acquiesced. The Munich Pact was hailed as 'Peace for our time', but proved a delusion. Stalin and Hitler signed a pact—the Molotov–Ribbentrop Pact. Hitler then demanded territory in Poland, and Britain and France declared war on Germany in September 1939; Italy joined on the German side.

It was taken for granted in London that the empire was part and parcel of the war effort. India, especially, would once again be crucial for the military effort, given the size and the fighting efficiency of the Indian army. There had been no self-government granted at the Centre, and the viceroy was still in charge of choosing some elected members and some officials as part of his Executive. Defence was one of the 'safeguards' in the 1935 Act. The Congress, however, took the position that India (in other words, the Congress) should have been consulted before it was committed to war. This may have been a radical position, but it was not realistic. Linlithgow, in stating the intention for future constitutional developments in India, went no further than what the 1935 Act offered. He was in no mood to make concessions and, even if he wanted to, Parliament back in London would never have backed him.

The Congress was, at this time, not unaware of the European dimensions of the problem. Nehru had been a frequent traveller to Europe, and had been in touch with socialist parties there. He had been moved by the Spanish Civil War, and even visited the battlegrounds. He knew that fascism was an illiberal force, which had to be fought. His colleagues in the Congress would have deferred to him in whatever course of action he suggested. For Nehru, anti-imperialism at home took precedence over anti-fascism in Europe. He had always been reluctant for the Congress to take office under the 1935 Act. He persuaded the Congress Working Committee to ask its ministries to resign, since the viceroy had not offered any advance on the status quo, such as a popular ministry at the Centre charged with war mobilization.

Once again, things were not straightforward. The Congress went on putting conditions to the viceroy as a price for its cooperation. The viceroy did not give much weight to the Congress position. The army was not under Congress control and even if a federation had come about with Congress control of the central assembly, the army would still not have been under its control. The Congress had no following in the army, which stayed remarkably loyal (except for the prisoners taken by the Japanese who formed the corps of the Indian National Army, which was still some years away—about which, more below). Congress agitation would not have affected the recruitment of the army, since the provinces where it took place were not under the Congress.

Gandhi's attitude to the war was, to put it most kindly, idiosyncratic, if not eccentric. He had been given, of late, to some shockingly heartless pronouncements—such as when he blamed India's sin of untouchability for the earthquake in Bihar in which 20,000 had died. This made even Nehru apoplectic: 'This was a staggering remark ... Anything more opposed to the scientific outlook it would be difficult to imagine ... The idea of sin and divine wrath and man's relative importance in the affairs of the universe—they take us back a few hundred years, when the Inquisition flourished in Europe and burned Giordano Bruno for his scientific heresy and sent many a witch to the stake!'[15]

This was not all. Now in his sixties, weakened by many fasts and his own experiments with esoteric natural physical cures, the Mahatma was increasingly unpredictable. Thus, when he suspended another Civil Disobedience movement in 1934, he cited the following as a reason:

A revealing information I got in the course of a conversation about a valued companion of long standing who was found reluctant to perform the full prison task, preferring his private studies to the allotted task. This was undoubtedly contrary to the rules of Satyagraha. More than the imperfection of the friend whom I love more than ever[,] it brought home to me my own imperfections. The friend said he had thought that I was aware of his weakness. I was blind. Blindness in a leader is unpardonable. I saw at once that I must for the time being remain the sole representative of civil resistance in action.[16]

This is the first clear public sign of Gandhi's belief that the ills of the world persisted because of some defect in his own character: 'Blindness in a leader is unpardonable.' This is very much a Christian, not a Hindu, doctrine. Krishna says to Arjuna in the *Bhagavad Gita* that whenever there is a lack of the right moral order (dharma), he takes birth to succour the virtuous and punish the evil ones. That is the task of God in Hinduism. But to take on the sins of the world on your own shoulders, or to cure its ills by better perfecting yourself, implies a special status for oneself. That is what Jesus is said to have done. Here are echoes of Gandhi's esoteric Christian past. This was to be his concern increasingly over the years till his death, as the world got worse and worse in his view.

Sitting in his jail cell while he read this, Nehru was baffled. All that had happened was that Mahadev Desai, Gandhi's devoted Secretary and amanuensis, had taken up the study of French while in prison. This was hardly the moral equivalent of a mob burning down a police station at Chauri Chaura, which had led to the suspension of the Non-cooperation movement, irrational though that decision was as well. It was, of course, the case that the movement was getting nowhere, and Willingdon was being much tougher than Irwin. But to make poor Mahadev Desai a scapegoat for his harmless interest in French was a cruel act, though swathed in protestations of love. No wonder he died young at the age of fifty, having served Gandhi devotedly half his life. As Nehru reflected, the Non-cooperation movement '... was a vast national movement involving scores of thousands directly and millions indirectly to be thrown out of gear because an individual has erred? This seemed to me a monstrous proposition and an immoral one.'[17]

'His increasingly obvious irrationality', as Kathryn Tidrick calls it, 'was in full flow during the war years.'[18] He just would not see the seriousness of the situation. In many ways he was a product of the Victorian era. Faced with the evils of Nazism and Hitler, he failed to see that this was a much different order of cruelty than what he had protested against. He thought Hitler may be amenable to non-violent protest. After all, he was a vegetarian and teetotaller. To quote Tidrick again, 'He admired Hitler for his "dash, energy, resourcefulness and capacity, his bravery, dedication, powers of concentration and organization, and unclouded intellect ... He has no vices. He has not married. His character is said to be clean. He is always alert".' She concludes, 'He had a fundamental incomprehension of how bad Hitler was'.[19]

Gandhi's idiosyncracy also undermined his credibility when he appealed to Britons to lay down their arms and 'invite Herr Hitler and Signor Mussolini to take what they want of the countries you call your possessions', to 'take possession of your beautiful island'. Let them 'occupy your homes' and if 'they do not give you a free passage out', 'the British should let themselves be slaughtered'.[20] Even his long-standing South African friend and admirer, Henry Pollak was offended by such callousness. He wrote a long and agonized letter to Gandhi:

And when I hear you echoing Jawaharlal's endless repetition of the mantram of 'British Imperialism', as though this had anything in common, either in theory or in practice, with the calculated bestiality and horror of Nazi torture of the unoffending Jews, or persecution and terrorism of the Czechs and the Poles; when I see you hesitate even for a moment in throwing all the forces of India into the balance in order to destroy for ever a truly 'Satanic Government' (to use an old and misapplied term of your own) I am amazed and shocked that either [illegible] ... you , trained in a knowledge of English and the use of language, should put your country to shame by confusing issues and misusing its trust in your guidance! If you had a drop of Jewish blood in you, you could not have rested until, without hatred and without a desire for vengeance, but from the deepest and holiest sense of duty such as Sri Krishna spoke to Arjuna, you had done your uttermost to destroy a locust regime that is seeking to devour every beautiful thing that mankind, intuitively realising its godly nature, has been developing during the ages of its development.[21]

Gandhi's reply in person to Pollak is quite short, but he refers to Pollak in his public reply in the *Harijan* of 15 December 1939. In the article he quotes excerpts from Pollak's letter, and then at the outset of his reply says, 'When in doubt on a matter involving no immorality either way, I toss and actually read in it divine guidance ... The Congress way was not only not immoral, for it, it was the only moral way.' After some further defence of the Congress position, he says, 'I do not lay down the law as you do about Nazism. Germans are as much human beings as you and I are. Nazism like other "isms" is a toy of today. It will share the same fate as other "isms".'[22]

In the long run, we are all dead, as an economist said; so a few millions dying is neither here nor there, seems to be Gandhi's message to Pollak. For Gandhi and the Congress, nothing could be more important than the national struggle. Yet, for Britain at this juncture, there was a life and death struggle going on. France had surrendered and in Europe only Britain was left to fight Hitler. Dunkirk had witnessed a messy, yet heroic effort by soldiers and civilians to escape the pursuing German soldiers across Normandy. Parliament was fed up with Chamberlain by April 1940. In a crucial speech from the Tory back benches, Leo Amery ended with Oliver Cromwell's exhortation to the Long Parliament, 'You have been here too long. In God's Name, go'. There was a power struggle in the British Cabinet where the appeasers, Chamberlain and Halifax were replaced by Churchill who became PM. Halifax was sent to the USA as ambassador, and Anthony Eden, who had resigned over Munich, became Foreign Secretary. Churchill presided over a coalition Cabinet with Attlee as Lord Privy Seal. Leo Amery became Secretary of State for India. There was total mobilization as bombs dropped over London, and thousands of children had to be evacuated away from their parents who stayed behind in London.

The Congress and Gandhi, in the meantime, had to do something to make their presence felt, but it was not clear what they could do. The Congress's strength was in mobilizing the masses in some sort of unarmed action, though, not necessarily non-violent as Gandhi would insist. But the Congress Working Committee, by itself, had already blown its one chance of making a public demonstration of its position by resigning rather than waiting to be sacked by the governor for taking a radical policy decision. All mass mobilization could only be done by Gandhi, medieval and unscientific though he might be.

So once again, Gandhi was left with the decision on the modalities of protest. He thought the war was the biggest challenge to his philosophy of non-violence. In September 1940 he said, 'If India can win *swaraj* non-violently even while this conflagration is going on, the latter is bound to be extinguished by that one event.'[23] This is an astonishing statement, and one cannot take it seriously. It was perhaps a hope rather than an expectation on his part. Yet, Gandhi did not trust a mass civil disobedience campaign, since he was not sure the protesters would follow his philosophy of non-violence. As in the Dandi march, he decided to select a few individuals whom he could trust to be reliable. So he chose individuals who met with his approval as being sound *brahmacharis*—Vinoba Bhave first and Nehru, a recent widower next. His search for perfection within himself was to focus on his being able to practise *brahmacharya*—abnegation from sexual, even sensual feelings and acts. Hence Vinoba, who was much like himself, and Nehru, who being a widower Gandhi presumed to be abnegating. Gandhi could not imagine extramarital sex, on Nehru's part or, indeed, of anyone else's. This is why he thought Hitler was a good man since he was unmarried. The satyagrahis got nowhere, as they were sent to jail before they could make any impact: Nehru for four years, which even Churchill, now PM, thought too much. Twenty thousand more satyagrahis followed, and then Gandhi saw the futility of the gesture and suspended the movement.

In its ineffectualness, the resignation of the Congress ministries was another 'Himalayan blunder'. As it happened, India's contribution to the war effort was superb, and may even have been a major reason for hurrying India's Independence. Some two-and-a-half million Indian soldiers and ancillary workers helped in the war effort. The Indian army was used to foreign deployments, and performed heroically in the Second World War. The payments for the materials bought by Britain for its war effort, some £1 billion in sterling balances (£100 billion in today's prices, roughly), were used by the Government of India after Independence. The presence or absence of Congress made little difference. So the resignation was, one has to say, a quixotic gesture. It harmed Congress in the medium run. For the next five years, Congress was in the wilderness, mounting lame satyagraha struggles or, in jail. Britain was under a major threat of being conquered, and there was no chance that Linlithgow would allow any disturbances. The strong-arm tactics, which began under Willingdon, continued under him. Time after time, attempts to mount a civil disobedience struggle were foreclosed at the outset, and the demonstrators locked up. The Congress was rendered impotent as the conflict raged in Europe. The stakes, which were high in September 1939, had increased after the fall of France, as Britain stood alone except for her empire, which was her only ally. As the war years passed, it looked less and less likely that the Congress gambit was the right one.

But then as luck would have it, within the next two years events in the wider world came to the rescue of the Congress.

THE CRIPPS MISSION

Two events helped Britain and—even more—the Congress. In June 1941 Hitler decided to invade Russia. He had signed the Molotov–Ribbentrop Pact, but this was just to win time while he sorted out his western front. He launched Operation Barbarossa and Britain could heave a sigh of relief as the fighting in Europe shifted eastwards, though it continued in North Africa. In December 1941 Japan attacked Pearl Harbour, and this brought USA into the war. A European war became a world war. This was a real bonus for the Congress, because the Americans had an anti-imperialist ideology in those days. They would fight, but not to shore up empires. American journalists—international figures including Louis Fischer, John Günther and William Shirer—had visited India and talked to Gandhi. India's case had been put before the Americans positively for the most part, but also negatively by Katharine Mayo in her book, *Mother India*. On balance, there was much sympathy for India and less so for Britain with whom, after all, the American colonists had fought to become independent. Churchill used his charm on FDR and got much help, but he had to accommodate the American demand that something be done about India. The alliance between the USSR, the USA and Britain meant that two out of three Allies were not friends of the British Empire.

It was in this context that Churchill was obliged by the Americans to show willing to discuss India's future. In December 1941, at their very first meeting, Roosevelt had raised the issue of India with Churchill. The Americans were not yet actively involved in the European conflict, but were willing to provide help to the British. Britain had been the sole European power fighting for a year and more on its own resources, and Churchill was an eager supplicant for help. Sir Tej Bahadur Sapru, along with his fellow Liberals, saw his chance and sent a telegram to Churchill in Washington appealing for a 'bold stroke [of] far-sighted statesmanship ... without delay'.[24] Having massaged Churchill's ego, they asked for a non-official national government subject to responsibility only to the Crown, and for the restoration of popular governments in provinces where there were none, that is, Congress provinces. This was a careful manoeuvre by loyal Indians who had accumulated a few goodwill points by their impeccable negotiating behaviour over the years. Sapru even conceded that the final constitutional arrangements could wait till after 'victory achieved in this titanic struggle against forces threatening civilisation'.[25]

Sapru managed to disseminate his telegram to the press around the world and sent the viceroy's private Secretary a copy. He knew the Labour members of the British Cabinet would be on his side. Attlee was, of course, strongly on the side of change in India, though not on Congress terms as he was worried about minority rights. Sir Stafford Cripps had also struck up a friendship with Nehru just before war broke out. He and Nehru were on the same wavelength, as they analysed the world through quasi-Marxian spectacles. They had corresponded since 1936, and Nehru had spent a weekend in 1938 with Cripps at his vast country mansion, Goodfellows, in Gloucestershire.

Cripps was a vegetarian teetotaller, but also a chain smoker; he was a barrister with a rich practice in commercial law and maverick enough to have been thrown out of the Labour Party, along with Aneurin Bevan, for his ultra-Left views. These were the years in which Stalin was on a charm offensive. In the early 1930s, all non-communist parties of the Left had been treated as enemies by the communists. In Germany the Communist Party allowed Hitler to gain power, since they were much more involved in their fight with the Socialist Party. Soon after his installation as chancellor, Hitler began an attack on all Left parties using the firebombing of the Reichstag building as his excuse. Stalin saw his error and launched the Popular Front, which was to unite all Left forces for an anti-fascist struggle. This was a very effective strategy, attracting many socialists and Social Democrats to Marxist ideas. Cripps and Bevan—and indeed, Nehru—were much taken by the Popular Front.[26]

Cripps had been sent to Moscow as a special envoy to parley with Stalin, and had won the confidence of the Russians. This meant that by the end of 1941 Britain had allies west and east, though Russia could not spare resources as USA could. Cripps became immensely popular in the country and, when he came back from Russia in early 1942, he was rated just below Anthony Eden as the man to succeed Churchill, should anything happen to the PM. Churchill was quite envious of Cripps's popularity. As he later recalled, 'There were some on the extreme Left who appeared to regard him as worth running as an alternative Prime Minister, and in these circles it was said that he would lead the new group of critics of the Government, which it hoped to organize into an effective force.'[27]

Churchill had to accommodate Cripps as the government was facing a no-confidence motion in the House of Commons in late January 1942. It won the vote handsomely. In the next Cabinet reshuffle Cripps was made Lord Privy Seal, and was seen as a senior member of the Cabinet. To mollify Attlee's displeasure at the promotion of a Labour Party renegade, Attlee was made deputy prime minister and leader in the House of Commons, a post previously held by Churchill himself.

In many ways Cripps was an English version of Gandhi in his food habits and his saintliness. 'He usually had one meal a day, consisting of vegetable, sour milk, wholemeal bread and butter, and an occasional baked potato.'[28] Sarojini Naidu, the poet and perhaps the only one with a sense of irreverent humour in the Congress party, had remarked that it was very expensive to maintain Gandhi in his poverty. Cripps's frugal eating habits were no less of a problem as the royal family discovered when he came to lunch after joining Cabinet, for he ate up their entire week's egg ration in one meal!

Once the war started, Stafford Cripps traded down from his large country residence, Goodfellows, to a smaller cottage, Filkins, in Oxfordshire. Though his home had ample proportions relative to his fellow barristers, for a man reputed to be making £50,000 at the Bar, it was modest. The Illustrated Weekly of India ran a picture under the caption 'Cripps's Cottage Home—as simple in its western way as Gandhi's hut'.[29] Churchill remarked of Cripps, 'He bore himself as though he had a message to deliver'.[30]

In the months which had elapsed since Pearl Harbour, Japan had swept through East and South-East Asia. It had invaded China in 1933 and Korea was its colony. Now, it scythed its way through Indo-China, and on 15 February 1942, Singapore fell. The war in Europe had come nearer to India. There was a serious possibility of a Japanese invasion of India. Previously, India had been a major source of supply of men and material, now it suddenly gained greater priority in the global strategic picture. Burma was to fall soon (in fact, Rangoon fell on 8 March 1942) and the North-East Frontier Area would become the battleground where the Japanese were halted.

Churchill announced, in the House of Commons on 11 March 1942, that the British government had decided to send Stafford Cripps to India to discuss a new draft declaration on British policy about India's future with major political leaders. This was, in a sense, Churchill's reply to Sapru's telegram. The American push was forceful. As Churchill wrote to Linlithgow, 'It would be impossible owing to unfortunate rumours and publicity, and the general American outlook, to stand on a purely negative attitude and the Cripps Mission is indispensable to prove our honesty of purpose ... If it is rejected by the Indian parties ... our sincerity will be proved to the world.'[31] Churchill had not changed his dogged opposition to giving up India. When, as a new Secretary of State for India, Amery tried to accommodate some of the demands Congress had made, Churchill told him he would 'rather go out in the wilderness and fight, than to admit a revolution which meant the end of the Imperial Crown in India'.[32] Cripps came to India on 23 March.

Churchill was shrewd in anticipating that the Indian parties—that is, the Congress—were more likely to reject than accept the Cripps Mission. It was yet another half-loaf and the Congress, with its well-known negotiating stance, was bound to ask for more, war or no war. What the Congress had not foreseen was that among the parties Cripps was to consult in India, Jinnah would be the sole Muslim spokesman. Since there was a war, the discussions of India's constitutional future could not be carried out with a new Round Table Conference in London. There was no time for elaborate and widespread consultations in India either. The 1937 elections had, in any case, narrowed down the list of parties who had any claim to represent Indian people. From now on, negotiations were around a small table rather than a large round one. Personalities mattered. This is where Jinnah's chance came.

CHAPTER 9

JINNAH'S HOUR

THE LAHORE RESOLUTION AND THE
RAMGARH RESPONSE

While the Congress had gone into self-imposed political exile, Jinnah had been following his game plan. At Lahore in March 1940, just over ten years since Nehru had led Congress members into taking a vow of purna swaraj, the Muslim League passed its famous Pakistan Resolution. The word Pakistan does not appear in the resolution itself, but the name—an invention of a Cambridge student, Chaudhary Rehmat Ali and Khwaja Abdur Rahman, a civil servant, while having refreshments at the Waldorf Astoria in the Aldwych—had been around since the early 1930s. (Across from the Indian High Commission at India House, there used to be a plaque on the wall outside the Waldorf Astoria commemorating this event, but it has disappeared lately.) The distinguished poet, lawyer and freedom fighter, Mohammed Iqbal had spoken of it at a Muslim League annual conference in Allahabad in 1930, but in terms of a 'North West Indian Muslim State'. The League could muster only seventy-five people to hear this historic speech as it was then a ramshackle outfit.

Iqbal had the rare distinction of writing songs which celebrated the glories of both nations—India and Pakistan. Iqbal's poem '*Saare jahan se achcha Hindostan hamara*' (Our Hindustan is better than any other country in the world) was much sung in India, as it could be sung by Muslims and Hindus alike since it was a secular song. Along with *Vande mataram*, it was sung on the 50th anniversary celebrations of Indian Independence in the Indian Parliament. He also wrote the national anthem of Pakistan. To complicate matters of identity, his family descended from Kashmiri Brahmins like Nehru's, but had converted to Islam.

The idea of Pakistan progressed further when Sir Abdullah Haroon, a prominent businessman and politician from Sind, proposed a separate clubbing together of the four Muslim majority provinces in the north-west of India. His ideas were soon taken up by some Aligarh intellectuals and discussed keenly in the corridors of the Muslim League's conferences. There is a long-standing notion among Muslims that the laws of the infidel should not be obeyed. During the Khilafat movement, even Maulana Azad spoke of the dual loyalty to the Osmani caliphate and also to India. This idea hovered around in some of the early Pakistani proposals. The experience of Congress majority rule sharpened this vision in the Muslim minority provinces, where the largest proportion of Muslim middle classes lived. Pakistan was, territorially, still a vague notion. Areas where Muslims had a substantial presence, though not with a majority, were more numerous than just the four states of the north-west and Bengal. Thus, apart from the areas of UP and Bihar, Hyderabad, the Nizam's kingdom, and the valley of Kashmir in the Jammu and Kashmir kingdom of Hari Singh had a large Muslim presence. Delhi was also much coveted as a Muslim city. Pakistan had an appeal precisely because of its vagueness and its fluid boundaries. Jinnah knew this. He had to build a political consensus around this vague but powerful notion.[1]

Jinnah had taken care to get Sir Sikandar Hayat and Fazlul Haq on board. He did not have the position within the Muslim League that Gandhi, or even Nehru, had in the Congress. This, despite the fact that his political career in India spanned a longer time—he had been with Tilak as far back as 1908. He was younger than Gandhi but older than Nehru, and had been a young rising star of the Congress in the first decade of the twentieth century. Unlike Gandhi, but like Nehru, he was a secular atheist and had quit Congress in 1921 because he could not abide Gandhi's religiosity which, in his opinion, had also encouraged Muslim obscurantists like the Ali brothers. He was shrewd enough to see that he would need to weave and tack if he wanted himself to be the sole spokesman for Muslims. He made himself uncharacteristically modest and pliable. At this juncture religion played little part as Jinnah needed not people like the Ali brothers, but those who wielded power in the Muslim majority provinces. He got Sir Sikandar Hayat to draft the Lahore Resolution, and Fazlul Haq to move it. Choudhry Khaliquzzaman, a veteran of the UP Muslim League and, until the breakdown of the coalition talks a member of the Congress as well, seconded the motion.

At this stage Pakistan was a scheme to use provincial autonomy, which had been granted in 1935 to group together Muslim majority provinces as a sub-federation within an All India federation. As the resolution demanded, 'geographically contiguous units are demarcated into regions which should be so constituted, with such territorial readjustments as may be necessary, that the areas in which the Muslims are numerically in a majority should be grouped to constitute "Independent States", in which the constituent units shall be autonomous and sovereign'.[2] There was, as yet, no idea of a partition of British India into two 'nation states'. The regions—note the plural—with Muslim majorities were to be 'independent states'—again plural. (Later in 1946, with the prospect of Pakistan nearer, Jinnah bullied the Muslim League leadership into changing the plural 'states' to a singular 'state'. This would later create trouble with East Pakistan.) The constituent units within the regions were to be 'autonomous and sovereign'. The 1935 Act signified that the Princely States would be individually autonomous and sovereign. So, in a way, this was just extending that idea to individual provinces, and then allowing them to group together.

At this point ideas about the kind of federation India was going to be were very vague, since everyone knew Parliament would have to legislate the next stage in any case. The princes' reluctance to join led to various suggestions that made the federation formula more flexible. The USSR Constitution of 1936 guaranteed—on paper at least—sovereign autonomy to each republic within the Union. Other federations, such as Australia, also had states as original members, which came together to create a federation. The USA started with thirteen original colonies, and went to war in 1861 to prevent secession by the South on the issue of states' rights. The Union was saved at an enormous cost in terms of human lives, but individual states, nonetheless, retained a lot of autonomy until the Great Depression necessitated the New Deal and a strong federal government.

That was not the kind of model India could follow. The British government had created a strongly centralized polity until the issue of Dominion Status came up. The provinces were creations of the Centre—as in the case of Sind and Orissa in 1936. The bulk of the nationalist movement was wedded to a strong Centre, which for them had priority over individual provinces. This was why the 1935 Act arrangement did not satisfy anyone. Jinnah saw that even if he did not succeed in having minority rights guaranteed, he could still carve off a sub-federation or two, where Muslims could live in relative autonomy from a Hindu majority Central government as long as the 1935 Act still held sway. It was a bargaining chip which Jinnah hoped would come in handy some day.

The Congress version of the history of the independence struggle refuses to accept that Pakistan was not just a fiendish plot by British imperialists who merely wanted to divide and rule. Thus, Jinnah is seen as a puppet or worse, a stooge, of the British. But there was a vacuum in politics created by the Congress's resignations. If there had to be negotiations at the All India level, with the princes out of the count for the time being, it had to be between the representatives of the two major 'communities' of British India. The bulk of Muslims lived in British India, not in the Princely States. The Congress argued that there was only one community in India—Indians, and the Congress was its sole representative. If there was a minority problem, it was entirely due to the presence of the imperialists. Once they departed the problem would solve itself. The solution was to grant independence first and let the Indians sort the problem out. The Congress proposed that a new constituent assembly would be elected, even accepting separate electorates for that purpose. If the minorities disagreed with the majority, a neutral arbitrator would decide, and the decision would be implemented. Gandhi had said this and Maulana Azad reiterated this in his presidential speech at the Congress's Ramgarh session in December 1940.

But after the elections of 1937, this was not a tenable claim. The Congress was the largest single party over all, and in a majority in five, or at most six (if Bombay was included, or even by a stretch seven if NWFP was counted) provinces. But its exclusion from the legislatures of the three Muslim majority provinces in the north-west and its minority position in Bengal meant that it could not be presumed to speak for Muslims. What was more, Jinnah could claim that the conduct of the Congress governments had been partisan towards the Hindu majority and negligent of Muslim grievances. How then could he trust that any award by a neutral arbitrator would be implemented, since a Hindu majority would be in power if the British left?

Thus, it is hardly sinister to say as Linlithgow told Jinnah in February 1940, 'British sympathy should not be expected for a party whose policy was one of sheer negation'. No prizes for guessing which party he meant. So, 'If [Jinnah] and his friends wanted to secure that the Muslim case should not go by default in the UK, it was really essential that they should formulate their plan in the near future'.[3] From the British point of view, no fresh proposals had been made since the Round Table Conference, where no agreement had been reached on the minority issue. The 1937 elections had shown the fragmentation in the Muslim vote between the provincial parties in Punjab, Bengal and Sind, and between the League and the Congress. The Congress 'negation' was well-known. What was the Muslim alternative? It is hardly plausible to believe that before Linlithgow mentioned this idea to Jinnah, the latter had not thought about it himself. He was miles smarter than 'Hopie', as the viceroy was known. Nor can we say that the whole resolution was inspired by Linlithgow, and put together in the one month between February and March (even allowing for an extra day due to leap year!) There is ample evidence regarding the ferment of ideas, among Muslim politicians and intellectuals, on the notion of Pakistan which need not all be attributed to the hidden hand of British imperialism.

Jinnah's speech at the Lahore Congress bears some careful rereading. He mentions the resolution in passing, but his perspective is an internationalist one (unlike Azad's speech at the Ramgarh Congress in December 1940 which was, in a way, the answer to Jinnah's speech), as illustrated by his mention of the question of Palestine and the rights of Arabs there. Jinnah mentions the League and himself as being involved in parleys with the government, and 'our negotiations are not concluded yet'. But he is pleased to report that he is now on an equal footing with the Congress as far as the British are concerned. His pent-up resentment and newly found joy are reflected equally:

> Up to the time of the declaration of the war, the Viceroy never thought of me, but of Gandhi and Gandhi alone ... Therefore when I got this invitation from the Viceroy along with Mr. Gandhi, I wondered within myself why I was so suddenly promoted and then I concluded that the answer was the 'All India Muslim League', whose President I happen to be. I believe that was the worst shock that the Congress High Command received, because it challenged their sole authority to speak on behalf of India.[4]

Jinnah added, 'We stand unequivocally for the freedom of India. But it must be the freedom of all India, and not the freedom of one section or, worse still, of the Congress caucus, and slavery for the Musulmans and other minorities.' The crucial change in Jinnah's argument comes when he asserts, 'It has always been taken for granted mistakenly that the Musulmans are a minority, and of course we have got used to it for such a long time that these settled notions are very difficult to remove. The Musulmans are not a minority. The Musulmans are a nation by any definition.'[5]

This is a tectonic shift in the argument about minorities. What is a nation? It can be defined by religion, language, a common history or even a common enemy. But in a multi-lingual, multi faith, multi-ethnic country like India, what could be the basis for defining a single over-arching nationhood? Jinnah chose territory to define Muslim nationhood and thereby created a problem for himself and the Muslims of India living in Muslim minority provinces. Thus, continuing the idea of Muslims as a nation, he says, 'We find that even according to the British Map of India, we occupy large parts of this country where the Musulmans are in a majority—such as Bengal, Punjab, NWFP, Sind and Baluchistan.'[6] Jinnah's problem, which bedevilled the entire debate on this issue and has not been settled till today, was that he was unclear as to whether he was defining a *nation* or a *nation state*. Muslims as a nation were scattered all over India. Why would one single out the majority provinces as *the* nation, leaving the rest—the majority of Indian Muslims—in the *other* nation. Since his objection was to a majoritarian Hindu domination over a Muslim minority, why did he choose a majoritarian definition for the Muslim nation?

The answer is that, as of 1940 Jinnah was not angling for a separate nation state; he was bargaining for minority rights deploying his theory of regional concentration. This has been argued by Ayesha Jalal but disputed by most Indian and many British and American Indianists.[7] But again, hindsight is very difficult to avoid here. One can only say that in 1940, the demand was for a grouping of autonomous provinces within an All India federation—perhaps more of a confederation—with a weak Centre and strong provinces. The Congress was determined to have a strong central authority in independent India; indeed, the Congress was fighting not just for strong independent India but for one under Congress rule. Ever since 1929 this had always been consistently its demand, as when it turned down the invitation to the Round Table Conference unless its condition of majority representation was met. This was what Gandhi claimed in his speech at the second Round Table Conference. Again, upon the declaration of the war, the Congress demanded a national government at the Centre. Simplified to its bare bones its narrative was—the Congress was Gandhi and Gandhi was India. It is this hegemonic position that Jinnah set out to undermine.

Azad's Ramgarh speech, delivered in December 1940, was the response of a prominent 'nationalist' Muslim to Jinnah. It is said that Nehru helped much with the draft of the speech, and it does reflect what the received syncretist view of Indian nationhood became. Azad blames the communal issue squarely on the British. 'For a hundred and fifty years British imperialism has pursued the policy of divide and rule, and by emphasising internal differences, sought to use various groups for the consolidation of its own power.' Yet within a few sentences, Azad seems to shift the blame to Indians. 'It is obvious that India, like other countries, has her internal problems. Of these, the communal problem is an important one. We do not and cannot expect the British Government to deny its existence ... Every step that we take by ignoring it will be a wrong step ... To admit its existence, however, does not mean that it should be used as a weapon against India's national freedom.'[8]

He then states the Congress position which differs from what Jinnah attributes to Gandhi. Indeed, had the Congress more fully articulated the Azad position, there could have been some compromise. Azad states two conditions worth quoting in full:

(i) Whatever constitution is adopted for India, there must be the fullest guarantee in it for the rights of and interests of the minorities.

(ii) The minorities should judge for themselves what safeguards are necessary for the protection of their rights and interests. The majority should not decide this. Therefore the decision in this respect must depend upon the consent of the minorities and not on a majority vote.[9]

This position could be read as the nearest the Congress got to a consociational stand. It could have meant that minority rights would be subject to a referendum in which the minorities alone would vote. Of course, Azad does not go on to elaborate what the majority would do should one of the minorities reject the guarantee and ask for more. In the resolution passed at the Ramgarh session, however, arbitration is mentioned as a way to settle differences, and a minority plebiscite is not. So, we are back to the Gandhi position which Jinnah had already rejected. The Congress was confident, at this stage, that it would be the prime negotiator for independence as and when it was offered by the British.

In his memoirs published posthumously, Azad does not dwell on his Ramgarh speech which has acquired an iconic status in the secularist canon. The speech is cited not for its approach on the minorities' rights issue, but more for its statement of the syncretist position. It is a sophisticated restatement of Sir Syed's 1883 speech:

> It was India's historic destiny that many human races and cultures and religions should flow to her, finding a home in her hospitable soil, and that many a caravan should find rest here. Even before the dawn of history, these caravans trekked into India and wave after wave of new-comers followed. The vast and fertile land gave welcome to all and took them to her bosom. One of the last of these caravans was that of the followers of Islam. This came here and settled for good. This led to a meeting of the culture-currents of two different races. Like Ganga and Jamuna, they flowed for a while through separate courses, but nature's immutable law brought them together and joined them in a sangam. This fusion was a notable event in history. Since then, destiny, in her own hidden way, began to fashion a new India in place of the old. We brought our treasures with us, and India too was full of the riches of her own precious heritage. We gave our wealth to her and she unlocked the doors of her own treasures to us. We gave her, what she needed most, the most precious of gifts from Islam's treasury, the message of democracy and human equality.[10]

The syncretic view thus stated is an almost mystical version of history. It is also peculiar in its final claim of the gift of democracy and human equality by Islam, since none of the Muslim rulers conferred any democracy or, even, a scintilla of equality on either their Muslim or their non-Muslim subjects. Democracy, such as it was, had to wait, alas, for the arrival of the last caravan which does not get a mention—that of the British imperialists. But if one is to use American analogies, the union of races seems neither a melting pot, nor yet a tossed salad. Azad speaks of 'We' having brought something to India and India giving something back to 'us'. The blending is an uneasy one, even in this account. It also leaves all of South India out. Soon, fine words were not to suffice; the language in the next few years was to be legalist and political.

JINNAH'S ONWARD MARCH

In the two years since the Lahore Resolution, Jinnah had been assiduously working away at establishing his right to be the sole person at the top table. He was not going to be completely successful in his ambition till 1946, but as a veteran of negotiations with the British (at the Round Table Conference) and with the Congress (in Lucknow in 1916 and during the formulation of the Nehru Report in 1928), he had some right to expect that he would be that person. He had one advantage which many people did not possess: his opponents, especially Nehru, did not take him seriously. Nehru had convinced himself, in any case, that the League was a reactionary collection of Muslim landlords of UP. He failed to see the profound change Jinnah was about to make to the League. Jinnah was not a landowner as many Muslim League grandees were, and his origins were quite humble. He had not the luxury of a rich father or the patronage of a powerful Mahatma as Nehru had. He was not young and handsome and a darling of the masses—yet. He was an Anglicized Muslim who had married a Parsi woman many years his junior, and then lost her ten years later. He was a lonely man, and developed a thick carapace of elegant suits and fine manners to hide or, even, protect his loneliness. But he was also a superb lawyer, perhaps the best in terms of legal practice of any of the leaders of India in the first half of the twentieth century. He was also a skilled negotiator.

Jinnah had a weak hand to play, but he knew how to play it well. The tactic was not to show his hand till the finale of the poker game. Or, perhaps, the key to his tactics is revealed by his approach to billiards, the only game he seems to have been fond of. A vivid description is captured in Saadat Hasan Manto's record of Jinnah's chauffeur:

> Twelve balls would be placed in front of the sahib and he would carefully choose three and then begin playing ... Sahib would place his cigar between his lips and study the position of the ball that he planned to hit. This would take several minutes, as he would examine it from every angle. He would weigh the cue in his hand, run it over his long and slim fingers as if it was a bow he was going to play a stringed instrument with, take aim and then stop short of executing the stroke because he had thought of a better angle. He only played his shot when he was fully satisfied that it was the right one.[11]

Jinnah's personal style, his immaculately tailored clothes, his cigar, his hauteur was such a contrast to Gandhi that none in the Congress could believe the Muslim masses would take to him. But Gandhi's style was undeniably, and deliberately, that of a poor Hindu villager with a dhoti and a bare chest. Muslims in villages and towns seldom wore such clothes, or exposed themselves above their midriff. One sees through the eyes of a young Muslim what it meant to have Jinnah as leader. The first time Mohammed Hanif Azad, who became his chauffeur and whose account of the billiards was cited above, saw Jinnah was at the 1937 Muslim League meeting in Delhi.

> He was in a phaeton drawn by six horses, and every leading Muslim League leader marched that day with us ... My response to that procession was deeply emotional. I was completely overwhelmed. I do not even remember now what exactly I felt when I first set eyes on Jinnah sahib. When I look back and analyse my reaction, I realize that I was so taken with him, even before I had seen him, that if someone had pointed at a man, any man, and said to me, "There goes your Quaid-e-Azam," I would have believed him immediately and felt deliriously happy. That's the way faith is. Pure and without a trace of doubt ... I got a chance to look at Jinnah sahib from many angles. Then suddenly a thought came to my mind. How could my Quaid, my Great Leader be so gaunt, so weak, so frail.[12]

Manto, perhaps the finest Urdu prose writer, distilled these impressions from Hanif Azad, and later reflected on this frailty and wrote, 'Come to think of it, the secret of Quaid-e-Azam's strong character lay in his physical infirmity. He was always conscious of his fragility and it was this awareness that was his greatest strength.'[13]

The Congress strategy at this juncture was to ask for a national government during the war and for total independence, regardless of the settlement of the Hindu–Muslim issue. Trust us, it said, and we will solve the problem of minorities which is, in any case, a pure creation of you imperialists, and your mere departure will ease its solution.

Nehru had some right to hope that his friend, Stafford Cripps would indeed bring such a plan. They had agreed to something similar at a weekend meeting at Goodfellows in 1938. It involved 'the recognition of the Congress as representing a united India.' There was, however, a snag. It required the 'installation in Britain of a sympathetic government, and presumably on the commitment of the Labour Party to such a deal'.[14] Powerful and popular though Cripps was, and despite the presence of the Labour Party in the Cabinet, the Conservative party still had a majority. 'And an Imperialist "die-hard" was the Prime Minister and the War Leader the country needed.'[15]

The Cripps plan, originally, was to make a declaration of HMG's intentions about India's future, which would, at least, appease the Americans. Rival drafts circulated within Whitehall and were sent across to the viceroy who was most hostile to the idea of any such declaration. Still Cripps was in the driving seat:

> Within the India Committee [of the Cabinet] he and Attlee could, in Churchill's absence, generally secure Amery's and Anderson's [Sir John Anderson was chancellor of the Exchequer] support to carry the plan forward, and within the War Cabinet, Attlee, Cripps and Anderson could expect little dissent from Bevin, Eden or Lyttleton, and only token head-shaking from Churchill. But at a meeting of the all Cabinet-rank ministers on 5 March, it was evident that the new policy initiative dismayed many Conservatives, who looked in vain to Churchill for reassurance, and a meeting of all Conservative backbench MPs gave Amery a rough ride, clearly believing that Government policy had been captured by its left-wing members.[16]

Cripps volunteered to go, convincing Churchill behind Amery's back during a lunch at Chequers. 'Churchill, who was tired of "trying to grasp the problem to which he had given little thought" and pained at "abandoning his old die hard position" now "resolved to get clear of it at all cost".'[17] With these reservations and doubts, it was no wonder that the drafting of Cripps's remit had to be careful. Cripps had ambitious plans for himself, but Amery was worried he could provoke the viceroy's resignation for which the Cabinet was not yet prepared. Churchill spoke to the House of Commons on 11 March of Cripps going 'to satisfy himself upon the spot by personal consultation that the declaration upon which we are agreed, and which we believe represents a just and final solution, will achieve its purpose.' But Churchill was explicit that Cripps's task was 'to procure the necessary measure of assent not only from the Hindu majority but also from those great minorities amongst whom the Muslims are the most numerous and on many grounds pre-eminent'.[18] Agatha Harrison, a long-time friend of India sitting in the gallery of the Commons, 'realised that the age of miracles has not passed'.[19]

Before miracles could deliver the promised goods, there was Linlithgow to consider. Churchill, wishing to keep him in line, assured him that 'the announcement of his mission will still febrile agitation and give time for the problem to be calmly solved or alternatively for the time being to be insoluble'.[20] Amery reassured the viceroy that while 'the choice of Cripps might upset the Muslims who will think we are selling out to Congress', on closer inspection it would be discovered 'that the nest contains the Pakistan cuckoo's egg'.[21] This may have been Tory skulduggery—of saying one thing to the Americans and the Left, and another to their friends—or merely a clever ploy to keep Linlithgow sweet. If Cripps' proposals had an in-built Pakistan option, it never rose to the top during the discussions but, of course, it stayed on the agenda from then on. The main purpose was to let the Americans and the Left wing be told by someone sympathetic that 'they must either find ways and means of compromising with the minority elements, or face the disadvantages of a divided India'.[22]

Cripps's biographer takes a more balanced view of the mission. He says that despite his 'agonized misgivings', Churchill knew that 'more was required than a mere propaganda ploy. Only an initiative with a real chance of success, however slight, would serve to improve the war situation, not only on the ground in Asia but in consolidating the grand alliance on which final victory depended.'[23] If anyone could make it work, it had to be Cripps. Success would help them both. Churchill realized that failure was risky since he could be blamed as well as Cripps.

Cripps arrived with a much more limited proposal than the Congress had expected. Gandhi, like his friend Agatha Harrison had hoped he would perform a miracle. Cripps had proposals for the 'Indianization' of the viceroy's executive council. The draft that he showed to Linlithgow had ten members for the viceroy's council. In a desire to make it representative it had four Congress and three Muslim League members, plus one Depressed Class, one Sikh and one co-opted. To mix the national–religious divide with the provincial situation, the draft said that each of the two main parties, the Congress and the Muslim League, had to have within its quota one each from among the provincial leaders. The Congress chose Rajagopalachari, the Madras chief minister and Jinnah chose Fazlul Haq, the Bengal chief minister. The others on the Congress list were Nehru, Azad and Patel. Jinnah had Khaliquzzaman; Azad took Asaf Ali as his interpreter since he was unsure of his ability to negotiate in English. Baldev Singh was the Sikh representative, Ambedkar represented the depressed classes and N.M. Joshi, the trade unionist, was the co-opted member. Gandhi came to Delhi and did not insist on Cripps going to Wardha.

But the snag was the defence portfolio. The Congress wanted it in Indian hands. With Japan approaching fast up the Burma road, Cripps and the chief of imperial staff in India, Archibald Alexander Wavell, were considering a switch of scarce aircraft capacity from Europe to the Asian theatre. The defence of India had moved up the list of priorities. The Congress had no expertise in defence whatsoever. Could the Allied powers risk handing over India's defence to amateurs, even if they were warm-hearted and sincere nationalists with the good of India at heart?

There was a so-called 'Pakistan' part of Cripps's declaration. This was the clause which said that in the forthcoming constitutional arrangements after the end of the Second World War, the provinces would be allowed the right of non-accession to the federation. This, however, never came up for serious debate.

The Congress was interested in the immediate situation and its demands for Indianization of viceroy's council, but with some added clout. Cripps, in an unguarded moment, said it would be like a Cabinet, which meant that decisions would be taken by a majority vote and not according to the governor general's sole power to overrule the majority, which is how the council used to work. Linlithgow did not want this at all.

Since Cripps did not have plenipotentiary powers, every wrinkle had to be cleared with Whitehall via telegraph. Still, Cripps was hopeful and extended his stay a second week from March into April. Gandhi had seen that the post-war proposals were not to his liking and he predicted failure for the mission, but his Congress colleagues persisted. His dismissal of the proposals as 'a post-dated cheque' has passed into history as a classic (though spoiled by the redundant addition 'on a failing bank' by reporters). He advised Cripps to take the next plane home.

When he met Jinnah, Cripps assured him that while he was known as a friend of the Congress, he meant to take all views into account. Jinnah held back from disputing with Cripps, shrewdly suspecting that the Congress was bound to reject the offer, and any opprobrium over the failure of the mission would fall on them. Jinnah focused on just one point of the agenda during the negotiations which ran on for five more years; he was never distracted by issues which were not related to Muslim rights.

It was Nehru who was much disappointed in his friend Cripps, a sentiment the latter reciprocated. Cripps could, at best, offer low-grade military supplies/commissariat type duties for the Indian member in charge of defence, even if it was not a Congress member. His hands were tied since the viceroy and the commander-in-chief had some say in the matter, and the viceroy was parleying with Whitehall behind Cripps's back. In rejecting the offer the first time around, the Congress raised issues such as there was no mention of independence even after the war, the fear of Pakistan, the latitude given to Princely States, but above all, the failure to understand the Congress's demands for defence, which could 'even at this grave eleventh hour ... galvanise the people of India to rise to the height of the occasion'.[24]

Eventually, the whole thing foundered not on the plans for post-war constitutional arrangements, but on the powers of the defence member of the viceroy's executive council and the status of the council itself. The Congress was eager to have the member be given substantial tasks. After much palaver, the member's role was left undefined, and that of the commander-in-chief was described in detail. But, there was still the issue of whether the council would become a Cabinet. The Congress wanted an ex-ante guarantee rather than let the process evolve over time.

Even a vigorous intervention by Roosevelt's emissary, Colonel Johnson, arriving in Delhi and ruffling the feathers of the viceregal peacock, was not enough. Cripps tried to go behind Linlithgow's back to the War Cabinet, but so did he, behind Cripps's back. There was, as Peter Clarke says, 'a vicious circle of disintegrating mutual confidence'.[25] The viceroy was in no mood to concede the cabinet-type arrangement that Congress insisted upon, and Churchill was happy to let him have his way. Much bad blood was spilt between Cripps and the viceroy, but Cripps returned home empty-handed. The *New York Times*, friendly towards India's aspiration until then, concluded that the fault lay with the Congress. As a historian of the British Empire tells us, 'The paper now saluted, "the effort of the British to adopt the fairest compromise"; it detected "a disheartening unreality in the response of some of the Indian leaders"; and dismissed Congress's reply to Cripps as "the repetition of slogans that have suddenly lost their meaning".'[26]

The Cripps Mission has been written off as a failure on all sides. But it was a rare moment which, had it been seized, would have given the Congress executive experience without yielding the parity in numbers to Jinnah, which the Congress had to do four years later. The nature of Cabinet responsibility could have been gained, in fact, by stretching the conventions, de facto, so as to reduce the powers of the viceroy, who very likely would not have been Linlithgow. But the Congress was not in a trusting mode; nor was it realistic. It was, in fact, both prickly and idealistic. Nehru was 'surprised at [Cripps's] woodenness and insensitiveness, in spite of his public smile',[27] and Cripps surmised that the rejection was because of Gandhi's stand on non-violence and hence he was reluctant to aid the Congress to take part in helping in the war. Cripps said, at a press conference in Delhi, that he thought the Indian leaders had missed 'an excellent offer'. He told one of his staff that Gandhi 'may be actually desirous to bring about a chaos, while he sits at Wardha eating vegetables'.[28] Rajagopalachari was the only one who favoured acceptance of the offer.

Azad says, in his memoirs, that Nehru wanted to accept Cripps's offer, as he was conscious of the need to fight the Fascists in Europe and Asia. He says of his friend, '[Nehru] was so impressed by China's struggle against Japan that he felt that the democracies must be supported at any cost. In fact, he felt genuine grief and anguish that India was not fighting by the side of democracies'. Azad was against acceptance and, as the Congress president throughout the war, he had some influence.

'The Congress stand was that India was willing to help Britain but could do so only as a free country.'[29]

Neither Nehru's anguish nor Azad's insistence had any relevance. India was fighting for the democracies with two-and-a-half million soldiers and a lot of material. It was the Congress which was not fighting. But by now, the Congress found it difficult to remember that it was not India. This arrogance was to cost the country dear.

Gandhi was blamed by the British and Churchill by the Indians, both, as it were, thought to be acting from behind the arras. Churchill wrote a scathing account of Gandhi's intentions at this time, in a passage for his history of the war, which he was prevailed upon to delete from the published version. He wrote that Gandhi 'did not reveal what was no doubt the truth, that, he was willing to give the Japanese free passage across India to join hands with the Germans in return for Japanese military aid to hold down Muslims and secure All India Dominion of the Hindu Raj.'[30] Churchill's Gandhi paranoia was incurable.

QUIT INDIA: AUGUST 1942

Cripps having departed, the Congress was back in a limbo. There was nothing to show for the hard line taken when resigning in 1939. Three years had gone by, the Japanese were at the door, and the British showed no sign of relenting. Even the Americans were unwilling to push much more, since they had a serious battle in the Pacific on their hands. Soon after, Hitler made the mistake of a U-boat attack on an American ship, and the USA declared war on Germany. Winning the war was priority. Post-war plans were being prepared; an Atlantic Charter was signed by Roosevelt and Churchill, regardless of the outstanding imperial issues.

The Congress had to do something to regain the initiative. The country was getting impatient. The younger generation was fed up with Gandhi's peaceful tactics. Subhash Bose, whom he had so ruthlessly removed from holding office, had started his own group—the Forward Bloc—which openly advocated a more violent struggle. Bose was arrested and put in jail in Calcutta, but escaped via Kabul to Germany in early 1941. It was known that Bose was looking for Axis support to mount a counteroffensive. It even seemed as if that could be the answer to India's helplessness.

Gandhi felt the urgency of the issue. The Congress had once again come to him for the next step in the struggle. His idiosyncratic view of the war meant that he thought the Japanese would not invade India if the British left. In his view the Japanese were fighting against the British, and not the Indians. How he explained to himself Japanese atrocities in

China, or any of the South-East Asian countries, is beyond comprehension. But all Congress leaders, except Nehru, Rajagopalachari and, perhaps, Azad—blindly put their faith in him. Patel, Prasad and Kripalani, at the top of the Congress tree, were unquestioning in their faith. Gandhi chose the most drastic action he could think of. He launched a final struggle to throw the British out of India. He somehow convinced himself that he would be allowed to launch a final non-violent struggle, somewhat like the Dandi march, his last great effort. He and his devoted followers had forgotten that while it brought great glory to Gandhi, the Gandhi–Irwin pact conceded none of the demands for which the march was launched, and the invitation to the Round Table Conference could have been had without going through all the trouble of making salt. It was the insistence of the Congress for majority representation which had caused them to boycott the first Round Table Conference, and Gandhi achieved little by his attendance at the second. But his fame was intact. The Dandi march had to be repeated; the British would yield. Gandhi had convinced himself that, with the Japanese at the door, the British would not suppress his movement. They would then be forced to depart by the strength of his movement, and the departure of the British would repel the Japanese. He sent out feelers to Linlithgow via Madeline Slade (Mirabehn), one of his devoted disciples. But she was rebuffed. Linlithgow was not playing this game.

Azad claims in his memoirs that he was sceptical—unlike Patel and Prasad. 'My own reading was completely different. I was convinced that in this critical stage of the war the Government would not tolerate any mass movement. It was a question of life and death for the British. They would therefore act swiftly and drastically.'[31]

But Azad was just the Congress president; Gandhi was the real leader and the only one whom all followed. Twenty years after he had cancelled the movement where he had promised swaraj within one year, Gandhi launched his last desperate struggle. Thus was born the Quit India resolution of the Congress on 8 August 1942. Gandhi said in his speech to the assembled members of the Congress in Bombay that he had written to Linlithgow saying there was still time for negotiations. He was fond of the viceroy; he had got to know his son and daughter-in-law intimately and they had even invited him for tea! He remained firmly loyal, but intransigent in his demand that the time had come for the British to quit and leave the Indians to face the Japanese. What would the viceroy's response be?

It is astonishing that Gandhi hoped even at this stage—after three years of Linlithgow's firm rejection of all overtures, including the latest from Madeline Slade—that there was any chance of negotiations, tea with the family or not. The Congress was going to launch yet another non-violent struggle. But Linlithgow did not negotiate. The entire Congress Working Committee was arrested on the early morning of 9 August, and locked up for the duration of the war. A fierce, violent struggle was launched by the now leaderless youth. They ripped up rail lines and destroyed power lines; they sabotaged war effort and led strikes in factories and mills. Freed of Gandhian leadership, the youth of India, many socialists among them, tried to throw the British out by violent means. The rebels were subjugated after a year of mayhem. Many such, as Jayprakash Narayan and Aruna Asaf Ali, earned their spurs in this battle. But again, as in 1857, the leaderless, badly under-armed army lost, and a harsh peace was imposed on India.

The Quit India movement has a great place in Congress mythology of the independence struggle. But it was a futile gesture as far as the party was concerned. Gandhi may have dreamt of the days of Gandhi–Irwin Pact, but this was not to be. It was a continuation of the series of Himalayan blunders, starting from the resignation of the Congress ministries in 1939. Congress spent the six years of war in a Walter Mitty-like state, and handed Jinnah a golden opportunity to build up his party while winning British sympathy, though without taking any official position in the viceroy's council.

So the Congress leadership spent the next two (Gandhi) or three (the rest of them) years in jail. Gandhi was taken to the Aga Khan's palace in Poona. The rest of them were put in Ahmednagar Fort. By now, the British were treating the Congress like a government-in-waiting. Prison can never be pleasant, but their needs were looked after. Azad reports how on the very first day, they made it clear that they would like china plates and not the iron ones on offer, and the cook had to be changed. Newspapers had to be delivered. Gandhi's wife, Kasturba was allowed to be with him, since she had got herself arrested on 9 August itself. Mahadev Desai arrived, but died soon after at the age of fifty after twenty-five years of devoted service to Gandhi. Sushila Nayar, who was a doctor, was there as was her brother Pyarelal, who replaced Mahadev as Gandhi's secretary.

Kasturba died in prison after sixty years of a turbulent marriage to Gandhi. They had both been only thirteen when they had got married, she older by six months and from a more prosperous family, much spoilt by her parents and brothers. He was possessive and jealous to begin with, but besotted with his new-found toy. He abandoned her to go to London, but did give her a son before leaving. As he pursued his career, she followed wherever he went. His whims ruled the family; he decided to wear Western clothes and she had to dress like a Parsi woman in a frock, socks and shoes. Then he got into hygiene and made her clean latrines, which nearly broke her. He took up his brahmacharya—

celibacy—without so much as discussing her wishes in the matter. As he changed his thoughts and his lifestyle, he unilaterally dragged her along. But, in fact, she was the more revolutionary of the two, since she had to change and adapt much more. After all, she only learned to read and write when in prison during one of his many movements. And she was the only one who could really stand up to him and whom he obeyed. She had to suffer the tragedy of their eldest son, Harilal's estrangement. She was Gandhi's pillar, though few realized this. She knew how much leeway to give to the endless stream of women who were attracted to him, even more because of his avowed brahmacharya. They bathed him, massaged his bare body and slept by him, keeping him warm—and fought among themselves for the privilege. They were the instruments through which he tested his powers of sexual abstinence. She knew when to get rid of someone who had become a nuisance, and who could be permitted to stay. As she lay dying, she told him she wanted to be wrapped in a khadi sari made from the yarn he had spun himself. It was a gesture of the abiding love she bore him. Her departure shattered him. For the first time in his life, he was all alone with no one to be his equal. He became even more eccentric than he had been since the early 1930s.

Nehru finished his great statement on Indian nationhood, *The Discovery of India*, while in jail. If there is a single book which tells us about undivided India before Independence, it is this. Nehru's analysis of Indian nationhood is unrivalled but, sadly, the India he 'discovered' was not the India he was going to lead at Independence.

SUBHASH CHANDRA BOSE AND THE INDIAN NATIONAL ARMY

Churchill's fear about Gandhi giving the Japanese free passage through India was uncalled for. But someone else did think about taking the help of Germany and Japan to wage an armed struggle for India's independence. Subhash Bose had already had a meteoric career in the Congress. He was a socialist and an internationalist. Younger than Nehru by eight years and twenty-eight years younger than Gandhi, he was impatient with Gandhi's methods and Nehru's acquiescence with them. He had been elected Congress president twice, but the second time Gandhi forced his resignation by asking his acolytes to resign from the Congress Working Committee through sheer strong-arm tactics, which could not be called democratic. Bose founded his own group, the Forward Bloc, and looked for a more active mode of struggle than the resignation and passive resistance policy which the Congress had adopted. He escaped from jail to Kabul, arriving there in January 1941; he reached Berlin in March 1941.

Bose's decision to seek Germany's help has tarred him with a Nazi brush ever since, and his name remains a controversial one, though fervent anti-Nehruvians worship him to this day. Germany had always attracted the more radical young Indian nationalists as an alternative European haven to the imperial power. Many who had got into trouble in England escaped to France or Germany. The earliest Indian communists—M.N. Roy and Virendra Chattopadhyaya (Chatto, as he was called), brother of Sarojini Naidu, had gone there during the First World War. Germany had also attracted Indian artists, such as Himansu Rai who made stunning films in Weimar Germany during the late twenties and early thirties. Subhash Bose had himself been to Germany during that time.

Bose, being a socialist, was anti-Nazi and is on record during the thirties for his opposition to Hitler. But he took the view that nationalism and anti-imperialism were more important than anti-Fascism. This was much as Nehru had done, but without seeking military help from the Axis powers, since he was more sensitive to the issue of Japanese atrocities in China. Bose did not get much help in Berlin, though he set up a Free India Centre and the Azad Hind Radio there. He established a government-in-exile, and chose the Tagore poem '*Jana gana mana*' as the anthem of free India—a choice which would be adopted by Nehru, later in 1947, in preference to *Vande mataram*. He declared Hindustani in Roman script to be India's national language, thus emulating the modernizing example of Kemal Ataturk. The national greeting he selected was *Jai Hind* (victory to India), and the Indian prime minister still ends the Independence day speech, from Delhi's Red Fort every year on 15 August, with this invocation.[32]

Bose met Joachim von Ribbentrop, Hitler's foreign minister, seven months after his arrival, and Hitler in May 1942. There was no meeting of minds. Hitler did not think Indians could govern themselves for the next 150 years, and did not want to challenge the British in their empire. He was still hoping to have a treaty with Britain so he could smash the USSR. Halifax (Irwin) would have been happy to go along, but Churchill was firmly against any compromise with Nazism, even when told that he could lose the empire in the process. So there was no rapport between the racist Führer and the proud nationalist Indian. Soon after his arrival, Bose had begun to form an Indian legion from Indian soldiers captured as prisoners of war by the Germans, and there were plans to deploy its 3000 troops in Afghanistan. But by December 1942, the battle of El Alamein had taken place, and the Germans had suffered reverse at Stalingrad. So that plan was abandoned because Germany had to move to a defensive strategy on both its western and eastern fronts.

The Japanese, who were rampaging through South-East Asia, also did not have India on their list of territories for their Co-Prosperity Sphere—as Japan called its empire in Asia; but on 16 February 1942 the chief of the Japanese army, Tojo announced Japan's support for India's struggle. The large Indian diaspora in East and South-East Asia had a leader in Rash Behari Bose, who had exiled himself to Japan thirty years previously. He was thrilled that Subhash Bose had escaped. Soon after the fall of Singapore in February 1942, a corps of Indian soldiers were taken prisoners of war, and the Japanese handed them over to a local Indian leader, Mohan Singh, to form a fighting division. Bose was transported to Singapore via a U-boat, which rendezvoused with a Japanese submarine at Madagascar and reached Singapore in May 1943.

Subhash Bose took over the Indian National Army (INA) and became active in fund raising and mobilizing diaspora support and recruitment. He was now called Netaji—'respected leader'. Of course, by this time, the Japanese were fighting a fierce war in the Pacific with the Americans. Just as Hitler had made a strategic blunder by attacking the USSR, so did Japan by attacking Pearl Harbour. Had these two actions not occurred, Germany would have kept a European empire, and Japan an Asian one. But, by the time an independent Indian government-in-exile was established on 21 October 1943, it was too late. Italy had already surrendered a month before, on 8 September. Japan recognized Bose's government two days later, and on 24 October 1943 Bose declared war on the Allies. The islands of Andaman and Nicobar, which the Japanese had captured, were handed over to the new government and Bose immediately renamed the Andaman Islands 'Shaheed' and the Nicobar Islands 'Swaraj'. Independent India did not adopt the new names in 1947.

Thai, Indonesian and Burmese nationalists had already established governments with Japanese support. Ba Maw and Aung San, leaders of the Burmese Independence Army, were not enamoured of the Indians, but had to cooperate with Japanese demands. Eventually, in March 1944, the Japanese launched an attack on India from the Burmese side. Operation Imphal lasted only four months from 15 March to 9 July 1944, but it was one of the most fiercely fought campaigns of the war. The Japanese army retained strategic and operational command. It is not clear whether the INA played a role in combat operations or were treated as coolies and sappers, as some reports have suggested.[33] As a sympathetic account says, 'An unofficial theory held widely by the Japanese is to regard the Imphal Operation as a brainchild of Netaji, who with his tremendous influence dragged the Japanese military into the disastrous adventure. An unofficial Indian theory, also circulating widely, holds that INA soldiers were expended like pawns in the wanton and reckless Japanese operation. Neither theory seems to be based on facts.'[34]

There was initial success. 'The Japanese-Indian offensive took the British by complete surprise. The Japanese and INA troops, mostly foot soldiers lacking vehicles and artillery, or any air support, literally galloped through mountains and jungles, smothering or routing the enemy on the way.'[35] They entered Indian territory early in April. They met Indians at the opposite end—the 2/5th Royal Gurkha Rifles and the 48th Indian Infantry Brigade. Kohima was captured on 6 April. Bose declared that the provisional government of India was fighting on, side by side with the Japanese army to liberate India.

After three months of holding Kohima and Imphal, the Japanese and INA were defeated. The INA's Kiani regiment was decimated, and some of its soldiers defected to the Indian army. As the official British-Indian version says:

> The Japanese commander of the Fifteenth Army had gambled for high stakes, and had lost ... His troops had indeed fought like heroes and covered themselves with glory ... But they had attacked prepared positions held by over 1,500,000 Allied troops with barely one-third of that strength. They had run out of ammunition in the middle of the battles ... Supplies of food and medicine were completely exhausted ... The Indian and British soldiers ... showed that they had mastered the difficult art of jungle warfare, and, given suitable circumstances, could defeat the flower of the Imperial armies face to face in the field.[36]

The short, fierce episode was sadly reminiscent of 1857 when one set of Indian soldiers defeated another set, both fighting with great bravery and loyalty to their oath.

The INA had no chance. They had been captured in early 1942, and had to wait two more years before seeing any action. In those two years they had little training, and their equipment was what they had been captured with. Their treatment by the Japanese left a lot to be desired as well. Bose exhorted the Japanese army to launch an attack on India as soon as possible. But the Japanese had their own agenda. They had not planned to invade India and, when they did so finally, it was as a desperate gesture to regain the initiative in the jungles of Manipur which they were losing in the Pacific. They used the INA badly.

Tojo was replaced soon after. The Thai collaborator, Pibulsongraam resigned on 20 July 1944. There was some idea that Bose might fly to the USSR and mount an offensive from the Afghan border (the USSR was not yet officially at war with Japan). But nothing came of it. The Burmese army turned coat in March 1945. By the summer of 1945 the Axis powers had lost and the Allies had won in a most decisive way. The news of the Holocaust, which emerged after the V-E Day, is now regarded as the most heinous act by any regime over an entire race.

Japanese atrocities in China and, indeed, in the rest of their empire during the 1933–45 period, were also shocking and are still unforgotten in China, Korea and other parts of Asia.

Bose died in a plane crash at Taipei airport on 18 August 1945. He was just forty-eight. His death has been denied—and is still denied in some quarters of India. He remains a romantic figure, an alternative to Gandhi and especially to Nehru, who is derided by some for his willingness to pursue peace in Kashmir in 1948 and for India's defeat to China in 1962. For some Indians Bose is the future that could have been. But he does remain compromised by his association with the German and Japanese regimes. He stretched the dictum 'My enemy's enemy is my friend' to its utmost. His intentions were honest, and his nationalism genuine and fierce, but he had no military experience whatsoever. This does not necessarily mean he could not have had military success. Leon Trotsky, the Bolshevik revolutionary, showed how quickly an intellectual can adapt himself to lead a spirited army in battle, against heavy odds, and win. Bose was a good leader as a fund-raiser and as an inspiration, but for military knowledge he depended on the Japanese. Whatever their merit, by the time he could persuade them to mount a campaign, the Japanese were already losing the war. It was too little too late.

Stories of the INA soldiers were received with great enthusiasm in India. Indeed, it was after they ceased to be active and were captured by the Allied forces that the INA became valuable to Indian nationalism. Their actual military achievements, which were few, if any, were hardly remembered. It was their gesture of defying the British and wearing military uniforms which excited the imagination of a nation which had little experience of arms and armaments in their civilian life. The INA soldiers were pardoned, but three officers were tried at the Red Fort; though convicted, they were not punished. By the end of their trial in 1946 the British were on their way out.

PASSAGE TO PAKISTAN

Gandhi came out of jail in May 1944. He had been weakened by the latest of his fasts, and the death of his beloved wife had been a blow. The rest of the Congress Working Committee was still in jail. But after recuperating in Bombay by the Juhu seaside, Gandhi initiated a dialogue with Jinnah. He took this initiative on his own, without consulting anyone else. Rajagopalachari (whose daughter Lakshmi had married Gandhi's son Devdas) had moved a resolution, in the Madras Congress legislature party and in the assembly itself after the collapse of the Cripps Mission in 1942, that Jinnah's demands be accommodated by the Congress. Azad had admonished him and Rajagopalachari had resigned from the Congress Working Committee. Rajaji, as he was known since the North Indians could not get their tongues around his polysyllabic South Indian name, was a pragmatic Right-wing politician and lawyer like most of the Congress leadership (Azad excepted). It is possible that his idea appealed to Gandhi while he thought about these matters in prison.

The offer of a dialogue was compounded with Gandhi choosing to address Jinnah by the title Jinnah's followers had given him—*Quaid-e Azam* ('great leader' in Urdu). Azad was most annoyed when he heard of Gandhi's offer. He called the invitation to Jinnah 'a great political blunder', and blamed 'a foolish but well intentioned woman called Amtus Salam [one of the women who devoted themselves to Gandhi]' for advising him to use that title. 'When Indian Muslims saw that Gandhiji also addressed Jinnah as *Qaid-e-Azam*, they felt that he must really be so ... I told my colleagues that Gandhiji was making a great mistake ... Jinnah exploited the situation fully and built up his own position ...'[37] (There is just a faint touch of envy in Azad's account here. Jinnah's title was one Azad may have coveted for himself from Indian Muslims.)

Along with Hindu Mahasabha leader, Veer Savarkar and Dalit leader, B.R. Ambedkar, Jinnah was another person over whom Gandhi's usually effective tactics and charm had no power. Gandhi tried to get under Jinnah's exterior persona by offering to talk in Gujarati, their common language. The shrewd lawyer that Jinnah was, he saw the trap and refused. His Gujarati lacked the subtlety which Gandhi's had. Gandhi wanted to extract Jinnah's demands so that he (Gandhi) could concede them. But Jinnah's entire approach had been that a guarantee by anyone in the Congress, including Gandhi, was worthless, since after independence it would be the Hindu majority which would have the decisive power. A guarantee given by Gandhi also had the problem that it could be rescinded if the 'inner voice' so decreed. After all, neither in Chauri Chaura, nor in the Mahadev Desai episode, was there any consultation with associates when Gandhi changed his mind. Jinnah knew his Gandhi well. He wanted the British to deliver his demands before they departed. Only the British Parliament could give what he wanted.

Jinnah was not alone in this. Muslim politicians who wanted a separate grouping of Muslim majority provinces—the so-called 'Pakistan'—were far keener for complete freedom from the Congress than from the British. They saw, much as Ambedkar and Ramaswamy Naicker, the Dravidian leader, did, that the British presence was a guarantee against Congress high-handedness. Where the Congress saw a seamless unity in a Congress-ruled India, Ambedkar and Naicker saw the many cleavages of religion, caste and region. Thus, Khaliquzzaman had said in February 1942, 'The Muslim demand is that Britain, after the war, should by an Act of Parliament, establish the zonal system, before considering further Swaraj. British control would be still required at the Centre—apparently for an indefinite period—since Defence and Foreign Policy [which is practically all the Centre would deal with] should still be in British hands.'[38]

Jinnah had not been idle during the time the Congress's leaders were in jail. He had built up his constituency and had brought many sceptical but articulate middle-class Muslims on board. Vagueness was his weapon, and he spelt out the notion of Pakistan leaving enough room for manoeuvre. This infuriated his co-locutors, but it was precisely what gave him the chance to make something out of an evanescent idea. The Gandhi–Jinnah talks ended in predictable failure, but it established Jinnah's status as equal to that of Gandhi's. Gandhi, of course, continued to assert that he was against Partition, but his gesture of September 1944 began the inexorable process whereby the Congress adapted itself to the two-nation theory, even while denying it all the time.

CHAPTER 10

THE ROAD TO PAKISTAN

END OF WAR IN ASIA

The outside world again intervened to restart the stalled machine of India's independence negotiations. The war in Europe was over by the spring of 1945 and Japan was on the retreat, though fighting a strong rearguard battle across the Pacific. Leo Amery, still the Secretary of State for India, announced in the House of Commons on 14 June 1945 that India would now be given the chance to take full part in the war effort that the Congress had asked for in 1942. So, here they were again, three years after the Cripps Mission, invited to resume negotiations on Cripps proposals. Wavell, who had replaced Linlithgow as viceroy, now saw his chance and summoned the main parties for a conference in Simla on 25 June. The prisoners were released and immediately treated like VIPs and ferried across to Simla. As Azad reports, 'He [Wavell] placed at our disposal an aeroplane which flew us to Ambala. From there we drove up to Simla ... Finally about 10 p.m. we reached Simla. We drove to the Savoy Hotel where rooms had been reserved for us.'[1]

From now on, the Congress Working Committee began to act like a shadow government. Churchill was still in power, but elections had been declared in Britain, and the British government in London was in a flux. The issues were the Cripps formula and the viceroy's executive council being converted to a cabinet-style operation. As Azad says:

> The Viceroy then described to me the details of his proposal. My first reaction was that it was not different in substance from the Cripps offer. There was however one material difference in the circumstances. The Cripps offer was made when the British were in dire need of Indian cooperation. Today the war was over in Europe and the Allies had triumphed over Hitler. The British Government had all the same repeated their earlier offer in an attempt to create a new political atmosphere in India.[2]

Azad does not see the irony of his statement. Cripps's offer was made in 1942 and repeated in 1945. The war in Europe had been won in the meantime, Indian, that is, Congress, cooperation or not. India had become an original signatory member of the United Nations in San Fransisco, just as it had been a member of the League of Nations. The British Cabinet had stuck to the path it had laid down in 1942, and the Congress's rejection had not mattered a jot to anyone except the Congress. The rejection of Cripps proposal was entirely in the pattern of usual Congress behaviour. But the proposal itself fitted into British Parliament's long-run behaviour as well. Ever since the 1917 statement by Edwin Montagu, Parliament had followed the course it had announced. This is, of course, not the official nationalist history which pits British intransigence against the brave struggle that the Congress put up over thirty, if not sixty, years to wrench independence from the reluctant imperialists.

In the broader context of the history of anti-colonial struggles, the Americans were the first and won their independence by military action. This was, perhaps, the fastest victory for any anti-colonial struggle, since between the Declaration of Independence in 1776 and the 1783 surrender at Yorktown, there was only a seven-year gap. The Irish case was a bit more complicated, since here it was a breakaway from a unified polity. From Gladstone's first attempt at legislating for Irish Home Rule in 1886, which split the Liberal Party, to Asquith's successful bill in 1914, and then independence in 1920 and partition in 1922, the gap is thirty-six years. India's journey of mass anti-colonial struggle began in 1917, or perhaps 1905 with the Bengal Partition, and it took forty-two years at the longest estimation or just thirty years at the shortest to succeed. If the Congress speeded up this process, it was not by much.

The Congress Working Committee, like the Bourbons who had learned nothing and forgotten nothing, resumed negotiations on the minutiae of how the viceroy would chair the council. Its resolution asked inter alia, 'If the Council arrived at a unanimous conclusion, would its decision be binding on the Viceroy or would the Viceroy have a veto even in such cases?' It added on the issue of cooperation in war effort, 'India would participate in the war against Japan not as a result of a British decision but by a vote of her own representatives.'[3]

There was no acknowledgement here that the Japanese attempt to invade Indian soil had been repulsed by a tough and brave campaign by Indian soldiers fighting under the Allied colours. The war with Japan was not yet over; it was expected to last some time longer, but the danger to India had passed. Indian soldiers were now recovering Burma and helping farther out in South-East Asia. There was also no recognition by the Congress of Allied victory in Europe over the forces of fascism.

The party's insularity at this crucial juncture is astonishing, as if the leadership's three years in jail had been spent in solitary confinement.

In any case, the Simla Conference failed. This time, however, the British were not to blame. It ended because of Jinnah's insistence that he alone could nominate a Muslim to the viceroy's council and this was, quite rightly, rejected by Wavell and the Congress. To quote Azad again, who was still the Congress president after six years, 'The Simla Conference marks a breakwater in Indian political history. This was the first time when negotiations failed, not on the basic political issue between India and Britain, but on the communal issue dividing different Indian groups.'[4] Jinnah had now come very near to the status which he had been aiming for. He controlled his party, and while other Muslims such as the Punjab and Bengal chief ministers were still influential, he was the sole national spokesman for the Muslims and acknowledged as such by the British as well as the Congress. Neither their condescension nor their contempt helped Congress leaders in neutralizing Jinnah. He kept his eyes firmly on the main chance while they enjoyed the trappings of British approval.

The failure of the Simla Conference did not matter. Yet again, events in Britain mattered more. The Labour Party came to power on 26 July 1945 with a landslide victory. The British voters may have loved Winston Churchill as a war leader, but they did not want him to be in charge of peacetime reconstruction. The war had radicalized many young soldiers and the experience of rationing had appealed to many as an example of cross-class solidarity. Labour Party leaders—Clement Attlee, Ernest Bevin, Stafford Cripps—had quietly delivered an efficient victory, leaving the grand rhetoric to Churchill. He was stunned at being defeated, but had to accept the verdict of the people.

The Labour Party manifesto had promised independence for India, and Attlee immediately set about trying to deliver it. It seems that Nehru and Gandhi did not expect the change of governing party to make much difference. This was either out of exasperation with Cripps or a failure to follow the changing fortunes of Labour Party during the war. It is also fashionable in a lot of the nationalist literature to have a monochrome, monolithic imperialist category. But it is a moot question: had Churchill won a similar landslide victory, would there have been any advance any time soon to India's freedom? It is said that the British left because they could no longer afford the empire after the costs of the war. If so, that contradicts what the same analysts often say too—that the imperialists benefited from the empire. The fact is that empires do not indulge in a careful cost–benefit calculation. J.A. Hobson, the pioneer theorist of imperialism, knew this and the sheer economic irrationality of empires exasperated him. Trade, in his opinion, was so much more lucrative than imperial territory, but the grandees of Europe always preferred territory to trade.

If acquiring empires was a process free of rational economic calculation, giving up empires proved to be even more so. French imperialism hung on in Indo-China till a military defeat in 1954, and in Algeria even more murderously till the 1960s. Belgium did not cease the occupation of Congo despite its defeat during the Second World War, and the Dutch, defeated by Hitler and despite having suffered a famine during the war, resumed their rule of Indonesia with the help of the British Indian army, who won it back from the Japanese. The Dutch had to be thrown out by Sukarno (the first president of Indonesia) with force. Closer home, Portugal stuck it out in Goa till the early 1960s and in Angola and Mozambique till much later. The Portuguese economy could ill afford such madness, but it took the death of dictator Salazar in 1970 and the removal of his successor, Caetano in the mid-1970s before Portugal retracted from its imperial concerns.

The British economy had a number of urgent problems which could have been given priority by the Attlee government. The welfare state had to be extended in accordance with the Beveridge Report, full employment had to be delivered after the harrowing experience of the Great Depression, the Bank of England as well as the coal, railway and steel industries had to be nationalized and the National Health Service had to be constructed. All this had been in the manifesto, but it put India on the front burner and Wavell was called back to take new instructions. In August 1945 the war with Japan ended as a result of the horrendous bombing of Hiroshima and Nagasaki, triggering a debate which has still not been settled as to the military, let alone the ethical, justification for the act. Wavell was recalled to London for new consultations, and found Attlee in as much of a hurry to give India its freedom as Churchill was for delay. 'They are obviously bent on handing over India to their Congress friends as soon as possible,' he recorded in his diary. Attlee wanted new elections by autumn, but Wavell demurred. He still went along with what Attlee wanted and in August, Wavell announced that general elections would be held again in early 1946 on the basis of the 1935 Act. This was the first time in nine years that Indian opinion was being consulted, albeit on a limited franchise. But this time the stakes were higher, because the elected members would also be the constituent assembly which would draft the Constitution of independent India.

Officially, at this stage, only the Cripps offer was on the table despite its rejection in June 1945. But the new government meant change. Attlee had made Pethick-Lawrence the new Secretary of State for India. He was known to be friendly to Indian views. Cripps also argued for a fresh approach and a new proposal. He felt that 'India was on the move again. The political stagnation of the war years had been replaced by an impatient mood of change, potentially violent in expression'.[5]

The elections were the key. The Congress was sure of winning, but it seriously underestimated the upsurge in Muslim League support. Nehru could not see any good in the League at all, nor gauge its chance of success. He thought the methods of the League 'strikingly similar to the Nazi technique' and the cry for Pakistan 'a sentimental slogan which they have got used to'. He did not think there was much in Jinnah's threat. Nehru still wanted a unitary Constitution and dismissed the idea of Muslim League resistance by saying 'There may be some petty riots in some cities'.[6]

Now, with the prospect of power approaching, the Congress shed its rebel image and became 'responsible'. When a revolt by Indian navy officers erupted in Bombay, Azad, as Congress president, was keen to inform the commander-in-chief, Lord Auchinleck that 'Congress has not approved of the action of the naval officers and has advised them to go back to work.'[7] In his own analysis Azad says, 'It was clear to me that this was not an appropriate time for any mass movement or direct action. We must now watch the course of events and carry on negotiations with the British government.'[8] The Congress did, however, turn out in full force when the British government decided to make an example and tried three officers of the INA. Even Nehru donned his barrister's gown and joined Bhulabhai Desai and others to argue their defence at the trial in Red Fort. The officers were convicted, but pardoned to the great joy of Indians everywhere.

In the election, Muslim League swept up bulk of the Muslim seats— 428 out of 482, and all thirty of the reserved seats in the Central Legislative Assembly. The Congress's claim to represent all Indian peoples was now hollow. Except for NWFP, where the Khudai Khidmatgars had managed a bare majority, the Congress had little to show by way of Muslim representation. Rafiq Zakaria, a hostile biographer of Jinnah, says of the results, 'Why ... did the Congress leadership succumb to Wavell and agree to the holding of fresh elections on restricted franchise which were bound to strengthen Jinnah's leadership?'[9] But the 1937 elections were on the same narrow franchise, and then the League had got only hundred seats. The difference lay in what Jinnah had been doing in the previous six years by way of mobilization. Taking a leaf from Gandhi, he had adopted the traditional Muslim dress, though stopped short of travelling third class in railways. He had befriended the religious elements in Muslim society whom he had previously held in contempt. Jinnah became a mass leader loved by Muslims everywhere across India, despite, or perhaps because of, his aloof air. But above all, he tempted the powerful provincial Muslim leaders with a promise of provincial autonomy as a solid part of his scheme. If the Congress wanted a unitary Constitution, Jinnah wanted a loose federation.

THE CABINET MISSION

Attlee concluded that he needed a new approach. Thus on 19 February 1946, he announced the Cabinet Mission consisting of Pethick-Lawrence, Cripps and A.V. Alexander. Cripps was now the president of the Board of Trade and could be spared only with great reluctance, since the problem of supplies was urgent for post-war British recovery. Alexander was the first lord of the admiralty, who came as a sound Labour man and also to look after any defence implications. The mission's task, as Attlee's biographer describes it, 'was to try to find agreement on principles and procedures which could lead to the setting up of the machinery by which the Indians *themselves* could establish the constitution of an independent India'.[10]

The big change was that from this point onwards the British Parliament would not legislate on its own. It would await a scheme agreed upon by Indians, and then discharge its formal duty of passing the legislation, which transferred power. The fact that independence was on offer was taken for granted by the British, though the Indians remained suspicious till the very end. Attlee clarified, in a series of statements, that while 'we cannot allow a minority to place their veto on the advance of the majority', it also meant that 'we must recognise that we cannot make Indians responsible for governing themselves and at the same time retain over here the responsibility for the treatment of minorities and the power to intervene on their behalf.'[11]

This made a crucial difference to Jinnah. He had hoped that the British Parliament would ensure the guarantees he wanted for the Muslims as a large minority in legislation, before leaving, rather than let Indians decide for themselves. His suspicions of the Congress majority in the Constituent Assembly meant that he would not enter it before he had secured what he wanted The Congress had envisaged a unitary Constitution, with a minority rights guarantee subject to arbitration if there was a disagreement. Jinnah had no faith in this procedure as once the British left, there would be no one to ensure delivery of such guarantees. He had said as much in Lahore in 1940.

In the event, the Cabinet Mission came nearest to squaring the circle. Maulana Azad claims credit for proposing a loose federation, with limited powers for the central authority and a substantial amount of autonomy for the provinces. Jinnah, with the Lahore 1940 proposals, should have been happy with such an arrangement. The Centre was to have Defence, External Affairs and Communications and the provinces the rest.

Azad claims that he had thought of the federal scheme by himself and proposed it to the Cabinet Mission. He had not informed his Congress colleagues earlier, but was able to persuade them of the merits of this scheme. There was a centralist unitary bias in the Congress, indeed in all Indian nationalist thought. The folklore version of Indian history says that India was subject to foreign invasion and rule whenever the Centre was not strong and there were rival powers. Since this was the rule rather than the exception in Indian (unlike, say, in Chinese) history, the nationalist desire was to reverse the course. No nationalist would admit that there was no such thing as a single India, qua polity, until after the British had fixed its boundaries in the late nineteenth century. South India had had no foreign invasion in its long history until Vasco da Gama arrived in 1498. But this was not part of the Congress nationalist narrative. Mughal rule—between Akbar's ascendancy, say by 1565 and up to Aurangzeb's death in 1707—was the only period where a strong central authority could be said to have prevailed. In terms of economic well being, there was always a debate regarding whether a weak central power was more conducive to prosperity, as I discussed earlier. But, here again, the new example of the planned economy of the USSR and, indeed, even the New Deal pointed to strong central powers for planning.

Thus, it was a major sacrifice for the Congress to agree to the federal scheme. By some miracle the League agreed as well. Between 24 March and 25 June 1946, the Cabinet Mission negotiated and somehow convinced all parties that the Constituent Assembly should frame the Constitution of new India on that basis. It was not easy. The sense of achievement was, however, short lived and the agreement unravelled soon after the mission left India. The details of the negotiations have fascinated historians and biographers of the principal players ever since. Azad's memoirs caused a sensation, when they were first published in 1959, by alleging that the best chance of keeping India united was missed when Nehru made an unfortunate statement after the departure of the mission, as we shall see later. On the other hand, Cripps's biographer calls the Cabinet Mission section 'Cripps versus Gandhi', and tells the story in over eighty pages.

The debate will never settle, but personalities apart, the issues were clear. India was to be independent but, at the same time, there had to be a formula to keep the two major communities together. The Congress wanted to be in charge of a unitary state with the minorities question left to an independent India's Constituent Assembly. Jinnah wanted guarantees on minority rights which would be binding on the Congress and the assembly. He preferred a loose federation to a unitary state. Ambedkar and Ramaswamy Naicker distrusted the Congress almost as much as Jinnah. They, too, wanted rights of the 'depressed classes' protected with an iron-clad guarantee. The hard task was to find a set of nuanced positions which would reconcile the conflicting perceptions of Indian nationhood held not only by the Congress and the League, but by those of the autonomous provinces and other minorities such as Sikhs, the depressed classes, the Christians, the Parsis, etc. as well.

The argument went back and forth in Delhi and Simla, and back again over those three long and hot months. Gandhi was not part of the Congress delegation but still made himself available for consultation after a special letter from Cripps. In Delhi Gandhi arrived 'on an officially commissioned special train and on arrival took up residence in the Harijan sweepers' quarters where a camp had been set up. The simplicity of the Mahatma's hut was juxtaposed with the installation of electricity, loudspeakers and telephones.'[12] Cripps went to see Gandhi soon after, arriving on 31 March and whisked him off to see Pethick-Lawrence. Cripps did not want a repeat of Gandhi's sabotage (as he thought) of his proposals in 1942. Wavell, as ever the simple military man wary of lawyers and politicians, said, 'I do not quite trust Cripps and wholly mistrust Gandhi.'[13]

Jinnah was going to be a major problem, now that he had proved his credentials in the elections as the representative of Indian Muslims. Cripps thought 'the one effective way of settling the matter was to get Jinnah and Gandhi to agree'. On meeting Jinnah, Cripps was pleased to note that 'he had got rid of his inferiority complex'.[14] Undaunted, the three ministers, Cripps, Pethick-Lawrence and Alexander, carried out 400 interviews between 26 March and 17 April. They drew up two plans. Plan A was for a federation along the lines of the 1935 Act, with a weak Centre and autonomous provinces. Plan B was for Partition in case that became necessary. To increase the acceptability of their federal plan—Plan A—they made Plan B—the Partition one—very unattractive to Jinnah. The obvious solution, in a case where each of two sides wants something badly, is to make sure neither gets their preferred option, and both have to accept the 'second best'. So, for Jinnah they proposed a bare Muslim-majority Pakistan with no additional areas, which was unattractive. For the Congress they proposed a Constituent Assembly, but without the option of having a unitary Constitution for independent India.

Nehru soon emerged as the man to talk to Jinnah. Azad had been the Congress president since 1939 as the Congress had not been able to meet and elect a successor. Now with independence looming, it was Nehru who proved to be the man of the hour. Others had their claim. Azad liked Nehru, but on reflection twelve years later, he says that he regretted not backing Sardar Patel. He was justified in feeling sorry for himself since the Congress president would be India's first prime minister. But Gandhi had chosen his man.

At the end of the first round, a three-tier structure began to emerge as a possible solution. There would be a group of provinces in Pakistan, another in Hindustan and overarching them would be the All India federation. The Congress could buy into a loose federation but not regional groupings. Jinnah knew this and refused to enter into any agreement till the Congress signed up the scheme of groups. 'Everything in the end turned,' Clarke says, 'on trust or its absence; but not as, in 1942, mistrust of Viceroy so much as mistrust between Congress and the League.'[15]

Exhausted, the mission retired to Kashmir and stayed with the maharaja where Pethick-Lawrence played snooker and Alexander, billiards, but Cripps, ever the puritan, worked hard forming new plans. Some schemes fell foul of Wavell, others of Nehru. Azad met Cripps behind the backs of his colleagues, and Cripps had an evening with Gandhi who 'regaled [him] with tea and honey—a good drink!' Gandhi was aware that Azad, and perhaps even Nehru, were making commitments behind his back. But, eventually, everyone agreed to a face-to-face meeting in the cooler climate of Simla.

The mission was at Viceregal Lodge, of course, and the delegates, four from the Congress and three from the League, were at the Savoy Hotel. 'Gandhi orbited the conference, eccentrically. He was not an official delegate, but he had been officially invited and accommodated along with his fifteen attendants. No sooner had they all settled in than all fifteen, with the exception of [Sudhir] Ghosh and Rajkumari Amrit Kaur, who in any case had her own house at Simla, were told to return to Delhi, so that the Mahatma could follow his own precept of relying on God.'[16] His proposal to settle the Congress–League dispute was, as ever, peculiarly his own. He said, 'We must choose between the two parties and then hand the matter over to one or the other of them to do entirely in their own way';[17] he called the three-tier plan worse than Pakistan.

Cripps also talked to God, but managed to bring forward a complex proposal: 'In effect, the Muslim League was asked to work within the framework of an All-India Union Government, while Congress was asked to accept Hindu–Muslim parity within it and the legitimacy of entering groups which might set up their own legislatures and executives.'[18] Gandhi, Azad and Nehru were willing to discuss this scheme. Nehru felt 'Congress should remain free to argue against grouping upon entering a Constituent Assembly'. When these proposals were published as a White Paper on 16 May, one innovation was that now independence was explicitly mentioned with the hope that India would stay in the Commonwealth. But the meat was in the Constituent Assembly idea, and its task of framing a Constitution for independent India.

Just as in 1942, the British prime minister back in London was keeping a close watch on the details of such negotiations. His biographer says, 'The exchange of dispatches between Attlee and the Cabinet mission indicates quite clearly that it was he who was in charge of Indian policy. It was essential ... for the mission to get the prime minister's assent to the proposals, but before he gave his permission Attlee sent back so many amendments that according to Wavell "Cripps and the Secretary of State became quite bellicose about it and even began to talk of resignation".'[19]

The mission thus added a three-fold regional sub-federation option. The autonomous provinces were put in one of the three, depending on their geographical location. Logically, region A would be where the Congress had its majority, which would be the middle of North India— the old 1857 territory plus the provinces of Bombay and Madras along with Orissa. Region B would comprise the Muslim majority provinces of Sind, Punjab, NWFP and Balochistan. Here the League had proved its majority in three out of four provinces, NWFP being the exception. Region C would include Bengal and Assam, the latter, while not a Muslim majority province was geographically contiguous to Bengal. The provinces were to be given no option about joining, but they could, if they wished, opt out after a while.

Gandhi saw the advantage to the Congress immediately. He said the proposals 'contained a seed to convert this land of sorrow into one without sorrow and suffering'. He had seen the crucial element, which had escaped the others. As Clarke says, 'What attracted less attention at the time was his [Gandhi's] assertion that, since the constituent assembly was necessarily a sovereign body, it was open to it to vary any of the provisions in the Statement, notably on grouping.'[20]

What was more, the sovereignty of the Constituent Assembly could not be constrained by any statement of the British any more. The train hurtling towards freedom was moving much too fast for that. The political parity between the Congress and the League, which Jinnah had wrested against all odds, meant that without his consent no such sovereign body could be set up. He was too shrewd a lawyer not to see the point that Gandhi had seen. He had never trusted the rights of Muslims to any constituent assembly where his side would be in a minority.

But Gandhi had a special position in Cripps's strategy, and he continued separate negotiations with him independently of the official delegates from the Congress and the League. Jinnah may have secured parity of delegates, but the Congress always had a trump card up its sleeve in the form of the Mahatma. Gandhi wrote to Cripps, asking for further clarifications of the statement about the freedom to reject or, at least, re-jig the grouping. The Congress leader in Assam, Gopinath Bardoloi had been unhappy about its inclusion in region C. The Congress wanted, at least, that any redefinition by the Constituent Assembly, as and when it started, worked. Even a staff member of the mission knew what was afoot. 'I smell trouble. The nasty old man has grasped that he can get what he asks for & so goes on asking for more and more.'[21] He was only reflecting what his bosses felt. Conceding what Gandhi was asking for meant that the Congress would hold on to its own region A and then nibble into what would otherwise have gone to Jinnah in region C and then, perhaps, would ask that NWFP be taken out of region B. The Cabinet Mission scheme would unravel. As Wavell noted in his diary after the mission received Gandhi's letter about clarifications, 'I have never seen three men taken more aback by this revelation of G. in his true colours'. Cripps, he noted, was 'shaken to the core' and 'quite *ahuri* ["outraged"].'[22] Cripps fell ill and had to recuperate in Willingdon Nursing Home for a fortnight. Isobel Cripps, his wife had to be flown in (much to the chagrin of Alexander who worried that his wife would feel deprived by this gesture), to nurse Cripps and be diplomatic with Gandhi.

JINNAH SQUARED

The crucial man now was Jinnah. The statement looked very much like offering the Pakistan the League had resolved on in 1940, a sub-federation within a confederate All India. Jinnah had, of course, complained that the word Pakistan was imposed on the League by the Hindu politicians of the Congress since the Lahore Resolution contained no such word. By 1946 he was quite used to the word, and happy to deploy it. But if he was to now finally declare his hand, he had to have one more card up his sleeve, just in case. This was the question of the viceroy's executive council which was, in the old Cripps 1942 proposal, rejected in Simla the previous year, but was now again under discussion under the title, interim government.

While Cripps was convalescing, Wavell further pursued the negotiations on the executive council which had gone on in parallel with the mission's work. Attlee was very keen to be seen handing over power; he had his own impatient backbenchers to satisfy. This would, then, become the first Cabinet of the proposed All India federation. Jinnah therefore insisted not only on parity, but on his right to nominate any and all Muslim members on it. This was a challenge to the secular credentials of the Congress, and a slap on the face of Azad as the senior most Congress Muslim leader. Jinnah was willing to accept six or seven Hindus (including one from the untouchables), five Muslim League ministers and two from other minorities, but not let Congress add one or two Muslims in place of Hindus. Azad had secretly told Cripps that he did not mind but wanted the news kept from the Old Man who, of course, found out and was furious with Azad. No one was sure if Gandhi wanted a Muslim on the Congress side or not. If he did, Jinnah would not agree.

Jinnah was able to persuade his colleagues in the League to agree to the mission's White Paper, issued on 16 May, by 6 June 1945. This was a very unusual move for him. He had always held back from revealing his hand till after the other side had displayed its. For Jinnah to have agreed to the Cabinet Mission scheme before Congress had declared its position, may have given Nehru and Gandhi the idea that, with Jinnah in the bag, they could turn the screw on the Constituent Assembly's powers. After all, they would have a majority there, even if Jinnah had won the reserved seats for Muslims.

Now the mission turned to the Congress to persuade it to agree. Gandhi remained a problem, but Alexander would not allow Cripps any more bilateral talks with him despite Cripps's belief that, 'Gandhi in his own peculiar way is at the moment fighting three-quarters on our side'.[23] Nehru encouraged Cripps 'to go ahead with the Scheme even if there was a refusal by Congress'. He had got the Constituent Assembly where Congress would have majority and be able to change the decisions of the Cabinet Mission. Nehru's current refusal centred on Jinnah's conditions for the interim government. One ploy that Gandhi pushed was to hand over all the seats on the interim government to the League. This was, in one way, madly generous but also shrewd because Gandhi knew, as did Jinnah, that with the Congress majority in the central assembly, a League Cabinet wouldn't get far.

A second statement was issued on 16 June declaring fourteen people would be invited to form the interim government—six Congress Hindus, five League Muslims and three from minorities. Gandhi then suggested, as was his due, that one of the six Congress 'Hindus' could be a Muslim. Cripps saw the nightmare of his 1942 failure return. He described this proposal as 'a completely new stunt idea introduced by Gandhi'. He continued, 'He is an unaccountable person and when he gets these ideas in his head is as stubborn as an ox because he is convinced that he is right and no arguments will move him.'[24]

By now, the Congress delegates were getting impatient for real power and the perks of office. Patel proved to be the realist. He and Rajaji roped in Nehru to oppose Gandhi and accept what the viceroy was proposing. Cripps saw the tension.

> I felt—and said—in 1942 that the only way we should get an agreement was if Congress would divorce themselves from Gandhi and that has again

proved to be the position though this time we hope that it will stick and will not be reversed as it was in 1942. I feel that now Congress are embarking on a constructive share of the government and are no longer to be oppositional, this divorce was almost inevitable though its repercussions, if it persists, may be difficult and dangerous.[25]

Divorce, alas, is never easy. The Working Committee had too many male versions of Gandhi's devoted women, who submitted to his every whim. Even Patel backtracked. But the Congress was, at last, happy with the White Paper of 16 May, even if not with the interim government proposals of 16 June. Then, Gandhi saw that elected members to the Constituent Assembly were to be grouped according to the regions to which they belonged—A, B or C, and had to give a commitment to attend their zonal group meetings. He found this unacceptable and threw a tantrum. It was late June, and Jinnah had signed up the 16 May Cabinet Mission settlement two weeks back. So Cripps and his fellow ministers went to see Gandhi early morning on 24 June. 'Gandhi who was enjoying his weekly twenty-four hours of silence had removed all but his loin-cloth and then sat right up in a divan chair, with his legs crossed, nodding and waggling his head as the case might be!' Alexander, who confided this to his diary, thought, 'I really believe that at 77 he is not able always to take things in and consequently he sticks to what is in his mind and so muddles it—which has disastrous results to everybody.'[26]

Alexander underestimated his (silent) interlocutor. Gandhi knew what he was up to, but he was now sensing the oncoming divorce proceedings. He finally wrote to Cripps in the early hours of 25 June; the letter, Cripps thought, 'showed signs of agitation'. Clarke describes it thus, 'The language was metaphorical: the light in the darkness had vanished, leaving a vacuum'. Gandhi admitted that while 'I must not act against my instincts', he 'had nothing tangible to prove that there were danger signals'.[27]

That was it, and on 25 June morning the Congress Working Committee agreed to the May 16 proposals. The Cabinet Mission had squared the circle. Cripps was still wary. 'I have just been called to the telephone [10 a.m.] to receive a message from the Maulana that "They have accepted the long term proposals" and the letter was being typed and would be with us in an hour ... I only hope that they have not filled it up with qualifications and reservations so that it really amounts to a rejection.'[28]

Kenneth Harris casts an interesting light on the proceedings in India from the London angle:

In his diary, Wavell deplored the mission's obsequiousness to the Congress, and attributed it with some justification to guidance coming from Attlee.

But Attlee's attitude, unlike that of Cripps, was not the result of a predilection for the Congress point of view. What Wavell failed to realize was that uppermost in Attlee's mind were two anxieties: that an independent Pakistan was not viable, and that the north-western part of the potential Pakistan was very close to Russian territory. In Attlee's view an independent India, controlled by Congress, was still the most desirable solution, and he knew that the American government 'concurred'.[29]

THINGS FALL APART

The mission left India on 29 June well satisfied with what it had achieved. Here was a blueprint for a united or All India federation, which was the climax of several years of face-to-face negotiations between the British and the Indian leadership going back to the first Round Table Conference. Azad described it in glowing terms in a speech to his Congress colleagues. 'The British acceptance of India's national demand as a result of non-violent agitation and negotiations was unprecedented in world history. A nation of forty crores was becoming independent through discussion and settlement and not as a result of military action. From this point of view alone, it would be sheer lunacy to underestimate our victory. I further pointed out that the Cabinet Mission had accepted in all essentials the Congress point of view.'[30]

But it was never implemented in full or in part. Within a year of the mission leaving India, a new constitutional settlement was put in place—hurriedly, some would say—which created a sovereign Pakistan and a sovereign India. The Partition of India, which had been talked about for ten years and more as a dreadful nightmare to be avoided at all costs, was agreed to by the Congress on 3 June 1947, having been already accepted by the League. Neither the 1935 Act nor the Cripps Plan nor yet the Cabinet Mission Plan, each of which were arrangements for an All India polity, came through. How had this happened?

The folklore in India, which persists to this day, blames either the British 'divide and rule', or, either as a creature of that policy or independently, Jinnah's venomous nature which was bent on a vivisection (a favourite word) of the motherland. It is said that Jinnah believed in the two-nation theory which the Congress had always rejected. In this account the Congress's hands were forced, the folklore argues, when the British favoured Jinnah as their puppet and made it accept Partition as a condition for freedom. The Pakistanis have a similar folklore, but in that narrative the brave and lonely Jinnah strives for Muslim nationhood and is thwarted at the last moment by the scheming British, who favour Nehru and cheat Jinnah of the whole Pakistan by dividing Punjab and Bengal. Folklores are never untrue, since they speak of a deep psychological need in the collective memory of a 'nation'. But they are not history and, while there is no single answer to the question why the dream of an All India was never realized, several answers are available.

Azad's account, which was first published in 1959 and then republished with some additional passages in 1988, lays the blame squarely on Nehru. The Congress delegates had accepted the scheme by 25 June, and then the All India Congress Committee (AICC) itself ratified it at its meeting in Bombay on 7 July. It was also the day on which Nehru formally took over from Azad the presidentship of the Congress. It is best to quote Azad on what happened next:

> On 10 July, Jawaharlal held a press conference in Bombay in which he made an astonishing statement. Some representatives asked him whether, with the passing of the Resolution by the AICC, the Congress had accepted the Plan in toto, including the composition of the Interim Government.
>
> Jawaharlal in reply stated that Congress would enter the Constituent Assembly 'completely unfettered by agreements and free to meet all situations as they arise'.
>
> Press representatives further asked if this meant that the Cabinet Mission Plan could be modified.
>
> Jawaharlal replied emphatically that the Congress had agreed only to participate in the Constituent Assembly and regarded itself free to change or modify the Cabinet Mission Plan as it thought best.[31]

In Azad's account, this statement came to Jinnah 'like a bombshell'. He proceeded to interpret this as the Congress's rejection of the plan, and convened a meeting of the League council on 27 July which duly passed a resolution rejecting the plan. The Congress Working Committee then reiterated their acceptance of the plan on 10 August. But it did not cut any ice.

As Azad says in his memoirs:

> Looking back after ten years, I concede that there was force in what Mr. Jinnah said. The Congress and the League were both parties to the agreement, and it was on the basis of distribution among the Centre, the Provinces and the Groups that the League had accepted the Plan. Congress was neither wise nor right in raising doubts. It should have accepted the Plan unequivocally if it stood for unity of India. Vacillation would give Mr. Jinnah the opportunity to divide India.[32]

Azad has been much criticized for his account which has been subjected to detailed analysis. But if we take the view of Cripps' biographer on board, it is astonishing that Azad was surprised. Gandhi had seen this opportunity early on after 16 May, as did Nehru who had seen that the sovereignty of the Constituent Assembly overrode any agreement. By convention, no Parliament can bind subsequent Parliaments who are free to change matters around. Nehru and Gandhi were using that British parliamentary convention as their weapon. The British Parliament could explicitly legislate the mission plan, but it could not bind the Constituent Assembly of independent India to do anything it did not want to do. If the Cabinet Mission had wanted to bind the Constituent Assembly to any preconditions, then the British Parliament would have had to pass a new Act, like the 1935 Act laying down the safeguards. But, by now, there was no appetite among the Labour majority in the House of Commons for such imperial oversight. Azad was right when he told his fellow Congress members that the mission had accepted the Congress view in all essentials. What he failed to see, despite his senior position in the party, was that the Congress wanted monopoly control of the government of India rather than just the unity of India with power sharing. Nehru and Gandhi thought they had got just that by agreeing with the plan, along with a nod and a wink from Cripps. From 1920 onwards the Congress had wanted to be the sole party in power when India became independent. They had not gone to jail for all those years to share power with the League or, indeed, any other minority party.

The problem was that while the others—Gandhi, Nehru, Patel and Jinnah—were barristers, Azad was a literary person, a genius though he was in his chosen field. This was an issue in which lawyers' minds get much pleasure with engaging. Once Jinnah had accepted the plan on 6 June, why did the mission spend nearly three weeks cajoling the Congress to agree to it and, in doing that, what promises were made which remain unrecorded? One thing is clear. The Congress wanted power as soon as possible. The condition that the mission imposed was accepting the plan. But then Gandhi and Nehru saw, and Cripps may even have pointed out, that accepting the plan did not commit the Congress to implementing it in full, if (a) it was in government with Nehru at its head and (b) it commanded a majority in the Constituent Assembly. The Congress had Jinnah exactly where they wanted him: in a weak bargaining position, despite his much vaunted negotiating skills.

Clarke, Cripps's biographer, is explicit on this tacit understanding: 'Cripps knew perfectly well that Congress's acceptance of his constitutional scheme [the statement of May 16] had been hedged about with potentially disabling reservations, notably over grouping of provinces. Gandhi's susceptibilities had been appeased on this point. Cripps, Pethick-Lawrence and Alexander too, it should not be forgotten, had refrained from exposing this ambiguity, treating it as a practical problem to be resolved by the increasing momentum of an actual transfer of power.' Wavell talked of 'the duplicity of Cripps', adding, however, 'I don't believe that by his code that he was doing anything dishonest, he was merely being clever'.[33]

Thus, Nehru was just articulating what he and Gandhi had been given to understand by Cripps. Attlee's attitude was cited above, which gave a higher weight to the Congress's control of government. Nehru knew that he was the chosen one, not just by Gandhi and the Congress, but by the British Labour Cabinet as well. Nehru had one thing going for him, which neither Jinnah nor Gandhi had and which the British loved. He had *class*; he had, after all, studied at Harrow and Trinity College, Cambridge. He had lived a life of luxury like many rich young blades during his Edwardian years in England. He could speak their language, and match them in their witticisms. He was one of them, and had the added advantage of being Indian and popular in India. The understanding he had reached with Cripps at Goodfellows in 1938 was now being implemented—that Congress was to be the sole authority if and when Labour would be in office in Britain with a solid majority.

Nehru was a liberal democrat, and believed in atomistic individual citizens, unattached to religion or region. He was a majoritarian, but not a Hindu majoritarian. He would have waited for the Constituent Assembly to come to its senses and legislate minority rights, rather than zones as the plan wanted. Pakistan, as a separate sovereign state, had not until now been on the table. Jinnah had been happy with the plan, but he had thought the British would stay around and enforce it. When he heard Nehru, he realized that he had been outwitted. His negotiating skills had run their course. He had to act fast.

The focus, meanwhile, had shifted to the issue of an interim government once the mission left. Wavell decided he could not wait for Jinnah's prior approval and invited Nehru, now the Congress president, to form the interim government on 12 August. Nehru invited Jinnah to take part in the government, and he declined since his conditions were not met. But this was just the last straw on Jinnah's back. He had, by then, been outwitted by Nehru about his agreement on the Cabinet Mission plan. Jinnah realized that if he was to reopen negotiations, he would have to copy the tactics Congress had been using since 1920, and get his supporters out on the streets. But he was not constrained by non-violence, and he did not have the time to play a long game. The clock was ticking towards freedom's midnight, though the date had not been set yet. He now declared 16 August as Direct Action Day. In many accounts this act, which unleashed a fresh bout of horrendous communal violence in Calcutta (by now Bengal had a Muslim League government), was the beginning of the end of any chance of a united India.

This is again hindsight. The riots in Calcutta were terrible, but other major cities, Bombay for example, did not experience much violence that day. By end of the month, however, the Calcutta riots led to some copycat riots in Bombay and then in other parts of the country, such as Noakhali in East Bengal where Muslims killed Hindus, and Bihar where

Hindus killed Muslims. Between 16 August 1946 and Independence exactly 365 days later, India was in a fairly continuous state of a very uncivil civil war.

Negotiations, however, continued. Formally, the Cabinet Mission plan was still on the table, and the British government did not have an alternative plan. On 24 August Wavell announced the plan for an interim government, and on 2 September the interim government took office with Nehru at its head. The Muslim League stayed out. But the horrendous massacres meant that something had to be done to resume talks.

Gandhi was now out of the loop. The tragedies in Calcutta, and then in Noakhali, convinced him more than ever that his life was about to end in failure. The Indians had not absorbed even an iota of his message of non-violence. As always, he acted; first to intervene, to place his body in the way of murderers, visiting them in their villages and reasoning with them, trying to make them repent and recant and pledge friendship with neighbours who did not share their religion. In Calcutta, he embarrassed Suhrawardy, who was now the chief minister and had become a loyal Muslim Leaguer, to help contain the riots.

But he also put himself to a severe test. He had to be an even better *brahmachari*, because his inner voice told him that his imperfections had caused the tragedies around him. But he was no Simon of the Stylites, the fourth century BC anchorite who sat on the top of a pillar and starved himself to death when he could not resist the attractions of a beautiful woman. Gandhi was active, moving about in Noakhali with his entourage, staying in one village one day and another the next. His life was much less private here than it was in the ashram or, even, in jail. His decision to persuade his young greatniece, Manu Gandhi, to sleep naked next to him in order to test his powers of resistance, caused a huge scandal, shocking even loyal Gandhians. One secretary walked off, and Sardar Patel wrote and admonished the Mahatma for undertaking this practice.

Manu Gandhi proved to be quite a tough person for her young age. She was told to join Gandhi's experiment only if she volunteered, and the meaning of what she was being asked to do was explained to her by her great, indeed Great, uncle. Only once did she walk away, but then she finally braved it out. This was, of course, not done in secret; Gandhi insisted on talking about it and writing about it in his weekly newspapers. In being explicit about his sexual (in)activity, Gandhi outdoes Casanova in the details with which he numbs his readers. What other seventy-seven-year-old would report in print that he had a wet dream in the early hours of the morning, or had an erection which he struggled to control?

This last episode of self-testing by Gandhi has led to much scandal and much misunderstanding. What Gandhi was doing in testing his powers of abstinence was in the tradition of Christian saints. It is not a part of Hinduism. Though unconventional sexual behaviour is part of every religion, there are as many arguments in Hinduism that encourage the indulgence of the senses as a path to attain God, as there are to deny them. In the epics, penance or *tapas* is practised by the great seers— *rishis*—as a means of attaining spiritual power. This reflects a primordial belief that expending the seminal fluid drains power from the male. To enhance power the fluid has to be stored, not expended—hence celibacy becomes imperative. As the body fills up—so goes the theory—with semen, the seer's power increases and finally becomes a threat to the gods. Then Indra, the king of the gods, sends a seductive *apsara* (nymph) to tempt the seer away from his penance. Usually Indra wins and one more threat is contained.

But the great seers were not doing penance to improve the world, but only to enhance their own spiritual power. Their penance had no consequences for the mundane sphere; only for the heavenly one. It was often assumed that Gandhi was behaving like a Hindu saint, but his logic was Christian. Just as Christ took on the sins of the world and by his sacrifice redeemed it, so Gandhi believed that his abstinence from all sexuality would save India. The world, however, continued to be imperfect. Mountbatten, the last viceroy, later in 1947 did pay Gandhi the complement of saying that the Mahatma's one-man band in the east of India had been more effective in saving lives than the army's had in Punjab. Mountbatten was being his usual charming self rather than factually accurate. But that is to run ahead of our story.

Wavell, ever the military man, had begun to make 'breakdown plans' which assumed the worst possible form. He wanted the Congress majority provinces to become independent and Muslim majority provinces to continue to be governed by the governor general. Attlee thought this was a mad scheme: 'Withdrawal from India would eventually become a necessity,' Attlee said, 'but if so, *all* India would be vacated, at the same time, not bit by bit, and as quickly as possible'. He asked Wavell to work on a political settlement instead.[34]

Atlee instructed Wavell to invite the League into the interim government to calm matters. Jinnah was persuaded to drop his claim to have the exclusive right to nominate Muslims, but was given five seats in the Cabinet. The Congress agreed to give up the Finance portfolio and some Congress ministers stepped down to accommodate League ministers. On 15 October 1946 the coalition Cabinet was formed with Nehru as PM, Patel as home minister, Liaqat Ali as finance minister, Rajagopalachari as education minister (replaced in January 1947 by Maulana Azad who stayed in the job till he died twelve years later) and Baldev Singh as defence minister. Jinnah perversely chose one Hindu, Jogendra Nath Mandal as a Muslim League nominee.

Attlee saw before most others that the Cabinet Mission plan, though formally on the table, would not ensure quick independence for India. 'The failure of the Cabinet mission taught Attlee three lessons which formed a turning point in his policy towards India: first, that in spite of their close relationship with the Labour Party, the Congress would not yield an inch to produce an agreement on India which fell short of their maximum terms; secondly, that the Muslim League was determined to obtain an independent Pakistan; thirdly, that Wavell's continued presence was an obstacle to further negotiations.'[35]

Yet, another attempt at negotiations was made in London in December 1946 with Nehru and Jinnah, with Baldev Singh representing the Sikhs. The issues were still the same as they were in July. Jinnah wanted a rigid scheme of zones unalterable by the Constituent Assembly after independence. This would assure him that minority (Muslim) rights would be safe at least in zones B and C. Congress wanted flexibility to change the zones so that Assam could opt out of zone C. Congress knew that once they got the assembly they could change things. But if there were to be pre-conditions, they wanted Assam out of Jinnah's clutches. Jinnah said there should be an option to opt *out* after the group Constitution was framed, but not opt in. This, Jinnah thought, was the Cabinet Mission's intention. Gandhi and Nehru had another interpretation, as they had raised the issue of Assam during their separate bilateral negotiations with Cripps and may have convinced him that there was a loophole.

Azad, who had staked his reputation on the mission plan, says in his memoirs, 'In fairness I have to admit that on this point Mr. Jinnah was on the whole right. Both justice and expediency demanded that Congress should have accepted the Plan unequivocally.'[36] Azad was wrong about one thing. Justice may have so required, but not expediency. Nehru and Gandhi were realists in politics, especially this close to the climax. The December meeting in London remained indecisive. Cripps said, 'It looked as if it had got beyond the possibilities of compromise'. The British Cabinet had to do something yet again to break the logjam.

THE FINAL ACT

The anxiety about how to end British rule in India was now occupying many minds in London. After the failure of the December 1946 meetings between Indian leaders and the British Cabinet's India Committee, Attlee met the King Emperor George VI, who confided in his diary, 'I told

[Attlee] I was very worried over the breakdown of the Indian leaders' talks, and that I could see no alternative to Civil War between Hindus and Muslims for which we should be held responsible ... Nehru's present policy seemed to be to secure complete domination by Congress throughout the Government of India. The Muslims would never stand for it and would probably fight for Pakistan which the Hindus dislike so much.'[37]

The December deadlock between Jinnah and Nehru convinced Attlee that a drastic shift in policy was required. Wavell had doubts that India could be held beyond March 1948 unless Britain were to reassert its authority and declare its intention to stay for fifteen more years. Attlee had made up his mind on an early withdrawal, but not an over-hasty retreat. The India Committee of the Cabinet decided before Christmas 1946 'that an early announcement of our intention to withdraw was the most hopeful means of inducing the Congress and the Muslim League to come to an agreement'.[38] A deadline by which the British would leave, whatever the Indians had decided, might concentrate minds in India and make the two rival parties agree on a modus vivendi.

Wavell would not do as the viceroy in charge of the final goodbye. Attlee chose the king's cousin and the Allied army's commander-in-chief in the East, Lord Mountbatten, in his place. Attlee wrote later, 'It was my own thought entirely to choose Mountbatten to negotiate India's independence. I knew his record in the war, and I decided he was the man to get good personal relations with the Indians, which he did. He and I agreed entirely.'[39] Years later Attlee told Kenneth Harris, his biographer, why he had chosen Mountbatten:

> We weren't getting anywhere. The only thing was that if we let the Congress have their way, the Muslims would start a war to get their Pakistan. Apart from that, nothing was in sight. Both parties were asking for everything and blaming us for not getting anything when they should have been blaming themselves. I decided there was only one thing to do—give them a deadline, and tell them 'on that date we go out. So you'd better get together right away'. It was the only thing that would bring them together ... Next thing was to find the right man to carry out the new policy. Dickie Mountbatten stood out a mile.[40]

Louis Mountbatten was also the one viceroy, though the last one, who had royal credentials. (Within a year of his arrival in India, his nephew Philip was to marry Elizabeth, the Princess of Wales, and become the Duke of Edinburgh, Royal Consort to Queen Elizabeth II.) He was used to command, and asked for plenipotentiary powers. Attlee gave him those powers, which had not been given to either Cripps in 1942 or the Cabinet Mission in 1946. No one had been given plenipotentiary powers in the twentieth century until then, and these powers allowed Mountbatten the leeway not to consult Whitehall on every move he made. Attlee was not worried. He never gambled, but in this case took a calculated risk. He reckoned that Mountbatten 'was too concerned about his reputation and his future career to commit the government to a hazardous step without consultation'.[41]

Attlee wrote to Mountbatten on 8 February that 'the definite objective of HMG [is] to obtain if possible a unitary government for all India in accordance with the Cabinet Mission's plan and you should do your utmost in your power to persuade all parties to work to this end'.[42] Mountbatten had his own ideas, though we only know of them from later recollections by himself or his staff. Alan Campbell-Johnson, who was his aide, recalls being told as early as 19 December that 'it was clear to him [Mountbatten] that there would have to be the earliest time limit for the transfer of power if his mission was not to be hopelessly compromised with Indian opinion from the outset.'[43] He was his own boss. He was either the most successful viceroy or a total disaster depending on one's views. In Britain he remains a much more controversial figure than in India, where he managed to be perhaps the only viceroy who elicited real affection. He is loathed in Pakistan—perhaps for the same reason that Indians love him.[44]

Before he arrived in India, the British Parliament had debated India yet again. This time it was to announce Mountbatten's appointment and the commitment to grant India independence by June 1948. In the Commons, Churchill defended Wavell since he was being abandoned by the Labour Party now, though he had only been 'the willing or unwilling agent of the Government in all the errors and mistakes into which they had been led'. Churchill added about the choice of Mountbatten, 'I am bound to say the whole thing wears the aspect of an attempt by the Government to make use of brilliant war figures to cover up a melancholy and disastrous transaction whose consequences will darken, aye, redden the coming years.'[45]

When Attlee replied, a witness who was watching the debate from the public gallery, wrote later, 'This man [Attlee] burns with a hidden fire and is sustained by a certain spiritual integrity which enables him to scale new heights when the great occasion demands. Churchill was raked with delicious irony'.[46] To Churchill Attlee said:

> In approaching this subject, we all have to recognize how little we know about India, and how soon what knowledge we have gets out of date. I ended my time on the Simon Commission nearly 18 years ago. I therefore hesitate to be dogmatic or prophetic about what may happen in India. In this, I admit, I differ from the leader of the Opposition. I think his practical acquaintance with India ended some fifty years ago. He formed some

strong opinions—I might almost say prejudices. They have remained with him ever since.[47]

But he admitted that 'a very grave fault of the reforms we have carried out over the years is that we have taught irresponsibility. All Indian politicians were permanently in opposition, and speaking with long experience, it is not always good to be in opposition.'[48]

Attlee ended by saying, 'We cannot wait. I would have liked a message to go from this House ... without a dissentient voice saying "It is our earnest will that the Indians should grasp now this great opportunity of showing that all of them, without distinction of creed, place the good of India's millions before the interests of any section whatever".'[49]

Mountbatten arrived on 20 March 1947 with a clear mandate to get out by June 1948. In theory, everything was the same as it was when the Cabinet Mission left. That was the only offer on the table, and an interim government had been formed under that plan. The December meeting in London had highlighted the differences in the interpretation of the plan as between the League and the Congress, or rather between Jinnah and Nehru (who now had Patel by his side stiffening his resolve to stand up to Jinnah). Mountbatten's potent weapon was the time deadline, and it is here that the compulsions came down on the principal players. But the compulsions pointed not towards the Cabinet Mission plan, but away from it. The reasons lay in the experience of sharing power.

Once the League joined the interim government, the Congress realized that one of their two holds on Jinnah, the control of the interim government, had become fragile. Liaqat Ali Khan, as finance minister, shocked the Congress by introducing a very radical budget, taxing excess profits. In doing so, he audaciously drew on speeches of the Congress leaders, especially Nehru, who had espoused socialist, anti-business policies since the Karachi Congress resolution of 1933. But that was then. Now the Congress had become a haven for industrialists and businessmen, who saw their advantage in supporting the oncoming men of power. Gandhi had always had the very public support of G.D. Birla and Jamnalal Bajaj as well as of the Ahmedabad textile magnates, Ambalal Sarabhai and Kasturbhai Lalbhai. Many industrialists and traders had made huge profits in war conditions, and were not about to be (even legitimately) robbed. The Liaqat Ali budget was not what they had donated all that money to the Congress for. Patel wanted out as soon as possible of the interim government and the entire set up of the Mission plan.

The experience of interim government convinced the Congress leadership more than ever that power sharing was not their style. The British tradition they had absorbed told them a majority party can form its own Cabinet and does not need to get into a coalition. That is why the Congress had refused coalition in 1937 in all the provinces where it had majority. The Congress was an inclusive party, but the inclusion was done by inducting members representing different regions and communities within it, while keeping the apex leadership firmly in elite hands. What was the point of independence if Liaqat Ali Khan was going to dictate economic policies, even if he cynically cited Congress scriptures?

Out on the streets of India, the communal situation was deteriorating fast. A bare calendar account shows destruction in Lahore and Amritsar in March and again in Lahore in May; by end of May in Gurgaon on the edges of Delhi, continuing in June in Punjab; again in Lahore and Calcutta between 1 and 10 July. Throughout this time Bengal (other than Calcutta) and Bihar were in flames.[50] By May it was clear that a division of India was now on the cards. The people of Punjab sensed the province was about to be divided, and anxiety and fear about where India would end and Pakistan begin, spread. Even so, until then no one had said the word 'Pakistan' officially, and even the major players were vague as to what partition would mean. There was a lingering hope that even after division, a single over-arching Central government would look after defence and communications and foreign policy, and that Hindustan and Pakistan would be under an All India Central government. The attachment to old places of residence was such that Suhrawardy, the Bengal chief minister, would not leave Calcutta even after Partition had been announced, and Jinnah hoped he would spend weekends in his Bombay house.

The only person who had foreseen that the creation of a Pakistan as a separate nation state could lead to mass migrations and much destruction, was not even a major player in the negotiations. Dr B.R. Ambedkar wrote a book, *Pakistan or the Partition of India* in 1940, and by 1946 the book was in its third edition. It is the only book, as far as I know, which explicitly talks about how human movements across new borders were inevitable if a formal division was carried out. Ambedkar drew on his extensive reading of the experience of Europe after the end of the First World War, especially in the areas of the former Austro-Hungarian Empire and the Ottoman Empire. As new nations were created, the persecution of the newly created minorities meant either their slaughter or their forced migration, or both. In all the writings on Partition before and, indeed, after the event few have noticed Ambedkar's warnings. The discussion is set on familiar lines—about united India versus communal division, two-nation theory versus the possibility of the Cabinet Mission plan. No preparation seems to have been made by the British government to foresee or forestall the carnage. Indeed, what could have been done was overtaken by the unseemly haste with which Mountbatten now moved to nail down the two sides to an agreement of some sort.

Azad tells the story of the events as they unfolded. Following Liaqat Ali's budget, he says:

> The Central government was paralysed as the Members of the Council pulled against one another ... A truly pathetic situation had developed as a result of our own foolish action in giving Finance to the Muslim League. Lord Mountbatten took full advantage of the situation. Because of the dissensions among the members, he slowly and gradually assumed full powers ... He also began to give a new turn to the political problem and tried to impress on both the Congress and the Muslim League the inevitability of Pakistan. He pleaded in favour of Pakistan and sowed the seeds of the idea in the minds of the Congress members of the Executive Council.[51]

Azad does not appreciate the irony in his statement that Mountbatten began taking over full power, since the Congress had always stopped short of entering the executive council in 1942 and 1945 because of their demand that the governor general/viceroy treat the council like a Cabinet. Now that it was a Cabinet, internal quarrels led the Cabinet to be converted back into a council.

As a naval man and with a winner's record to defend, Mountbatten believed in dispatch. He did not waste time like Cripps, drafting and redrafting plans. He made a quick inspection of the situation and by 19 April—within three weeks of his arrival—he had concluded that further talks with the Congress and the League would not lead to any progress towards the implementation of the Cabinet Mission plan. It was time to cut losses and move on. This was how he thought of the idea of the two units to which power could be transferred. If anyone is the 'father' of Pakistan, it is Mountbatten. Or, perhaps, he was the just the surgeon who performed the Caesarean operation.

The seeds Mountbatten had sown among the Congress members of the interim government had fallen on receptive soil. Fed up with Liaqat Ali, the Congress was seeking a way out. It saw that exclusive power could only be had outside the Cabinet Mission plan framework. Sardar Patel was the first to bite Mountbatten's bait (to change the analogy from horticulture to angling). 'Till perhaps the very end Pakistan was for Jinnah a bargaining counter, but in fighting for Pakistan he had overreached himself. His action had so irritated Sardar Patel that the Sardar was now a believer in partition.'[52]

With Patel on his side, Mountbatten directed his and his wife Edwina's charm to the task of winning over Nehru. An affair between Nehru and Edwina has been rumoured ever since. Some prudish minds have tried to insinuate that 'nothing really happened between them', but whether two grown-up, mature adults did or did not do 'it' is neither possible nor necessary to establish. Given their records, it is more likely than not. But what matters is the final result, and that was Nehru being won over to the idea of Pakistan.

It may even be said that Nehru was already willing to reject the Cabinet Mission plan and by April 1947, he recognized he would not be able to control the Constituent Assembly if the executive council could be rendered dysfunctional by the minority party. Nehru wanted power to mould India according to his ideas; he did not want obstacles in his way. He was amenable to giving up provinces which the Congress would never win. Even NWFP was being lost each day as the Red Shirts fought to maintain their slender lead in the assembly. Once he was rid of these provinces, then the hold of the Congress over the legislature and the executive would be that much more secure.

The British Cabinet had received the first plans for Partition from Mountbatten by the beginning of May, and its India Committee approved them on 8 May. On 10 May Mountbatten showed the plans to Nehru. Since Nehru balked at first, saying the plan 'would lead to the Balkanization of India', Mountbatten flew to London on 14 May to discuss his next step. He revised his plan and got Nehru and Jinnah to approve. The Princely States, which had been left out of the discussion thus far, would have the right to join either India or Pakistan. They would choose by royal whim—no voting would take place in any Princely State to decide which unit to join. In the discussions of the 1935 Act the Congress had criticized the fact that the choice to join the federation was left to the whim of the rulers rather than through a plebiscite among the people of the Princely States. But again that was then, and now the caravan had moved on. Time was running out in any case, and no other choice could be permitted to the princes.

The Cabinet was most cooperative. Lord Listowel, now the Secretary of State for India and the last one to hold the position (and indeed outlive all other participants in the discussions as he lingered on daily at his perch in the House of Lords till the late 1990s where I saw him myself) said, 'We could hardly do less than agree without a murmur to a scheme that had the blessing of both the Viceroy and the two communities.' The India Committee discussed the plan on 27 May, Attlee having 'successfully injected a sense of utmost urgency into his colleagues'. Cabinet approved the same day and Attlee announced that Mountbatten was to return and make a last formal attempt to preserve a united India and then, since that was bound to fail, announce the Partition plan.

Azad, for his part, was still hoping that the Cabinet Mission scheme would be implemented. He even argued for a two-year delay, during which the League could be persuaded to see reason. He tried to enlist Gandhi, knowing the revulsion the prospect of division caused him. Gandhi sympathized, but did not help reverse the solution he knew his two most trusted Congressmen—Nehru and Patel—wanted. As Azad recalls, 'I realised that if a decision was taken now, partition was inevitable but a better solution might emerge after a year or two. Gandhiji did not reject my suggestion but neither did he indicate any enthusiasm for it.'[53] India's fate was now accepted by its staunchest guardians.

Mountbatten spoke to the Indian leaders on 2 June, and by 3 June both parties had agreed. Attlee could, therefore, later that day make to the House of Commons the historic announcement. Churchill was moved to pay a tribute to Attlee. 'The Prime Minister said that credit was due to the Viceroy. There are matters about which it is extremely difficult to form decided opinions now, but if the hopes that are contained in this declaration are borne out, great credit will indeed be due to the Viceroy and not only to the Viceroy, but to the Prime Minister who advised the British government to appoint him.'[54]

The Congress got the exclusive control it wanted, and it also got the decision to split Punjab and Bengal between the two nation states. This was because each assembly had a choice and in those two, a partition of the province itself was an extra choice. Jinnah ended up with a 'moth-eaten Pakistan'. India inherited the old title of British India, and called itself India (or Bharat, as some purists added in the Constituent Assembly, enabling Pakistan for many years to deny the title India to the new polity by calling it Bharat). In a subtle way, the retention of the name India has perpetuated the impression that what was India was partitioned, its left and right limbs hacked off. Had a different name been imposed—Hindustan for instance or even Bharat, but not India—it would have been seen as the birth of two nations out of one territory which had been forcibly united by a foreign power, and not the tragic division of a single nation.

A live link up from Westminster, where Prime Minister Attlee was making the announcement to the assembled benches of the House of Commons, was relayed via Delhi across the Indian empire's 1.8 million square miles, twenty times the size of Britain itself. After Attlee's announcement, Mountbatten spoke followed by Nehru, Jinnah and Baldev Singh for the Sikhs. As Khwaja Ahmad Abbas, a renowned Urdu writer as well as a film director and screen play writer described it, 'Literally millions all over the yet-India sat glued to their own or their neighbours' radio sets, for the fate of India was to be decided that day. From Peshawar to Travancore, from Karachi to Shillong, India became an enormous collective ear, waiting for the broadcasts breathlessly, helplessly and hopelessly.[55]

Attlee announced that power would be handed over before 30 June 1948, but the next day at a press conference Mountbatten upped the ante and said 15 August 1947 would be the date. His announcement caused consternation in Delhi and London. Listowel tried to get Attlee to question this decision, worried that Parliament might not agree to so rapid a timetable for legislation. 'Attlee was imperturbable. His instruction, written in his own hand, was "Accept Viceroy's proposal".'[56]

Mountbatten's decision, to hasten the grant of independence by more than ten months, has been much criticized. It did not give time for the careful preparation of such matters as the drawing of boundaries, which were announced late on 16 August. Cyril Radcliffe, the judge who drew them up for Punjab, albeit with local advisers, had no first-hand experience of these matters. As Azad recalls:

> Mr. Radcliff was then in Simla. He accepted the appointment but suggested that he would start the survey in early July. He pointed out that it would be an impossible task to undertake a field survey in the Punjab in the heat of June and in any case July meant a delay of only three or four weeks. Lord Mountbatten told him that he was not prepared for even one day's delay and any suggestion about three or four weeks' postponement was simply out of the question. His orders were carried out.[57]

Even so, the time was very short.

Immeasurable misery was caused to thousands of families as widespread violence broke out across the two provinces, which everyone knew would be divided—Punjab and Bengal. The decision had to be formally made since each assembly was to vote separately on the issue of whether to stay in India or join Pakistan. There were only ten weeks left to Independence Day after 4 June.

The Bengal legislature decided on 20 June, meeting separately according to whether they represented Hindu or Muslim majority constituencies, to partition Bengal. Ninety 'Hindu' members chose India (that is, to stay in the existing Constituent Assembly), among them the young Jyoti Basu, who would, thirty years later, become the first democratically elected communist chief minister of West Bengal, and also the longest-serving chief minister—a period of twenty-five years. Hundred and twenty-six opted for the new Constituent Assembly (that is, Pakistan). Then each group met again. The Hindu group voted by 58 to 21 for Partition and the Muslim group voted against by 106 to 35. By the stated rules either group could force Partition—and the Hindu group had its way.

As Leonard Gordon has put it, 'Thus the Congress–Mahasabha alliance successfully manoeuvred to keep West Bengal as a Hindu-majority province within a divided India. Given the limited choice before them, the Hindu Bengalis voted to split Bengal and remain part of the larger political entity, India.'[58] Thus two generations after the agitation by their grandparents against Curzon's plan to divide Bengal, the Bengali Hindus voted for Curzon. The Muslim majority was happy to join Pakistan, but also wanted to keep Bengal undivided. This was not to be; here was the proof of the astute negotiating techniques of Gandhi and Nehru in scuttling the Cabinet Mission plan. Bengal Hindus got the sort of effective parity for a minority which Jinnah had been seeking during the discussions of the Nehru Report in 1928, and which the Congress, egged on by the Hindu Mahasabha, refused him.

Once again, though now for the last time, the British Parliament had to gird its loins to legislate on India. Given what Mountbatten had said, time was short. If the 1935 Act had been taken up at a level of detail which was unprecedented, this time every device was used to make it quick. Cripps prevailed upon the Cabinet to allow Nehru a glimpse of the draft bill. But there was still the Conservative Opposition to bring on board. 'To cover their political nakedness, and to keep Churchill quiet, the Conservatives clutched at the fact that the measure provided for Dominion status within the British Commonwealth. But despite their objections, which Attlee faced down, the title was simply, "Indian Independence Bill", as Cripps had wished.'[59]

The hero was definitely Attlee at this stage. 'The legislative feat required to put the Indian Independence Act on the statute book in time for the transfer of power on 15 August was prodigious. No comparable piece of British legislation was drafted, debated and passed into law in so short a time.'[60] The bill went from its first reading (a short formal affair) to its second reading within the shortest period of time permitted—one week. Having had a second reading on 10 July where Harold Macmillan, a future Conservative prime minister, congratulated Attlee 'on the lucidity, moderation and dignity with which he has performed his formidable task', the bill had an unopposed third reading on 14 July and passed. Attlee said, 'In parting with this Bill from this House, I do it not with a feeling of elation, but with a feeling of responsibility, some feeling of anxiety, but also with an unquenchable hope that these things will work out for the good of all the people of India.'[61] In the House of Lords debate Lord Samuel, a member of the Liberal Party, said, 'This Bill is a moral to all future generations; it is a Treaty of Peace without a war'.[62]

He was only half right. It was peace between All India and Britain, but a war within All India among Indians who were no longer Indians, but Indians and Pakistanis. Within the month that was left, there was mayhem. Whatever officials and leaders may have envisaged at the top and in the Centre or in the provincial capitals, there was an orgy of decentralized violence where neighbours broke friendships of decades and looted and killed and burnt. Women suffered more as they were either the victims of rape by the other community, or killed to save the honour of the clan by their own. Many were forcibly converted, abducted and subjected to various abuses. Trains crowded with anxious passengers, and plying the very short distance between Lahore and Amritsar, arrived packed with none alive. Khushwant Singh, India's leading writer has captured this horror vividly in his classic novel, *Train to Pakistan*.

There is no accurate count of how many died during the Partition mayhem; perhaps as few as half-a-million; perhaps several times that number. Millions moved across the borders, Hindu Sindhis from Sind to Bombay or Delhi, Punjabi Hindus and Sikhs mainly across to East Punjab or to Delhi and later all over the country. Bengali Hindus from East Bengal to West Bengal, but mainly to the railway platform in Howrah, where they lived in tents for years. Muslims from UP and Bihar went to either West or East Pakistan respectively, and from East Punjab to West Punjab, which was now in Pakistan. They had lost their land and jewellery and all their possessions, they had lost their dignity and peace of mind. Even sixty years on, the wounds of Partition have not healed; the horrible memories have not been obliterated.[63]

But even so, this was a North Indian affair. Elsewhere across India Partition had no immediate impact. But there was another dimension to the Mountbatten decision, which also requires some discussion. The question of the Princely States had loomed large at the Round Table Conference and in the 1935 Act. The princes had shown insufficient enthusiasm to join the federation proposed in the 1935 Act. The Act had, in fact, promised them a lot of clout in the federation, with seats in both houses of the Indian Parliament and, since the prospect for India then was only Dominion Status, they could have consolidated their position before any eventual independence. They did not join partly because they thought they could get better conditions if they held out— perhaps even independent sovereign status—or, because their friends in the Conservative party in Britain egged them on to stay out. In either case, they made a Himalayan blunder of their own.

Many princes had fought in the First World War, but warfare in those days was still a leisurely activity for the officer class and creature comforts assured for even minor royalty. The Second World War was more professional and hangers-on were not welcome. So the princes had, by and large, sat out the war. But afterwards, once the Labour Party came to power, there was no sympathy whatsoever for them. Mountbatten told the politicians first about the impending changes and only then informed the princes that they, too, had to choose and choose quickly whether they wanted to join India or Pakistan. The power of paramountcy under which their relations with the Crown were defined, was passed over, de facto if not de jure, to the two independent Dominion Status entities. Mountbatten as a viceroy and one with royal connections could afford to be particularly ruthless in telling the princes that their time was up. Sardar Patel as the home minister, with the astute V.P. Menon at his side, now began to exercise his extensive powers on the princes.

Most chose on the grounds of geography since there was not much leeway. The kingdoms located adjacent to Hindu majority areas of British India went to India, and those adjacent to the Muslim majority provinces, to Pakistan Three held out. Junagadh was a small principality in the Kathiawar region of Bombay province which had a Muslim nawab and a Hindu majority population. The Nizam of Hyderabad was an important Muslim ruler and the oldest ally of the British. He, too, had a Hindu majority population. His kingdom was large enough to be a nation state on its own, and he had hired some clever lawyers (among them Walter Moncton, KC who later became a minister in the 1951 Conservative government) to probe into his claim for independence. The Maharaja of Jammu and Kashmir, conversely, was a Hindu king with a majority Muslim population in the valley of Kashmir, and a largely Hindu one in Jammu, with Ladakh, the mountainous third part, largely Buddhist. His was the only kingdom which was adjacent to both India and Pakistan as they began to take shape. He thought he had some bargaining power with the two new governments. This was to leave a long and bitter legacy after 1947, which to this day remains a major obstacle to friendly relations between the two countries.

These three princes tried in their own ways to seek a 'third way', but eventually failed. Their story is part of the story of independent India. Partition has marked the history of India after Independence. The Congress discussed the Partition at an agonizing meeting on 14–15 June and Ram Manohar Lohia, a perennial radical socialist, then a young man, has recorded how Gandhi sat silent and Nehru and Patel did most of the talking. Azad quietly smoked away, and only the younger generation of Congress socialists voiced any opposition. Yet, the agony remained even after the horrendous immediate effect of Partition had passed, and a semblance of recovery had been achieved. The idea that the party which had been wedded to a vision of a united India and had an ideology of nationalism which emphasized the syncretic Hindu–Muslim bond, had agreed to a partition based on religion, has been an awkward fact to explain away. Later in the early fifties, the Congress rewrote history and argued that it had never accepted the two-nation theory. That may be so—though there is evidence against this contention—but they certainly embraced its practice. They shifted the responsibility for the Partition on the British and Jinnah, whose joint and several machinations were blamed for forcing the vivisection of the motherland.

But the question has to be posed to the Muslim League as well. What did it gain by winning Pakistan? After all, what was partitioned into three sections was the Muslim population of India, the largest single concentration of Muslims anywhere in the world till then. Pakistan itself had two widely separated parts, West and East Pakistan, the latter more populous than the former. The Muslim population was fractured and the Muslim culture of North India—fashioned over a thousand years, rich in its many achievements in music, painting, cuisine, textiles and architecture—rendered lame by the removal of its legitimacy. Perhaps, Jinnah never did want a separate independent sovereign state for the Muslims, but only guarantees for their rights. He played a long game, but at the end declared his hand too soon and was then driven by the Congress to accept his 'moth-eaten Pakistan'.

Way back in April 1946, during the Cabinet Mission's marathon negotiations, Maulana Azad had issued a statement warning of the consequences on the Muslim community should the proposed zonal arrangement take place:

> Let us consider dispassionately the consequences which will follow if we give effect to the Pakistan scheme. India will be divided into two states, one with a majority of Muslims and the other of Hindus. In the Hindustan State there will remain three and-a-half crores of Muslims scattered in small minorities all over the land. With 17 per cent in UP, 12 per cent in Bihar and 9 per cent in Madras, they will be weaker than they are today in the Hindu majority provinces. They have had their homelands in these regions for almost a thousand years and built up well known centres of Muslim culture and civilisation there.
>
> They will awaken overnight and discover that they have become alien and foreigners. Backward industrially, educationally and economically, they will be left to the mercies of what would become an unadulterated Hindu raj.[64]

Azad was speaking of zonal arrangements, but his prophetic words anticipated what would happen to Muslims of India when the even greater displacement of Partition look place.

WHY DID PAKISTAN/PARTITION HAPPEN?

The Partition was not an accident. It became a reality very quickly, having been used as a threat by Jinnah to make the Congress come to the table. Pakistan was not a legal possibility on the table as an offer until mid-April 1947, but was signed and sealed by 3 June 1947 and delivered by British Parliament on 14 July. Was it always a secret plan of the fiendish British, buried deep in their files ever since the Aga Khan led a Muslim delegation to Lord Morley in 1907, if not before? Was it a diabolical plot hatched by an amoral and ambitious Jinnah? Or, was it simply, as Nehru told Leonard Mosley, that they were all getting old and tired and wanted an end to the bickering?

My argument has been that the narratives of nationhood that were put forward were inadequate to command total support across the entire territory which came to be defined as India sometime around the late-nineteenth century. This India was an administrative creation of the British as a political unity (leaving the question of Princely States aside for the moment). The consciousness of nationhood was founded on the unpleasant fact of foreign creation of the motherland. The foreign role in creation of the nation had to be denied or, at best, reduced or negated. A history of the nation had to be forged; nationalism had to create a history of the nation that was timeless, indeed primordial. Ah, there was the rub! The farther back in time one went to create the story of the nation, the more partial it became. Religion became central to the national story except that there were, at least, two religions which could tell a story.

The shock of modernity, which came along with imperialism, led to religious reaction in the form of revivalism or reform in Hinduism as well as Islam. The reactions took different forms in different regions with very few 'All India' movements. These religious reactions laid the proto-nationalist foundations of the Indian 'nation' before a secular, elite nationalism was constructed by the Congress from 1885 onwards. The Congress was the only 'All India' body. The religious movements, both Hindu and Muslim, were regional or, at most, confined to North India.

But the Congress also resorted to religion when it needed to expand its base after the 1905 Partition of Bengal. The moderates, who were constitutionalists, were loyal yet secular. The radicals of Punjab, Maharashtra and Bengal, who were militant, were steeped in their own regional versions of Hinduism—the Arya Samaj in Punjab, the revival of Ganesh worship in Maharashtra and of Kali worship in Bengal. The moderates managed the Lucknow Pact in 1916, the highpoint of their secular constitutional approach. But Gandhi rejected this. He built a bridge by fashioning a loyal but oppositionist movement, which alternated between the streets and the conference table to get its way. He used a powerful religious idiom which eschewed the orthodox Hinduism of Lajpat Rai, Tilak and Aurobindo Ghose, and accommodated Islam in an ecumenical way.

His ecumenism worked in his first struggle in the early 1920s but after the collapse of the Khilafat movement, there was an increasing alienation of the Muslims from the Congress. This has been hotly contested by the Congress version of Indian independence movement's history, but the results of 1937 and, even more, of the 1946 elections, leaves no doubt in any neutral observer's mind. It was only after the unsuccessful Khilafat movement and the exodus of Muslims from the Congress that the syncretic story was pushed to the fore. Maulana Azad himself had subscribed to a stronger pan-Islamist theory of Muslim nationhood in India during the Khilafat agitation. It was after the movement's failure that he began to fashion an alternative narrative. He used elements of the story of Hindu–Muslim unity which were put forward by Sir Syed Ahmad in the late nineteenth century. But even Sir Syed had increasingly abandoned this story as pressures from Hindu/Hindi nationalists began to erode the economic space the Muslims had.

Thus the syncretic narrative had become not so much an 'Indian' as a Congress narrative. Congress thought it was India. Jinnah took his chance when Congress went into the wilderness after 1939 for six years. By the time the negotiations resumed after the war, the ground had shifted from beneath the feet of all the nationalists. Neither the Muslim League nor the Congress got what they wanted. Partition was a bad compromise but then none other was viable. This, at least, became clear after the Cabinet Mission plan failed to secure acceptance by the two parties. The leaders divided up the spoils of the empire; it is the masses who paid the price for their intransigence.

CHAPTER 11

POLITICAL ECONOMY OF EMPIRE AND NATION

THE OTHER NARRATIVE OF NATIONALISM

Religion was one axis along which Indian nationhood became increasingly identified as independence approached. This, of course, was not the way the Congress began in 1885. It had a political economy critique of British rule which did not dwell on religion or region, but on the dual and dialectical relation between empire and the (putative) nation. But even this 'secular' narrative became fragmented as independence approached, more because of the differences within the Congress about the nature of the imperial economic relation than due to differences between the Congress and the League. Was it imperialism Indians needed to be rid of, or was it capitalism itself? Luckily for the Congress, there was never the time to settle the issue and when Independence came there were, at least, two views on the political economy question as there were on the religious issue. It is worth looking at the way these differences were articulated to see why the economic legacy of imperialism was, and is still, disputed.

The narrative the Congress drew on to unite Indians was a nationalist economic narrative fashioned in the first twenty years of its life, a critique of the British rule as being un-British. Central to the critique was the theory of the 'drain' which Dadabhai Naoroji pioneered. This held that the British were draining away valuable economic surplus from India which, if retained at home, could alleviate India's poverty. The Congress also added demands for tariff protection for India's nascent modern industry, and a devaluation of the rupee vis-à-vis the pound sterling. The issue of the exchange rate was not just a technical one. It concerned the burdens of imports and exports on parts of the Indian economy which were exposed to international trade.

The British India government was interested in maintaining a high value of the rupee relative to the pound sterling. In this, British business interests who exported to India concurred. It made British exports cheap for Indians to buy. The Indians buyers of British cloth and other imports also liked a high rupee for the same reason. The value of the pound sterling was fixed in terms of gold. The rupee was freely minted from silver, hence the rate of exchange depended on the bimetallic price ratio of gold to silver. But silver was depreciating in the 1880s, and hence the rupee fell against the pound. This hurt British exporters and the British Indian government simultaneously. The former found the market for their goods falling, and the latter had to ship more rupees to pay for the dues it had to pay in pound sterling.

After 1893 the government fixed a rate of 1s 4d per rupee (or 15 rupees to one pound) and stopped free minting. This meant that it had to pay fewer rupees to service the home charges—pensions of retired officials, stores purchased in the UK, etc. which was at the heart of the drain debate. If drain was the issue, an overvalued rupee kept more of India's surplus at home. But while Calcutta wanted an overvalued rupee, the newly emerging Indian industrial classes and, indeed, the farmers who exported food grains wanted a cheap rupee so that they could sell more abroad. Thus, the new industrial classes argued for a policy which would drain more rupees per pound of home charges. But this contradiction was not recognized at the time, either by the nationalists or by the British. A Royal Commission, which had Lord Kilbracken (Arthur Godley who served twenty-five years as permanent Secretary at the India Office) as chairman, and the economist, John Maynard Keynes as Secretary, recommended an even higher rate of two schillings per rupee (10 rupees per pound). The war intervened and this change did not happen.

After 1905, for a while the economic critique added the boycott of foreign imports—swadeshi—in addition to tariff protection to its repertoire.[1] Yet, this was a strategy that ultimately worked in the elite's favour, since the beneficiaries of the tariffs and of rupee devaluation would be the urban better-off, while the poor would lose out since the foreign cloth which was being burned was cheaper than its domestic variant, at least then.

After the First World War and Jallinawala Bagh, the nationalist narrative became more critical. While tariff autonomy had been granted, the rupee devaluation debate continued. But Gandhi introduced a different set of themes in the critique which divided, rather than united, the nationalist forces. Gandhi's critique embraced not just the impact of un-British rule on the domestic economy, but a rejection of all modernization, all industry, whether under Indian or British ownership. It was not imperialism, but modern industry which, in his view, had impoverished India. Though he later modified this stand, his economic approach remained focussed on cotton spinning and 'managing' poverty (harnessing prohibition, sexual abstinence to control population growth, cottage industries, etc.) rather than overcoming it by using the instruments of modernization.

Gandhi struck a radical chord when he took up the legitimate grievances of peasants, the first Congress leader to do so. In Champaran, Bihar, and then in the Kheda district of Gujarat, he championed peasant demands for remission of revenue. This kept the focus on the British rule as an enemy of the poor peasant. He continued this on many other occasions in Bardoli, Gujarat, and elsewhere, but restricted himself to revenue strikes and avoided rent strikes. This was because rent strikes would hurt the landlords as well and he did not want antagonism among Indians, whatever their class position. The younger generation of Nehru and the socialists wanted land reform, abolition of zamindari and a struggle against agrarian exploitation. Nehru's focus was the United Provinces (UP), but the land reform agitation also spread to Bihar. Bengal had its own agitation, but here the Congress was on the side of the Hindu landlords, and it was Muslim parties, such as the Krishak Praja Party, which took the lead. This twin track approach—the conservative all class-alliance of Gandhi and the radical anti-feudal programme of Nehru—lived in an uneasy partnership till Independence. It definitely put the Congress on the side of the peasant and against the government, but it could also be divisive as in UP, where landlords were more often Muslim rather than Hindu.

Bengal

Bengal had descended from prosperity to misery in the period between 1905 and 1947. The nineteenth century had been a period of economic prosperity and cultural efflorescence. Bengal had also then provided the political leadership of India. The miseries of the early decades of Company rule had been forgotten. Calcutta was one of the leading cities of the empire, a blend of British, Awadhi Muslim and Bengali Hindu cultures. Romesh Chandra Dutt, who wrote a fine two-volume economic history of India during the Victorian era, praises Bengal's zamindari system and criticizes the ryotwari on the grounds that with zamindari and a fixed revenue demand, the surplus stayed within Bengal as it grew; in ryotwari the government siphoned it off.

Bombay province had witnessed the Deccan riots in the 1870s and a severe famine in 1899. Bengal, by contrast, had not had a famine since the terrible days of 1769–70. But by the middle of the 1930s, no one would have endorsed Dutt's praise of the zamindari system.

For the twentieth century was different. Bengal's rice and jute economy collapsed in the Great Depression. Population expansion and ecological degradation, as well as periodic shifts in flows of the many river tributaries of the Ganga did much damage to livelihoods. In 1943, while facing an imminent Japanese invasion, a decision to seize all small boats as a precautionary measure to deny them to the Japanese, destroyed the means of livelihood of thousands of fishermen. Wartime emergency diverted grain supply to the urban centres where the armed forces had priority. Bengal suffered one of the worst famines of modern times, and as many as three to four million people may have died in it. The principal reason we now know, thanks to Amartya Sen's seminal work, was not so much shortage of food supply as the collapse of the income earning abilities of non-farming families.[2]

As Bengal declined economically, its situation was reflected in its political fortunes. The leading province of the nationalist movement for nearly a hundred years since Raja Rammohun Roy, by the time C.R. Das died in 1925, Bengal's star was waning and that of North India and Bombay province rising. The political trajectory of Subhash Bose was illustrative of this decline. He had a meteoric rise and then was ruthlessly removed by Gandhi, when the latter felt threatened by his radicalism. Bose sought help abroad, and though he tried his best, had no success. His memory as a future that might have been, is also Bengal's lament for a past that did not last.

Bengal had become a dysfunctional province economically by the mid-twentieth century. Its one main industry, jute, was in a declining market as cheaper substitutes were available, and the mainly British owners liquidated their capital rather than expanding—as was the case with cotton textiles in Bombay and Ahmedabad. Partition was another blow, and neither East Bengal nor West Bengal recovered its economic prosperity for the rest of the twentieth century.

World economic conditions were changing as was Britain's relative economic standing. Much of the nineteenth century saw a steadily growing British economy enjoying a declining farm imports bill as food prices fell thanks to imports from Australia, New Zealand and Eastern and Central Europe, while it exported its manufactures to markets around the world. British banking and the financial services the city of London offered also generated a healthy foreign income flow, and the gold standard was informally managed by the Bank of England. India enjoyed its connection with the British economy (though this was contested later by the nationalists), and the economy grew at between 0.5 and 1 per cent per capita per annum. The fledgling manufacturing industry grew at a staggering rate of 8 per cent per annum between 1860 and 1900. The moderation of the Congress critique and its interest in a low rupee was for the rapid growth of this industry. In the inter-war period, the British economy lost its lead. An attempt to restore the gold standard at too high an exchange rate while Churchill was the chancellor of the Exchequer, depressed the British economy from 1925 onwards. India was dragged along with this disastrous policy, and the rupee was valued further upwards at 1s 6d (thirteen and a half rupees per pound).

The 'drain', which was the subject of much debate, was only 3 per cent of the GDP or about half of the balance of trade surplus which India enjoyed during the 1860–1914 period. It declined in the inter-war period to around 1 to 1.5 per cent. Even so, it was an unrequited transfer from a very poor economy.[3]

THE GREAT DEPRESSION AND THE CRISIS OF CAPITALISM

In 1929 the entire capitalist system was convulsed in a depression. For India, the hardships of high exchange rate and a depressed British market were compounded by falling prices of exports of agricultural products. By 1933 the index number of prices was 40 per cent below its level in 1929, more than in the US (31 per cent), UK (25 per cent), Australia (22 per cent) or Japan (18.5 per cent). Cotton prices were down from Rs 0.70 per pound in the 1920s to Rs 0.22 by 1930. Wheat prices fell from Rs 5 to Rs 2 per maund.[4]

It was this background of a failing capitalist system and the heavy suffering caused to the farmers, which gave the Congress's economic policy its radical edge. The pro-capitalist tone of the Congress moderates of the late nineteenth and early twentieth centuries was no longer justified. While no estimates of national income were available then, we now know from a range of estimates that between 1900 and 1947 per capita income grew, at best, at 0.5 per cent per annum or as little at 0.1 per cent, which is as good as zero. Agriculture, which had grown at 1 per cent per annum in total and 0.6 per cent per capita from 1860 to 1900, slowed to 0.31 per cent in total and declined by 0.5 per cent per capita per annum in the 1900–47 period.

Thus, just at the time when the Congress became a politically radical mass party, the economic case for radicalism was also reinforced. It was Nehru who in the early 1930s fashioned an economic critique which not only opposed imperialism, but capitalism as well, without rejecting modernization. The Indian state, when independent, was to develop India on its path to a modern prosperous economy by containing both domestic and foreign capitalism and taking a lead in fashioning a socialist plan for industrial growth. Nehru's Congress colleagues were much more guarded than he was, and stayed friendly with the Indian industrialists who had joined the Congress. But they let him take the lead in these matters when power was a distant prospect. Nehru did, however, have the support of the young Congress socialists and, along with Subhash Bose, began work on the National Planning Committee of the Congress Party, established in 1938 during Bose's presidency.

This meant that there emerged a two-pronged narrative of economic nationalism. The moderate Right-wing Congressmen wanted the British to give way to Indian capitalism, which was being denied its space by the British. The Congress socialists, much influenced by the Popular Front variant of Leninism, wanted a root and branch rejection of capitalism and feudalism in all its forms. The original Congress story said that Indians were united as one because they were all subjects of imperial exploitation, but for the socialists the exploiters were not just the British, but the native industrialists and landlords as well. The Muslim League was on the side of landlords in North India and on the side of poor peasants in Bengal. But on the whole it was against any story of exploitation, whether imperialist or capitalist. Its concern was with the alleged or real exploitation of Muslims by Hindus. Thus, neither religion nor the economic narrative provided sufficient cement to keep All India together. Nehru went on thinking, perhaps even hoping, that the religious divide would vanish once economic independence was gained. He never got his chance to test the hypothesis.

GANDHI: THE NATION

What ultimately united the various factions within the Congress was Gandhi's persona. He became the one unifying message through his life of simplicity, identifying with the poorest Indian through the way he dressed and his saintly demeanour. His life and his struggles became the story of why India was a nation. He empowered Indians by making them fearless while facing lathi charges. He took them in thousands along with him to prison, and the certificate of incarceration gave the Congress its perfect legitimacy to claim power when it came. The sacrifice of the founding generation of Congress leaders, whatever the differences among them, became the uniting story of Indian nationhood.

It was not sufficient, however, when it collided with the Muslim League story. This developed very late—from 1937 onwards—when the League began to make itself into a mass All India party. Jinnah leveraged Muslim grievances in UP and Bihar to fashion a new critique of Hindu majoritarianism. His most powerful, if negative, contribution was to question the national character of the Congress narrative. He demythified Gandhi, casting him as a Hindu leader. He scorned the simple lifestyle and the habits of travelling third class in trains. His own style was to adopt what every other leader in India had done since time immemorial—put a distance between himself and his followers. This did not hurt him, whatever the Congress may have said. His aloof style and abstemious habits, which was the only thing in which he resembled Gandhi, only strengthened his Muslim mass following.

Jinnah came through from behind, when the Congress was sulking after resignations from ministries or in jail after the Quit India movement. By 1945, when discussions resumed, the Congress narrative had been enfeebled. The Congress was stunned at the change, and shocked with the results of the 1946 elections. A party which they had dismissed as an elite party of landlords and reactionaries had become the largest party for Muslims in the elections, which legitimated its claim to be *the* party speaking for Muslims; perhaps not the sole party, but still the largest one.

It was the suddenness of this change which fractured the Congress narrative based on Gandhi's persona. By meeting Jinnah and failing to move him, Gandhi gave Jinnah parity of status and inadvertently cast himself exactly as Jinnah wanted—a Hindu leader. In his defence, one can only say that he was now seventy-five and weakened after yet another spell in jail. He had lost his wife of sixty years and his trusted lieutenant, Mahadev Desai. But from then on Jinnah was there, not just because of the viceroy, but the Mahatma as well. By then, in 1944, the independence of India was a foregone conclusion, if not its date. The final outcome was going to hinge on a few personalities and their negotiating abilities. The masses played the role of a Greek chorus. There has been much wishful thinking, and even writing on the Indian Left, elevating various popular events as radical forces (the Naval Mutiny, for instance, in February 1946) which are said to have driven the British and the Indian nationalist leaders to the final decision. But, in the end, the decision to grant India independence, when it was done with a Partition, was not a subaltern one; it was the haute elite, a mere dozen people, who did it.

Jinnah's narrative was also defective. He began with a constitutionalist position which was secular (he was, after all, a prominent Congress moderate before Gandhi arrived on the scene) and focussed on minority rights. After his failure to move the Congress in the Nehru Report, he retired from the scene for a while only to return when elections became a possibility, bringing with them the prospect of real power in the provinces. He did not succeed at first, but exploited the opening the Congress gave him brilliantly. Yet, in the end, he got what he did not really wish, and thereby harmed the Muslim nation in India. His mistake was to underestimate Gandhi when it came to closed-door negotiations. Gandhi and Nehru outsmarted him after he agreed to the Cabinet Mission plan before they had committed the Congress. His demands for separate zones were pruned, and he had to take a sovereign state with the two largest Muslim majority provinces cut in halves. The British favoured the Congress—Gandhi and Nehru and Patel—in the final stages after Labour came to power in Westminster. They had always had a soft spot for them, and gave the Congress what it wanted—exclusive control over the bulk of the Indian territory (two-thirds of the 1.8 million square miles), the title of India and continuity with the raj. This was because the Congress talked the language of secular politics, a language the Labour Party shared. They had their religious believers too, Cripps being the most prominent. He kept his religion private, separate from his politics. But what the British could not abide, having Ireland on their doorstep, was anyone who brought the weapon of religion into politics. Jinnah was the bad boy; he became the bully who was sent off with a moth-eaten state.

The Congress got what it wanted, and then continued to complain for decades after Independence that they were robbed of their cherished dream of a united India. At the end they did not fight for it, but for exclusive power; they gave up united India for Congress raj which became a proud successor of the British raj, emphasizing continuity. This was best reflected in the appointment of Mountbatten as independent India's first governor general. Mountbatten, more than anyone else, drove Partition through between mid-April and late May, and then delivered a chaotic and bloody independence—an independent, yet Dominion Status nation. He had hoped to be the governor general of both dominions, but Jinnah, by then, had seen through the façade. He knew who had cheated him of his prize. He consoled himself by becoming governor general of Pakistan himself, the first Indian and, indeed, the first Pakistani as he became after he took over, to do so.

Again, it was Attlee who put it in his typical direct fashion:

> For him [Mountbatten] to accept an invitation to be the first Governor General of an independent India was a great boost for Britain, and for the Commonwealth. I thought it would do more than anything to keep India in the Commonwealth. If he had refused the job, it would have worsened relations between India and Pakistan—Nehru would have said Jinnah's *volte-face* had driven Mountbatten out of India. It was essential for him to stay. Both countries trusted him. If Mountbatten had left India, it would have looked like a victory for that twister, Jinnah.[5]

Interestingly, when Attlee says Mountbatten was trusted by both countries, he does not mean India and Pakistan; he means India and Britain. All had been forgiven and forgotten. Independent India was all right; it was one of us, Attlee seems to say. Gandhi's loyalist opposition tactics had paid off. In nineteenth century Britain, the Chartists had pioneered the tactics of peaceful mass protest to demand rights from the Parliament. They had organized the disenfranchised working masses, organized what was until then the largest petition presented to the British Parliament. Though they lost and their movement petered out after 1848, their example lived on. The British trade union movement had always used those tactics, though without the spiritual paraphernalia of Gandhi. As a student for the Bar during the late 1880s and early 1890s, Gandhi was witness to the rising power of the trade union movement, and his fellow vegetarians, who were socialists, would have been active in it. Peaceful and organized mass protest defying unjust laws was the principal weapon which had made the British trade union movement the despair of the Marxists of the Social Democratic Federation led by H.M. Hyndman in the 1880s, and later still of the Bolsheviks when they came to power. It was Gandhi who was able to deliver the best results of peaceful mass protest. By coating a British tradition in spirituality he made it seem genuinely Indian.

Punjab

The tragedy of the Partition is very much a Punjab story. The vast literature on Partition on both sides of the border is disproportionately focussed on Punjab rather than Bengal. Punjab had been the success story of British rule, especially in the twentieth century. The system of canals that were constructed and the resultant rise in cultivation turned Punjab into an agricultural miracle province. Army recruitment helped and the Punjabi became synonymous with an enterprising, energetic person though also a lovable figure of fun, if a Sikh. Punjab had its own 'school' of administrators starting with the Lawrence brothers, John and Henry, who had been involved in its conquest and one of whom became a viceroy. Punjab's steadfastness during 1857 was much appreciated and rewarded. During the twentieth century, the British legislated debt relief and other reforms to help the agriculturist. The alienation of Land Act 1900 forbade urban dwellers from buying rural land. Punjab farmers were the backbone of the army and they, in turn, were treated especially well, with protection against money lenders as well as against the urban commercial classes.

Punjab had three major communities—Muslims, Hindus and Sikhs. There was much intermingling between the Hindus and Sikhs. It was not unusual for a Hindu family to dedicate one of their sons to the Sikh faith. Sikhism has a democratic structure in which the devotees control the places of worship—the gurudwara. The control of the gurudwaras had passed into the hands of the Hindu mahants in the late nineteenth century. The struggle by the Sikhs, to wrest control away from the Hindu mahants and into the hands of the devotees, became an important part of the Sikh renaissance in the early twentieth century nationalist movement. The Punjabi Hindus were mainly Arya Samajists. The Muslims of rural west Punjab were much influenced by the Sufi movement, with its lineage of saints who inherited the leadership of the followers who worshipped at the tombs of the revered founders of the dargahs. In these matters, the belief systems were much similar to traditional Hinduism, though not the revivalist Arya Samaj. Urban Muslims, on the other hand, were attracted to the more doctrinal tendencies such as Deobandi, which elevated the Qur'an to an indisputable authority, rather than to the mysticism which the rural Muslims believed in.[6]

Punjab prospered in the twentieth century though the Great Depression hit farmers' incomes badly. The Unionist Party represented the powerful rural interests, and used the religious hierarchy to keep the farmers (few of whom had franchise even in 1946) attached to them. The tenants were mostly Muslim, but some were Hindus and Sikhs. The Unionists were loyal to the British who returned the favour with generous treatment. It was the crisis in the leadership of the Unionist Party with the death of Sir Sikandar Hayat, and the steady penetration of Muslim League into urban areas of West Punjab, which impacted on the fortunes of the party in the early 1940s.

West Punjab had large landholders, while peasant proprietors were much more prevalent in the East. The peasant proprietors were mainly Hindus and the farmers were Hindus, Sikhs and Muslims. Hindus and Muslims shared Urdu as a common language, while Gurumukhi was the script for the Sikhs as their holy books are written in Gurumukhi. Although the Congress took part in the reform movement for the Sikh gurudwaras, the party had a very marginal presence in Punjab.

The Unionist Party would have been able to keep Punjab together and, perhaps, even tilted the balance in favour of the Cabinet Mission plan. But Sir Sikandar Hayat died before the crucial moment of decision-making, and his successors could not stand up to the powerful personality of Jinnah. Punjab became divided since neither the Congress nor the Muslim League had deep roots in its politics. To them Punjab was a territory, not a nation. It thus became two instead of remaining one.

WHY PAKISTAN: A DIFFERENT PERSPECTIVE

All the debates and discussions about why Pakistan happened have concentrated on the religious minority issue, whether genuine or conjured up by the British and/or Jinnah. A totally different explanation, indeed a 'materialist' one has been offered by the prominent Pakistani barrister and intellectual, Aitzaz Ahsan. In his book, *The Indus Saga*, he has advanced the thesis that there was a fundamental difference in terms of social formation between what became India and what became Pakistan.[7]

Ahsan argues that what became India after 1947 was much more advanced in its progress towards a 'bourgeois' economy than Pakistan after 1971. His analysis is not Marxist by any description, and his writing is entirely based on his own thinking, using very little jargon. He is, if anything, a liberal intellectual. In his view, India had been conquered by the British between 1765 and 1818, the Battle of Buxar and the Fourth Maratha War. The three presidency capitals were in India rather than Pakistan. This is where new higher educational institutions were set up early on and universities established in the 1850s. Modern industry began in Ahmedabad in the 1850s and spread to Bombay and Calcutta, and later to Kanpur. Commercial banking had developed fast.

It was this bourgeois society which the Congress tapped into as it began its life in 1885, but even more so after the advent of Gandhi. Their demands against the British were for tariff protection and devaluation of the rupee, in other words, to make the British get out of the way of the Indian bourgeoisie who wanted room for growth.

The Punjab, Sind and North-West were tamed much later in the 1840s and after. The loyalty of soldiers from Punjab in 1857 had never been forgotten, and the British saw to it that none of the 'modernizing' influences affected the area. The British encouraged the rural elite to consolidate their authority, and there was little encouragement for the urban elites to claim power. The Unionist Party in Punjab as well as the Sind United Party were not mass formations, but led and controlled by the rural elite and, on occasion, by a commercial magnate such as Sir Abdullah Haroon, a self-made industrialist who had campaigned for the separation of Sind from the Bombay province, a demand which was granted in 1936. The recruitment of soldiers for the Indian army was done here, and the British wanted to ensure that the soldiers would be sturdy sons of the soil, and not like the argumentative urban babus of Calcutta. Thus, the social formation of what became Pakistan was feudal and military, run by civil servants who co-opted the elite and kept them happy.

Such bourgeoisie as had developed within Muslim society were in UP, Bihar and Bombay. These were the urban government servants, merchants and traders, with a smattering of lawyers. They were the passive beneficiaries of the bourgeois development in India. The Muslim League had recruited them, but until after 1937 they had little say in how the League was run. They were the big losers from the Partition.

Thus, in essence, the two parts of British India were so unevenly developed with such contrasting social formations that there were, in effect, two nations, not because of religion but because of material factors.

Ahsan's thesis is a very enticing one, and it has also the merit that it can explain the contrasting fortunes of democracy in India and Pakistan. It also does not rely on personalities and ideological factors.[8] I am quite attracted by it.

A parallel case is that of Ireland. It is often assumed by nationalists and, indeed, was by the Congress, that if there is a unified territory, there can be only one nation in it. Ireland is an island, but the Northern part of it, Ulster, had a different formation since the sixteenth century. It was Protestant and Scottish and industrial, while the South was Celtic and Catholic and agrarian. Irish nationalism still denies the existence of two nations in Ireland, and fought very hard against it. The division, which took place after the end of the civil war in 1920–22, was always blamed on the perfidious British who divide and rule. But, after seventy-five years of denial and thirty years of 'troubles', the reconciliation in Northern Ireland took place when the Irish Republic admitted that the North could exist independently. The Ulster Protestants, in turn, recognized the right of the minority Catholics to live and work as equal citizens.

It is thus plausible to argue that in the single territory of British India there was, indeed, more than one nation. But, then, why stop at two nations? Jinnah's two nations became three in 1971. So, the thesis of uneven development, of feudal and bourgeois formations slotting neatly into Pakistan and India, is too convenient to be convincing. For one thing, the theory of uneven development extends even within region A— India as it became after 1947—in which the South or the North-East was much less developed than the core territory around Bombay and Calcutta in terms of industrial development. Even UP and Bihar lagged behind the Bombay and Bengal provinces. Within Pakistan, Punjab was much more developed than Sind or NWFP or Balochistan.

In fact, most nations, as they have developed, have carried such unevenness within them. Even Britain has, to this day, a much more highly developed south-east region relative to Wales and Scotland, or even the north-east of England. America had a developed north-east and west coast, and a relatively less developed south until very recently. It is the task of politics to bind together such disparate formations within a single union and give each enough to prevent a breakaway, which Pakistan failed to do vis-à-vis East Pakistan. That was due to the lack of a democratic politics. The larger territory of All India could have provided opportunities for areas of Pakistan to industrialize, if they could have exerted the pressures of democratic politics. This is the way the relatively less industrialized areas of the south of India caught up with the western states of Gujarat and Maharashtra.

Ahsan's thesis deserves a much more detailed response than I have managed here. It certainly is the only innovative, non-religious explanation of why Pakistan became a fact.

COUNTERFACTUAL BOX

Could the Partition Have Been Averted?

A perennial question of modern Indian history which comes up again and again is: Could the Partition have been averted?

There were two chances for that possibility. One was the implementation of the All India federation proposed in the Government of India Act 1935. This had been crafted over seven years of debate and discussion with a large degree of Indian participation (Congress excepted). The federation would have had a weak Centre dealing with defence, foreign policy and communication, perhaps currency as well. The provinces of British India would have had a lot of autonomy and control over various departments. The Native States, the ones which voluntarily joined, would have retained their autonomy within the overall paramountcy of the Centre. They had representation in the central legislature in both houses, and could have chosen to nominate or elect their delegates. There would have been Native States which did not join the federation. It is not clear what their constitutional position would have been, but with Dominion Status for British India and for such Princely States that joined, there would still be 'safeguards' and the British could have kept paramountcy in relation to these states in their hands, or passed them on to the federation.

If we can avoid hindsight, this may not have been such a bad solution. Initially, it would have been a weak federation but, over time, it could have led to a stronger and closer Union. The example of the United States of America is apposite here. After 1783 America had a Constitution which created a Confederate State. This Constitution gave a lot of autonomy to the individual states, and soon proved unworkable. There were farmers' revolts about refusal to settle their debts, incurred during the inflation-ridden War of Independence, in more deflationary post-war years. In 1789 America gave itself a new Constitution which has stood the test of time. It began, even so, with many powers for the states, and only after the Civil War did the balance begin to shift in favour of the federal government. It was the New Deal which equipped the USA with a powerful federal government and the Second World War strengthened it. Thus, the USA evolved over the two centuries between 1783 with a Confederate America with a weak Centre, and 1945 with a powerful federal arm for the federation.

The advantage for the 1935 Act was that, if an All India federation had been set up, it would have forced the debate about the minorities along constitutional channels. The Muslim League was yet a small, elite party, and with Princely States to constrain the popular politicians, it could have stayed the break-up which eventually came. It would not have been the India we know now, but if you can visualize a weak Centre enfolding India, Pakistan and Bangladesh as they are now, it begins to look possible.

There has been much more debate about the opportunity lost with the Cabinet Mission plan. Maulana Azad has been the only person who openly suggested that the Congress had deliberately thrown away the chance to have a united India. It is true that as events unfolded, the possibility of both sides sticking to their formal acceptance was present. Now again, suspending hindsight, if that possibility had been turned into an actuality, what would have been the nature of the All India federation Mark 2?

One presumes that by then, the Native States question would have been dealt with. Although there is little mention of it in the debates surrounding the Cabinet Mission, with the Labour Party in power, the princes would have been told to sign up. As there would have been only one federation, they could only sign up with that. The choice would have been about which zone to join and, even there, geographical proximity rather than anything else would have been the norm. Hyderabad was too far away from zone B and C to be able to join these Muslim-majority zones, and Jammu and Kashmir could have been part of zone A or B.

The real difficulty with the Cabinet Mission plan is to envisage how the Constituent Assembly would have framed the Constitution. Unlike the 1935 Act, which could have been implemented as early as 1938, if the princes had not behaved stupidly, by 1946 much poison had spread in the body politic. With six provinces in zones B and C (assuming Assam would have stayed in zone C) and six in zone A, it would have been a close run thing between the majority Hindu provinces and majority Muslim provinces. If Bengal and Punjab had stayed undivided, the power of the Muslim minority would have been greater than their numbers relative to the total population. This may not have been a bad thing for the unity of India. If, for example, the Upper House had been arranged according to the US Senate principle with equal representation for each province, then the minority would have achieved parity. If, however, the Congress would have driven home its majority based on the 1946 electorate, then endless disputes would have resulted. Both Pakistan, as it was between 1947 and 1971, and Sri Lanka, as it has been in the last twenty-five years, do not give us much confidence.

For the Cabinet Mission plan to succeed, the Congress would have had to really embrace power-sharing. Jinnah would have been required to genuinely use the arbitration procedure to settle minority/majority disputes in Constitution making. Again, things could have worked out over time. There are examples on either side. Tito united the Balkan nations into a single Yugoslavia, and it lasted for almost fifty years before breaking up in ethnic cleansing and much bitterness. There was no such 'Strong Man' available in 1946 who could have united the rival factions in India. Belgium has survived for many years with two antagonistic communities—Flemish and Waloons, speaking two different languages, Flemish and French—often at loggerheads with each other. Each political party has a French and Flemish variant. There are always fragile coalitions and twice, in 1968 and again in 2008, Belgium has come close to breaking up.

Thus, it is possible that a united India could have been preserved, but it would have looked very unlike what it is today. The agony over India breaking up has never been shared by Pakistan or, even, Bangladesh. There is perhaps a message here for Indians.

INDEPENDENCE AT LAST

On Independence Day Gandhi stayed far away from the celebrations, and fasted. Nehru delivered his famous speech chronicling how India had made a 'tryst with Destiny' many years ago and how 'at the stroke of the midnight hour, when the World sleeps' (in fact, most of it was wide awake being daytime for them) they had fulfilled their pledge 'not wholly or in full measure, but very substantially'. Sarojini Naidu, during the day of 15 August, struck a cosmopolitan note as she thanked 'the scholars of Europe who restored to us our pride and ancient culture, to the antiquarian and the archaeologist who had discovered for us our own ruined cities, to the missionaries of all countries who chose the life of poverty in far-off villages and served the poor and the needy and the desolate. To all we owe thanks.' There was a sense of occasion and, indeed, of celebration despite the bloodshed. After all, the bloodshed was not new and would recur. Independence comes but once in a nation's lifetime.[9]

The departing rulers were happy too. Atlee wrote to his brother about the event, 'I doubt if things will go awfully easily now ... but at least we have come out with honour instead, as at one time seemed likely, of being pushed out ignominiously with the whole country in a state of confusion.' Mountbatten wrote to him, 'The man who made it possible was you yourself. Without your original guidance and your unwavering support nothing could have been accomplished out here.'[10]

A hundred and ninety years after Plassey, or ninety years after the failed rebellion of 1857, the British gave up their rule over India. As Sarojini Naidu, a poet as much as a freedom fighter, reminded her listeners on the All India Radio on 15 August, 'And it seems somehow poetical, it seems somehow romantic, it seems somehow logical that the great-grandson of Queen Victoria, Louis Mountbatten, should have, by grace and generosity, dissolved the empire that Disraeli built for her.'[11]

Within three years more India shed its Dominion Status and became a sovereign democratic republic. Yet, it was not an independent republic. It remained part of the Commonwealth. Thus, after all, when independence came economic independence came for the old Congress leaders or even for Gandhians, but not for Nehruvian socialists. It did not come for those who had staked their mast with a syncretic India. For them they got a 'moth-eaten' India, as much as Jinnah got his 'nation' but not as much of it as he would have liked. India did not go back to what it was in 1750 or in 1050. It was bigger than ever before as an independent entity, but for many it was still smaller than how they had conceived it—their 'All India'. The democratic Republic of India occupied a larger territory under a single rule than any previous emperor, Hindu or Muslim, had managed. That was, perhaps, not a small achivement. The task was now to keep it together and revive its reputation as the Golden Hind.

PART II

CHAPTER 12

INDEPENDENT INDIA: THE NEHRU YEARS

NEHRU AT THE HELM

Jawaharlal Nehru addressing the members of the Constituent Assembly, now also the Parliament of independent India, on the midnight of 14/15 August spoke of the nation that was coming into being:

> At the dawn of history India started on her unending quest, and trackless centuries are filled with her striving and the grandeur of her success and her failures. Through good and ill fortune alike she has never lost sight of that quest or forgotten the ideals which gave her strength. We end today a period of ill fortune and India discovers herself again.[1]

India's first prime minister had thought deeply about India's history, her quests and her ideals. During the three years he spent in Ahmednagar Fort prison, Nehru wrote his masterly book, *The Discovery of India*. But the India he had discovered was not the India he welcomed that fateful night. The largest and most populous possession of the British Empire, the jewel in the Crown, was now free India. But although she was still the largest post-colonial nation, she did not have the full territory her leaders had visualized when they were fighting for her freedom. She had, nonetheless, fought an exemplary fight, combining not so much non-violent, as unarmed mass agitation along with masterly negotiations—and a dash of incendiary violence. Independent India's great advantage was that she came into being equipped with a formidable team of leaders who were ready to rule just as if they had always been in power. The man chosen to lead them was, of course, Jawaharlal Nehru.

His father may have asked him to take up the Science Tripos and become a barrister like himself, or even nudged him towards the ICS, but he would not have been at his best—as he had already shown by his performance as a barrister. Ever since he met Gandhi and dedicated himself—dragging his father—to him and to the fight for independence, Nehru could not have wanted anything else. The first struggle he took up was the agitation against the Rowlatt Act. He did not take office after the 1937 elections, as leading a provincial government was too narrow for his ambition. After his inspiring pledge of purna swaraj at the Lahore Congress in December 1929, there was never any doubt that he was the heir to the Mahatma and the future leader of India, especially young India which was straining at the leash for radical change.

Now nearly two decades after that pledge, and having spent nine of his politically active thirty years in prison, Nehru was ready. At fifty-eight he was not old for the job—Churchill had to wait till he was sixty-five to become Britain's wartime prime minister, a job he alone could do at that time, and in that place. Nehru was to enjoy the longest continuous tenure as prime minister—seventeen years—longer than any governor general of India since 1765—before he died at the age of seventy-five. He had used his last prison term well: to reflect not just on the history of the nation he was sure to lead, but also on the many urgent tasks that would be waiting for him. Keenly interested in India's economic problems from the late 1920s, he had insisted on framing the resolution for the 1930 Karachi Congress which formulated the economic policy—and this at a time when many Congress leaders thought these were distractions. A mere critique of the British depredations would have sufficed for most of them, but Nehru, along with Subhash Bose, created the National Planning Committee of the Congress. After Bose's departure abroad, Nehru continued to take an interest in its workings, and was able to draw upon this knowledge for his writings in prison.

Nehru was a modernist and an internationalist—as well as a fierce nationalist. But among fellow Congress leaders of comparable seniority, he was an anomaly; he was an atheist and, unlike them, who were much influenced by Gandhi's asceticism, he was a sensualist who liked and enjoyed the good things of life. He was devoted to the Mahatma, but absorbed little of his economic or social philosophy. He was impatient with the old, the slow and moribund aspects of Indian society, especially when they were defended by his fellow Congressmen. He bristled with ideas and had a short temper. He was aware that he had a tendency to being dictatorial and had written about this, objectively in the third person, in an anonymous article in 1937. And yet, he was a democrat in belief and practice, willing to be swayed by the majority if, after his best attempts at persuasion, it disagreed with him.

In the Cabinet that he headed, he had only one equal—Sardar Vallabhbhai Patel, who was older and held beliefs and qualities that were diametrically opposed. Patel was from a peasant caste of Gujarat; he was a nationalist and a devotee of Gandhi, though he did not take the full paraphernalia of the Mahatma's spiritual baggage seriously. He was, moreover, a Right-wing conservative in social and economic matters. If Nehru was an idealist and could move crowds, Patel got things done quietly and ruthlessly. This was evident from the way he had, between the end of June and the middle of August, mopped up most of the Princely States into the new India. He did this so efficiently that it seemed easy: it was not, but it was absolutely crucial to the establishment of India as a single nation state. Indeed, the one state that was not integrated on his watch—Jammu and Kashmir—continues to be a trouble even now, after over sixty years of Independence.

THE AFTERMATH OF PARTITION

The most urgent problem facing the new government was not long-term social or economic reform, but the relief and rehabilitation of refugees from Partition. Patel was determined to punish the Muslim community which was, in his view, responsible for the division of the country. Nehru was conscious of the millions still left behind, who had been Indians the week before and continued to be so. Jinnah's two nations had become two nation states, but while one was predominantly Muslim with a small and eventually dwindling non-Muslim minority, India still had a large Muslim population which had stayed behind.

The division notwithstanding, India did well out of the Partition in a material sense. It had 70 per cent of the area, 99 per cent of the industrial capacity and around 75 per cent of the population of All India, including a third of its Muslim population. In Bengal it kept most of the industry, mainly jute manufacture, which was located in West Bengal, though the fields supplying raw jute were now in East Pakistan. Assam was cut off from its natural corridor to Bengal down the river Brahmaputra, which now flowed into East Pakistan. The bulk of the civil service was non-Muslim, as was the leadership in the army. Only 101, that is 18.4 per cent of the total strength of the Indian Civil Service (ICS) and Imperial Police (IP) officers were Muslim, ninety-five of whom opted for Pakistan. British ICS and IP officers stayed on in Pakistan, but they were not needed in India.[2]

Though people celebrated the birth of the independent nation, a feeling of resentment and anger at what had happened was palpable. It resulted in India dragging her feet when it came to the division of assets between the two new states that came out of British India. And Muslims in Delhi and across North India were fearful of their safety—Sardar Patel, now the home minister, was definitely not playing on their side. Nehru and Patel had differences on this crucial question and it was a question that would never leave the front stage—the position of the

Muslims in India. Were they full citizens at home? Or, were they merely those who had stayed behind when they should have followed their leader, Mohammad Ali Jinnah?

Maulana Azad, who more than anyone else in the Congress leadership had resisted the Partition and, indeed, had the most to lose, expressed his bitterness to the Indian Muslims about how some of them had been enticed by the siren song of Jinnah. In a speech at the Jama Masjid in Delhi on 23 October 1947, he said:

> Do you remember? I hailed you, you cut off my tongue; I picked up my pen, you severed my hand; I wanted to move forward, you broke off my legs; I tried to turn over, and you injured my back. When the bitter political games of the last seven years were at their peak, I tried to wake you up at every danger signal. You not only ignored my call but revived all the past traditions of neglect and denial. As a result the same perils surround you today, whose onset had previously diverted you from the righteous path.[3]

He added, 'I am an orphan in my own motherland.' He had anticipated how Indian Muslims would feel. He had even warned them before the event in 1946 when the Cabinet Mission plan had been put forward—how Muslims left in Hindu majority provinces would fare when the Muslim majority provinces had formed a separate block. He was the highest-ranking Muslim in India's political leadership after 1947. After his death in 1959, no other Muslim was to attain his stature in any subsequent Cabinet of India. Muslims were shunted off to positions of higher status but no power—as president or vice-president, or placed in largely ceremonial posts in the Cabinet.

Interestingly, the Hindu Mahasabha and the Right-wing Hindu organization, the Rashtriya Swayamsevak Sangh (RSS), too, were bitterly opposed to Partition. As Hindu majoritarians, they had looked forward to independence as payback time after a thousand years of Muslim rule. Islam, they argued, had many homes around the world, so Muslims could go elsewhere; and Muslims in India were traitors and fifth columnists (fifty years on the same argument would be extended to Indian Christians, resulting in sporadic killings and burnings by groups loosely identified with the Hindu fundamentalist cause). According to this school of thought, as the religious centres of Hinduism were all in India, it was the homeland of Hindus, doubly so after Independence. There was much sympathy within the Congress hierarchy for the Mahasabha view; indeed, there had always been. Things were delicate, and a clash between Nehru and Patel seemed very likely.

It took a fast by Gandhi on 18 January 1948 to make the government realize its responsibilities. He insisted that Pakistan be given its just share of the assets. This was to be his last fast. On 30 January 1948, within six months of Independence, Gandhi was assassinated by Nathuram Godse, who had been a RSS volunteer. He fired three bullets at point blank range when Gandhi was at his daily prayer meeting in the grounds of Birla House. Just before his death he had persuaded Patel that he and Nehru should cooperate and not quarrel. In death as in life, he did not fail to serve his country. His death reconciled the two leaders, and the beginnings of independent India were assured a united leadership. Patel as home minister was much blamed for the lapse in security for Gandhi, but everyone knew that the Mahatma prided himself on his openness to all comers. Patel was genuinely grieved; he modified his anti-Muslim stance considerably after the death of Gandhi.

Gandhi had already been out of the loop of Congress leadership since the end of the Cabinet Mission plan. He had agreed to the Partition by his presence at the Congress Working Committee meeting of 14–15 June 1947. He wanted the Congress to disband itself as a political party and become a social service agency. But he misunderstood the nature of the machine he had helped create. The Congress had become an election-winning and power-using mechanism. India is what it is today, good and bad, because the Congress was what it was at that time, and it did not follow the Mahatma's advice. They had benefited from his guidance on earlier occasions but, lately, he had been sidelined. He was redundant. He had done his job. He had delivered Independence. He could now be the Father of the Nation and spin his charka in peace.

But Gandhi had his heart elsewhere—with the sufferers of communal violence in East Bengal and Bihar. He was preparing to go to Punjab, but the communal violence in Delhi kept him in the capital. One fast followed another, and by the time he had settled the division of assets, his killers were no longer ready to wait any more. His death was a shock, but also a relief. Had he lived to be 125 years old—as he once declared—he would have still been around in the 1990s. He would have become hoarse with giving advice which would have been ignored time and again. His death gave independent India, and especially the Congress, an immensely powerful unifying symbol, indeed the only one which still commands a substantial majority support. His name is invoked in times of trouble, his face smiles from currency notes whose principal use is to fuel the corruption he would deplore; but, lately, at the beginning of the twenty-first century, even the young have been introduced to his message via Bollywood. *Gandhigiri*, the practice of loving your enemy into agreement with you, is the rage.

SECULARISM OR RELIGIOUS TOLERANCE?

Gandhi's death also renewed the Congress' faith in a tolerant and accommodating attitude towards the Muslim community. This became known as secularism, and is one of the pillars on which Nehru reconstructed the identity of post-Partition India as a nation. What Nehru meant by secularism, as an atheist much influenced by Western liberal thought, was a separation of the public and private spaces confining religion strictly to the private sphere. Queen Victoria's declaration in 1858 had promised non-interference in the religions of her subjects, and the British Indian state had practised that stringently, discouraging Christian missionaries clamouring for official support. As in many other matters, continuity was to be the keyword here as far as Nehru was concerned. He wished his fellow citizens to see the immense damage that religious differences had visited upon All India, and would have liked them to refrain from all further indulgence in sectarian thought.

But he was whistling in the wind. The narrative the Congress had championed of a syncretic India lay in tatters once Pakistan had been agreed upon. But the secular mindset now became doubly necessary to maintain peace and harmony and to provide safety to the millions of Muslims in India. Nehru's greatest challenge was to be able to strengthen syncreticism and build a new narrative for Indian nationhood. Gandhi's death was an immense help because the assassins were identified with the Hindu Mahasabha and the RSS. The Mahasabha leader, Veer Savarkar, was implicated in the conspiracy to kill Gandhi, but later acquitted at the trial. His narrative of Indian nationhood which identified its roots in Hindu religion and culture—Hindutva—had, no doubt, been one of the many ingredients which went into the alternative narrative to the Congress' syncretist one. There were informal moves from within the Congress for a merger with the Mahasabha/RSS just after Independence, but Gandhi's death put a stop to that. The RSS just narrowly escaped a permanent ban, and had to agree to withdraw from political activities. Instead, it sponsored a political party, the Jan Sangh which later became the Bharatiya Janata Party (BJP).

The rest of the Congress' Hindu leadership, Nehru apart, did not sign up to his secularism but, adopted a stance of religious tolerance—what is called *sarvadharmasamabhav* in Sanskrit. Though it means viewing all religions with similar regard, it inevitably became the case that some religions were more tolerated than others, especially the majority religion, Hinduism. Congress Muslims underplayed their religiosity and became champions of Nehruvian secularism. After Nehru's death, the tolerance for other religions became a matter of political calculation rather than one of principle.

WRITING THE CONSTITUTION

Independent India was framing its Constitution in the Constituent Assembly. This was the enduring fruit of the Cabinet Mission which designated the assembly elected in 1946 as also charged with this task. The Muslim League had boycotted it and, consequently, there were few elected Muslims on it. The Congress top leadership was there in full force, including Nehru, Patel, Pant and Azad while Rajendra Prasad was elected to preside over it. The Congress tried to be inclusive of all elements of national life. Women were recruited from within its ranks— Rajkumari Amrit Kaur who was also the health minister; Hansa Mehta, president of the All India Women's Conference in 1945, whose husband Dr Jivraj Mehta was a politician as well as a doctor, and had been Gandhi's physician; Sucheta Kripalani, another half of a Congress couple, although fiercely independent of her husband, J.B. Kripalani; and, of course, one of the most prominent women members of the Congress, Sarojini Naidu. The Congress invited distinguished leaders from other parties and prominent Indians who belonged to no political party, such as Dr Sarvepalli Radhakrishnan, the philosopher who had been an Oxford professor, and the great lawyer, Alladi Krishnaswamy Iyer. But the most significant personality in the Constitution-making excercise was B.R. Ambedkar, the Dalit leader who had never forgiven the Congress and Gandhi for their role in the Poona Pact negotiations. Ambedkar would become the leading architect of the Constitution and India's first law minister.

The paramount concern of all those who gathered to write a Constitution for the new nation state was India's unity and territorial integrity. The fear of Balkanization, especially after Partition, was very strong. Thus, a Constitution was written which consciously avoided all ideas of a weak Centre and powerful autonomous provinces. Gandhi had suggested that India should be a collection of village republics, highly decentralized and eschewing modernity. This idea was firmly rejected by his own followers: India became a union rather than a federation or a confederation. As the objective resolution moved by Nehru in the Constituent Assembly, four days after its inauguration on 9 December 1946, said, 'The territories that now comprise British India, the territories that now form the Indian states, and such other parts as are outside British India and the states as well as such other territories as are willing to be constituted into the Independent Sovereign India shall be a Union of them all.'[4]

The reference to 'such other parts as are outside' is to the two colonies on Indian soil—a Portuguese enclave in the west of India which covered three locations: Diu, Daman and Goa; and a French colony near Madras in Pondicherry which had provided sanctuary for the fiery young rebel, Aurobindo Ghose before he turned spiritual. These two colonies were to get back to India in contrasting ways. Pondicherry was ceded voluntarily by France in 1954. The Portuguese held out and India had to move in military force to 'liberate' Goa in December 1961—not, however, with the universal support of its people. I will return to the Goa problem later on.

The anxiety about Balkanization meant that while the structure would be federal, it would have a unitary bias. The Centre would have the authority to make and unmake provinces, unlike in federations such as Australia and the US where the individual provinces/states were the original members who created the federation. New states could be admitted into the US only after approval of the existing members, and the federal government could not redraw the boundaries of any state. India would be different since the powers to make and unmake states were found at the beginning of the Constitution, as Articles 2 and 3.

The Centre was constructed along the lines of the Westminster Constitution, with a ceremonial president who would act on the advice of his council of ministers who commanded a majority in the directly elected chamber, the Lok Sabha. In each constituent unit, a similar arrangement was followed. There were some 'Union Territories' which were more directly ruled. The example of the Government of India Act 1935 was very useful in arranging the administrative structure of the Union, especially with regard to the financial arrangements between the Centre and the provinces, though the degree of autonomy the Act had given to the provinces was curtailed. The Centre had the power to suspend the government in the provinces by declaring President's rule (echoes of paramountcy) if it held that the law and order situation so required it. There was also a provision, echoing the British raj, confirming 'the central government's authority to administer in a unitary fashion the entire country'.[5]

The Constitution renewed the iron framework which the British administration had created, but it festooned it with democratic freedoms. The most revolutionary act of the Constituent Assembly was to provide for universal adult franchise without any literacy or property qualifications. There was no tradition of democracy in India before the arrival of the British, though there were a few republics in what is now the state of Bihar in the middle of the first millennium BCE. Hindu society was characterized by a strict hierarchy of caste and, beyond the pale of the system were the depressed classes/Dalits. Then there were tribes which were regarded as being even further from the mainstream Hindu society of the plains. Muslim society, though in principle egalitarian, was feudal and hierarchical. The British had only gradually expanded the franchise in India, much as they had done at home. But Indians absorbed the lessons of British history and the value of democracy. If in 1857 there was a movement to restore the Mughal Empire, now no one argued for anything that outdated. There were always lingering demands for a 'strong man', but the Congress tradition of consensual democratic leadership (the Mahatma excepted as always) won out.

Ceylon (Sri Lanka) was the only exception among Britain's colonies to be encouraged to ask for, and granted, adult franchise as early as 1932, sixteen years before it obtained Dominion Status. It had made a tremendous difference to the health and social welfare levels of its people. The Sinhalese elite, which obtained those concessions and, later, led the country after Dominion Status, was collaborative, not combative.

Democracy, even with a limited franchise, had been at home in India since before the twentieth century. Reform associations had been formed which had imbibed the British practice of passing resolutions and petitioning the government for change. These voluntary activities, beginning in the first half of the nineteenth century in Bengal and spreading to the other presidencies, had matured into the establishment of the Congress in 1885. Legislators had been co-opted, first indirectly elected and then directly elected over the years; they had mastered the procedures and practices of the British Parliament. India was well prepared to exercise parliamentary government.[6]

Yet, while familiarity with procedures was one thing, what India had not known—and therefore it was a considerable gamble—was the exercise of universal adult franchise. This was a potentially explosive weapon. How would the millions of downtrodden Indians, who had suffered not just a couple of centuries of foreign rule, but millennia of oppression from their fellow Indians, all with the sanction of religion and culture enforced by local kings and potentates, use this new power? How much would they challenge the domestic 'colonial' powers—the caste elite, the landlords and the princes—who had historically oppressed them? How would they express their self interests and how would they translate their needs into political demands? What political agents—political parties, leaders, associations—would fill the gap between the ordinary voter and the legislator pretending to be an assiduous student of Erskine May?

The Constitution had not just granted franchise, it had also recognized that citizens of free India had certain fundamental rights. Both the British example of 1688 and the American example of 1789 had been harnessed. The tradition of Common Law had been ingrained in Indian law courts, and precedents of British judgements were valid here. Thus a written and an unwritten culture of fundamental rights was fitted to the new Indian republic at its very birth. This was a result of the

Congress having been, for decades, a mass party which may have had an elite leadership, but identified with the poorest. This was Gandhi's legacy.

In addition to fundamental rights, the Constitution also put in aspirations. These came more from the modernizing influence of Western liberal and social democratic—and even socialist—thought than from Gandhian influence, though his pet project of prohibition found its way into the Directive Principles of State Policy. The newly independent India was convinced that the state was the key to its future—its security, prosperity and capacity for achieving justice and equity. In what had been for millennia a stateless society or, at least, one with a weak, remote and not very caring political order, people had got by without much help. They experienced political power, if at all, in repressive forms from the local landlords or priests who could be sure of sanctions from higher authority. This is why stories such as the emperor Jahangir meting out justice against his own queen are so rare and memorable. The state aspired to be, or rather its subjects hoped it would be, *maa-baap* (mother and father) of its people, but the actual practice of pre-British states and even contemporary Princely States, with some notable exceptions, left much to be desired (not all parents are kind to their children, after all). In that context, the new Indian state was a revolutionary institution since it engaged itself as the servant of the people who had guaranteed rights, and who had been promised that certain aspirations would be fulfilled.

There was, and still remains, a tension between the fundamental rights and the desire to right old wrongs, as reflected in the Directive Principles. This was felt not just with regard to the right to private property implying no acquisition without compensation, but also with the rights to free speech and free expression of beliefs. Tensions arose regarding the reform of landholdings or the takeover of private businesses, and also when the exercise of free speech came into conflict with what the government of the day viewed as a threat to national unity and integrity. While India follows the Westminister model, the position of the Executive is much more powerful than in Britain. This is because the legislature which checked the Executive in the British context was, by and large, in the first forty years dominated by a single party. A rare Opposition MP, occasionally, held up the Executive to scrutiny. The Second Chamber, which in the UK is unelected and acts as a second stop on the Executive, is indirectly elected in India and much less given to detailed scrutiny of legislation. The Indian Executive had its priority cut out—the unity and integrity of India had to win every time, and if the judiciary came in the way as defender of the Constitution, the response was clear. The Indian Parliament led by the Executive used the privileges of the British

Parliament, which with an unwritten Constitution, could always rewrite the law. Thus, India acquired itself a written Constitution, but unlike in the US, the Constitution could be trumped by legislation which the Indian Parliament could declare to be above the Constitution. It could amend and has, since, amended the Constitution many more times, in the sixty years since 1949, than the US Constitution has in 220 years.[7]

Dr B.R. Ambedkar, who as an untouchable had climbed the long distance from the bottom of the pile to become a member of the Constituent Assembly, brought an awareness of India's millions of ordinary downtrodden people for whose protection the exercise was being undertaken. He was uniquely qualified to assess the contradictions in the elite Constituent Assembly—elected from a limited franchise and now sitting in Delhi, busy building a nation on paper—from the viewpoint of those they were building it for. He saw that the Constitution created in the political sphere equal citizens on the principle of one person one vote, but in the social and economic spheres, there were gross inequalities not just of income and wealth, but of status based on the gender, caste and religion of the citizens. Even the elite, who claimed to be radical and to speak on behalf of the downtrodden, presumed their right to rule on behalf of, and in the interest of, the poor majority. The poor majority would discover, sooner or later, that there was a self justifying trap here which the elite often sprung on them. The elite assured them that it alone could deliver equality, but to do that it must preserve its monopoly on power. The poor soon learned to use their voting power in ways which were often subversive of the well-meaning attempts by their superiors to help them, and this only increased over the years since Independence. The challenge to the Indian state was to find a method to accommodate these contradictions, and learn to diminish the distance between political and socio-economic status.

SECURING UNITY AND INTEGRITY

Difficult as these tasks were, and despite the high expectations and the attendant impatience which Independence obviously aroused, the people at the helm had one overriding priority. This was to secure India's unity and territorial integrity. This was certainly influenced by the scarring experience of the Partition, but also by a reading of India's long history which was riddled with internal quarrels and fragmented polities, short-lived large kingdoms and dissolute dynasties. The new rulers were aware that keeping India one was their first and foremost responsibility. In this the massive presence of the Congress party, and its dominance over the Constituent and legislative assemblies, helped enormously. It was the Congress and, indeed, Nehru who had the task of delivering Indian unity.

The dangers were many. To begin with, there was the existence of a hostile neighbour. Pakistan had emerged at a late stage in the negotiations for independence as a negation of India. Soon after August 1947, the problem of the accession of Jammu and Kashmir made the two countries permanent enemies. Nations often define themselves by their Other, their pet enemy. In England's notion of nationhood, its enmity with France, during the eight centuries between 1066 and 1815, was crucial. This was despite the fact that the Norman Conquest of 1066 had given England Norman, that is, French kings, and for three centuries after that English aristocratic families were part of the royalty of France; as for example, Henry II's queen, Eleanor of Aquitaine. There was a Hundred Years War between the English and the French in the fourteenth and fifteenth centuries and the French became the Other, especially after Henry VIII took the English Church out of the Catholic order. Wars with France and Spain, another Catholic country, built up English perceptions of nationhood. It was only in 1801 that the King of England (then George III—who lost the American colonies) gave up the title of King of France, which Edward III had claimed in the fourteenth century. The French and the British made an *entente cordiale* later in the nineteenth century, and it held through both world wars. The French–German battles from 1870 to 1945, with the twin territories of Alsace and Lorraine changing hands back and forth, shaped German nationalism. It was only after 1945 that sense prevailed and economic cooperation replaced quarrels about land.

India, similarly, defined its nationhood by its hostility to Pakistan, but the danger inherent in that was to the millions of Indian Muslims. So, while maintaining its vigilance against the external enemy (who helped cohere the nation), India had to shelter the Indian Muslims from any perception that they were just Pakistanis who had not left. This has proved to be the most difficult task. Nehru's secularism was one strategy which worked while he was alive, but the problem haunts India till today.

Nehru attempted to construct a new India institutionally, as well as by persistently projecting his idea of India. If Gandhi was India before Independence, Nehru became India—in a similar, but not equal sense—immediately after Independence. He was everywhere and was expected to do everything. The writer, Aubrey Menen recalls Nehru plonking out the tune of the national anthem, *Jana gana mana* on the piano with one finger for someone who had to train the army's and other bands for the Independence celebrations. He had to choose the national dress and the national bird. Writers, film-makers, soldiers, scientists, quacks—all rushed to him for approval of their latest wheeze. When Vladimir Nabokov's *Lolita* was published and the censors were not sure what to do, it was

Nehru who had to read it, along with President Radhakrishnan, and give his judgement that the nation's morals were safe if they read the novel. When after twelve years at the top and then seventy years old, he proposed to retire and make room for someone else, his party and his country were horrified at the idea. He was allowed a short holiday in the hills, which he utilized to put together some of his correspondence into *A Bunch of Old Letters*. He never could or did stop. His favourite lines were from Robert Frost:

The woods are lovely, dark and deep,
But I have promises to keep,
And miles to go before I sleep.

At the highest—Indian—level, the promise was to include Muslims into the new India as full citizens, and to do this knowing that the bitterness caused by the Partition and the enmity with Pakistan would make the task difficult. If India was an old country whose story went back thousands of years to 'the dawn of history' as he had said, did Independence not signal the return of the original majority—in other words, the Hindus? Why after centuries of foreign rule—not just since the battle of Plassey but since the incursion of Mahmud of Ghazni in the ninth century—could Hindus not take charge of their country? Why was the majority denied power in a democracy? This was the narrative propagated by the Hindu Mahasabha and the RSS, and would persist as a constant challenge to the Congress narrative of secularism.

Beyond that, India's borders had been defined by the British raj. The Congress had chosen continuity, and not rupture, to define the new nation. British institutions and practices—the civil services, the law, the language, the parliamentary procedures—were taken over wholesale to smooth the transition to an independent India. The Congress, more or less, dropped whatever anti-colonial radicalism it had after 1945.

India was friendly with China and recognized the People's Republic soon after October 1949. Nehru championed China's case for a UN seat and welcomed Zhou En-lai to the Afro-Asian Summit in Bandung, Indonesia in 1955. But India also allowed the Dalai Lama asylum, when he left Tibet as a protest against the assertion of China's sovereignty over Tibet, in 1959. While New Delhi did not back the Dalai Lama's case for an independent Tibet, it let him stay with his retinue in India. This ambiguity was to lead, in 1962, to the most serious military conflict India had faced since Independence, and the only one in which it was decisively defeated. Indian reluctance to accommodate what the Chinese thought were their legitimate grievances against British imperialism, surprised the Chinese; the Chinese resorted to arms. The swift retribution and the humiliating unilateral withdrawal, rather than continued negotiations, shocked the Indians. This episode created the most serious crisis of Nehru's premiership and, indeed, may have hastened his death.

If the frontier with Tibet was a cause for unease for the new nation, the border areas of the North-East brought their own set of problems. The regions of Manipur and Nagaland fell within the North-East Frontier area, and were a source of bewilderment to most people in India. The lack of integration of Manipuris and Nagas with the rest of the country mirrored the distance between the upper castes and the local untouchables in Hindu society. India's new rulers had to convince the Nagas and others that they were part of the national narrative; it was clear—to some at least—that unless a new narrative could be fashioned, Nagaland would be the scene of a continual low-intensity war, one that would continue for decades. And this happened. As a recent article on the North-East has stated, 'Ever since its litigious incorporation into the independent republic of India, the region has alternately challenged Indian nation-building processes and pushed constitutional politics to its limits, with violent and tragic consequences.'[8]

As for the three 'protected' kingdoms—Nepal, Bhutan and Sikkim—on the Himalayan borders, India behaved very much as the British Empire did. Its relations with Nepal were high-handed until China acquired an interest in Tibet which was much more active and permanent. This restrained India's Nepal policy. Sikkim was absorbed into India. Bhutan retains its independence as of now.

THE CLEAVAGES WITHIN

But if trouble lurked on India's external land boundaries, the internal borders, both physical and social, were no less porous. As we have already seen, provincial identities had grown over a century and more of British rule, in many cases recovered and renewed, and in other cases newly acquired. Macaulay's hope, that those who were taught English would stimulate new developments in their native languages, was amply fulfilled. These revived and modernized languages had given a big boost to local nationalisms, and the Congress from 1920 onwards had constituted its provincial offices along linguistic lines. Some areas such as Tamil Nadu had an autonomous history going back thousands of years. As I have argued above, the Congress story of why All India was a nation had no room for South India or North-East India. Here again, there was the need for a new rhetoric to be fashioned so that India, the new India, could have an idea of being a nation.

This was to lead to at least two serious confrontations. The first was the agitation in South India against the adoption of Hindi as the sole national language in 1965, as had been decided by the Constituent

Assembly. It had been a controversial debate, since the final decision of the assembly was that there would be no official resolution from any committee of the assembly, but a private members' motion which would be put to vote. There has been a persistent rumour that the decision to make Hindi the sole official language was carried by a narrow majority of one. This was a half-truth. In the Congress legislative party, the motion to make Hindi rather than Hindustani the sole national language was carried by the margin of only a single vote. Nehru and Azad voted with the minority in favour of Hindustani, since that choice would have preserved the Urdu script as a possible vehicle for writing the language. But the conservative Hindu forces of North India, deeply embedded in the Congress, had invested much energy in Hindi and the Devnagari script. They won, but just. It was this margin which persuaded the Congress leadership not to make the resolution an official one, but ask some members to move a private motion. The private motion was carried in the Constituent Assembly by a large margin.

Hindi was not as developed a language as Bengali or Tamil, or even Gujarati and Marathi. It was Gandhi's idea that India should have a single national language, and that it should be Hindi/Hindustani. The idea of Hindi as the sole national language offended many in the South. Their languages not only had different scripts—not Devnagari in which Hindi was being projected—but also completely different vocabularies which, while loosely connected to Sanskrit in some cases, had their own histories. Languages were not just cultural artefacts but also a passport to jobs, especially in government offices. Indians from the South had taken to English as their passport to any place in India before 1947. The Constitution resolved to have Hindi as the sole national language of India, but allowed for a transition period of fifteen years while English shared the stature of national language

This led to a widespread protest in the South, but especially in the Madras province (Tamil Nadu) where it was led by the Dravida Munnetra Kazhagam, which translates as the Dravida Progressive Federation and was known by the initials DMK. The DMK was the successor of the anti-Brahmin Justice Party. E.V. Ramaswamy Naicker had started the Dravida Kazhagam (DK) party and had argued for a rationalist radical programme for the upliftment of the lower castes. He was at one with B.R. Ambedkar in opposing Gandhi and the Congress before Independence. Later, his most charismatic follower, a pioneer of the Tamil cinema, C.N. Annadurai built up an electoral party, the DMK, which became the principal opposition party to the Congress in Tamil Nadu, and one which eventually displaced the Congress from there. In April 1962 as an MP, Annadurai spoke in the Lok Sabha, three years before the deadline for the adoption of Hindi, for self-determination of

Dravida Nadu, the homeland of the Dravidian people. This was 'a country', he said, 'a part [of which] in India now, but which I think is of a different stock, not necessarily antagonistic'. He demanded separation, though reassuring his fellow MPs that 'our separation is entirely different from the Partition which has brought about Pakistan'. He cited the view of many in Madras province that they were ruled by 'northern imperialism', and warned that 'the natural unity that we found when we were opposing the British is not to be construed as a permanent affair'.[9] As it happened, some months after he spoke, the India–China border conflict united the entire Indian nation from north to south and east to west. The government also passed a law making it illegal to argue for secession. Later, English was given an indefinite extension as a joint language with Hindi for official purposes, and individual states could also use their local language. The Hindi language issue was thus settled amicably.

The other serious challenge to India's unity was in the 1970s and 1980s when the Sikh demand for a homeland—Khalistan—would become a serious issue. The Partition had been argued for on the basis of a two-nation theory, but in Punjab there were three such nations—Hindus, Muslims and Sikhs. The Sikhs had always felt that they had been short-changed in the division of Punjab, and the consciousness of a Sikh homeland in Punjab, the land where Sikhism was born and where most Sikhs live, became intense, especially after Pakistan split and Bangladesh was created as a separate Bengali Muslim nation in 1971. National liberation movements had been in the forefront of news since the 1960s, with Vietnam as well as the struggle of the Palestine people in the Middle East well documented. The viability of a small state could no longer be easily questioned as new nations sprang up in Africa as well. All this fuelled the movement for a separate Sikh homeland.

It led to a virtual civil war between the supporters of Khalistan, aided and abetted by the Sikh diaspora, and the Government of India. It led to a military attack by the Indian Army on the holiest shrine of the Sikhs—the Golden Temple in Amritsar. The defeat and death of sant Bhindranwale, the leader of the Khalistan movement, led to the assassination of Indira Gandhi, India's second longest serving prime minister, by her own Sikh bodyguards in 1984 as revenge. Anti-Sikh riots in Delhi followed the assassination in which three thousand Sikhs died, while the police and other government agencies looked away. In 2005 the first Sikh prime minister of India, Dr Manmohan Singh apologized to the Sikhs for this atrocity. Court cases are still pending.

There were, yet, other internal 'proletariats' to bring on board. Class cleavages were a part of the rhetoric of the Congress Left, and the vocabulary of anti-feudalism and anti-capitalism slipped off Nehru's tongue effortlessly. He had some, but not many, friends who shared such views. The Communist Party had recovered its revolutionary appetite once the Second World War was over, and it planned many movements in the countryside and in cities, as it thought (or, rather, was told) that India was ripe for revolution and that Congress's was a reactionary regime. Their slogan was '*Azadi jhuthi hai*'—freedom is a lie. They branded the government 'as the Government of national surrender, of collaborators, a Government of national compromise'. Just as the Congress had nourished grandiose notions during the war that its cooperation was crucial for Allied victory, the Communist Party of India (CPI) believed that its support or its withdrawal would have grave consequences for the new government.

> We then said: Here is a national movement; strengthen it and fight for it. We tried to make the Congress the basis of the anti-imperialist front. Later on when we said Congress-League-Communist joint front, it was our idea of the maximum unity and mobilisation of the people for the purpose of the common fight against imperialism. Today, the Bourgeois leadership is no longer oppositional, because the Bourgeois leadership is collaborationist, the main brunt of the fight falls on the Party of the working class ... Our task therefore is one of fighting its policy, of defeating its policy.[10]

The CPI conveniently forgot that it had collaborated with the British once the USSR became an ally after June 1941.

There had been clearly a shift in Comintern policy and Stalin had decided that India could be ripe for revolution. (India was not. China was. Stalin chose the wrong country and the Chinese communists surprised everyone, including Stalin, by coming to power in 1949.) The Communist Party launched a revolutionary struggle in February 1948. The main form it took was a peasant war in Telangana, part of the old state of Hyderabad. Its attempts to call a general strike in the industrial cities failed miserably, and the Telangana struggle petered out after two years. Soon Stalin changed his mind, and the CPI began its phase of collaborating with the Congress, but only the 'progressive elements' within it, reminiscent of the Congress befriending the Labour Party Left-wingers such as Cripps. It was only in 1955 that the CPI recognized that the independent Indian state was genuinely free, and after some more years it reconciled itself to the parliamentary path.[11]

The Socialist Party had been established in 1934 within the Congress, but upon Independence with new elections looming, the Congress decided to discourage other political parties inside its ranks. It would no longer be the umbrella organization under which many different political parties could unite to fight foreign rule. The Congress would become a political party on its own, while keeping the same name. The Congress socialists had a choice of staying in and aiding Nehru, or going out and striking a more radical tone. They now seceded from the Congress. Unlike the CPI, which was very much a plant bred in the hothouse of international communism, the Socialist Party had deeper roots and was a much more original radical formation. Its leaders—Jayprakash Narayan, Achyut Patwardhan, Ram Manohar Lohia, Narendra Dev, Ashok Mehta—had a record of long participation in the freedom struggle and going to jail, but also contributing to the Nehru wing's policy ideas. The Socialist Party merged with the Kisan Mazdoor Praja party, formed by J.B. Kripalani, a Congress veteran and a Gandhian, who opposed the Congress's shift towards a Hindu conservative stance. The Praja Socialist Party was a major force in the 1950s, but eventually foundered on the contradictions between a class-based social democratic approach and a conciliatory Gandhian one. The Congress mopped up many of its members in the 1960s. Jayprakash Narayan quit politics to pursue a Gandhian programme, and the Praja Socialist Party split several ways several times. Only Ram Manohar Lohia left a legacy which I shall examine later.

There were, of course, serious class cleavages in India, but they did not fit the standard Leninist model invoked by the communist parties. The organized working class—employed in factories, mills and large enterprises—was minuscule in relation to the total working population. The largest part of the non-agricultural labour force was in the informal sector characterized in Leninist lore as 'lumpen proletariat'. The majority of workers in the orgnanized sector was employed in government jobs, where they had tenure and regular increments in pay, but they were also very well organized for 'industrial' action and formed the backbone of many trade unions. But even at their largest, the organized workers did not exceed 15 per cent of the total labour force. In the rural areas, agrarian relations differed from region to region given the variety of tenure systems. They included landlords, large or medium or small farmers who owned land, tenant farmers, share croppers and landless labourers and, indeed, many layers in between. The Left parties did little empirical investigation, and class analysis in India remained primitive until modern social scientists came on the scene. Indian analysts, for instance D.D. Kosambi and A.R. Desai, did some pioneering work in the fields; international scholars who did early and seminal work on Indian conditions include Charles Bettelheim from France and Jan Breman from the Netherlands. American scholars, too, were amongst the earliest to study India.[12]

In fact, Indian and Western sociologists played a major part in illuminating the structure and trends in Hindu society. Indeed, one could say that the study of Indian society made its own distinct contribution to the creation of modern sociology. Scholars such as Louis Dumont from France, G.M. Carstairs and David Pocock from UK, Milton Singer and David Mandelbaum from the US and India's own G.S. Ghurye, M.N. Srinivas and Irawati Karve enhanced our knowledge of India. It was left to an American to link the social cleavages to the democratic politics in the provinces. When in 1960 Selig Harrison wrote his *India: The Most Dangerous Decades*, he incited a barrage of vituperation, and suspicions as to his presumption as a foreigner, and an American at that, to question India's seamless unity, abounded. But when he pointed out how Andhra politics was a tussle between two caste groups, the Kammas and the Reddys, how Karnataka politics was a struggle between the Lingayats and Vokkaligas and so on, state by state, he was only being the first person to report what is now routine fare in Indian electoral politics. But for a new nation to admit of such cleavages to a foreigner was unthinkable.

Social or caste cleavages were unfashionable in the socialist/communist analysis of India's problems. Ever since the days of Jotirao Phule and the anti-Brahmin, later Dravida, movement in Tamil Nadu, it was the caste cleavages that were highlighted by radical forces fighting for the ritually defined downtrodden. This was not always acknowledged by the elite leadership which expressed its radical colours in anti-colonial or, even, anti-capitalist rhetoric. Gandhi, with his strategy of cross-class and cross-caste alliances, and his attempts to involve caste Hindus in reforming untouchability consensually, had tried to contain this explosion. But it was only a matter of time before the numerous downtrodden groups came to assert their rights for social equality. Ambedkar had struggled for the rights of his people, and was impatient with Gandhi and Congress in their upper-caste Hindu attitude towards social change. His slogan 'Educate, Agitate, Organize' had been taken to heart by many of his fellow 'depressed', who later called themselves Dalits (literally, 'the ground-down ones'). Untouchability was formally 'abolished' in the Constitution of India (Article 17) in the early 1950s, but that was no more meaningful than the abolition of slavery in the US in 1864. The long struggle, which took another hundred years in the US—to translate the legal abolition of slavery into status equality for the Black Americans (and is still not over)—was still ahead of India. It would be Ambedkar who would gain in stature as that struggle intensified.

But the simple caste Hindu/untouchable distinction was just one cleavage. There were further ones within the caste Hindu structure, as, for instance, the gap between the three upper or forward castes and the Shudra or backward castes. As the democratic system struck roots in India, the sheer numerical strength of the Other Backward Castes (OBC), as the non-Dalit, non-Forward castes are called, began to make its influence felt in Indian politics. The Brahmin elite, which had the reins of leadership firmly in its hands in the early years after Independence, began to see a challenge from the lower orders, though it was not until 1978 that a OBC politician, Charan Singh, a Jat, became prime minister of India—though briefly. This was unlike what the Hindu Mahasabha had envisaged, though it was what Jinnah had feared—there was no solid Hindu majority, whatever the numbers, since Hindu society survived on its many cellular divisions. Building a unified Hindu vote bank remained a big worry for the Hindu parties. This lack of unity remains an advantage for the secular cause.

Ram Manohar Lohia was among the first to see that these social cleavages were fertile grounds for mobilizing the people for a radical transformation of the Indian society, and possibly more effective than a class conflict approach. His analysis was not universally accepted since much of what he was saying was more applicable to North India, especially the 1857 territory, than to South India where the radical movements were already a century old. But he did become very influential when he argued that it was necessary to build an anti-Congress coalition if India was going to throw off the elite ruling formation of upper-caste politicians, rich landlords and businessmen—which he felt the Congress represented. Anti-Congressism, as this philosophy was called, was to prove a potent rallying factor after Nehru's death.

Newly independent India also faced the problem of reconciling the various provincial 'nations', which historically had often been enemies of each other and nurtured old resentments. These were in addition to the over-arching Hindu–Muslim differences. The problem was to convince every citizen that they were all equal in the new free India. The seventeenth century Maratha warrior, Shivaji, for example, was a hero in Maharashtra, but feared and loathed in Bengal and Gujarat for his frequent raids. Aurangzeb, the last of the great Mughal emperors, ruled India for forty years and his rule is the last by an Indian ruler over such a large swathe of the Indian subcontinent till 1947. Yet, he is condemned as intolerant, tyrannical and almost un-Indian by the secularists. Muslim kings began to be divided into 'good' (in other words, tolerant of Hindus) and 'bad' (taking the propagation of Islam as their mission). No similar classification was made for Hindu kings since if they displayed anti-Muslim sentiments, as some Rajput kings did—the Sisodias, for example, who defied Akbar's policy of Hindu–Muslim reconciliation— they were praised for their valour and patriotism in standing up to the Mughals. While Nehru was alive, the Hindu–Muslim cleavage was kept under control and a syncretic Indian history was constructed, for example, by K.M. Panikkar, whose book I have cited. But provincial quarrels were another matter as they had not been part of the nationalist narrative. Many such issues came to the fore when, in the mid-1950s, against Nehru's wishes, there were proposals to reorganize the boundaries of provinces along linguistic lines. This was not a new demand since the Congress had organized its provincial offices along linguistic lines, anticipating the redrawing of provincial boundaries as and when independence came.

The Partition experience was so fraught that any further redrawing of boundaries was thought unwise. A Congress committee comprising Jawaharlal Nehru, Vallabhbhai Patel and Congress party president, Pattabhi Sitaraimayya was formed, and reiterated caution. But the demand for a Telugu-speaking Andhra Pradesh to be formed out of the northern parts of Madras province and Hyderabad was acknowledged. Nehru was still doubtful. He feared Balkanization, but his hand was forced when Potti Sriramulu—an activist for the establishment of Andhra Pradesh—went on a fast and died. This led to a violent reaction which could not be resisted. Andhra was created in 1953.

The States Reorganization Commission was appointed to propose other such linguistic states. It reported in 1955 and had several suggestions on the redrawing of boundaries to form unilingual states. Many such demands were granted. Long-time residents in a province suddenly found themselves part of a minority language group as the dominant language group won majority status. The rights of all people as Indian citizens to live and work anywhere had to be maintained by curbing attempts by majority linguistic groups to impose 'non-tariff barriers' on the employment or advancement of minority groups. It is a sore point which flares up again and again even fifty years after the establishment of such states. The most contentious was the division of Bombay province between a Marathi-speaking state—Maharashtra—and a Gujarati-speaking one—Gujarat. In this case the multilingual, cosmopolitan city of Bombay was at issue. Marathi-speaking people were the largest single group, but not a majority. There were other minorities who had significantly contributed to Bombay's economy and culture: Gujaratis, Hindu as well as Muslim; Parsis who also spoke Gujarati, but in their own special way; Punjabis who then dominated the cinema industry; people from the southern states who had migrated in search of jobs; Sindhis who had just migrated from Sind; Christians of all denominations including Goan Catholics, Kerala Syrian Christians, Anglo-Indians; and, of course, a small enclave of foreigners settled permanently. Bombay was unique until Independence, but democracy made number counting important. There was even a proposal to make it a city state. Nehru refused a division in the mid-1950s, but had to concede when a popular agitation in Maharashtra led to a severe election loss for the Congress in the 1957 elections. The two states were inaugurated in 1960 with Bombay going to Maharashtra.

The provinces knew little about each other once you got beyond the English-speaking elite. Their arts and their histories and their literatures had to be given room to flourish, but in a way which enhanced India's unity, not detract from it. They had cohabited in the same territorial space and, in some sense, shared a common religion or social system—such as the caste system—but there were historical memories of old wrongs and perceived or imagined differences in economic circumstances between neighbouring linguistic groups, as, for example, between Gujarati- and Marathi-speaking communities in Bombay. India has, in this sense, many sub-nations and they have to accommodate each other in as non-antagonistic manner as is feasible and consistent with an All India federation. Democracy has been both a problem—since numbers matter and majorities batten down on minorities—and a solvent, since no linguistic community, even a majority one, is so homogenous that it can win power on its own. Alliances have to be made across linguistic groups as across castes and classes. India's democracy bears a chaotic look because it has had to cope with such multiple class and social cleavages, as well as sub-nationalities within a Union.

FASHIONING THE NATION

Nehru used the machinery and the resources of the government he was heading to create identifiable agencies whose task would be to generate a sense of belonging together. Thus, he created the three Akademis—a suitable transliteration of Academies—for literature (Sahitya), fine arts (Lalit Kala), and music and theatre (Sangeet Natak), whose remit was to bring together classical and folk art forms, promote music and dance, and encourage cross translation between various languages so that their literary heritages were accessible to all Indians. Many became aware of the South Indian dances, Bharatanatyam and Kathakali or the North Indian Kathak or the North-Eastern Manipuri as diverse expressions of an Indian aesthetic for the first time. Northerners came to appreciate the subtleties of Carnatic music, as Southerners learnt to admire North Indian music. The enjoyment of such fine things was democratized. Arts were subsidized for popular dissemination and All India radio, with its monopoly, was compelled to play only classical and not film music (thus driving many young people to Radio Ceylon or Radio Pakistan which played Indian film music freely).

The annual celebrations marking the Republic Day on 26 January were used to invite folk dancers from various parts of India, especially the remote areas of North-East, to participate in the parade. Indians, who frequented the cinema halls in their millions every week, saw Indian News Reviews prepared by the Films Division of India, which made many documentaries illustrating the rich diversity of India. They learnt about events at home and abroad, and were fed regularly with excerpts from the prime minister's speeches. For someone who grew up in the 1950s, it was most educational. Indians became aware of the size and the plural culture of their country, of the many languages and different modes of dress and behaviour, of the range of features and pigments from the fairest Kashmiris to the darkest tribal people.

Nehru fashioned the Congress into an inclusive image of India. Each province had its local Congress leader who headed the government along with the Provincial Congress Committee (PCC), which had a chairman not always on friendly terms with the chief minister. Within a province the Congress organization went down to the district level, mimicking the administrative structure, with functioning offices and elected leaders. There would be a flow upwards along party channels of information about people's needs and demands, and down would come, via the government channel, the implementation of the policies responding to those needs. It was an elite leadership at each stage, but, as one went down the ladder, the elite became more locally rooted. Each cleavage had its representative in the Congress. The untouchables had Jagjivan Ram who rivalled Ambedkar as a leader of his people. The Muslims had Azad, of course, and Asaf Ali, Rafi Ahmad Kidwai and other 'Congress Muslims'. B.C. Roy led West Bengal, though here the Congress was weak. After serving as the successor to Mountbatten as governor general, Rajagopalachari went on to become the chief minister of Madras province, Gobind Ballabh Pant took care of UP (now called Uttar Pradesh) and Rajendra Prasad, who chaired the Constituent Assembly and became India's first President, looked after Bihar's interests at the Centre. When Andhra was formed, T. Prakasam became its leader after a lifetime of service in the Madras cadre of the Congress. B.G. Kher, who had become the leader in Bombay province after the 1937 elections, continued after Independence, and he was succeeded as chief minister by Morarji Desai, a Gujarati Congress leader.

In all the three general elections he fought, Nehru delivered success at the Centre and in every state except Kerala. The Congress polled about 45 to 48 per cent of the votes cast (the turnout was in the 60–65 per cent range) and, thanks to a divided opposition and the first-past-the post system, won a much larger share of the seats in the Lok Sabha than their vote percentage indicated—averaging 350–80 out of 510 seats. As of today, Nehru is the only leader of the Congress or, indeed, of any Indian political party to deliver three consecutive general election victories. Thus, for the first seventeen years while he was prime minister, India had a single dominant party rule. The government machinery ran in sync with the party machinery, though a distance was kept to separate the two, at least while Nehru was around. Few democracies, none in a post-colonial context, had such a dual domination of the Executive and the political party culture (Japan and Mexico are the only two parallels). Only communist countries managed something more integrated between party and government, but then they were not democracies.

Given such dominance, India could easily have slipped into single-party rule as many ex-British colonies in Africa did. It did not, primarily because Nehru was a scrupulous democrat. He was often criticized for not doing enough to encourage the growth of opposition parties. But his reply was that he did try his best, but their frequent splits and walk-outs were not of much help. He reinforced the contribution of G.V. Mavlankar, an Independent and the first Speaker of the Lok Sabha, to establish a good parliamentary culture and encourage the government benches to work harmoniously with the Opposition.

He took on the role of a teacher to the nation and to his colleagues, inevitably, given his somewhat hectoring style. A Canadian diplomat, who was high commissioner for Canada in India between 1952 and 1957, writes of Nehru's 'stream-of-consciousness speeches, occasionally dull, but usually illuminating and moving ... the way in which he revelled in the endless adventure of politics, revelled in whirling, restless, relentless activity, the activity of the creative, practical politician who conceived his task to be to prod, push, pull, cajole, lead India out of the bullock-cart and cow-dung age into the age of jet airplanes and nuclear energy'.[13] Nehru wrote to the chief ministers of the provinces every fortnight, informing them about national and international developments. He was India's window to the world and, as foreign minister throughout his tenure, fashioned India into a serious player on the international scene. Thanks to him, India played a major part in the decolonization committee of the UN, making sure that its own record of success in the anti-colonial struggle also benefited other colonies. Nehru made Indians proud by creating a distinctive foreign policy which was neither pro-Western, though India's British legacy had been widely absorbed and projected, nor pro-Soviet Union, though the long association of the Great Game with India's borders ensured that Russia was never to be ignored by India. His idea of 'non-alignment' rather than 'neutrality' appealed to the Indian elite, since it was like one of those subtle philosophical distinctions Sankaracharya would have made in his battles with his Buddhist rivals.

The Non-Aligned Movement (NAM) which Nehru fashioned, along with fellow leaders of the African and Asian countries, was born in Bandung in 1955 at a conference of newly independent African and Asian nations. India saw a constant stream of foreign leaders—North Vietnam's Ho Chi Minh and Ghana's Nkrumah. I remember waving to them myself in the streets of Bombay in the 1950s. Soviet leaders, Khruschev and Bulganin came as did Yugoslavia's Tito, boosting the image of the communists and helping India establish its non-aligned image (somewhat tarnished when it failed to criticize the USSR for its intervention in Hungary in 1956, while condemning the British–French invasion of Egypt to 'save' the Suez canal). Indians could see that their country had a dignity and a place in the family of nations. While they never lost the sense that Western imperialists were 'out to get them', it was more because there was an urge to highlight the anti-colonial radicalism which the Congress had laid claim to, but forgotten when Independence came. After all, joining the Commonwealth committed India to be a part of the West, indeed of the ex-imperial family of nations. The communists, who had also aligned themselves with the Congress, paraded their radical pretensions, and wanted to give Nehru a Left-wing sheen. The contradictions between the continuity with the empire and the pretensions to a non-aligned, indeed a pro-Soviet, stance, were exposed in 1962 when India had its border dispute with China. There was then an unseemly and uncoordinated rush to the US embassy to seek military help. J.K. Galbraith the US ambassador had chosen that week to catch up on some theatre in London to the intense annoyance of President Kennedy.

JAMMU AND KASHMIR

It was the question of Jammu and Kashmir (J&K), though always called the Kashmir problem, which brought out the full paranoia of Indians against the international system. As a native state Jammu and Kashmir had to choose which Dominion Status country they wanted to join— India or Pakistan. Its ruler was Hindu and, as I have said before, the valley of Kashmir had a Muslim majority, while Jammu was largely Hindu and the sparsely populated Ladakh region predominantly Buddhist. Maharaja Hari Singh waited to drive a better bargain, since he was perched on the borders of both region A and region B. Pakistan had seen Congress send its volunteers into Junagadh (Gujarat) and destabilize it enough to send the nawab into exile. So Pakistan sent an incursion of Pathan 'irregulars' to take the Valley. Under paramountcy, a breakdown of law and order could allow the governor general to take over a Princely State. It was unclear, however, which government had the paramountcy rights here—India or Pakistan. As the irregular army approached the capital Srinagar, the maharaja could see that he was about to lose his kingdom, and he signalled to India that he was willing to sign the Instrument of Accession of his kingdom with India. Patel and Nehru sent troops, which were airlifted, and repulsed the march of the 'irregulars' on Srinagar. In December 1948, a ceasefire was called after an appeal to the UN, which marked a line separating the two armies: the Indian Army and the 'irregulars', now bolstered by the Pakistan Army.

Nehru was, and continues to be, much criticized for taking the Kashmir question to the UN. There are insinuations that Mountbatten, playing the Great Game for the British, forced Nehru to do so; Patel would never have halted the march of Indian troops short of the full recovery of the entire territory of J&K. Nehru is criticized for agreeing to the UN resolution asking for a plebiscite to determine the future of Kashmir after the withdrawal of troops by both countries. He himself was bitter that the UN, in whom he had put his faith, saw the dispute as not about the illegality of the aggression of Pathan irregulars backed by Pakistan on J&K, but as a dispute between two sovereign nations and members of the UN. Britain and the US are blamed to this day in India for the UN decision. The UN, much respected otherwise in India, could never be loved because of its stance on Kashmir. The patriotic Indian was, and has been, convinced that the UN interfered in India's internal affairs and that, had it not been for Nehru's weakness, there would never have been a ceasefire short of a total victory.

The integration of J&K into the Indian Union became an issue. The Congress had supported a plebiscite of the people of the Princely State even before the war. Now, there was a UN resolution on the issue. Sheikh Abdullah, the charismatic leader of Kashmir and the chairman of the National Conference, a secular political party which had been agitating for a democratic Kashmir since the early 1930s, was a friend of Nehru and popular in India. He believed he had assurances that the state would receive special treatment, and eventually be integrated only after a special treaty between India and Pakistan. The Constituent Assembly added an Article—370—in the Constitution enshrining the unique position of Kashmir in the Indian Union. Kashmir was allowed to form its own Constitution. Its head of government was not just a chief minister as elsewhere in India but a prime minister, a position which Sheikh Abdullah assumed.

But Article 370 was in part XI of the Constitution, which dealt with Temporary and Transitional Provisions. Abdullah wanted the arrangement to be permanent. In 1953 he began to demand a formal negotiation between India and Pakistan to achieve this. This was required to rejoin the two separated parts of the Valley. He wanted an 'iron-clad guarantee of autonomy'. He was accused of fomenting secession from India, arrested and held without trial, off and on for many years. The Constitution of J&K was subordinated to the Constitution of India by a hand-picked leadership passing a resolution in the assembly to the effect that the state 'is and shall be an integral part of the Union of India'. Article 370 remained in place.

Nehru's behaviour towards Abdullah was nothing short of squalid, and there can have been no justification for it in law. Kashmir became a totem for Nehru's secularism, since its Muslim majority had to be made to stay in India just to show the world how secular India was. There were, no doubt, considerations of security—the Great Game was one and, subsequently, the Cold War which had brought Pakistan to the US camp—which added to Nehru's self-righteousness. In a sense, this was Nehru taking up the viceregal mantle and treating a native princedom in a high-handed fashion. Dalhousie would have approved. Abdullah is reported to have shed tears when he was allowed out of prison to attend Nehru's funeral. He was crying as much for a flawed friend as for his own loss.

Whatever the justice of the many claims, Kashmir festers like an open sore which heals for a while, and then flares up again. There can be little doubt that had it not been a Princely State but a part of British India, it would have gone to Pakistan on the principles agreed on 3 June. Perhaps, it would have been partitioned as Punjab and Bengal were, and Jammu and Ladakh may have come to India and Kashmir to Pakistan. Even to say as much would be regarded as heresy in India, which considers the inclusion of J&K into India—an integral part of the Union of India no less—vital to India's own sense of being a nation. Kashmir has become a talisman of India's secularism, of its commitment to keep Muslims happy within India, a Hindu majority country.

REFORM AND REVERSAL

It was this solid start of the first seventeen years of Independence when Nehru was prime minister, as well as the long apprenticeship in representative politics before Independence, which gave India its taste for democratic politics. At the same time, the various strengths and limitations of both Nehru and the Congress shaped the future trajectory of India. Nehru was a liberal individualist with socialist ideas. He wanted radical reform in the social and economic life of Indians. He meant by that a root and branch reform of the Hindu society, a radical overhaul of the land ownership system, and the imposing of limits on private enterprise in the industrial and commercial spheres.

His fellow Congressmen, especially the leaders of his generation—Patel, Prasad, Kripalani, Rajagopalachari—were social conservatives who had been radicalized by Gandhi, but only radicalized politically for the cause of independence. They were converted to Gandhi's vision of a consensual reform of Hindu society and of doing 'something' to relieve poverty, but here again only by harnessing a cross-class alliance, with the landowners and industrialists firmly in the saddle.

Nehru's allies in his fight against the conservative forces were the socialists and some younger Congressmen such as Asaf Ali, Rafi Ahmad Kidwai and Sampurnanand. But he also proved a worthy heir of Gandhi. Patel died in December 1950 and Nehru strong-armed the Hindu conservative, Purushottam Das Tandon who had been elected Congress president, off his perch. Nehru became president of the Congress and prime minister in 1951, on the eve of the first general elections. He was to be the unchallenged power for the rest of the 1950s in the Congress as well as in the government.

But he did suffer one major reverse. This was in his bid to reform the laws of family and property among the Hindus. It was an essential step if Hindu society was to be modernized. It was also the first chance in thousands of years for a government of India to tackle the reform of Indian society, a large part of which was Hindu. Napoleon did it for the French nation by leaving behind his monumental Code Napoleon which rationalized the entire corpus of ancient French laws. Ataturk did the same for Turkey. At the minimum, the different systems prevalent in different parts of India about property inheritance—the *dayabhaga* and the *mitakshari*—a result of the fragmentation of political authority over the territory of what had now, at last, become a single nation state, had to be reconciled. A committee appointed before Independence under the chairmanship of Sir Benegal Narasimha Rao, himself a technical adviser to the Constituent Assembly, had proposed a Hindu Code Bill. Ambedkar, who had been much more concerned with reforming Hindu society than Nehru was over the years, moved the bill in 1948.

There was massive opposition from the Congress ranks. Rajendra Prasad who presided over the assembly, was dead against it, as were Patel, Rajagopalachari and many others. Nehru had invested much more energy in economic reform ideas than in social reform. He had probably imagined that social reform would be a much easier task, since his socialist thinking rang alarm bells about class antagonisms but not caste ones. But Gandhi had schooled his lieutenants in rearguard action against root and branch reform of Hindu society, while retaining the best intentions. He had not wanted a fight against untouchability, and never against caste. Nehru and Ambedkar had to abandon the Hindu Code Bill in 1951. Ambedkar resigned as the law minister in disgust. Nehru learned his lesson. Amedkar, later, led his people out of Hinduism to a mass conversion to Buddhism before he died in 1956.

There were deeper reasons for Nehru's defeat. The British Indian state had been frightened off social reform after 1857. The Clapham sect radicalism of William Bentinck was put down as one of the reasons why the natives were antagonistic to the empire. From then on, social reform was left to 'civil society' as one would call it today. Private collective action against child marriage or for widow remarriage was pushed by social reform groups. Har Bilas Sarda succeeded in introducing a bill against child marriage in the central legislative assembly in 1927. This had become the Sarda Act in 1929. But this was a rare example of private action reaching legislative maturity.[14]

People who believed that revival of Hindu society and its old norms was an assertion of an anti-colonial nationalism outnumbered those who wanted a Western-style modernization of Hindu society. Gandhi was a good example of someone who was anti-colonial but also anti-Western, as far as modernization was concerned. In Muslim society, the movement against reform and the belief that sharia law should be implemented was and, indeed is, to this day strong. The reform of Muslim family law was never on the cards, and some people, even today, berate Nehru for his asymmetric criticism of Hindu social practices and indulgence towards the Muslim ones. This, they say, is a violation of secularism. Nehru was, of course, pushing modernization of the majority community as it was more urgent in his view, but he was not to succeed. The Hindu Code Bill had to be broken up into separate bills and modified to assuage conservative sentiments, before it was passed in 1955.

THE GOLDEN TRIANGLE

The politics of India during the Nehru years and, indeed, until the end of Congress majority rule in 1989, was directed almost entirely to the maintenance of national unity or integrity. This worked through three basic mechanisms which formed a kind of 'golden triangle'[15] which underpinned the politics of the state: first, a *revolutionary* political commitment to universal adult franchise-based parliamentary democracy; second, a *conservative* avoidance of social reform; and, third, a *reformist* economic policy based on planning and state initiative for economic development. It was these three which determined the successes and failures of India in its sixty years' trajectory as an independent nation.

The revolutionary political commitment framed the context in which the two other mechanisms operated. The social conservatism resulted in the persistence of caste and untouchability in Hindu society and conservatism in the Muslim. It led to the democratic use of social backwardness as a political weapon. Castes became foci of vote banks and political alliances, and instead of Nehru's vision of a *modernist rational* society, India became a *modernized conservative* society. (The distinction between modernity and modernization is a critical one. The former involves a critical rational attitude about society while the latter is an instrumental use of modern technology without commitment to the scientific spirit.) Yet through it all, despite many vicissitudes, India remained a united and territorially integrated state unlike its neighbour Pakistan which split in 1971, or Sri Lanka where a bloody civil war between a Tamil minority and the Sinhalese majority continued for twenty-five years.

It was economic reform which became Nehru's major preoccupation after his efforts at social reform were impeded. Here he was in a commanding position. The narrative of India's economic problems was fashioned by the Congress in two phases, as I have described earlier. The nineteenth century Congress moderates wanted tariff reform and a cheap rupee, along with Indianization of public services. Dadabhai Naoroji had also fashioned a critique based on the notion of a drain of surplus from India to Britain. The inter-war critique was much more severe and blamed the British for deindustrialization and for the neglect, if not ruination, of Indian agriculture. This critique in the hands of the Congress Left was anti-capitalist—they distrusted private business as an agent for India's economic advance. It was also informed by the Comintern critique of British imperialism fashioned mainly by Rajani Palme Dutt, a prominent British communist with an Indian father and Swedish mother, who devoted his whole life to the Communist Party. His book *India Today* became the Bible for Indian radicals.

There seemed to be a universal agreement among Indian nationalists, politicians as well as businessmen that India needed industrialization, and that a leading role had to be taken by the state. Planning was in the air and India was to be a planned economy. The national planning committee encouraged thinking about planning among India's leaders. The businessmen produced the Bombay plan. The Left wing had the People's plan. Even the Gandhians produced a plan.

Nehru established the Planning Commission almost immediately upon Independence. He became the chairman of the commission. Yet, he made it clear that he was not an ex-officio chairman. This was revealed when the First Five Year Plan document carried a letter at the outset from the chairman of the Planning Commission (J. Nehru) to the prime minister of India (J. Nehru), submitting the plan for his consideration. This was also Nehru's way of inculcating proper procedures in government functioning. A series of Five Year Plans has been launched since, the prime minister has always assumed the chairmanship of the Planning Commission and it has become a fixture of India's economic policy-making structure.

An industrial policy resolution was passed in 1948 and another in 1956, laying down the areas reserved for the state in which it was to be the sole agent of industrial production. The private sector was to be the junior partner. There were to be heavy industries first and, later, consumer goods industries. Having been a colony dependent upon a highly industrialized nation, Indian nationalists decided that power came from industrialization. They were also much impressed by the example of the Soviet Union and Japan.

The nationalists, however, concluded, with less justification, that India had to be self-sufficient in all its industrial needs rather than rely on international trade. This avoidance of international trade was fuelled by the prevailing view attributed to Raul Prebisch, a Latin American economist and Hans Singer, a British economist, who argued that terms of trade for primary products were deteriorating in a secular (that is, long run) trend vis-à-vis manufactured products. Thus, a country specializing in exports of primary products was unlikely to make enough to finance imports of manufactured goods. There was, accordingly, a prevailing pessimism about India's chances of exporting enough to finance imports of machinery. India's share of world trade had been as high as 7 per cent in the nineteenth century. But the Great Depression left bitter memories, with its accompanying collapse of agricultural prices. India's export surplus was also much lower in the first half of the twentieth century than it had been fifty years before.

As far as foreign capital was concerned, India had accumulated the large amount of sterling balances during the war—Rs 17,240 million (£1.15 billion, which would be around £100 billion in today's money). This gave credence to the drain argument since this surplus was now at India's disposal. There seemed to be no need for outside capital to help India's development plans. In the first five years after Independence, much of the money was spent on helping Indian capitalists buy off the British owners of factories and firms in India. Thus, there was a net outflow of capital from India. The new government spent the money, in the words of the finance minister, C.D. Deshmukh, 'as if there was no tomorrow'.[16]

Self-sufficiency became a major planning goal, both in the financing of the plans, as well as in minimal reliance on imports. India's strategy was shared by many similarly large, poor countries, and it was called Import Substitution Industrialization (ISI). This required stopping imports of consumer goods or machines to produce indigenous consumer goods. It meant importing machines to make machines which, in turn, would make other machines to produce consumer goods. Steel factories would link to machine tools and heavy machinery making, which would then make machines which, for example, textile mills could use rather than import.

India was not devoid of modern industry at the time of Independence. Indeed, India began acquiring modern industry in the mid-nineteenth century, well before most European countries. But the early rapid growth of modern industry in the 1860–1900 period had not kept pace in the twentieth century, especially during the depression. India had a wartime revival of manufacturing and, by 1947, was the seventh-largest country in terms of volume of industrial output, though in terms of the total economy it was still a small sector. Of course, this was post-war period and many Axis countries had their industry destroyed. This may have boosted India's rank somewhat, but even so, India was not 'de-industrialized' as nationalists have argued. India had one of the largest private business classes of any colonial country; it had a world-class cotton textile industry and a virtual monopoly over jute manufacturing. There were steel, cement and glass manufacturing companies, but Indian industry fell short of what was needed in quantity as well as quality. Nehru confessed in Parliament that he preferred the imported Gillette 'safety razor blades', since Indian blades were low quality. Till the mid-1950s, no bicycle was manufactured in India. Industry had to have priority. It was a moot question whether the need was for heavy industry or light. Other Asain countries—Malaysia and South Korea, for example, who developed later avoided India's choice and industrialized much faster than India.

Agriculture underwent drastic reform of land tenure rights, and farmers were encouraged to pool the fragmented bits of land so as to make cooperative agriculture feasible and realize the economies of large-scale farming. The nationalist critique of colonial rule gave the impression, even to the nationalists themselves, that once the foreigners had left, prosperity would return. There would be no more drain of India's wealth. In farming a similar idea prevailed that the poverty of the cultivator was due to the draining of surplus by the landlords and their agents. So the emphasis was on tenurial reform rather than on raising productivity as such. Soon after Independence, food grains output stagnated, but in 1954 the harvest reached a level 20 per cent above its 1950 level. This allowed Nehru, perhaps prematurely, to shift plan investment allocations much more towards industry than agriculture in the Second Five Year Plan. This relative shift of emphasis was to trouble India for the next ten years. The output of food grains, as an index of how cheaply food could be provided for cities, became a major issue. This was crucial if the development plan was to shift workers from low productivity agriculture to high productivity industry. In 1947 the output per worker in agriculture was Rs 423, in manufacturing Rs 1605, in small-scale and cottage industry Rs 776 and in services Rs 1094.

India had been a low-productivity country throughout its history. The size of the population, however, made total income quite large despite the low per capita level. Angus Maddison has estimated that for the 250 years between 1600 and 1850, per capita income did not change at all.

It began to grow at a slow pace of 0.5 to 1 per cent per annum in the next half century, and under 0.5 per cent for the first fifty years of the twentieth century. But since the kings and landlords and the temples were both efficient and ruthless in extracting the surplus, an impression of enormous wealth was created in the minds of travellers and chroniclers who merely saw the royal parades and processions. Also until around 1850, the population had been static or rising extremely slowly. Thus, the 140–50 million people who lived in the sixteenth to eighteenth centuries were well provided for, with surplus land as and when their old farms became less fertile. Kings would give concessions to attract people to farm virgin land. The Hindustani word for population—*abaadi*—is also the word for prosperity. For kings and landlords, more people meant more output and more surplus to extract. Thus India was, through the centuries, a poor country with rich rulers.

It was to modernize India and make it an industrial and, therefore, rich and powerful country that the national planning committee had been set up by the Congress in 1938 with experts as well as politicians, trade union representatives and businessmen—as Nehru put it 'a strange assortment of different types'. But this was just a stocktaking exercise before independence and before a free nation took up its urgent tasks. Bose and Nehru had no time for Gandhi's rural utopia. The resolution setting up the National Planning Committee had said, 'the problem of poverty and unemployment, of national defence and economic regeneration in general cannot be solved without industrialisation. As a step towards such industrialisation, a comprehensive scheme of national planning should be formulated. This scheme should provide for the development of heavy key industries, medium scale industries, and cottage industries.'[17]

But industrialization was a means to an end. 'That aim was declared to be to ensure an adequate standard of living for the masses, in other words, to get rid of the appalling poverty of the people. The irreducible minimum, in terms of money, had been estimated by economists at figures varying from Rs 15 to Rs 25 per capita per month.' The growth target was set. 'We calculated that a really progressive standard of living would necessitate the increase of national wealth by 500 to 600 per cent. That was however too big a jump for us, and we aimed at a 200 to 300 per cent increase within ten years.'[18]

The reality was much less shining than the ambition. The formulators of the NPC targets were dreamers. They set targets that aimed to double or treble the total national income in ten years—implying an annual growth rate of national income of either 7 (doubling) or 10 per cent (trebling) per annum. But such optimism was forgivable—the pioneering planners did not realize the size of the challenge. Economists had just begun to grapple with the theory of economic growth in the late 1940s. The simple and, rather mechanical, calculations required for achieving a target rate of growth involved calculating the savings ratio and what was called the capital output ratio. The combination of these two variables told the planner what growth rate was achievable. Few countries, even including developed countries, had such information readily available. India was one of the pioneers in terms of national income statistics. Yet, the NPC did not have such information. The Planning Commission became one of the first institutions to grapple with the new discipline of development economics, and India became a laboratory as well as a generator of new ideas on development.

It has to be said that economic policy was the biggest failure of Nehru and, indeed, of the Congress. During the forty-two years of its rule as the single majority party, from 1947 to 1989 (two years excepted), it was in command, it had the best expertise and it had willing workers. But neither the ambition of providing the masses with a minimum standard of Rs 15–25 per month, nor the income growth target of 200–300 per cent in ten years was, or indeed has been, realized. National income took nineteen years to double between 1950–51 and 1969–70, and another nineteen to double again in 1988–89.

Nehru himself was a witness to a good decade of growth in India. The First Five Year Plan, which was hastily thrown together from existing schemes of irrigation and public works, etc., led to a national income growth of 18 per cent over the five years. The much more ambitious Second Five Year Plan was formulated by Prof. P.C. Mahalnaobis, a world renowned statistician who laid down a growth plan for Indian economy with emphasis on heavy industry. The Mahalanobis model acquired immense appeal for India's intellectuals. Here was an entirely original Indian economic contribution, even more exciting because it had been anticipated by a Soviet economist, Grigorii-Alexandrovic Fel'dman in the 1920s, but rediscovered in the West only in the mid-1940s. Mahalanobis had not read it as he was not an economist. Nehru backed Mahalanobis to the hilt, and the model became a part of Left ideology in India. To doubt its priorities for heavy industry and to argue for more investment in agriculture and consumer goods industries became a byword for Rightist economics. From its inception in 1955 till the late 1980s, the Mahalanobis strategy remained an unquestioned tenet of India's economic policy. It was a very costly innovation for the Indian masses.

The strategy turned out to be too ambitious. Savings to finance the investment were lacking; the sterling balances had disappeared by 1955, the drain proved to be an overestimate. The 'internal' drain in the form of the incomes of landlords and princes proved difficult to tax, though

Nehru did seek the help of the Cambridge economist, Nicholas Kaldor who advocated wealth tax and an expenditure tax. The Indian state was too soft to be extortionate, and India had to rely on foreign aid to bridge the gap between its investment plans and its available savings. The second plan had to be pruned two years after its launch, and India began to depend on US food aid under US PL 480 and also on foreign aid from various countries—the Soviet Union, the UK, Germany and the USA. But all this aid was provided by the donors for their own political ends; they certainly never questioned India's approach to planning. The Second Five Year Plan saw growth at 23 per cent, slightly higher than in the first Five Year Plan. Over the decade of planning, 1951–61, national income grew at an average of 4.5 per cent per annum. If growth had continued at that rate, the GDP would have doubled in sixteen years.

But the pattern of growth was grossly distorted. The emphasis on heavy industries and the neglect of agriculture meant that the growth in income did not translate into growth in employment for the mass of workers. It created jobs for the educated urban elite who were recruited into the new public sector industries and higher education institutions. Government bureaucracy expanded and its members led a privileged life of guaranteed lifetime job tenure, with a steady increase in salaries keeping pace with inflation. Employment in the manufacturing industry was limited to the new capital goods industries which only took in highly skilled workers. The older existing manufacturing industry was restricted in its ability to expand output, because planning had decreed that additional consumer goods output should be made by small-scale and cottage industries. It is easy for non-economists to think that small-scale industries are less capital intensive than large-scale factories. But the economies of scale which manufacturing can bring to production allow it to save on capital per unit of output much more than small-scale industries. Labour is much more productive with machine spinning and weaving than with a spinning wheel and a handloom. But Gandhian dogma was catered to and, thus, at both the consumer goods and the capital goods end, India adopted capital intensive policies which, as a poor country, it could ill afford. Thus growth was lower than what it could have been.

This elitist growth pattern was justified in the name of a socialist pattern of society, which was declared the Congress's policy aim at the Avadi Congress Conference in 1955. This was the apogee of Nehru's power over his party. Few in the Congress were socialists, but if it meant a larger public sector and thus greater powers of patronage, they were happy to go along. The Left parties were supportive, of course, and the communists lauded Nehru for following the Soviet Union's example in planning.

Nehru had his own reasons for following the capital intensive path. The NPC resolution mentioned national defence as one aim of planning. Nehru wished India to be self-sufficient in production of its defence requirements. He said this explicitly to Marie Seton, a well-known writer on cinema who was frequently his guest while in India. 'Thinking of the development of defence production as a means of expanding India's public sector, Nehru said, "You cannot develop an isolated industry without a general background of industrial development." Nehru's immediate objective was to build up heavy industry to ensure self-reliance in general economic development. This remark was made in Lok Sabha in January 1957.'[19]

This is not surprising since national integrity was always the top priority and all other decisions followed from that. Thus, India was able to be a nuclear power by 1974, thanks to the atomic energy policy which Nehru began and carefully nurtured. India had an aircraft factory, factories for machine tools and heavy electrical goods and, of course, steel factories—three, in fact, established with help from Soviet Union (Bhilai), Germany (Rourkela) and UK (Durgapur). The Indian Institute of Technology (IIT) was established as an apex higher education college and many more proliferated. To this day, being admitted to an IIT remains a cherished ambition for India's young men and women.

India's private sector industrialists who had been avid supporters of Gandhi and Congress, found themselves under attack as indulging in monopolistic and restrictive practices. The shortage of foreign exchange which hit planning in 1957 led to a strict regime where each import required permits, and any expansion of output had to obtain a licence. India failed to benefit from an enterprising native industrial class, as the Leftist bias in economic policy increased in the second half of the 1950s and even more so in the 1960s and 1970s. The failure of the plans to achieve targets did not lead to a questioning of planning strategy; it merely led to a further restriction of private sector.

India did acquire a large apparatus of basic industries. But this was at an enormous cost in terms of alternatives foregone—higher growth rate, more employment, more food and consumer goods. This large basic industry sector was a matter of great national pride, especially when India's arch enemy, Pakistan, signed up to be an ally of the US and received massive military and other aid. There was always a rhetoric of removing poverty, but the emphasis was on modernization and national defence and national self-sufficiency. The poor could wait.

NEHRU AT THE TOP

By 1957, the tenth anniversary of Indian Independence, Nehru was towering above all others. He had steered India through its post-Partition trauma, schooled it in democracy and launched planned economic development. He had made India an international presence, if not a power, and mediated in disputes in Korea and Indo-China as a non-aligned but friendly country to all sides. Nehru won the second general elections handsomely. He was able to induct his long-time friend, the London-based, Left-wing firebrand, Krishna Menon into the Cabinet, after securing his nomination and then election as an MP from Bombay north. Menon had been nursing the India League which had worked for Indian independence through many decades in London. He had befriended Nehru during the latter's visits to London, and looked after his publishing matters almost like an agent. He had been made the first high commissioner for independent India in the UK, but got embroiled in a scandal about the purchase of jeeps for India. Menon was useful to Nehru as they spoke the same language of Anglophile Fabians, though Menon was farther to the Left. He represented India at the UN and cast the infamous vote with the Soviet Union at the time of the Hungarian uprising in 1956. He redeemed himself by putting up a fierce defence of India's position on Kashmir in the UN Security Council, when Pakistan brought up the issue. Menon was something of a pin-up, thanks to his strong defence of India and for being fashionably Left-wing. Nehru welcomed a socialist ally to the Cabinet.

The brand of progress that Menon and Nehru espoused was much helped by the Bombay film industry. Hindi cinema has had an uncanny way of telling the nation's story even as it entertains a large semi-literate audience, only a fraction of which speaks the language in which the films are written. In their loud, obvious ways, they tell the stories people love to see again and again—simple romances with larger-than-life heroes and obviously evil villains. The hope inspired by the first ten years of Independence was reflected in the films which Bombay was making. If in the 1940s the hero and his love faced a tragic future often ending in death for one or both of them, helpless in the face of the society or the world which crushed them, by the mid-1950s heroes were fighters and winners. They exuded confidence; they could win battles and the love of their life. Typical of this new genre was a 1957 film, *Naya Daur* (the New Way), in which Dilip Kumar, an iconic film star known for his tragic roles, played the driver of a horse-drawn carriage about to be made redundant by a bus brought in by the local landlord who believes in progress and mechanization. The hero summons his village friends to help build a road which will take his carriage, but not the bus. At the end, progress is reconciled with mechanization; both the bus and the carriage have a place in the new India. Along the way there is romance, some rivalry for the favours of the leading lady, and many songs and dances. But the message is that new India is in control of its destiny.

There were other voices, mainly from the Left, which expressed their disappointment at the lack of a more radical overhaul of the old order. Guru Dutt, a popular director and actor made *Pyaasa* (The Parched One) in 1956, where the protagonist is a poet whose poems are exploited by his grasping publisher, who though earlier neglectful realizes he can make a huge profit from them because of the poet's (alleged) death. Only a prostitute stands selflessly by the poet as people all around seek to exploit him. At the end he leaves the cruel city along with his loved one, denouncing the selfish and corrupt society that surrounds him. In a famous film poem, the songwriter Sahir Ludhianwi, who belonged to the Progressive Writers guild, a communist cultural group, challenges those who can still take any pride in India to show their faces in public. Similarly also in 1957, in the epic film *Mother India*, Nargis, who later became the first film star to receive the state honour of Padma Shree, portrays the struggles of a farmer's wife and a mother—debt ridden and alone, she still emerges triumphant through her tragedies. There was much hope though some disappointment in that decade, a decade which Nehru straddled like a Colossus.[20]

The year 1957 was also one in which the Second Five Year Plan, which had just been launched the previous year and given Nehru the satisfaction of seeing his dreams being fulfilled, became a source for the beginnings of his woes. It was scaled down due to a shortage of foreign exchange. Indian businessmen and consumers had foreseen the coming shortage and ordered so many imports that a sudden shortage of foreign exchange was the result. The pruning of the plan exposed a serious flaw in the economic management of the country. The shortage of foreign exchange was a part of an overall shortfall of savings, both domestic and foreign, to match the ambitious investment plans. India had to resort to deficit financing, flooding the banks with government paper, and to foreign aid.

It was in agriculture that, perhaps, the biggest failure of Indian policy was seen. Spectacular irrigation dams had been built on the model of the US' Tennesse Valley Authority, hailed by Nehru as modern India's temples. But the fragmentation of cultivable land into many small parcels and the primitive tools and techniques were not touched. It was thought that once the cultivator was the owner of his land, all problems would be resolved. The problem, of course, was not that the surplus which was once taken away was now with the cultivator, but that it was a meagre surplus either way.

The answer to greater productivity was seen to be in pooling land together and making the use of tractors and other heavy machinery more economical. The Congress had resolved, in its Agrarian Reforms Committee in 1949, that cooperative farming was the solution. Nehru pinned his hopes on this through much of his tenure at the top. Many economists and—especially—Left intellectuals wanted rapid consolidation of the cultivating units, even using force if necessary. China had shown, soon after its 1949 revolution, how agrarian reform could abolish private property in land, establish village level cooperation and, indeed, move on to communes. The Chinese example was urged upon India by an official delegation which had been sent to study its agricultural policy. The Chinese had done their land reform, but also transformed the production processes in the countryside. India had reformed tenure, but left the farmer to his devices. Would India follow the Chinese path?

This did not happen. This was because once land reform, however imperfect, had happened, the new owners of land—even small tracts of land—began to be immensely suspicious of any scheme to make them give up control over their possessions. The Congress had attracted supporters from conservative rural segments ever since the peasant agitations launched by Gandhi and Patel. Now, a new generation of leaders had sprung up within the Congress to look after the interests of farmers. Charan Singh who was a Jat, and as such represented a farmer community of north India, was a leader in Uttar Pradesh. He emerged as the principal opponent of the Chinese solution as well as the cooperative path. He had some reason to doubt the wisdom of the policy of consolidation, as it soon emerged.

The farm management surveys of the Planning Commission, which were carried out in the mid-1950s, concluded, after studying extensive empirical data, that large farms were not more productive than small farms, thus knocking down a holy tenet of Left-wing thinking on agriculture which was much influenced by Lenin's work on Russian agriculture. Lenin had favoured large farms and mechanization. Stalin had implemented this policy in his disastrous collectivization experiment, which deprived the Soviet Union of an efficient agriculture for decades. A.V. Chayanov, another Russian agrarian economist whose work had a much sounder empirical basis, was hardly known in India. Chayanov was able to appreciate the superior mode of production that the small cultivator represented. There followed an agonized debate among Indian intellectuals and economists (mainly in the pages of the *Economic Weekly* and the *Economic and Political Weekly*) over two decades as to how to understand this departure from accepted wisdom. This finding was, however, grist to the mill for Charan Singh and the conservative forces. At a Congress conference in 1959, Nehru was forced to abandon the cooperative solution.[21]

The battle for the owner–cultivator had been won, but the issue of productivity remained. Also, by this time the growth of population and the lack of employment opportunities in the non-agricultural sectors meant that landless workers had become a big issue in the countryside. They needed work which could extend round the year, but agriculture, with its low productivity and use of primitive technology, was unable to provide it. India faced a severe shortage of food in the late 1950s. The Ford Foundation issued a report on India's deficiency in this regard, as did a government committee appointed under the chairmanship of Ashok Mehta, a socialist intellectual. As the 1950s ended, food supply became a live issue in Indian politics.

Food grain output was about forty-five million tons in 1950. It stagnated for the next three years, but in 1954 there was a good harvest of fifty-four million tons. Yet again, the output stagnated for the next four years at or below the 1954 level. In 1959 it rose again to fifty-nine million tons, continued rising for the next two years to fall again in the following two till 1964. Thus, until Nehru's death, the food problem had not been sorted out, and the Indian economy remained a gamble on the monsoon.

Nehru's defeat by Charan Singh was a portent of the changes which were occurring. The first generation of national leaders had been All India figures. But now, a new generation of leaders rooted in a particular state or region, or even community, was emerging. In Tamil Nadu it was Kamaraj Nadar who displaced Rajagopalachari, the latter having abandoned the Congress and started the Swatantra Party which was strongly opposed to Nehruvian socialism. Kamaraj spoke little English and no Hindi, but he ruled Tamil Nadu like his fiefdom. Similarly, West Bengal had Atulya Ghosh, and in Bombay S.K. Patil and Morarji Desai were the new leaders. Many of these leaders had rural roots and were aware of agricultural interests. They were not Westernized, and had not been abroad to study. They were not barristers, but professional politicians. They were, in other words, utterly unlike Nehru.

NEHRU OVER THE TOP

Nehru was seventy years old in 1959. This would have been a good age for him to retire, and give up the prime ministership he had held for twelve years. There was, however, no presumed successor in sight, and there was panic in the Congress party and, indeed, the country when he suggested stepping down. He was persuaded to stay; but in many ways, his last five years in power were a contrast to his previous twelve. While he continued to be at the top and, indeed, delivered for the Congress a third successive general elections victory, his word was no longer law.

He was defeated by Charan Singh. He had to concede the demands for separate states of Maharashtra and Gujarat with Bombay going to the former by 1960. He was forced to accommodate Morarji Desai, a known Right-winger, as his finance minister.

Public life had deteriorated on his watch, though no one blamed him for it. Corruption entered the Indian political scene in a serious way. There is an apocryphal story that around the time of his seventieth birthday, Nehru asked a friend of his—Sri Prakash who was governor of Punjab—whether it was true that there was a lot of corruption in India. Sri Prakash is reported to have answered, 'I don't take bribes, but I can't get along without giving them.'[22] The vast system of public bodies and regulations and permits and licences which was Nehru's legacy in India, was to become a breeding ground for corruption. After Nehru's departure it only grew even faster.

It was his son-in-law, Feroze Gandhi who exposed one instance of the use of public funds, held by the government-owned Life Insurance Corporation, to shore up the companies of a businessman called Mundhra who was on the brink of insolvency. Feroze Gandhi as a Congress MP acted like a fierce Opposition critic and made the government institute an inquiry into the affair. But this was a lone episode in which Parliament acted to correct the Executive.

Nehru had blotted his democratic record by intervening in the workings of the first democratically elected communist government in the world. Kerala, a state made up from the Princely States of Travancore and Cochin and British Malabar, was a Malayalam-speaking state formed as a result of the linguistic reorganization. In 1957 it elected a communist majority government. This being the height of the Cold War, immense propaganda commenced against the government on the grounds of its discrimination against the Christian Church, its bias in education, etc. Indira Gandhi, Nehru's daughter had just been elected Congress president. She persuaded her father that the popular agitation against the Kerala government (which it had handled in much the same way that all Indian authorities did) had used excessive cruelty, and that law and order had broken down. Her advice was that President's rule should be imposed under Article 356. Nehru reluctantly agreed—though he should not have. As Granville Austin has said, 'Over the years, President's Rule became extremely controversial because it was thought often to have been used to serve central government convenience or political party interests, not to protect constitutional governance and sound administration.'[23]

Nehru could be said to have inaugurated this tendency. The problem was, of course, that while framing the Constitution, the firm expectation was that the Congress would rule at the Centre and in all the states and forever. The arrangements were for a single centralized federation, however contradictory that may sound. Once non-Congress parties began to be elected, it strained the democratic credentials of the Congress. It was very easy for a Congress government at the Centre to convince itself that non-Congress governments were not fit to rule as viceroys used to do with Native Princes. Dalhousie lurks behind Article 356.

The victory over the Communist Party was short lived and pyrrhic. Kerala went on to enjoy many more episodes of Communist rule. It was an early, and somewhat sinister, introduction to Indira Gandhi's political tactics. It was her arrival in Indian politics, as president of the Congress, which gave the country a foretaste of her limited commitment to democracy and total focus on power for the Congress party. Her claim to becoming Congress president was based solely on the fact that she was her father's daughter and looked after him. That and the accident that she had married someone with the last name spelled the same way as the Mahatma (on the Mahatma's own advice one should add).

As ten years of planning were about to come to an end, criticism began about its effect on the economy. The first objection was that the 45 per cent growth in national income, while welcome, had resulted in an uneven distribution of its fruits. Nehru had been keen on equality, but had not made it his policy goal. His efforts to tax the rich via a wealth tax proposed by Kaldor had failed. Agricultural income had been declared by the Constitution as exempt from income tax, a declaration based on the romantic notion that all farmers were poor. There were plenty of opportunities to convert income into agricultural income, or to just stick to cash payments which would escape the tax net. A 'Black economy' began to grow and soon all durables, especially real estate and other purchases, were made in cash. Prices were understated in 'white' money, and the submerged parts of the price were collected in black. After a parliamentary debate, a commission was appointed under the chairmanship of Mahalanobis to inquire into income distribution. Nothing much came of the report.

But the more serious criticism was about the neglect of agriculture. The rural interest in Indian politics was finding its voice. Given the diversity of land tenures in India, it was finding its voice in different ways in different provinces. Thus while no national agricultural lobby was ever formed, provincial Congress leaders, and even some Opposition leaders, began to voice their objections to the excessive emphasis on industry at the expense of agriculture. Nehru had sanctioned the downgrading of sectoral allocation to agriculture and irrigation from 33 per cent in the first plan to 20 per cent in the second, while industry and transport went up from 31 per cent to 52 per cent. The resulting crisis in food supplies and the inflation which began to be a problem, were evidence enough that all was not well with the strategy. Since 1959 the Swatantra Party established by Rajagopalachari, an old Congress hand, and Minoo Masani, a former socialist, had propagated an unashamedly pro-capitalist line that sought to reverse the Nehruvian march of socialism.

One instance of the Congress's changing profile was the stand India took on the India–Tibet border issue. This border was the one which Col Francis Younghusband had forced on the Chinese when leading the British expedition to Tibet in 1904. But independent India decided not to view the border as the outcome of an imperialist attack. The Chinese had expected that India, as a fellow Asian nation which had also experienced colonialism, would amend the boundary.

The dominance of Left thinking in economic and foreign policy matters was well entrenched. The Mahalanobis model was a Soviet-type strategy, and Krishna Menon was casting India's vote in defence of Soviet suppression of the Hungarian Revolution. It was an external event, but one which brought the Left's position into question. The Dalai Lama escaped from Tibet and arrived in India in March 1959. The border with China had been a simmering issue for some time. Nehru seriously misjudged the Chinese and let his faith in their good intentions be the father to his diplomatic strategy. No one in the Cabinet could stand up to him as Patel would once have done. They fell in line with the prime minister's wishes; after all, Nehru had held the external affairs portfolio since 1947. His naivety was to prove costly for India. For the Chinese, the whole point of being a resurgent nation was to correct historic anomalies and insults. Reclaiming their old suzerainty over Tibet and correcting the border imposed on them by the British were integral to this policy. India's borders had been defined by the British, and India under the Congress was proud to make them its own. This was a clash of Indian and Chinese nationalisms, but the romantic that he was, Nehru continued to believe that Asian nations having suffered under imperialism, would never fight each other. He believed he had a peace treaty—a *panchsheel*—agreement with China.

Left to himself, Nehru might have conceded the Chinese demands for border adjustments. He had even said that the disputed region of Aksai Chin was one 'where not a blade of grass grew'. (The retort by an MP was to point to his own bald head, and by implication Nehru's, and ask if the fact that no hair grew on it made his head expendable.) India eventually lost 12,000 square miles of territory to China in the Aksai Chin area. On the eastern side, 50,000 square miles of disputed territory lay between Assam and Tibet. But Nehru now faced a much stronger opposition from the Swatantra Party as well as from the Jan Sangh, the

Hindu nationalist party which was the creation of the RSS. Atal Bihari Vajpayee was one of the few Jan Sangh MPs in the House, and he was an effective parliamentary speaker who could stand up to Nehru on matters of foreign policy. Krishna Menon, as minister for defence, was also making himself unpopular by his excessive interference in the army and his insistence that weapons be manufactured in India and not imported. The chief of the Indian Army resigned in protest at Menon's behaviour, and this caused quite a stir.

Nehru released the correspondence between India and China about the border dispute in 1959 after border clashes became frequent. It was obvious that he had been naive in his dealings with Beijing. J.B. Kripalani, another Congress veteran now in Praja Socialist Party, criticized Nehru in the Lok Sabha. 'In spite of the agreement and the Panchsheel, aggression on our borders began three months after the signing of the Treaty, as pointed out in the White Paper. It has since been going on and it has been increasing . . . Our territories have been occupied, our people have been kidnapped, our guards have been fired at, taxes have been collected, roads have been built leading towards India'. He concluded by urging the government to be firm, adding that, 'Their vacillation and the Prime Minister's varying statements confuse the public minds. A confused people cannot be ready for emergency.'[24]

Alas, not just the people, but the government itself was ill prepared for an emergency. Nehru was driven by pressure from the Opposition as well as his own party to 'do something' about the border. He ordered the soldiers to remove the Chinese outposts. The result was catastrophic. The Chinese army had been well entrenched in the region for many years, and was suitably prepared for mountain warfare. The Indian Army was both unused to such conditions and ill-equipped. It was entirely unrealistic of Nehru to consider border warfare as a routine matter. Krishna Menon's favoured military man, B.M. Kaul also fed this fanciful strategy. In October 1962, when Indian soldiers tried to re-take the Thag La ridge, they were repulsed. The Chinese also attacked across the Eastern front. Then they stopped as suddenly as they had attacked. The battle lasted only five days, and the unilateral cessation of hostilities by the Chinese was even more humiliating than the defeat.

Zhou En-lai wrote to Nehru urging negotiations, adding that their common enemy was imperialism. He advocated withdrawal by both sides from the line of fighting. Nehru was distraught, bitter at the betrayal by the man he thought had been his friend. 'Nothing in my long political career has hurt me more and grieved me more.'[25] The price had to be paid in the form of removal of Krishna Menon from the post of minister. But there was also an unorganized rush to seek Western arms aid. Nehru's non-aligned policy was in shreds. Western help was indeed available from the US, the UK, Canada and France.

China resumed hostilities on the Eastern front in November. Again, there was a rout and once more within ten days, the Chinese army stopped unilaterally. India lost soldiers in hundreds, if not thousands. Many were taken prisoner, and many more injured. The Indian Army had no suitable clothes for combat at high altitude, no motorized weapon systems appropriate for the icy conditions. It was yet another throwback to the days of Plassey and Assaye, when a disciplined and well-prepared army beat one of brave, but unprepared, soldiers. The Indian Army was never to forget this defeat.

But the response of the public was magnificent. The defeat united Indians. They realized that the India they loved was defined in terms of geography and territory, more than in terms of culture, language or religion. The hopelessly outgunned soldiers were celebrated as martyrs. Yet again, as often before, the film industry played an important part in the way the story of the nation was told. The defeat by China elicited a poem from a well-known Hindi cinema songwriter, Pradip, and India's most famous playback singer, Lata Mangeshkar sang it. It was a moving and simple tribute to those who had fallen. When Lata Mangeshkar sang it in front of a large gathering, Nehru, who was present, was moved to tears. The opening lines of the poem are remembered to this day on patriotic occasions:

Ai mere watan ke logon, zara aankh mein bhar lo pani
Jo shaheed hue hain unki, zara yaad karo kurbani.

(Oh people of my homeland, let tears well up in your eyes
Think for a moment of the sacrifice of those martyrs for your cause.)

One consequence of the disaster was that the areas of Aksai Chin, Ladakh and Tawang were no longer considered alien by the wider Indian nation. Despite their remoteness, they became the heart of India. Indian blood had been shed and would be shed again, if needed, for their defence. Tamil Nadu's recent upsurge for secession from India immediately stopped. Even though people saw that Nehru had been weak, they rushed to his defence. He was a broken man after 1962, but he was not arraigned for India's defeat. Indeed, no one was tried or even charged with neglect. Krishna Menon remains to this day a figure defended by the Left, but largely forgotten in the rest of the political spectrum.

There had been one short campaign which completed India's quest for the removal of Western powers from its soil. The Portuguese colonies of Diu, Daman and Goa were scattered across the west coast. There had been no willingness on the part of the Portuguese to leave voluntarily as the French had done. So India, swiftly and with minimal loss of life, took over these territories in December 1961. This gesture was partly to secure an election victory in 1962, especially for Krishna Menon who was once again contesting from Bombay north. Although Kripalani opposed him, Nehru's reputation was still sound in early 1962, and Menon won. This was perhaps the last hurrah for Nehru and Menon. The problem of integrating Goa and the other Portuguese colonies into the national narrative was not foreseen as a serious one. After all, Goans were natives of Konkan, a coastal region along the western coast of India adjoining Maharashtra and Karnataka. But Goa, the largest of the three colonies, had been colonized for 450 years, longer than the British had been in India. They had not been part of the nationalist narrative, since Portuguese colonialism had not been taken seriously by the nationalist movement. Were the Goans Konkanis, and, if so, were they, along with other people of the Konkan in Maharashtra, part of the latter? Or were they, instead, part of Karnataka, which lay to the south and the east? Were they unique, since a large proportion, though not a majority, were Christians—the largest Christian minority in terms of proportion of total population of any state? Goa was to go through many such questions about its identity, and still does.

Nehru died a broken man in May 1964, after a stroke which left him much weakened. His reputation was high even though he had led India to its humiliating military defeat in his last years. His legacy was the top-heavy industrialization of India, the message of secularism as a building block for the nation and the habits of rationality and modernity that he tried to inculcate in Indians, though less-than-successfully. He gave India some permanent values to cherish—a belief in democracy, pride in its nationhood, an ambition to scale heights so India can take its rightful place in the community of nations and an internationalism in its outlook on the world. If he is no longer the dominant influence, his legacy still invites champions who think he showed India the right way to be.

CHAPTER 13

HEIRS AND SUCCESSORS

TOWARDS THE LATE 1950s, as it became obvious that not even Nehru would be around for ever, both within and outside India a debate began about his likely successors. Many articles were written and even a book—by the Canadian journalist, Wells Hangen—speculating on the likely successors and even predicting chaos, no matter who succeeded him. Perhaps, Nehru's proudest boast was that he had so built the Indian democracy that he was dispensable. Before he died, he tried to clear a way for his likely successor by inviting senior Cabinet members and chief ministers, who were likely rivals, to quit office and devote themselves to rebuilding the Congress. The Kamaraj Plan, as this was called after Kamaraj Nadar, the Congress president, was a transparent ruse on Nehru's part. When it came to getting his way, Nehru was no match for his mentor, Gandhi. But he was indulged—Morarji Desai, the Congressman he liked least, resigned, as did Lal Bahadur Shastri, his favourite.

AFTER NEHRU, WHO?

Upon Nehru's death, the Congress parliamentary party met and proceeded to elect its new leader. Preliminary negotiations had narrowed the choice down to a single candidate, Lal Bahadur Shastri. Shastri had been a successful Cabinet minister and, uniquely among all his colleagues, had demitted office once before. He had resigned as railway minister, accepting responsibility for a train accident in which many people had died. Shastri was a complete contrast to Nehru—a modest man, short of stature and simple of habits. He had no 'presence', but commanded much respect among his colleagues.

The Congress leadership, Kamaraj Nadar, Atulya Ghosh and S.K. Patil, was now collectively known as the Syndicate. It was widely expected that the new prime minister would share power with the

Syndicate, who had not only delivered the job but had managed to keep Morarji Desai out. Yet, Shastri was to prove his mettle in many ways. Though a faithful protégé of Nehru, he proved his ability to chart out an independent path for India. The Third Five Year Plan had been launched in 1961, but had run into problems. Actual growth fell way short of targets in the first two years. The Left in the Congress party and outside wanted to increase the size rather than prune it—their logic being that the five-year targets could be met in the remaining three years only if more resources were thrown in. Shastri initiated a revision of the planning strategy. He suspended work on the Fourth Five Year Plan which would have started in 1966, and inaugurated a series of annual plans.

This was not his only innovation. Agriculture also began to get greater attention under Shastri. C. Subramanian, his minister for agriculture, proved a success when he initiated a revolution in cultivation practice. The favoured mechanical/physical strategy required larger cultivating units and tractors. Recognizing that the cultivation unit would remain small, Subramanian switched to improving productivity by biological/chemical innovations. Fertilizers were deployed and luckily for India, the Rockefeller Foundation supported the International Rice Research Institute in the Philippines, and was able to pioneer high yield variety seeds for rice. Wheat would soon experience a similar revolution. The Green Revolution came to India—and the demand for drastic land reform, for Chinese-style communes etc., took a back seat. This was a truly revolutionary change in the Indian countryside. The British had neglected agriculture except to tidy up the property rights structure and make revenue collection efficient. They did some amount of canal building—more than the Mughals at any rate—but even so, productivity remained low. The sharp increase in the population growth rate during the first half of the twentieth century, when the Indian population increased from 220 million in 1901 to 350 million in 1951, put a greater burden of people on land and reduced wages. Since 1951, the population has trebled. The Green Revolution removed the constraint of food grain availability. If people are still starving, it is because they lack incomes, not because there is no food for them. India became a food surplus country after the 1960s with much food being wasted in government-owned warehouses, a position unimaginable in the 1950s. After centuries, Indian agriculture had turned into a profitable activity for the cultivator. Capitalism had come to Indian agriculture at last.

As I wrote in 1975:

> Instead of underestimating the incidence of the Green Revolution, we should look at the inherent contradictions which will attend upon its success. The Green Revolution will spur the accumulation process in the

countryside and strengthen capitalist relations. The distribution of cultivated land (owned and leased) may become even more unequal than before. But its most important effect will be to replace the pre-capitalist economic relationships, such as share-cropping, by wage earning. The encouragement to multiple cropping that the Green Revolution gives will generate a more even flow of labour-demand on the larger farms and lead to the gradual formation of a wage-earning proletariat finally divested of all control over means of production such as land.[1]

But before that could happen, India went through two bad harvests in succession. Both 1965–66 and 1966–67 were low output years for food grains. Food grain output, which had reached 67.5 million tons in 1964–65 from its level of 45 million tons in 1950–51, went down to 54.5 million tons in 1965–66 and 55.8 million tons in 1966–67. India had become dependent on US wheat imports under PL 480. The wheat had to be paid for in rupees which led to complacency rather than urgency in the Nehruvian circles. The Americans urged India to devote more resources to its own agriculture rather than rely on US supplies. The shift to more resources in agriculture could not have come sooner. Dogma was abandoned and the strategy adopted was to let larger farmers run ahead in raising their output. The regions which were better adapted to the new technology were allowed to go forward without any qualms about spreading the investment over all regions. It was Shastri's great contribution to reverse Nehru's anti-agricultural bias and rescue Indian agriculture from its perennial backwardness, much romanticized by the Gandhians and the socialists.

Shastri suspected Nehruvian grand plans:

> No doubt we have to have bigger projects, bigger industries, basic industries, but it is a matter of the highest importance that we look to the common man, the weakest element of the society. When we think in terms of the common man, we have to think of his food, his clothing, his shelter, medical facilities, recreation for the children. These are some of the basic necessities of life which everyone needs, and more so in the rural areas. We cannot ignore this fact in whatever we may plan, and however big our plan might be. We cannot go on doing things which do not touch the common man, which do not touch the weaker element in our society.[2]

This was a change of emphasis and the objectives of planning, had it been pursued, would have revolutionized economic planning in India. Instead of the military industrial complex, it would have helped living standards and employment. Indeed, India lost twenty-five years before it abandoned big plans. And it took until the twenty-first century for the Congress to champion the *aam admi* and *roti, kapda, makaan*.

Shastri also did two other things which cemented the Indian nation. He faced the full eruption of the agitation on the adoption of Hindi as the sole national language. There was much resentment in the South, but he was able to smooth things over. Nehru had piloted the Official Languages Act in 1963, which did say that English may be used after 1965 when the switchover to Hindi as the sole national language was scheduled. But the people in the South, especially Tamil Nadu, were having none of it. Two men set themselves on fire on Republic Day 1965. Prominent Congressmen, including members of the Syndicate, urged some compromise on the issue, but Morarji Desai as deputy prime minister was all for enforcing the law. Shastri mediated and promised that English could be used in inter-state communication or an English translation provided. English was also retained as a language of public services examinations. A deeply divisive issue between the North and the South was diffused.

I was witness to the transformation of Shastri's image from a non-entity to a hero. During a short visit to India in the summer of 1965, I watched as Indian cinema audiences laughed when they saw him in their weekly newsreel. Here was a short, simple man receiving salute from tall soldiers, and frankly, it looked a bit anomalous: after the handsome Pandit Nehru who could look viceregal, Shastri was just your man-next-door, and Indians expected a more impressive figure. But that was July. By August a war had broken out with Pakistan, and Shastri's response had been much more forthright and aggressive than Nehru's would have been. Kashmir was once again the cause of trouble. Sheikh Abdullah, now released, had gone to Mecca and London, but also to Algiers where he met Zhou En-lai. This inflamed passions against him in India, and he was arrested on his return. He was suspected of being in cahoots with the Chinese and being a Muslim leader of disputed territory, prima facie, a traitor.

While Sheikh Abdullah was abroad during April 1965, a clash had occurred in the Rann of Kutch between Indian and Pakistani soldiers. Now after his arrest, Pakistan believed the Valley would be ripe for revolt against India if its army crossed the Line of Control. The Indian Army was taken by surprise. The Pakistan Army had better equipment in terms of American tanks which were crucial for the mountain terrain in Kashmir. But then Shastri extended the campaign to another front, and the Indian Army attacked across the Punjab border, almost reaching Lahore. This widening of the war brought immediate results: the UN intervened and a ceasefire was signed on 22 September 1965. Shastri was now the hero, and cinema audiences applauded when he appeared on the screen. Shastri had restored—at least partially—Indian pride in its own army after the China humiliation.

There followed an India–Pakistan truce meeting mediated by the Soviet PM, Alexei Kosygin in the Central Asian city of Tashkent.

General Ayub Khan, the Pakistani president, a Pathan soldier, standing over six feet in his boots met the diminutive five-foot-something civilian from India on equal terms. Indeed, Shastri could even think of himself as the victorious party, though he did not push matters. A treaty was signed on 10 January 1966, but that night in Tashkent, Shastri died suddenly. It was an event of great importance and has invited much speculation as to why he died. He had previously suffered two heart attacks. He had been through a tough time and the negotiations in Tashkent had been gruelling, lasting a week and many hours per day. There are rumours that his food may have been poisoned by someone who wished to push a Leftist agenda. It is much more likely that the explanation is a simple heart attack. Upon his death, the Syndicate elected Nehru's daughter, Indira Gandhi who was then minister for information and broadcasting in Shastri's Cabinet, to the post of prime ministership.

COUNTERFACTUAL BOX

Had Shastri Lived

Lal Bahadur Shastri had a very short innings—only twenty-month long. He has been almost wiped out from India's history which goes smoothly from Nehru to Gandhi. Dynastic rule seems inevitable. But had Shastri lived, and let us assume at least a full term after the 1967 elections, he would have served eight years before he went, say in 1972. What would that have done to India?

He may have charted the Congress's path away from a dynastic course and could have let it be a normal, democratically run party, which it had been until then and ceased to be soon after. Congress was always an umbrella organization where power was shared. Nehru's brief years, between the death of Patel and his defeat by Charan Singh on the issue of cooperative farming in 1959, was a short interlude. Shastri had kept the Congress party together by adopting a collegial style but with firm leadership on key questions, such as national security. Like the Liberal Democratic Party of Japan and the Institutional Revolutionary Party of Mexico, both of which have a long record of one-party dominance in a democratic set up, Congress could have stayed a broad-based party including rival groups and tendencies, sharing power. It would have given much better governance than what happened.

But Shastri's importance goes beyond that.

Shastri was a change agent. Few saw it because they were still dazzled by Nehru's style and personality. Yet, he changed the course of Indian polity in a number of vital ways. He tilted more towards the American side. He was more decisive in defending India's military interests. He was more rooted in Indian soil. Only he could have coined the slogan 'Jai jawan, jai kisan'. This simultaneous celebration of the soldier and the farmer is uniquely his legacy to India. He was the first to give these two sections their due prominence.

But, most significantly, he grasped the need to shift the emphasis in planning from heavy industry to agriculture and from grand plans to modest annual plans. Shastri's policy was disliked by the Left. He was accused of deviating from Nehruvian policies, and he defended himself in the Lok Sabha on 18 September 1964: 'To my mind, socialism in India must mean a better deal for the great mass of our people who are engaged in the various factories and the middle classes who have suffered much during the period of rising prices.'[3]

What Shastri was thinking about is what many East Asian and South-East Asian countries accomplished during the 1960s and 1970s. Taiwan, South Korea, Malaysia and Indonesia, which were all poorer and less industrialized than India as of 1960, surpassed India in living standards by following a policy of light industries and concentrating on agriculture and exporting. They managed in the 1960s, and even more during the 1970s, to emerge as Asian Tigers (along with the two island economies, Hong Kong and Singapore), while India continued at its elephantine pace until 1991. Had Shastri lived, India would not have lost twenty-five years of economic growth. India would not have as many poor as it did in 1991, or even today, and perhaps fewer large factories making loss-making industrial products.

In 1991, India resumed on the path Shastri would have taken in the late 1960s. By then, much lasting damage had been done.

The resumption of Nehru family in the top seat of power has made dynastic succession seem inevitable. It has even been argued, somewhat fallaciously, that dynastic politics is embedded in Indian culture. But it came about as an accident—and triggered by Shastri's sudden death. Had he lived, Shastri would have established a proper democratic succession. He has now been almost airbrushed out of India's modern history, which sets a seamless sequence of Nehru–Gandhi rule from 1947 to 1989, but for a small break of two years after the Emergency. Shastri is the unnecessary punctuation, a semi-colon, or perhaps just a hyphen. It was not until 1977 that someone other than a member of the Nehru family again became prime minister. Then the dynasty resumed in 1980 for another nine years with Rajiv Gandhi succeeding his mother, Indira Gandhi when she was assassinated in 1984. From 1989 to 2004 the dynasty was out of office. Today, the dynasty has revived—Sonia Gandhi, Rajiv Gandhi's widow is president of the Congress party and the power behind the throne; her son Rahul Gandhi, the fourth generation pretender to the throne, is waiting in the wings.

INDIRA GANDHI: A DUMB DOLL?

In denying Morarji Desai once more his legitimate claim to succeed Shastri as PM, the Syndicate thought they were choosing a novice, a *goongi gudia*—a dumb doll. Indira had been Congress president when she helped topple Kerala's communist government in the late 1950s. She had no mass base in the party, and her single claim to prime ministership was that she was Nehru's daughter and was called Gandhi. In a largely illiterate nation the two names were national brands, and few cared that she was not the Mahatma's daughter or that her husband was a Parsi as long as he was called Gandhi.

Indira Gandhi was to surprise everyone, including the Syndicate, by proving a decisive and strong and—some say—destructive political leader. If Nehru had laid solid foundations for Indian democracy, she tested them to their limits. She restructured not only the Congress party, but the political party system itself. She used ideological rhetoric and strategic alliances with the Left parties to usher in a populist culture in Indian democracy, and nearly took it to the authoritarian limit. She almost got away with it but, luckily for India, halted short of the ultimate step of suspending liberal democratic practices. Yet, she remains a popular prime minister, and in polls of India's best prime minister frequently surpasses her father. This is because she made executive power decisive and subordinated legislatures and even the judicial courts, using a doctrine of popular mandate. Had her prime ministerial tenure not been interrupted, India could easily have become a 'people's democracy'.

Her first few years were hesitant and uncertain. Upon taking up office, she had to confront some of the worst problems India had ever faced. The year she became prime minister was the second consecutive year of famine. India's balance of trade was in deficit, and a critique of Nehruvian planning priorities was mounting at home and abroad. India had tied its currency to the sterling and followed the devaluation of the pound in 1949. Now the pound sterling itself was under much pressure, and was to be devalued in 1967. India faced even greater pressures, and Indira Gandhi had to sanction a devaluation of the rupee in March 1966 of around 60 per cent relative to the dollar—from Rs 4.76 to Rs 7.50. The International Monetary Fund and the World Bank had orchestrated the move, though even they were surprised by the magnitude of the devaluation. There was a promise from them that India would receive a large aid package, the devaluation being a signal of India's readiness to adopt other market-driven policies.

There was a real chance that Shastri's modification of Nehru's priorities by shifting resources to agriculture and scaling down the size of plans, followed by Indira Gandhi's devaluation of the rupee, could have embarked India on policies which later proved so successful in other Asian economies. India's relations with the USA could also have improved.

But Indira was less sure of herself than Shastri. Facing criticism at home from Left politicians such as Krishna Menon, she soon began speaking against US involvement in Vietnam and siding with the USSR in its anti-US pronouncements. Lyndon Johnson, who had just received her and promised help, was furious. But he seriously misjudged India's nationalist pride. He thought he could take advantage of US food aid to India and the relative immaturity of Indira Gandhi. He wanted India to support the US war in Vietnam. Johnson kept India on a short leash, releasing food aid on a month-by-month basis against the advice of Chester Bowles, his ambassador to India. The idea was to make India bend to US foreign policy needs in South-East Asia.

Indira Gandhi refused, falling back on Nehru's non-alignment doctrine. She could not have granted Johnson's wishes even had she desired. Shastri could have just about managed that on the back of his Tashkent gains, but he was gone. The Congress was in a fragile position and in the elections of 1967, the first without Nehru to lead them, it did very badly. The Lok Sabha majority was small—only 55 per cent of the seats with 40 per cent of the votes. Congress got only 284 seats, down from 361 in 1962. The future fragmentation of party strength got a preview in 1967 with communists (42), socialists (36), Swatantra (44) and Jan Sangh (35) all gaining seats, and the category 'Regional and Other parties' (44) doing as well as the best of the opposition parties. In a number of states, Lohia's anti-Congressism worked—and non-Congress coalitions came to power. In Tamil Nadu the DMK came to power, and a Dravidian party has stayed in power since, in one way or another. Supporting the USA in such circumstances would have been suicidal.

Johnson is alleged to have forced the World Bank to renege on its promise to deliver an aid package as a reward for the devaluation. This was the decisive moment when Indira Gandhi swung to the Left. She had arrived with no ideological baggage. She was happy to inherit her father's Leftish mantle, and consult the Left coterie in New Delhi which used to worship her father. P.N. Haksar, who became her principal adviser, had a LSE education of the Harold Laski vintage, and carried the full Fabian baggage of the days when the Soviet Union was an ally of the British. He is often seen as her *eminence grise*. Now she took decisive steps to rid herself of her patrons in the Syndicate. In 1969, two years after the elections, Indira Gandhi, the scourge of the Communist Party in 1959, began her socialist life.

INDIRA GANDHI'S LEFT TURN

The Communist analysis of the Congress was that it was a bourgeois nationalist party and, hence, not to be trusted to bring about the much needed revolution. But the Congress had some radical elements, and the communists felt impelled to support them. Nehru was, of course, the principal such element. His high reputation with the Soviet Union, the presence of Krishna Menon by his side and his endorsement of planning were all plus factors. Yet Nehru was a democrat first, and socialist second. He was also restrained in his anti-business attitude. Thus, he only nationalized two private sector entities—the Imperial Bank and the life insurance industry. With Indira Gandhi's need for Left support, the climate was to turn much more anti-business.

The sudden death of President Zakir Hussain created a vacancy for the top spot. Indira Gandhi used the pretext of the presidential election to split the Congress party. She put forward her candidate, V.V. Giri, a veteran labour leader and already vice-president against the official Congress candidate, Sanjeeva Reddy. At the Bangalore meeting of the Congress, she also proposed the nationalization of banks and, since Morarji Desai was known to be against it, sacked him as her finance minister. This was a declaration of war as far as the Syndicate was concerned. But luckily for her and unfortunately for them, her candidate won the election, in which the central as well as all state legislature members voted. Indira Gandhi proved that in a national test, she was more popular than her rivals. There was no stopping her now.

She took over fourteen banks by an ordinance. I.G. Patel, who had been the government's chief economic adviser and had been moved, as a rare case, to the civil service cadre as special Secretary to the ministry of finance, had a ringside seat to these developments. Many years later, after he had served with distinction as the governor of the Reserve Bank of India and director of the London School of Economics, he wrote an account of his years as a policy maker. His account of the bank nationalization episode is fascinating:

> It was, I think, later in July 1969 that I was sent for once again. No one else was present. Without any fanfare, she asked me whether banking was under my charge. On my telling her it was, she simply said: 'For political reasons, it has been decided to nationalize the banks. You have to prepare within 24 hours the bill, a note for the Cabinet and a speech for me to make to the nation on the radio tomorrow evening. Can you do it and make sure there is no leak?' There was no pretence that this was not a political decision, and the message was clear that no argument from me was required.[4]

Luckily for Patel, he knew that a draft bill nationalizing banks was in the files of the Reserve Bank of India (RBI). He asked the RBI governor, L.K. Jha, a former adviser to Indira Gandhi, along with the officer who had the only copy of the draft bill on his file, to come to Delhi. They worked through the night and fourteen banks, which accounted for 85–90 per cent of total deposits, were nationalized. Patel writes that he added a sentence to Indira Gandhi's radio speech, 'This is not the first step in a new wave of nationalization. This, in fact, is the culmination of the process which began with the nationalization of Life Insurance and the Imperial Bank to occupy the commanding heights of finance.'[5] Though she did not alter anything in the speech Patel had written, it was he who was whistling in the wind. What had begun was an inexorable Leftward shift in policy.

Raj Thapar, who along with her husband, Romesh Thapar was quite close to Indira Gandhi, gives an insider's account of this episode in her memoirs:

> Haksar had prepared a scheme for taking over the banks—it then seemed to him, and to all of us, that this could be the beginning of the quiet revolution. Morarji had been resisting. He favoured what he called the 'social control' of banks and experience showed that his idea was more sensible in the circumstances. Indira was not really concerned with nationalisation or social control. Her passion was to remove Morarji Desai from Finance Ministership, not because he didn't handle the portfolio well but because his presence there was a constant reminder that she could be threatened, opposed, even thrown out. She needed a reason. Romesh had warned her time and time again that to be credible you had to fight on issues which concerned the people. And this was one such.[6]

The Supreme Court ruled the nationalization as contrary to fundamental rights, but Indira Gandhi renewed the ordinance and, later, had a bill passed because the judgement had recognized that 'The Legislature is the best judge of what is good for the community, by whose suffrage it comes into existence.'[7]

Yet the more profound, long-term effect was the break up of the Congress party. For eighty-four years, it had been a part of India's political life, a consensual gathering of differing views, which were united on the aim of India's independence and, after 1947, on India's democratic progress. In 1920, Mahatma Gandhi had turned the Congress from an umbrella organization of annual meetings to a proper party with mass membership. But even so, many other parties continued to belong to the Congress. After 1947, the Congress told other parties to leave and fought the elections on its own. Now twenty-two years on, there was a split. It began the process of fragmentation of India's political structures.

Perhaps, such a split was inevitable. Nehru had provided the unifying narrative of Indian nationhood by his presence, his vision and his untiring efforts to state and re-state the narrative of India's nationhood. His story had begun to fall apart by the end of his days. He had encountered opposition on the ideological front from Charan Singh from within the Congress and from the Swatantra Party from outside. He had lost face in the China debacle, and the savage way in which his detractors rounded on Krishna Menon gave a foretaste of how faction-ridden politics was going to be the future. There was also the fact that while the development model adopted by Nehru may have yielded shining factories to make steel and machines and given jobs to the educated upper-caste and upper-class youth, it had left the bulk of India's population out of the charmed circle of prosperity. Nehru was the first political leader to articulate the notion of 'trickle down', yet there was little employment creation for the unskilled workers in the informal sector. Nor was there any significant advance in primary or secondary education for the mass of the people, even though elite institutions, such as the Indian Institute of Technology, were created. Land reform had created a class of small and medium farmers—'bullock capitalists', but the landless labourers were increasing in number. Growth had been far too slow, and far too tied in with industrial and military needs to benefit the poorest. Subaltern anger was bound to increase, and crystallize itself in political parties.

Already by 1967, many opposition parties had formed coalitions to defeat the Congress. Many such coalitions proved unstable. These were regional parties or caste parties or even linguistic community parties which began to emerge, and their perspective on India's needs and problems was definably local. Such parties were either formed to represent a single interest, or the regional offices of national parties were captured by one caste group or another—the Jats in UP and Haryana, the Yadavs and Kurmis in Bihar, the Vokkaligas in Karnataka, the Vellalas in Tamil Nadu, the Kammas and Reddys in Andhra Pradesh, and so on. Worse yet was the rise of sub-nationalist parties which carved out local linguistic majorities as new nations and pursued exclusionary politics. The Shiv Sena, which was a proto-fascist organization in Bombay, for example advanced the rights of Marathi-speaking citizens of Bombay against other citizens who did not speak Marathi or had migrated from outside Maharashtra, a state set up only in 1960.

There were not many parties which could claim to be 'All India', as well as non-caste-based. Besides the Congress, these parties included the Jan Sangh which had a Hindu nationalist agenda and the Communist Party of India, now split in two—the Communist Party of India (CPI) and the Communist Party of India (Marxist) (CPI (M))—thanks to the China–Soviet Union dispute. The Swatantra Party was the only secular Rightist ideological party as it championed a liberal approach to economic policy. Along the way, the Praja Socialist Party had split and been partially absorbed in the Congress, and the rump had gone to the Lohiaite Socialist Party. Now, with the split in the Congress party where the breakaway factions distinguished themselves by adding various letters—for example the Congress (O) (the 'O' standing for organization, not old as some maintained), the Congress (R), the 'R' standing for reformed or, later, the Congress (I), the 'I' standing for Indira—the party itself became a source of further fragmentation.

Indira Gandhi claimed the legacy of the original Congress, more as an inheritance due to whose daughter she was than anything else. But she also caught the imagination of a younger India which was more impatient for change. Already in the late 1960s, a new, even more Leftist communist party—the Marxist-Leninist (CPI(ML)) had taken birth in West Bengal, where in the village of Naxalbari in the Darjeeling area, young communists began to organize the landless labourers to seize land from landlords by force. The Green Revolution had not yet touched West Bengal; indeed, the local radical parties were hostile to it. So the rural employment situation had not been transformed as in Punjab and Haryana. Land hunger was thus more acute. This Maoist peasant war strategy alarmed not just the Congress government at the Centre, but also the United Left Front government in West Bengal in which the CPI(M) was a partner. There was trouble not just in West Bengal but also in Andhra Pradesh, which had been the site of the old Telangana peasant rebellion in the late 1940s. The Naxalites, as the new communists came to be called, were dealt with utmost force, even as young college students from middle-class families gave up the prospects of stable, secure careers and joined the movement. For a while India seemed to be aflame.

Indira Gandhi sought an alliance with CPI, which was then still the larger of the Communist Party factions. She moved from bank nationalization to the abolition of the privy purses (a regular and substantial annual income provided by the government to erstwhile royalty), which had been part of the agreement with the princes when they gave up their kingdoms and joined the Indian Union. This was a confiscatory move and, as such, contrary to the Constitution. The purses had been exempt from income tax as part of the original agreement but, in the new radical mood, such feudal privileges seemed out of sync with Indira Gandhi's recent commitment to socialism. The government moved the twenty-fourth amendment bill in the Lok Sabha in May 1970. To be fair to Indira Gandhi, there had been a movement in the undivided Congress in 1963, when Kamaraj and Atulya Ghosh—two doughty members of the Syndicate—had broached the issue at AICC meetings. Nehru had been unhappy with these purses, but had failed to push the issue which had, after all, been settled quite openly and after consultation with the Constituent Assembly by Sardar Patel. Thus, it required a constitutional amendment to deprive the princes of their annual purses.

The amendment was in conflict with the fundamental right to private property guaranteed by the Constitution, as well as two or three Articles which dealt with the privy purses, which the amendment removed. The issue of the fundamental right to private property had already reached the Supreme Court earlier in the 1960s in a well publicized case known as Golak Nath, in which a family of landowners had challenged the Punjab government's decision to divest them of 'surplus land' according to a land reform Act. The court had then ruled that the decision was not justified. The government had wanted for some time to find a way of removing this obstacle to radical redistributive land reform policies. The Privy Purses Bill passed in Lok Sabha with two thirds majority, but failed in the Rajya Sabha. The government swiftly found a loophole which allowed the President to 'derecognize' the princes. Within twenty-four hours of the bill's defeat in the Rajya Sabha, the order was flown to President V.V. Giri, who promptly signed it. This cloak-and-dagger operation, typical of many of Indira Gandhi's acts, was challenged as unconstitutional by the princes and many MPs who had opposed the original bill.

The Supreme Court with its eleven judge-bench ruled the 'de-recognition order as unconstitutional' with a majority of nine to two, thirteen weeks after the Rajya Sabha decision. Nine days later, Mrs Gandhi asked the President to dissolve the Parliament, and decided to go to the people. In her broadcast to the nation announcing new elections, she said she wanted power to satisfy people's aspirations 'for a just social order', and while her move had been 'welcomed by large masses of people throughout the country ... reactionary forces have not hesitated to obstruct these urgent and vitally necessary measures'.[8]

INDIRA GANDHI: THE RADICAL POPULIST

Her instincts were sound. Indira Gandhi knew that her move to abolish the privy purses, however precipitate and procedurally clumsy, commanded a majority even in the old, undivided Congress and, by implication, in the country. Most of her opponents were appalled at her methods, not her purpose. But instead of proposing compromises, they challenged her. She was incensed and, henceforth, adopted a doctrine of the popular mandate, which said that a government popularly elected and backed by a parliamentary majority had the right to override all constraints on executive power. She tested the limits of the Constitution and, indeed, of India's democratic polity itself. This was a consequence of the uneasy combination of a Westminster model of Executive and legislature, but also of a US-style written Constitution. In British practice, Parliament can legislate as it pleases as long as both Houses pass a bill. The unwritten Constitution only implies that it can be easily amended. The founding fathers of the Indian Constitution had envisaged a Constitution as a 'cornerstone of the nation', but, at the same time, wanted to assert parliamentary sovereignty in order to allow Parliament to alter the face of India's social and economic life. The consensus of the 1950s had, however, already broken down as Indira Gandhi sought to speed up change.

She was opposed by a grand alliance of opposition parties including the Jan Sangh, Swatantra, Congress (O) and the Lohiaite socialists, as well as regional parties. Their slogan was '*Indira hatao*' (remove Indira) which she countered with '*Garibi hatao*' (remove poverty). Her shrewdness in choosing such a slogan shows how out of touch her old opponents were. The problem was, of course, that the Nehruvian model had done nothing to reduce poverty though it had built up an industrial structure of machine-making. Only improvements in agriculture had relieved the food constraint and created job opportunities in regions where the Green Revolution had been implemented. Yet, she chose to deepen the Nehruvian model; her popular appeal and, indeed, the climate of opinion not just in India but around the world—the anti-Vietnam war movement, the student revolutions in the USA and France, the Black Power movement and Prague Spring—was such that a Leftward move seemed the only one possible. The gains in terms of removing poverty were to prove less than expected. This only spurred her on to further populist radical measures.

She won 352 out of 518 seats, with the CPI(M) the next largest party with twenty-five seats. Indira Gandhi had become the undisputed leader of Congress and, indeed, India. She led a party which was her own creation, thanks to her bold moves in 1969 and her decision to move it to the Left. The Congress(R), as the party was called, became a personalized party, something Nehru would have never permitted. She now had the votes to abolish the privy purses. In December 1971, the constitutional amendment was passed in the Lok Sabha by a majority of 381 to six, and in Rajya Sabha by 167 to seven.

But between the time of her election victory and the passage of the bill, Indira Gandhi had accomplished something which gave her a permanent place in the hearts of Indians. Since its creation Pakistan had been an uneasy cohabitation of two regions far apart—West Pakistan consisting of (West) Punjab, Sind, Balochistan and NWFP, and East Pakistan, which was East Bengal before 1947. The latter was more populous and preferred to have Bengali, rather than Urdu, as their national language. But while India managed to solve its language differences, Pakistan could not. Since independence, it had been a democracy only for a brief period, and since the late 1950s had become a dictatorship. From early on the Muslim League, the party that had fought for Pakistan, had discovered that it had no roots in either West or East Pakistan. Jinnah died a year after Independence and his successor, Liaqat Ali Khan was assassinated soon after. There followed an uneasy coalition of civil servants and army generals, mostly from Punjab and NWFP, who ruled Pakistan. The East Pakistanis had a meagre presence in the civil service and practically none in the army. The Pathans and the Punjabis had scant respect for the Bengalis who had become their fellow citizens. In 1958 General Ayub Khan seized power and became the President of Pakistan, but his setback in the 1965 war led to his replacement by General Yahya Khan who also became President and, in effect, imposed military rule on Pakistan. It was only in 1970 that Pakistan had its first general elections based on universal adult franchise.

In that election Zulfiqar Ali Bhutto's Pakistan People's Party won eighty-eight out of 144 seats in West Pakistan, but Mujibur Rahman's Awami League Party won 165 out of 167 seats in East Pakistan. The West Pakistani contempt for their Bengali fellow Pakistanis was ill-concealed, and in order to prevent the writing of a federal Constitution with equal status for East and West Pakistan, Yahya Khan suspended the results, arrested Mujib and sent the army to occupy East Pakistan— which it did with horrendous brutality. In the resulting civil war that followed, the Mukti Bahini—the liberation army for Bangladesh, as the new entity wished to be named—fought the Pakistan Army. The flood of refugees entering India gave Indira Gandhi the excuse to send the Indian Army to the Bengal border. Her case was helped by Pakistan attacking parts of Kashmir and Punjab on 3 December 1971.

By this time in the sequence of events, China's support for Pakistan in this conflict was out in the open—as was the USA's. The Soviet Union was on India's side. Pakistan had, perhaps, hoped that broadening the war on the western front would bring in the UN, or that China would open a new front in the north. Neither event happened, and the Indian Army went into East Pakistan. By 6 December 1971, India had recognized the Republic of Bangladesh and despite US threats to deploy the Seventh Fleet, the Indian Army decisively defeated the Pakistan Army. On 16 December 1971, General Niazi of the Pakistan Army signed a document of surrender with Lt General J.S. Aurora of the Indian army's Eastern Command.

Indira Gandhi had achieved the impossible. She had dismembered India's main enemy, permanently reduced its territory and humiliated it militarily. The attack, though swift, was planned well in advance. It was launched in winter, well after the monsoon—as an attack was difficult to mount during the rains, given the country's marshy terrain. The added advantage of winter was that snow in the Himalayas made a

Chinese advance unlikely. The strategy proved that Indira Gandhi was better than either Nehru or Shastri when it came to deploying force. The campaign, short as it was, had to be conducted in the teeth of American opposition and in violation of the UN charter. In Pakistan the event was seen as the first defeat of Muslim armies by a Hindu army in a thousand years, which was obviously a myth. India did not see the victory in terms of a Hindu nation—the war was seen as extending a helping hand to distressed East Bengal. India did not occupy Bangladesh for any length of time and the new republic was set up soon after the surrender of General Niazi.

The liberation of Bangladesh did several things for Indira Gandhi and India. It removed any residual feelings of inferiority about Indian army's fighting powers. Indira Gandhi also laid to rest, the idea that being non-aligned meant India would not take up arms when it suited her national interest. It further distanced India from the US—at least while Richard Nixon was in power. India signed a treaty with the USSR which guaranteed defence cooperation. Nevertheless, India was not irrevocably 'lost' to the US as China had been for two decades after the Second World War. India always had one foot in the Western camp, as a result of its membership in the Commonwealth, its English usage and the preference of its intellectuals on both the Left and Right for Western universities. Yet, it took India and the USA many more years, in fact decades, to become friends.

The dismemberment of Pakistan, the much vaunted 'homeland' of South Asia's Muslims was noted by Muslims in India as well. Pakistan, far from being a haven for all Muslims, turned out to be a Punjabi monopoly with Sindhi support. For Indian Muslims, the lesson was clear—better the devil they knew than the one in the distance. This allowed Indira Gandhi to defuse the Kashmir issue, and she allowed Sheikh Abdullah to return to Kashmir. It was obvious that Pakistan could not come and liberate the Valley, even if it wished to do so, after its military defeat in East Bengal.

There was some speculation during 1971 when the Mukti Bahini was fighting, and even more after India's successful intervention, that a United Red Bengal might emerge from the crisis. West Bengal was going through its 'red' phase, which was to last beyond the end of the century. At that time, under attack from the Naxalites, the CPI/CPI(M) leaders could not hide their enthusiasm for such a project. But the Bangladesh revolution was a nationalist, not a socialist one. In 1905, when Bengal was first partitioned, the Muslims of East Bengal had been short-changed by the Indian nationalist movement, which was largely Hindu bhadralok led. Forty years later, they seemed to have drawn another short straw. Now at last, having shed their blood once again, the East

Bengalis could not be tempted to lose their nationhood. Bengal, like Punjab, remained split, and its two parts never did come together, nor did they prosper separately. Bangladesh was to be born destitute, despite the myth that its riches were being taken away by the West Pakistanis. It remained dependent on foreign aid for a long time before it emerged from extreme poverty. Bangladesh was yet another illustration of the fallacy of the theory that colonized countries were poor because of a transfer of surplus from them. When the transfer stayed at home, the poverty was still obvious, since the root cause of poverty was the smallness of the surplus and not its transfer abroad.

The second, more important, effect of the Bangladesh war was that Indira Gandhi's delusions of omnipotence increased. She was now very popular and, having arrived at the top after a bruising battle with her opponents both within and outside India, she began to establish a combative style of leadership. It was, of course, highly personalized. There was never a coterie around Nehru which had extra-constitutional powers or even much influence. India Gandhi concentrated all power within the Congress party in her hands, and did the same with the Cabinet. This meant that both the party and the Cabinet ceased to function democratically. The members of her Cabinet were, by and large, not colleagues any longer, but sycophants and hangers-on. When Dev Kant Baruah, a puppet president of the Congress said, 'Indira is India and India is Indira', the bankruptcy of the Congress ideology was visible to all. The Congress did not have regular inner party elections any more. It became India Gandhi's plaything. If Nehru was a viceroy, though a scrupulously democratic one, his daughter was a Mughal empress. Her younger son, Sanjay, took full advantage of her mother's position, and extracted a large tract of land for his pet private project of a people's car. Various intellectuals of a Left disposition became members of her kitchen Cabinet. Romesh and Raj Thapar, Left intellectuals and innovative as writers and publishers (I have quoted from Raj Thapar's memoirs before), were one such couple. Dom Moraes, a poet and journalist was another. Mohan Kumarmangalam, who was a prominent member of the Communist Party, was also very influential, along with P.N. Haksar. Corruption now became second nature to Congress leaders. It was 'deeply entrenched and institutionalised', P.N. Haksar told her and, indeed, it became necessary to bolster party coffers.[9]

India, far from being Indira, was still a largely poor country. The first twenty-five years of Independence had built factories for steel and machinery, it had even relieved the acute shortage of food grains, but it had not tackled the poverty of the country. National income did double over nineteen years between 1950 and 1969, but per capita income had grown just about 25 per cent. In 1971 two economists, Dandekar and Rath, from the Gokhale Institute of Economics and Politics in Pune, published the first estimate of the extent of poverty in India—a task which the Planning Commission should have undertaken right from the start—and measured its performance against the yardstick of poverty reduction. What it showed was that, rhetoric notwithstanding, development had been about building up the military–industrial complex of India as an insurance against foreign attacks or interference, and had not addressed removal of poverty.

The measurement of poverty is more an art than a science. But the basic idea is that, there is a definable minimum level of expenditure required to provide the people with a tolerable life. Those people whose expenditure is below that level are counted as poor, or as is now fashionable 'below the poverty line' (BPL). The minimum level which the Pune authors used as a marker was quite modest—Rs 324 per annum or Rs 27 per month for rural population and Rs 489 per annum or Rs 41 per month for urban dwellers. By this marker, they concluded that 40 per cent of the rural and 50 per cent of the urban population were poor, that is had a standard of living below the minimum. This was, if anything, an underestimate of the true extent of poverty. If we take the standard the national planning committee had set itself, Rs 15 or 20 per month at 1938 prices and adjust it for inflation between 1938 and 1971, the poverty line would be much higher and many more people would have been judged to be below the poverty line, nearer 60–70 per cent. Indira Gandhi had radical ambitions, but these took the form of attacking the large incomes of the princes and nationalizing the private sector—fashionable policy actions in those days, but having little impact on reduction of poverty.

HUBRIS

The persistence of poverty and, indeed, underdevelopment gave rise to the belief in the government that the problem was not in their policies, but obstacles placed by the Constitution, whose guardian was the Judiciary. The doctrine of mandate told Indira Gandhi that she had permission from the people to change the Constitution and challenge the Judiciary. Since she had been elected by a minority of voters, around 40 per cent in a turnout of 70 per cent her mandate was really from about 30 per cent of the electorate. Yet, this was never said, and she proceeded to interfere with the accepted traditions of selecting Chief Justice of the Supreme Court, by elevating one judge over the head of several senior ones. She needed poodles in important places to do her bidding.

It was the Judiciary which was to prove her nemesis. By 1973, the weak performance of the Indian economy in the previous few years and the quadrupling of oil prices brought a big wave of inflation. Popular agitation began against the price rises and rising unemployment, which was the result of the weakening of growth. In Ahmedabad a student-led movement soon attracted much wider support. The Nav Nirman (New Dispensation) movement was a popular radical development which went against Indira Gandhi's image. Jayaprakash Narayan (known universally as JP), the man many had hoped would succeed Nehru, had retired from active politics, but continued to comment on the state of the country. He had been increasingly unhappy about Indira Gandhi's highly autocratic style and had objected to her interference in Supreme Court promotions. The Gujarat movement spread to Bihar, where it was led by the student wing of the Jan Sangh. The Jan Sangh had a medium-sized presence in the Lok Sabha. Its twenty-two seats made it the third highest after Congress and CPI(M). Yet, it was dismissed with contempt by the Congress and Left for its Hindu nationalist views. Now, it was to cash in on this popular upsurge. It had learnt that Left-wing tactics of mass agitation could be deployed by any party. In Gujarat and Bihar the students led a movement from below, which did not buy into the Leftist rhetoric of Indira Gandhi. Now JP came out of retirement to lead the Bihar movement on the condition that it should be non-violent. He was fighting 'corruption and misgovernment and blackmarketing, profiteering and hoarding'. By March 1974, India was seething with mass movements against Congress governments in the provinces. And the movements were collectively called the JP movement.

Indira Gandhi did not immediately appreciate the depth of the resentment. She played another master stroke in May 1974 by staging a nuclear explosion, announcing to the world India's emergence as a nuclear power. The military–industrial complex thus remained the top priority of the Nehru–Gandhi vision of India's development. Nehru had laid the foundations of India's nuclear research capabilities by setting up the Atomic Energy Commission under the leadership of Homi Bhabha, who proved to be as good a manager as he was a scientist. The facilities were ostensibly peaceful and India had received help from Canada, among others, to set up reactors. It was always a secret agenda in Indian nationalist vision that, if necessary, India could develop a bomb. Indira realized this dream. But the real economy was in trouble. There was a national strike by railway workers. Since the railways were in public ownership, this cast the Indian government in the unwelcome role of an exploitative boss. The strike was effective and the Army was called out to suppress it—which it did, brutally. Indira Gandhi also looked on as JP was attacked by the police and had to be moved to a hospital. She had used the instruments inherited from the British to great effect.

The movement did not abate and JP led a march on Delhi on 6 March 1975. The slogan, though not actually used, could have been '*Indira hatao*'. What shook Indira Gandhi up, however, was a ruling by the Allahabad High Court in a case filed by Raj Narain, who had stood unsuccessfully against her in the 1971 elections. Narain alleged that Indira Gandhi had used the state machinery illegally during her re-lection campaign. The judgement, delivered on 12 June 1975, indicted her on two of the fourteen charges. One was that she had allowed the UP government to make the platforms from which she addressed crowds and second, a government employee helped her during her campaign. Her election was declared null and void. These charges were, at one level, quite trivial. As the *Times* of London said, 'It was like dismissing the Prime Minister for a traffic offence.'[10] Still, it was the magnificence of the law and its ability to subject even a prime minister to its authority, which was impressive.

The Delhi establishment least expected such a judgement. To quote Raj Thapar again:

> On the face of it, there was nothing particularly incriminating. Everyone did the same, every single politician violated or rather, flouted all the election laws quite openly and government candidates had a distinct advantage ... the government machinery just swung into operation at a moment's notice ... She had been accused of using Yashpal Kapur for electioneering when he held a government post. She tried hard to persuade Haksar to put in a backdated letter in the file dismissing Yashpal which Haksar naturally refused. She herself had to face the court and ended by making contradictory statements—but despite all of that, no one for a second thought that she could possibly lose the case. Familiar with the kind of corrupt power she was coming to wield, this made no sense at all.[11]

This was the final confrontation. The head of the Executive, who had abrogated to herself overweening powers, claiming a popular mandate thanks to a large majority in the legislature to override the Judiciary and rewrite the Constitution, and a Judiciary which stuck to the letter of the law. Of course, all around India there was evidence of the fragility of the mandate Indira Gandhi was claiming. In Gujarat, where the initial agitation in 1973 had led to the dismissal of the Congress government and the imposition of President's rule, fresh elections had been allowed in 1975 and a coalition of many parties under the name 'Janata' led by Morarji Desai, Indira Gandhi's *bete noire*, was in the lead, even as the Allahabad High Court passed the judgement on Indira Gandhi. The Supreme Court, while opening the hearing, ruled that the PM could not vote in the Lok Sabha pending its decision.

Indira Gandhi reacted to this decision, mild as it was, with a quite disproportionate severity. Her father would have submitted to such a decision and stood down from office until the final verdict. It was most likely that the Supreme Court would consider the High Court judgement too harsh, given the minor nature of the charges, which were upheld. But that was not Indira Gandhi's way. She did not feel as secure in her position as her father would have done. She now felt extremely threatened. JP had already planned a huge demonstration on 25 June and Morarji Desai told the Italian journalist, Oriana Fallaci, 'We intend to overthrow her, to force her to resign. For good. The lady won't survive this movement of ours.'[12] She had always been a lonely person, having grown up in a large house with a mother who was deeply unhappy and a father who was more often in jail, or on a political campaign, than at home. Now, in her mid-fifties, she had lost her husband from whom she had anyway been distanced since she always gave her father priority over him. Once her father was gone, she had her sycophants, but she knew enough to sense that they would desert her the moment she lost power.

She was losing some of her friends. Raj Thapar quotes from her diary of 18 August 1974:

> Have been trying to unravel the political illogic that seems to prevail—why every opposition party keeps splitting like the aged hairs on a balding head when the need of the hour is just the reverse—and I have come to a sad, sad conclusion. We were wrong. We were wrong in supporting Mrs G. as the catalyst—she was not capable of it ... Mrs G only had the will for what now seems to be a passion for personal power ... A little building of her own power, a few slogans which might have been initiated by a genuine desire for reform and change but were so parroty that they finally became mere vote gathering chants, a little deterioration in the economic situation, a little shift here and there , a gradual sinking into the bog, a few cries for help to the countries that can help, but never clear directions, clear goals, clear assessment.[13]

If she could not vote in Lok Sabha and was replaced even temporarily, pending the Supreme Court decision, it was not clear whether she would ever come back. Indira Gandhi had the fragility of a Louis Bonaparte, popular for now, but uncertain of the permanence of her hold on the seat of power. She fell back on her own family. Her two adult sons, Sanjay and Rajiv, lived with her in the prime ministerial house along with their wives: Sanjay's wife, Maneka, and Rajiv's wife, Sonia—an Italian whom Rajiv had met while doing an apprenticeship in Cambridge. Indira Gandhi turned to her younger son, Sanjay. His advice was unequivocal: she had to defy the courts.

Romesh Thapar who had been close to Indira Gandhi, once tried to advise her that 'if she stepped down, then appealed to the Supreme Court, held elections, she would romp home after establishing democratic norm'. But she would not see him and did not follow his advice even when conveyed via a deputy. 'Sanjay had set up a command post at the house ... All orders were being issued from there. Indira was no longer in control.'[14]

On 25 June 1975 Indira Gandhi declared a state of Emergency which President Fakhruddin Ali Ahmad was happy to sign into law. The electricity supply to the offices of all Delhi newspapers was cut off, major Opposition leaders, JP and Morarji Desai among them, were among the 900 arrested and fundamental rights were suspended. It was almost like Quit India and the British Empire. Indira Gandhi was convinced, as dictators often are, that if she were to quit there would be no one else to lead India and restore order amid the unrest. The fact that she was the prime cause of the unrest did not occur to her. Having hollowed out the Congress party, there was no one in her Cabinet to challenge her. 'These, then, were the men who ruled India and her 570 million people, stricken and paralysed with fear when two sentences from a Jagjivan Ram or a Chavan could have transformed the situation. She must have expected those sentences, that frightened child in her, but when they never came she knew that Sanjay was right when he told her that "if one kicked them hard, they wouldn't even squeak".'[15]

The Emergency was the first fundamental crisis in Indian democracy. A democracy of more than twenty-five years' standing, with a history of five well-conducted general elections, found itself with a government with a decisive majority unable to rule within the accepted constitutional norms. The crisis was, of course, due to the failure of economic policy to change the lives of the overwhelming majority for the better. In fighting for independence, the Congress had played on the contrast between an exploitative foreign rule, which had de-industrialized and impoverished India, and the promise that once India was independent, the Congress could be trusted to deliver a better life for all. This was Gandhi's vision of uplifting the least advantaged person; this was Nehru's rhetoric of a socialist pattern for society. Twenty-five years on, the Indian ruling classes had failed spectacularly to deliver on their promise.

The most charitable excuse one can make for the appalling failure of the Congress to deliver economic growth would be to admit that national security was always the top priority. The vision of heavy industrial development borrowed from the Soviet Union, and the employment opportunities it generated for the elite, kept the upper castes/classes well-fed and proud of their nation. The less fortunate in the rural areas and in the fast-growing cities had to do with crumbs as they fell from the top table. But growth at 4.5 per cent during Nehru's tenure, as capital intensive as it was, allowed little, if anything, to trickle down. After Nehru's death and particularly after Indira's Left-wing swing, growth collapsed. So the average for 1950–69 was under 4 per cent, and by the end of the 1970s the 1950–80 average growth rate fell to 3.5 per cent per annum. Indira Gandhi's socialism was much more costly than her father's, and at a GDP growth rate roughly 1.5 per cent less per annum over her first eight years in power, the slowdown meant a compound loss of income of 15 per cent or so for the entire country, compared to what it could have been even with the moderate growth rate that Nehru had delivered. Of course, slower growth meant an even worse life for the less well off—the majority of the Indian population, not the elite.

Thus, the public reaction to Indira Gandhi's policies was not fomented from abroad, as her paranoia led her to allege repeatedly. It was entirely home-made. The reaction of the citizenry was unerring. The backward castes had benefited somewhat from the Green Revolution as they were the cultivators in North India. This was Charan Singh's constituency. But the growing ranks of landless workers, often scheduled castes and tribes, were left out. There was little violent class conflict outside the Naxal regions. In the cities, the 10 per cent of workers employed in organized industries, private and public, were unionized and their ranks supported the Left parties in their class war rhetoric. But the bulk of the workers—around 90 per cent—were in the informal sectors.

After five general elections, the Indian masses had learnt that they could not rely on parties which were organized along Western ideologies. They resorted to their caste associations. The elite factions had already done this. The American author, Selig Harrison had shown in his 1960 book, *India: The Most Dangerous Decades* how in many states the political divisions were along caste factions. Now, the non-elite sections began to organize aggressively. The scheduled castes redefined themselves not as untouchables or Harijans, but as Dalits. The backward castes— the Jats in Punjab and Haryana, the Yadavs in UP and Bihar, the Patidars in Gujarat, the Marathas in Maharashtra—all became politically organized to lobby for their share in what was a very slowly expanding cake. Good incomes and careers came from government jobs. Political patronage was the key whereby caste leaders could extend benefits to their communities, while also consolidating their own positions. The private sector was not a growth area; the public sector was. Political office also allowed many opportunities to exploit the power to grant permits and licences and allocate quotas to enrich one's coffers. The caste leader had to finance his own party and this required money. His private wealth and his party's were the same. If Indira Gandhi could run the Congress as her own family fiefdom, so went the argument, then others could as well.

The ferment was not restricted to backward and scheduled castes.

Through the 1970s, there began a number of local struggles by tribals against the state encroachments on their common property in forest lands; small farmers and tenants also rebelled against land-grabbing by bigger farmers with political clout. Each struggle was small and local, and the linkages between them were not sufficiently articulated to build a national movement. Lokayan, as the wider movement came to be known, was a potent radical force. North and South India were different in this regard. In North India the onset of Congress rule had strengthened the Brahmins and associated upper castes, and they had kept the rural hinterland illiterate as a matter of policy. In Congress strongholds such as UP and Bihar, the economic devastation as a result of Brahmin domination has left scars which remain to this day. Once the lower orders got organized they began to shove the Brahmin elite aside, and with that Congress began to lose UP. Caste oppression did not abate as far as the backward castes and the Dalits were concerned. Lalu Prasad Yadav, who rose to prominence as a student leader in the 1970s and later became Bihar's chief minister, recalls how he was beaten up by the local thakurs for the 'audacity' of wearing a clean ironed shirt in public. In 1977, when Ambedkar's birth anniversary was celebrated in Agra by taking out an elephant procession with his pictures at the top, the upper castes rioted and broke up the procession. Dalit cottages were burned and after some days the army had to be called to restore order. Bihar became a byword for backwardness rather than the land that produced great leaders such as Rajendra Prasad and JP. The feudal masters formed a private army, Ranvir Sena, in Bihar to intimidate the lower castes and Dalits who were their tenants or landless labourers. The harrowing account of the violence and rape suffered by women in these states— Bihar, Madhya Pradesh, Rajasthan, Uttar Pradesh (which came to be known later by their first few letters joined together as an acronym BIMARU, meaning 'sick' in Hindi) was dramatically depicted in the film *Bandit Queen* based on the life of Phoolan Devi. The Congress gave its Brahmin leadership in these areas a free hand to do as they liked. In areas such as Rajasthan, the Congress had absorbed the old feudal classes, who donned khadi dress and continued in their privileged positions. At the Centre, the Congress mouthed radical slogans and preached socialism, but at the grassroots it condoned and consolidated the old order. The privy purses issue was a smoke screen.

In the South, the long-established anti-Brahmin movement did not allow such oppression. The DMK and its offshoot, the AIADMK, had a bilateral monopoly of power between them in Tamil Nadu and threw the Congress out. In Kerala the Communist Party retained its dominance, and even the Congress had to be a progressive formation there. In Andhra Pradesh, local Telugu nationalism was about to displace the

Congress, but this was more a case of caste factional politics rather than a progressive movement. Thus, instead of the old Kamma–Reddy factionalism within the Congress party, there emerged a new movement, Telugu Desam, which was spearheaded by N.T. Rama Rao, a popular film star. Karanataka showed the possibility of a reformist movement even within the Congress with Devraj Urs, who became chief minister.

The Congress had recruited an elite across each region, much as the British had done, to keep itself in power. It had also sheltered the scheduled castes and Muslims as homogenous vote banks. So at least until 1971, it could poll around 40 per cent of the popular vote, and with a divided opposition, romp home with a much larger share of seats than votes. This perpetuated its power and it held on to its collaborators by extending the fruits of patronage. The Congress looked after its own.

What the Congress had also done, however, was to strengthen the coercive powers of the state. The restrictive laws passed by the British, the Defence of the Realm Act, for instance, came back under other names—Preventive Detention Act, Maintanance of Internal Security Act (MISA) for example. After 1962 an uneasy suspension of the Right to Free Speech was introduced to prohibit anti-national speeches and writings. Speeches like Annadurai's speech in Lok Sabha in 1962 demanding secession by the South were no longer to be permitted. In 1971 during the Bangladesh war, the Emergency provision, Article 352 had been used since there was an external threat. That restriction had not been lifted by the time Indira Gandhi called the Emergency. Haksar, who had been abroad before the Emergency was declared, came back and when told by Romesh Thapar that an Emergency had been declared said, 'There can't be another Emergency. There is already one.'[16] Even as a high official little did he know of the extent of New Delhi's powers. The Government of India could always revert to imperial style of rule even after Independence. This time around the clause 'armed rebellion' was invoked from the same Article. But, while the British governor general in Delhi had a British Parliament as a distant but real check on arbitrariness, an elected Indian prime minister with a supine majority in Parliament had no such check to prevent her from assuming dictatorial powers. There was no doubt that for the first time since Independence, India faced serious unrest. This was not a problem of one of the many sub-nations of India—Kashmir or Nagaland or the reluctant South of India unwilling to accept Hindi as a national language. This was a crisis across India, a protest movement, whose roots lay in the economic failure of the Congress rule.

The Emergency lasted till February 1977. The power of Sanjay Gandhi grew as he became the de facto chief executive, while his mother was the presiding deity. She convinced herself that her motives were of the purest, and even old friends of her father such as the British Labour Party MP Michael Foot, an old-fashioned champion of liberty and socialism, were beguiled into accepting her story. The Soviet Union was, of course, happy to find a new convert to 'people's democracy'. The CPI faithfully supported Indira Gandhi.

What the Emergency did was to make Right-wing parties the champions of the people for the first time in India's political history. Until the Emergency, the Congress had the monopoly of virtue as far as being a friend of the people was concerned. Given its increasingly Leftist rhetoric, the communist parties, despite their limited popular appeal, could join the Congress bandwagon. The Right-wing formations were derided for being ideologically anti-modern and religious/communal (the Jan Sangh, for example) or for catering to the vested interests of the minority rich (for instance the Swatantra Party). The rump of the defeated old Congress was also tarred with the anti-people brush. Now, however, it was these Right-wing formations which bore the brunt of the government's arbitrary powers and its violence. The old Congressmen whom Indira had ousted, the Jan Sangh and the Swatantra were upholding the Constitution, while Indira Gandhi and her Left coterie were subverting it. Unintentionally, Indira Gandhi made Right-wing parties, especially the Jan Sangh which later became the BJP, a permanent and respectable feature of India's political life.

This was because the experience of fighting foreign rule was vivid in popular memory, and there was no perceived dishonour in going to jail while resisting arbitrary laws. Gandhi's followers were Right-wing in one sense, but they were dedicated champions of fundamental rights and justice. Thus, the attacks on freedom of the press were met with enough resistance so as to make it clear that the newspapers, which were still available, were being published under censorship. Some veteran publishers, such as Ramnath Goenka who published the *Indian Express*, defied the government by refusing to submit to censorship, often leaving pages blank to indicate the hand of the censors. The *Hindustan Times* was the only Delhi newspaper to come out on the day after Emergency, though its few sheets were confiscated. Later, it became the favoured mouthpiece. Sanjay had I.K. Gujral, the minister for Information and Broadcasting removed days after Emergency was declared as he was insufficiently repressive. The *Times of India* was loyal and Khushwant Singh, the renowned author and editor of the *Illustrated Weekly of India*, became an enthusiastic supporter of the Emergency.

People opposed to the Emergency devised various small ways of subverting and registering disapproval. The government tried to censor the *Seminar*, the monthly publication edited by the Thapars, but they ignored the threat and survived. The armed forces deliberately honoured

Romesh Thapar by asking him to speak at National Defence College, knowing that he was against Indira Gandhi's policies. Most Indians found that, when push came to shove, they had a real desire for liberty, and were willing to fight for it. The simple idea that the poor preferred bread and circuses to freedom was exploded in India.

In the event, the Emergency provided neither bread nor circuses. The twenty-point programme recited the usual mantras for fundamental change. But if Indira Gandhi was going to deliver change, she had ample opportunity to do so with a willing majority in Parliament and Congress governments in power across India. Parliament willingly passed constitutional amendments to bar courts from questioning the prime minister's election and even extending its own life. This is a freedom that even the House of Commons does not have under the unwritten British Constitution. The House of Lords, with lifetime tenure for its unelected members, is the jealous guard against the popular chamber extending its own life. India, which had been a shining exception to Third World penchant for dictatorship, had lost this precious asset.

Even so, the Emergency did not lack admirers then and later. Dom Moraes, who wrote an affectionate biography of Indira Gandhi, gives what is a most typical defence of an authoritarian rule:

> Three beneficial results came from the imposition of emergency. The first was that the Indian population as a whole became very aware that it inhabited a governed country, a fact it had recently needed to know. The second was that it became aware that the government of the country was by and large for the people, for under MISA a large number of smugglers and tax defalcators were imprisoned, and a rigorous control of commodity prices enforced so that the cost of living went down. Third property and life became much safer, for the penalties for crime increased and murder, robbery, theft and rape which had become very common in the country while the police were dealing with political agitation against a background of high prices, low wages, and unemployment, decreased in incidence.[17]

The real question is why Indira Gandhi could not do any of this when she had a more than two-thirds majority in Lok Sabha and all the repressive powers at her disposal. One may also ask whether the people of India, who were so enlightened about their governance thanks to the Emergency, preferred anarchy and disorder when they voted for the Janata Party and threw Indira Gandhi out. It could be that their daily experience was different from what Moraes imagined it to be.

Sanjay Gandhi abrogated immense power to himself, and in one or two cases inflicted immense suffering on the people—for instance he initiated programmes of forced sterilization which targeted Muslim men and tribals and, indeed, the poor in towns and villages ostensibly for purposes of population control. It is estimated that in the first five months of the Emergency, 3.7 million and, by its end, as many as twenty-three million men were forcibly sterilized. There was also an attempt at slum clearance of Muslim hutments at Turkman Gate in Delhi which was more a communalist move than urban renewal. An estimated 150,000 shacks of the poor people were bulldozed and many died, though the numbers vary from six to 150 depending on the source.[18] Sanjay Gandhi's behaviour, which defied all norms of constitutionality and even decency, showed the real dangers that a populist demagogue can lead a country into. It was not just that he amassed a lot of wealth via his car factory, but that he built his own version of gangster rule which, because of his mother's position, was beyond criticism or justice.

NEMESIS

What persuaded Indira Gandhi to dissolve Parliament and call new elections in January 1977 remains a mystery. She had sought a legal extension of the election date when it was due in February 1976. She could not face another extension, though in November 1976 she had won a full twelve-month extension. She could have won the first time around in February 1976 since she would have kept to the democratic timetable and thus resolved the Emergency. Sanjay is known to have been dead against his mother's desire to re-legitimize her rule. He wanted to perpetuate her rule forever as did B.K. Nehru, India's then high commissioner in London. Sanjay had clearly not been consulted on calling the elections by his mother, or if he had been, she did not follow his advice. But Indira Gandhi lacked cynicism; she quite possibly genuinely believed that she was doing what she did in the national interest. She was of the generation which read and was affected by foreign newspapers, especially the British press in which her father's old friends had been raising their voices against her descent into dictatorship. Her friend, Dorothy Norman had initiated a letter against the Emergency signed by many American intellectuals and writers, among them Linus Pauling, John Updike and Noam Chomsky. It is possible that the steady drip of this criticism finally got to her. She believed her sycophants and her own propaganda. She was confident of winning the elections. A charitable—and not implausible view—is that the democratic instinct was too deeply embedded in her, and that she always saw the Emergency as a temporary measure.

In the event, she faced a united Opposition, which came together in a hastily built-up coalition of several parties—remnants of the old Congress led by Morarji Desai, the Jan Sangh, the Swatantra Party, the Lohia-inspired Socialist Party and Charan Singh, the old nemesis of Nehru on the land ownership issue, who now had his own caste-based party—the Bharatiya Lok Dal. Overseeing all this activity was JP himself. This was his finest hour. He had flirted with, but shied away from, real commitment to political power. He had, in one sense, wasted his abilities and short-changed the many who had joined his socialist banner in the 1930s and later. Instead, he had been seduced by Gandhian ideas of retreat from politics, and thus he had been reduced to being an occasional, if uncomfortable, irritant to his friends in active politics to whom he sent periodic missives of disapproval.

But now his charisma was put to use to get together a coalition which defeated the Congress in the general elections. Indira Gandhi lost her Rae Bareily seat to Raj Narain, her old rival, and was out of Parliament. The Congress lost 200 seats and was left with only 153, while the Janata Party won 292. It proceeded to take office. For the first time since 1947, the Congress was not in power in Delhi. Indira Gandhi had managed to lose her bequest by her arrogance. There was an air of national liberation when her defeat was announced. From a triumphant victory in 1971, bolstered by victory of the Indian Army in East Pakistan and the exploding of a nuclear device, she was now down and out. The Emergency had given her, at most, one extra year in power as elections were due in 1976. It was a costly mistake.

COUNTERFACTUAL BOX

Had the Emergency Not Been Declared

Indira Gandhi had no need to declare the Emergency. She had a majority in the Lok Sabha and most Congress candidates were of her choosing. There already was an Emergency in existence to protect India against external aggression. She could have stepped down. Among her friends, Romesh and Raj Thapar had warned her that her lawyer, Rajani Patel was incompetent and corrupt, and that she could lose the case because he was not a constitutional lawyer. But even so, no Supreme Court could have removed her from office. The charges which had been sustained were minor; the gap between the civil servant Yashpal's resignation and his helping Indira Gandhi's campaign was only six days. At the worst she may have had to fight a by-election within six months and she would have romped home.

Let us assume the worst. Suppose she had to demit and someone else, say Jagjivan Ram or Chavan had become PM. This was hardly a disaster. Both had long experience of Cabinet government and both were unifiers. They may have been willing to hand power back to her when she returned to the Lok Sabha. If not, she could have then split the party again as she did in 1978 and the bulk of Congress(R) would have gone with her as it did after 1978.

Indeed, since the adverse judgment had been given in June 1975 and Supreme Court would have delivered its judgement a month or so later, she could have dissolved Parliament pro tem and then called an election had the judgment gone against her. This would have given her almost five years since her last election in 1971.

Any of these alternatives would have preserved India's democracy much better. The rise of the BJP as it became could have been prevented, or at least, delayed. The fragmentation of Indian party system which followed the Janata experience of 1977–79 could also have been prevented or, again, at least delayed.

Almost any alternative to what she actually did would have harmed India much less.

TOO MANY CHIEFS

Fortunately for Indira Gandhi, her opponents proved miserably incompetent. They did reverse the constitutional violations she had promulgated but, beyond that, there was little to cheer the voters. There was ideological confusion among the various parties and they had not agreed on a common programme prior to the elections, which might have given them a basis on which to reconcile their often conflicting worldviews. The Janata Party was in office for two years, but not in power. Morarji Desai, widely regarded as an unbending, conceited moralist, finally became prime minister after two previous attempts. The Dalit leader, Jagjivan Ram had jumped ship from Indira's Cabinet months before the elections and formed yet another Congress faction which he joined to the Janata Party. He became deputy prime minister. Charan Singh, because of his mass following in the North, had successfully insisted on being given the rank of deputy prime minister as well. The Cabinet included George Fernandes, a Lohiaite socialist with solid roots in Bombay as a trade union leader. The Janata Party turned out to be a mixture of Gandhians, Nehruvians, Lohiaites and just hangers-on.

The Janata government went through two prime ministers—Morarji Desai and Charan Singh—and, by the end of 1979, it had unravelled. It had made foolish attempts to try Indira Gandhi, which she cleverly frustrated. Congress had split once more in 1978, with Indira Gandhi inaugurating Congress(I) and her rivals starting Congress(S), S for Swaran Singh who had been her cabinet minister. She came back into Lok Sabha in November 1978 from a seat in Karnataka. The South had not rejected the Congress in the same way as North India had done. Here again, the social distance between North and South becomes clear. The South, even in states where a Congress government was in power, was never as badly behaved as in UP, Bihar and Rajasthan. These regional differences had persisted and become sharper after Independence, as the growth rate, slow as it was, threw up opportunities for the old elites to recruit new followers and advance regional causes. The Planning Commission had committed itself to eliminating regional inequalities. This allowed it to locate industries far away from the most cost-efficient locations and led to even more resource-wasting policies, such as the uniform pricing of coal without regard for transport costs from mine to final use. But this had the consequence of strengthening regional power elites. Many new industrial projects were located in the South—lignite in Tamil Nadu, aircraft production in Karnataka which allowed small and medium firms to raise supply components along with a new entrepreneurial class.

The one contribution of the Janata government, apart from showing that the Congress could be defeated, was to champion the rights of the Dalits and landless workers. This intensified caste wars in UP and Bihar. Attacks on untouchables increased sharply during the tenure of the Janata government. The oppressive peace of Congress rule was broken, and the more deprived sections began to fight their masters The Janata government decided to examine the pattern of social injustice and appointed a commission under the chairmanship of B.P. Mandal. The commission's remit was to inquire into the nature of social discrimination in India and recommend the policies required to overcome it. The Mandal Commission Report was delivered after the end of the Janata's term in power and it was not to be implemented until the Congress had been defeated once again. But that was still some time in the future.

The Janata experience in power did, however, have one significant legacy: this was the survival and growth of the Jan Sangh. The party had joined the Janata coalition and its leader, Atal Bihari Vajpayee had won praise for his excellent conduct of foreign policy as foreign minister, especially with regard to Pakistan and China. Vajpayee had been a long-time Jan Sangh MP, and was a superb Hindi orator as well as a reputed poet. However, during the Janata's term in government, voices from outside as well as from within the coalition were raised against the Jan Sangh's double allegiance—to Janata and to what many regarded as the Jan Sangh's parent organisation, the RSS. Increasingly, pressure built up on the Jan Sangh to sever its ties with the RSS. Vajpayee refused and left the Janata party, founding the Bharatiya Janata Party (BJP). This proved to be a much more respectable vehicle for the Hindu nationalism which remained the main plank of the party's ideology. The BJP managed to accrue to itself the credit for having fought the Emergency (in its Jan Sangh avatar), when its leaders went to jail in large numbers, and additionally it gained credit for being effective in government.

GANDHI REDUX

Indira Gandhi returned to power in January 1980. Once again, it was not the popularity of the Congress, but the fragmented nature of the Opposition which allowed her to win. The Janata party split into two at the end of the two-year experience—the two segments called themselves Janata (Secular) and Janata (United) respectively. Further splits occurred, amoeba-like—and the resulting sub-factions were each more recognizable from the leader's name appended to them rather than for any significant ideological nuances. Indira Gandhi's action in splitting the original Congress and her personalizing of party rule began a fashion which has proved irresistible. With a divided Janata, the Congress, despite polling only 36 per cent of the vote, regained its old 350 plus seats, one more than it did in 1971.

The re-elected Indira Gandhi was a chastened woman, and had clearly reflected on her rejection by the people. She changed the course of the Congress in some significant matters, imposing an even more personal style of leadership which unfortunately has persisted to this day. She also became more centrist and less shrilly Left-wing. The Congress had regained the loyalty of the untouchables as Jagjivan Ram had returned to the fold; the Muslims had also gone back to the Congress after Sanjay Gandhi apologized for his outrages. But the loyalty of the Hindu vote, especially that of the upper castes, was less certain with the upsurge of the BJP. Indira Gandhi began to display her religiosity by talking to priests and holy men and being seen at temples around India. Her father was an atheist as well as a secularist. She, too, had been one too until political compulsions, or perhaps, the trauma of defeat and the sudden and violent death of Sanjay, led her to religion.

Katherine Frank has a different view of Indira Gandhi's religiosity. 'Though she presented a secular façade and claimed to have only the vaguest of spiritual beliefs, Indira had always been superstitious—a legacy no doubt of her maternal [sic] grandmother Swarup Rani Nehru, as well as her mother. Indira had irritated Nehru, for example, by refusing to move to Teen Murti House until the exact auspicious time and date.'[19] Whatever the true nature of her religiosity, the effect on policy was profound. Secularism, from now on, was to mean a balance in indulging the two major religions, rather than the exclusion of religion from public life Also, from here on, most public functions began to acquire a Hindu aura with lamps being lit at the start of each event, marigold garlands for every important guest and often an invocation in Sanskrit. Nehru would have hated such displays. There were none in the 1950s while he was around.

The biggest change was in economic policy. The Congress had been wedded to the doctrine of national self-sufficiency. This meant minimal reliance on foreign borrowing, especially from private sources. India had been a major recipient of foreign aid from the USA, the USSR, the UK and West Germany. In per capita terms, this was not much and, even then, it came with strings attached. But there had been a constant shortage of investment. Much capital was wasted in setting up units for heavy electrical companies, machine tools and aircraft industries, all in the public sector. This was a deliberate rejection of the benefits of the international division of labour. National pride preferred an expensive home-made item to an imported one, especially from neo-colonial Western economies. The cost in terms of slow growth was high. The average growth rate of real GDP for 1950–80, also called in economics jargon the 'secular' rate of growth, was only 3.5 per cent, and per capita growth was 1.25 per cent. This was duly damned by Raj Krishna, a rare economist with wit, as the 'Hindu' (as opposed to 'secular') rate of growth.

Indira Gandhi sought and obtained a large loan from the International Monetary Fund. This was partly to cope with the balance of payment consequences of the second oil shock. But it was also to signal to the world that there was a change of economic philosophy. Yet, given her power base on the Left, she did not dismantle the many public sector units, nor did she change the licence-permit raj, as India's economic structure had come to be known. The infusion of aid relaxed the import constraint and more efficient machines could now be imported. The Indian economy began its journey away from the abysmal Hindu rate of growth. It allowed the Congress a respite from the India-wide social protests which had overwhelmed Indira Gandhi during the mid-1970s.

HOW MANY NATIONS WITHIN INDIA?

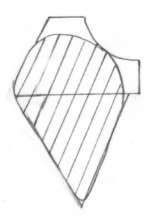

What hit her instead was a sub-nationalist problem. For the thirty-three years since Independence, many of India's intractable problems had been on its borders—Kashmir, Nagaland, Aksai Chin/Arunachal. The rest of India, if one leaves aside the North-East region, forms a sort of oval shape like a rugby football. In this rugby football, there had not been a sub-nationalism which had ever threatened India's security. Even the agitation in South India on Hindi had been civic and unarmed, though not non-violent. Now, for the first time, India faced an internal civil war in Punjab, a border area, of course, but previously well-integrated into India. The roots of the crisis lay, like much else, in India in the Partition of 1947.

In the grand narrative of Indian nationalism before Independence, there were two communities—Hindus and Muslims. Even as the Congress denied taking a religious view of India, it put at the centre of its narrative the syncretic nature of the Indian civilization as it had grown through history. It was a largely North Indian story, but that was not the only problem. The Government of India Act 1935 would have given a lot of autonomy to provinces such as Punjab and Bengal. But that was no longer on the cards once the Second World War begun. As the debate sharpened in the two years after the Labour Party came to office in UK in July 1945, the outcome of an actual division of India, largely theoretical till then, gained inevitability. But even then, what Jinnah had envisaged was a territory that comprised at least undivided Punjab and Bengal, as well as Sind, Balochistan and NWFP with perhaps Assam thrown in as well—in short regions A and C of the Cabinet Mission plan. But the Congress managed to insist on separate voting by districts in the Muslim majority and Hindu majority areas, and Punjab and Bengal were split.

Bengal did split, but then twenty-five years later East Bengal undid the Partition's divisions and became an independent nation. In Punjab there had always been not two but three communities—Sikhs being the third. Their interests were not taken into account and they were bracketed along with the Hindus as one community. The Sikh religion originated separately, in the teachings of Guru Nanak, as a synthesis of the best of Hinduism and Islam. The Sikhs had fought many battles with the Mughal Empire, and several of their ten gurus had faced persecution by the Mughals and had become martyrs in the Sikh cause. The last and tenth guru, Guru Gobind Singh, was martyred by Aurangzeb, the last of the great Mughal emperors. The Sikhs, thus, had a martial reputation and they inhabited the region through which many invaders had entered India. They had a much sharper sense of their religion and their 'race'. Many Hindu families often had one son who was brought up as a Sikh, so there was no racial difference between the communities. But their religion, and its injunction regarding what to wear and what to bear by way of arms, gave the Sikhs a distinct identity.

It was, however, a game of numbers, and the Congress wanted Sikhs on the Hindu side, even as it denied any division of India on a religious basis. The Sikhs vacated West Punjab where some of the best agricultural land had been their possession. They joined their East Punjab brethren, and remade their lives. Many settled abroad in the West, in the USA, the UK and Canada, and successfully established themselves in professions and businesses. The many mergers and splits of the Princely States and the linguistic reorganizations within India, which took place between 1947 and 1970, ended up in Punjab going to the Sikhs and Haryana going to the Punjabi Hindus, though, of course, each state had other communities as well. Chandigarh, the futuristic capital city built by the great French architect, Le Corbusier, was shared between the two states, and there were endless disputes about sharing of river waters.

The Sikhs were neither poor nor neglected. There had been Sikhs in the Cabinet since before Independence, and the community was well represented in the armed forces. Punjab prospered, especially after the Green Revolution. But despite their relative affluence, a latent anger simmered in the community. The Sikh religion has a holy book, the *Granth Sahib* at its centre, and an order of priests and gurudwaras or community places of worship. The lay community has an active role in determining who controls the gurudwaras. Indeed, after decades of having ceded authority to Hindu Mahants or priests, the Sikh community regained control as the result of a mass movement, which merged with the independence movement. The Shiromani Gurudwara Prabandhak Committee (SGPC) was a vital part of the Sikh community, since it was the apex body controlling the process through which the community determined the conduct of their gurudwaras. Thus, battles over identity and nationhood within the Sikh community often centred on getting elected to the SGPC. The Akali Dal party, a fusion of a political and a religious movement, contested elections alongside the Congress and other parties, but its ties to the SGPC were more intimate.

The Akali Dal had to compete in Punjab's political arena with the Congress and the Jan Sangh, which had made inroads into the Hindu and, to some extent, the Sikh vote banks. The Akali Dal dreamt of reviving the empire of the legendary Sikh king, Maharaja Ranjit Singh, who had established an empire in North India the early eighteenth century. The Akali Dal aspired to bring within its control at least part of that territory which lay within the boundaries of post-Independence India. Thus, it claimed some parts of the neighbouring state of Haryana. Such inter-state disputes about small bits of territory were not unusual at that time, nor were water disputes. What was different about Sikhs was that of the many communities in India, they had all the elements that were needed for being defined as a nation. They had a language— Punjabi, with its own distinctive script, Gurumukhi; they had a religion which coincided with ethnicity, and a single region which the community identified as its 'home'. In this respect, they were somewhat similar to the East Pakistani Bengalis.

As often happens in tightly knit religious communities, the seeds of trouble were sown by a dissident religious movement. The Nirankaris were a deviant sect because they believed that there was a living guru. This was in marked contrast to the Sikh ideology which worshipped the ten gurus who had lived between the sixteenth and eighteenth centuries. The Nirankaris—who were regarded as heretics by the Sikhs—had gathered in the holy city of Amritsar in April 1978, and this was widely perceived as a sign of weakness on the part of the SGPC and Akali Dal. Punjab witnessed the emergence of a charismatic leader, Sant Jarnail Singh Bhindranwale who challenged the Akali Dal, asserting that they had reduced Sikhs to the status of 'slaves in India'. What was needed, he argued Savonarola-style in 1978, was purity and a return to the fundamental religion.

There was nothing unusual in this sudden challenge, as holy men (Bhindranwale was a religious leader—a sant—after all) often preach such doctrines. What gave his call resonance was a crisis among the diaspora Sikhs who felt their identity was under threat since they were living abroad; they were ripe for a purifying movement. They conducted themselves much more strictly on their visits back home to the Sikh holy city of Amritsar, the site of the Golden Temple, and their piety much impressed the locals. Indira Gandhi, the then leader of the Opposition, regarded Bhindranwale as a welcome counter to the Akali Dal, and by all accounts actively encouraged his movement. This was in line with her favoured tactic of setting up counterpoints to her enemies in the hope of weakening them. She could not have anticipated the eventual outcome of this strategy.

Bhindranwale was no one's puppet; he was to prove an independent and powerful leader. He was charismatic and it was more than likely that he had designs on leadership of the SGPC. He was not a separatist to begin with—just engaged in an internal feud with the Akali Dal. Yet, he ended up asserting the demand for Khalistan, the land of the Khalsa, the Sikh nation. This had first come in June 1980 from the diaspora, articulated by the leader of the Khalistan movement—Jagjit Singh Chauhan—who was living in the UK. By then Indira Gandhi was back in power, and was focussed on making trouble for the Akalis who were the opposition party in Punjab, while the Congress was in power. The Akali Dal was worried about Bhindranwale, who had leveraged his holy status into acquiring a dedicated following which was willing to kill, and some spectacular murders did occur. The Delhi and the Punjab governments dithered about bringing Bhindranwale to book and, when they tried, the hunter lost to the hunted. Bhindranwale became a cult figure and asserted the demand for a separate Sikh homeland.

ENDGAME

The Akali Dal was under pressure to follow suit as it was being outflanked on the Sikh nationalist front. They increased their demands on Delhi, and even threatened to stop food grains leaving Punjab. Bhindranwale, meanwhile, condoned the killing by Sikhs who were in the police and, of course, Hindus. By 1983, President's rule had to be imposed in Punjab; Bhindranwale took refuge in the Akal Takht housed within the large complex of buildings in the Golden Temple. He barricaded himself there, and reinforced his position with military throroughness. He was defying the powers that be. As the Akali Dal tried to match him in militancy, Indira Gandhi decided that this was a challenge to the integrity of India which had to be met with maximum force.

In early June 1984, the Indian Army attacked the Golden Temple with tanks to break down the barricades and managed to kill Bhindranwale and his associates. This was an extreme act, conducted, as it was, in the precincts of the Sikhs' holiest shrine. But its use as a military base to defy the nation state was not something any prime minister could negotiate with. India has always put its territorial integrity as its number one priority. Also, given the example of Pakistan's dismemberment, Indira Gandhi could not afford to hesitate; Punjab was, after all, on the border with Pakistan. India had seen a constant interplay of war and truce with the Nagas in the North-East as well as in Kashmir. The Punjab situation appeared fraught with the possibility of secession. With regard to the North-East and Kashmir, there had been no compromise. But these were peripheral areas, with long histories of insurgency; Punjab was a different matter. This was India, by any definition. There was never any question of granting Khalistan, or even substantial autonomy to Punjab. The Union was paramount.

In the end, Indian Army lost four officers and seventy-nine soldiers. For the Bhindranwale group, the losses were in hundreds or, some say, thousands. The army's Sikh officers did their duty, including Major General Brar who led the assault. General Aurora, who was the superior officer, said, 'The army was used to finish a problem created by the government. This is the kind of action that is going to ruin the army.'[20] He was, fortunately, wrong. The army was not ruined. It was Indira Gandhi who paid for her decision with her life. On 31 October 1984 she was gunned down in her garden by her Sikh bodyguards. She was sixty-seven, younger than her father when he died.

The assassination of Indira Gandhi was the first of a major Indian leader since that of the Mahatma. But in South Asia as a region, this was no longer rare. Pakistan had lost Liaqat Ali Khan early in its independent existence. Zulfiqar Ali Bhutto had been hanged by Zia-Ul-Haq on the flimsiest of grounds. In Bangladesh Mujibur Rahman, the founder of Bangladesh, had been brutally murdered inside his official residence. In Sri Lanka S.W.R.D. Bandaranaike had been killed in full public view by a lapsed Buddhist monk. The land of Buddha and Gandhi, whatever its claims, is a very violent place.

Had Indira Gandhi lived she would, no doubt, have been re-elected. While the multiplicities of conflict and cleavages grew rather than diminished, as Indians took their battle for resources into the public arena, she was still able to manage a national discourse which commanded attention. She could have been prime minister for longer than her father, though he had never suffered an electoral defeat as she had. She managed a total of sixteen years to his seventeen. Between them, father and daughter, led India for thirty-three of its first thirty-seven years While Nehru dug the deep foundations of Indian democracy, she tested them to destruction, but, in the end, gave them new strength by her Emergency misadventure. Indians realized that they valued their freedoms much more than a cynical world had given them credit for. They surprised her and she, in turn, surprised them by calling elections in 1977.

Indira Gandhi remains a difficult person to evaluate. She was the last 'strong' leader India has had; some would say the only such leader. In her reaction to the challenges posed by the regional nationalist movements—Bangladesh and Khalistan—she showed her willingness to take extreme risks and decisive action. But, she failed on the economic front, and though the second phase of her office was better than the first, the many troubles she faced were largely due to her economic failure.

She is also the last leader who could articulate an All India vision. Despite her many unnecessary provocations and divisive battles with her party and others, she had the confidence that she articulated a vision which Indians shared. She was never perceived as representing a region or a caste or a religion or a partial narrative of what India was about. This could be because her generation had grown up while Gandhi was alive and a strong voice; it could be because of the long tradition of fighting for India, which her grandfather had started. Whatever it was, and a flawed leader though she was, she still remains the last genuinely national personality in modern Indian history.

She hollowed out the Congress, so that from being a well-organized political party with internal democracy and a plurality of views, it became a personal fiefdom where below the leader were sycophants. If anyone rose high enough to be on her radar, she cut him or her down to size. Apart from her son, that is. But Sanjay died in a plane crash in

June 1980. She had persuaded her elder son, Rajiv, to step into the supportive role. Rajiv, unusually in the Nehru family, was the first since Motilal Nehru to earn a living—he was a qualified commercial pilot. But he, despite the fears of his Italian-born wife Sonia and his own reluctance, had to walk the plank of Indian electoral politics and become an MP. Now, the supine Congress party, shocked by Indira Gandhi's sudden death, offered him the prime ministership. Indira had reduced India to the status of a monarchic democracy.

THE SIKH POGROM

What happened once the news of Indira Gandhi's death spread was a sense of immense tragedy and great shame for the nation. In those days, before 24x7 news channels and with government monopoly of TV and radio, the news took many hours to travel. But in Delhi, mobs of Hindus, led in many cases by officials of Congress party, unleashed a massacre of Sikhs, which can only be called a pogrom. Around 3000 Sikhs died in three days of unrelenting violence, while the machinery of law and order looked on. Not a single non-Sikh casualty was recorded. Rajiv Gandhi's smug comment on the situation was, 'When a big tree falls, the earth shakes.' The task of recording what happened and who were the culpable people was left largely to unofficial groups in civil society, and even after twenty-five years the known culprits, among them prominent Congress MPs and even Union ministers, have not been brought to justice.

Punjab became a battleground and all Sikhs were suspected of anti-national sentiments, even though the President of India at that time was a Sikh, Giani Zail Singh. (This much confused a BBC commentator covering Indira Gandhi's funeral since he wondered why a terrorist-like person was in the centre of the ceremony.) Punjab had to be 'pacified' with some severity. Another generation of young 'Khalistanis' had to be gunned down. Even as elections were held, the streets remained violent. The pacification of Punjab was a police operation led by J.S. Ribeiro, a Christian along with a Sikh official, K.P.S. Gill. Together, they ensured that the dissidents were systematically flushed out. The fact that Sikhs are now reconciled to the Indian Union and have largely forgiven their fellow Indians, is a tribute to their character and magnanimity. The demand for Khalistan has now receded to a few groups outside India and there is little, if any, enthusiasm for the idea in Punjab. But, as recently as 2008, Indira Gandhi's killers were honoured in many Sikh homes, and there was a demand for the recognition of Bhindranwale as an official Sikh icon.

A DEVIL'S COCKTAIL

Indira Gandhi's legacy to her son was a devil's cocktail of problems. She had, of course, been its victim. Yet, she had tried her best to tackle them. They remained and, in some cases, grew as time went on. It is time to take stock of them.

Economic growth was higher, but, as yet, no solvent for the many conflicts which raged. Electoral majorities in Delhi were no guarantee for peace around the country. By now the pattern of the conflicts in India was clear. There were national problems in the sense that they were not region specific. There were region specific sub-nationalisms. There were inter-regional conflicts and intra-regional ones. There were conflicts within each community, Hindu and Muslim, and no doubt, other minorities such as Sikhs. These took social, economic and religious forms, and often, though not invariably, were violent.

At the apex there was the 'macro' issue of Hindu–Muslim division. This was inherited from the Partition and was central to the narrative of Indian nationhood. Nehru had managed to contain the conflict and so had Indira Gandhi. But, by now, the rise of the BJP and the increasing prosperity of the middle classes (predominantly Hindu with Muslims largely absent) were complimenting each other to create a confident assertion of Hindu national identity. Also, as in the case of the Sikhs, a prosperous Hindu disapora, anxious about its identity, was pouring money into religious movements and also in the RSS and BJP. The oil price rise had enriched orthodox Muslim states like Saudi Arabia, who saw it as their duty to spread their preferred version of Wahhabism, a fundamentalist sect of Sunni Islam. Many new madrasas—religious schools which provided free education for the young—came up, and there was a move to convert more people to Islam. This was a worldwide phenomenon, but its repercussions were felt sharply in India and, also across the border, in Pakistan. Pakistan was caught in the late 1980s and early 1990s in the Afghan rebellion against the Soviet presence, and the Americans were happy to finance the fight which was led by Muslim fundamentalist groups known as the Taliban—'students'. Thus, the Hindu–Muslim issue was being changed by the international context.

There were always the sub-nationalist conflicts at the periphery— Kashmir and Nagaland, Mizo and Bodo tribal areas in the North-East. These were dealt with by a combination of force and concessions—the latter an attempt to admit people into the overall democratic life of India. These struggles had existed since 1947 and were tough to end. Added to this was the sub-nationalist sentiment within the 'rugby ball'— the growing consciousness of regional identity in Punjab, Tamil Nadu and other states during the 1970s and 1980s where the increasing income (however slowly it increased) created identity movements— Telugu Desam, Asom Gana Parishad (AGP) and Shiv Sena which insisted on more power for the states. This often took the form of demands for relaxing the rules about allocation of resources between the Centre and the states. Non-Congress governments, in states such as West Bengal and Kerala, often felt they received unfair treatment. The rules which existed on the statute books were being distorted by politics. What was needed was a new politics of federalism. But the Congress had a unitarian view of India, preferably ruled all over by the party itself. It resisted any such demands. The states made angry demonstrations, both within their region and in Delhi. These seldom took a violent turn, Punjab being the exception.

There were subaltern conflicts which did not have a specific geographical concentration, but were spread around the country. Such were the struggles which the scheduled castes and tribes (SC/ST) had to engage in to assert their rights as equal citizens against the local elites. These were age-old, but given a new dimension by the progress of some members of the community, which inspired others. Reservations had been granted in the Constitution for the SC/ST in higher educational institutions and in government jobs. After thirty plus years, a literate middle class was forming in these communities, and it provided the front line activists for the status battles. These were Ambedkar's children.

There were battles between the upper castes and the lower or backward castes especially in North India, where status inequalities were ruthlessly asserted by the upper castes with the sanction of Hinduism behind them. In Bihar and Madhya Pradesh, there were large tracts of tribal settlements, often in areas rich in mineral resources, where the original inhabitants saw that the only way to obtain their fair share of the public resources was to have their own state. Such were the movements for Jharkhand and Chhatisgarh. There were also the problems of a linguistic majority wishing to exclude the 'outsiders' from economic opportunities, as with the Shiv Sena in Maharashtra and the Assamese with Biharis and Bengalis working in their provinces.

It would be a cliché to say that all these conflicts were just the epiphenomenal versions of the underlying economic class conflict. There were, of course, massive differences between the rich and the poor, and the poor were still the majority of India's population. But there was no chance of a mobilization of the poor across the country as a revolutionary force. The economic conflicts were intersected by the regional dimensions, since, even after three decades of Independence, there was not a single national economy in India. There were many obstacles to the nation-wide movement of goods and services imposed by the dirigiste economic logic. The rural poor were stuck in a local backward agricultural economy despite some areas of Green Revolution. They were engaged in local battles, where their caste status and their religion often determined their allies or their enemies.

The backward castes in Bihar and UP and, indeed, much of the 1857 territory, had done well economically from agricultural growth, even though it was hardly rapid. They received subsidies by way of guaranteed prices for their output and subsidies for their inputs, along with easy loans from nationalized banks as long as they had a caste agent in local politics. But socially they were treated with contempt by the upper castes. They fought with the upper castes for status equality, while oppressing the Dalits who were often their farm workers. Armed gangs of upper caste landlords, such as the Ranvir Sena, in Bihar, battled the rising lower orders, often literally. The Naxalites flourished in such areas as well as in the rural/tribal areas, which were the poorest and often both hilly and arid.

In urban areas, in the organized sector, unionized labour often engaged in long strikes as in the Bombay textile industry, which went through a two-year long strike in the early 1980s, ruining both capital and labour. But this was only the tip of the iceberg as the organized sector accounted for about 10 per cent of the labour force, and much of it was in the public sector. In the informal sector, health and safety were precarious at the best of times, and there was neither job tenure nor the freedom to unionize. Yet, the worst case of health hazard was in a multinational, when the Union Carbide factory in Bhopal released toxic gases in an accident which killed 400 immediately and 2000 eventually— a shaming example of an uncaring multinational company, moving its polluting plants away from where the laws are strict, exporting it to where poverty and corruption allowed unhindered activity.

Despite such a long litany of troubles, India somehow managed to conduct a normal political life that was open and democratic. Disputes did get settled, if only temporarily. Lives were lost or ruined, but there were also achievements. The size and complexity of the country give it an aura of a functioning anarchy. Yet, it must be remembered that India has had the experience of a viable over-arching state only for a fraction of its long history. The open society with its press and other media, a tradition now over a hundred years old, a cumbersome and overburdened, yet functioning, legal system built on the ideas of the rule of law, all provide a formal envelope for the resolution of many such conflicts. The rest are dealt with in the time honoured way of Indian society, which Hegel labelled 'Oriental Despotism' and Marx called the 'Asiatic Mode of Production'—a world where political authority is remote and does not touch the lives of ordinary people.

RAJIV GANDHI

Before its recent reform which abolished the hereditary principle, some of the youngest members of the House of Lords had come by the hereditary route. The rest of us life peers had to wait much of our working life to make the grade. Thus, the one advantage of heredity as a principle of succession is that one may occasionally get a much younger person to occupy an important post. Rajiv Gandhi, prime minister while still under forty, was such a person. He was, of all the five prime ministers India had had till then, the least prepared. He had shown no interest in politics throughout his adult life, and shunned the privileges which his mother's position would have allowed him to enjoy. He was also one of the few MPs who had been out and about in the real world of timetables and deadlines and punctuality and performance. He had not assumed the top status in his job where he was a middle-ranking pilot with Indian Airlines. He had no ideological baggage, and was naturally pragmatic. His friends were from the corporate world, and it was to them that he looked for guidance. This was the computer generation now suddenly finding itself at the top.

Rajiv Gandhi also had the room for manoeuvre. Elections called in December 1984 had given the Congress, for the first time, nearly 50 per cent of the votes cast and 401 seats; Rajiv had done better than his mother or his grandfather. Yet, this was the sympathy vote for his recently assassinated mother rather than a positive vote for him. He immediately worked out a compromise in Punjab with the Akali Dal. Assembly elections were held, and the Akali Dal handsomely won a majority despite the fact that their leader, Sant Longowal had recently been murdered by a dissident youth. Chandigarh was promised to Punjab, and prisoners were released. For a while Punjab was normal.

The North-East region had been feeling neglected. A powerful students' movement in Assam had been protesting about immigrant Bangladeshis who were competing for their jobs. The usual flurry of strikes and processions and train wreckage followed. Assam had, for long, been dominated by Bengal and by British tea planters. Now there was a demand for local autonomy and some control over its economy. Indira Gandhi had contained the demands, Rajiv now proceeded to meet them. Elections were held in which the party formed by the students, the Asom Gana Parishad defeated the Congress. As a relatively young leader, Rajiv seemed to have been less worried by the fears of Balkanization which had haunted the generations of his mother and grandfather. He also seemed to be happy to concede that non-Congress parties could come to power in the provinces. Rajiv Gandhi brought a relaxed feel to the Union government after his mother's overbearing imperial style. But it did not work any better than his mother's approach.

A long struggle had been waged by the Mizoram National Front (MNF) led by Laldenga. A ceasefire was signed in June 1986 with the MNF, and Laldenga became the chief minister. India found that the solution to the many sub-national demands was a judicious combination of force and democracy. Rajiv Gandhi, being of the new confident generation, could see the futility of imposing a uniform identity on all, as he did in Mizoram. The answer was to accommodate specific sub-national identities within the overarching Indian identity. This required the region to be part of the federal democratic polity and not resort to armed violence. The North-East Frontier area was to see a proliferation of states—Arunachal Pradesh (1987), Assam, Mizoram (1987), Tripura (1972), Manipur (1972), Meghalaya (1972) and Nagaland (1963). India had boasted about unity in diversity, yet the elite of the Indo-Gangetic plains, who had told the story of Indian nationhood, had not realized the full extent of the diversity. It had to acknowledge the plurality of India, while creating a unity.

Rajiv Gandhi's lasting contribution remains a change of vision about India's economy. He was much more business-minded, much more managerial, and did not have the visceral dislike of the private sector which his mother and his grandfather had. By this time, the thinking about economic policy was fast changing. In the developed countries, Keynesian nostrums had lost appeal and free market monetarism was ruling the roost with Reagan and Thatcher leading. Nearer home, the Asian Tigers were showing how export-led industrialization could yield miracle growth rates. Import substitution was losing out to export promotion. In China, Deng Xiao Ping had shocked his comrades by setting the practical goal of a result-oriented policy as the preferred option. It was no longer wrong to be rich. This made Rajiv's policy much more mainstream than before. This was, of course, not the view of the entrenched Left.

He pursued a much more explicit programme of deregulating the economy, relaxing the constraints which had been imposed much to India's economic detriment. He did this not as an ideological shift away from his mother's position, but as a practical move. His first budget introduced by V.P. Singh, whom he had chosen as finance minister, liberalized the trade regime reducing import duties and giving export incentives. Many sectors were deregulated and freed from the licence-permit stranglehold. Tax rates were reduced, with the prime minister arguing that this was good for tackling corruption.

India's middle class, now 100 million or so strong, liked what they got. They could now afford consumer durables—cars, TVs, scooters, apartments. People openly talked of 'Bel-India'—an economy the size of Belgium and France within India, which was now welcome and not suppressed despite the radical Left slogans about increasing gap between the rich and the poor. The economy responded, and growth picked up to above 5 per cent. Population growth had slowed down as a result of the long-standing policy of promoting family planning, which resulted in the growth of per capita incomes.

But while Rajiv Gandhi coped with the many troubles on his plate as best as he could, he had to resolve wider disputes as well. Sri Lanka had been independent since 1948, and had a Constitution drafted by the British which incorporated many fine features of the Westminster model. But in the 1950s an Oxford-trained radical member of the landed elite, Solomon Bandaranaike became prime minister, and installed the idea of Sinhalese citizenship and championed Sinhala as the official language. This deprived the substantial Tamil-speaking minority of its right to education in Tamil, or the advantage they had had of English education. Some Tamil workers had gone there from India to labour in the tea plantations. But many more, especially in the North, had been living in Ceylon (as it was called) for centuries; these were middle-class, articulate citizens, much envied by the Sinhala speakers.

The sudden demotion of the largest minority caused shock, and negotiations continued between the two communities for many years. The Sri Lankan situation was reminiscent of the pre-Independence arguments between Congress and Jinnah. Jinnah's fears of a majority reneging on a promise given before the departure of the British were realized in Sri Lanka. There were also echoes of the Hindi agitation in India in the 1960s, which in India was peacefully settled, as well as similarities with the secession of Bangladesh, which had also hinged on the linguistic rights of a community. The Tamils wanted their minority rights guaranteed by the Constitution as it was (until rewritten by the Sinhalese majority). It took twenty-five years before a total breakdown occurred. A civil war started in which a movement for a Tamil nation Liberation Tigers of Tamil Eelam—took to arms against the Sinhalese majority. Given the large Tamil population in Tamil Nadu, which is very close to the Tamil areas of Sri Lanka, there were bound to be complications. Indian Tamil sympathies were with the rebels, but New Delhi had to side with the sovereign Sri Lankan state.

Rajiv Gandhi was persuaded to send an Indian military force to keep peace in Sri Lanka during one of the phases of the civil war. This was partly a throwback to pre-Independence days when the Indian army was the bulwark for peace in regions ranging from East Africa and the Middle East to South-East Asia. India had now become sufficiently confident of its military prowess to aspire to the status of regional hegemon. In the event, the Indian army won a pyrrhic victory, and the Tamil guerrilla army, while contained, was never defeated. After three years the Indian Peace Keeping Force was withdrawn. The war ended many years later in a bloody defeat for the LTTE (Tamil Tigers) in May 2009. V. Prabhakaran was killed along with many of his followers, and a horrendous refugee resettlement problem threatened to overwhelm Sri Lanka.

Rajiv Gandhi's good record in economic policy was negated by three decisions which had long-term consequences on Indian politics. First was a move to overturn a decision by the Judiciary, which upheld the rights of a divorced Muslim woman to alimony payments from her former husband. The Shah Bano case, as it became known, was a shock for orthodox Muslim men, but quite in line with the human rights orientation of the Indian Constitution. Rajiv Gandhi, however, succumbed to pressure from the guardians of the Congress's Muslim vote bank and legislated that the orthodox male-dominant position should be enshrined in the law of modern India. His claims to modernity and progressiveness were ruined, and the move also inflamed Hindu sentiments who felt that while his grandfather had wanted to reform Hindu law, Rajiv was quite happy to play the religious orthodoxy card where Muslim sentiments were concerned. This, indeed, was double-standard secularism or, in what became a famous slogan for the BJP, pseudo-secularism.

As if to compensate for this, Rajiv made a concession to the Hindu orthodox position. Ayodhya is the city which, according to the Hindu epic, *Ramayana*, is the birthplace of the God-hero, Rama. Whatever the status of the epic, as history or fiction, this is a deeply-held belief among Hindus. On this site, a mosque was built in the sixteenth century during the reign of Babur. The mosque, named Babri Masjid (Babur's Mosque), was in disuse by the time of Independence. There had been a move to install idols of Rama, as a token of the original holy status of the site, when Nehru was prime minister. The issue first surfaced in 1949 when someone, possibly the district collector, had turned a blind eye to the installation of idols in the disused mosque. This was discovered, and in the ensuing controversy, Nehru had ruled the act illegal and wanted the idols removed. But Sardar Patel and the then chief minister of UP, Gobind Ballabh Pant, were inclined to live with the *fait accompli*. A compromise was worked out—worship of the idols would be allowed one day in the year, and the rest of the time the place would be locked.

In the new climate, with Hinduism in ascendance as a political programme of the BJP, the stir to install the icons took a much more popular militant form. There were now several Hindu bodies which were more openly and aggressively religious than the RSS or the BJP. One such was the Vishwa Hindu Parishad (World Hindu Congress) known as the VHP. It had made the liberation of Rama's birthplace the principal plank of its programme. There was a move in the courts to allow the opening of the locks and the worship of Ram *lalla* (the child Rama). It was widely believed that Delhi let it be known that the court should allow this installation, and this was duly done with an unusually swift implementation of the judgement. Now there was a small Hindu temple dedicated to Rama in his birthplace—*Ramjanmabhoomi*—right inside the mosque complex. It was a sop to the orthodox Hindu sentiment. Secularism now meant catering to the orthodoxies of both major religious communities. Popular as the gesture was, it was to sow seeds of discord for years to come.

MR CLEAN NO MORE

What really doomed Rajiv's tenure, however, was a charge of corruption which his ex-finance minister brought against him and the government. V.P. Singh was known for his integrity. A minor *raja* (large landowner), he had been head-hunted by Rajiv for his incorruptibility. He had, however, taken his brief far too seriously for a Congressman, and raided business houses for tax evasion. He was moved to the defence ministry and later sacked. On his dismissal he alleged that a Swedish company, Bofors had won a large defence order for guns, worth Rs 143 billion (just under $20 billion at the then exchange rate), by paying about $500 million in bribes to the upper echelons of the government, including the prime minister himself. India had become one of the largest purchasers of arms from abroad. In this respect, Nehru's dreams of self-sufficiency had been abandoned. Incredible amounts of scarce capital could have been deployed to pursue employment-intensive growth if the arms had been purchased abroad right from the outset. The arms trade is always a murky business with huge mark-ups, opaque pricing, gullible governments—who purchase more for prestige than for effect—and shady middlemen who make a living by bribing both sides of the transaction.[21]

The news had first come out on Swedish radio, and one of the alleged middlemen was an Italian called Ottavio Quattrochi. Given Rajiv's wife's Italian origins, the media had a field day with the scandal. Rajiv, who had been labelled Mr Clean when he took office, now saw himself being sullied in public by his former colleague, V.P. Singh. Singh resigned from the Congress and from Parliament and contested his old seat under a new banner, the Jan Morcha. He was re-elected. The Bofors incident was used as the platform to unite the old Janata Party, the Jan Morcha and other anti-Congress stragglers. Rajiv faced a united Opposition.

His response was to reverse his liberal record and scramble back on to his mother's bandwagon—restrictions on press freedom, dropping liberal economic policies and grandstanding in international affairs. It did not do him any good. In the 1989 elections the Congress lost massively, returning only 197 seats, the Janata Dal won 142 and BJP's tally was eighty-six seats. The Congress had done better than in 1977, but did not attempt to form a coalition government with Left parties and others. V.P. Singh became prime minister at the head of a coalition government.

Rajiv's defeat was, to some extent, self-inflicted. His inexperience, which was an advantage at the outset, became a burden later when he had to rely on the advice of the old stalwarts in matters non-economic. His knowledge of recent history was scant and he is supposed to have asked his advisers, who were talking of the Mahalanobis framework, to fetch Mahalanobis to meet him. He had to be gently told that the 'Professor' had died some years previously. In any case, there was now a sea change in Indian politics. Rajiv was the last person to win a decisive majority for a single party, and, indeed, a majority as large as his has not been seen before or since. One could say that the changeover was not too soon. It was delayed by the incompetence of the first Janata coalition in 1977, and its failure to present a united front in the 1979 elections. Indira Gandhi had destroyed the original Congress party and its Centrist orientation. Her strategy worked once in 1971, but the damage was done. The Congress was never again to be the same broad-based party which could appeal to all shades of Indians. Indian democracy lost its super stability which Nehru had bequeathed to his successors.

The aberration was the return of Congress with a large majority, while polling less than 40 per cent of votes, in 1979. Rajiv's election in 1984 was due to the sympathy vote following his mother's assassination. Thus, what happened in 1989 was just ten years away from when it could have happened for the first time, The old Congress magic had vanished during the mid-1970s as Indira Gandhi was forced to ride roughshod over opposition within and without Parliament. India had become too diverse, too confident about its rights, too impatient with a party which had signally failed to deliver the goods. The much-vaunted sacrifices for the Independence movement, which the Congress and the Nehru–Gandhi family had made, were no longer encashable in the electoral marketplace. Half of India had been born since 1947 and did not recall the indignities of foreign rule. The year 1989 was Nehru's birth centenary and, fittingly, the Indian public bade his heirs a long goodbye.

Rajiv Gandhi was in office for only five years, and he was never to be prime minister again. The intervention in Sri Lanka cost him his life as suicide bombers from the LTTE, the Tamil nationalist movement, killed him while he was campaigning for the 1991 elections in

Sriperumbadur in Tamil Nadu. His death was uncannily similar to his mother's. He was also killed by a sub-nationalist movement, but this time a Sri Lankan, rather than an Indian, one. He was forty-six when he died, older than his brother, but much younger than his mother or his grandfather. His lasting legacy was to jolt India out of the Fabian socialist/East European state capitalist cul-de-sac. He did not quite finish the task of liberalizing the Indian economy, and lost his nerve in the final year of his prime ministership. But he will always be remembered for what he could have been, as a promise unfulfilled. Had he lived and won power again, he could have ushered in a generational change in the personnel of Indian politics. His death gave a fresh lease of life to the gerontocracy. He was widely mourned, and there were few who bore any grudges against him. He was a prime minister by accident of death, and he died as a result of a similar accident.

CHAPTER 14

SEARCH FOR STABILITY, 1989–2004

DRIFT AND DISASTER

The years following 1989 were very different from the forty-two years of Independence that went before. In the first forty-two years, India had six prime ministers: Jawaharlal Nehru, Lal Bahadur Shastri, Indira Gandhi, Morarji Desai, Charan Singh and Rajiv Gandhi. Of these, three had served thirty-eight years between them. The following twenty years saw seven prime ministers: V.P. Singh, Chandra Shekhar, Narasimha Rao, I.K. Gujral, Deve Gowda, Atal Bihari Vajpayee and Manmohan Singh. Nine elections were held in the first forty-two years: 1952, 1957, 1962, 1967, 1971, 1977, 1979, 1984 and 1989. In the following twenty years there were six: 1991, 1996, 1998, 1999, 2004 and 2009.

If there is a pattern to this, it is one of alteration between a Janata-like short-lived, unstable coalition that followed the 1977 elections, and longer, stable coalitions which gave the ruling alliance at least five years in office. The key is the size of the largest single party in the coalition, and whether the coalition commands a majority by itself or requires support 'from outside'. In a Lok Sabha of 545 seats, since two seats are reserved for the Anglo-Indian community the effective electoral number is 543, and a majority of 272 is necessary. No single party has obtained that many seats since 1989. The best on offer was the Congress at 244 in 1991, once again helped by the sympathy vote of Rajiv's assassination in mid-election campaign. Neither the Congress nor their close rival, the BJP was to see 200 seats again (until the 2009 elections about which more in Chapter 16.). The BJP managed 182 in 1998 and 1999. The Congress declined to 140 in 1996 from 244 in 1991, then 141 in 1998 and an even more catastrophic 114 in 1999 when Sonia Gandhi's bid to topple the National Democratic Alliance (NDA) government resulted in another election and a big setback for the Congress. In 2004 Congress surprised everyone by winning 145 seats, seven more than the BJP and went on to form the coalition, United Progressive Alliance (UPA).

The Congress had lost its dominant position in Indian politics. It had to reluctantly share the top slot with the BJP. The rise and growth of the BJP is the story of the years since 1975. Once reviled for its association with the RSS, which was tarred with Gandhi's assassination, it transformed itself during the Emergency. As the BJP rather than the Jan Sangh, its cadre assiduously worked away at a campaign undermining the official ideology of secularism, which the Congress had established as a fulcrum of the narrative of Indian nationhood. It exposed this Congress practice in office as pseudo-secularism, blamed the Congress for a lack of balance in its dealings with Hindus and Muslims, and projected the idea that the majority community was deprived in the land of its own origin. Many were convinced by this message. Why was it, the BJP asked, that Muslims got a subsidy for going to Mecca on Haj? Why did Hindus not have such a subsidy to visit their holy places? Did secularism mean ignoring Hinduism and pandering to the preachers of Islam? The BJP then built an alternative narrative around the concept of Hindutva—the idea of a notion of Indian-ness which based itself cleverly, not on the religion of Hinduism per se, but on the fact that the word 'Hindu' also stood for all who lived in the land of the Indus. It was the Hindu Mahasabha founder, Veer Savarkar who had first developed the idea of Hindutva. The model the BJP used was the state of Israel which proudly asserts its Jewishness, not so much as a religion but as the identity of nationhood. While its detractors criticized Hindutva for its anti-Muslim bias, many in the majority community bought into the notion that in a democracy the majority had the right to define nationhood on its own terms.

The decline of the Congress thus brought out the fragility of its nationalist narrative, the Nehruvian story of a syncretic India where Hinduism and Islam were joined in a seamless union, and secularism rather than religion, any religion, was the foundation of nationhood. There were now competing narratives of nationalism. The Congress and the BJP commanded the largest following, but neither persuaded the majority of the nation. Hindu society is built on hierarchy and cellular division. Though Hindus comprise over 80 per cent of the population, they cannot all be mobilized under the Hindutva banner. The consequence is a proliferation of regional, sub-nationalist narratives which coexist— somewhat uneasily—with the supra-national All India narratives.

The decline of the Congress also led to the fragmentation of the political party structure across India. Ever since the Congress split in 1969, parties had proliferated which attached certain letters in parentheses to their names. The Congress was (R) and (N); then (R) became (I). The

Janata split into (S) and (U). New fragments came out of the Lohia-inspired Socialist Party which became the Samajwadi Party (SP) in UP, the Rashtriya Janata Dal (RJD) in Bihar and the Samata Party, also North India based. In Tamil Nadu, the Dravida Munnetra Kazhagam (DMK) split into the DMK and the All India Anna Dravida Munnetra Kazhagam (AIADMK). Regional parties such as Andhra Pradesh's Telugu Desam Party (TDP), Assam's Asom Gana Parishad (AGP), Maharashtra's Shiv Sena, Jharkhand's Jharkhand Mukti Morcha (JMM) added to the variety. The UP-based SP and the Bihar-based RJD were parties of the Yadav caste groups, similar to the Bharatiya Lok Dal, a Jat party founded by Charan Singh. Parties on the Left included the Communist Party of India (CPI) and Communist Party of India (Marxist) (CPI(M)), the Forward Bloc (FB) and the Revolutionary Socialist Party (RSP). Ambedkar's Republican Party had once represented the non-Congress Dalit vote bank. To this was added a new party, the Bahujan Samaj Party (BSP) founded by Kanshi Ram along with the dynamic woman leader, Mayawati.

The ideological veneer of these parties was thin. They were mostly small clientelist parties defining their base in terms of caste groups—Yadavs, Jats, Dalits, or regions—Andhra Pradesh (TDP), Assam (AGP), for instance. One line across was secular versus communal. The BJP and its associates such as the Shiv Sena were cast as communal. The Congress, the Left and many of the fragments of Janata and Lohiaite parties, were secular. This meant that they sought Muslim votes actively or, rather, that Muslims trusted them to be their agents. Being secular did not prevent them from being casteist, which only a Hindu party can be. But there was another axis apart from the anti-BJP one. This was the old Lohia idea of anti-Congressism. Here, the BJP was eager to join the Left parties on occasion, as well as join hands with the various Janata parties when the need arose. The politics of the 1990s veered between anti-BJP and anti-Congress axes, leading to much ideological cross-dressing.

The Indian Constitution had envisaged a strong Centre which would preserve the Union with an iron rod, disciplining the constituent states if they fell out of line. The hope, indeed, the expectation, of the founding fathers was that the Congress would be in power for evermore at the Centre and in all the states. This assumption had begun to slip by the mid-1950s when Kerala voted for the communists. After 1967 there were many non-Congress coalitions, but none that lasted long. The Congress remained the sole national party. After 1977 there were further fissures as not only did the Congress split, but the larger part under Indira Gandhi lost power. This meant that the more draconian powers of the Centre, the power to impose President's rule for instance, were often driven by the electoral considerations of the party in power at the Centre. President's rule became a useful means of dealing with a troublesome rival party in power at the state level. Worse was to follow—fragile coalitions at the Centre were held to ransom by crucial coalition partners. These parties usually had strong regional bases, but their few seats at the Centre allowed them to wag the dog of the ruling coalition and make it impose President's rule for regional electoral interests. Despite the bruising experience of the Emergency, there was no appetite for restricting the powers of the Lok Sabha. Each party saw that its turn would come some day, and such powers would be useful.

The V.P. Singh government of 1989 was a re-run of the Janata government of 1977, except that it was a tragedy rather than a farce. One of the most fundamental decisions of the V.P. Singh government was to implement the Backward Classes (Mandal) Commission Report. This commission, appointed by the Janata government, had reported by 1980, but its report was shelved by the Congress. The commission recommended that reservations in higher educational institutions and government jobs, which had been given to the SC/ST in the Constitution (initially, it was for a limited period of fifteen years but was later extended) should also be available to what it called the Other Backward Castes (OBC). Since the SC/ST had 22.5 per cent reservations in all educational seats and jobs, the Mandal Commission said a further 27 per cent should be given to the OBC. After an extensive investigation, it listed 3743 jatis (sub-castes) which fell within the deprived category. The enumeration was based on the 1931 census, since caste data had not been collected in subsequent censuses.

The Mandal Commission not only argued for affirmative action to combat discrimination and deprivation, but also advocated the use of caste status as the best indicator of such deprivation. In the early years of the independence movement, and even in the Nehru era, the ideal had been to create a casteless/classless society. By making caste a passport to reservations, the Mandal Commission entrenched caste as a permanent feature of society. Now, there was an incentive to treasure caste membership as a badge of backwardness. Unlike race, caste is not a physical marker and can be disowned if required. When caste Hindus converted to other religions they lost their caste but not their economic and social deprivation. The Mandal Commission was thus privileging Hindu society as especially marked for favourable treatment in case of deprivation. Some Christian 'castes' of Kerala, however, were listed among the eligible OBCs. Muslims in India also have 'castes', but they did not qualify.

The rationale behind the demand for such reservations was the slow growth of the Indian economy over the previous forty years. Access to higher education provided entry to government jobs, and if, somehow, such jobs could also be additionally ensured, then the claimant was on to a tenured, well-paid job with an inflation-indexed salary, not to mention the many opportunities for receiving bribes. There had been a de facto 'reservation' for the upper castes for such jobs as they were better educated, better connected, though most of them undoubtedly believed that it was merit which had got them where they were. But political power had been passing from the minority upper castes to the majority OBCs across India, but especially in the North. Now the power of the Yadav parties in UP and Bihar lent some clout to the Mandal recommendations. In South India the anti-Brahmin movement had long preceded Independence, and the Mandal recommendations caused no trouble.

There was widespread protest across North India by upper-caste youth, and some examples of self-immolations, strikes, riots, etc. As usual in Indian controversies, someone moved the court, and the Supreme Court gave a stay order pending its judgement. The V.P. Singh government did not last long, nor did the Chandra Shekhar one, which had come to power with outside support from the Congress. New elections were held in 1991 in which Congress won 244 seats, partly as a result of Rajiv Gandhi's assassination. Rajiv Gandhi's widow, Sonia Gandhi was offered the prime ministership, but she declined as she was even less interested in politics than her husband, and she had two children to bring up. The job went to P.V. Narasimha Rao, a politician from Andhra Pradesh who had been home minister at the time of the anti-Sikh pogroms in Delhi. He had been in the top echelons of the Congress for a long time. He was a linguist, and became the first South Indian to become prime minister of India. Seven out of the eight previous PMs had been from UP, the exception being Morarji Desai. Rao thus became only the second Congressman from outside the Nehru family to become PM after Shastri.

Both the Congress and BJP had been shy of endorsing the Mandal recommendations. They were, after all, competing for upper-caste votes and had Brahmin leadership. (Rajiv Gandhi's father was a Parsi, but Feroze Gandhi has been written out of the family's history. Rajiv is considered a Hindu and a Brahmin like his mother and grandfather.) The Congress had catered to upper-caste needs and desires for forty years. Now it had to change its tune to stay alive. In UP and Bihar, the Yadav parties—the SP and the RJD—led by Mulayam Singh Yadav and Lalu Prasad Yadav respectively, had established dominance in what used to be Congress strongholds. They not only had majority Hindu OBC votes, but were also favoured by the Muslims. Electoral compulsions dictated that Congress accommodate the OBCs.

Narasimha Rao implemented the Mandal Commission recommendations in 1991; the total reservations went up to 49.5 per cent. The upper-caste middle classes now had to concede that they would be crowded out of the elite institutions of higher education and government jobs; the democratic compulsions of majority voting were beginning to come home to them. In any other polity, a privileged class would have fought hard to retain its perks. The Indian middle classes lacked cohesion and no party, not even the BJP promised to rescind Mandal. Luckily for them, something else happened which relieved their distress.

ECONOMIC RENAISSANCE

Rajiv Gandhi had continued the policy of borrowing from abroad to lift the import constraint on the economy by extending the lending sources to private lenders, in addition to the IMF and World Bank. This had boosted growth, but he had not reformed the economy sufficiently and its export orientation was still weak. India piled up foreign debt of $70 billion of which $30 billion was owed to private creditors, many of them NRI (Non-Resident Indians). Much of this was serviceable, thanks to the remittances of Indian workers abroad, especially in the oil-exporting Gulf countries. India's remittances totalled $2 billion at this stage. But then Iraq invaded Kuwait, and war broke out between the UN-sanctioned forces led by USA and Iraq. The flow of remittances dried up and India hit the buffers. By mid-1991, the foreign exchange reserves were only sufficient for two weeks' imports. India had the humiliating experience of having to pawn its gold reserves, physically transferring them to London to obtain short term credit. IMF credits followed. Normally, it is enough to pledge the gold stock by giving proof of its existence in a store within the borrowing country. But India had to transfer the gold physically. Indicative of the state of the country, the van carrying the gold to the airport for loading on to an aircraft broke down en route.

India was lucky in its adversity. A new non-dynasty prime minister had already chosen a seasoned economist who had been a technocrat as well as an academic—Dr Manmohan Singh. He had a BA from Britain's Cambridge University and had written his DPhil thesis at Oxford on the subject of exports. He had taught in Punjab and Delhi universities, and had also been a high official in the ministries of commerce and finance. He had held the posts of governor of the Reserve Bank of India and deputy chairman of the Planning Commission. Most recently, he had been in Geneva as Secretary of the South Commission and had seen, first-hand, the new liberalizing trends in economic policy. Eastern Europe had already left the Soviet camp after the fall of the Berlin Wall in September 1989, and the USSR was on its last legs. Manmohan Singh was given his head by Rao and told to be bold since the hour demanded it. Singh surprised everyone by seizing his chance, belying his cautious, self-effacing exterior persona.

The rupee was devalued and the old licence-permit raj began to be dismantled. Import quotas were converted into tariffs and tariffs were put on a downward escalator. India began to liberalize its economy and adopt market-friendly policies after forty-four years of rejection and restricted growth. In some ways this was a revolutionary act of economic policymaking. In fact, India was beginning to question the entire nationalist story of why India was poor. The reasons were not in British rule or, even, de-industrialization. They were in India's mistaken reading of its own economic history and its suppression of its own entrepreneurial class.

India was, after all, one of the earliest countries to have modern factory production, railways and modern banking, as well as property rights and the rule of law. Despite overall poverty and illiteracy, its small elite was large enough to be able to provide the personnel for modern corporations. Old business families had adapted to Western practices and textile mills had sprung up all over the country. Sir Jamshedji Tata had shown enterprise by building a steel mill in face of British scepticism in the early twentieth century, and there was a can-do attitude among India's business classes, despite a hostile foreign government. The Depression and nationalist struggle shaped the vision of the Congress and, in Nehru's case, this was exacerbated by his visceral dislike of private business. So upon Independence, even though India possessed a most enterprising group of businessmen, they were restricted in what they could produce, and how much, and by what technology, and at what price they could sell their products. The private sector was hobbled by quotas, licences, permits and, in general, infantilized.

Such policies were in fashion, of course. The teaching of economics at Cambridge, UK, where many of India's top economists were trained, particularly exaggerated market failure and the need to replace government control on the market. In the UK itself, this had marginal influence as there were other economic schools around, such as Oxford and LSE which favoured a more free market approach. But the LSE had its Left-wing influence on many students who were enthralled by Harold Laski, a professor and a prominent socialist of his times. In India, the effects of the combination of Cambridge economics and LSE politics were devastating. For the first thirty years, policy makers made a virtue of perversely interfering with market prices, and the greater the distance was between market prices and controlled ones, the more vindicated they felt. The most charitable thing one can say is that Nehru years were better than the Indira Gandhi years. Economic dogma became much harder in her regime.

The policy makers did not have to suffer the consequences of their actions. It was the unemployed and the poor who did. Now, the release of the energy of the economy was like a miracle cure. It coincided with the new phase of globalization when private capital began to flow much more to emerging economies, and markets in the rich countries opened up to imports from around the world, thanks to the new GATT/WTO framework. India, which had been crippled by export pessimism, now yielded to export optimism. In particular, India was able to win export orders in software services, where its familiarity with English and its large pool of literate and numerate graduates was a winning card.

Industries were de-licensed and opened to private capital, domestic and foreign. The old, established economic coterie warned of a debt trap and predicted a meltdown. Socialism, the great Nehru–Gandhi legacy, was being abandoned. But Rao persisted and backed his finance minister. There were now enough graduates from US universities, (among them Dr C. Rangarajan, the governor of the Reserve Bank of India who had a doctorate from the University of Pennsylvania), who had absorbed the free market message to lend support. After a difficult first year, growth rates bounced up to above 6 per cent, an unprecedented level. If 1972– 82 had registered a dismal 3.5 per cent, and 1982–92 5.2 per cent, the decade of 1992–2002 achieved 6 per cent. Per capita income growth rate rose from1.2 per cent to 3 and, finally, 3.9 per cent.

India was just a late arrival on the Asian economic miracle bandwagon. South Korea and Taiwan, Singapore and Hong Kong had shown the way in the 1970s by adopting aggressive export-led industrial growth policies. They had used public taxes and subsidies wisely to encourage profitable and competitive enterprises. In the 1980s China joined Malaysia, Indonesia, Thailand and the Philippines on the same path. Asia, which had been proverbially a poor, overpopulated continent, was now in the vanguard of emerging economies and ahead of Latin America on manufacturing exports and, of course, Africa. It had high savings ratios, high literacy (except India) and habits of hard work and family security nets. Asian capitalism made waves, and the West began to take note as it came to invest and profit from the Asian miracle. During the late1960s, there was a fashionable Leninist–Maoist prediction that the communist revolution would come out of the East and swamp the West. A revolution did come out of the East, and it did impress, if not, as yet, overwhelm the West, but it was Asian capitalism that did it, not Asian communism. When it finally came, it swept over Mao's China as well.

Even so, the Rao government had to overcome much political resistance to such policies. The Left parties were against them, and the regional and caste parties had no interest in growth, only in redistributive populism. As Somnath Chatterjee, leader of the CPI(M) speaking in Lok Sabha in March 1992, said of the President's address to both houses of Parliament, 'If one goes through the Address, one hears the voice, not of the President of a vibrant and progressive India, but the voice of a President of a country which has lost its self-reliance and self-dignity . . . The Address is the product of a Government which is in bondage, a Government which is on leash led by the nose by the combine of Bush, Camdessus and Preston who have become the arbiters of our nation.'[1] (Bush is President George H.W. Bush, Camdessus is Michel Camdessus, Managing Director of IMF, and Preston is William Preston, President of World Bank.)

The BJP was broadly supportive of the liberalization, but reluctant to give up its oppositionist stance. It flirted for a while with being a champion of Nehruvian policies, which it had always opposed. It had an ultra-nationalist faction from the RSS, which wanted to exclude all foreign capital from India. This led to the launch of Swadesh Jagaran Manch (National Awakening Platform), which, in many ways, mirrored Left policies. It was only their Hindu extremist agenda which made the saffron forces anathema for the reds. Indian liberal reform, the admitting of foreign firms into India, was resisted for a while, even by Indian capitalists who formed the Bombay Club to urge the government to hasten slowly. Luckily, they were ignored, and then they rose magnificently to the challenge of competing with the best from abroad.

There was less boldness in reforming the peculiar laws which restrict hiring and firing in large firms—large firms being defined as those employing more than a hundred workers. These laws have prevented India from starting low-tech industries which can employ large numbers of unskilled or semi-skilled manual workers. China has invested a lot of its resources in these sectors, and won export markets abroad. It was also the strategy of the other Asian Tigers such as Malaysia, Taiwan, Indonesia, all of whom had much lower level of industrialization than India at the time of their independence. Protecting jobs in the privileged organized sector is what the Indian Left calls socialism, and that is the way it has been for sixty years in India. There was also opposition to the 'divesting' of publicly-owned firms to the private sector—'privatization' being too charged a word for India's politicians. The problem is that the myriad loss-making enterprises in the public sector are hard to sell, and the Left regards the profitable ones as too precious—indeed as precious as *navaratna*s (jewels)—to be sold.

After three years of reform, Rao became cautious and pulled back his finance minister. Yet, enough had been done to change the climate of opinion. Results followed quickly, and businesses were won over. There was here an escape for the middle classes. They could leave the race for government jobs to the SC/ST and OBC, since there were now better-paying private sector jobs. There was also enough money and sufficient relaxation of foreign exchange rules to enable the middle classes to send their children abroad to study. The shock of Mandal was softened. But this also meant that the middle class withdrew from politics, leaving it to the professional politician, who had, more often than not, joined politics to make money. Soon, criminal elements entered politics as agents for the various caste factions and sat in the legislatures with impunity and even, in a few cases, with immunity. The quality of Indian politics began to slide.

THE RAMA REVOLUTION

The biggest crisis the Rao government faced was, predictably, on the Hindu–Muslim front. Rajiv Gandhi had allowed the unlocking of the corner of Babri Masjid where the installation of the Ram lalla idols had been carried out in 1949. This legacy now came back to haunt Rao. Rajiv's concession had inflamed passions rather than doused them. The BJP and the VHP, along with the RSS (known collectively as the *parivar*, or family) had made the liberation of the site, Ramjanmabhoomi, their major goal. The BJP had increased its parliamentary strength from a meagre two in 1984 to eighty-six in 1989. It was now within the sight of ruling Delhi. The temple–mosque (mandir–masjid) issue was the launching pad. The first step in this campaign was in 1990 when the vice chairman of the BJP, L.K. Advani embarked on a *rath-yatra*, a journey in a souped-up Toyota van dressed up as a chariot which was redolent of the old epics. He travelled 6000 miles through North India, from the Somnath temple in Gujarat to Ayodhya, to highlight the issue. V.P. Singh could not deal with this defiant gesture as he needed BJP support to stay in office. Lalu Yadav, the chief minister of Bihar, proved his secular credentials by arresting Advani when he was passing through Bihar. Many VHP volunteers went to the Ayodhya site to rebuild the temple; they were called *kar sevak*s—literally 'servants engaged in a holy task'. Their goal was to destroy the old mosque and build a temple in its place. This was a fundamental defiance of the secular nature of the Indian state. Mulayam Singh Yadav, the chief minister of UP and, like Lalu Yadav, a fellow traveller on the secular path, detained them en route, and those who reached Ayodhya were tear-gassed.

The battle lines were now drawn. Indian politics in the 1990s were to swivel around the secular–communal divide, and anti-Congressism was joined by anti-BJPism. In 1991 the BJP increased its presence in the Lok sabha to 120 seats. It won Uttar Pradesh as well as Madhya Pradesh,

Rajasthan and Himachal Pradesh. Except for Bihar, the old 1857 region was now a BJP stronghold. Rama, the god–king was obviously a good electoral asset. The Congress was in power in Delhi, and knew the crisis would recur. It also knew that the UP government was now on the side of the demolishers. But Rao was cautious rather than decisive. Some accuse him of being in sympathy with the cause. His record during the Delhi anti-Sikh pogrom of 1984 did not inspire much confidence. While Indira Gandhi and, even perhaps, Rajiv Gandhi would have put on a show of force, Rao tried to placate the VHP. But the parivar had the bit between its teeth now. On 6 December 1992, after publicly announcing the event, the VHP and the Bajrang Dal—the latter in the forefront—attacked the mosque and demolished it. The government TV channel, Doordarshan did not carry the footage, but CNN and BBC—widely available in India—did.

It was an ironic rerun of the demolition of the Berlin Wall. The UP government had played host to the rioters and kept the police on a leash. Central government security units were ordered to stay away from the spot by the Delhi government. It was not a spontaneous act, but meticulously planned. No one was charged at the time, and none has been as yet punished seventeen years later. Arun Shourie, an intellectual in the BJP, wrote of the event, 'Hindus have now realised that they are in very large numbers, that their sentiment is shared by those who man the apparatus of the state and that they can bend the state to their will.'[2]

This was the most blatant act of defiance of the law in modern Indian history, and the Indian state had stood by helpless or, worse still, approving. In the following month, communal riots broke out all over India. Muslims felt, for the first time in sixty years, that they were orphans in India, whatever the amended preamble to the Constitution might say about its being a secular socialist democratic republic. Indeed, 1992 was the watershed for Indian nationhood when the Congress, as the guardian of the Nehruvian narrative, gave up its time-honoured role. From this point, it would be the OBC parties of the Yadavs as well as the Left who would be the unfailing champions of the Muslim minority.

Matters did not improve during the month-long mayhem. In Bombay (now Mumbai, thanks to the Shiv Sena insisting on Marathi re-labelling everywhere), the ruling Congress government also abandoned the Muslims to their fate. The police intervened, often feebly, and their inclination appeared more to arrest Muslims rather than check the Hindu mob. It was the Delhi 1984 anti-Sikh saga all over again; only the victimized minority was the largest in India. India's 140 million Muslims, the second largest concentration of Muslims in the world, had to defend themselves from this point on. Eventually the army had to intervene, and it took ten days to bring the riots under control. It is estimated that 2000 died across North India and Gujarat; 800 were killed in Mumbai of whom 600 were Muslims. I was in Bombay at the time, delivering a public lecture[3] where I spoke in favour of the economic reforms. My hosts insisted that I go from my downtown hotel, the Taj (which was later attacked by terrorists in November 2008), to the airport only with an army escort. It was a chilling experience in a city where I had spent eleven happy years.

The global climate was changing in another sinister way. The war against the Soviet Union in Afghanistan had successfully concluded in favour of the many Afghan groups which had fought the Russian occupation. The group which was ultimately victorious was the Islamic fundamentalist Taliban. American aid had created the monster it would have to fight in the 1990s. During the Afghan war the Americans had used Pakistan as a base to pass arms and ammunition to the guerrilla groups. And the war situation had resulted—inevitably—in a surge of drug trafficking. In 1988 President Zia-ul-Haq had died in a plane crash which, by all accounts, was a conspiracy. His death brought democracy back to Pakistan, but the influence of fundamentalist Islamic forces on Pakistan also increased. This allowed many guerrilla forces from Afghanistan to switch their operations to the Kashmir border with India. Jammu and Kashmir had gone through an election in 1987, but even after fifteen years of peace, Delhi could not resist rigging the poll to ensure a victory for the party of Sheikh Abdullah, now headed by his son, Farooq Abdullah. This was the signal for much local unrest signalled by the rise of openly separatist parties, including the Jammu and Kashmir Liberation Front (JKLF), and the infiltration of terrorist groups such as Jaish-e-Mohammad (JeM) and others across the Line of Control (LOC) into the Indian side of Kashmir. The 1991 war against Iraq in the wake of its invasion of Kuwait—Operation Desert Storm— led to further retaliation from Islamist groups in Kashmir, as also across the world.

In New York, in 1993, there was an attempt to blow up the World Trade Centre by driving a van loaded with explosives. This was the advent of the global Islamist movement led by Osama Bin Laden. India was added to the many centres which were to be targets of the terror threat. Kashmir had become part of the global struggle that the Islamists were fighting against the infidels, and after Babri Masjid, they directed their sights to the rest of India as well. In March 1993 bombs exploded in Mumbai's commercial centre. The death toll was 300, and responsibility was claimed by a local gang leader, Dawood Ibrahim, who managed to escape to Pakistan. Unlike in the December riots, this time the police quickly arrested many Muslims who were charged with acts of terrorism. A prominent film star, Sanjay Dutt, was arrested. Sanjay Dutt is the son of one of Bollywood's most famous star couples. His mother, Nargis, a Muslim, was a legendary film heroine; his father, Sunil Dutt, a Hindu, was also a very successful actor who later became a Congress MP. The trials took place thirteen years later, and the final verdict is still not out. For the December 1992 riots, a commission of inquiry was appointed under the chairmanship of Justice Srikrishna; his report listed the likely culprits, but they are too powerful in Mumbai politics to be brought to book.[4]

THE FRACTURED POLITY

After the demolition of the Babri Masjid, Indian politics lost its innocence. And due to trends which had been gathering pace since the mid-1970s, it also became fractured. In 1996 the Congress lost its place as the largest single party, ceding the position to the BJP which won 161 seats. A new era dawned in which only fragile coalitions could hold office. The BJP formed a government which lasted only thirteen days, and was replaced by a rag-tag coalition of Left parties and several regional parties, united solely on the platform of being anti-BJP. The Congress did not join the coalition. The Congress had now declined from 401 seats in 1984 to 140 seats in 1996, but it still hoped that in another election it would regain its status as the sole dominant party. It had lost UP and Bihar—Muslim voters abandoned the Congress after the Babri Masjid episode. The upper-caste Hindus, once a Congress vote bank, had defected to the BJP and the OBCs had their own Yadavs to back. It was only thanks to the South that Congress survived at all.

From this time on there would not only be no single party governments, but even the two major national parties, the Congress and the BJP, saw their share of the votes sink. The overwhelming advantage of the first past the post system, which gave the Congress a disproportionate share of the seats relative to the share of votes over forty years, was triggered by a vote share of 30 per cent or above. By the 1990s no party could aspire to such a large share. Smaller parties had a field day. Their narrow clientelist concerns now moved centre stage. Kanshi Ram, a Dalit intellectual, who had built up the Bahujan Samaj Party (BSP), a Dalit party in UP, argued that the lower orders of Indian society had nothing to lose, indeed much to gain, from such a fractured polity. They could leverage their small number of seats to secure effective gains in the allocation of public goods and patronage. Stable, one party-dominated governments were upper-caste monopolies which, according to him, neglected his people.[5]

It is a profound insight. This is, in one sense, the happy result of fifty years of electoral practice which had schooled those who would never have had any clout in any previous age of Indian history, British, Mughal, Afghan or Hindu. Now they could leverage their small numbers into enough seats to make or break coalitions. This meant a proliferation of identities for Indian citizens. No longer was one just an Indian, but a Dalit or OBC, and even within that large group a Yadav or a Jat or a Kurmi. Or one was Muslim, a precarious identity which required the protection of a strong agent party. The Brahmin vote coalesced with similar upper-caste ones and chose among the supplicant parties for their preference. The Mandal process, along with the sluggish economic growth of the first thirty if not forty years after Independence, and the ease of mobilization thanks to the huge growth in local language press and, after 1991, private TV channels resulted in many such small crystals of identity which could claim a political party at the national and/or the regional level. The Indian national narrative was beginning to fragment into many shards.

The 1996–98 interregnum was yet another Janata-type fiasco. Two prime ministers, I.K. Gujral and Deve Gowda were added to the ever lengthening list of Indian PMs. India was becoming like the Fourth Republic in France or, even, Italy which went through governments at astonishing speed. Jyoti Basu—the veteran leader of the CPI(M) and the politician with the longest record of serving as chief minister of West Bengal or, indeed, of any state in India—was suggested as the best candidate for the PM position, and so he would have been. But his party resolved not to let him have the job which it later regretted. Jyoti Basu as PM could have held the coalition together much better than either of the other two did. The government may even have lasted longer than two years. The United Left governments slowed down but did not reverse the economic reforms. This was largely due to P. Chidambaram who had been minister of commerce in the Rao government and a part of the reform team. His small breakaway party in Tamil Nadu had joined the 1996 coalition, and he was made the finance minister. He tried his best to keep the Left detractors of the reforms at bay. They made a very generous settlement for public employees' pay in exceeding the recommendations of the statutory Pay Commission. This triggered large deficits in the budgets at the Centre and in the states. But after having followed this scorched earth policy, the government was finally replaced in the 1998 elections.

The efforts to have an anti-BJP coalition did not work, and BJP came to power with 182 seats and the support of many minor parties such as the Telugu Desam, the Samata Party, the DMK, among others. Congress went up from 140 to 141 seats, and this despite the entry of Sonia Gandhi, Rajiv's widow into politics. The old firm was back in action after seven years of withdrawal. Sonia Gandhi tried in her first year as

MP to have a no-confidence motion passed against the NDA, as the BJP-led coalition was called. She succeeded, but could not show that she had the numbers to form an alternative government. New elections were called, in which the BJP repeated its 182 seats. The Congress sunk to 114 seats, its lowest tally in fifty-one years.

The BJP was tied down by its coalition partners, which included some secular parties. The conduct of coalitions was now being systematized. There was a common agreed programme between the partners with a point person who managed the politics of the coalition. The veteran socialist, George Fernandes of the Samata Party performed this role in the NDA, monitoring the implementation of the common programme. The BJP had to abandon some of its cherished Hindutva goals, including rebuilding the Ayodhya temple. The whole temple issue was now tied down in Supreme Court and was to fester without conclusion. This was perhaps one positive outcome of the fractured polity: no party had sufficient strength to ride roughshod over Parliament as Indira Gandhi did.

Atal Bihari Vajpayee proved to be a conciliatory figure, though the Opposition accused him of being just the mask (*mukhota*) covering the Hindu fundamentalist BJP. The BJP tested a nuclear device and India openly joined the nuclear club in 1998. Pakistan responded by exploding its own nuclear device. The India–Pakistan border region was now classified by the US National Security Council as one of the most dangerous in the world. A meeting took place in Lahore, Pakistan, soon after the nuclear tests in February 1999 between the two prime ministers, Pakistan's Nawaz Sharif and India's A.B. Vajpayee. Vajpayee had been a reconciliatory foreign minister during the first Janata government, and he reached out again.

Three months later, there was a serious military confrontation between the two countries, the first since 1971. Pakistan managed to surprise India by occupying the heights of the Kargil mountains on the Indian side. The war that followed began with an attack to repulse enemy troops who had made deep incursions into the Indian territory. In 1962 the Chinese had succeeded; in 1999 the Pakistan Army did not. The war came as a rude shock to India, coming so soon after Vajpayee's placatory gesture in travelling to Lahore, but there is some evidence that Sharif may not have been kept informed by his army. Sharif was soon overthrown in a military coup by General Pervez Musharraf who had led the Kargil assault. Pakistan became a dictatorship again after ten years of an uneasy democracy.

For India, a war on the border has always been a national integration event. A war with Pakistan was likely to be more fraught after the Babri Masjid incident, but the national joy at the victory and the sorrow for the 500 soldiers dead were genuine. In a fractured polity with competing narratives of nationhood, the army is one institution which is genuinely national and loved as such. For India territorial integrity remains the one theme that binds.

KASHMIR: THE PERENNIAL PROBLEM

Vajpayee surprised everyone by not giving up on a dialogue with Pakistan on matters of mutual concern. For Pakistan Kashmir remains the central, if not the sole, problem. It was not until I spent a month in Islamabad in the summer of 1998, during the last months of Nawaz Sharif's regime, that I realized how much Pakistani nationalist imagination is engaged with Kashmir. It almost defines its national identity, though more because Pakistan does not have Kashmir. Almost all Pakistanis think it obvious that Kashmir should belong to Pakistan, and cannot understand why the world does not see the justice of its claims. Pakistan refers repeatedly to the UN resolutions of 1948 which have been ignored by India. But it knows, and Kargil brought home to it once more, that a military victory over India leading to the possession of Kashmir is well-nigh impossible. The non-solution of the Kashmir problem eats away at Pakistan's sense of its nationhood.

India, on the other hand, is more concerned with the vulnerability of Kashmir to terrorist infiltration from across the border, and the likelihood of secessionist groups within its side of the border getting an upper hand. For India the possession of Kashmir is a proof of its secularism, or its ability to give the large Muslim minority a sense of belonging. To that end, it is willing to station a large number of troops in the Valley to make sure that the situation does not get out of control. The desire to micromanage Kashmir's democracy is intense, even to the point of making the entire effort ineffective. Most Indians cannot abide the thought that within their borders in Kashmir, there are actually people who would rather join Pakistan or even seek independence from India. India also knows that it has Kashmir in its possession, and there is little that anyone can do about it. It is India's international image that is sullied by Kashmir, because of its image as a militarily-occupied region and because of the many violations of human rights that routinely occur there. Though few Indians would admit it—and some perhaps are unaware of it—the ruling elite knows it well enough.

Within the state of Jammu and Kashmir there is a further distance between the largely Hindu Jammu area and the Muslim Valley. There have been bitter complaints by the pandits, the community traditionally based in and around Jammu, that they have been displaced from their homes and that Congress governments tolerated such anti-Hindu behaviour in order to appease the Muslims. But the BJP also did not change the situation when it came to power. The issue is thus both internally divisive within Jammu and Kashmir and also within India along the communal–secular divide. India wants the world to believe that Jammu and Kashmir is a multi-religious, democratic province. To international observers or likely mediators, it says bluntly that it is a problem for bilateral solution. The British Labour Party politician, Robin Cook, when he became Foreign Secretary, thought he could offer to solve the problem. In Britain the Labour Party itself had had views from both sides represented by the diaspora—Pakistani and Indian immigrants—immigrants from Mirpur which is in Pakistan Occupied Kashmir (called 'Azad Kashmir' in Pakistan) as well from the Indian side of Kashmir (known as 'Held Kashmir' in Pakistan). The Kashmir issue figured regularly at the annual conference of the Labour Party. Cook, an intellectual, felt he had the empathy, and as Foreign Secretary of the former imperial power, was in a position to tackle the perennial problem. He was most politely told to mind his own business when he visited India in 1997.

President Musharraf and the Indian prime minister, Vajpayee met in Agra in January 2001. The occasion was symbolic rather than substantial. Yet, the fact that the dialogue took place was in itself a positive step. The terrorist attacks in Kashmir continued, and there was an assault on the Indian Parliament building in December 2001. Though the attackers were killed by the police guarding the building, it was a bold move. Also during the NDA/BJP tenure, a stunning hijack had taken place of an Indian aircraft, IC-814 on its way from Kathmandu to Delhi which was diverted to Kandahar. To get the hostages back, the foreign minister, Jaswant Singh was forced to negotiate and release Maulana Massod Azhar, leader of the terrorist group Jaish-e-Mohammad, who had been previously jailed in India for terrorist offences.

These events had a double impact. First: the official dialogue, once opened, continued despite strains from the frequent terrorist attacks (and did so until the Mumbai attacks of November 2008). Vajpayee cemented his reputation as an international statesman who could rise above the routine Muslim-bashing sentiments of his party. It showed that BJP could afford to parley with Pakistan since it had a 'tough' image. The Congress, until then, was reputed to have some degree of guilt about Kashmir as it was under Nehru that the problem was left unresolved in the first instance. Second: when it came to terrorism, India was exposed as a soft state.

India's attitude to terrorism is influenced by its own internal Hindu–Muslim divide. Since the Islamist terrorists are Muslims and also much given to a display of religious sentiments, India's Muslims are put on the defensive. For the secularist, the first concern, when faced with news of a terrorist attack, is to ensure that no communal violence erupts as a result. So the first response is denial of Muslim involvement and/or attribution of responsibility for the act to the police, calling it a 'fake encounter' etc. For the Hindu nationalist, such acts of terrorism are just another proof that all Muslims are traitors and agents of Pakistan. These two attitudes are represented by political parties which arrange themselves on the secular–communal axes. The terrorist is not just a criminal to be convicted regardless of his religion; he becomes a political football in India, for either side to score points.

A THRIVING ECONOMY

The reform process was given a further push by the NDA/BJP government. For once, business had a government in charge which had little truck with old Left dogma and no ideological commitment to Nehruvian policies. The political weakness of successive governments proved a boon for the private sector. Once the Rao government had opened the bottle, the genie had escaped and no one had the power to put it back. Successive governments pushed reforms along and saw much prosperity. India began to feel confident and good about itself. Centuries-old feelings of victimhood vis-à-vis the West began to go away as India began to register victories abroad: Indian women won Miss World and Miss Universe contests; Indian software firms became global competitors for outsourced business; and Hindustani films, known as Bollywood, began to penetrate the Western market, thanks to the large and prosperous diaspora whose own stories Bollywood began to relate. The three Bs— Beauty, Bytes and Bollywood—worked like a tonic to the Indian psyche.

India's GDP growth rate kept up. The average 6 per cent was maintained against much scepticism from the old guard, who were still sad that the Nehru–Gandhi path had been abandoned. The government had a successful disinvestment programme, and steadily relaxed the limits on the share of foreign capital in Indian industrial sectors. As the new century and, indeed, the new millennium opened, India was back to what it must have been like in the sixteenth century at the time of the arrival of the Portuguese—a global trading nation with a reputation for efficiency where foreigners flocked to make money. India's rise followed the much more spectacular rise of China, but now India and China began to be bracketed together as miracle economies.

Indian business responded to the opening up of the economy magnificently. Old business houses, which had been around for a century and more and had survived lean times during the Nehru–Gandhi era, now managed to throw up a new generation of young managers from within their ranks who could take on the global competition challenge. The Bombay Club of fearful entrepreneurs was a thing of the past. Now, in automobile parts, in IT and communications, in the drugs and fashion industries, India was making its mark. New entrepreneurs and world class managers emerged to take Indian business to new frontiers across the globe. Globalization proved to be good for India. Indian businesses began to take over companies abroad. Tata took over Tetley Tea and Corus, a merger of British Steel and a Dutch company. L.N. Mittal became the largest steel producer in the world by a suitable series of mergers and acquisitions.

The Indian government had long taken an active part in the production and distribution of goods which could be made as well by private as by public enterprise. This was not the most efficient use of resources. Its choice of sectors to invest in and its rigid labour laws, between them, had meant that manufacturing had stagnated at 25 per cent of the economy in terms of its share of GDP, providing largely skilled employment in the capital intensive industries. Agriculture was now 20 per cent but 60 per cent of the population depended on it, while services had grown to account for 55 per cent of the output with only 20 per cent of the labour force employed in it. The services sector had thrived because of government neglect; it was not part of the planners' vision which engaged only with industrial machinery. But this meant that the bulk of the economy was stuck in low productivity agriculture, and this is where poverty was concentrated. Agriculture grew at most at 4 per cent, frequently even slower. In any case, unless many of the rural poor were moved to full-time industrial jobs, they were not likely to escape poverty.

Economists began to study poverty and its root causes seriously in the 1970s. The realization soon came that redistribution of existing income, even if feasible, did not provide a sustainable cure for poverty. The cure was in equipping the poor with access to education and skills, which made them employable. Being in paid work was the most reliable antidote to poverty. This required good health and access to the places where the jobs were. So good health care and an infrastructure which allowed the poor to get to places where work was available, were other necessary elements in any anti-poverty programme. The Indian government was against any relaxation of labour laws and, therefore, there was little possibility of providing unskilled and semi-skilled people with good round-the-year jobs. Most anti-poverty programmes gave some help to small farmers and subsidies, which provided employment more as relief schemes than as regular paid work. A lot of money spent on fighting poverty did not actually reach the poor, but was gobbled up along the way by the bureaucracy. Rajiv Gandhi once publicly stated that of every rupee spent on an anti-poverty programme by the government, only 15 per cent reached the poor. His statement was based on research he had commissioned, and it was never challenged. It was also not followed up to improve the trickle down.

A larger proportion of government subsidies went to the better-off in both rural and urban areas. In a poor country, many more can use the rhetoric of poverty and redistribution than is strictly deserved. So farmers had guaranteed output prices, subsidized supplies of fertilizers (home-made, so expensive relative to imports), water (thereby leading to overuse and consequent depletion of the water table in many regions) and power (leading to large registered losses by state-owned electricity companies). Urban middle classes had subsidized petrol for their cars, which meant that the government-owned oil companies had to be advanced money to meet the deficits (the latest estimate of the subsidy in 2008 was $50 billion). Bank loans were given at subsidized rates to farmers (given away by politicians at loan *melas*—literally 'fairs') as well as to public sector companies, most of whom were loss-making. One estimate in 2000 was that government subsidies to the middle classes cost 15 per cent of the GDP.[6]

The Indian policy makers meant well but they were stuck in an old model. They asserted that the state was a better provider of 'goods and services' than the market, but did not see that that statement is not universally valid. There are things that the state can do better than the market, and vice versa. The Indian state manufactured industrial products at a high cost, which could be better made privately. The fact that they were more expensive than what could be bought internationally, required tariff barriers and import quotas to keep the cheaper goods out. But at the same time, farmers were insulated from the markets by restrictions placed on the flow of agricultural products even within the country. They could not export, even if they could get a better price abroad. It was when India signed the WTO treaty in 1994 that the calculations of tariff burdens on different sectors revealed that agriculture was subject to a *negative* tariff of 45 per cent matching a similar positive protection for industry. Thus, India's poor farmers were paying for the expensive industrial baubles, which the planner had produced, to satisfy the conceit of the upper-caste/upper-class nationalists. Of course, those who were making such policies had no idea the damage they were causing. But the truth, when it was revealed, did surprise many policy makers.

While the state had made things which the private sector could have made better and cheaper, it had neglected the tasks that the private sector finds difficult to perform—providing primary and secondary education, primary health care and provision of clean water. Governments in the states, whose responsibility it was to provide education for children, misused the opportunity by appointing their chosen party members and their relations to posts of teachers. The task of such teachers was not to be at school to teach, but stick around and serve party political masters. North India was the worst culprit in this respect. The reason was the familiar one—lack of a social revolution empowering the lower castes in the North, unlike the century-long experience of the anti-Brahmin movement in the South. The upper castes secured their power by keeping the lower castes in darkness. Then, during the 1990s and later, private schools became available; poor parents would rather pay to send their children to private schools where a teacher was actually present, than to a free government school. Of course, the government school had full registers: officially, state schools educate everyone—except that they don't.

The Indian state had also neglected providing infrastructure which would connect villages to local town markets and to each other. While telephones were a government monopoly, they were a privilege to have. It was not until the introduction of mobile telephones with private providers by the BJP/NDA government, that the villagers became connected. Roads were lacking for round the year transport, and so were schools, hospitals and easily accessible supplies of fuel and clean water. The daily fetching of water and fuel falls on women, adding to their work burden and inhibiting their education or earning power. Most of the thinking on economic policy in India during the period, where it was supposed to be socialist, ignored the gender dimension of policies. Rural women were the most disadvantaged in terms of literacy, health and work burden.

In 1990 the United Nations Development Programme introduced the concept of human development, which was measured by a Human Development Index. This index was meant to evaluate to what extent a country had travelled the distance between being underdeveloped and developed. The concept put as much emphasis on health and education as on income. Adding together well-calibrated measures of life expectancy, school enrolment and adult literacy, along with income, countries were ranked by their score on the index. India was, and has always been, low in the human development category, at a rank of between 120 and 130 among about 160 countries. India did not do much better than Pakistan, was far worse than Sri Lanka and, of course, China. South-East Asian countries, such as Malaysia and Indonesia, were also way above India in the Human Development Index rankings. Of course, India and Pakistan have the nuclear bomb, which the South-East Asian countries choose not to afford.

Despite these lacunae, there was a dent into India's horrendous poverty numbers. One reason for the change was the continuity of reform policies, albeit at differing pace from one year to the next since 1991. The cumulative impact of a growth rate of 6 per cent plus began to be felt, even on the poorest. Trickle down is, after all, better assured if the water being poured down is a flood rather than a ripple in the first place. India has a series of poverty estimates based on a poverty standard which was fixed in 1972 and has been revised upwards in the light of inflation. A National Sample Survey (NSS) is conducted every five years or so to measure the extent of poverty across rural and urban India. Whenever the results are released, heated scholarly debates take place among the economists and the policy makers. The Left is watchful of any spurious drop in poverty, ever ready to point to flaws in the statistical methodology. The reformers are happy to parade the new successes. International experts take part in these debates, and the results are compared to the other estimates such as those of the World Bank.

For 2004–05, the poverty level for urban people was Rs 552 and for rural India Rs 363 per person per month. The World Bank uses a different poverty standard of $1 per day per person, defined in terms of Purchasing Power Parity (PPP) which makes the estimates internationally comparable. The absolute level of poverty in India as a proportion of the population depends on which standard you choose, but the movements over time in each standard are remarkably similar.[7]

A broad consensual result can be stated as saying that during the decade 1993–94 to 2004–05, the percentage of people below the poverty line (also called the 'head count'), as measured by the NSS, fell from around the mid-thirties (36 per cent) to around the mid-twenties. Here, there are two rival estimates based on different methodologies of recording the expenditure data of households. The differences are arcane and need not detain us. But the result is either 21.8 per cent or 27.5 per cent. As the table below shows, the World Bank results are similar in terms of broad trends, but higher in absolute numbers. Thus poverty comes down from 41.8 per cent to 34.4 per cent using $1 a day standard. To show the fragility of the measurement of poverty, I cite the latest estimates by World Bank which have caused much controversy. It adjusts the $1 a day of 1993 to be worth $1.25 in 2004 terms, instead of $1.08 as it did previously. The upgrade is because the dollar had depreciated relative to the Hong Kong dollar, and Hong Kong prices are used as Hong Kong is the most open market economy. This measure gives a higher 60 per cent estimate for 1993 since the poverty level is higher. But even here, the drop over the ten years is clear. Whichever way it is measured, the proportion of poor in India came down over the ten years of reform. Since however the total population has also risen over those years, the number of poor is still large.

There is unevenness among the different communities as far as poverty is concerned. Thus while the overall incidence is about 22 per cent, the poor SC/ST are 36.4 per cent and 34.8 per cent in urban and rural areas respectively, while poor Muslims are 38.4 per cent and 26.9 per cent in urban and rural areas as proportion of their total numbers. The OBC are somewhere in between, being 25.1 per cent in urban and 19.5 per cent in rural areas.[8]

Poverty Estimates
(percentage of total population below the poverty line)

Agency	1993/94	2004/05
GOI	36	21.8/27.5
WB	41.8	34.4 ($1.08 PPP/1993$)
WB	60	42 ($1.25PPP/2005$)

Key: GOI: Government of India; WB: World Bank

CONCLUSION

The drift in politics may have been caused by the slow pace of the reduction in poverty. Of course, the fact that the growth upturn after 1991, and especially after 1998, speeded up the rate of reduction in poverty did not impact on politics immediately. Even in pure economic relationships there are long lags between cause and effect. How the resurgence of the Indian economy, after forty plus years of stagnation, would shape its politics and how soon it would do so, remained open questions. India had to cope with some persistent recurring rigidities along with some exciting new trends as the twenty-first century unfolded.

CHAPTER 15

GLOBALIZING INDIA

THE ECONOMY MAY have been undergoing a renaissance, but the polity was marching resolutely backwards to the past. Once again, the Ayodhya temple issue flared up. VHP and its associates had been disappointed by the unwillingness of the NDA/BJP to pursue the temple building issue. But they continued to gather volunteers who took part in building bits and pieces of the final structure, believing it would eventually be part of the new temple that would stand at the site of the old mosque. The actual question of whether this was legally possible was stuck in the courts. But that did not stop much activity. Volunteers—kar sevaks—came from all parts of India, but especially from BJP-ruled states such as Gujarat. They did their work on the temple structure for a while and then returned home.

THE TEN-YEARLY POGROM

One such group was returning from Ayodhya to Ahmedabad by train, when at Godhra station in Gujarat there was an altercation. The story of what happened next is disputed, but the end result was that a carriage was set on fire in which fifty-nine of the kar sevaks died. This happened on 27 February 2002. There followed days of communal riots across Gujarat, a state the BJP had ruled for several years. During the riots, about two thousand Muslims died. Women were raped and Muslim houses burnt, Muslim shops looted and a general economic boycott was forced on the minority community after the riots. The main trouble spots were the capital city of Ahmedabad, Vadodara, Surat and Godhra itself. The police seem once again to have stood by, or actively joined the mob. Reports indicate that in many cases, the mob had a printed list of addresses to identify Muslim houses, which they used. The rioters were middle-class Gujarati Hindus, normally the gentlest of people. Narendra

Modi, the chief minister of Gujarat came in for much criticism, and many hold him culpable for what happened.

The events in Gujarat have been described as genocide; but a more appropriate term would be a pogrom, since this was a short, well-directed episode of violence against a single community. It had all the signs of a planned, if not officially sanctioned, attack. Some Hindus died, but the ratio of Muslims to Hindus was five to one, whereas their proportions in the population are exactly the reverse. The army was called in after some days, and regained control. Many court cases have followed, but far too few given the enormity of what happened. Narendra Modi justified the riots by saying that every action had its own reaction—implying that the burning of the railway carriage in Godhra, allegedly the work of local Muslims, deserved a bloody response.

Atal Bihari Vajpayee, as prime minister, was reportedly deeply upset by the Gujarat riots. He attempted to admonish Modi by reminding him of his *raja dharma*—his duty as a ruler according to classical Hindu doctrine. But the admonition was too feeble to impress either the person to whom it was directed, or the many who were angry, whom it was meant to appease. Vajpayee later changed his tune and blamed the Muslims. He said, 'Wherever Muslims are, they do not want to live with others peacefully.' Vajpayee's reputation as a national statesman, who was capable of rising above the pettiness of his party, was tarnished by the Gujarat episode. He looked weak, ineffective and, then, vindictive. That said, the similarities between Delhi 1984, Bombay 1993 and Gujarat 2002 were uncanny. In each case the executive in power, bolstered by a majority in the legislature, in face of a sudden traumatic event, let loose the fury of a mob, while keeping the police passive. All three were well planned, if at short notice, and led by 'respectable' legislators and members of municipal councils and community leaders almost invariably Hindu. The Bombay and Gujarat riots were shown on 24x7 TV channels, unlike the Delhi riots. India's capacity for officially sanctioned pogroms is a tragic development.

INDIA SHINING

The BJP/NDA government lasted six years in the two phases, winning two elections, one in 1998 and the second in 1999. In a way, Indians were reassured. The fears that the BJP was a fascist party and that, if it ever came to power even with a minority share of the votes, it would do what Hitler did in Germany, proved unjustified. Such fears were frequently expressed by sincere 'secularists' in the early 1990s when the BJP began to get larger number of seats. Yet, they were unfounded. India was a much more robust democracy than Weimar Germany. Gujarat was the one major blot on its record, and this was more a case of a party which could not, or would not, discipline one of its provincial stars. The growth of regional power vis-à-vis Delhi was a phenomenon unforeseen by the makers of the Constitution. India seemed to be returning to the 1935 Act situation which had granted a lot of provincial autonomy. Regional governments could not be forced to adhere to a national policy they did not like except under duress. In the case of the three pogroms—1984, 1993, 2002, the army had to be called in to quell the riots, and assure mark of duress necessary to make recalcitrant regions obey rules of law. As for the 1984 riots, Delhi is both a regional government and the capital city, so the tragedy was doubly unnecessary. Demands for devolution of power from the Centre to the states had gathered pace during the 1990s, and state governments such as the CPI(M)-led one in West Bengal, for instance, had many complaints. Now, even within ruling parties such as the Congress and the BJP, there was much dissidence between Centre and states. The halcyon days when Indira Gandhi could make or unmake chief ministers as she pleased, were gone. The states did not wish to take up the burden of taxation, but they did want a guaranteed and increasing share of the total federal revenues. The Constitution stipulates that a finance commission would report on this issue every five years, and the drift has been very strong towards increasing states' resources. The states' borrowing is covered by the Union guarantee, but the Centre cannot discipline the states about their deficits or debts. Even if such powers were available to the Centre, in the fragile world of coalition politics, this luxury is not available to Union finance ministers. There have been many attempts made by admonition and legislation to bring the overall deficit under control, but the wish, as always, runs ahead of achievement.

As India became subject to global scrutiny from markets and investors, there was a desire, on the part of the Centre at least, to reduce the deficit. What helped was the robust growth performance, which improved the revenue collections. The GDP growth rate began to climb from 6 per cent towards 8 per cent and above. In early 2004 this rate of growth tempted the BJP-led NDA to call general elections, which were, in fact, not due till later in the year. It campaigned on the slogan of 'India Shining', a confident message of a prosperous India displayed in TV commercials which showed mobile telephony in rural India and wide national highways on which happy and satisfied citizens were travelling. That confident message, it was thought, along with the prestige of a nuclear power overseen by a benevolent prime minister, who was, by and large, liked across the nation, would ensure the NDA's re-election.

The BJP had fought elections successfully at the state level on the slogan of '*sadak–bijli–pani*'—roads, electricity, water—and '*roti–kapda–*

makaan'—bread, cloth and a house. The idea this was meant to convey was that the BJP was not a party of temples and religion, but a practical, down-to-earth organization which could deliver basic amenities. The BJP had also given up its long-held ideas of how India should be a unitary state, and granted the demands in three instances to break up larger units and set up smaller states. Thus in Bihar, the tribal area of Jharkhand was carved out as a separate state. In Madhya Pradesh, Chhatisgarh was a similar tribal area, and was made a separate state and Uttarakhand was set up by breaking off parts of UP. This was done because the new buzzword was good governance, and the hope was that smaller states would have governments that would be nearer to the people.

Rajiv Gandhi had pushed the idea of village self-government which was enshrined in the Directive Principles of State Policy in the Constitution. Panchayat raj, or self-government at the village level, had required amendments to the Constitution—the seventy-third and seventy-fourth—to be implemented. These amendments were passed after Rajiv Gandhi's death by the Rao government in 1993. This was a bold experiment in grass-roots government, and it was enhanced by one-third reservations for women in the village panchayat. Of course, it was one thing to set up institutions, and another to invest them with real power. The states which were intermediate between the Centre and the village panchayats were unwilling to concede their functions or resources. A move to break up big states and set up smaller ones, frowned upon by Nehru's generation, was now found a good way to create many smaller institutions at different levels of aggregation. India had overcome the fears of Balkanization. The BJP's reversal was a sure sign of this maturity. Good governance and meeting the basic demands for public facilities were now the slogans for the BJP.

The Congress had been out of power for eight years and was now led by Sonia Gandhi. She had plunged into politics in 1998 when she could see the old party losing its grip. She was an even greater novice in politics than her husband had been when he became MP. She was, moreover, foreign-born, even though she had lived in India for over thirty years by the time she entered politics. Nevertheless, the orthodox Hindu voter and certainly many politicians felt their xenophobia rise when contemplating this foreign woman as a possible ruler of India. Sonia had to teach herself not just Hindi, but the local political patois, as well as the cunning ways in which the largely masculine world of Indian politics operated. She had one advantage, however. Everyone underestimated her.

The Congress slogan was about the aam aadmi—the common man. It argued that the gains from reform and globalization had gone to the better off, and not to the common people. This was truer of the rural areas where agricultural growth had not kept pace with overall economic growth. Urban areas had enjoyed a boom thanks to IT exports and many new services, which employed educated people. Cities such as Bangalore and Hyderabad and Cochin had flourished as much as Mumbai and Delhi. But the hinterland had lagged behind. Or so it seemed. Poverty numbers, when they did come out later, showed little distance between the percentage of rural and urban poor.

This was a clever strategy to dramatize the distance between the prosperous, middle-class urban India and the poorer, deprived rural India. The Constitution names the Union as 'India, that is Bharat', 'Bharat' being the name the orthodox Hindu members of the Constituent Assembly preferred to 'Hindustan', which was the commonly used Hindi/Urdu name for the nation. Now, the Congress popularized a contrast between what India had gained, but what Bharat had been denied. Thus, according to this message, the Hindu champions of the BJP had neglected Bharat while pandering to India. Henceforward, economic policies of liberalization and reform had to meet the test of whether they benefited Bharat as well as India. The idea was now firmly established that development had to be 'inclusive', if it was to benefit both Bharat and India.

Sonia Gandhi proved an indefatigable campaigner. What she may have lacked in eloquence, she made up with energy. She travelled to many rural areas. Vajpayee was, by now, in frail health and remained in elder statesman mode, only making certain big set speeches. In the event, in May 2004 Sonia Gandhi stunned India and the world by upsetting all the predictions and winning more seats than the BJP: the Congress won 145 seats to the BJP's 138. The Congress had gambled by not entering into any pre-poll alliances, but now it quickly found partners. It had enough to muster 223 seats. Left parties won their best number of seats: CPI(M) had forty-three, ten more than previously and CPI won ten, six more than in 1999. Along with their allies, Forward Bloc and RSP who together added twelve more, the Left parties agreed, on the basis of a Common Minimum Programme, to support the United Progressive Alliance, as the Congress-led coalition was called, from the outside. Sonia Gandhi further wrong-footed the hysterical BJP propaganda about the prospect of a foreigner becoming PM by sidestepping the job and giving it to Dr Manmohan Singh, who had joined the Congress during his tenure as finance minister in the 1991–96 Congress government. Sonia Gandhi was the Congress president, but she moved the motion proposing Singh at the Congress parliamentary party meeting. She became the convenor of the UPA, the job George Fernandes had performed in the BJP-led NDA coalition. This was a shrewd move because Singh, as a technocrat, was better as a non-political chief executive, leaving the political horse-trading to Sonia Gandhi, who had by now learned the art.

COUNTERFACTUAL BOX

If BJP/NDA Had Won in 2004

The BJP did not expect to lose the elections. Its long and steady rise in Indian politics since its nadir in 1984, when it got only two seats, was spectacular. Its Lok Sabha strength in subsequent elections went up to 85 (1989), 120 (1991), 161 (1996) and 182 (1998–99). This was a result of some hard grass-roots work among the Hindu urban middle-class households to get legitimacy for its ideas. When it shed its narrow economic nationalism and embraced reform, it looked like having acquired a winning combination—modern economics, traditional politics. Its coalition partners had kept it from pursuing its most extreme ideas, such as rebuilding the temple. It was expecting a renewal of its mandate.

Had BJP/NDA won in 2004, it would have given BJP a truly national status. It could have become like Congress—'a natural governing party'. It is a moot question, therefore, if BJP would have been tempted to move India much more into a Hindu majoritarian direction. During 1998–2004, it had tried to rewrite textbooks of history taught in schools and, no doubt, this trend would have continued. A renewal may also have emboldened it to build the temple had its strength increased vis-à-vis its partners. The position of minorities, especially Muslims, would have been rendered precarious. Even the tolerance of modern Westernizing trends would have come under attack as became frequent in BJP-ruled states.

Yet, much of the psychology of such extremist movements was based on a feeling of resentment, of being excluded from power. Once BJP saw that it could come to power legitimately through the ballot box, such resentment could have subsided. Governing is a sobering experience since it teaches a party that what it thought it could do when outside, is never as easy as it seems when in power.

It is an open question, therefore, whether India would have been a more divided society as a result, or whether the experience of power would have mollified the feelings of resentment on which the party mobilized its cadres. The unexpected defeat plus the retirement of Vajpayee posed significant challenges for BJP to reassemble its forces for another victory in the future.

CONGRESS REDUX

For the Congress it was like old times again, being in power after a break of eight years. It had been out of power ten of the previous fifteen years. Even now, its majority was fragile and dependent on the Left parties who chose not to join the government but lend support. The defeat of the BJP led to a major assessment of the reasons for its failure, and this thinking influenced the conduct of the Congress-led UPA government. Since the BJP had paraded India Shining and lost, while the Left had gathered sixty-five seats—its largest-ever total—it seemed voters had rejected liberal economic reforms and were ready to return to the Nehruvian days. The Congress had pioneered the reforms, and the man who could claim due credit was now prime minister. It had to tread carefully. While not disowning, or much less, reversing the reforms, it was obliged to pursue many populist policies which, often, were more show than substance.

A more careful reading of the results had shown that the reversal of the BJP's fortunes were more due to what happened to its coalition partners than its own actions. The BJP did lose forty-five seats and the Congress gained thirty one. So, the two national parties, together, lost their support and had a bare majority in Lok Sabha. Even so, had they formed a coalition, India would have had a super-stable grand coalition, much like Germany has done twice in the post-war period. As it happened, the two major parties are still too unsure of each other to risk such a coalition (though I did publicly advocate it at the time). The BJP had switched its ally in Tamil Nadu from the DMK to the then-ruling AIADMK. There is a phenomenon well known in Indian electoral lore as anti-incumbency. As Yogendra Yadav notes in the *Economic and Political Weekly*, voters tend to throw out governments-in-power more often than not. This is just what happened to the AIADMK. The same fate visited Andhra Pradesh's Telugu Desam Party (TDP) whose chief minister, Chandrababu Naidu, despite his exemplary record as a chief executive who could deliver good development and clean government, lost to the Congress.

It was this complicated mathematics of small parties winning or losing locally, which added up to the defeat of the NDA. Yet, the climate was very strong for 'progressive', that is, statist, policies to be brought back. The actual record shows much greater continuity between the two coalitions—the NDA and the UPA—than any rupture. There have been populist interventions such as the National Rural Employment Guarantee Act (NREGA), which ensures a hundred days of employment to a member of a rural family if no one else in the family is employed. This is a minimal employment subsidy. Its implementation has run into the usual criticisms of corruption and ineffectiveness, but its presence has been felt across the country, especially in providing work for women.

The GDP growth record has been spectacular given India's past record. From 2003–04 to 2007–08, the growth and inflation stayed good. India was the second-fastest growing economy after China for the first few years of the twenty-first century. After doubling every nineteen years in the first thirty-eight years, the GDP doubled in eleven years after

1988. At 9 per cent per annum, it would take only eight years for the GDP to double. After decades of lethargy, Indian economy was picking up speed at last.

Indian economic growth in the twenty-first century was much more solidly based on private sector performance. While the Planning Commission still brings out Five Year Plans, it is more of a macroeconomic projection and forecasting body which also has a large discretionary amount to allocate to states for their projects. It gives expert advice on issues such as environment and energy. It no longer engages in a detailed industry-by-industry plan as was the practice in the 1950s and 1960s, when the glamour was of larger and larger input–output tables being used to chart the course of the economy. The economy refused to grow at the pace the planner had set for it, which only made the planner revise the plans in a more ambitious direction. Now, the competitive strength of a dynamic private sector dovetailed with a rapidly growing global economy. Globalization was the cause of a fifteen-year boom in the world economy from 1992 to 2007. India was riding on top of this big crest.

Growth and Inflation 2003/04–2007/08[1]
(in annual percentage rates)

Year	GDPg	WPIg
2003/04	8.5	5.4
2004/05	7.5	6.4
2005/06	9.4	4.4
2006/07	9.6	5.4
2007/08	9.0	4.7

Key: GDP: Gross Domestic Product; WPI: Wholesale Price Index.

INDIA IN THE GLOBAL POLITY

The demise of the Soviet Union in 1991 had created a vacuum in the global polity. What had been since 1945 a balance of terror in the Cold War with two superpowers, was now replaced by a single hyper-power, the USA. India had been assiduously friendly towards the USSR, its Left parties had basked in the glow of that policy and the ideological predilections of the intellectuals in India, who were pro-Marxist rather than pro-Western. Now, the Wizard of Oz had been exposed as just a frightened old man pulling strings. USSR was no longer an economic giant as it fell apart into its constituent units. Russia became an unstable pluto-kleptocratic state under Yeltsin. America seemed to have the chance to rebuild the world in its own image. India faced some searching choices as to how it would make a smooth transition from a bipolar world, where it could display its non-alignment, to one where the West was in charge.

It had its ambitions to fulfil as a global power—which is what it perceived itself to be. After the end of the Cold War, it could see itself as a leader of the Non-Aligned Movement, though it was not clear what it could be non-aligned against, unless this was merely a fig-leaf for being anti-American. India was the leader of the Third World group of seventy-seven in the UN and played a big role in WTO as well. It aspired to be a permanent member of the UN Security Council and joined the demand, made by many in the General Assembly, for a restructuring of the 1945 architecture which had given the world the UN–IMF–World Bank set of institutions. But to achieve its aims, India had to seek not the popular support of Third World countries in the UN General Assembly, but the discreet approval of the superpowers. Its attempt to nominate Shashi Tharoor, a high-level Indian UN official, for the Secretary General's post, ended in failure. China made its disapproval clear and Ban Ki Moon became the UN Secretary General. India did, however, secure the Secretary Generalship of the Commonwealth for its High Commissioner to the UK, Kamalesh Sharma. India knew it had to get up the ladder of power to superpower status. In the unipolar world, this meant India had to reconsider its tactics.

Given its democratic institutions, its free press and fundamental rights of free speech, its use of English language and its open society, India is more a Western society than a communist one. Its fierce nationalist pride, however, wanted to insist on its uniqueness, its rejection of all alternatives and a desire for an Indian Way. The commercial logic of emergent India was, however, quite willing to go where the business was. Outsourcing by Western firms became big business for India's IT sector. Indian students were in major universities in Anglophone countries—Canada, Australia, UK and USA. The diaspora was getting bigger and more visible in the economic and political lives of their chosen homelands.

Indo-US relations had been fraught since the days of Indira Gandhi. Even after the liberal economic reform, India could not mend its fences with the USA. The relationship became more relaxed, but the US preference for Pakistan remained. The Afghanistan campaign in the 1980s, and later the Islamist attacks on New York, Kenya and elsewhere had made the US aware of the Muslim presence. It chose to harness Pakistan to its 'war on terror', as it had been an ally and made fewer difficulties about morals and principles. But President Zia-ul-Haq had tried to install an orthodox Islamic regime in Pakistan as a way of legitimizing his dictatorship. By the 1990s, Pakistan had many deeply embedded agencies whose ideology was Islamist. Its secret service, the Inter Services Intelligence (ISI) as well as the lower echelons of the army were said to be infiltrated by Islamist influence.[2]

India had the reputation of having a large Muslim population which had, by and large, steered clear of joining Islamist terrorist groups. In Kashmir India suffered from cross-border infiltration by jihadi groups which had trained on the Afghanistan–Pakistan border (also in Punjab and the Pakistan side of Kashmir). But Indians did not have much to do with such groups. Even the March 1993 Bombay blasts were blamed on Bombay gangland Muslims rather than ideologically motivated Islamists. India seemed a haven where, rarely among nations with large Muslim populations, a democratic regime functioned in which Muslims played a full and active part.

This is one reason why the US began to look at India as a possible ally after years of prickly relations. But the explosion of nuclear device in 1998 postponed a rapprochement, as the Clinton presidency had to impose sanctions on both India and Pakistan for having violated the norms of the international nuclear community. India had been a champion of disarmament for many decades. Rajiv Gandhi was just the latest PM in 1988 to make a major proposal for a complete elimination of nuclear weapons at a peace initiative in Stockholm. Yet, India had refused to sign the Comprehensive Test Ban Treaty (CTBT) or the Non-Proliferation Treaty (NPT). Bill Clinton visited India in his last year as President, the first US President to do so since President Carter in January 1978 during the tenure of the Janata regime.

The BJP had been openly friendly with the US, except for its fervent nationalist wish to make India a nuclear power. It also opened friendly relations with Israel. It was a peculiarity of the Congress's non-alignment policy and, perhaps, also a perverse result of its secularism, that India had always tilted towards Muslim nations of the Middle East and had even, at one stage, tried to join the Organization of Islamic States (OIC).

Fortunately it was not successful, which saved it from being the first and only secular socialist state to be a member of the OIC. India also took the side of the Palestine Liberation Organization (PLO) in the Israel–Palestine dispute—all this despite India having voted for the founding of the state of Israel in the UN in 1948. Now, the BJP opened up a channel for friendly relations and also military hardware purchases. This did not escape the attention of the State Department.

It was 9/11 which made America aware that the world outside its borders could impinge on its own security. While it had been hailed as a superpower and, indeed, was able to throw its weight about freely in the 1990s, now there was the challenge of global Islamist terror which required a fresh approach to international relations. With George W. Bush's presidency, there was also a 'Neo-Con' thrust about spreading democracy around the world as a way of making America safer. In simple realpolitik terms, America was becoming aware of the rise of China as a superpower on the economic as much as on the military front. In Richard Nixon's days, it had seen China as an antidote to the USSR. Now with USSR having disintegrated and China looming large, America could see that it would need allies in Asia just in case something went awry in its relations with China.

It is said that George W. Bush, in his simple-minded way noticed that India had over a billion people, just as China had. India was emerging on US radar screen, not just as a nuclear power, but also as a vibrant market economy. India was obviously one strategic partner USA could acquire to meet its 'just in case' need to have an insurance policy against China. Of course, India was suspicious of American foreign policy bias towards Pakistan. India would not join the American crusade in Iraq or Afghanistan, during the first phase of the war against the Taliban. The visceral anti-Americanism of India's Left and even some centrist nationalist circles, is of long standing. Nehru was never comfortable with American capitalism and its cold war policies. Indira Gandhi had been insulted by Johnson and Nixon. India needed to be wooed by America, if it wanted a strategic relationship rather than just friendship. The US had to balance its pro-India tilt carefully.

It finally came down to personal chemistry. Vajpayee had an almost sphinx-like personal style of communication (as I can attest first hand). Western leaders, such as Blair and Clinton, found it difficult to relate to him, despite their admiration for him. Manmohan Singh proved to be a very different kettle of fish. George W. Bush took to this articulate but deliberate interlocutor, who was well aware of the global dimension of economic as well as foreign policies. Singh had matured beyond his initial technocrat persona, and now as PM was ready to make his mark on India's history. He had already decided to continue and deepen the dialogue on Kashmir with Pakistan, and was hoping to tackle it in a serious manner. He now saw a chance to advance India's status in the world.

In a meeting in 2005 in Washington DC, Bush and Singh agreed on an Indo-US nuclear deal. India had been a pariah of the international nuclear club, and had been deprived of any nuclear fuel supply by the Nuclear Supplier Group (NSG). The regime was closely monitored by the International Atomic Energy Authority (IAEA), which inspects nuclear reactors to make sure they are used only for peaceful purposes. India had stayed out of any inspection regime, and with the boycott needed to get back into the club of nuclear nations. The many nuclear nations which had eschewed military use were jealous of the rights of the NSG. Now USA offered to intervene on India's behalf, if India would join in a strategic partnership. To lift the ban on supplying fuel to India, Bush had to have legislation sent to the US Congress and passed. He then had to commit American help to convince NSG to lift the ban on supplies to India.

Within India the deal was not universally popular. Having lost its much vaunted national self-sufficiency in economic matters, the Left and many of the Nehru tradition were extremely averse to letting America dictate India's nuclear policy. Even though deprived of a steady supply of nuclear fuel, Indian nationalists were not sure that America's meddling was worth the resumption of supply. Since the Congress-led UPA coalition was dependent on Left support for its majority and subject to a Common Minimum Programme (though the deal had not been anticipated at the time of victory in 2004), there was a special concern that even if the Americans were willing to concede India's demands, India could reject the deal.

India went through an intense debate about the deal. It was like the Cripps Mission all over again, with people debating the minutiae of the drafts of American legislation. The UPA position was that the deal would make it possible for India to increase its energy supply for the future, when its oil and gas resources would be inadequate and its coal reserves could run into the restrictions of the Kyoto carbon emission agreement. The opponents of the deal were not fooled; they wanted to ensure that no foreign power, certainly not America, could veto India's sovereign right to test nuclear weapons as and when it wanted to. The anti-nuclear lobby in India, that opposes the military or peaceful uses of nuclear power, is not significant. It was the issue of India's sovereignty being under threat that brought the Left and the BJP together, for once.

The ability of the Indian elite to absorb intricate details of obscure scientific and military matters is admirable. The public debate about the deal with its US Congressional legislation such as the Hyde Act and the 123 Agreement occupied large swathes of daily newspapers and weeklies. For once the Congress party had to actually prove that it was not about to pawn India's sovereignty, or mortgage its independence in foreign policy making to secure the deal. In the event, the issue paralysed the UPA coalition since the Left warned that it would strongly oppose the deal. Between August 2007 and July 2008 there was a stalemate, during which policy making virtually ceased, as the coalition could not secure agreement on the decision. Sonia Gandhi, as a naturally risk-averse person, was unsure whether the deal was worth a defeat in a parliamentary confidence vote or, worse still, an election defeat. But Singh seems to have proved to be of sterner stuff than many anticipated. He convinced

Sonia Gandhi that the gamble was winnable, and that the UPA should call the bluff on their erstwhile partners.

The Americans maintained their keenness for the deal. The government was able to display the superbly trained diplomatic corps that India had, which dealt with the internal as well as the international discussions deftly. The IAEA was squared, and the deal was proceeding by the summer of 2008 to its consummation. The Left officially withdrew its support from the UPA coalition. The government faced a trust motion in the Lok Sabha on 22–23 July 2008 where the arithmetic looked distinctly against it.

The trust vote was a rare event in Lok Sabha. The BJP-led NDA had faced a no confidence motion in Lok Sabha in 1999 and lost it by just one vote, but returned to power in the ensuing elections. Now it was the UPA's turn to face a trust vote which, if the government had lost, would still leave it a chance to seek a confidence vote, which the Left had promised to support since it did not want BJP to come to power. Yet, it would be a humiliation for Singh, Sonia Gandhi and the UPA. The debate lasted two days and was quite charged. But on the second day, the event descended from a drama into a farce as some MPs alleged that they had been offered sacks of thousand rupee notes to the extent of forty million, as an inducement to change sides. This was later revealed to be the result of a planned sting which was to be televised live while the debate on the trust vote was going on. Thanks to a counter-sting, the TV channel pulled out. Then the frustrated BJP MPs, who were supposed to be part of the deal, sneaked in the sacks past guards in Lok Sabha. Indian TV viewers, as well as the watching world, saw the whole squalid spectacle. Proceedings had to be suspended by Speaker Somnath Chatterjee who was himself in trouble because, as a member of the CPI(M), he had defied party discipline and decided to refrain from voting, which is the Speaker's normal practice. He was expelled from the CPI(M).

The government won the trust vote comfortably. It had secured the defection or, at least, the abstention, of enough BJP MPs to win. It had cooked up a last-minute coalition with Mulayam Singh Yadav's Samajwadi Party, which gave it just the numbers to partially make up for the loss of the Left. The defections did the rest. The NSG soon approved India's deal, and the US Congress even in the midst of a financial meltdown to occupy their minds, sent the bill for the President's signature.

The Indo-US nuclear deal was the sign that India had arrived on the global super power stage though, as yet, it was not centre stage. When Bush spent some time calling up leaders around the world to argue India's case before the NSG, India seemed to have turned full circle in its relations with the US since the days of Lyndon Johnson. The reluctant manner of India's parliamentarians in welcoming the deal added, rather than detracted, from India's reputation. Here was proof again, if proof were needed, of India's robust democracy. The UPA government and Dr Singh insisted that here was a solution to India's energy supply problems. There is a distinct possibility that the deal will mean much more than just energy supplies. It may well usher in a new phase of India's membership in the Western alliance. Lal Bahadur Shastri had attempted a slight tilt towards USA while not losing the friendship with the Soviet Union. Now with no Soviet Union around, it made sense to be friendly with the remaining superpower. Singh is, in many ways, much like Shastri. He is modest and self-effacing, but with a steely determination when he means it. He surprised everyone by his willingness to take his government to the brink in defence of the nuclear deal.

THE CENTRE CANNOT HOLD

The President of the USA often finds that he can accomplish more abroad than at home. Abroad, he is made welcome by grateful hosts. At home, he faces a hostile Congress, regardless of the party composition at any time. Such is also the fate of the Indian prime minister. A prosperous economy and a successful diplomatic deal were not enough to give the UPA coalition or Manmohan Singh a quiet life. Congress, with only 145 seats out of the necessary 273, was facing multiple problems. In individual states, powerful allies such as DMK in Tamil Nadu would insist on running their own show, and wanting their men and women in key Cabinet positions at the Centre. Indeed, a family quarrel of Chief Minister Karunanidhi led to the summary dismissal of his nephew, Dayanidhi Maran, a highly successful minister for telecommunications. The prime minister could not retain a valued colleague; he was subject to diktat from coalition partners. Court cases against Cabinet members such as Lalu Prasad Yadav, railways minister and former chief minister of Bihar, had to be allowed to run on without any loss of office or, even, influence. The health minister, Ramadoss carried on a personal feud with the head of the All India Institute of Medical Sciences (AIIMS), India's premier medical institution. At the nadir of the quarrel, the government was forced to pass an ordinance to curtail the tenure of the AIIMS head, Dr Venugopal, since the courts had ruled against the minister. As the few seats of the health minister's party were critical to the survival of the coalition, he was untouchable.

A more serious development was the growth of Naxalite groups across the east-central states of India, from Bihar to Chhatisgarh down to Orissa and Andhra Pradesh. As many as one in six districts of India were said to be subject to Naxalite attacks on the police and the local landlords. This was an armed guerrilla movement, open and political, unlike terrorism. Maoist groups had been waging a civil war in Nepal for many years and in 2007 succeeded in removing the king and establishing a republic through cooperation with democratic parties. The Nepalese Maoists took to the ballot box, dropped their arms and proceeded to become part of the democratic political process. Their Indian colleagues are still at the armed struggle phase. Of course, the Naxalites are marginal to the larger Indian reality, but they have stayed the course and have been hard to eliminate from their strongholds. Their appeal is to the tribal populations which live in hilly and arid lands, or who scratch a living from forests which used to be common property. These have been nationalized and given over to private contractors to exploit for timber and minerals, thus depriving the poor of access to fuel or fruit. There are also landless Dalit labourers who are at the bottom of the agrarian economy of what are stagnant economic regions. Such groups are fertile grounds for mobilization by the Naxalites, who fight on their behalf.

The quality of local police action depended greatly on the level of provisioning, much affected by corruption and the ubiquitous low morale, thanks to much political interference in appointments and promotions. As governments change, either because of the anti-incumbency factor or because fragile coalitions break up as small parties defect, seeking a better bargain, the incoming government routinely sacks or transfers police officers who have served the previous regime. 'Regime revenge', as the phenomenon is called, is populist, but not conducive to good governance. Police officials are always watching their backs to check whether their political masters are happy or not. It does not make for effectiveness when fighting a dedicated guerrilla army. An awareness that the fight requires as much positive development as a police force, has surfaced. The battle for hearts and minds has focussed on an organization called Selva Judum, emphasizing collective effort for security and development. The battles with the Naxalites coexist with the conduct of elections in these areas, but the persistence of Naxalite threat is stubborn. More security personnel have died in the Naxal battles than in Jammu and Kashmir in recent years.

Kashmir itself continues to be a site for worry. Manmohan Singh continued the dialogue with Pakistan and many Confidence Building Measures (CBMs), such as bus connections across the LoC and from Amritsar to Lahore, were inaugurated. A railway link, the Samjhauta Express continues to run, though it has once been a target of terrorist bombs. Elections had been held in Kashmir in 2002 which had led to the formation of a popular government. The Congress was in alliance with the People's Democratic Party (PDP) led by Mufti Mohammad Sayeed and formed the government, sharing the chief ministership in turns and also ministerial berths. Singh has allowed the many dissident groups in Kashmir—the separatist ones fighting for Kashmiri independence as well as those wishing to join Pakistan—permission to meet and debate with parties in Delhi and even travel to Pakistan. This did not stop the terrorist attacks, but reduced their incidence. Jammu and Kashmir seemed almost normal for a while.

Then, a surprising fracas broke out which led to the resignation of the chief minister, Ghulam Nabi Azad, a Congressman. The issue was an obscure one. A holy site for Hindu pilgrims—the Amarnath shrine—is in the Valley of Kashmir, where the local Muslim population has traditionally helped the pilgrims cope with the steep climb up to the cave in the mountains where the shrine is located, by providing food and shelter. The board running the pilgrimage was awarded use of some land by the governor of Kashmir, with the approval of the government. Then some local opposition started saying that this was alienation of land belonging to the Kashmiris. Hindus in Jammu began an agitation insisting that the land transfer be retained. It became a Hindu–Muslim battle, as also BJP–Congress, and Congress against the Muslim parties in the Valley. A blockade in Jammu prevented trucks loaded with fresh fruit from going to the markets in Punjab and farther south leading to economic distress; and the only way around the blockade seemed to be the route across the LoC, through the Pakistani side of Kashmir. Then, the separatist parties got their wind up, began waving the Pakistan flag and asking for secession. The situation became tense during the summer of 2008. It soon settled down, however, because the bottom line was that it was a fake battle orchestrated because of the nearness of elections which were scheduled for November–December 2008. Through the summer the Congress-led UPA showed masterly inactivity, since many vote banks with opposing demands were at stake. The entire battle was allowed to take its course, unlike in previous years when Delhi would have stepped in right at the start. In November, elections began to be held in the first of its many phases which spread into December. The turnout was 60 per cent, despite the boycott by separatist groups.

Almost concurrently with the Amarnath dispute, there was a vicious religious war in the Kandamahal district of Orissa. Here a Hindu holy man, Swami Lakshmananand Saraswati was brutally murdered by some gunmen, who fled away on a motorbike. The police failed to apprehend them. One rumour had it that the Naxalites may have done the deed. But immediately, Bajrang Dal started attacks on Christians, especially recent converts. Their huts were burned and they were attacked. There was retaliation. The dispute, which had religious overtones, was also shaped by reservation rights of the recently converted Christians. When they were Hindu Dalits, they had Mandal rights which they lost on becoming Christians. What happened is a bit murky. India's Constitution guarantees the right to practice the religion of your choice and also allows conversion. Some states have passed laws banning conversion if undue force or monetary payments are used as inducement. But many Hindus regard all Christians in India as formerly Hindus who have been forcibly converted or bribed with money. Thus, Hindu–Christian conversion battles have become more frequent. The BJP had come to power in Karnataka, their first southern state. Almost immediately, at least as a coincidence if not direct causation, Christian converts were attacked.

The freedom to practice and propagate one's religion is among the fundamental rights in the Constitution. Yet, there is resentment in the Hindutva circles about conversions. In 1981, soon after Indira Gandhi's return to power, the village of Meenakshipuram (in Tamil Nadu) made news by the fact that its entire 1000-strong Dalit community converted to Islam and changed the village name to Rehmatnagar. The cry of 'Hinduism in danger', which had not been raised when Ambedkar took his flock into Buddhism, resulted. This was Arab money pouring in from the Gulf, it was alleged. The asymmetry of Non-Resident Indian (NRI)—which is largely Hindu—money being used for Hindu conversions, and the enmity to 'foreign' money for other conversions remains strong.

Some states have legislation which forbids the use of coercion or bribery when converting people. This has almost become the standard excuse for Hindus to attack conversions. But Hindus have, at the same time, been active in Gujarat and elsewhere converting, or rather 'repurifying', as they put it, tribals into joining the Hindu fold. These activities are carried out openly, and often with blatant inducements, especially when the BJP happens to be in power in the state.

THE RISE OF TERRORISM

Through the UPA's tenure, terrorism has become a major issue. Terrorist bombs have exploded in Mumbai, Jaipur, Delhi, Hyderabad, Bangalore, Ahmedabad, in some cities more than once and, of course, in Kashmir. There is evidence here of Indian Muslims taking on the terrorist mantle, either on their own or in collaboration with Islamist groups from abroad. This development of an India-based Islamist terrorism has confounded the secularism ideology The Student Islamic Movement of India (SIMI) has often been cited for its possible involvement. Revenge for the Babri Masjid demolition and the post-Godhra killings have been aired as motives, though no one knows for sure. Yet, many secularists in India have a fundamentalist tendency as well, which firmly believes that every police 'encounter' with Muslim terrorists is fake and has been generated by communalists. There is a strongly held belief, for instance, that the one person—Afzal Guru—who has been convicted of the attack on the Indian Parliament of 2001, is innocent, and his conviction is the result of a state-instigated frame up. Afzal Guru's death sentence has been stayed pending appeal, and the Congress-led UPA government has taken its time in dealing with his case. Demands to ban SIMI or declare it a terrorist organization were resisted by members of the UPA cabinet, including the secularist stalwart, Lalu Prasad Yadav. In September 2008, the Delhi police cornered some suspected terrorists in a heavily Muslim area near the Jamia Milia University. The encounter, in a place called Batla House, resulted in the death of a police inspector, Mohan Chand Sharma. The tragedy became an occasion for partisan bickering, with the BJP hailing Sharma as a martyr and some secularists muttering about a fake encounter. On 8 December 2008, the Supreme Court dismissed a public interest litigation seeking a judicial inquiry into the Batla House encounter and also the death of Inspector Sharma. A sceptical bench said to the petitioner, 'So you say that policemen went there to shoot themselves? Go and tell the police if you have information about the encounter.'

These quarrels are reminiscent of the differences in the perception of crime by America's Black and White communities in some inner cities in the 1970s and the 1980s. Black leaders took every encounter as police misbehaviour rather than a Black person's infringement of the law. The White community was split between the liberal East Coast establishment which was apologetic about Black crime, while the Republican Party missed no chance implying that the Black American had done nothing to deserve the civil rights conferred on him. George H.W. Bush fought the 1988 US presidential election on an insinuation that his Democratic rival, Michael Dukakis, would let loose convicts like Willie Horton, who had been released by Dukakis when he was governor of Massachusetts and had re-offended. The Willie Horton campaign was a classic smear, and it worked.

India's counter-terrorism machinery is hobbled by the fact that law and order is a state subject and not a central one. The Centre does look after national security in terms of external attacks and aggression, but individual states have their own legislation to counter terrorism. There is a lack of coordination as well as serious under-funding and lack of training. In a way, tackling terrorism is a problem for India, given the Hindu–Muslim dimension. Partition does, after more than sixty years, continue to wreak its revenge on Indian politics.

The UPA has taken the view that fighting terrorism is not a matter of draconian laws, but of removing the grievances that lead to it. It is also more convenient to blame Pakistan rather than home-grown terrorists. There is no cross-party consensus on this issue, as it runs across the secular–communal divide. It is even difficult for politicians to agree that a terrorist should be treated as a criminal and dealt with as required by the law, rather than regarded as a Muslim and hence carrying the burden of communal discrimination on his shoulder. In October 2008, when police discovered that a bomb attack on Malegaon may have been carried out by 'Hindu' terrorists, there was undisguised glee on part of the secular parties that this time the BJP had been caught with its clients at fault. The BJP, alas, despite its long-standing stance of toughness on terrorism, took the view that as the court case was still pending, they would not comment on the case. The parivar furiously denied that Hindu terrorists existed, maintaining that Hindus were not capable of such acts. They accused the Anti-Terrorism Squad (ATS) of framing the people arrested—and thus became a mirror image of the fundamentalist secularists.

UPSURGE OF THE UNDERPRIVILEGED

The dialectic of Indian democracy is such, however, that the same weakness which cripples the fight against terrorism, also releases energies of groups, which have waited, centuries, if not millennia, for their turn at the top table. The most remarkable phenomenon of the last two decades is, no doubt, the emergence of a woman Dalit leader, Mayawati, a protégé of Kanshi Ram, who founded the Bahujan Samaj Party. Mayawati won the UP elections outright in 2007, wresting power from the Samajwadi Party government led by Mulayam Singh Yadav. This was a stunning result. The BJP was expected to win the elections and then form a coalition with the Samajwadi Party (SP). The BJP plan was for the SP to then withdraw its support from the UPA-led coalition, and thus lead to an early general elections. The Congress, which was a marginal presence in UP, saw the SP as its partner, and hoped to win a few seats with its help. In fact, Mayawati and her BSP trounced both BJP and SP and won an outright majority.

Mayawati is a phenomenon in Indian politics, not only because of what she symbolizes but also because of her distinctive style. As a woman and a Dalit, she carries a double handicap in a caste-ridden patriarchal society. Her style is 'in-your-face'—aggressive rather than humble gratitude for the distance she has travelled. Kanshi Ram, in the long tradition of the nineteenth-century anti-caste reformers such as Jotirao Phule and twentieth-century reformers such as Ambedkar and Ramaswamy Naicker, began to attack the hoary myths of India's ancient cultural and philosophical traditions at its roots. Indian nationalism takes great pride in the old Sanskrit *Veda*s, the *Upanishad*s and the epics. The very length of the tradition is, for the nationalist, a slap in the face of the barbaric Westerners who had not seen such splendour till many centuries later. Left and Right, Nehruvians and Hindutva champions, communist atheists and devout believers, were as one on the 'wonder that was India'. Kanshi Ram and Mayawati carried the battle against this heritage right into the heart of this cherished narrative. They denounced much of this paraphernalia as Brahminical, and hence hostile to the Dalits who were among the original inhabitants of India. The slogan was to denounce *Manuwad*, the ideology attributed to Manu whose *Manusmriti* is the foundational text of the laws and norms of Hindu society. Since the book enshrines the caste hierarchy, the domination of Brahmins and the low ranking of the Shudras and the Dalits, there was no reason for a Dalit intellectual to enthuse about it. Indeed, like Ambedkar the Dalit political tradition departed sharply from the Congress–BJP consensus on the greatness of ancient Hindu traditions.

Mayawati reached much higher than her mentor. She is a fiery speaker and an astute politician. She rejoices in her position and displays the gifts she receives from her followers—gold, jewellery and clothes—quite openly. She boasts of how much money she has collected for her party funds from donations. She had used her earlier brief stints, as minister or chief minister in coalition governments in UP, to install large statues of Ambedkar and Kanshi Ram. Now, she also had huge statues of herself built. Public institutions—universities, hospitals, parks—have been renamed after Ambedkar and Kanshi Ram. Considering that the renaming of Marathawada University as Babasaheb Ambedkar University led to extensive riots across Maharashtra as recently as 1978, in which 5000 Dalits were rendered homeless, the Dalit movement has indeed come a long way. In Agra in UP, also in 1978, an attempt was made to celebrate Ambedkar's birthday by taking out a procession that included an elephant carrying his picture, as is the practice with upper-caste leaders. This is associated with kings and gods. The ensuing riots led to clashes which required the army to intervene. Much worse occured in Belchi, a village in Bihar, where nine Dalits were burnt to death by an upper-caste mob. This was in May 1977, soon after the Janata government had come to power. The now dethroned Indira Gandhi shamed the new government by visiting the area herself. Thus, given this quite recent history of Dalit oppression, Mayawati's achievements are indeed impressive. Whether this achievement can also be taken a step further, to integrate the Dalits fully into Indian society and make them feel accepted by the caste Hindus, remains a challenge for the Dalit movement.

As chief minister of India's largest state with eighty seats in the Lok

Sabha at stake, Mayawati was expected to be a crucial power broker for the general elections due in 2009. Given the fragility of the two national parties as to their share of the vote and seats, it seemed not unlikely that she would be the pivotal person to do a bargain with, if she had even forty UP seats under her control. She sought to take the BSP beyond UP, wherever there is a Dalit vote, and made small dents in north Indian states such as Delhi, Rajasthan and Madhya Pradesh. She also astutely made pacts with Brahmin vote banks, since their common enemy is seen to be the OBCs. At the time of the trust vote in Lok Sabha in July 2008, the Left parties and many who had been previously with the NDA coalition, had declared her to be their prime ministerial choice as and when general elections were held. Even to be considered a prime ministerial candidate, albeit by a somewhat loose alliance of minor parties, is a remarkable feat of achievement for which one needs to congratulate not only the woman herself, but also India's democracy. During the first Janata government when Morarji Desai was proving unpopular even among his Cabinet colleagues, Janata Party wanted the Dalit leader, Jagjivan Ram, to be PM. It is rumoured that Charan Singh threatened to walk out of the coalition and, indeed, did so saying he was going to stop a *bhangi*—a pejorative term signifying the lowest among the Dalits—from becoming prime minister. This despite the long tenure Jagjivan Ram had had in the Congress and his long stint as Cabinet minister in many Congress governments. Jagjivan Ram, who had left Indira's Congress just before the 1977 elections, went back realizing that he would never be PM of India. Mayawati roused a lot of hopes among the Dalits that she may yet fulfil his dream.

RETURN TO RAMA

Some things never change and one of them is the belief of the BJP and its parivar that whatever else may divide Hindus, the legend of Ramachandra as depicted in the epic *Ramayana* will prove a unifying theme. The Palk strait separating Sri Lanka and India is a difficult sea course to traverse. Ships going from the western parts of India to the eastern coast have to go around the southern tip of Sri Lanka. There was a scheme to dredge the sea course to speed up maritime traffic. The proposal had the support of the Tamil Nadu government in whose neighbourhood the project was located. By the lore of the epic, however, Rama had built a bridge across that sea course to invade Lanka where the villain, Ravana who had abducted his wife, Sita, ruled. It was called Ramsetu—'the Rama bridge'. Thus, the site was holy since the god–hero had sanctified it with his bridge. The bridge was built by the monkey army which helped Rama, and one of that army's leaders,

Hanuman (also called Bajrang from whom the Bajrang Dal derives its name) is a popular deity. The entire project had been launched during the BJP-led NDA government's tenure, but that was conveniently forgotten. People claimed, in a bizarre combination of modern technology and ancient lore, that photographs taken by NASA space satellites clearly showed the bridge lying at the bottom of the sea. Hindu fundamentalists had learnt a lot from their Christian counterparts in the US in this respect.

The government deposed before the Supreme Court that they did not accept the historic existence of Rama or his construction, and asked the court to dismiss a BJP petition against the Setu Samudram Project. All hell broke loose as the BJP/VHP accused the UPA of denying a basic tenet of Hindu faith. They promised to launch a nationwide agitation to defend the bridge, and prevent any construction. Karunanidhi, the Tamil Nadu chief minister, then waded into the controversy by saying that there was no support for the story and, after all, how could Rama have built a bridge? Was he, asked the CM, a qualified engineer? Karunanidhi had been schooled in the tradition of a strong anti-Ramayana ideology since Ramaswamy Naicker, the founding father of the Dravida movement, had written a strong critique of the epic denouncing it as a story of fair-skinned Northerners exploiting the dark Southerners and conquering them by trickery.[3]

Karunanidhi was a strong ally of the UPA coalition, and Tamil Nadu had a lot of business at stake from the project. There were ecological arguments against draining the sea channel, but they got little play. The UPA government, however, got nervous, and returned to the court stating that it did, indeed, believe in the historical existence and divinity of Ramachandra and that the entire subject would be referred to an expert committee to report later, that is after the next general elections.

The entire episode showed the fragility of the polity or, at least, the risk averseness of the Congress. Here was the law minister of a secular socialist republic deposing before its Supreme Court the government's belief in the godhood and historical existence of the hero of an epic. There is plenty of scholarly evidence that the epic, *Ramayana*, generally accepted as written between 1000 and 1500 BCE, as it is now available in the Sanskrit Valmiki version, has been added to and expanded since its first draft in which the hero was human and not divine. Over the centuries Rama has become more and more god-like till his final apotheosis, by about the fifteenth century, as an incarnation of the god Vishnu. The Hindi version by Tulsidas does, indeed, treat him as a god, yet, there are, at least, a thousand *Ramayana*s available in which the story is told in many variants. The Hindus lack a single Book which characterizes the Abrahamic faiths, but Hindutva-supporting politicians dearly wish they could conjure up one Book which would serve the unifying purpose. The *Bhagavad Gita* is one such text, but it is dry and philosophical. The mass of devotees need something more interesting, and there is no doubt that the *Ramayana* has fascinated generations of Indians forever.[4]

But the episode, also again in a dialectical way, illustrated the strength of India, since there is no possibility of uniting Hindus, North and South, around any one Book. Hindus are unlikely to constitute a monolithic majority which was Jinnah's nightmare. The myriad divisions of caste also help to prevent the construction of an overarching coalition of Hindus which could dominate the rest. There is an uncanny anticipation of the importance of multiple small groups in a democracy in an essay by James Madison, the fourth President of the US. At the Philadelphia convention gathered in 1787 to write a new Constitution for the young republic, three political essayists, Madison, Alexander Hamilton (who became the first Secretary of the Treasury under George Washington) and John Jay (the first Chief Justice of the US Supreme Court) anonymously published what has come to be known as the Federalist Papers. James Madison, in the tenth essay of this collection, took up the issue of what makes democracies stable or collapse into autocracy. He wrote:

> The smaller the society, the fewer probably will be the distinct parties and interests comprising it; the fewer the distinct parties and interests, the more frequently will a majority be found of the same party; and the smaller the number of individuals comprising a majority, and the smaller the compass within which they are placed, the more easily will they concert and execute their plans of oppression. Extend the sphere and you take in a greater variety of parties and interests you make it less probable that a majority of the whole will have a common motive to invade the rights of other citizens.[5]

Madison's argument that a country where there is no single powerful majority community, but lots of small groups which compete and collude with each other, would strengthen a democracy has been vindicated in India. It is because there is no permanent majority to oppress minorities that a large degree of tolerance prevails. Sri Lanka's recent history is an illustration of how a permanent majority (Sinhala speakers) can oppress a minority (Tamil speakers) until it drives the minority into a military confrontation. If democracy is absent, a minority can oppress a majority. West Pakistan's Punjabi elite did that to its East Pakistani majority till the Bangladesh war settled the matter. Iraq's Sunni population, despite being a minority, allowed Saddam Hussein as a dictator to practice a virtual genocide on its Shia majority.

INDIA HELPS BHARAT

The strong trend of GDP growth for the fifteen years since 1992 had, by 2007, made the budget constraint much more relaxed. The UPA government, under the finance ministership of P. Chidambaram, also used IT expertise to rationalize tax collection by giving each income tax payer a number which had to be cited in all transactions to avoid tax avoidance and also to streamline tax information. Revenues began to pile up, growing at a phenomenal 20 per cent per year in the first four years of the UPA regime. The Centre as well as the states could now pursue inclusive development, if they wished. This gave rise to a new class of state chief ministers who were willing to play the good governance card to deliver power and roads and education.

The most surprising chief minister in this respect was none other than Narendra Modi, widely held to be responsible for the 2002 Gujarat riots. He had been re-elected eight months after the riots with a two-thirds majority. The riots had clearly not hurt him with the Hindu electorate. But when it came to re-election in 2007, he was playing the good governance card much more than the communal card. He did criticize the UPA for its laxity on terrorism and fulminated against Pakistan as the source of all terrorism, but his record on delivery of electricity and water and schools was thought to be exemplary. The Rajiv Gandhi Foundation, which carries out policy-oriented research, ranked Gujarat at the top in a league table of Indian states in 2007. The Congress and the secular parties wanted the Gujarat voter to remember Modi's actions after Godhra: Sonia Gandhi, in a visit to Gujarat during her campaign, denounced him and his party as *maut ke saudagar* (merchants of death). This rebounded, because it introduced the communal issue much more prominently than had been the case till then. The Congress had a weak team in Gujarat and had failed to build up a sufficiently strong opposition to Modi. It relied on divisions within the BJP to promote ex-BJP candidates. But the robust growth performance and Modi's good governance reputation gave him another stunning victory, where he retained a two-thirds majority in the assembly. Modi has still to answer for the 2002 riots, and there is an atmosphere of intimidation in Gujarat thanks to the permissive attitude displayed towards violent Hindutva gangs. These gangs unleash violence against Muslim artists and cinema actors and break up meetings which are anti-Modi. But the electoral verdict has strengthened Modi's hands, as well as his chances of leading the BJP at the national level sooner rather than later.

Robust growth in regions like Gujarat is contrasted with the stagnation and despair in some of the cotton-growing districts of Maharashtra,

Andhra Pradesh, Madhya Pradesh, Chhatisgarh and Karnataka. In the five years, 1997 to 2001, no less than 15,747 suicides by farmers were recorded per year on average in these regions. The numbers rose to 17,336 in 2002–07. The ten year total is 182,936. In the dry cotton-growing region of Vidarbha, which is part of Maharashtra, 4238 farmers committed suicides in 2007 alone. The critics of liberalization blame these suicides on Genetically Modified (GM) seeds which, they say, have been forced on the farmers who have incurred debts in the hope of large gains. The technology of new GM seeds has somehow failed them in yielding a higher output, and/or the higher output has earned low incomes since, cotton prices have been adversely affected. Most of the suicides seem to be due to indebtedness. The puzzle is that public sector banks were supposed to advance rural credit as one of the tasks especially assigned to them at the moment of nationalization in 1969. In Punjab and Haryana, loan melas were held frequently, when political leaders would spray loans like confetti, no questions asked. The callous and uncaring reaction of local leadership in Vidarbha was exposed when, during the summer of 2007, the then chief minister of Maharashtra, Vilasrao Deshmukh, joked that these farmers were very clever and adulterated their cotton crop to cheat. A Union minister, Shankarsingh Vaghela, travelling along with the CM in a helicopter above the arid region, laughed and said that Gujarat farmers were hard working but Vidarbha farmers were lazy. Political neglect and cynicism cannot be ruled out as a contributing factor, but the expectation among the farmers and the larger public was that the caring Congress regime would, over the decades, look after farmers. Yet, there are still stories of farmers caught in the vice-like grip pf local moneylenders who charge exorbitant interest rates, as they have been since the mid-nineteenth century.[6]

The banks seem, in many cases, to be too bureaucratic and inflexible, and their procedures require too much form filling. The local moneylender knows his customer intimately and can supply ready cash when needed, since he follows the fortunes of his borrowers. He can also vary the terms and conditions of loans. The need is to be able to match the flexibility of the moneylender in a way which improves the availability of credit, without creating moral hazard. The UPA government had made attempts in the summer of 2007 to install relief schemes. Dr Manmohan Singh went to the region and announced relief worth Rs 30 billion. But the money seems not to have trickled down. In the summer of 2008, the finance minister announced a debt relief scheme of Rs 600 billion to compensate the banks for non-payment of debts owed by farmers. This was a classic example of the large revenues earned from a booming India Inc. to help out Bharat Ltd. As 2008 progressed, the farmers' suicide issue went off the headlines.

BHARAT BITES INDIA

Yet, universal peace has not been declared between India and Bharat. West Bengal has been ruled by a communist-led government since 1977. Jyoti Basu had led his party to victory in three elections. The CPI(M) attitude upon coming to power was hostile to private capital, and inclined to give trade unions their head. Industrial disputes went up sharply. A new technique of intimidation, *gherao* had been innovated in West Bengal in the late 1960s, when Naxalism first captured the imagination of the Left. Workers surrounded their employers in their office, preventing any exit. This type of intimidation became much more frequent with the Left-led government. Much industry was shut down and new investment failed to come to West Bengal. To their credit the Left government had pursued a radical land reform programme, and also installed panchayat governments before the Rajiv Gandhi initiative was mooted. West Bengal had been already battered by a decline through much of the first half of the twentieth century and because of the Partition. Now, the state went into a sharp industrial downturn.

It was in the 1990s that along with the reforms at the national level, the CPI(M) government also began to attract outside investors from both within and outside India. Things were however slow to move, and trust in the CPI(M)'s intentions was lacking. When Jyoti Basu retired, he was replaced by Buddhadev Bhattacharya who became a poster boy of the new reforms. He was openly welcoming of outside investments and offered attractive conditions for new projects to locate to West Bengal. In this he was following the new model chief ministers, such as Chandrababu Naidu of Andhra Pradesh or Narendra Modi of Gujarat, who would go abroad and sign Memoranda of Understanding (MOUs), offering red carpet treatment to investors. The overall responsibility for allowing foreign investment is still with the Centre and not with the states, but this would be a crucial first step.

A vital help that the state can render is to buy land for the industrial project. The purchase of land is governed by a 1894 Act which permits the state to buy land from its owners by offering compensation and, even if the seller disagrees, the state has 'eminent domain' to be able to take the land for public projects. The legislation was originally introduced for railway construction. While the public good is served, the private property rights of the seller are abridged. But what worked in the late nineteenth, or even much of the twentieth century, no longer works in an India which has tasted democratic freedoms for sixty years. There was immediate opposition to two of the West Bengal government's schemes, one at Nandigram where an Indonesian company was given land, and the other at Singur where Ratan Tata promised to locate his most dazzling innovation, the Nano—the Rs 100,000 car. It made a big sensation when the car was unveiled, and the first batch of cars was to roll out of Singur in late 2008.

There came a taste of the medicine CPI(M) cadres had been dishing out to industrial owners in the 1980s. A farmers' movement began in Nandigram in 2007. There were physical battles between the farmers opposing the setting up of the project, and the CPI(M) cadres who fought them with police help. This was illegal usurpation of state powers by a political party and Mamata Banerjee, who had set up her own faction outside the Congress—the Trinamul Congress—led the fight back. Mamata Banerjee had been staunchly anti-communist, but had had little success challenging Left hegemony in West Bengal. Now she saw her chance. The Buddhadev Bhattacharya government lost much face in the Nandigram episode, but it returned to power with a huge majority in the state elections in 2007. Then the battle moved to Singur, where, again, a minority of farmers who had not consented to sale of their land but had been overruled, decided with Banerjee's help to blockade access to the factory site. The Kolkata High Court had ruled that there was nothing illegal done by the West Bengal government in acquiring the 1000 acres for the Nano project. Given the history of CPI(M) and of Kolkata, many intellectuals denounced the concessions made to Ratan Tata by the government. After three decades of destruction of West Bengal industry, the appetite still existed for more of the same.

Soon, there was physical danger to Tata workers as the summer of 2008 progressed. Ratan Tata gave notice that he could quit the site. Attempts were made to negotiate a via media. Banerjee's demand was that one-third of the area, which was the share of the nay-sayers, should be set aside from the site and given over to them; she had mobilized them and represented their interests, which were hostile to the project This hostility was a sign of the despair of West Bengal farmers who had seen little industry, and saw no alternative to cultivation during their lifetime. They could not and would not trust the promise, either from Ratan Tata or the chief minister, that the Nano project would generate jobs for them and their children. Mediation by the West Bengal governor, Gopalkrishna Gandhi, himself a grandson of the Mahatma, was to no avail. In late September 2008, Ratan Tata pulled out of Singur, and among many offers he received from states who wished to host the re-located Nano project, he chose Gujarat. Modi had notched up one more triumph.

Singur brought out all the contradictions of India versus Bharat. There was a political angle since an ambitious politician, Mamata Banerjee, had used the dissatisfaction of farmers to sabotage a large project. Her hope was that when the general elections came in the summer of 2009, she could wrest some seats from the CPI(M). Since the Left had withdrawn support from the UPA in early July, Delhi did not lift a finger to save this most prestigious project; if anything, it connived with Banerjee to derail it. Yet, this was the West Bengal's past blocking its future. What Mamata Banerjee did was routine practice when CPI(M) was anti-business. Now twenty-five years on, the sides had changed. The desperation of the underdeveloped and hopeless farmers of West Bengal was also a palpable fact. The cynical truth is that if Mamata Banerjee were to come to power on the back of the protest and invite investment back to West Bengal, the CPI(M) would, no doubt, pay her back with the same coin.

Yet, what the episode tells us is that the right of private property in land needs better protection than what the Constitution gives. The property owner is no longer the ogre that the founding fathers imagined, and to whom they were hostile. He, or even she, is often a small farmer, a widow whose only asset is the piece of land. Such a person is bound to be cautious and reluctant to sell their possession; the state can, of course, bully them, but that is hardly just. Voluntary consent should be necessary before someone is deprived of their land in any free society. The mistake is to give the state such a powerful role. If land buying and selling were left to private agents, there would not be the asymmetry of power which the state introduces in its transactions. After 115 years, India needs to ditch the 1894 land legislation, and introduce land transaction procedures which are more in keeping with its democratic culture.

WAITING FOR GODOT

As the summer of 2008 passed, the febrile atmosphere of Indian politics became even more edgy. The prime minister had the privilege of speaking from the Red Fort for the fifth time on August 2008, once more than even Rajiv Gandhi. But the prospect of the elections, sometime before May 2009, was preoccupying everyone. Since the August of 2007, the UPA government had treaded water as it tried to keep the Left on its side. Many decisions were postponed—such as further liberalizing reforms in insurance and media ownership by foreign firms, the entry of foreign universities in higher education and reform of land and labour legislation. Elections were also due in a number of states in late 2008. The BJP had captured Karnataka by the summer of 2008, its first outright win in one of the four southern states. In Madhya Pradesh, Rajasthan and Chattisgarh, it was defending its majority, while the Congress had Delhi to secure for a record third straight win for its chief minister, Sheila Dixit. These elections would be read as auguries for the bigger battle in 2009.

The UPA government had lost some of its shine since inflation had gone into double digits. Indian voters are very inflation averse. One factor which had harmed the NDA coalition in 2004 was a sudden rise in the price of onions, a daily item of consumption for the poor and better-off alike. By the time the onion price came down, it was too late. The UPA tried to argue that the inflation was imported from abroad, thanks to the sharp rise in commodity prices especially oil and food grains. But the voter was right to feel sceptical. The same government was saying by the summer that the meltdown in financial markets in USA and Europe would not affect India as it was insulated, thanks to the caution in fully opening up the capital markets. Meanwhile, the Left which had been nursing its bruises after the trust vote, felt vindicated by the turmoil in the markets. In a heady atmosphere of capitalism collapsing and even George Bush buying up banks in distress, it seemed India's socialist ways could still enjoy a revival. Even Nicolas Sarkozy, the conservative President of France, was seen carrying around a copy of *Das Kapital*.

Team Manmohan, as the triumvirate of the prime minister, the finance minister and the deputy chairman of the Planning Commission, Dr Montek Singh Ahluwalia were known, did not trumpet any abandonment of reform. The financial meltdown was more serious than anyone had anticipated. It would require drastic restructuring of the international financial architecture. China and Japan but India also, as countries with healthy reserves of foreign exchange, were potential creditors who could lend to the IMF, enabling it to mount more rescue attempts of financial systems in Iceland, Hungary and, no doubt, many more. The demands for the reform of the global governance structure last agreed upon in 1945, had been gaining momentum for some time. The crisis exposed the shift in the balance of economic power from the West to the East. Asia's moment had come.

There was also much questioning of the free market philosophy, as preached by Thatcher–Reagan generation ideologues, which was still dominant. Alan Greenspan, the recent ex-chairman of the US Federal Reserve, was one such person. He had put his faith in the ability of private banks and hedge funds to self regulate. Now, as Lehman Brothers collapsed in mid-September 2008, the mood was getting anti-Greenspan. Banks had to be recapitalized if they were not to go under. It was even possible that they would have to be taken over by the state, albeit temporarily. At the same time as the financial meltdown, there was a crisis in the real economy. The Western countries had resolved to use massive fiscal and monetary intervention to get out of the recession before it could become a depression. Not just Karl Marx, even John Maynard Keynes was making a comeback.

India was affected as the industrial growth rate had already slowed down earlier in the year. The government hoped that India would have a mild growth slowdown, say from the heights of 9 per cent plus to around 7 or 7.5 per cent. Everyday was bringing bad news. The stock market had seen euphoric heights thanks to a lot of foreign money seeking high returns; the Bombay sensex had gone up from around 4000 when Dr Manmohan Singh became PM in May 2004, to 20,000 by mid-2008. Now it was trading below 10,000. Money was draining out of India. The basic mistake had been to liberalize the short-term flow of foreign money for portfolio purposes, and put obstacles on long-term foreign capital which came for investment in productive assets. Now the fast money was going and the slow money would be discouraged by foreign investors' own problems back home, as well as the sight of someone like Ratan Tata being unable to do lawful business, thanks to the fractured politics of India.

Bad economic news can be good politics as long as the news is really bad. This was what Gordon Brown, the UK prime minister, found during September 2008 as his fortunes prospered in inverse proportion to the state of the economy. In times of trouble, people prefer the incumbent. Dr Manmohan Singh also had the advantage of being known as an economist of vast experience. The BJP had problems proving that it had an alternative policy which could do better. The fact is that there had been a bipartisan consensus on the economy between the two national parties, though they dared not admit it publicly. The BJP had also thrown away a chance of sticking by the UPA when the Left abandoned it on the nuclear deal issue. The deal could have as easily been done by the BJP-led NDA as by the Congress-led UPA. The defeat in the trust vote left the BJP looking foolish, since its own MPs had crossed sides.

Its best bet was to bash the UPA on the question of national security. This was eventually a tonic for its anti-Muslim stance. It could sound tough on law and order, and accuse the UPA of pandering to the terrorists in the name of secularism. L.K. Advani, who had succeeded Vajpayee as leader of the BJP and of the NDA as well, was now designated prime minister-in-waiting. It was a ploy to project him as a strong man—*lohapurush* (iron man) in contrast to the mild-mannered Dr Singh. Advani had already had his own baptism of fire at the hands of the fundamentalists of the parivar. He had gone to Karachi from where his family hailed, and while speaking at a public meeting, had said that Jinnah was a much misunderstood man since he was quite secular. Jinnah's famous speech to Pakistan Constituent Assembly on 11 August 1947 was proof of his tolerance towards, indeed disinterest in, all religions.

Historical revisionism is all right for scholars, but bad for leaders of parties, especially newly chosen ones. Advani had to retract his statement, despite insisting that he had pretty much said the same in Delhi a few years ago when he was home minister during the NDA government. Vajpayee would have gotten away with it, but Advani had a hard-line reputation in the parivar. He had tried to put on the statesman's mantle far too soon. It was this fragility in his position which led Advani in November 2008 to react to the arrest by the ATS of some Hindu 'holy' people, one a woman self-styled as a *sadhvi*—'a woman saint'—and the other an army officer, as possible conspirators in a bomb blast in Malegaon, a town home to many Muslims, many of whom were hurt in the attack. The case was still being investigated and evidence was still coming in. A likely associate of the group, which had allegedly carried out the deed, was Pravin Togadia, the head of the VHP. The BJP president, Rajnath Singh had been caught on camera on a previous occasion talking in a friendly manner to the woman under investigation. Neither was being investigated by the ATS.

Many in the parivar reacted with shock and anger and, much like the secular fundamentalists did with Muslim suspects, denied that Hindus could be terrorists at all. The usual line in many previous cases, which many have adopted, is to say that the terrorist has no religion, whatever she or he may profess. This certainly is an effective way to separate the Islamist ideologue terrorist from an Islamic devout believer. But while it is one thing for various unofficial people to sound off against the ATS, accusing it of bias and playing politics, when Advani got onto the bandwagon, he made a serious error of judgement. A potential PM has to take the view that the law must be allowed to take its course, and no one is guilty till so proved in a court of law. He accused the police of torturing the woman who had been arrested, and also denounced the ATS.

There were other contenders for the prime ministerial post. The Third Force, as the anti-Congress and anti-BJP brigade styled itself, had chosen Mayawati as its leader on the eve of the trust vote. Preparations continued for pre-election agreement among the several parties—the Left, the BSP, the Telugu Desam, the AIADMK et al. Barack Obama's victory in the US presidential elections had raised the question of who could be India's Obama. Mayawati was certainly a likely candidate for the slot given her Dalit origins and the long distance she had to travel to get to the top. If Mayawati were by some chance to become prime minister of India, it would, indeed, be a world turned not 'upside down' so much, as 'right side up'. It would be the apotheosis of hundreds of years of struggle for equality of social status for the downtrodden of India.

At the other end of the privilege spectrum was Rahul Gandhi, the son of Rajiv and Sonia Gandhi. In the tradition of a monarchic democracy, he has the mantle waiting to fall on him. By all accounts he is a reluctant recruit to the political battlefield, as much as his father and mother had been at different times in their lives. His younger sister, Priyanka, was once expected to inherit the mantle, as she shows a flair for politics which reminds many of her grandmother, Indira Gandhi. But the decision has been to induct the son, not the daughter. Rahul Gandhi has been an MP since 2004 and has engaged himself in rebuilding the Congress. He is supposed to be encouraging younger people to join the party and to refurbish its internal democracy. The Congress has been unwilling to name him as the next prime minister.

But even as the summer turned into autumn, India and the world was in for a shock.

CHAPTER 16

WHOSE INDIA? WHICH INDIA?

IT IS RECORDED that on 25 November 1510, Alfonso Albuquerque invaded Goa. This was a more crucially significant event than Vasco da Gama's entry into India in 1498. Before the Mughals and, of course, two centuries and more before the English had any conquest to register, the Portuguese had a conquest thanks to Albuquerque. India had had its history littered with foreign incursions, but they had been by land, mostly from the north-western frontier with Afghanistan. The attack from the sea was to change India's destiny, though few could have accorded the small attack on the west coast much attention. The Portuguese Empire was to last for 450 years, longer than the French, the Danish, the Dutch and, of course, the British.

For the Portuguese, as for the Spanish, the maritime adventure was a part of the ongoing battle with the Muslims, who had only recently been driven out of Iberia. There would be many more years of Christian–Muslim war till the decisive battle of Lepanto in 1571. Alfonso reported back to King Manuel of Portugal:

> Our Lord helped us to do this job better than we had planned or expected. Over 300 'Turks' [this is what the Portuguese called Muslim Goans] died and till Benastery and Gandauly the roads were strewn with dead bodies and others lay wounded and dying. Several died while trying to cross the river with horses. I had the city put to fire and sword. During four days our men made the city bleed. No moor was given a chance to escape alive.
>
> They were driven into mosques which were then set ablaze. I ordered that the land cultivators and the Brahmins should not be killed. Nearly six thousand moors, men and women, were killed. No burial place or houses belonging to Muslims were left standing. Anyone caught is fried alive.[1]

Four hundred and ninety-eight years later, on 26 November 2008 at 9.25 p.m., Bombay/Mumbai was to witness an attack which lasted sixty hours. The victims were ecumenical—Hindu, Muslim, Jew, Sikh, Buddhist and Christian. They came from around the world and from around

India. That was more because of what Bombay is than anything else. The terrorists knew that. Bombay is at once a global city and an Indian city, though for some local politicians, it ought to be a Marathi-speaking village where outsiders are unwelcome. Hence its name Mumbai. But that does not change the nature of the city.

Bombay was to face an attack this time from the global Islamist movement; led by Al-Qaeda with its many franchised terrorist groups, all invoking some Islamic religious image of the army (*lashkar*), struggle (*jihad*), holy warrior (*mujahideen*), or taking the name of the Prophet Muhammad or even of Allah. Global Islamism, however, is a parasitic political ideology feeding on religious imagery. It wants to resume the thousand-year (on and off) war of Islam and the West. For Al-Qaeda, the war stopped briefly after the collapse of the Ottoman Empire and the abolition of the caliphate; it has just resumed seventy years on. Al-Qaeda struck New York and Washington, London, Madrid and Bali. It now came to India, which it has always considered to be part of the West, the 'Other', which has to be defeated or converted to Islam. Kashmir is part of the cauldron of Muslim issues which Al-Qaeda hopes to keep on the boil with violence. The idea came to Osama Bin Laden when USSR was defeated in Afghanistan. The West seemed the next easy target for the Islamist jihadis. Bosnia, Chechnya, Philippines, Palestine and Iraq, along with Kashmir and Indonesia, were all in the frame. Global Islamism is a parody of global capitalism.

Bombay was no stranger to terrorism. Only two years previously, the local commuter trains had been ripped apart by bombs and 183 people had died. There had been more blasts at other times with Pakistan-based groups, and even some Indian ones, claiming responsibility. But this was different. In scale, in thoroughness, in intensity and in cruelty, this was more an act of war than of terrorism. Bombay, indeed India, seemed to be held hostage for sixty hours.

The first stop of the attackers was the Taj Mahal hotel, a beautiful haven of luxury and elegance, which has stood at the Gateway of India since 1903. The Taj is a meeting place for Bombayites and a lot of multinational businessmen passing through. No one understood initially whether this was just one of the many 'routine' terrorist attacks India has seen plenty of, or something on a much more serious scale. It emerged later that this was a meticulously planned, well-resourced attack by a commando-style, well-trained and superbly fit, well-armed squad of perhaps only ten fighters. The Victoria Terminus (VT, renamed Chhatrapati Shivaji Terminus after the iconic Maratha hero of the seventeenth century) was next. At 9.50 p.m., it was attacked by two young men in blue fatigues with AK-56 and AK-47 plus RDX, 2000 rounds of ammunition, bombs and hand grenades. In all, fifty-nine people died at VT before the attackers moved on.

The terrorists then turned to the Cama Hospital (an example of Parsi charitable work) nearby and, along the way, killed the head of the ATS, Hemant Karkare as well as his colleagues, Vijay Salaskar and Ashok Kamte, who died almost at the outset of the attack. Hemant Karkare had been, until that morning, subject to a political attack by the parivar and the Shiv Sena, the local guardians of Marathi pride. They had threatened dire consequences if he persisted with his investigations into 'Hindu' terrorists. The Shiv Sena mouthpiece, *Saamna* had editorialized, 'This is nothing but a ploy to defame Hindutva by the people in the ATS who have taken a "supari" [a 'mafia like contract to kill'] for this. On such officers we spit, we spit.'[2]

These ATS and police officers died before they could be spat upon by the Shiv Sena or the VHP. Their bodies were thrown out of the police van which the two terrorists commandeered. In all, fourteen policemen died during the siege.[3]

The security response was woefully inadequate. For once, this was a tragedy caught on TV cameras and even mobile telephones. News came out and, across Bombay and India, people began to realize the enormity of the event. The electronic media were there 24x7, and the men and women covering the events worked non-stop. They were the only 'public' voice speaking to the nation and the world. The political system had failed totally. As one protester, after the event, said on a placard she was carrying, 'Terrorists strike at 9 p.m., Cabinet meets at 2 p.m.' The Union home minister, Shivraj Patil, had been the centre of criticism through the year as India faced one terrorist attack after another. His attitude showed the total unpreparedness of the counter-terrorism machinery.

Political India was preoccupied with its main activity—elections. Elections were due or taking place in Jammu and Kashmir, Madhya Pradesh, Rajasthan, Delhi, Mizoram and Chhatisgarh. Advani, the leader of the Opposition, did go and meet the prime minister almost immediately on the night of the 26th, but neither appeared before the public. Madhya Pradesh was voting on 27 November, the next day, and that was perhaps the only charitable reason why the prime minister did not speak to the nation till the evening of the 27th. The National Security Adviser, M.K. Narayanan, was at a party and, upon hearing the news, saw no reason to return to his office. The alphabet soup of security agencies—Research and Analysis Wing (RAW), Intelligence Bureau (IB), Defence Intelligence Agency (DIA), Joint Intelligence Committee (JIC), National Technical Research Organization (NTRO) and the National Security Council (NSC)—failed to garner advance information, pass it on or act upon it. When finally the prime minister and Sonia Gandhi did visit Bombay, Advani failed to accompany them, travelling separately. Manmohan Singh convened an all-party meeting after the attack ended, but Advani chose to go campaigning in Rajasthan which would vote on 4 December. Unity of purpose was hard to discern among the electoral concerns of the politicians.

The final toll was put at 173 dead and 288 injured.

CHIEFS FAIL INDIANS

The public outrage only barely exceeded its grief. There were candlelit vigils and processions; there were agonized blogs. Why had the politicians failed the people? The Bombay middle classes, like their counterparts all over India, had abandoned politics to the grubby politicians, but now they wanted answers. Shivraj Patil resigned as home minister over the weekend. P. Chidambaram, the finance minister, took over his portfolio. The Maharashtra chief minister and deputy chief minister took their time resigning, and even more time was taken finding their replacements as the equations of caste and coalition came into play. Seven days later, Bombay had a chief minister and on Monday, 8 December at 4.50 p.m. Ashok Chavan took oath.

The shock of the attack on Indian soil was palpable to the citizens, but the politicians failed to empathize. Indians know that their leaders are not evil, just corrupt and often incompetent. Over the years the middle classes have fallen behind in their share of those actually voting, while the poor have kept up their participation at a higher level than the middle classes. The poor voters elect their leaders for handouts, and the middle class thinks they don't need them. Thus, they pay little attention to the failure of their elected representatives. Such failure is almost predictable from the thousand delays in tackling other myriad problems Indians face. The macho posturing of a nuclear power was no compensation against ten young men as they took a corner of Bombay, which was iconic. The Gateway of India says it all.

The cumbersome ways of Indian politics were in full view. There were full-page advertisements in the newspapers seeking votes for BJP against the backdrop of the bloody act. The Congress lay low lest it attract more opprobrium, and talked only of the need for all-party unity. But in the meantime, results of the state elections began to come in. By Monday 8 December, just ten days after the attack, it was the triumph of Sheila Dixit in Delhi, winning a third term for the Congress and the capture of Rajasthan by the Congress, which made the headlines. The BJP retained Madhya Pradesh and Chhatisgarh where development-oriented governments beat the incumbent jinx. In Mizoram the Mizo National Front lost after ten years in power and the Congress won overwhelmingly—just twenty years after the guerrilla warfare that had ravaged the state. There was relief in UPA circles that neither terrorism nor inflation had hurt the Congress. The BJP had gambled on a 'soft on terror' plank but it did them no good.

There had been hope that Indian politicians would sink their differences about Muslim terrorism and Hindu terrorism and try and define a common story of what was under attack. This did not happen. What served the same purpose, as far as politicians were concerned, was Pakistan bashing. Immediately after the Bombay attacks, there was the cry that Pakistan had been behind them. Lashkar-e-Taiba (LeT), a Pakistan-based terrorist group, and Jamat-ud-Dawa, its 'civilian' front, were named as the agents. The ISI or its retired personnel were named as trainers of the ten young men. Indian TV channels were ready for war as the rhetoric became shriller. It is always easy to shift the blame from one's own incompetence to the evil designs of the Old Enemy. Lacking a truly unifying narrative, the politicians know that they can always fall back on Pakistan.

WHO AND WHAT IS INDIA?

The 26/11 events highlighted, more sharply than anything else could have done, the one question I have been raising throughout this book. The standard narratives—Nehruvian syncretic/secular or Hindutva— proved inadequate. Even more tragic was the absence of politicians as guardians of India's flame. For the previous few years, the Indian success story had been getting more and more hyped up. 'India Unbound', 'India Shining', 'Incredible India', 'The Fastest Growing and the Largest Free Market Democracy', etc. were the eye-catching slogans. Here was a different India: a somnolent, soft, dysfunctional India; a badly trained, under-armed India, unable to defend itself. What had happened to the miracle story?

The Lok Sabha had witnessed embarrassing scenes at its previous session when the trust vote was taken. Now, it met again for the final phase of the winter session on 10 December. There was a show of unity, but it was for fighting Pakistan. Is India defined more by Pakistan than by itself?

THE ARGUMENT REVISITED

India was first defined, I argued, by the 'Other', which was the foreign presence. It was the historical accident of the European presence in India, from the sixteenth century onwards, which began to shape India as we know it today. Before then it was a society and a culture, perhaps more than one society and culture, but not a nation. Of course, the

Europeans came pursuing their war against the Muslims as Albuquerque says explicitly. It was the Arabs (Turks as the Portuguese called them) who had control of the Indian Ocean trade, which the Portuguese contested. They won the contest thanks to their superior military technology. The contest did not end there. Its focus shifted later to Europe again. But in India the Europeans settled down to pursue trade, and functioned like the scores of Indian kingdoms aligning or fighting the rest regardless of religion.

There was no need to define an Indian nation, or even worry about its territorial boundaries till the mid-nineteenth century. By then two things had happened. In Europe the British had defeated the French and subordinated the Portuguese and the Dutch to their purposes. India had small foreign enclaves where the French, the Portuguese and the Dutch had possession, but the rest of India was either British or 'native'. It was the defeat of the 1857 Mutiny/Revolution/Rebellion—call it what you will—which sealed the fact that a sovereign Indian dynasty—Hindu or Muslim—would never rule over substantial parts of India. Denied the chance of being a dynastic empire or kingdom, India had then to invent itself as a nation.

The tools to define India as a nation had been made available by foreign rulers. Macaulay had opened up the treasures of Western knowledge to a much wider audience than had been the case earlier. Isolated scholars, such as Rammohun Roy, could communicate in English as in Persian, but few others could. Indeed, other than the Brahmins who could read Sanskrit, the Kayasthas and other writer castes, and a parallel group of Muslim elite who knew Arabic and Persian, the bulk of the country could neither read nor write. Yet, the few who learnt English at Elphinstone, Presidency and St Xavier's colleges, formed the elite brigade of Indian nationalism. The foreigners, with their intrepid curiosity, dug up monuments, collected manuscripts, attempted translations and began to reconstruct a rudimentary account of India's past.

The avant-garde of Indian nationalism were clever; indeed they were soon showing themselves to be better than their rulers and teachers. They absorbed the Western lore and threw it back at the rulers, accusing them of un-British rule. They knew their Burke and Pitt, and recited them back. The rulers challenged them to prove that India was indeed a nation, and not just a hotch-potch of religions and regions and languages. Christian evangelists, who had fought and won access to India from the British Parliament after decades of assiduous propaganda, had long denounced Hinduism as an area of darkness. They had been engaged in a contest with Islam since the Arab armies swept into Mediterranean Europe in the eighth century.

The shock of 1857 was such for the British that they decided to give up any scheme of reform of Indian society, and forbade the various Christian denominations from aggressive conversion. Victoria's proclamation promised equal treatment and protection for all religions. The British state may have an established Church, but British India was going to be a secular state. Yet, the critique of religion had sunk home for the Indians. They had to respond.

Hindus reacted with the dual strategy of reform and revival. They all took pride in the hoary old lineage of Hinduism and the great books which had poetry, epic stories and high philosophy. The revivalists, though, were fighting Islam as well as Christianity. The reformers were fighting the British and, to that end, wanted all hands on the deck. They were happy to recruit Muslims. The Muslims had their own long history of fighting British rule, which began with the breakdown of the Mughal Empire. Here, the revivalist and reformist duality was reproduced. The difference was that for the Muslims, this was not just an Indian struggle, but a struggle which stretched across the Muslim world whose centre was the Ottoman Empire. As the largest concentration of Muslims in the world, India had a special place both for theological and political leadership.[4]

The Congress was a broad tent, when it started in 1885, for all the Westernized elite who wished to reform British rule. By 1905, when it began battling the British rule thanks to the Bengal Partition, its radical wing chose a Hindu religious narrative to mobilize the young and middle-class people. The moderates relied on gentle persuasion and patient petitioning. They stuck to a non-religious idiom. The moderates could claim a victory since the Morley–Minto reforms opened up a parliamentary path for British India. Along with it came the question of how India was to be represented. Who were the Indians? The Muslim leadership, alarmed by the bold stand of the Congress petitioning the government for jobs and tariff protection and arguing about the value of the rupee, saw the Bengal agitation as directed against them and sought and obtained separate electorates for themselves in the new reforms. The Bengal Partition was annulled and Muslims lost the one gain they had made in decades of British rule. The Congress faced the challenge of deciding who it represented—India or just the Hindus. Jinnah at the Lucknow Congress of 1916 made an attempt to fuse together the Congress and the Muslim League in a pact embodying the moderate strategy. But Gandhi's strategy of mass mobilization was to render such legislative arrangements irrelevant. The rift which then began between the two religious narratives of nationhood was to shape the next forty years. Despite Gandhi's efforts in 1920 to recruit the Khilafat issue to the Indian anti-British struggle, the union proved temporary. But the Congress's hegemony was established, and its narrative became the nationalist narrative.

Once India had contributed to the war effort in the First World War as had the White colonies, it was clear that sooner or later the British would transfer power in a limited way, at least making India a Dominion Status country. This was implicit in Montagu's speech in 1917. What Gandhi did in 1922, by suspending the Non-cooperation movement due to Chauri Chaura, was to show that the Congress was a 'responsible opposition' to HMG. He had studied his British parliamentary and political history and already rehearsed his techniques of civil unarmed disobedience in South Africa. From then till 1935, there was a pirouette of advance and withdrawal, of acceptance and rejection. The blueprint of an independent India was implicit in the Government of India Act 1935. The issue was the pace of the transfer of power, not its likelihood. By 1937 the Congress had taken part in provincial elections and accepted that it had to apprentice itself for power. The Congress's decision to resign at the outbreak of the war began its period of impotence. The Quit India movement was a mistake in as much as it cost the Congress three years of absence from the fray. It did, however, burnish its anti-colonial credentials. Still, for the Congress, its wish for hegemony was paramount, and it was its desire for monopoly of power that shaped the negotiations between 1944 and 1947. The Congress accepted the Partition despite its later denial. It wanted to rule India on its own terms. Jinnah overreached himself and, as I have argued, was outsmarted by Gandhi and Nehru. He got a moth-eaten Pakistan, which became even more so in 1971. The Congress won most of India—the commercially prosperous and more populous and fertile parts.

In 1947 the Congress took power from the British with a show of continuity rather than rupture. Old antagonisms were forgotten and Mountbatten became a hero. The Indian Civil Service was kept intact, and Sardar Patel and Nehru saw to it that the transfer of power was smooth. The new government of India exercised paramountcy with all the finesse of Dalhousie. Except for the severing of its limbs in the north-west and in Bengal, India was one. The new state was secular just as its predecessor was; not for the sake of ideology, but as a prudent practice.

The past is prologue, but in our case it will not go away. The narrative of Indian nationhood that the Congress had presented was a North Indian one and also elitist in terms of membership—the Hindu upper castes, the Muslim aristocracy and the rich middle class were the members. It had many challengers. It was contested by Hindu Mahasabha which defined India as a Hindu nation, sharing the Congress's upper-caste elitism, but excluding the Muslim aristocracy and middle class. The

Muslim League had championed an elitist approach to seek minority rights for Muslims by being loyal to the British. It did not have its own narrative of Indian nationhood; it just did not accept the narrative the Congress offered. The Partition removed the Muslim League's challenge along with half of India's Muslim population, and strengthened the Mahasabha's position. Only Gandhi's assassination and Nehru's towering personality kept it at bay. Nehru revived and refurbished the Congress narrative. He became, in effect, the narrative of Indian nationhood after 1947 by his speeches and his actions. Above all, he was aware that the fragmented Muslim population left behind would need special protection against a majoritarian logic, which democracy privileges.

The other narrative which was subdued was the Dalit/anti-Brahmin narrative from the South and the Deccan. Here was a hundred years of questioning of the 'Wonder that was India'. It had benefited from the British window on Western rationalism and notions of egalitarianism, so foreign to Hindu society. Jotirao Phule and Ambedkar and Ramaswamy Naicker were the subaltern subversive narrators of this story. Gandhi's accommodation of Ambedkar had been uneasy and grudging. The issue would not go away by just a fast or two. This challenge was also part of a broader one against reading Indian history from a North Indian, Indo-Gangetic perspective.

It was in this context that Pakistan and its provoking a dispute over Kashmir proved crucial to Indian nationalism. However awkward it was that a Muslim nation, formerly part of the national narrative, was now an enemy, Pakistan focussed India's attention on the one element which became central to its narrative of nationhood. This was territorial integrity. The Congress had little military imagination before Independence (Subhash Bose apart), since it knew that it would inherit the territory of British India, along with its borders and its army. But after Partition, territory became a uniting theme for the nation. Not giving up Kashmir was the big theme. Pakistan cemented India, as indeed, the theme of Kashmir cemented Pakistan.

Territory was also at issue in the 1962 war with China. India had decided to defend the British imperial boundaries as its own and no questions were negotiable. The Chinese viewed them as products of past injustices of the British meted out on the Chinese, which needed to be redressed; the Indians saw their boundaries as age-old and inviolable. The same was the case in the North-East. Here was a region which had never been a part of the grand narrative of Indian nationhood—Nehruvian, Hindutva or Dalit/anti-Brahmin. Even the national anthem has no mention of Assam or its great river, the Brahmaputra, though it does mention Sind. The long struggle to tame the Nagas, Mizos, Bodos and other tribes and induct them into the Indian Union has been occupying Indian governments ever since 1947. But territory it is and it is India's.

It was the unravelling of the Congress's hegemony soon after Nehru's death which gave voices to the other narratives. It began with the anti-Hindi agitation in the South. Kashmir had to be found a better deal than Nehru had offered. But Indira Gandhi destroyed the original Congress, and released many regional and caste tendencies which were in the broad tent. Her imperial manner succeeded for a while, especially thanks to the Bangladesh War. By 1975, the advantage Indira Gandhi had got by splitting the Congress and sharpening her populist radical rhetoric was eroded. Nehru's India ended in 1975 with the Emergency. While Nehru was prime minister, he established certain norms and practices whereby the Judiciary, the army and the police, and the civil services were insulated from politics. Indira Gandhi began to invade that neutral public place. She invoked the doctrine of mandate, which meant she could override the Judiciary and the Constitution. She also argued that all appointments in the civil services were subject to a loyalty to the elected leader rule. The Congress also stopped having any procedures by which inner party elections took place openly and democratically.

Indira Gandhi also made secularism an ideology, part of her radicalism/populism, and even introduced an amendment to the Constitution to add the words secular and socialist in the preamble to 'Sovereign Democratic Republic of India'. Secularism was no longer for all Indians; it was a badge of being Congress and Left-wing. India became officially secular just when it ceased to be so in practice. The Janata government, in its brief period of power, removed some of the worst damage she had done. But later populist governments could follow her example, and did so at state levels.

Indira Gandhi came back and kept the Congress in power till 1989, as much by her death as by her life. But this was a false autumn. She began to indulge all religions, but especially Hinduism and Islam openly, as part of the public life. Rajiv did much worse by his concessions to the orthodoxies of both major religions. Secularism was now a tattered garment. The state did not stand above the religious divisions but treated them as equal claimants to its attention. The same was to happen to other divisions. The Indian state had to use force much more often to quell the 'million mutinies'. The winter of discontent was soon to commence.

There is also the economic dimension of the Congress hegemonic discourse, which is germane to my argument. The anxiety about territorial integrity and the desire for a monopoly of power, induced a centralizing and military–industrial bias to the development efforts of the first thirty years. India chose a top-heavy growth, but failed to provide employment or literacy or health facilities for the masses. India could make a nuclear bomb, but not connect rural India with urban India by roads. The Hindu rate of growth was a matter of choice exercised by the elite, who did not have to pay its cost. It took Indira and Rajiv Gandhi's limited efforts to escape the stranglehold of the Mahalanobis strategy which brought some relief during the 1980s. But it was not enough; four decades of stagnation drove India's economy to its fateful wreck in 1991.

MANY PARTIES, MANY NARRATIVES

It is the last twenty years which have shown that India needs to fashion a new narrative of nationhood. The anxieties of the earlier generation— that if there was not a single hegemonic account India would break up— have, as yet, not been realized. India survived the anti-Hindi agitation, troubles in Kashmir and the North-East. Even Khalistan, the biggest challenge to the notion of Indian nationhood, was contained, though at the cost of much blood. The key has been that India is large and diverse. None of the many mutinies occupied a large slice of Indian territory. Most of India was at peace or only mildly troubled, even while a certain region was in revolt.

The lessons of recent history, however, warn against any false hopes. Large federations have had a bad time recently. Within the last twenty years, two mighty federations, the USSR and Yugoslavia have imploded, the latter violently. Both were strong, and exemplified an alternative possibility of a non-capitalist, non-liberal polity. The USSR was just under seventy-five years old (or under sixty since its Constitution was proclaimed in 1935). Yugoslavia was not much older than India. Nearer home, Pakistan split in 1971 and Sri Lanka has had a civil war for twenty-five years. What, then, has kept India together?

What helped again was the global context. The struggle for equality of social status had sparked off movements for civil rights in the US— anti-racism, feminism, human rights for indigenous peoples. Class war was now displaced; the socialism/capitalism dichotomy was not the theatre of battle any longer. The end of the Cold War, with the collapse of the Berlin Wall, released enormous energy across the world and myriad movements developed. It also opened up the scope for a new global phase of capitalism. India was to benefit from both these trends— struggles for social equality and the liberalization of the economy.

The dominant ideology of nationalism, which Congress as well as Hindutva forces had championed, was for control from the top around a single narrative. To begin with, there was a struggle between the two rival narratives to establish sole control. Secularism versus communalism became the axis along which parties were ranged. The upsurge of

Hindutva ideology took the Congress and its partners on the Left by surprise. They had imagined that Hindutva was outdated, medieval, obscurantist and hardly likely to acquire mass appeal. But religion had been a part and parcel of Indian politics since the days of Tilak. Gandhi deployed religious imagery to great power and while he was ecumenical, after 1922 few Muslims followed him. Nehru was an exception. Being an atheist and a rationalist, he downplayed religion successfully during his tenure. But none of his fellow Congress members took his brand of secularism seriously. What remained in face of the Hindutva challenge was that the Congress could assure Muslims that they would be looked after as a special case. Rajiv Gandhi was even willing to side with orthodox misogynist Muslim clergy to deprive Shah Bano of her hard judgement for maintenance. Secularism was for the men; deprivation for women.

Thus the Hindu–Muslim fissure opened up again. Was secularism a strict separation between religion and the state, or was it an even-handed treatment of all religions, but with a special concern for the largest minority? Was it just an excuse for the elite in power to trash Hinduism, while treating Islam with elaborate respect? These questions began to be aired. Increasing prosperity, meanwhile, had allowed Indians to indulge in conspicuous consumption. One of the major consumer items was religiosity or spirituality. Gurus and swamis and sants proliferated. They had thousands of patrons who wished to display their devotion. Houses became decorated with little temples and statues and icons. Festivals for Ganesha became larger and louder popular events each passing year. Indeed, Ganesha has become a secular god for all of India whom Muslims, Christians as well Hindus are happy to worship. Religion could not be kept out of India, any more than it could be in America. But the US has a strict separation between the Church and the state. The President may take his oath and swear by God, but the US as a government cannot spend any money on any religious activity. India has secularism, but fuzzy boundaries as to what can and cannot be done by the state. The practice has been to spend on each community as much as the electorate could bear. The government does subsidize the Haj pilgrimage for Muslims, and treats the Hindu joint family as an allowable tax shelter. Of course, each community thinks the other gets more.

Hindu–Muslim tension has become the principal source of violence in India for the last twenty years. The demise of Nehruvian secularism in 1975 and the myriad compromises made since then for electoral reasons, have made secularism a political football. The BJP has aggressively argued against it, and its parivar has decided to use religion openly as a mobilization card. The Congress stands by the Muslims when it sees an electoral advantage, but is ready to abandon them when convenient. The result is a violation of the public space. Hence the Babri Masjid conflicts and consequent riots of December 1992, January 1993 and March 1993 in Bombay, the Gujarat riots of 2002 and the fractured debate on terrorism. India has found no overarching narrative to contain this divide. Secularists are disheartened. Secularism is now just the bid for Muslim votes and, as such, has been taken over by caste parties (such as OBC parties of the Yadavs in UP and Bihar) and non-Hindu religious bodies. It has lost all coherence. Worse still, it has brought about an idea that Indians are not equal before the law. Hence, the bitter debates around 'encounter killings' by the police where Muslims have been killed, and the new bitterness about Hindu terrorists. Immunity is sought for each community, even as its members defy the law.

But, there have also been the fissures caused by the reservations debate. On one hand, it is the Indianization of affirmative action. Since Hindu society is hierarchical and caste is the marker for status as well as life chances, it is convenient to use caste labels to dole out ameliorative policies. The SC/ST reservations, initially for fifteen years, have been extended indefinitely. But for this 22 per cent minority, their deprivation is irrefutably due to their forced existence on the margins of society. They had no chance of upward mobility till the British came, and not much even then. For the castes within the Hindu varna system, mobility has been uneven but not impossible. The uplift of the Patidars of Gujarat, the Jats of Haryana and UP, the Yadavs of UP and Bihar, are all evidence of this.[5]

In seeking to extend reservations to 27.5 per cent more, the Indian system had despaired of economic advance coming from any source other than state patronage. The economic failure of the Congress in its forty years is, of course, the structural cause for this despair. Yet, the Congress's misguided policy has been easier to redress and has been revised since 1991; the entrenchment of Mandal will be much harder to remove. This is because it solidifies the identities of social backwardness and valorizes them by making them a passport to public goods. Then the ballot box cements them into vote banks, and democracy does the rest. The egalitarian logic of the Constitution presumes an individualistic basis for each citizen's rights. The practice is that individuals are now seen through the prism of their religious or caste 'community'.

Thus, the masjid–mandir division, added to the Mandal one, makes India a fragmented polity. Citizens are not just Indians, but hyphenated ones—as OBC-Indians, Muslim-Indians, SC/ST-Indians and so on. It is then just another step to labelling citizens by the language they speak or the province they originate from. Regional nationalism had always run parallel with Indian nationalism, but had been suppressed during the negotiations for Independence. Had India been a confederation as envisaged by the 1935 Act, such local nationalism would have flourished as the Centre would have had a much smaller presence and states a lot of autonomy.

Independence came with a centralizing top-down mentality, and Delhi continued to behave like an imperial headquarters as it had done since the twelfth century when the Delhi Sultanate was established. Yet, the linguistic reorganization of the states, the anti-Hindi agitation, the many struggles in the North-East, in Jammu and Kashmir and the Khalistan movement in Punjab, have all shown that sub-nationalisms flourish. The Constitution cannot accommodate this; politics, however, since 1989 has had to come to terms with it. The single narrative of the Congress no longer commands loyalty. The single narrative of the BJP parivar does not either, as the Ramsetu controversy showed.

If Indians are not Indians, but Muslims and Hindus and OBCs and SC/STs, why can they not be further divided into, for instance, Marathi-speaking-Hindu-non-Brahmin Marathas, who are distinct and deserving special treatment in their 'own' state of Maharashtra? This is precisely what the Shiv Sena and its offshoot, the Maharashtra Navnirman Sena, have argued. They want North Indians working in Bombay to cede jobs to Marathi speakers. They wish to muscle them out of Bombay. The Shiv Sena also had argued about the intrusive South Indians, who were taking away 'our jobs' in the 1960s. Such fascist populism has been accommodated rather than opposed by the Congress due to electoral considerations. The Assamese have targeted Biharis working in their state. They also complain about illegal migration from Bangladesh—so all Bengali speakers are under scrutiny there.

WHO THEN IS AN INDIAN? WHAT IS INDIA?

India has survived scaremongers, predicting the return of imperialism, break-ups, Balkanization, secessions and the end of democracy, since its birth as a nation state in 1947. It has managed to become an economic success story belying the pessimism of the pioneers of the nationalist movement. Does it, however, face a new danger? Did the events of 26/11 and the inability of the political system to speak to the people or for the people raise the old questions again, only in a new form?

Is India's political fracturing since 1989 an irreversible phenomenon? Will it cause a serious disruption among Indians along the cleavages of caste, language, religion, region and class? Or, can we say that the economic renaissance of India is the fruit of the end of a single party hegemony; that it has downgraded the Indian state and stopped it from blocking economic progress? Will an increasing prosperity be the solvent for such divisions as people find attractive life chances in the private sector and leave behind the fight for political patronage? What and how can we reconcile economic success and political dysfunction in India?

Indians appear to have lost a unity of identity, except when it concerns an external enemy. Pakistan, or even China, cannot be relied upon to keep Indian identity as one. There has to be a better answer than that. What is the basis for a new narrative of Indian nationhood, which can deliver such an identity even without the unifying presence of an alien 'Other'?

VERDICT 2009: A NEW START FOR INDIA?

The general elections held in five phases during April–May 2009 provided a surprising answer to these questions. While it is as yet premature to discern long-run trends from such recent results, a tentative answer has to be made. India's 700 million voters managed to score a 60 per cent turnout and then deliver a decisive verdict. The elections returned the UPA with a larger plurality than had been anticipated by any of the many experts. The Congress on its own gained sixty-one seats more than its tally in 2004. It had been selective in making pre-poll alliances, shedding many who were part of outgoing governments such as RJD, the party of Bihar's Lalu Prasad Yadav. Its main partners were the DMK in Tamil Nadu and the Trinamul Congress in West Bengal. Its coalition partners added another fifty-six seats to its own 206 to reach a total of 262. This gave it a commanding position to claim power as it fell only eleven short of a majority. The RJD and the SP had formed a Fourth Front, but won only twenty-eight seats and offered support to the UPA.

Other identity-based parties, most notably the BSP which Mayawati led, also failed to win as many seats as they had hoped. Mayawati and the Congress shared—almost equally—the eighty seats from UP; her dreams of being prime minister at the head of the Third Front along with the Left parties, were shattered. The CPI(M) got only sixteen and the CPI four seats, the lowest since 1952. The Third Front, a rag-tag coalition at best, got only seventy-nine seats, considerably less than the number required to block both the UPA and the NDA from forming a government. The Lohiaite concept, of a non-Congress–non-BJP coalition governing India, was decisively defeated.

The BJP won 112 seats, twenty-six less than its score in 2004, and its partners in the NDA added forty-eight more. UPA, with 262 seats, had a lead of 102 over the NDA. This second successive defeat for the BJP-led NDA has inaugurated a crisis in the BJP. At 112 its numbers are the lowest since 1991. One of its coalition partners, the Janata Dal(U) in power in Bihar, managed to increase its tally from twelve to twenty. The Bihar chief minister, Nitish Kumar had set an example of good governance while not abandoning identity politics. In Orissa the Biju Janata Dal (BJD), an erstwhile partner of the BJP, also increased its tally from eleven to thirteen, thus cementing the position of Navin Patnaik, the chief minister of Orissa.

India has now guaranteed itself a stable government for a further five years. Despite the fragmentation of the party political structure in the post-Mandal years since 1989, the NDA and the UPA would have ruled as single-party coalitions from 1998 till 2014 on current expectations. Indeed, only four out of the twenty years since 1989 have seen 'Third Front' coalitions—1989–91 and 1996–98. The two national parties, the Congress and the BJP, had together totalled 282 seats in 1989, the lowest since 1952 when the Congress alone got 364. This total fluctuated over the next few elections as 364 (1991), 301 (1996), 323 (1998), 296 (1999) and 283 (2004). Now, the combined tally of the two national parties had risen again to 318. This can be interpreted as a swing back in favour of national versus regional parties. Of course, neither of the two national parties has a presence in all states. Each uses regional partners where its presence is small. Thus, Congress uses the DMK in Tamil Nadu and the Trinamul Congress in West Bengal as major partners. The BJP has the Shiv Sena in Maharashtra and the Akali Dal in Punjab.

One clear trend which was reflected in the state elections in November–December 2008 was reinforced in 2009. This was the success of parties which delivered good governance. As I have described before, those state governments which used their larger revenues to improve the provision of public goods and services defied the anti-incumbency rule. This was the case with the BJP in Madhya Pradesh and Chattisgarh, and the Congress in Delhi. The JD(U) in Bihar and the BJD in Orissa showed the importance of development, as did the Congress in Andhra Pradesh and the DMK in Tamil Nadu. The fruits of economic reform have compensated for the fissures of identity politics.

Indeed, the success of the UPA can also be seen as a reward for delivery of good growth rate for four out of five years (till the global recession reduced the growth rate to around 5 per cent), as well as the rural employment scheme, NREGA, and a generous debt waiver scheme worth Rs 600 billion which relieved rural distress. The response to the 26/11 outrage had been measured, and though the issue has not yet been resolved between Pakistan and India, at least they have not gone to war with each other.

It is tempting to think of the Congress's return to 200-plus seats as the vindication of the Nehruvian vision of Indian nationhood. The BJP clearly failed to engage the voters with its emphasis on terrorism, and its casting the UPA government and especially Prime Minister Manmohan Singh as weak. It hesitated in pushing an aggressive Hindutva message with Ramsetu and anti-Muslim rhetoric, though individually Narendra Modi and Varun Gandhi (the son of Sanjay Gandhi) did indulge in such rhetoric. The BJP faces a crisis of identity and, like many opposition parties which have tasted the fruits of office, needs to resolve this urgently. But at 112 seats, one cannot say that its vision is vanquished totally. It is in power in Gujarat, Madhya Pradesh, Chattisgarh, Karnataka, Uttarakhand, Bihar (with the JD(U)) and Punjab (with the Akali Dal).

Neither the Left with its anti-American vision nor the rest of the Third Front could command much support nationally. Nonetheless, in Punjab, Bihar, UP, Orissa and Tamil Nadu, regional parties are in power, whether singly or as a national partner in a coalition. These states represent 200 out of 543 seats in the Lok Sabha. In Jammu and Kashmir the National Conference is in power, while Kerala and West Bengal have communist governments, though after these parliamentary elections their position is precarious. There is, thus, still a great deal of regional specificity in governments.

Can we say, then, that the Indian nation is now firmly re-established? Can we assert that the single nationalist narrative of the Nehruvian variety is now back in dominance? Has India resolved its contradictions? Or, do the developments tell us a different story?

The argument against declaring a victory for a single Nehruvian narrative can be seen in the way the two national parties have performed in recent years. We looked at the sum of their seats above; the difference is equally informative. Thus since 1989, the Congress minus the BJP score has been 112 (1990), 122 (1991), –21 (1996), –41 (1998), –68 (1999), 7 (2004), 94 (2009). What we are seeing here is a cycle rather than a trend. The combined total of the two major parties fluctuates; since 2004 it has been on the rise. The difference seems to be in the Congress's favour right now, but for how long?

Yet, the lessons of the last twenty years, indeed the last sixty years, are that, perhaps, the obsession with a single overarching narrative— Nehruvian or Hindutva—is unwarranted. India's history and even more its people, have been charting a course which can be read differently.

RECASTING THE NARRATIVE OF NATIONHOOD

We need to rethink the history and origins of India as a nation state. India is an old civilization, but a young nation. As a nation it is, at most, 150 years old, but as a nation state it is only sixty-two years old. Its birthmarks as a nation were affected by its origins in a reactive response to a foreign presence. This is what led the elite to seek an old and continuous history of India qua nation, rather than as a civilization or a culture. This is why single overarching narratives had to be constructed, which related uncomfortably to the actual fragmented historical experience. India was not a single nation, unlike China, through most of its history. To invent a Hindu India of old lineage, or invent a syncretic India of Hindu–Muslim melange, are flawed exercises. The reason for their falseness is that each narrative denies the 'Indian-ness' (*bharatiyata/ hindustaniyat*) of a substantial part of contemporary India—either the South, the North-East, the Muslims, the tribal people, the Dalits or the many other minorities—Sikhs, Christians, Parsis, Jews, Jains, Buddhists.

Think, instead, of India as a creature of the 150 years since 1857. There was no Indian nation before then. What the rebels fought for in 1857 was the Mughal Empire or a revival of the Maratha dream of *Hindu-pata-padshahi*. It was confined to the Indo-Gangetic plains, and did not spread beyond. Troops from Punjab and Peshawar and Bombay fought the troops from Awadh and Meerut and Barrackpore. The former were led by the British and the latter by, well, no one in particular. As in 26/11, the sepoys had to fight for themselves; the few 'leaders' who claimed credit led from behind, not from the front. The so-called leaders were brave and they deserve tribute, but not for a vision or even talent for fighting the British. It is a story good for sentiment, not for serious nation building.

The 1857 experience had two effects. The British became socially conservative and politically cautious. But for the new generation of Indians, it removed forever the idea of an Indian king. From now on, India would be a republic. India would be a modern nation, whenever it became an independent nation state.

This India, the new nation state which was born in 1947, should be seen as an unprecedented construction, bigger than any previous empire in the area. No one, after all, had brought the Tamils and the Assamese and the Gujaratis and the Punjabis together under *one sovereign* domain, along with the Indo-Gangetic plains. These regions had never shared a single administrative structure, a single system of law or a single native or foreign Hindu or Muslim rule. British India excluded the native states, and while it gave India an administrative unity, it was an alien rule which had to go. India as a nation state was a new phenomenon. Other empires also existed which brought together many languages and many peoples. The Austro-Hungarian Empire or the Ottoman Empire were large collections of nations. Neither had any movement which sought to define a single supra-nationality over the entire region. After the First World War, they both broke up into many nations. Both were pre-capitalist constructs, and they were also non-democratic.

India is different. It became a colony simultaneously with the Industrial Revolution. The colonizer was also the winner in the European wars which spanned the eighteenth century. The modernization of Britian was parallel with that of India. Law and the civil services and the idea that the state was concerned with the welfare of the people, was an idea first formulated by Bentinck, which went back to Britain after having come to India via Bentham. India was, thus, a creature of global capitalism harnessed to the winner country. It was also harnessed to a democracy which, uniquely in Europe, had fashioned its own peaceable way of reform. India inherited that uniqueness through the work of an England-trained barrister—Mohandas Karamchand Gandhi. It is this democratic framework, imbibed by India alone among the modern colonies over a century and more, which has made it a success story.

AMERICA AS A MIRROR FOR INDIA

India is by reason of its plurality much like the USA. America is an older nation state than India, but the civilization from which it claims its origins—the European civilization—is younger than the Indian civilization. America's first struggle for nationhood was like India's, just thirty years long between the first protests about arbitrary taxation via the surrender of Cornwallis at Yorktown in 1783, and the adoption of the Constitution in Philadelphia in 1787. But, as the nation grew, it has had to come to terms with its own diversity. Indeed, America acknowledged some aspects of its diversity—the melting pot formed to absorb White immigrants from Europe. But it struggled, for its whole history, to accommodate the involuntary slaves who arrived from Africa, not to mention the native Americans (once called 'Indians') against whom the settlers fought many wars.

America saw its history as that of a White nation, to which immigrants from all over Europe had come. It thought of itself, at the beginning of its nationhood, as a White Anglo-Saxon Protestant nation. Then, perhaps, as White and Protestant, once Germans and Scandinavians came, and as White and Christian when Catholics came from Ireland, Italy and Mexico. It was not until 1960 that a Catholic could become President of the United States. By the 1980s, there were demands that American history be rewritten to acknowledge the contribution of the Black Americans. Even what the former slaves were called—from negroes to coloured people to Black to people of colour to African–American—changed, and each label was fiercely defended, just as in India the caste system's pariahs became untouchables or depressed classes and then Harijans, scheduled castes, then Dalits. Then again, the decimation of the native Americans had to be acknowledged as a cruel and unjust act in founding of the nation. The preservation of their rich languages, the collective rights they had in their lands and the beauty of their art came to the fore in the late twentieth century. Now Hispanic Americans have added a major language—Spanish—to America's political discourse. Even 233 years since the Declaration of Independence, America is defining and redefining itself. The election of Barack Hussein Obama is another milestone in this never-ending journey.

America had to fight a bloody civil war after seventy years of its existence as a nation, in which it lost more people than any war since. The war was fought on the question of the rights of the states as against the Union. Slavery was the root issue, but Lincoln did not abolish slavery till well into the American Civil War. The Union was the important story. But USA had to come to terms with the consequences of late abolition of slavery in the mid-twentieth century. America also fought its own native peoples in a continuous set of wars, which have not had the same status as the civil war. But many Americans—White and Native—died in those wars. Since then America has had to rewrite its own history to acknowledge that America is as much a product of Europe as of Africa and indeed of America itself, thanks to the native American tribes. It is, thus, an even more diverse nation now than it was when it adopted *E pluribus unum* at its birth. It has had to accommodate African–Americans and native Americans as equal citizens, with the same body of civil rights as the White Americans who arrived at various times from Europe. It has done all that within the framework of its original Constitution, thanks to a vibrant democratic practice.

America has had to battle constantly to accommodate the diversity of its people. On vital issues such as the right of a mother to abortion (Roe vs Wade), the opinion both popular and judicial has swayed one way and then another. There is no definite final solution to such a problem, because each generation has different values. The question of Muslim or Hindu private law, and its compatibility with a single citizenship, will also go on being a controversial one for India with no definite solution. But as long as we are agreed on the process by which disputes are settled—the legal constitutional norms and processes—there is no need for finality.

Take the issue of creationism in the USA. This was 'settled' in the Tennessee Monkey Trials in the 1920s with Clarence Darrow arguing for freedom of the teacher to teach Darwin, and William Jennings Bryan arguing for the Christian orthodox view. Today it is back again, being fought on campuses and in print and TV. A nation sure of itself is not afraid of such disputes.

The analogy of India and America is not exact. But it is the recognition of the even richer diversity than the pre-1947 nationalist imagination acknowledged—the Dalits, the various tribal/hill peoples of India, the Nagas, Khasis, Goros, Bodos, Mizos, Bhils, Santals—which has enriched the Indian notion of nationhood. The Sikhs have as much right to be included in the overarching narrative as the Hindus and Muslims. Their tragedy in the Partition and their struggles around the issue of a separate nationhood need to be integrated as part of the story of building the Indian nation, and not as a subversive act. The battles in the North-East must have a similar status. Indian history, even today, is too much about the plains and not the hills, about the 'settled' communities and not the 'nomadic' ones. It is too much about who was ruling in Delhi than about the entire country. Time has come to remedy this lacuna.

A MULTI-NATIONAL DEMOCRATIC POLITY

'Unity in diversity' is a slogan which many countries have used. USA has E pluribus unum. India does so too. But the starting point of India's national narratives has been unity *overriding* diversity. The search for a single central unitary identity wrecked the subcontinent twice—in 1947 and 1971. It has also caused many battles across India in Kashmir, Punjab and the North-East. It has been at the heart of the secularism–communalism divide. So, why not start with diversity?

India is a collection of many nations. It is a multi-national polity, uniquely among modern democracies. These many nations are defined by religion and by region, by language and ethnicity, along with the differences of caste and class. Many regions are large enough to be substantial nation states in their own right. They are together by an accident of history. But having stayed together for sixty years, it should now be possible to search for a non-unitary narrative to cement the Union. India is at once Hindu and Muslim and Jewish and Punjabi and Tamil and Mizo and Brahmin and Dalit and Tribal, hill peoples and plains people. No single overarching shared history united these many nations *before* the last sixty years.

What is now common is that all individuals, as Indians, are willing to coexist under the same legal and constitutional system. All regions have agreed to be part of the Union, some after a long struggle. All take part in the vibrant democratic process. It is this democratic process which has been the binding experience, an experience which was never part of the past of the subcontinent, no matter how far back you go. India is neither secular nor communal. It is the collection of, probably, most religious people anywhere with a bewildering variety of religions. Yet, that should not be any cause of anxiety if we live within the rule of law. I don't need you to be secular or religious; I just do not want you to interfere with my right to be what I want to be. I do not want anyone to impose a false 'Indian' identity on me as a Hindu and hence a native, or non-Hindu and so a foreigner. As a Muslim I do not want to be patronized by secularists, who just turn up for iftar parties to show how broad-minded they are. As a Muslim I do not wish to receive a fatwa by some imam for joining a Ganesh festival. I do not want you to think I am foreign because I am a Christian or a Jew. I may be a proud Malyalee as well. You may think I look Chinese but I am merely a Ladakhi or from Arunachal. My language as a Naga or Khasi or Santhal is not even listed in the eighth schedule, but I am still an Indian and my language is also an Indian language.

Every Indian is an individual with defined fundamental rights, which the state is committed to protect. The individual citizen and not any 'community' is the beginning and the end of the definition of who is an Indian, who is a constituent member of the Union. I may be a Muslim and need my right to worship as one. Or, I may need protection as one born Muslim who turns apostate. I do not want my Book burnt or my paintings trashed because some hoodlums may decide I am not a good Muslim or a good Indian. I insist that the state protect me against these invasions of my private space. As a woman, I may be happy to identify with my cultural group or rebel and be different. My rebellion could be against female foeticide, which may be 'cultural practice' in my community, or dowry or right to divorce. My right to enter a temple should not be defined by my caste or even by my religion, much less by my gender. Gods should not be threatened by my natural physiological processes. If the temple or mosque or Church partakes of any public facility such as access to public roads, water, electricity or garbage collection by the local municipality, I should have the right of access. These are public places and hence it is my right as a citizen to access them.

In return, I am subject to the law of the land. The rule of law states that I am innocent until proven guilty. Neither the Hindu concept of dharma, nor any Islamic notion of justice that I am aware of, treats all as equals regardless of religion, gender or age. Thus, it is my equality before the law as a citizen of India which is the unifying story. I have then the right to live in any part of India free of discrimination, regardless of the majority language. The laws have been passed by legislatures elected democratically. Hence, they are binding on me. I have the right to protest and agitate to change the law by all lawful means.

This may mean a rethinking of reservations. They should be on common universal criteria of income and social deprivation rather than jati labels. It may mean rethinking the status of private law as more and more Hindus or Muslims may want to live in both communities by intermarrying, for instance. Or, they may wish not to be labelled Hindu or Muslim but just as citizens of no faith. Individuals should not be 'assigned' to the community in which they were born. They should choose to identify wherever they wish to be. It will not happen overnight, and not even in ten years. But once we begin thinking in another way, the possibilities open up.

India does not need a long hoary history during which it has to be shown as having been a single entity, one single homogenous people, by accident of birth or religion. Its sixty years of democratic existence as a multi-national polity—a unique event in modern history—is proof enough of its nationhood. The difficult task will be to shed the pre-1947 baggage. That was before India, just the prologue.

This is not an easy option as a narrative of the nation. But it is, in my view, the only one which is sustainable. It will mean clearing a lot of the historical debris. But almost nine-tenths of Indians have been born since Independence, and a majority since Indira Gandhi died. Eighteen-year-olds, born since Rajiv Gandhi's death, make up 40 per cent of the population. There are people who still recall the old battles—1942, the Partition, the creation of linguistic states. But to most Indians, India, as it is today, is the only India they know. It is the India they love and are loyal to. It is that India which needs a story, and not the India which was created to tell the British why we were a nation. The identities which were crystallized before 1947, which are meant to define the India which Nehru 'discovered' before 1947, were not relevant to the India he led. He helped make the transition to the new, the only India, by building the one solid block which makes post-1947 India different from all that went before, and from Pakistan as well. That building block is democracy, rooted in a Constitution which the Constituent Assembly members—the founding parents—gave their fellow citizens. Nehru's legacy is, therefore, not the vision of a syncretic India which, for the many reasons I have outlined, is no longer viable, if it ever was. His legacy is democracy, which even his successors could not destroy.

India is a nation of its billion common citizens living under a Constitution in a vibrant, thriving democracy. It is time to rediscover this India.

NOTES

INTRODUCTION: INDIA AT SIXTY

1. 'March of the Red Army', *Indian Express*, 22 July 2007.
2. Ramchandra Guha, *India after Gandhi: The History of the World's Largest Democracy*, Picador, 2007.
3. John Keay, *India: A History*, HarperCollins, 2000.

1. THE VASCO DA GAMA MOMENT

1. Carlo Cipolla, *Guns, Sails and Empires: Technological Innovation and the Early Phase of European Expansion 1400–1700*, Pantheon, 1966.
2. John Keay, *The Honourable Company: A History of the English East India Company*, HarperCollins, 1991, p. 72.
3. Ross Dunn, *The Adventures of Ibn Battuta*, University of California Press, 2004.
4. Keay, *The Honourable Company*.
5. Burton Stein, *A History of India*, Wiley Blackwell, 2003, p. 111.
6. K.M. Sen, *Hinduism*, Penguin, 2005; K.M. Panikkar, *A Survey of Indian History*, Asia Publishing House, 1964. Nirad Chaudhuri, however, disagrees with this view in his book, *Hinduism: A Religion to Live By*, Oxford, 1979.
7. N.N. Bhattacharya, *Buddhism in the History of Indian Ideas*, Manohar, 1993, p. 55.
8. Louis Dumont, *Homo Hierarchicus: The Caste System and Its Implications*, University of Chicago Press, 1980.
9. Dunn, *The Adventures*, p. 199.
10. Ibid., p. 202.
11. S. Moosvi, 'The Indian Economic Experience 1600–1900' in *The Making of History: Essays Presented to Irfan Habib*, edited by K.N. Panikkar, Terence J. Byres and Utsa Patnaik, Anthem Press, 2002, p. 331.
12. Ashok Desai, 'Population and Standards of Living in Akbar's Time', *Indian Economic and Social History Review*, March 1972. Grain prices from Tapan Raychaudhuri's chapter 'Non-Agricultural Production in Mughal India', p. 284 and the comment on Desai's wage data from Irfan Habib's chapter 'Monetary System and Prices', p. 378, footnote 2, both from *The Cambridge Economic History of India*, edited by Tapan Raychaudhuri and Irfan Habib, vol. 1, Cambridge University Press, 1982.

13. Keay, *The Honourable Company*.
14. H. Fukazawa in Raychaudhuri and Habib, *The Cambridge Economic History*, pp. 312–13.
15. C.J. Fuller, 'Misconceiving the Grain Heap: A Critique of the Concept of the Indian Jajmani System' in *Money and the Morality of Exchange*, edited by Maurice Bloch and Jonathan Parry, Cambridge University Press, 1989.
16. H. Fukazawa, 'Standard of Living: Maharashtra and the Deccan' in Raychaudhuri and Habib, *The Cambridge Economic History*, p. 476.
17. Om Prakash, *European Commercial Enterprise in Pre-Colonial India*, Cambridge University Press, 1998, p. 64.
18. John H. Parry, *Trade and Dominion: The European Overseas Empires in the Eighteenth Century*, Weidenfeld and Nicolson, 2000.
19. Tapan Raychaudhuri, *Jan Company in Coromandel 1605–1690: A Study of the Interrelations of European Commerce and Traditional Economics*, S'–Gravenhage, 1962.
20. Robert B. Ekelund and Robert D. Tollison in *Politicized Economies: Monarchy, Monopoly and Mercantilism*, Texas A&M University Press, 1997. Ekelund and Tollison blame rent-seeking and mercantilism, but they extend their analysis to all mercantilist countries including England.
21. Angus Maddison, *The World Economy: A Millennial Perspective*, OECD, 2001.
22. Prakash, *European Commercial Enterprise*, p. 316.
23. Ibid., p. 339.
24. Maddison, *The World Economy*, p. 112.
25. Prakash, *European Commercial Enterprise*, pp. 349–50.
26. Habib, 'Monetary System', pp. 363–79.
27. Parry, *Trade and Dominion*, p. 159.
28. Burton Stein, 'A Decade of Historical Efflorescence', *South Asia Research*, vol. 10, November 1990, p. 133, cited by Prakash in *European Commercial Enterprise*, p. 345.
29. D. Morris, 'Towards a Reinterpretation of 19th Century Indian Economic History', reprinted along with a comment by Tapan Raychaudhuri in *Indian Economic and Social History Review*, March 1968.
30. Maddison, *The World Economy*, Tables 1–7c, p. 35.
31. Andre Gunder Frank, *Capitalism and Underdevelopment in Latin America: Historical Studies of Chile and Brazil*, Monthly Review Press, 1967; Paul Baran, *The Political Economy of Growth*, Monthly Review Press, 1960. See also Meghnad Desai, 'War and Imperialism' in *Marx's Revenge: The Resurgence of Capitalism and the Death of Statist Socialism*, Verso, 2002.

2. THE ENGLISH TURN

1. Parry, *Trade and Dominion*, pp. 4–5.
2. For a succinct definition and bibliography, see Ernest Gellner, 'Nationalism' in *The Blackwell Dictionary of Modern Social Thought*, edited by William Outhwaite, Blackwell, 1993, pp. 422–24.
3. Parry, *Trade and Dominion*, p. 3.
4. Keay, *The Honourable Company*, pp. 321–22.

5. Biplab Dasgupta, 'Palashi: The Inside Story of a Betrayal in the Making of History' in *The Making of History*, edited by K.N. Panikkar et. al.
6. Dasgupta, 'Palashi', p. 229.
7. Ibid., p. 209.
8. Parry, *Trade and Dominion*, p. 166.
9. Keay, *The Honourable Company*, p. 392, citing R.B. Barnett, *North India between Empires: Awadh, the Mughals and the British 1720–1801*, University of California Press, 1980.
10. Keay, *The Honourable Company*, p. 377.
11. Ibid., p. 375.
12. James Mill, *The History of British India*, vol. 4, Baldwin, Cradock, and Joy, 1826, p. 307.
13. Mill, *The History*, p. 308.
14. Mill, *The History*, p. 314.
15. Adam Smith, *The Wealth of Nations*, vol. 4, Glasgow bicentenary edition, University of Glasgow Press, 1976, p. 527.
16. 1757 minute from law officers quoted in *The Cambridge Shorter History of India*, edited by H.H. Dodwell, vol. 5, Cambridge University Press, 1929, p. 593.
17. K.M. Panikkar, *A Survey*, p. 209.
18. Keay, *The Honourable Company*, pp. 394–95.
19. Margery Sabin, *Dissenters and Mavericks: Writings about India in English 1765–2000*, Oxford University Press, 2002, p. 50.
20. Ibid., p. 51.
21. Ibid.
22. Mill, *The History*.
23. Ibid., p. 71.
24. Ibid., footnote 77.
25. 'Warren Hastings' in *The Works of Lord Macaulay*, vol. 5, edited by his sister, Lady Trevelyan, Longman, Green and Co., 1875, p. 633.
26. Mill, *The History*, pp. 77–78.
27. Ibid.
28. Lady Trevelyan, *The Works*.
29. Ibid.
30. Sabin, *Dissenters and Mavericks*, p. 48.

3. REVENUE, REFORM AND RENAISSANCE

1. Nicholas Dirks, *The Scandal of Empire: India and the Creation of Imperial Britain*, Harvard University Press, 2006.
2. Bernard Cohn, *Colonialism and its Forms of Knowledge: The British in India*, Princeton University Press, 1996.
3. Introduction to *Education and Colonial Knowledge*, vol. 3 of *Britain in India 1765–1905*, edited by John Marriott and Bhaskar Mukhopadhyay, Pickering and Chatto Publishers, 2006.
4. Rammohun Roy's letter is reprinted in Marriott and Mukhopadhyay, *Britain in India*, pp. 135–39.
5. Richard Reeves, *John Stuart Mill: Victorian Firebrand*, Atlantic Books, 2007, p. 259.

6. Paul Johnson, *The Birth of the Modern: World Society 1815–1830*, Weidenfeld and Nicolson, 1991, pp. 350–51.
7. Cohn, *Colonialism and its Forms*, p. 4.
8. John Keay, *India Discovered: The Recovery of a Lost Civilization*, HarperCollins, 1981; and Charles Allen, *The Buddha and the Sahibs: The Men Who Discovered India's Lost Religion*, John Murray Publishers, 2002.
9. Stuart Blackburn, *Print, Folklore, and Nationalism in Colonial South India*, Permanent Black, 2003.
10. Max Boot, *War Made New: Technology, Warfare and the Course of History 1500 to Today*, Gotham Books, 2006.
11. Even so, this was a high rate of loss for the British mainly due to the mistake by Lt Col Orrock in attacking the fortified village of Asaye which he had been told to avoid. Every officer of the 74th regiment was either killed or wounded.
12. Boot, *War Made New*, pp. 82–83.
13. Ibid., p. 85.
14. Ibid., p. 101.
15. C. Ross, *The Correspondence of Charles, First Marquis Cornwallis*, John Murray Publishers, 1859.
16. All quotes concerning Bentinck's rule are from John Rosselli, *Lord William Bentinck: The Making of a Liberal Economist 1774–1839*, University of California Press, 1974, pp. 141–42.
17. Charles Ross (ed.), *Correspondence of Charles, First Marquis Cornwallis*, John Murray Publishers, 1859, p. 193.
18. See Eric Stokes, B. Chaudhuri, H. Fukazawa and Dharma Kumar, 'Agrarian Relations' in *The Cambridge Economic History of India*, edited by Dharma Kumar and Meghnad Desai, Cambridge University Press, 1983, p. 86.
19. Ranajit Guha, *A Rule of Property for Bengal: An Essay on the Idea of Permanent Settlement*, Duke University Press, 1996.
20. Rosselli, *Lord William Bentinck*.
21. Reeves, *John Stuart Mill*, p. 339.
22. Ibid., pp. 330–40.
23. Lady Trevelyan, *The Works*.
24. Rosselli, *Lord William Bentinck*, p. 186.
25. Ibid., pp. 191–92.
26. Ashis Nandy, 'Sati: A Nineteenth Century Tale of Women, Violence and Protest' in *At the Edge of Psychology: Essays in Politics and Culture*, edited by Ashis Nandy, Oxford University Press, 1990, pp. 1–32.
27. Introduction to *Education and Colonial Knowledge*, p. xxii.
28. Thomas Babington Macaulay, 'Minute on Education', *Language in India*, vol. 3, http://www.languageindia.com/april2003/macaulay.html#minute, 2 February 1835.
29. Reeves, *John Stuart Mill*.
30. Macaulay, 'Minute'.
31. While this is the accepted view of the Arab influence on Western

Renaissance, recently some authors have doubted this construction. See *Aristote au Mont Saint-Michel, Les Racines Grecques de l'Europe Chretienne* by Sylvain Gouguenheim, Seuil, 2008.

32. Sir George Trevelyan, *The Life and Letters of Lord Macaulay*, Longmans Green, 1908.
33. Macaulay, 'Minute'.
34. Ibid.
35. Ibid.
36. Ibid.
37. Ibid.
38. Ibid.
39. Ibid.
40. Reeves, *John Stuart Mill*, quoting a letter of Mill written in 1837, p. 101.
41. Ibid.
42. Trevelyan, *The Life and Letters*.
43. Ibid.
44. Ibid.
45. Ibid.
46. Ibid.
47. Macaulay, 'Minute'.

4. THE GREAT DIVIDE: FROM COMPANY TO CROWN

1. George Dodd, *The History of the Indian Revolt and of the Expeditions to Persia, China, and Japan 1856–7–8*, W. and R. Chambers, 1859.
2. Ibid.
3. Italics mine. Ibid.
4. Ibid.
5. Rosselli, *Lord William Bentinck*, p. 182.
6. Dodd, *The History of the Indian Revolt*, p. 23.
7. Achyut Yagnik and Suchitra Sheth, *The Shaping of Modern Gujarat*, Penguin, 2005, pp. 90–91.
8. I have discussed the developments in my *Marx's Revenge*.
9. Panikkar, *A Survey*, p. 208.
10. Ibid., p. 209.
11. See, for example, the details of revolt in Gujarat in Yagnik and Sheth, *The Shaping*, pp. 90–96.
12. Panikkar, *A Survey*, p. 215.
13. Andrew Roberts, *Salisbury: Victorian Titan*, Weidenfeld and Nicolson, 1999, pp. 85–86.
14. Ibid.
15. Shireen Moosvi, 'The Indian Economic Experience 1600–1900' in *The Making of History*, edited by Panikkar et. al., p. 347.

5. THE SETTLEMENT

1. George Nathaniel Curzon, 'Speech on India', University of California Libraries, http://www.archive.org/details/speechesonindiad00curzrich.
2. Dodwell, *The Cambridge Shorter History*, vol. 6, p. 546.

3. Kenneth Rose, *King George V*, Weidenfeld and Nicolson, 1983, p. 66.
4. Sumit Sarkar, *Modern India 1885–1947*, Macmillan, 1983, p. 140.
5. *Time*.
6. Rose, *King George V*, pp. 134–35.
7. Keay quoting John Buchan, *The Honourable Company*, pp. 470–71.
8. Italics mine. House of Commons Hansard ('Debates'), vol. 86, cols 1695–98.
9. Ibid.
10. Ibid.
11. Ibid.
12. The most recent and, perhaps, the most original biography of Gandhi is by Kathryn Tidrick, *Gandhi: A Political and Spiritual Life*, I.B. Tauris, 2006. I make extensive use of it in what follows.
13. Rushbrook Williams, 'India and the War' in Dodwell, *The Cambridge Shorter History*, p. 476.
14. Commons Hansard.
15. Ibid.
16. Ibid.
17. Ibid.
18. Ibid.
19. Ibid.
20. For more information, see Sarvepalli Gopal, 'Churchill and India' in *Churchill*, edited by Robert Blake and William Roger Louis, Oxford University Press, 1993, pp. 457–71; and Martin Gilbert, *Winston S. Churchill*, vol. 4, Heinemann, 1977, chapter 23.
21. Commons Hansard, vol. 116, col. 622.
22. Ibid.
23. Ibid., col. 2315.
24. Aurobindo Ghose, 'Rishi Bankim', 1907, reproduced in Sri Aurobindo Birth Centenary Library, vol. 17, Sri Aurobindo Ashram Trust, Pondicherry, 1972, p. 347; quoted from Rachael Fabish, 'The Political Goddess: Aurobindo's Use of Bengali Sakta Tantrism to Justify Political Violence in the Indian Anti-Colonial Movement', *Journal of South Asian Studies*, vol. 30, no. 2, 2007, pp. 269–92.
25. Rajmohan Gandhi, *Mohandas: A True Story of a Man, His People and an Empire*, Penguin, 2006, p. 244; also see my 'Gandhi and Gandhi', *IIC Quarterly*, Autumn 2007, pp. 46–61.
26. Gandhi, *Mohandas*, p. 266.

6. WESTMINSTER TAKES CHARGE

1. Katharine Adeney, *Federalism and Ethnic Conflict Regulation in India and Pakistan*, Palgrave Macmillan, 2007.
2. H.N. Mitra (ed.), *The Govt. of India Act 1919: Rules Thereunder and Govt. Reports 1920*, Internet Archive, http://www.archive.org/stream/govtofindiaact19029669mbp/govtofindiaact19029669mbp_djvu.txt.
3. Kenneth Harris, *Attlee*, Weidenfeld and Nicolson, 1982, p. 77.
4. Ibid.

5. Ibid.
6. Sarkar, *Modern India*, quoting Uma Kaura, 'Muslims and Indian Nationalism', 1977.
7. Australia, New Zealand and Canada are still governed under that system.
8. Ramsay MacDonald, *The Awakening of India*, Hodder and Stoughton, 1911.
9. Commons Hansard, col. 1307, 7 November 1929.
10. Ibid.
11. Ibid.
12. Ibid.
13. Ibid., col. 1312, 7 November 1929.
14. Ibid., col. 1314, 7 November 1929.
15. Ibid.
16. Ibid., col. 1326, 7 November 1929.
17. Ibid., col. 1328, 7 November 1929.
18. Ibid.
19. Ibid.
20. Ibid.
21. Ibid.
22. Mohandas K. Gandhi, *The Collected Works of Mahatma Gandhi*, vol. 48, Publications Division, Government of India, 2000, p. 397, note 473.
23. Tidrick, *Gandhi*, p. 221, citing Gandhi, *The Collected Works*, vol. 36, p. 282.
24. Sarkar, *Modern India*, p. 282, quoting from the English journal published by Gandhi, *Young India*, September 1929.
25. Proceedings, Indian Round Table Conference, Command 3778, His Majesty's Stationery Office, London, 1931.
26. Ibid.
27. Ibid.
28. Ibid.
29. The Simon Commission gives the population of depressed classes in British India as 43.6 million, 19 per cent of the total population and 28.5 per cent of the Hindu population; Simon Commission, part 1, chapter 4, p. 40.
30. Proceedings, Indian Round Table Conference.
31. Ibid.
32. Ibid.
33. Ibid.
34. Ibid.
35. David Marquand, *Ramsay MacDonald: A Biography*, Jonathan Cape, 1977.
36. W. Wedgewood Benn, *The Indian Round Table Conference in International Affairs*, vol. 10, no. 2, March 1931, pp. 145–59.
37. Ibid.
38. Robert Rhodes James (ed.), *Winston Churchill: His Complete Speeches*, vol. 5, Chelsea House Publishers, 1974, p. 4983.

7. GANDHI, IRWIN AND CHURCHILL

1. David Marquand, *Ramsay MacDonald*.
2. James, *Winston Churchill*.
3. Robert Rhodes James, *Churchill: A Study in Failure 1900–1939*, Penguin, 1981.
4. House of Commons speech on 22 March 1931, reprinted in James, *Winston Churchill*, p. 4994.
5. Ibid., p. 4995.
6. Geoffrey Ashe, *Gandhi: A Study in Revolution*, Stein & Day, 1968.
7. Speech at Albert Hall, 18 March 1931, reprinted in James, *Winston Churchill*, p. 5007.
8. Ibid.
9. Lord Butler, *The Art of the Possible: The Memoirs of Lord Butler*, Hamish Hamilton, 1971, p. 41.
10. Tidrick, *Gandhi*, pp. 235–45.
11. Gandhi, *The Collected Works*.
12. Ibid.
13. Ibid.
14. Ibid., vol. 51, pp. 338–42.
15. Ibid.
16. Tidrick, *Gandhi*, p. 246.
17. Gandhi, *The Collected Works*, vol. 53, pp. 269–92.
18. Ibid.
19. Butler, *The Art of the Possible*, p. 48.
20. *Sunday Times*.
21. Marquand, *Ramsay MacDonald*, p. 707.
22. Tidrick, *Gandhi*, p. 259.
23. Ibid.
24. Narahari Parikh (ed.), *Mahadevbhaini Diary*, vol. 1, Mahadev Desai Centenary Committee, Navjivan Prakashan, 1948, p. 68.
25. Italics mine. Christophe Jaffrelot, *Dr. Ambedkar and Untouchability: Fighting the Indian Caste System*, CERI Series, Columbia University Press, 2004, p. 23.
26. Translation from the Gujarati mine. Parikh, *Mahadevbhaini Diary*, vol. 2, 1949, p. 23. The word 'Hindutva' is in the original.
27. Translation from the Gujarati mine. Chittaranjan Dadubhai Desai, *India's Freedom Reassessed: The Legacy of the Desais and Patels of Gujarat*, Book Guild Publishers, 2007. The letter is published as a photocopy of the original letter to the author's father.
28. John Swift, *Labour in Crisis: Clement Attlee and the Labour Party in Opposition 1931–40*, Palgrave, 2001.
29. Clement Attlee, 'Joint Select Committee on Indian Constitutional Reform', draft report, HMSO, pp. 253–87.
30. Ibid.
31. Ibid.
32. Ibid.
33. Ibid.
34. All quotations of House of Commons second reading debate from Commons Hansard, vol. 297, cols 1162–63, February 1935.

35. Ibid., cols 1167–75
36. Ibid.
37. Ibid.
38. Ibid.
39. House of Commons speech on 11 February 1935, reprinted in James, *Winston Churchill*, p. 5481.
40. Ibid., p. 5478.
41. Ibid.
42. Ibid.
43. Ibid.
44. Ibid.
45. Ibid.
46. Ibid.
47. Ibid.
48. Butler, *The Art of the Possible*, p. 60.

8. THE RUPTURE

1. Dinshaw Wacha, 'Moving the Congress Resolution on Military Expenditure' in *The Penguin Book of Modern Indian Speeches*, edited by Rakesh Batabyal, Penguin, 2007, p. 58.
2. Italics mine. Ibid., p. 13.
3. K.M. Panikkar takes very much this view in his *A Survey*.
4. Batabyal, *Modern Indian Speeches*, p. 13.
5. Aijaz Ahmad, 'Azad's Careers: Roads Taken and Not Taken' in *Lineages of the Present: Political Essays*, Tulika, 2006, pp. 133–90.
6. Ahmad, *Lineages of the Present*, p. 169.
7. For definitions of consociationalism and references, see Katharine Adeney, 'Constitutional Centring: Nation Formation and Consociational Federalism in India and Pakistan' in *Commonwealth and Comparative Politics*, vol. 40, no. 3, 2002, pp. 8–33.
8. Batabyal, *Modern Indian Speeches*, p. 19.
9. Ibid.
10. Anthony Low, *Britain and Indian Nationalism: The Imprint of Ambiguity 1929–1942*, chapter 7, Cambridge University Press, 1997, pp. 268–302.
11. Rafiq Zakaria, *The Man Who Divided India: An Insight into Jinnah's Leadership and its Aftermath*, Popular Prakashan, 2001, p. 70. As the title indicates, this is a version of why Partition happened according to the Congress, written by a prominent Muslim Congressman.
12. Ayesha Jalal, *The Sole Spokesman: Jinnah, the Muslim League and the Demand for Pakistan*, Cambridge University Press, 1985; see also my essay 'Communalism, Secularism and the Dilemma of Indian Nationhood' in Meghnad Desai, *Development and Nationhood: Essays in the Political Economy of South Asia*, Oxford University Press, 2005, pp. 232–63.
13. Sarkar, *Modern India*, p. 356, quoting Kaura, 'Muslims and Indian Nationalism', p. 123. For a detailed account of this period and subsequent developments, see Mushirul Hasan (ed.), *India's Partition: Process, Strategy and Mobilization*, Oxford University Press, 2001.
14. For more details, see my *Marx's Revenge*.

15. Jawaharlal Nehru, *An Autobiography: Jawaharlal Nehru*, Penguin, 2004. p. 507.
16. Gandhi, *The Collected Works*.
17. Jawaharlal Nehru, *An Autobiography*, p. 522.
18. Tidrick, *Gandhi*, p. 268.
19. Ibid., p. 289.
20. Ibid., p. 290, quoting from *Harijan*, 2 July 1940.
21. Gandhi, *The Collected Works*, vol. 77, appendices 1402–08.
22. Ibid., p. 148.
23. Ibid.
24. Low, *Britain and Indian Nationalism*, chapter 8.
25. Ibid.
26. See my *Marx's Revenge*.
27. Peter Clarke, *The Cripps Version: The Life of Sir Stafford Cripps*, Penguin, 2002.
28. Ibid.
29. Ibid., p. 262.
30. Ibid., p. 264.
31. Low, *Britain and Indian Nationalism*, chapter 1, pp. 394–95.
32. Ibid.

9. JINNAH'S HOUR

1. R.J. Moore, 'Jinnah and the Pakistan Demand', *Modern Asian Studies*, vol. 17, no. 4, pp. 529–61, reprinted in Hasan, *India's Partition*, pp. 160–97.
2. Moore, 'Jinnah' in Hasan, *India's Partition*.
3. Sarkar, *Modern India*, p. 379, quoting Kaura, 'Muslims and Indian Nationalism', p. 149.
4. Moore, 'Jinnah' in Hasan, *India's Partition*, pp. 45–46.
5. Ibid.
6. Ibid.
7. Asim Roy cites the literature in his review article on Jalal, 'The High Politics of India's Partition: The Revisionist Perspective', *Modern Asian Studies*, vol. 24, no. 2, 1990, pp. 384–415, reprinted in Hasan, *India's Partition*, pp. 102–32.
8. Hasan, *India's Partition*.
9. Ibid., pp. 60–61.
10. Ibid, p. 67.
11. Saadat Hasan Manto, 'Jinnah Sahib' in *Bitter Fruit: The Very Best of Saadat Hasan Manto*, edited by Khalid Hasan, Penguin, 2008, pp. 424–25.
12. Ibid., p. 416.
13. Ibid., p. 421.
14. Clarke, *The Cripps Version*, p. 118.
15. Ibid.
16. Ibid., pp. 284–85; inset quotes from Amery's diary, 8 March 1942.
17. Ibid.

18. Ibid.
19. Ibid., pp. 285–87.
20. Ibid.
21. Ibid.
22. Ibid., p. 288.
23. Ibid., p. 291.
24. Ibid.
25. Ibid.
26. Peter Clarke, *The Last Thousand Days of the British Empire*, Penguin, 2007, p. 23.
27. Clarke, *The Cripps Version*.
28. Ibid.
29. Maulana Abul Kalam Azad, *India Wins Freedom*, Orient Longman, 1998, pp. 65–66.
30. Clarke, *The Cripps Version*, p. 324.
31. Azad, *India Wins Freedom*, p. 76.
32. For Bose and the INA in above and much that follows, I use Sisir K. Bose, A. Werth and S.A. Ayer (ed.), *A Beacon Across Asia: A Biography of Subhas Chandra Bose*, Orient Longman, 1973, especially chapters 4 and 5, pp. 116–231.
33. Patrick French, *Liberty or Death: India's Journey to Independence and Division*, HarperCollins, 1998; Christopher Bayley and Tim Harper, *Forgotten Wars: Freedom and Revolution in Southeast Asia*, Harvard University Press, 2007.
34. Bose et. al., *A Beacon Across Asia*, p. 198.
35. Ibid.
36. Ibid., pp. 210–11.
37. Azad, *India Wins Freedom*, pp. 96–97. I have kept the spelling of Quaid as Azad gives it, though Manto's translator cited above has it differently.
38. Hasan, *India's Partition*, p. 187.

10. THE ROAD TO PAKISTAN

1. Azad, *India Wins Freedom*, p. 111.
2. Ibid., p. 113.
3. Ibid.
4. Ibid.
5. Clarke, *The Cripps Version*, pp. 402–03.
6. Ibid., pp. 403–04.
7. Azad, *India Wins Freedom*, pp. 140–41.
8. Ibid.
9. Zakaria, *The Man Who Divided India*, p. 105.
10. Harris, *Attlee*, p. 367.
11. Ibid.
12. Clarke, *The Cripps Version*.
13. Ibid.
14. Ibid.
15. Ibid., p. 417.

16. Ibid., p. 423.
17. Ibid.
18. Ibid.
19. Harris, *Attlee*, p. 368.
20. Clarke, *The Cripps Version*, p. 433.
21. Ibid.
22. Ibid., p. 434.
23. Ibid., p. 443.
24. Ibid., p. 447.
25. Ibid., p. 448, quoting Cripps's diary.
26. Ibid.
27. Ibid., pp. 452–53.
28. Ibid.
29. Harris, *Attlee*, p. 369.
30. Azad, *India Wins Freedom*, p. 164.
31. Ibid., pp. 164–65.
32. Ibid., p. 185.
33. Clarke, *The Cripps Version*, pp. 459–60.
34. Harris, *Attlee*, pp. 370–71.
35. Ibid.
36. Azad, *India Wins Freedom*.
37. Harris, *Attlee*, p. 372.
38. Ibid.
39. Ibid.
40. Ibid., p. 373. Mountbatten has claimed credit for suggesting a deadline, but Harris is certain that it was Attlee's idea.
41. Ibid.
42. Ibid.
43. Ibid.
44. Leonard Mosley in *The Last Days of the British Raj*, Harcourt, Brace and World, 1962, is critical of Mountbatten while Philip Ziegler, in *Mountbatten: The Official Biography*, Weidenfeld and Nicolson, 1971, is complimentary.
45. Commons Hansard.
46. Ibid.
47. Harris, *Attlee*.
48. Ibid.
49. Ibid., pp. 380–81.
50. Yasmin Khan, *The Great Partition: The Making of India and Pakistan*, Penguin, 2007, pp. xviii–xix.
51. Azad, *India Wins Freedom*, p. 197.
52. Ibid.
53. Azad, *India Wins Freedom*.
54. Commons Hansard.
55. Khan, *The Great Partition*, pp. 1–2.
56. Clarke, *The Cripps Version*.
57. Azad, *India Wins Freedom*.

58. Leonard A. Gordon, *Brothers Against the Raj: A Biography of Indian Nationalists Sarat and Subhas Chandra Bose*, Rupa, 1997.
59. Clarke, *The Cripps Version*, p. 475.
60. Harris, *Attlee*.
61. Ibid.
62. Ibid., p. 384.
63. For a moving personal story of one family, that of Balraj Dutt, who later as Sunil Dutt became a famous actor in Hindustani cinema, then an MP and a minister in the 2004 Congress coalition government, see Kishwar Desai, *Darlingji: The True Love Story of Nargis and Sunil Dutt*, HarperCollins, 2007.
64. Azad, *India Wins Freedom*, p. 151.

11. POLITICAL ECONOMY OF EMPIRE AND NATION

1. Rabindranath Tagore's unhappiness at the Bengal Partition agitation and the burning of foreign cloth, etc. is reflected in his novel *Ghare Baire*, later made into a film by Satyajit Ray as *Home and the World*.
2. Amartya Sen, *Poverty and Famines: An Essay on Entitlement and Deprivation*, Clarendon Press, 1983. See also Paul R. Greenhough, *Prosperity and Misery in Modern Bengal: The Famine of 1943–44*, Oxford University Press, 1982; and R.C. Dutt, *The Economic History of India under Early British Rule*, Routledge, 2001.
3. The data on income, the drain and manufacturing growth are from P.R. Brahmananda, *Money, Income, Prices in 19th Century India: A Historical, Quantitative and Theoretical Study*, Himalaya Publishing House, 2001.
4. Data from Dietmar Rothermund, *India in the Great Depression 1929–1939*, Manohar, 1992.
5. Harris, *Attlee*, p. 384.
6. David Gilmartin, 'Religious Leadership and the Pakistan Movement in the Punjab', *Modern Asian Studies*, vol. 13, no. 3, 1979, pp. 485–517, reprinted in Hasan, *India's Partition*, pp. 198–232.
7. He confines his arguments to Pakistan after 1971 and does not deal with Bangladesh. Aitzaz Ahsan, *The Indus Saga: From Pataliputra to Partition*, Roli Books, 2000.
8. See essays by Meghnad Desai, 'Why Is India a Democracy?' and Aitzaz Ahsan, 'Why Pakistan Is Not a Democracy' in David Page (ed.), *Divided by Democracy*, Roli Books, 2005.
9. Batabyal, *Modern Indian Speeches*, pp. 327–31.
10. Harris, *Attlee*, p. 385.
11. Batabyal, *Modern Indian Speeches*, p. 328.

12. INDEPENDENT INDIA: THE NEHRU YEARS

1. Batabyal, *Modern Indian Speeches*.
2. Data are from Meghnad Desai, 'South Asia: Economic Stagnation and Economic Change', 1999, reprinted in Desai, *Development and Nationhood*,

pp. 269–89; and Philip Oldenburg, *The Puzzle of Why India Is a Democracy and Pakistan Is Not*, unpublished, 2008. I am grateful to Philip Oldenburg for giving me access to his paper.

3. Batabyal, *Modern Indian Speeches*, p. 334.

4. Ibid.

5. Granville Austin, *Working a Democratic Constitution: A History of the Indian Experience*, Oxford University Press, 1999, p. 594.

6. I have discussed this in greater detail in my essay 'Why Is India a Democracy?'

7. Austin, *Working a Democratic Constitution*; see especially the concluding chapter, 'A Nation's Progress', pp. 633–69.

8. Sanjoy Barbora, 'Under the Invisibility Cloak: Re-imagining the "Northeast"', *Biblio*, vol. 13, nos 5–6, May–June 2008, p. 15.

9. Batabyal, *Modern Indian Speeches*.

10. B.T. Ranadive, 'Opening Report on Draft Political Thesis', reprinted in Batabyal, *Modern Indian Speeches*, pp. 338–40.

11. Raj Thapar has a very amusing account of the high hopes the communists had in their call for a general strike in Bombay and their surprise when revolution did not break out. See Raj Thapar, *All These Years: A Memoir*, Penguin, 1991.

12. For a sketch of some of the issues, see the contributions in Meghnad Desai, Ashok Rudra and Suzanne Rudolph (eds), *Agrarian Power and Agricultural Productivity in South Asia*, University of California Press, 1984. Also, a somewhat earlier and rather general text, Meghnad Desai, 'Vortex in India', *New Left Review*, vol. 61, May–June 1970.

13. Khushwant Singh, *Why I Supported the Emergency: Essays and Profiles*, Penguin, 2009.

14. See K.M. Panikkar (under pen-name 'Chanakya'), *Indian Revolution*, Asia Publishing House, 1955. Check for an account of the voluntary activity for social reform in the 1857–1947 period.

15. I put forward the notion of a golden triangle in my K.R. Narayanan lecture, 'Democracy and Development: India 1947–2002' at the Australian National University in Canberra, Australia; and it is reprinted in Desai, *Development and Nationhood*, pp. 94–104.

16. See Meghnad Desai, 'Drains, Hoards and Foreigners: Does the Nineteenth Century Indian Economy Have Any Lessons for the Twenty-first Century India?', first P.R. Brahmananda lecture, Reserve Bank of India, 20 September 2004.

17. All quotes concerning the National Planning Committee from Jawaharlal Nehru, *The Discovery of India*, Penguin, 2004, pp. 435–38.

18. Ibid.

19. Marie Seton, *Panditji: A Portrait of Jawaharlal Nehru*, Denis Dobson, 1967, p. 238.

20. I have written about cinema and politics in the Nehru era in *Nehru's Hero: Dilip Kumar in the Life of India*, Roli Books, 2004. For the life and career of Nargis, who later became a member of the Rajya Sabha, see Kishwar Desai, *Darlingji*.

21. D. Thorner, B. Kerblay, R.E.F. Smith (eds), *A.V. Chayanov, On the Theory of the Peasant Economy*, Homewood, 1966; Lenin's ideas are contained in many of Chayanov's articles. For details, see Meghnad Desai (ed.), *Lenin's Economic Writings*, Lawrence and Wishart, 1989.
22. Seton, *Panditji*.
23. Austin, *Working a Democratic Constitution*, p. 157.
24. Batabyal, *Modern Indian Speeches*, pp. 631–39.
25. Seton, *Panditji*.

13. HEIRS AND SUCCESSORS

1. Meghnad Desai, 'India: Emerging Contradictions of Slow Capitalist Development', in *Explosion in a Subcontinent*, edited by Robin Blackburn, Penguin and *New Left Review*, 1975, pp. 11–50.
2. Lok Sabha debates of 21 February 1965.
3. Ibid.
4. I.G. Patel, *Glimpses of Indian Economic Policy: An Insider's View*, Oxford University Press, 2002, pp. 135–36.
5. Ibid.
6. Raj Thapar, *All These Years*, p. 312.
7. Austin, *Working a Democratic Constitution*, p. 217.
8. Ibid., pp. 220–33. All details about the legal aspects of this issue are from this book.
9. Guha, *India after Gandhi*, p. 470.
10. Katherine Frank, *Indira: The Life of Indira Nehru Gandhi*, HarperCollins, 2001, p. 372.
11. Thapar, *All These Years*, p. 397.
12. Frank, *Indira*, p. 374.
13. Thapar, *All These Years*, p. 386.
14. Ibid., p. 405.
15. Ibid., p. 408.
16. Ibid.
17. Dom Moraes, *Indira Gandhi*, Little, Brown, 1980, p. 223.
18. Frank, *Indira*, p. 407.
19. Ibid., p. 448.
20. Guha, *India after Gandhi*, p. 568.
21. Details of Bofors are from N. Ram, 'Know Your Bofors: The Facts, the Issues, and What Lies Ahead', *Frontline*, vol. 16, no. 24, 13–26 November 1999.

14. SEARCH FOR STABILITY, 1989–2004

1. Somnath Chatterjee, 'Surrendering Self-Reliance', Lok Sabha speech of 4 March 1992, reproduced in Batabyal, *Modern Indian Speeches*, p. 603.
2. Guha, *India after Gandhi*, p. 640, has the full reference.
3. The lecture, 'Capitalism, Socialism and the Indian Economy', EXIM Bank Lecture, January 1993, is reproduced in Desai, *Development and Nationhood*.

4. For the ideology of global Islamism, see Meghnad Desai, *Rethinking Islamism*, I.B. Tauris, 2006. For details about the December 1992 riots in Bombay, see Rajdeep Sardesai, 'Anatomy of a Riot', *Times of India*, 13 December 1992, and for the aftermath of the riots, see Jyoti Punwani, 'A Conspiracy of Silence', *Hindu*, 8 January 2003. Both have been reproduced in Nirmala Lakshman (ed.), *Writing a Nation: An Anthology of Indian Journalism*, Rupa & Co., 2007.

5. Personally heard at a seminar on 'Political Stability' in the Rajiv Gandhi Foundation in August 1997.

6. Sudipto Mundle and M. Govinda Rao, 'Issues in Fiscal Policy', in *The Indian Economy: Problems and Prospects*, edited by Bimal Jalan, Penguin, 1992.

7. PPP is a method which takes a basket of basic consumer goods and prices in an economy which is the most free of trade distortions, at present assumed to be Hong Kong. Having priced the basket, it is then compared to how much it would cost in each local currency. The ratio of the value of the two baskets determines the PPP exchange rate for the local economy, which differs from the market exchange rate. Then it is translated into the US dollar based on the Hong Kong dollar–US dollar market exchange rate.

8. Data from the Sachar Committee Report, Ministry of Minority Affairs, Government of India.

15. GLOBALIZING INDIA

1. *Economic Times*, 1 September 2008.

2. Note that the word 'Islamist' refers to a political ideology, and the word 'Islamic' to religious beliefs and practices. For details, see my *Rethinking Islamism*.

3. Ramaswamy Naicker's position on the *Ramayana* and, indeed, his strongly rationalistic atheism is well described in Paula Richman (ed.), *Ramayana in Many Ramayanas: The Diversity of a Narrative Tradition in South Asia*, University of California Press, 1991; see also Paula Richman and V. Geetha, 'A View from the South: Ramasami's Public Critique of Religion', in *The Crisis of Secularism in India*, edited by Anuradha Dingwaney Needham and Rajeswari Sunder Rajan, Permanent Black, 2007.

4. I have written about this in 'The God that Divides', *Little Magazine*, 2009.

5. Isaac Kramnick (ed.), *The Federalist Papers*, Penguin, 1987, p. 127.

6. Farmers' suicide data from *Hindu*, 12 December 2008.

16. WHOSE INDIA? WHICH INDIA?

1. Teotonio R. de Souza, 'Never the Same Again', *Herald*, 6 December 2008.

2. *Saamna*.

3. The sources for this account are the daily newspapers of the days: *Times of India, Indian Express, Hindu, Asian Age*; and some weekly magazines: *India Today, Outlook, Week*.

4. See Muzaffar Alam, *The Languages of Political Islam in India 1200–1800*, Permanent Black, 2004.
5. F.G. Bailey, *Caste and the Economic Frontier*, Manchester University Press, 1971; and David Pocock, *Kanbi and Patidar: Study of the Patidar Community of Gujarat*, Oxford University Press, 1972, provided such evidence in the early 1960s.

INDEX

Abdali, Ahmad Shah, 41, 56, 80
Abdullah, Farooq, 399
Abdullah, Sheikh, 318–19, 342, 354, 399
Acts: 1773 and 1784, 58, 59; (1909),133
Advaita, doctrine of, 27
Advani, L.K., 397, 440, 445–46
affirmative action. *See* reservation policies
Afghanistan, 8, 23, 32, 56, 72, 101, 150, 194–95, 236, 421, 443–44; war against Soviet Union, 193, 399
Afro-Asian Summit, Bandung (1905), 305
Agrarian Reforms Committee, 331
agriculture, 36, 43, 47, 47, 69, 84, 119, 186, 189, 191, 209–10, 216, 234–36, 280, 284, 322–24, 326, 340–41, 344–45, 352; backwardness, 341; economy, 380; mode of production, 26; neglect, 327; non-agricultural labour force, 310; policy, 331, 334;—failure, 330; primitive technology, 332; prices, 166, 280, 323; reforms, 324, 340
Ahsan, Aitzaz, 285, 287
Ain-i-Akbari, 34
Aix-La Chapelle Treaty, 51
Akali Dal, 373, 375, 381, 458.
   See also Sikhs
Akbar, 24, 30, 34, 36, 37, 41, 75, 87, 96, 195, 248, 312
Aksai Chin border dispute, 32, 335, 337, 371
Al-Azhar, 96
Albuquerque, Alfonso, 443, 448
Alexander, A.V., 247, 249, 250, 253, 254, 257
Ali brothers, 198, 220
Ali, Aruna Asaf, 234
Ali, Asaf, 229, 315, 320
Ali, Maulana Shaukat, 142, 145, 163, 177, 178
All India Anna Dravida Munnettra Kazhagam (AIADMK), 362, 390, 417, 441
All India federation of British India, 185

All India Institute of Medical Sciences (AIIMS), 424
All India States Peoples' Conference (1927), 157
All India Women's Conference (AIWC), 299
Allahabad Treaty, 54, 102, 108
Allied Powers, Allies, 131, 141, 210, 229, 237–38, 242–43, 262
Al-Qaeda, 444
Amarnath shrine, 426
Ambedkar, Bhimrao Ramji, 13–14, 74, 166, 168–69, 182–84, 185, 198, 203, 229, 240, 248, 265, 299, 303, 307, 311, 315, 320, 362, 379, 390, 427, 429–30, 451
Amery, Lord Leo, 213, 218, 228, 242
Amherst, Lord, 74, 101
Amrit ·Kaur, Rajkumari 250, 299
Amtus Salam, 240
Andaman and Nicobar Islands, 126, 194; captured by Japanese, 237
Andhra Pradesh (AP), 313, 349, 362, 390, 435–36; Naxalite movement, 424
Anglo-Afghan War (1893), 32
Anglo-Dutch War, 44
Anglo-French wars, 40, 81, 87; peace treaty, 51
Anglo-Gurkha War, 1814–16, 100
Anglo-Indians, 180, 195, 202, 313, 388
Anglo-Maratha War, Fourth, 1818, 72, 285
Annadurai, C.N., 307, 363
Ansari, Abdul Hameed, 166
Anti-Terrorist Squad (ATS), 429, 441, 445
Anushilan (Bengali youth movement), 126
Arabian Sea, 21, 23, 37
Arabs (Turks), 13, 23, 448
Archaeological Survey of India (ASI), 11
Archipelago, 46–47
Arthashastra, 8
Arunachal Pradesh, 9, 32, 371, 382
Arya Samaj, 97, 121, 274, 284; movement, 201
Aryans. *See* Indo-Europeans

National Security Council, 402; PL-480 food aid, 327, 341; slavery, 311; support/aid to Pakistan, 353, 419; terrorists' attack on World Trade Centre (WTC) (11/09/2001), 399, 420; war on terror, 419. *See also* slavery
unity and integrity, 303–06
Universal adult suffrage, 159
untouchability, untouchables, 143, 176, 180, 181–84, 211, 252, 320, 321, 361
Upanishads, 26, 98, 430
Urdu, 115–16
Uttar Pradesh/United Provinces (UP), 9, 45, 103, 361–62, 368, 397; backward castes, 380, 392; fractured polity, 400–03; politics, 390, 392; Ramjanmabhoomi temple movement, 4–5, 397–400
Uttarakhand, 103, 459

Vaishyas, 27, 28
Vajpayee, Atal Bihari, 336, 369, 388, 402–04, 412, 415–16, 421, 440–41
Vande mataram, 208, 219, 236
varna system. *See* caste
Vedas, Vedic, 26, 430; Brahmanism, 25–28, 195, 196; nature-gods, 26; religious tradition, 26
Vegetarian Society, 135
Vellalas, 349
Vellore Fort, 82, 86
Versailles Conference, 131, 168
Victoria, Queen, 80, 104, 106, 298, 290; Proclamation, 126, 449
Vidarbha, farmers suicide, 435
Vietnam, 45; US war, 346, 352
Vijaynagar Empire, 30, 37, 41
village self-government, 414
Vindhyas, 41, 201
Vishnu, 25, 27, 432
Vishwa Hindu Parishad (VHP), 384, 397, 398, 432, 445
Vivekananda, Swami, 142–43
Vokkaligas, 311, 349
voting rights, 119

Wahhabism, 378
Wajid Ali Shah, Nawab of Awadh, 103

Walpole, Robert, 51, 59
Washington, George, 433
Waterloo, 17, 71, 166
Wavell, Archibald Alexander, 229, 242, 244–46, 249–52, 254–55, 257–63
Wellesley Arthur, 72, 78, 79–81
West Bengal, 436–38, 457, 458, 459
West Essex Conservative Association, 171
Western, 1, 379; education, 99, 113; imperialism, 46; liberalism, 175
Westernization, 92, 142
Westminster, 48, 61, 132, 149*ff*, 186, 268, 282, 302, 383; model of Executive and legislature, 351
Whig/Tory distinction, 70, 71
White colonies, 132
widow remarriage, 321
Wilberforce, William, 70, 71, 81
Wilkes, John, 58, 63
Williams, Rushbrook, 137
Willingdon, Lord, 176, 181, 212, 214
Wilson, Hyman Horace, 65, 89
Wollstonecraft, Mary, 60, 81
women's education, 97
Wood, Edward. *See* Irwin, Lord
World Bank, 345, 346, 393, 396, 409
World Council of Religions, 142
World Trade Organization (WTO), 39, 407: GATT, 395
World Wars: First (Great War), 42, 114, 124–25, 129, 130, 134, 136–37, 236, 265, 277, 450, 460;— aftermath, 130–34; Second, 17, 71, 166, 191, 214, 230, 245, 271, 309, 354, 372

Yadav, Lalu Prasad, 362, 392, 397, 424, 428, 457
Yadav, Mulayam Singh, 392, 397, 423
Yadavs, 349, 361, 390, 392, 398, 401, 455
Yeltsin, Boris, 418
Younghusband, Francis, 32, 194
Yugoslavia, 199, 289, 317, 453

zamindari, zamindars, 83–85, 200, 278
Zetland, Lord, 205, 209
Zhou En-lai, 305, 336, 342
Zia-ul-Haq, 376, 399, 419
Zulu rebellion, 127